Read
Write
Connect

Read

Write

Connect

Second Edition

Read
Write
Connect

A Guide to College
Reading and Writing

Kathleen Green
Pasadena City College

Amy Lawlor
City College of San Francisco

bedford/st.martin's
Macmillan Learning

Boston | New York

For Bedford/St. Martin's

Vice President, Editorial, Macmillan Learning Humanities: Edwin Hill
Editorial Director, English: Karen S. Henry
Executive Editor: Karita dos Santos
Senior Developmental Editor: Caroline Thompson
Assistant Editor: Cara Kaufman
Senior Production Editor: Kendra LeFleur
Media Producer: Sarah O'Connor
Production Supervisor: Lisa McDowell
Marketing Manager: Joy Fisher Williams
Copy Editor: Susan Zorn
Indexer: Jake Kawatski
Photo Editor: Martha Friedman
Photo Researcher: Sheri Blaney
Permissions Manager: Kalina K. Ingham
Permissions Editor: Kathleen Karcher
Senior Art Director: Anna Palchik
Text Design: Jerilyn Bockorick
Cover Design: John Callahan
Cover Art/Cover Photo: robodread/Shutterstock
Composition: Cenevo Publisher Services
Printing and Binding: RR Donnelley and Sons

Manufactured in the United States of America.

1 0 9 8 7 6
f e d c b a

For information, write: Bedford/St. Martin's, 75 Arlington Street, Boston, MA 02116
  (617-399-4000)

ISBN 978-1-319-03596-9

Acknowledgments
Text acknowledgments and copyrights appear at the back of the book on pages 738–39, which constitute an extension of the copyright page. Art acknowledgments and copyrights appear on the same page as the art selections they cover.

Preface

B orn out of our collective years of experience in the classroom, as well as countless hours of one-on-one tutoring sessions with inquisitive students in office hours and tutoring centers, *Read, Write, Connect* helps students understand that being a good writer requires being a good reader, both of published texts and one's own writing. With lots of guidance and practice in both reading and writing, *Read, Write, Connect* is designed to help students meet the challenges of college courses that require them to integrate reading and writing skills and make connections among a wide variety of texts.

Our students are like most college students: diverse in their backgrounds and experiences, varied in their educational and career interests, and eager for challenging work that will inspire them. We wrote *Read, Write, Connect* for them. Our guiding principles in deciding what to include in this book have been the questions: "Do students need help with that?" "Is that the way you explain it in class?" and "Does it work?" As a result, the explanations in the book are student-centered and eminently practical.

In preparing this second edition of *Read, Write, Connect*, we gathered feedback from instructors teaching the book as well as from our students. We streamlined some of the content and added new material, including a full chapter on strategies for reading textbooks, more discussion of how to read and write about visuals and charts, and more paragraph editing exercises for sentence-level concerns. We also added a new thematic unit of readings as well as new readings in the existing units. Some content from the previous edition's e-Pages has been moved into the print book. The result of these changes is a text that is now even better equipped to meet the needs of quickly evolving developmental composition curricula.

Organization

In order to meaningfully integrate the recursive processes of reading and writing, *Read, Write, Connect*'s design and organization take a steep departure from traditional rhetorics.

PART 1: THE WALK-THROUGH

Designed as a walk-through of the entire reading and writing process, Chapters 1–4 guide students step-by-step from pre-reading to proofreading, beginning with how to read actively and ending with revising and proofreading their first out-of-class essay. The walk-through forms the basis of a strong reading and writing practice that students will follow not only in subsequent essays, but ideally in all of their college courses requiring reading and writing. We begin with a brief article by Carol S. Dweck that can be used as an ice-breaker to introduce the concept of the growth mindset, which sets the tone for a process-oriented classroom. The major theme of the walk-through, financial literacy, has been tweaked to better address issues of college students, with an overall emphasis on financial literacy across various life stages. We consistently receive positive feedback from instructors and students regarding the topic of financial literacy and find that it has broad appeal as the first thematic unit of the book. While instructors do not have to assign all the readings in the walk-through, we find it helpful to assign as many as possible so that students have weighty enough readings with which to learn and practice new skills, and so that they have sufficient schema to write meaningfully about the topic.

PART 2: READING AND WRITING WORKSHOPS

The workshop chapters (Chapters 5–23) offer a deeper understanding of the reading and writing processes by focusing on and expanding coverage of specific topics that many students need to practice more deeply to master—such as note taking, essay organization and outlining, and vocabulary building. The workshops offer tremendous flexibility to instructors, who can assign them at any point in the semester to emphasize a particular topic in more depth for the class as a whole or for an individual student struggling with a particular concept. The instruction, examples, and practice exercises make the workshop chapters fairly self-contained; as such, they can serve as the focus of classroom instruction or for independent practice. By making connections between the initial lessons of the semester and the more advanced lessons and activities of the workshops, students can reflect on the increasing sophistication of their writing and reading skills as well as the recursive nature of the reading and writing processes. The workshops also address integrated reading and writing instruction in a natural way that makes sense in the classroom.

PART 3: THEMATIC READINGS

The thematic reading units combine readings from a variety of sources into a conversation around a popular theme that most college students will find relevant and thought provoking. The themes cover many disciplines and interests, ranging from business and finance to the arts to psychology and science, so they will appeal to students with a variety of career interests and majors. Chapter 2 in Part 1 contains readings on the theme of Money, Wealth, and Financial Literacy, and Part 3 (Chapters 24–26) includes three additional themes—Curiosity, Public Art, and Fame and Celebrity. Each of the thematic reading units, class-tested by us to assure they work both together and individually for students at this level, includes texts of varying lengths drawn from a variety of sources. The units are designed to be flexible so that an instructor can assign all or a few of the readings.

PART 4: GRAMMAR, STYLE, AND MECHANICS WORKSHOPS

The grammar section of *Read, Write, Connect* (Chapters 27–41) begins with a workshop that encourages students to take stock of their strengths and weaknesses as writers. Chapter 27 leads students through the process of identifying the errors that they commonly make, studying the rules about their errors, recording those errors and notes about how to fix them in a personalized Grammar Log, and undertaking systematic practice in editing for those particular errors. The remainder of the grammar workshops offer focused instruction and practice in the areas of grammar and mechanics. While many instructors may spend some class time with those chapters that cover the major errors, such as fragments, the chapters can also be studied individually, on an as-needed basis. Like the rest of the book, this section explains how to find and fix errors in a student-friendly, straightforward manner. All the grammar workshops have detailed explanations as well as realistic examples, practice exercises, helpful tips, and chapter reviews.

Features

"PRACTICE IT" ACTIVITIES

Students need to practice the techniques of successful readers and writers, so we created the Practice It activities to provide lower-stakes assignments that prepare them for their larger assignments and offer them an immediate opportunity to apply what they learn to a concrete, real-life practice of reading or writing. These activities are deeply embedded in the instruction—often asking students to refer to the readings in the themed chapters for models, or requiring them to apply what they learn to their own assignments. Such activities are designed to offer authentic and useful practice to students, and can be assigned individually or to the class as a whole, as homework or as in-class activities. We numbered the Practice Its in the second edition to make them easier to assign.

TIPS

Practical in nature, these helpful tips appear in the margin and guide students so that they can avoid repeating some common mistakes that our students have made over the years. They also provide students with an easier way to perform a task in the writing or reading process.

VOCABULARY PRACTICE

Read, Write, Connect addresses vocabulary in several ways. Students are instructed to mark, look up, and write definitions for unfamiliar words they encounter as part of annotating. In all the readings, potentially unfamiliar words are marked with a dotted underscore and repeated in the margin. Students are prompted to look up the words they don't know and fill in the definitions in their own words. Additionally, Chapter 9 is devoted entirely to vocabulary building.

COMPREHENSION AND DISCUSSION QUESTIONS

Each reading selection in the thematic units is followed by comprehension questions and discussion questions. Both types of questions are open-ended to take students beyond a search for "correct" answers and toward deeper thinking about the ideas in the readings.

STEP-BY-STEP HELP FOR WRITING ABOUT THE READINGS

Each thematic reading unit closes with strategies for synthesizing the readings, a step-by-step guide to writing an essay, a variety of writing assignments in different modes, and a list of online and media resources to spark further ideas.

New to This Edition

The second edition offers new chapters and new features devoted to stronger, more integrated coverage of reading; expanded coverage of research and grammar; and exciting new readings, class-tested with our own students.

MODEL READING STRATEGIES

A new feature, Model Reading Strategies, visually demonstrates possible approaches to key reading selections. One selection in each thematic unit of readings is visually annotated to demonstrate an active reading strategy such as using context clues to understand vocabulary, mapping the structure of a text, asking questions, or connecting images to text. This features gives students a foothold on more challenging readings and models a variety of ways to approach other texts they will encounter. To explore this feature, see pages 46, 449, 486, and 551.

ADVICE FOR READING TEXTBOOKS

A new Chapter 6, Reading Textbooks, helps students get the most out of textbook reading assignments by introducing them to pre-reading, annotating, and other strategies as well as showing them how to use common textbook features effectively. Additional sample readings from textbooks have been incorporated into the thematic reading units, retaining their original design whenever possible. These readings are called out in the table of contents and in the text with the textbook icon shown in the margin.

STRATEGIES FOR USING VISUALS IN READING AND WRITING

Many of our students are visual learners, and we also find that developing students often struggle to map out their ideas, so we explain and model throughout the book many visual techniques for reading comprehension and textual analysis including mapping and charting. We have expanded Chapter 5 on active reading with advice for reading charts, graphs, infographics, photos, and videos. Visuals and graphic organizers are incorporated throughout the book.

NEW READING SELECTIONS

An engaging new unit of readings on the theme of curiosity invites students to consider the connections between curiosity and their own learning. Other thematic units have been updated with new readings on financial literacy, fame, and public art. The new readings update the discussions and also provide a wider variety of types of sources (such as infographics, excerpts from scholarly journals, and excerpts from textbooks). We class test all of the readings with our own students, so we can be sure these are readings students will *want* to read and write about.

EXPANDED GRAMMAR COVERAGE

Instructors who taught with the first edition told us that additional grammar exercises would be helpful, so we have added paragraph-editing Practice It exercises for each grammar topic. The Practice Its are numbered in this edition to make them easier to assign. We have also strengthened our grammar coverage with new chapters on basic sentence components, sentence structure, and major verb errors, and expanded discussions of misplaced and dangling modifiers.

MORE HELP WITH RESEARCH

A new chapter on APA documentation and expanded discussions of avoiding plagiarism provide stronger support in this edition for students writing source-based essays. Advice for documenting sources in MLA style has been updated in accordance with 2016 MLA guidelines.

NEW CHAPTER REVIEWS

Our new Chapter Review feature promotes metacognition and can help with student learning outcomes (SLO) assessment by prompting students to paraphrase what they've learned and reflect on it in their own words, in writing, at the end of each chapter.

Acknowledgments

The following reviewers were very helpful during the revision of this book: Jean Armstrong, Delaware Technical Community College; Jenny Billings Beaver, Rowan Cabarrus Community College; Tiffany Daniel, Oconee Fall Line Technical College; Kimberly Koledoye, Houston Community College; Diane Lerma, Palo Alto College; Daryl Long, Waubonsee Community College; Barbara Overgaard, Pikes Peak Community College; Dorothy Reade, Lone Star System–North Harris; Lelamay Seely, Chaffey College; Cheryle Snead-Greene, Prairie View A&M University; Matilda Staudt, Palo Alto College; Minnie Thomas, Texas Southern University; Tondalaya VanLear, Dabney S. Lancaster Community College; and Jonathan Wise, Asheville-Buncombe Technical Community College.

Working with a publishing company that values collaboration as much as Bedford/St. Martin's, necessarily we have many people to thank. Among them, we owe a deep debt of gratitude to those who helped breathe life into the first edition of this book: Nick Carbone, Kimberly Hampton, Alexis Walker, Ellen Darion, Joan Feinberg, and Denise Wydra. Without them, we would never have started on this journey. This second edition of the book has been inspired by Vivian Garcia, Executive Editor, our supporter and friend, and Edwin Hill, Vice President Editorial, Humanities, whose practical advice has kept us on track. Our profound thanks go to the many people whose efforts have helped us to look polished: Kendra LeFleur, Senior Production Editor; Cara Kaufman, Assistant Editor; Anna Palchik, Senior Art Director; Susan Zorn, copyeditor; Sheri Blaney and Kathleen Karcher for art and text permissions research, respectively; and Joy Fisher Williams, marketing manager. We would also like to especially thank our editor Caroline Thompson, who has given us excellent guidance and advice for the second edition of this book.

And finally, to all of our students, who have been guinea pigs and sources of inspiration, we owe the deepest thanks. Every time we tried to explain something and didn't get through, and a student had the strength of mind and purpose to say "Wait, that doesn't make sense" or "This reading is boring" made us better teachers, teachers who had to reach down a little deeper to find a way to explain it all better.

Amy would like to thank her many students over the years who have given her as many opportunities to learn as to teach. She would also like to thank her many colleagues who have offered inspiration, courage, guidance, humor and, on countless occasions, copies of excellent handouts! She is grateful especially to her parents, Marty and Bill, who were her first and continue to be her most important teachers. She would also like to thank her brothers and sister and friends who have supported her and keep asking "When can we see the book?" And finally, she would like to thank Brian and Gracie for their tireless support, love, and understanding while she was buried in the writing of this book.

Kathy would like to thank the students of Pasadena City College, particularly her student veterans, who taught her how to teach developing students. She would also like to thank all the marvelous colleagues and fellow teachers whose passion for developing writers is a constant source of inspiration. Finally, the biggest thanks go to Jo, Hana, and Ben, for their extreme patience and understanding and their amazing ability to read hand signals during conference calls.

Kathleen Green
Amy Lawlor

Get the Most Out of Your Course with *Read, Write, Connect*

Bedford/St. Martin's offers resources and format choices that help you and your students get even more out of your book and course. To learn more about or to order any of the following products, contact your Bedford/St. Martin's sales representative, e-mail sales support (sales_support@ bfwpub.com), or visit the Web site at **macmillanlearning.com**.

CHOOSE FROM ALTERNATIVE FORMATS OF *READ, WRITE, CONNECT*

Bedford/St. Martin's offers a range of affordable formats, allowing students to choose the one that works best for them. For details, visit **macmillanlearning.com.**

- *Paperback*   To order the paperback edition, use ISBN 978-1-319-03596-9.

- *Loose-leaf edition*   The loose-leaf edition does not have a traditional binding; its pages are loose and hole-punched to provide flexibility and a low price to students. To order the loose-leaf edition, use ISBN 978-1-319-03642-3.

- *Other popular e-book formats*   *Read, Write, Connect* is available in a variety of e-book formats. For details about our e-book partners, visit **macmillanlearning.com/ebooks**.

SELECT VALUE PACKAGES

Add value to your text by packaging one of the following resources with *Read, Write, Connect.* To learn more about package options for any of the following products, contact your Bedford/St. Martin's sales representative or visit **macmillanlearning.com.**

LaunchPad Solo for Readers and Writers allows students to work on whatever they need help with the most. At home or in class, students learn at their own pace, with instruction tailored to each student's unique needs. *LaunchPad Solo for Readers and Writers* features:

- *Pre-built units that support a learning arc.* Each easy-to-assign unit is comprised of a pre-test check, multimedia instruction and assessment, and a post-test that assesses what students have learned about critical reading, writing process, using sources, grammar, style, mechanics, and help for multilingual writers.

- *A video introduction to many topics.* Introductions offer an overview of the unit's topic, and many include a brief, accessible video to illustrate the concepts at hand.

- *Adaptive quizzing for targeted learning.* Most units include LearningCurve, game-like adaptive quizzing that focuses on the areas in which each student needs the most help.

- *The ability to monitor student progress.* Use our gradebook to see which students are on track and which need additional help with specific topics.

LaunchPad Solo for Readers and Writers can be **packaged at a significant discount**. Order ISBN 978-1-319-10376-7 to package LaunchPad Solo with *Read, Write, Connect* to ensure your students can take full advantage. Visit **macmillanlearning.com/readwrite** for more information.

Writer's Help 2.0 is a powerful online writing resource that helps students find answers whether they are searching for writing advice on their own or as part of an assignment.

- *Smart search.* Built on research with more than 1,600 student writers, the smart search in *Writer's Help* provides reliable results even when students use novice terms, such as flow and unstuck.

- *Trusted content from our best-selling handbooks.* Choose *Writer's Help 2.0, Hacker Version* or *Writer's Help 2.0, Lunsford Version* and ensure that students have clear advice and examples for all of their writing questions.

- *Adaptive exercises that engage students. Writer's Help* includes *LearningCurve*, game-like online quizzing that adapts to what students already know and helps them focus on what they need to learn.

Student access is packaged with *Read, Write, Connect* at a significant discount. Contact your sales representative for a package ISBN to ensure your students have easy access to online writing support. Students who rent a book or buy a used book can purchase access to *Writer's Help 2.0* at **macmillanlearning.com/writershelp2**. **Instructors** may request free access by registering as an instructor at macmillanlearning.com/writershelp2. For technical support, visit macmillanlearning.com/getsupport.

Portfolio Keeping, **Third Edition, by Nedra Reynolds and Elizabeth Davis,** provides all the information students need to use the portfolio method successfully in a writing course. Portfolio Teaching, a companion guide for instructors, provides the practical information instructors and writing program administrators need to use the portfolio method successfully in a writing course. To order Portfolio Keeping packaged with this text, contact your sale representative for a package ISBN.

LearningCurve for Readers and Writers, Bedford/St. Martin's adaptive quizzing program, quickly learns what students already know and helps them practice what they don't yet understand. Game-like quizzing motivates students to engage with their course, and reporting tools help teachers discern their students' needs. *LearningCurve for Readers and Writers* can be packaged with *Read, Write, Connect* at a significant discount. An activation code is required. To order *LearningCurve* packaged with the print book, contact your sales representative for a package ISBN. For details, visit **learningcurveworks.com.**

The Bedford/St. Martin's ESL Workbook includes a broad range of exercises covering grammar issues for multilingual students of varying language skills and backgrounds. Answers are at the back. To order the ESL Workbook packaged with the print book, contact your sales representative for a package ISBN.

Bedford/St. Martin's Planner includes everything that students need to plan and use their time effectively, with advice on preparing schedules and to-do lists plus blank schedules and calendars (monthly and weekly). The planner fits easily into a backpack or purse, so students can take it anywhere. To order the Planner packaged with the print book, contact your sales representative for a package ISBN.

INSTRUCTOR RESOURCES
macmillanlearning.com

You have a lot to do in your course. Bedford/St. Martin's wants to make it easy for you to find the support you need—and to get it quickly.

The Instructor's Edition of *Read, Write, Connect* includes the complete text of the student edition plus the instructor's manual, including suggested responses for all the Comprehension Questions and Practice It activities. To order the Instructor's Edition, contact your Macmillan sales representative or use ISBN 978-1-319-03640-9.

The Instructor's Manual for *Read, Write, Connect* is available as a PDF that can be downloaded from the Bedford/St. Martin's online catalog at the URL above. Visit the instructor resources tab for *Read, Write, Connect.* The manual offers sample syllabi, tips for teaching the course and insights into teaching each chapter, and suggested responses for Comprehension Questions and Practice It activities.

Join Our Community! At Bedford, providing support to teachers and their students who choose our books and digital tools is our first priority. The Bedford/St. Martin's English Community is now our home for professional resources, featuring Bedford *Bits*, our popular blog site offering new ideas for the composition classroom and composition teachers. Connect and converse with a growing team of Bedford authors and top scholars who blog on *Bits*: Barclay Barrios, Steve Bernhardt, Susan Bernstein, Traci Gardner, Elizabeth Losh, Andrea Lunsford, Jack Solomon, Elizabeth Wardle, and Donna Winchell, among others. In addition, you'll find an expanding collection of resources that support your teaching. Download titles from our professional resource series to support your teaching, review projects in the pipeline, sign up for professional development webinars, start a discussion, ask a question, and follow your favorite members. Visit **community. macmillan.com** to join the conversation with your fellow teachers.

Teaching with LaunchPad Solo for Readers and Writers

Pairing *Read, Write, Connect* with *LaunchPad Solo for Readers and Writers* helps students succeed at their own pace.

You can use *LaunchPad Solo for Readers and Writers* to integrate skills-based practice into your teaching with *Read, Write, Connect,* allowing you to more efficiently track students' progress with reading, writing, and grammar skills in an active learning arc that complements the book. To package *LaunchPad Solo for Readers and Writers* with *Read, Write, Connect* at a significant discount, use ISBN 978-1-319-10376-7.

Assigning a project for which students will need to develop a strong thesis?

Start with the unit on thesis statements in *LaunchPad Solo for Readers and Writers* to assess what students know. Before turning to Chapter 11: Thesis and Main Idea in *Read, Write, Connect,* have students complete the pre-test to get perspective on what they already know. With this insight, you can meet them where they are.

Then, from *Read, Write, Connect,* assign appropriate Practice It activities based on the results of the pre-test. For example, if the pre-test shows that many students cannot identify strong thesis statements, you might choose to spend considerable class time on Practice It 11.2, which asks students to analyze and revise thesis statements.

practice it 11.2   Improving Weak Thesis Statements

Evaluate the following four working thesis statements about fame and celebrity. What works and what needs more work for each thesis statement? Analyze each one based on these criteria:

• Is it an arguable claim? (Would some people disagree with it? Can it be supported by evidence?)
• Is it clearly and specifically phrased?
• Does it address the question or task of the assignment?
• Is it a statement (*not* a question)?

1. The question is, what is fame?
2. This essay will explore the downsides of celebrity and why we still want it despite the negatives.

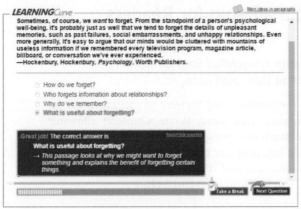

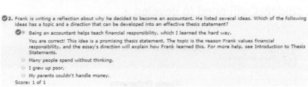

In the writing lab or at home, students can practice finding the main point in readings using LearningCurve, game-like adaptive quizzing.

If assigned, the post-test asks students to apply what they've learned in the skill unit to different writing situations. You can use results from the post-test to determine whether some students will require more help as they begin building theses for their projects.

For more information about *LaunchPad Solo for Readers and Writers*, visit **macmillanlearning.com/readwrite**. To sign up for WebEx trainings with pedagogical specialists and access round-the-clock tech support, visit **macmillanlearning.com/support**.

Brief Contents

Contents

Read
Write
Connect

Read

Write

Connect

These chapters are designed as a walk-through of the core reading and writing steps that form the basis of a strong reading and writing practice. Whether you've never written an essay or you are a pro, these chapters walk you through every step of the process.

part one

From Pre-Reading to Proofreading: The Reading and Writing Processes

1

Reading and Responding to College Texts

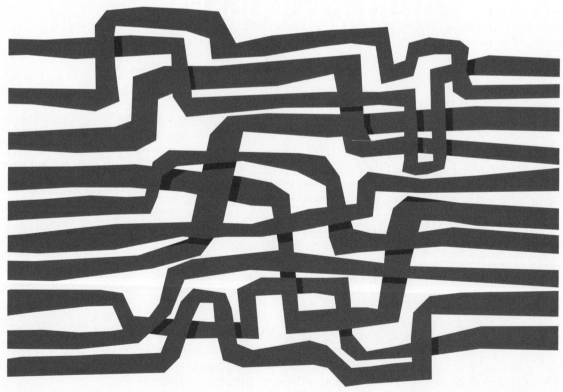

©robodread/Shutterstock

You already know how to read and write. But do you know how to read and write well? How many times have you read something, only to forget a few days or even minutes later what you just read? Have you ever studied for a test but blanked out when it came time to write your answers? Do you know how to write with your own voice about what you read? *Read, Write, Connect* is designed to help you think critically and become a more effective and efficient reader and writer and to prepare you for college work.

This book's central premise is that reading and writing are both processes. No one is born a good writer or a good reader. There are many steps to reading and writing well, and all students can learn those steps, practice them, and improve their reading, critical thinking, and writing. Unfortunately, there is no "quick fix" to learning how to read and write well, but we believe that when you see reading and writing as processes and practice the steps outlined in this book, you'll make serious progress as a reader, writer, and thinker.

This chapter gives a quick overview of active reading and summary writing to jump-start your college semester and to get you into the college "mind-set." The rest of the book goes into far more detail about these important skills. This chapter includes a short article that provides valuable information on the learning process and can give you a quick introduction to the skills of pre-reading, annotating, and summarizing, which are the foundation of college-level work.

LaunchPad Solo
macmillan learning

Visit **LaunchPad Solo for Readers and Writers > Overview: Reading** for extra practice in the skills covered in this chapter.

How to Approach a Text: Pre-Reading Strategies

Strong readers don't just begin reading at the first sentence. They follow a process. Very experienced readers follow the process almost automatically, so they may not even be aware of what they are doing. It makes them look naturally "smart," but actually they just have had a lot of practice at something everyone can learn. The first step in the process is called pre-reading because you do it before you actually start to read. We'll begin with two basic pre-reading techniques: taking stock of what you already know about a topic and previewing the text.

▶ For more on pre-reading and becoming a strong reader, see Chapter 5, Active Reading Strategies.

TAKING STOCK OF WHAT YOU ALREADY KNOW ABOUT A TOPIC

To get you thinking about the selections you'll read later on, complete the following Practice It activity. Don't worry; this is not a formal writing assignment to be graded. You don't need to worry about organization or writing the perfect sentence. This sort of writing is called *freewriting*, and its purpose is to help you generate as many ideas as possible.

▶ For more on freewriting, see Chapter 10, Pre-Writing.

practice it 1.1 Taking Stock of What You Already Know

Spend ten minutes writing nonstop about one or more of the questions below:

- What does it mean to be smart?
- What does it mean to be a good student?
- How do you feel when you struggle with something you are learning?
- Think of a time you overcame a difficult problem in life or at school. How did you handle the problem? What helped you to bounce back afterward?
- Recall a time when someone's praise really mattered to you. Describe what happened. What did the person say? How did it make you feel?

Read over what you have written and reflect on it. Highlight or underline any particularly good points or ideas that you generated. Add any additional thoughts that come to you. What three or four words come to your mind when you think about learning, overcoming obstacles, and praise? Write them down.

You've just practiced one of the most effective techniques for becoming a strong college reader. Why is taking stock of what you know so helpful? Consider for a moment all the knowledge and information you hold in your mind. Readers understand and remember what they read much better when they can connect the reading to what they already know. So by thinking about what you already know of the topic you are going to read about, you are drawing from all the knowledge and information you already have and getting ready to understand the reading and make connections.

PREVIEWING THE TEXT

Previewing means flipping through the reading to get a sense of what it might be about, how it is organized (into sections or paragraphs), how long it is, and what tools the writer has provided to help you read it. (You probably already check the length of assigned readings, just to see what you're in for!) Previewing the text in this way will help you understand the scope of the topic and the organization of the text. Previewing a reading takes very little time, and it really helps you understand the material.

Why is previewing so effective? Imagine you have to go someplace in an unfamiliar part of town. You may have a rough idea of how to get there, but looking up the route on a map will give you a clear picture of how to get from where you are to where you want to end up, and it will let you know what landmarks to look for along the way so you will know you are on the right path. Similarly, previewing a text before reading it will give you a map of the text. What points will it cover to get you from the introduction to the conclusion? Previewing will tell you what main points (landmarks) you should be noticing along the way.

To use another analogy, think back to your first day of college or of a new job. Probably much of that first day is one big blank because you were so overwhelmed by all the new information. Something similar happens with reading. Plunging into a reading without previewing it is like dropping in on an event without prior preparation: It's easy to overlook the main points and get lost in the details. Getting a sense of the big picture before you read will prepare you to absorb the information right away.

practice it 1.2 Previewing the Text

Previewing the text is quick. Practice right now with Carol S. Dweck's article "The Perils and Promises of Praise" on pages 6–13. You can do this by yourself or with some classmates, or even as a whole class. Keep these questions in front of you as you work. Here's how to do it:

Step 1: Look at the title of the text. Based on the title, what might you predict the article will be about? Look for words that suggest an opinion or point of view (words like "best" or "against"), a topic range (words like "from _____ to _____"), or titles that ask questions.

Step 2: Find out where the text was published. What does this tell you about the audience and purpose? Is this a reading intended for students, parents, or teachers? How will the intended audience shape the information presented?

Step 3: Flip through the pages of the article. How long is it? How is it laid out? What kinds of pictures does it have? Is the reading broken up by sections or paragraphs? Are there any section headings? If so, what do they tell you about the subtopic of each section? What kind of information is at the end of the article? What can you learn about the author, topic, audience, and/or purpose of the text?

Step 4: Quickly skim the first paragraph. What did you learn? What do you expect the article will discuss?

Step 5: Quickly skim the last paragraph. What did you learn? What point(s) do you think Dweck is going to make?

Step 6: Check whether there are any comprehension or discussion questions at the end of the reading. If so, read those before you read the article. The questions will clue you in on what important points or ideas you should be looking for in the text.

Step 7: Take a few minutes to write what you learned in the margins of the text. (That's right: Write your thoughts directly on the pages of your book.) Writing down what you learned will help you make sense of the text, even if you are just guessing or making predictions.

SCHOLARLY ARTICLE

Dr. Carol S. Dweck is the Lewis and Virginia Eaton Professor of Psychology at Stanford University, where she researches motivation and success. She has published widely in both scholarly and popular arenas. Since publishing the following article in the journal *Educational Leadership* in October 2007, she has played an enormous role in helping teachers rethink how they react to students. Her work is regularly cited in educational, parenting, business, and psychology contexts.

Some difficult words and phrases are noted in the margins. Look up the ones you don't know and write their definitions in your own words in the space provided. The first one has been done for you.

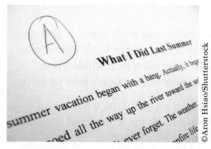 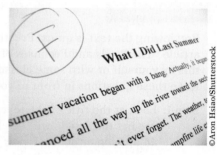

CAROL S. DWECK

The Perils and Promises of Praise

The wrong kind of praise creates self-defeating behavior. The right kind motivates students to learn.

We often hear these days that we've produced a generation of young people who can't get through the day without an award. They expect success because they're special, not because they've worked hard.

Is this true? Have we <u>inadvertently</u> done something to hold back our students?

inadvertently: *without meaning to*

I think educators commonly hold two beliefs that do just that. Many believe that (1) praising students' intelligence builds their confidence and motivation to learn, and (2) students' <u>inherent</u> intelligence is the major cause of their achievement in school. Our research has shown that the first belief is false and that the second can be harmful—even for the most competent students.

inherent:

As a psychologist, I have studied student motivation for more than thirty-five years. My graduate students and I have looked at thousands of

children, asking why some enjoy learning, even when it's hard, and why
they are resilient in the face of obstacles. We have learned a great deal.   **resilient:**
Research shows us how to praise students in ways that yield motivation
and resilience. In addition, specific interventions can reverse a student's
slide into failure during the vulnerable period of adolescence.   **vulnerable:**

Fixed or Malleable?

Praise is intricately connected to how students view their intelligence.   5
Some students believe that their intellectual ability is a fixed trait.
They have a certain amount of intelligence, and that's that. Students
with this fixed mind-set become excessively concerned with how smart   **intricately:**
they are, seeking tasks that will prove their intelligence and avoiding
ones that might not (Dweck, 1999, 2006). The desire to learn takes a
backseat.

Other students believe that their intellectual ability is something
they can develop through effort and education. They don't necessarily
believe that anyone can become an Einstein or a Mozart, but they do
understand that even Einstein and Mozart had to put in years of effort to
become who they were. When students believe that they can develop
their intelligence, they focus on doing just that. Not worrying about how
smart they will appear, they take on challenges and stick to them (Dweck,
1999, 2006).

More and more research in psychology and neuroscience supports the   **neuroscience:**
growth mind-set. We are discovering that the brain has more plasticity
over time than we ever imagined (Doidge, 2007); that fundamental
aspects of intelligence can be enhanced through learning (Sternberg,   **plasticity:**
2005); and that dedication and persistence in the face of obstacles are
key ingredients in outstanding achievement (Ericsson, Charness,
Feltovich, & Hoffman, 2006).

Alfred Binet (1909/1973), the inventor of the IQ test, had a strong
growth mind-set. He believed that education could transform the basic
capacity to learn. Far from intending to measure fixed intelligence, he
meant his test to be a tool for identifying students who were not profiting
from the public school curriculum so that other courses of study could be
devised to foster their intellectual growth.

The Two Faces of Effort

The fixed and growth mind-sets create two different psychological worlds.
In the fixed mind-set, students care first and foremost about how they'll
be judged: smart or not smart. Repeatedly, students with this mind-set
reject opportunities to learn if they might make mistakes (Hong, Chiu,
Dweck, Lin, & Wan, 1999; Mueller & Dweck, 1998). When they do make
mistakes or reveal deficiencies, rather than correct them, they try to hide
them (Nussbaum & Dweck, 2007).

They are also afraid of effort because effort makes them feel dumb.   10
They believe that if you have the ability, you shouldn't need effort
(Blackwell, Trzesniewski, & Dweck, 2007), that ability should bring
success all by itself. This is one of the worst beliefs that students can
hold. It can cause many bright students to stop working in school when
the curriculum becomes challenging.

Finally, students in the fixed
mind-set don't recover well from
setbacks. When they hit a setback
in school, they *decrease* their
efforts and consider cheating
(Blackwell et al., 2007). The idea
of fixed intelligence does not
offer them viable ways to
improve.

viable:

Let's get inside the head of a
student with a fixed mind-set as he sits in his classroom, confronted with
algebra for the first time. Up until then, he has breezed through math.
Even when he barely paid attention in class and skimped on his homework, he always got As. But this is different. It's hard. The student feels
anxious and thinks, "What if I'm not as good at math as I thought? What
if other kids understand it and I don't?" At some level, he realizes that he
has two choices: try hard, or turn off. His interest in math begins to wane,
and his attention wanders. He tells himself, "Who cares about this stuff?
It's for nerds. I could do it if I wanted to, but it's so boring. You don't see
CEOs and sports stars solving for *x* and *y*."

wane:

By contrast, in the growth mind-set, students care about learning.
When they make a mistake or exhibit a deficiency, they correct it
(Blackwell et al., 2007; Nussbaum & Dweck, 2007). For them, effort is a
positive thing: It ignites their intelligence and causes it to grow. In the
face of failure, these students escalate their efforts and look for new
learning strategies.

escalate:

Let's look at another student—one who has a growth mind-set—
having her first encounter with algebra. She finds it new, hard, and
confusing, unlike anything else she has ever learned. But she's determined to understand it. She listens to everything the teacher says, asks
the teacher questions after class, and takes her textbook home and reads
the chapter over twice. As she begins to get it, she feels exhilarated. A
new world of math opens up for her.

exhilarated:

It is not surprising, then, that when we have followed students over   15
challenging school transitions or courses, we find that those with growth
mind-sets outperform their classmates with fixed mind-sets—even when
they entered with equal skills and knowledge. A growth mind-set fosters
the growth of ability over time (Blackwell et al., 2007; Mangels, Butterfield,
Lamb, Good, & Dweck, 2006; see also Grant & Dweck, 2003).

The Effects of Praise

Many educators have hoped to maximize students' confidence in their abilities, their enjoyment of learning, and their ability to thrive in school by praising their intelligence. We've studied the effects of this kind of praise in children as young as four years old and as old as adolescence, in students in inner-city and rural settings, and in students of different ethnicities—and we've consistently found the same thing (Cimpian, Arce, Markman, & Dweck, 2007; Kamins & Dweck, 1999; Mueller & Dweck, 1998): Praising students' intelligence gives them a short burst of pride, followed by a long string of negative consequences.

In many of our studies (see Mueller & Dweck, 1998), fifth-grade students worked on a task, and after the first set of problems, the teacher praised some of them for their intelligence ("You must be smart at these problems") and others for their effort ("You must have worked hard at these problems"). We then assessed the students' mind-sets. In one study, we asked students to agree or disagree with mind-set statements, such as, "Your intelligence is something basic about you that you can't really change." Students praised for intelligence agreed with statements like these more than students praised for effort did. In another study, we asked students to define intelligence. Students praised for intelligence made significantly more references to innate, fixed capacity, whereas the students praised for effort made more references to skills, knowledge, and areas they could change through effort and learning. Thus, we found that praise for intelligence tended to put students in a fixed mind-set (intelligence is fixed, and you have it), whereas praise for effort tended to put them in a growth mind-set (you're developing these skills because you're working hard).

innate:

We then offered students a chance to work on either a challenging task that they could learn from or an easy one that ensured error-free performance. Most of those praised for intelligence wanted the easy task, whereas most of those praised for effort wanted the challenging task and the opportunity to learn.

Next, the students worked on some challenging problems. As a group, students who had been praised for their intelligence *lost* their confidence in their ability and their enjoyment of the task as soon as they began to struggle with the problem. If success meant they were smart, then struggling meant they were not. The whole point of intelligence praise is to boost confidence and motivation, but both were gone in a flash. Only the effort-praised kids remained, on the whole, confident and eager.

When the problems were made somewhat easier again, students praised for intelligence did poorly, having lost their confidence and motivation. As a group, they did worse than they had done initially on these same types of problems. The students praised for effort showed excellent performance and continued to improve.

20

Finally, when asked to report their scores (anonymously), almost 40 percent of the intelligence-praised students lied. Apparently, their egos were so wrapped up in their performance that they couldn't admit mistakes. Only about 10 percent of the effort-praised students saw fit to **falsify:** falsify their results.

Praising students for their intelligence, then, hands them not motivation and resilience but a fixed mind-set with all its vulnerability. In **perseverance:** contrast, effort or "process" praise (praise for engagement, perseverance, strategies, improvement, and the like) fosters hardy motivation. It tells **hardy:** students what they've done to be successful and what they need to do to be successful again in the future. Process praise sounds like this:

Cardinal/RF/Corbis

- You really studied for your English test, and your improvement shows it. You read the material over several times, outlined it, and tested yourself on it. That really worked!
- I like the way you tried all kinds of strategies on that math problem until you finally got it.
- It was a long, hard assignment, but you stuck to it and got it done. You stayed at your desk, kept up your concentration, and kept working. That's great!
- I like that you took on that challenging project for your science class. It will take a lot of work—doing the research, designing the machine, buying the parts, and building it. You're going to learn a lot of great things.

What about a student who gets an A without trying? I would say, "All right, that was too easy for you. Let's do something more challenging that you can learn from." We don't want to make something done quickly and easily the basis for our admiration.

What about a student who works hard and *doesn't* do well? I would say, "I liked the effort you put in. Let's work together some more and figure out what you don't understand." Process praise keeps students focused, not on something called ability that they may or may not have and that magically creates success or failure, but on processes they can all engage in to learn.

Motivated to Learn

Finding that a growth mind-set creates motivation and resilience—and leads to higher achievement—we sought to develop an intervention that would teach this mind-set to students. We decided to aim our intervention at students who were making the transition to seventh grade because this is a time of great vulnerability. School often gets more difficult in seventh grade, grading becomes more <u>stringent</u>, and the environment becomes more impersonal. Many students take stock of themselves and their intellectual abilities at this time and decide whether they want to be involved with school. Not surprisingly, it is often a time of disengagement and plunging achievement.

stringent:

We performed our intervention in a New York City junior high school in which many students were struggling with the transition and were showing plummeting grades. If students learned a growth mind-set, we reasoned, they might be able to meet this challenge with increased, rather than decreased, effort. We therefore developed an eight-session workshop in which both the control group and the growth-mind-set group learned study skills, time management techniques, and memory strategies (Blackwell et al., 2007). However, in the growth-mind-set intervention, students also learned about their brains and what they could do to make their intelligence grow.

25

They learned that the brain is like a muscle—the more they exercise it, the stronger it becomes. They learned that every time they try hard and learn something new, their brain forms new connections that, over time, make them smarter. They learned that intellectual development is not the natural unfolding of intelligence, but rather the formation of new connections brought about through effort and learning.

Students were <u>riveted</u> by this information. The idea that their intellectual growth was largely in their hands fascinated them. In fact, even the most disruptive students suddenly sat still and took notice, with the most unruly boy of the lot looking up at us and saying, "You mean I don't have to be dumb?"

riveted:

Indeed, the growth-mind-set message appeared to unleash students' motivation. Although both groups had experienced a steep decline in their math grades during their first months of junior high, those receiving the growth-mind-set intervention showed a significant rebound. Their math grades improved. Those in the control group, despite their excellent study skills intervention, continued their decline.

What's more, the teachers—who were unaware that the intervention workshops differed—singled out three times as many students in the growth-mind-set intervention as showing marked changes in motivation. These students had a heightened desire to work hard and learn. One striking example was the boy who thought he was dumb. Before this experience, he had never put in any extra effort and often didn't turn his homework in on time. As a result of the training, he worked for hours one evening to finish an assignment early so that his teacher could review it and give him a chance to revise it. He earned a B+ on the assignment (he had been getting Cs and lower previously).

Other researchers have obtained similar findings with a growth-mind-set intervention. Working with junior high school students, Good,

30

Aronson, and Inzlicht (2003) found an increase in math and English achievement test scores; working with college students, Aronson, Fried, and Good (2002) found an increase in students' valuing of academics, their enjoyment of schoolwork, and their grade point averages.

facilitate:

To facilitate delivery of the growth-mind-set workshop to students, we developed an interactive computer-based version of the intervention called *Brainology*. Students work through six modules, learning about the brain, visiting virtual brain labs, doing virtual brain experiments, seeing how the brain changes with learning, and learning how they can make their brains work better and grow smarter.

We tested our initial version in twenty New York City schools, with encouraging results. Almost all students (anonymously polled) reported changes in their study habits and motivation to learn resulting directly from their learning of the growth mind-set. One student noted that as a result of the animation she had seen about the brain, she could actually

neurons:

"picture the neurons growing bigger as they make more connections." One student referred to the value of effort: "If you do not give up and you keep studying, you can find your way through."

Adolescents often see school as a place where they perform for teachers who then judge them. The growth mind-set changes that perspective and makes school a place where students vigorously engage in learning for their own benefit.

Going Forward

Our research shows that educators cannot hand students confidence on a silver platter by praising their intelligence. Instead, we can help them gain the tools they need to maintain their confidence in learning by keeping them focused on the *process* of achievement.

Maybe we have produced a generation of students who are more   35
dependent, fragile, and entitled than previous generations. If so, it's time for us to adopt a growth mind-set and learn from our mistakes. It's time to deliver interventions that will truly boost students' motivation, resilience, and learning.

References

Aronson, J., Fried, C., & Good, C. (2002). Reducing the effects of stereotype threat on African American college students by shaping theories of intelligence. *Journal of Experimental Social Psychology, 38*, 113–125.

Binet, A. (1909/1973). *Les idées modernes sur les enfants* [Modern ideas on children]. Paris, France: Flammarion. (Original work published 1909).

Blackwell, L., Trzesniewski, K., & Dweck, C. S. (2007). Implicit theories of intelligence predict achievement across an adolescent transition: A longitudinal study and an intervention. *Child Development, 78*, 246–263.

Cimpian, A., Arce, H., Markman, E. M., & Dweck, C. S. (2007). Subtle linguistic cues impact children's motivation. *Psychological Science, 18*, 314–316.

Doidge, N. (2007). *The brain that changes itself: Stories of personal triumph from the frontiers of brain science.* New York, NY: Viking.

Dweck, C. S. (1999). *Self-theories: Their role in motivation, personality, and development.* Philadelphia, PA: Taylor and Francis/Psychology Press.

Dweck, C. S. (2006). *Mindset: The new psychology of success.* New York, NY: Random House.

Ericsson, K. A., Charness, N., Feltovich, P. J., & Hoffman, R. R. (Eds.). (2006). *The Cambridge handbook of expertise and expert performance.* New York, NY: Cambridge University Press.

Good, C., Aronson, J., & Inzlicht, M. (2003). Improving adolescents' standardized test performance: An intervention to reduce the effects of stereotype threat. *Journal of Applied Developmental Psychology, 24,* 645–662.

Grant, H., & Dweck, C. S. (2003). Clarifying achievement goals and their impact. *Journal of Personality and Social Psychology, 85,* 541–553.

Hong, Y. Y., Chiu, C., Dweck, C. S., Lin, D., & Wan, W. (1999). Implicit theories, attributions, and coping: A meaning system approach. *Journal of Personality and Social Psychology, 77,* 588–599.

Kamins, M., & Dweck, C. S. (1999). Person vs. process praise and criticism: Implications for contingent self-worth and coping. *Developmental Psychology, 35,* 835–847.

Mangels, J. A., Butterfield, B., Lamb, J., Good, C. D., & Dweck, C. S. (2006). Why do beliefs about intelligence influence learning success? A social-cognitive-neuroscience model. *Social, Cognitive, and Affective Neuroscience, 1,* 75–86.

Mueller, C. M., & Dweck, C. S. (1998). Intelligence praise can undermine motivation and performance. *Journal of Personality and Social Psychology, 75,* 33–52.

Nussbaum, A. D., & Dweck, C. S. (2007). Defensiveness vs. remediation: Self-theories and modes of self-esteem maintenance. *Personality and Social Psychology Bulletin.*

Sternberg, R. (2005). Intelligence, competence, and expertise. In A. Elliot & C. S. Dweck (Eds.), *The handbook of competence and motivation* (pp. 15–30). New York, NY: Guilford Press.

COMPREHENSION QUESTIONS

1. What sort of research study did Dweck and her colleagues conduct? How did they design the study? Who participated? What were they trying to discover?

2. How does a fixed mind-set differ from a growth mind-set?

3. What kinds of praise encourage a growth mind-set?

4. What does "resilience" mean, and why is it so important to learning?

5. What does Dweck suggest about people who like to be challenged versus those who prefer to take on easy tasks?

6. Why did Dweck and her colleagues decide to focus on seventh graders in the study described in the "Motivated to Learn" section?

DISCUSSION QUESTIONS

1. How does a person develop a fixed mind-set or a growth mind-set?

2. Do you believe that praising students' intelligence does more harm than good? Why or why not?

3. Do you think the study would have had different results if it had been conducted in a different area, such as a rural or suburban location? Why?

4. Can a person change from a fixed mind-set into a growth mind-set? How?

5. What can a parent do to create a growth mind-set? What can a teacher or coach do? What can a student do?

6. Is it possible to have a dual mind-set? Explain.

7. Is the IQ test relevant today? Why or why not?

TIP
Use highlighters sparingly. When most of a page is highlighted, essentially nothing is: All you end up with is a brightly colored page. Highlighters also discourage more in-depth annotation. If you have a pen or pencil in your hand instead, you are likely to make notes in the margins.

Annotating While You Read

Strong readers read actively rather than passively. Passive readers scan the words on the page, but after reading a sentence or two, can't remember what they've just read. (Sound familiar?) Active readers, on the other hand, do a number of things to keep them engaged and focused, and to help them understand and remember what they have read. When you listen to a story your friend is telling you, do you find yourself nodding your head and maybe adding comments like "Really? He said that?" or "I know what you mean" or "That's too bad"? If you hear something you don't understand, you probably ask for clarification: "What do you mean you couldn't find your car? Was it gone or had you just forgotten where you parked it?" These are all signs of active listening.

Active readers do the same kinds of things when they read. Although the author isn't present to answer our questions or notice if we are nodding our heads in agreement, by responding in this way—especially in writing, through annotations—we are participating in a conversation. The most common active reading strategy is annotating your text.

ACTIVE READERS ANNOTATE

Annotating—writing in your book in a specific and productive way—may be difficult for you to wrap your mind around, especially if you are a new college student. From elementary school through high school, students are told over and over again not to write in their books. Get ready for a change: The best readers write in their books constantly, and in college your professors will expect you to write in your books. Once you can shift your mind-set into finding this acceptable, you'll see that annotating helps you process and remember information, study for tests, and write papers. There are many ways to annotate, and you will find your own style of annotation with practice.

RECORDING YOUR THOUGHTS ABOUT THE TEXT

Another reason to annotate is to record your ideas as they come to you, particularly the first time you read something. Briefly write your thoughts in the margins near the sentences that inspired your reaction. Do you agree or disagree with what the author has to say? Why? How does the reading make you feel? What does it make you think? Chances are the reading is making you feel something, so start with that.

Recording your honest personal reactions to the text can help you later when you analyze the reading. You often start with an emotional response, but then you think through the reasons for your response.

Sample Reactions

Huh?	Yes! I agree!	No! I disagree!
How can that be?	Exciting!	Losing interest . . .
Really?!	Interesting!	Frustrating!
Lacking support	This sounds like me	I don't think so
Don't get it . . .	Good point	Funny
Confusing	Sad :(	Why?
How?		

Another type of annotation helps you draw connections between your previous experiences and the reading. Readers frequently compare and contrast what the reading says to what they already know. While reading, you may compare people you know to those described in the text. You might also relate information you've learned in other classes or through personal experience to what you are reading.

Sample Connections

Sounds like my brother
Like the theory of motivation from psychology class
Like the Golden Rule—do unto others
Happened to me once—but turned out differently

Connecting the ideas in a reading to other things you have read or studied becomes increasingly helpful as you move on in college. You will get more out of your studies when you see the connections between, for instance, your psychology and English class readings, or your math and business class.

ASKING QUESTIONS ABOUT THE TEXT

Strong readers also make note of any questions they have about the text while annotating. You may think you already know a lot about the topic of the reading, but finding some questions to ask about the text helps you identify what you don't understand and sparks your critical thinking about a topic. Thinking over your questions, talking about them in class, and asking for clarification about them will all increase your comprehension of the text.

Sample Questions

What does "peril" mean?
Can someone have both a fixed and a growth mind-set?
How does she come to that conclusion?
How does this apply to me?

Your instructor will likely ask the class what questions you have about the reading; here's your chance to keep track of those questions.

IDENTIFYING NEW WORDS

▶ For more strategies for learning new words, see Chapter 9, Vocabulary Building.

As part of annotating, make sure to underline or circle any words you don't know. Sometimes you can figure out the meaning of a word by examining the words or phrases near it in the sentence or paragraph; we call this looking at context clues. If you can't figure out a word's meaning this way, look it up in a dictionary and write the meaning in the margin in your own words. Keep a glossary of new vocabulary and key terms in your notebook or make flash cards of important vocabulary words as you read. Every time you see a new vocabulary word, in addition to writing the definition in your own words in the margin, add it to your list or make a flash card for it, and note the page number of your reading or textbook so that you can find it again later if necessary. This is a great way to build your vocabulary.

EXAMPLE OF ANNOTATING

An example of one student's annotations to part of Carol S. Dweck's article "The Perils and Promises of Praise" follows. Note how the student recorded her thoughts, asked questions, and identified new words.

CAROL S. DWECK

The (Perils) and Promises of Praise
(dangers)

The wrong kind of praise creates self-defeating behavior.
The right kind motivates students to learn.

I didn't know there was a wrong kind of praise…?

We often hear these days that we've produced a generation of young people who can't get through the day without an award. They expect success because they're special, not because they've worked hard.

Is this true? Have we inadvertently done something to hold back our students?

I think educators commonly hold two beliefs that do just that. Many believe that (1) praising students' intelligence builds their confidence and motivation to learn, and (2) students' inherent intelligence is the major cause of their achievement in school. Our research has shown that the first belief is false and that the second can be harmful—even for the most competent students.

As a psychologist, I have studied student motivation for more than thirty-five years. My graduate students and I have looked at thousands of children, asking why some enjoy learning, even when it's hard, and why they are resilient in the face of obstacles. We have learned a great deal. Research shows us how to praise students in ways that yield motivation and resilience. In addition, specific interventions can reverse a student's slide into failure during the vulnerable period of adolescence.

Fixed or Malleable? *able to be molded*

Praise is intricately connected to how students view their intelligence. Some students believe that their intellectual ability is a fixed trait. They have a certain amount of intelligence, and that's that. Students with this fixed mind-set become excessively concerned with how smart they are, seeking tasks that will prove their intelligence and avoiding ones that might not (Dweck, 1999, 2006). The desire to learn takes a backseat.

Other students believe that their intellectual ability is something they can develop through effort and education. They don't necessarily believe that anyone can become an Einstein or a Mozart, but they do understand that even Einstein and Mozart had to put in years of effort to become who they were. When students believe that they can develop their intelligence, they focus on doing just that. Not worrying about how smart they will appear, they take on challenges and stick to them (Dweck, 1999, 2006).

More and more research in psychology and neuroscience supports the growth mind-set. We are discovering that the brain has more plasticity over time than we ever imagined (Doidge, 2007); that fundamental aspects of intelligence can be enhanced through learning (Sternberg, 2005); and that dedication and

doesn't it?

really?

expert

able to bounce back

5

true!

what does that mean?

persistence in the face of obstacles are key ingredients in outstanding achievement (Ericsson, Charness, Feltovich, & Hoffman, 2006).

Alfred Binet (1909/1973), the inventor of the IQ test, had a strong growth mind-set. He believed that education could transform the basic capacity to learn. Far from intending to measure fixed intelligence, he meant his test to be a tool for identifying students who were not profiting from the public school curriculum so that other courses of study could be devised to foster their intellectual growth.

interesting!

The Two Faces of Effort

The fixed and growth mind-sets create two different psychological worlds. In the fixed mind-set, students care first and foremost about how they'll be judged: smart or not smart. Repeatedly, students with this mind-set reject opportunities to learn if they might make mistakes (Hong, Chiu, Dweck, Lin, & Wan, 1999; Mueller & Dweck, 1998). When they do make mistakes or reveal deficiencies, rather than correct them, they try to hide them (Nussbaum & Dweck, 2007).

isn't praise/feedback from teachers also important?

They are also afraid of effort because effort makes them feel   10
dumb. They believe that if you have the ability, you shouldn't need effort (Blackwell, Trzesniewski, & Dweck, 2007), that ability should bring success all by itself. This is one of the worst beliefs that students can hold. It can cause many bright students to stop working in school when the curriculum becomes challenging.

I never thought about that—but true!

---

practice it 1.3   Annotating the Text

Ready to try your hand at annotating? Let's review first:

- You've done freewriting on what you think about intelligence, praise, and motivation, key topics Dweck covers in her article.
- You've previewed the text to see how long it is, how it's structured, and what the introduction and conclusion might cover.
- You've learned how to annotate to keep track of your reactions to the text.
- You've learned how to annotate to ask questions of the text and make note of unfamiliar words.

Now, carefully reread Carol S. Dweck's article "The Perils and Promises of Praise," on pages 6–13. Annotate the text by writing your questions and reactions in the margins as you read.

practice it 1.4   Reflecting on Your Reactions and Questions

Now that you have practiced recording your reactions and asking questions of the text in your annotations, share and compare your reactions with other students. Then, on your own, write a one-paragraph reader response that describes your initial thoughts about Dweck's points.

Finding Main Ideas and Supporting Evidence

After you have read and annotated to record your reactions and questions, it's time to identify the main ideas and support in the reading. Well-constructed readings generally have one main idea and support for that idea. Marking these elements in the text as you read will help you understand the text better and recall it more effectively later. An experienced college reader can probably record reactions, ask questions, and read for main ideas—all at the same time. However, for now, we have separated those steps.

WHAT IS THE MAIN IDEA?

Nonfiction essays in a newspaper, magazine, or textbook are generally persuasive or informative, so the main idea will usually be the overall point that the author is trying to get across. We often call this the thesis. Sometimes the thesis is stated directly (this is called an explicit thesis) and can be found right away. In many types of writing, though, the thesis is not clearly indicated. It is not stated directly, but is instead implied, or suggested. It can take some practice to determine the thesis in those cases.

▶ You'll learn more about implied main ideas in Chapter 11, Thesis and Main Idea.

WHAT IS SUPPORT?

Support is the evidence that the author uses to develop and prove the main idea. A reading's main idea is usually broken down into a series of major points, which in turn will be supported by evidence. When you write an essay, you support your main idea or thesis with a variety of information, which is generally made up of facts, details, examples, explanations, statistics, quotations, paraphrases, and anecdotes. To find the support in a reading, look for this kind of information. Often, readers can pick out the examples and evidence and then work backward from there to figure out what main idea the examples illustrate. If that works better for you, especially with those difficult readings where the thesis or main idea is implied rather than stated directly, then begin with the support and work your way backward to the main idea.

▶ For more on paraphrases and anecdotes, see Chapter 4, Revising, Editing, and Proofreading.

HOW DO YOU FIND THE THESIS, MAJOR POINTS, AND SUPPORT IN AN ESSAY OR ARTICLE?

STEP 1: Find the thesis.   Begin by rereading the introduction and conclusion, looking for the main idea. Ask yourself what overall point the author makes or proves. Try to find an explicit thesis in the introduction of the reading. Sometimes it's there; other times, the main idea is nicely summed up in the conclusion.

If you have trouble locating the main idea, perhaps it is not stated explicitly and is only implied. If that's the case, you need to read the text again carefully, asking yourself what the purpose of the reading is. If you can answer that question, you've probably found the main idea. Try to write it in your own words in a sentence or two. Run your ideas by your instructor or classmates to see if they agree and to help you make your ideas more clear.

Another trick for finding the main idea is to look at the title of the article or chapter. If the title is a question, the thesis might be the answer to the question. If the title is not in the form of a question, turn it into a question and see if the answer is the main idea of the reading. For example, Dweck's title "The Perils and Promises of Praise" can be phrased as "What are the perils and promises of praise?"

If you are still having trouble locating the main idea, take your reading to a tutor or visit your instructor during his or her office hours to get help.

▶ **For more about structure, see Chapter 14, Essay Organization and Outlining.**

STEP 2: Find the major points by looking at the structure of the reading.   The reading is probably broken down into chunks of some sort. Are there subheadings dividing sections or just paragraphs? If it is not divided into clear sections, can you determine where the reading shifts from one major point to the next? Can you group the paragraphs together in some way to identify when the author covers one major point and then moves on to a new point? Looking at the structure in this way helps you break the main idea down into smaller parts. You will see how one major point leads to another and to another. All the section or paragraph points together support the overall thesis. Some authors indicate the major points or topics by grouping the paragraphs into sections with headings. These headings can give you a clue about the major points or topics covered.

For example, Dweck's article is divided into the following sections:

Introductory paragraphs
Fixed or Malleable?
The Two Faces of Effort
The Effects of Praise
Motivated to Learn
Going Forward

What major points or topics does Dweck emphasize through these headings?

STEP 3: **Find the main ideas by figuring out the main point of each paragraph.** You can usually figure out the main point of each paragraph by finding the topic sentence. Often, the topic sentence is the first sentence of a paragraph, but sometimes it is elsewhere. The topic sentence is the "umbrella" sentence that all the other sentences relate to or support.

▶ For more on topic sentences, see Chapter 13, Topic Sentences and Paragraphs.

If you can't find a topic sentence, the topic sentence may be in a previous paragraph, or maybe the author hasn't written one. In newspaper or magazine writing, frequently two or three paragraphs support one major point from a previous paragraph. In these cases, finding the topic sentence might mean looking in a preceding paragraph. Some paragraphs, however, have what is called an implied topic sentence, meaning the author did not include it in the paragraph but kept one in mind as the paragraph was written. In these cases, ask yourself what overall point is being made by that paragraph and then write a "nutshell summary" in the margin, jotting it down in a phrase or sentence. Making nutshell summaries for all the paragraphs gives you a rough outline of the whole essay. If you still can't find the main point of the paragraph, move on to the next step, and then work your way backwards to this step again.

When you come to a part of a reading that is hard to understand, it's easier to figure it out if you slow down, figure out the topic sentence or main point of each paragraph, and then put all the topic sentences into your own words. This helps you find and keep track of the major points as you go through the reading. It's like you're building a wooden footbridge, one plank of wood at a time. If you understand this point, and then the next one, and the next one, eventually you will put them all together and understand the whole reading.

Here's a sample student nutshell summary of a short passage from Dweck's article.

Fixed or Malleable?

Praise is intricately connected to how students view their intelligence. Some students believe that their intellectual ability is a fixed trait. They have a certain amount of intelligence and that's that. Students with this fixed mind-set become excessively concerned with how smart they are, seeking tasks that will prove their intelligence and avoiding ones that might not (Dweck, 1999, 2006). The desire to learn takes a backseat.

Other students believe that their intellectual ability is something they can develop through effort and education. They don't necessarily believe that anyone can become an Einstein or a Mozart, but they do understand that even Einstein and Mozart had to put in years of effort to become who they were. When students believe that they can develop their intelligence, they focus on doing just that. Not worrying about how smart they will appear, they take on challenges and stick to them (Dweck, 1999, 2006).

Nutshell Summaries

praise can cause students to think of their intelligence as set in stone

some students don't care how they look—they know they can learn through trying *research shows brains keep growing if we keep trying*

More and more research in psychology and neuroscience supports the growth mind-set. We are discovering that the brain has more plasticity over time than we ever imagined (Doidge, 2007); that fundamental aspects of intelligence can be enhanced through learning (Steinberg, 2005); and that dedication and persistence in the face of obstacles are key ingredients in outstanding achievement (Ericsson, Charness, Feltovich, & Hoffman, 2006).

Binet originally thought of IQ as a way to figure out who needed help, not label people as smart or stupid!

Alfred Binet (1909/1973), the inventor of the IQ test, had a strong growth mind-set. He believed that education could transform the basic capacity to learn. Far from intending to measure fixed intelligence, he meant his test to be a tool for identifying students who were not profiting from the public school curriculum so that other courses of study could be devised to foster their intellectual growth.

STEP 4: **Find the support.**   Underline or make a vertical line in the margin next to any facts, statistics, examples, and quotes. These pieces of evidence probably support a point the author is making. Ask yourself what the author is trying to say about that fact (or statistic or quote). The support can be easier to identify than the main idea, so if you have trouble locating the main idea, you might have better luck by looking for the support first. A good trick is to ask yourself: What does this fact/example/ statistic show? The answer will likely be the thesis or a major point.

In the following paragraphs from Dweck's essay, we have underlined the evidence and examples.

Students were riveted by this information. The idea that their intellectual growth was largely in their hands fascinated them. In fact, even the most disruptive students suddenly sat still and took notice, with the most unruly boy of the lot looking up at us and saying, "You mean I don't have to be dumb?"

Indeed, the growth-mind-set message appeared to unleash students' motivation. Although both groups had experienced a steep decline in their math grades during their first months of junior high, those receiving the growth-mind-set intervention showed a significant rebound. Their math grades improved. Those in the control group, despite their excellent study skills intervention, continued to decline.

STEP 5: **Check your accuracy.**   Look back at your answers to the comprehension and discussion questions that followed the reading. If you skipped any, see if you can answer them now that you have read the article more critically. Compare your ideas about the reading's thesis and main point to the ideas that were raised in the comprehension and discussion questions. Can the questions help you fill in any gaps in your understanding of the article now?

When reading to find the main idea and support, follow the steps and keep working with the text until you get it. Some readings are structured in such a way that the main idea is obvious. With others, you have to work a little harder to figure it out. Let's practice now with Dweck's article "The Perils and Promises of Praise," which you have already read carefully.

---

practice it 1.5   Finding the Main Idea

Follow the steps listed above to find the thesis and main points of "The Perils and Promises of Praise." Try to summarize the main point of each subsection in one sentence. For instance, for the "Fixed or Malleable?" section, you might write, "Some students believe intelligence is fixed, but others believe intelligence can grow and be developed." Write a summary of each section, making sure that your summaries do not just restate the thesis but adequately cover the specific ideas in that section.

Thesis: _____

Main point of "Fixed or Malleable?" section: _____

Main point of "The Two Faces of Effort" section: _____

Main point of "The Effects of Praise" section: _____

Main point of "Motivated to Learn" section: _____

Main point of "Going Forward" section: _____

Compare your ideas with your classmates' responses. If you had very different ideas about the thesis or main points, reread the article with the various responses in mind. Which ideas are a better fit? Why?

Writing a Summary

Being able to summarize a text you have read—or a presentation you have seen, or anything else for that matter—is one of the most funda-mental skills of college life and a very important post-reading strategy. Once you become comfortable writing summaries, you will begin to feel more at ease with college readings. Writing a summary helps you clarify and remember what you read. Summary skills will help you in just about every career too, because summarizing is something you will do pretty much on a daily basis: You might summarize a complex problem for your boss, summarize a patient's symptoms for another doctor or nurse, or summarize your own work for your coworkers or clients.

So what makes a good summary? Good summaries restate in your own words the major points contained in a text. They do not include your opinion or reaction to the text (no "I" statements). They present a lot of complex information in a clear, coherent, brief way. A summary is much shorter than the original and includes only the most important points, not specific details. For example, a one-sentence summary of the story of *Romeo and Juliet* might read:

> William Shakespeare's tragic play *Romeo and Juliet* tells the story of two teenagers in love who end up dying because their families forbid their relationship.

Although the length of your summary will depend on the length of the text you are summarizing, summaries are often a single paragraph. Here is a one-paragraph summary of *Romeo and Juliet*:

> *Romeo and Juliet* is William Shakespeare's tragic play about two teen-agers in love against the wishes of their families. The problem is their families were feuding and wouldn't let them get married, but against their parents' wishes, they got married in secret. After a fight breaks out, Romeo kills Tybalt, Juliet's cousin, and is banned from the city, and Juliet's family wants her to marry another boy, Paris. To avoid having to marry Paris, Juliet fakes her death by drinking a sleeping potion, thinking that she will be able to run away with Romeo after her family mourns her. However, Romeo finds her and, thinking she is really dead, he kills himself. Juliet wakes up from her fake death and sees that Romeo is, in fact, really dead, and so she kills herself for real. The families are distraught and realize that their feud caused these deaths and agree to fight no more.

While this summary isn't perfect, this student did a good job of putting the main points of the play in his own words and staying concise.

HOW DO YOU WRITE A SUMMARY?

STEP 1: **Look at your annotations.**   Skim over any marginal notes that identify the main point of a paragraph or section. Make a list of the main points. (If you skipped annotating for any reason, you will quickly discover how difficult it is to write a summary without a thorough understanding of the reading. You'll have to go back and reread, annotating carefully. Get help from an instructor or a friend if you don't understand the material after several attempts to master it.)

STEP 2: **Make a list of all the key terms.**   This will jog your memory about important points and give you some terminology to use in your summary. For instance, for Dweck's article, you might include words like *fixed mind-set, growth mind-set, resilience, motivation,* and *praise.* This list is not complete, so go ahead now and add other key concept words that you believe are important.

STEP 3: **Draft a summary of the central idea and main points.**   Cover up the text so that you can't see it. Then, in your own words, write down a sentence or two that states the main idea (thesis) of the text. Once you have something written down, look back at the text and see how well you got the author's main idea across and if you have forgotten anything. Skim through your annotations or use your list of main points, and restate the main points in your own words. Look at your list of key terms for ideas of what else to include.

Read your summary over several times to make sure you have included all the main points, have not included details or examples, and have put the author's ideas into your own words. Check to be sure you haven't included your thoughts or opinions. Add and delete as needed until you feel confident about your summary paragraph.

STEP 4: **Write an introductory sentence.**   In your introductory sentence, mention the author's full name and the full title of the original text with a very general statement about the purpose of the text. It might sound something like this:

> In her article "The Perils and Promises of Praise," Carol S. Dweck presents research on how to praise students appropriately to help them become motivated learners.

STEP 5: **Reread and revise.**   Read over and revise your summary a few more times so that it reads smoothly, makes sense, and is entirely in your own words. Try reading it out loud, too, to catch any errors you might have made. Realize that everyone will summarize a reading slightly differently, though all summaries should include the same major points.

practice it 1.6   Writing a Summary

Follow the preceding steps to write a summary of "The Perils and Promises of Praise." Then use the summary checklist that follows to help you revise it.

summary checklist

☐ Does the summary include the full name of the article and the full name of the author?

☐ Is the summary an objective statement of Dweck's ideas, rather than a subjective response (your opinions, thoughts, or feelings)? Remember, you shouldn't use "I" in a summary.

continued ❯

☐ Does it have an introductory sentence that states the main idea of the text in your own words?

☐ Does it use the vocabulary words and key concepts from the text, such as *fixed mind-set* and other words?

☐ Does it include all the major points of the reading? Is it missing any important points? What more should be included?

☐ Does the summary go into too much detail anywhere? What could be cut?

☐ Does the paragraph feel coherent and finished? How might you make it better?

---

practice it 1.7   Bringing a College Mind-Set to Writing

In this chapter, you have been introduced to some fundamental reading and writing skills, and you have read Dweck's research on student motivation. Now you can put those skills and ideas into practice by writing a short essay for one of the following assignments:

1. Examine your experiences as a student. Do you think you have a fixed or growth mind-set? In explaining why, be sure to discuss what messages you have received from others (teachers, parents, peers) about your potential, as well as how you have responded when faced with challenges in school.
2. Write about a time you have been resilient and adopted a growth mind-set in the face of adversity. Describe what happened, and then explain how you might apply that life lesson to your future academic success.

---

chapter review

In the following chart, fill in the second column to record in your own words the important skills included in this chapter. Then assess yourself to determine whether you are still developing the skill or feel you have mastered it. If you are still developing the skill, make some notes about what you need to work on to master it in the future. If you believe you have already mastered it, explain why.

Skills and concepts covered in this chapter	Explanation in your own words	I'm developing this skill and need to work on . . .	I believe I have mastered this skill because . . .
Pre-reading			
Annotating			
Finding main ideas and supporting evidence			
Writing a summary			

2

Active and Critical Reading

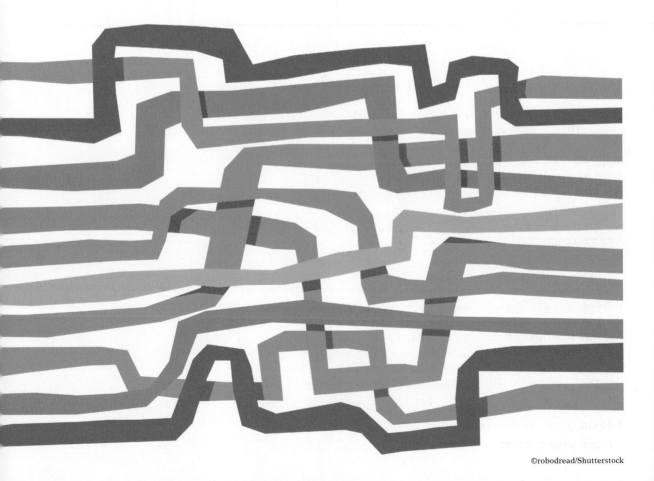

©robodread/Shutterstock

Chapter 1 introduced a few key strategies for college-level reading and writing: pre-reading, annotating, and summarizing. Chapter 2 gives you more practice with those skills and adds new techniques, as you move from comprehending and summarizing your readings to reading them critically. To practice all of these skills, you'll work with a number of reading selections on the topics of financial literacy (an understanding of personal money topics, like saving, budgeting, and planning), money, and wealth.

LaunchPad Solo
macmillan learning

Visit **LaunchPad Solo for Readers and Writers > Active Reading** and **Critical Reading** for extra practice in the skills covered in this chapter.

---

practice it 2.1 Previewing the Chapter

Take a few minutes to preview this chapter. Note its content, structure, and features. What can you learn from the titles of the readings? How do the opening pages of this chapter help you predict the topic, audience, and purpose? What do you already know about financial literacy? Overall, what do you expect to learn about critical reading or the other topics covered in this chapter? Make a list of your predictions.

Reading Critically

Reading critically means reading closely, asking questions, and thinking about what you're reading. Critical reading helps you move beyond merely understanding (or comprehending) what authors are saying; it helps you analyze how they say it and evaluate whether or not they do a good job. When you read and think critically, you analyze by looking at how the author established the text's purpose, argument, evidence, and audience. You also evaluate the text when you establish your own opinion about how well the author achieved his or her purpose in writing. Analyzing and evaluating prepare you to write essays about what you have read, and they are skills that strong readers practice regularly.

For most essays that you write in college, you read about or research a topic extensively before writing about it. These readings will give you substantial information and background knowledge on a topic, but in most cases the writing you do in response has to go beyond merely reporting this information. Instead, you will be expected to contribute your own ideas on the topic, joining the conversation that the articles and books have already begun.

The good news is that in Chapter 1 you already learned and practiced several key steps necessary for getting into conversation with other texts:

- Taking stock of what you already know
- Previewing the text

- Annotating to respond, ask questions, identify and define new words, and find main ideas and support
- Summarizing the text you have read

The next step to learn and practice is how to read critically by analyzing or evaluating the strengths and weaknesses of a piece of writing. Using the strategies described in the following paragraphs will help you do so.

Reading With and Against the Grain

READ WITH THE GRAIN

You bring some relevant ideas and opinions to most of the reading that you do. Critical college readers are open-minded and consider the strengths and weaknesses of a piece of writing, whether they agree or disagree with some (or all) of its ideas. To read with the grain, try to share the author's point of view (or that of people likely to agree with him or her) as much as possible. Whether you personally agree, disagree, or are neutral on the topic at hand, reading with the grain helps you understand the topic as your author sees it, and possibly enrich or even alter your perspective on it.

To read with the grain, assume the author is a reasonable person, and ask yourself why he or she takes a particular position. Why is the position compelling and the support convincing? Even if you remain unconvinced of the author's main point, trying to read with the grain makes it more likely that you will honestly acknowledge any solid supporting points, examples, or evidence the author includes. If you're still unconvinced of the main idea but you do find some interesting evidence, ask yourself whether this evidence would support a slightly different point from the one the author is making. In other words, is there common ground to be found between your perspective and the author's perspective? Take notes on what you discover.

If you already agree with an author's main point, it won't be very difficult for him or her to win you over. Most likely, you will find the evidence and examples very convincing because you already see things from the same perspective; however, that doesn't necessarily mean the author has done a great job of making his or her case in writing.

READ AGAINST THE GRAIN

To read against the grain, read the text skeptically—that is, read it as if you don't agree with the author's point. This will give you a better perspective when evaluating how well the author has supported his or her points and whether the author offers credible support or evidence. Try to see things from a viewpoint different from or opposite to that of the author. Ask critical questions of the text. Is the support provided convincing? Has the author left out important points or perspectives? Does the author have any hidden bias or preexisting beliefs about the subject matter that influence the way he or she presents it? As always, take notes on your responses to the text.

COMPARE YOUR NOTES

After making serious efforts to read both with and against the grain, compare your notes on each approach. These notes will help you do a thorough job of thinking critically about the strengths and weaknesses of the text as a whole. Form a careful response to each of the following questions:

- Does the main idea represent a reasonable perspective on the topic?
- Is the evidence used to support the main idea persuasive and credible? Is there enough evidence to support the point?
- Does the author have any biases that you can detect, or is the material fairly and objectively presented?

As usual, save these notes and ideas; they come in handy when you start to write your own essay.

> **practice it 2.2**   Reading With and Against the Grain
>
> Here is a short passage from the magazine article "Teach Your Children the Building Blocks of Finance," by Sherie Holder and Kenneth Meeks (the complete article appears on p. 35). Read this passage from the middle of the article, and then follow the steps listed.
>
> **Show children how to pay bills.** With so many people paying bills online, this is an opportunity to get children involved. Show them how money is deposited into an account, and how you're subtracting from those dollars to pay your obligations for gas, the lights, and food.
>
> [Single-mother Yvette] Saul discusses her finances with her daughter because it gives her a better sense of household expenses. When Saul receives her paycheck, she sits down with [her daughter] Savannah on a monthly basis and explains her income and the expenses she has to meet. "I would sit down with Savannah every month when I pay my bills and she
>
> *continued* ❯

would pull out her calculator and start adding things up. It becomes like a game to her but her thought process is moving."

According to [certified financial planner Gwendolyn] Kirkland, this is good for children to see. "This makes it real to the children—the specific dollars you have left in your account," says Kirkland. "This instills an appreciation for what it takes to run a household." Savannah sees exactly where her mother's money is going.

STEP 1: Read the paragraphs "with the grain." Look for the strengths in what Holder and Meeks write. What examples do they use that you find particularly persuasive? In the margin of the page, make some annotations commenting on the points, examples, or evidence. An example of a "with the grain" comment might be: "This is a good real-life example of managing money."

STEP 2: Reread the paragraphs "against the grain." Now, look again at the same paragraphs, but this time try to poke holes in the ideas. Are there places where the authors have not provided enough explanation or examples? Are their points well supported? If not, what other information might you need to be convinced to see things from their point of view? Can you detect any bias in the writing? Make some annotations in the right-hand margin pointing out what might be flaws or weaknesses in the presentation of the material. An example of an "against the grain" comment might be: "Young children shouldn't be stressed out by their family's finances. Let them be kids."

STEP 3: Compare your notes. Now, compare your notes from reading with and against the grain (the left and right margins), and make a list of the strengths and weaknesses of this particular passage.

Readings on Money, Wealth, and Financial Literacy

Money drives many of our decisions and behaviors, from what we eat for breakfast to what we choose to do with our lives. Even those people who choose their life paths without considering how much money they'll make, like monks and artists, do so partly because they understand how money influences us. For those millions of people who live at or near the poverty level and want to do better, money is certainly one of the major concerns of daily life. Even middle-class people often struggle to live happily within their means—to spend less than they make and put some money aside for emergencies. Financial well-being isn't important only for individuals, either. A healthy economy is important for all of us, and when our national and global economies are in trouble, our local communities suffer too.

Despite the importance of money in our personal lives and our society at large, many of us have major misconceptions about money and wealth. Few students are offered financial management courses in grade school or high school. Many Americans—even highly educated ones—are financially illiterate. We might confuse the cost of an item with its value. We might struggle to figure out the relationship between money and happiness. We might have no meaningful information about how to save and spend. These problems affect many Americans, no matter how much money they actually have in the bank—or at home in a sock drawer.

The readings in this unit invite you to think about what money and wealth mean to you personally and to Americans as a group. These resources provide some factual information about the basics of the economy and personal finance, ask you to think about your own priorities and values, and challenge you to consider the philosophical issues surrounding money and our world.

To get the most out of the collection of texts that follow, annotate them using the steps outlined in Chapter 1 (pp. 14–16). Your annotations will help you answer the questions and complete the activities that follow each reading. Remember to read with and against the grain as you annotate.

---

practice it 2.3 Considering What You Already Know

Below is a list of pre-reading questions for you to answer, either in your notebook or in group discussion, to determine your knowledge of, and biases about, money.

- What are your own experiences with money? What do you wish for yourself in terms of money? What sacrifices might you be willing to make to attain your goals?

- How have the costs of college surprised you? What resources are you using to pay for college?

- Do you know people who have money troubles? What are some obvious causes of those troubles? What are some of the underlying causes?

- How is money represented in the media? What television shows or movies have you seen that focus on money and wealth? What sorts of messages do those examples send to their audiences?

continued ❯

- What do you know about how our economy works? List the economic terms that you can define or that you want to know more about.

- How have you learned about money? How have you learned about the economy?

- What does it mean to be wealthy or poor? What characteristics do you use to determine someone's economic status?

MAGAZINE

This article is from the magazine *Black Enterprise*, which offers news and advice about business and personal finance for African American entre-preneurs. This particular article (published on February 6, 2006) uses real-life people as examples to illustrate its points. The authors, Sherie Holder and Kenneth Meeks, are freelance writers who have written other articles as well as several books on topics ranging from NASCAR to racial profiling. Since writing this article, Meeks has become a supervising editor for *Black Enterprise*.

Some difficult words and phrases are noted in the margins. Look up the ones you don't know, and write their definitions in your own words in the space provided. The first one has been done for you.

practice it 2.4 Pre-Reading

Before you begin reading, do the following:

- **Look at the layout of the article.** Consider the pictures, headings, bolded lines, and other graphic features. What do they tell you about the topic, audience, and purpose of the article?

- **Note your first impression.** Do you want to read this article? Why or why not? Write down your feelings in the margins near the top of the article.

- **Think about your own knowledge, experience, and biases.** Do you believe in giving children allowances or not? Did your parent(s) tell you much about the family finances when you were growing up? Why or why not? How well did your older family members teach you about managing money? What could they have done differently? Freewrite for five minutes on these questions in your notebook.

- **Turn the title into a question.** For example, you might ask, "How can you teach your children the building blocks of finance?" or "Why should you teach your children the building blocks of finance?" As you read, look to see how and where the authors attempt to answer your question.

SHERIE HOLDER AND KENNETH MEEKS

Teach Your Children the Building Blocks of Finance

As a thirty-seven-year-old single mother, Yvette Saul knows that the key to her financial empowerment starts with her ability to create and maintain a savings initiative and to adequately manage her family's finances. And while she didn't learn this as a child, she is determined to make sure that her eleven-year-old daughter, Savannah Gay, learns the concept of proper money management. By educating her daughter at an early age, Saul is ensuring that little Savannah is more inclined to practice sound budgeting as she gets older. In doing so, Saul is adopting Declaration of Financial <u>Empowerment</u> principle No. 7: to provide access to programs that will educate my children about business and finance.

empowerment: *the giving of power*

"It's extremely important for me to teach her about money and financial planning," says Saul. "Although money is not the root of happiness, it certainly is the pathway to happiness by being fiscally responsible as an adult."

In a <u>turbulent</u> economic environment, and with the uncertain future of Social Security, it's even more important that parents pass on the basics of personal finance. The learning

©Steve Widoff, Widoff Photo

Saul and her daughter, Savannah, meet regularly to discuss financial matters.

turbulent:

process should start when you're a child. Parents have to teach children the value of money and guide them in their spending, encourage them to save, explore <u>entrepreneurship</u> opportunities, and expose them to solid financial planning. By using a few of the principles found in our Black Wealth Initiative, we offer you a step-by-step guide to help start your children down the right path.

entrepreneurship:

Open a savings account and show children how to save. Since the age of five, when Savannah opened her first savings account with $100, she has been on a path toward saving and money management. And while she is <u>tucking</u> away 40% of her $20 weekly allowance into a savings account, Savannah is following DOFE principle No. 2: to save and invest 10% to 15% of my after-tax income. Savannah has spent some of the money while on family vacations and on other personal items. She currently has about $700 in her account. According to New York City–based financial consultant Ivanhoe Ffriend, of Ffriend

tucking:

underscore:

budget:

credit:

overextended:

cornerstone:

Enterprises, parents cannot underscore enough the importance of exposing their children to the sacrifices that go into planning the family budget. The value of money can be taught early on by teaching children how to bargain shop or collect coupons.

Teach children to respect the value of money. A child's attitude toward money will determine how he or she uses it in life, according to Laura Levine, executive director of Jumpstart Coalition, a Washington, D.C.–based national organization that develops standards to teach kids about finance in grades K–12. "A lot of times it's a value decision, but we encourage parents to include a lesson at home that teaches their children about the value of money."   5

Inspire children to budget. Getting children to track their own spending is a great way to start and follow DOFE principle No. 4: to engage in sound budget, credit, and tax management practices. Parents might have to give children an incentive to keep track of their expenses, such as a financial reward or a day off from chores. Showing them the importance of budgeting for items they need versus spending extravagantly is critical.

"Children must realize that there is an inflow and an outflow of money and you don't want the outflow to be greater than the inflow or else we become financially overextended," says Gwendolyn Kirkland, a certified financial planner at Kirkland, Turnbo & Associates, in Chicago. "A budget establishes financial boundaries. So when they're asking for different things, parents can say they either budgeted or they didn't budget for it."

Encourage children under the age of eight to divide money into different categories. Perhaps they should have one piggy bank for saving and another piggy bank for spending. By the time your child turns nine, talk to him or her about creating a small budget to keep track of income and expenses. Teenagers should already understand the basics of personal finance and budgeting and be allowed to make their own financial decisions, with your guidance. By then, budgets should be a cornerstone of their money management.

The Lipfords encourage their children to earn money rather than receive an allowance.

©Keith Lanpher Photography

Plant the seeds of entrepreneurship. Not all children receive weekly allowances. When Angelina and Marvin Lipford, of Hampton, Virginia, were married twenty years ago, they entered into their marriage carting around $15,000 to $20,000 worth of credit card and student loan debt. They spent the first five years of their marriage paying off the debt along with the accompanying high interest rates. The couple was determined to keep their three children from falling into the same trap.

Knowing the financial sacrifices they had to make early in their marriage, the Lipfords are making sure their three children keep a tight rein on their finances and avoid the same pitfalls. They have an eighteen-year-old daughter, Jasmine, who is attending Howard University on a basketball scholarship; a fifteen-year-old son, Marvin Jr., who is a sophomore in high school; and a nine-year-old, Nehemiah. A natural progression in teaching their children the building blocks of finances was to encourage their children to either work, as Jasmine had done before going to college, or to start their own business. Instead of giving their children allowances, the Lipfords encouraged them to earn their own money by doing chores around the house. It was on a pay-per-work arrangement. And if the children asked their parents for additional money, they were required to pay their parents back with interest.

This arrangement encouraged Marvin Jr. to earn money on his own. In 2002, he took the financial and entrepreneurial lessons he learned from attending a weeklong financial camp to cut grass during the summer months using his father's lawn mower. This past summer, he charged $20 a yard and earned $1,000, which he put into his savings account.

Show children how to pay bills. With so many people paying bills online, this is an opportunity to get children involved. Show them how money is deposited into an account, and how you're subtracting from those dollars to pay your obligations for gas, the lights, and food.

Saul discusses her finances with her daughter because it gives her a better sense of household expenses. When Saul receives her paycheck, she sits down with Savannah on a monthly basis and explains her income and the expenses she has to meet. "I would sit down with Savannah every month when I pay my bills and she would pull out her calculator and start adding things up. It becomes like a game to her but her thought process is moving."

According to Kirkland, this is good for children to see. "This makes it real to the children—the specific dollars you have left in your account," says Kirkland. "This instills an appreciation for what it takes to run a household." Savannah sees exactly where her mother's money is going.

Expose your children to investing. Many people can go online to monitor their 401(k) account, change the contribution they make, and change their asset allocation. This is an excellent time to introduce children to this concept.

Kirkland suggests getting children to invest early and to invest in what they know or what they use. As an example of practicing DOFE principle No. 6: to be proactive and knowledgeable about investing, money management, and consumer issues, Kirkland suggests giving stock as a gift to children when they turn twelve. "If it's something that they wear, they want, they eat, something

rein:

instills:

proactive:

10

15

custodial account:

tax-deferred:

defer:

parliamentary:

that they can relate to, buying stock in that company introduces them to the concept of ownership. You own a part of this company."

While parents will have to open a custodial account for children under eighteen, the process of doing it together exposes young people to investing.

Kirkland suggests introducing children to other tax-deferred investment vehicles, such as a 529 Plan. "While control of the 529 Plan rests with the parents, the benefit is that it is tax-deferred," he explains. "One of the things a child will learn early on is that wherever it is legitimate, they should defer taxes as much as possible, so they can have more income in the future."

Hold family financial meetings. On a regular basis, parents should hold meetings where family finances are discussed. Go over spending habits with your children. Examine how they track their spending and what they spend money on. Let the kids explain why they are making certain purchases, and make the total family finances a discussion with input from everyone. Use the same principles, standards, and parliamentary procedures that a board of directors in any multimillion-dollar corporation might use. This is the meeting where you, as a family, map out long-term and short-term financial goals and develop strategies to accomplish those goals. This is also a good time to invite a professional financial planner to attend and let him or her offer individual professional help.

These are but a few of the tips to teach your children about money manage- 20 ment. There are other everyday practices you can do, from reading the business or money section of the local newspaper with your children, to watching television programs that follow the market and our national economy. Have discussions about what's in the financial news. It's important to do something that puts your children on the correct path to good money management. And as always, follow the coverage of our Black Wealth Initiative. For a Wealth Building Kit or to open a ShareBuilder Custodial Account for your child (an online brokerage account), visit blackenterprise.com.

▶ **For more on audience and purpose, see Chapter 7, Audience, Purpose, and Topic.**

practice it 2.5 Post-Reading

Review the article again and underline any particular sentences that indicate that the audience for this article is parents. Without the images and the title, how clear is the intended audience? What types of words and examples reveal the intended audience?

COMPREHENSION QUESTIONS

1. What is Social Security?

2. What is a 401(k)?

3. What does "financial empowerment" mean?

4. What does "entrepreneurship" mean?

5. According to the article, what are the best ways to teach children about money?

DISCUSSION QUESTIONS

1. Why do many parents prefer not to discuss their finances with their children?

2. Do you think children should be given a set allowance for doing regular chores, or should they earn money for each individual chore? Why?

3. Who else outside of the intended audience for this article might find the information helpful or interesting?

4. Why do you think the article begins with the story of Yvette Saul?

5. Besides the personal examples, what other types of evidence does the article include? What pieces of evidence do you find most convincing?

6. The article refers to the "Declaration of Financial Empowerment" but never explains it. How does the context of the article help you determine what this is?

TEXTBOOK

For All Practical Purposes: Mathematical Literacy in Today's World is a leading introductory college mathematics textbook for liberal arts students with a focus on applied mathematics and mathematical literacy. The text is cowritten by members of COMAP, the Consortium for Mathematics and Its Applications. The following chapter was authored by Paul J. Campbell, a professor of mathematics at Beloit College in Wisconsin. This excerpt covers some key components of financial literacy, including explanations of simple and compound interest.

practice it 2.6   Pre-Reading

As a math textbook chapter, this reading selection applies algebra to real-world situations. Preview the textbook excerpt and then brainstorm a list of all the ways you use math in your everyday life. Spend about five to ten minutes generating this list, and be sure to think outside the box.

22

Borrowing Models

Paul J. Campbell

I n the previous chapter, we looked at consumer financial models for saving and formulas for calculating the amount accumulated. Savings or investments would not earn interest unless they could be loaned to someone to make productive use of the money.

In this chapter, we examine the other side of consumer finance—borrowing. You may have a student loan, you are likely going to need to borrow (or have already borrowed) to buy a car, you will almost certainly borrow if you buy a house or apartment, and you are borrowing if you use a credit card. For any such loan, you pay "finance charges," which include interest and perhaps other "fees" as well. We investigate and compare some common kinds of loans.

Section 22.1 (re)acquaints you briefly with simple interest, while Section 22.2 does the same with compound interest, in the contexts of student loans and credit cards. Section 22.3 considers "conventional" loans (such as the mortgage on a house), reviews the savings formula from Chapter 21, and derives from it the formula for the payment on a conventional loan. Finally, Section 22.4 investigates annuities, one of the ways that you can receive the grand prize in a lottery and a way of providing for retirement and old age. If you have a grasp of the ideas behind compound interest and can use the compound interest formula (page 772) and the savings formula (page 781), which we repeat shortly for your convenience, you can proceed with this chapter without first reading Chapter 21.

22.1 Simple Interest

The amount of **interest** charged on a loan is determined by the **principal**, by the amount borrowed, and by the method used to calculate the interest. With **simple interest**, the borrower pays a fixed amount of interest for each period of the loan. The interest rate is usually quoted as an annual rate.

For a principal P and an annual rate of interest r, the interest owed after t years is

$$I = Prt$$

and the total amount A due on the loan is

$$A = P(1 + rt)$$

EXAMPLE 1
Simple Interest on a Federal Direct Student Loan

The U.S. Department of Education offers Stafford Federal Direct Loans to students to use for tuition, fees, housing, and textbooks (such as this one), with repayment deferred until after graduation. For students with financial need, subsidized loans are available, at a lower interest rate (3.40% for 2011–2012), and the federal government pays the interest while the student is in school, unemployed, or experiencing economic hardship.

However, any eligible student can take out an unsubsidized Stafford loan, at 6.8% interest, in which interest is charged from when you receive the loan until it is repaid in full. One option is to pay each quarter the interest due, and defer paying back the principal until six months (the "grace period") after you leave school.

Suppose that you took out an unsubsidized Stafford loan for $5500 (the maximum amount for a first-year student) on September 1, 2011, before your freshman year and you plan to pay the interest as you go and begin paying back the principal on December 1, 2015, after graduating on June 1, 2015 (so you will have had the loan for 4 years + 3 months = 51 months).

How much is the monthly interest, how much total interest will you have paid over the 51 months, and how much will you owe when you start to pay back the loan?

SOLUTION We have $P = \$5500$ and $r = 6.8\% = 0.068$, and for one quarter, we have $t = 0.25$ years. So the interest for one quarter is $I = Prt = \$5500 \times 0.068 \times 0.25 = \$93.50$. Over the 51 months (17 quarters), you will have paid $17 \times \$93.50 = \$1589.50$; and you still will owe the original principal of $5500. If you had not paid the interest as you went along, you would owe the principal of $5500 plus the accumulated simple interest of $1589.50, for a total of $7089.50. (Actually, the amount of a quarterly payment varies slightly with the number of days since the previous payment.)

22.2 Compound Interest

Compounding is the calculation of interest on interest. A common example is the balance on a credit card. So long as there is an outstanding balance, the interest owed is calculated on the entire balance, including any part of it that was previously calculated as interest and added to the balance in earlier months.

EXAMPLE 2
Credit Card Interest

Suppose that you owe $1000 on your credit card, the company charges 1.5% interest per month, and you just let the balance ride. How much interest do you pay in the first year?

SOLUTION Your interest the first month is 1.5% of $1000, or $0.015 \times \$1000 = \$15$. The new balance owed is $(1 + 0.015) \times \$1000 = \$1015$. Your interest the second month is not 1.5% of $1000, or $15 (as would be the case for simple interest), but 1.5% of $1015, or $0.015 \times \$1015 = \$15.23$. Therefore, the new balance for the second month is

$$(1 + 0.015) \times \$1015 = \$(1 + 0.015) \times (1 + 0.015) \times \$1000 = \$1030.23$$

rounded (up) to the nearest cent. (We are not factoring in the extra charges for your failure to make minimum payments, which would add up pretty fast!) After 12 months of letting the balance ride, it becomes

$$(1.015)^{12} \times \$1000 = \$1195.62$$

(where we neglect the rounding of interest to the nearest cent that occurs at each billing). In other words, the actual interest for the year comes to $195.62, which is 19.562% of $1000. So, although the quoted rate of interest is 1.5% per month, which seems as if it should amount to $12 \times 1.5 = 18\%$ per year, the effective interest rate is actually greater. (Actually, credit cards charge interest by the day, so the interest rate for a month will vary with the number of days in the month.)

We apply two formulas from Chapter 21: the **compound interest formula** (page 772) and the **savings formula** (page 781), phrasing them for loans. Here is the compound interest formula, followed by an example:

Compound Interest Formula   RULE

If a principal P is loaned at interest rate i per compounding period, then after n compounding periods (with no repayment), the amount owed is

$$A = P(1 + i)^n$$

This formula just generalizes what we saw happen with the credit card balance. We give the formula in a slightly more elaborate version below, to make the connection to multiple compoundings per year.

General Compound Interest Formula   RULE

For a principal P loaned

- at a nominal annual rate of interest rate r
- with m compounding periods per year (so the interest rate $i = r/m$ per compounding period), the amount owed
- after t years (hence $n = mt$ compounding periods) with no payment of interest or principal is

$$A = P(1 + i)^n = P\left(1 + \frac{r}{m}\right)^{mt}$$

EXAMPLE 3
Not Repaying a Guaranteed Student Loan

Before July 1, 2010, another kind of student loan was available (and you may have one). That was a "federal guaranteed student loan," under which you got your loan not from the government but from a bank. If you failed to pay back the loan, the bank was paid by the federal government instead. (In other words, the bank charged an origination fee for the loan and then earned interest on it with no risk to the bank; because this arrangement did not seem fair, the Obama administration abolished this kind of loan.)

With a guaranteed student loan, if you do not make the payments due, the interest continues to accumulate and is usually *capitalized* every quarter. That means that the interest during each quarter is simple interest on the amount due at the beginning of the quarter, and at the end of the quarter, that interest is added to the amount due. In other words, the compounding period is one quarter.

Suppose that six months after you graduate, when you begin to have to make payments on your student loans, you owe $5000 on your guaranteed student loan at 6.8% interest per year. However, you aren't able to find a job, so you fail to make any payments for the next nine months. (This would be very foolish, since after 270 days of nonpayment, the loan would be in default and all kinds of bad things would happen!) How much would you owe then?

SOLUTION The principal P is $5000. The quarterly interest rate is $i = 6.8\%/4 = 1.7\%$ and there are $n = 3$ compounding periods. The compound interest formula gives the amount owed as $A = \$5000(1 + 0.017)^3 = \$5259.36$.

Terminology for Loan Rates

The interest on a loan depends on whether compounding is done and how the interest is calculated. Just like the Truth in Savings Act mentioned in Chapter 21 (on page 771), the Truth in Lending Act establishes terminology and calculation methods for interest.

A **nominal rate** is any stated rate of interest for a specified length of time. For instance, a nominal rate could be a 1.5% monthly rate on a credit card balance. By itself, such a rate does not indicate or take into account whether or how often interest is compounded.

The **effective rate** *takes into account compounding.* It is the rate of simple interest that would realize exactly as much interest over the same period of time.

We saw that $1000 at a yearly interest rate of 18% (a nominal rate), calculated as 1.5% per month compounded monthly, yields $195.62 in interest owed at the end of the year, which is 19.562% of the original principal. Hence, the effective annual rate is 19.562%. In other words, a $1000 loan at simple interest of 19.562% for one year would owe exactly the same interest.

Finally, when stated per year ("annualized"), the effective rate is called the **effective annual rate**. (In connection with savings, the effective annual rate is the annual percentage yield of Chapter 21, discussed on page 771.)

To keep the rates straight, we use i for a nominal rate for the specified **compounding period**—such as a day, month, or year—*within which no compounding is done*; this rate is the effective rate for that length of time. For a nominal rate compounded m times per year, we have $i = r/m$. For that $1000 credit card balance at 18% compounded monthly, we have $r = 18\%$ and $m = 12$, so $i = 1.5\%$ per month.

The Truth in Lending Act introduced the term **annual percentage rate (APR)**.

Annual Percentage Rate (APR)   DEFINITION

The **annual percentage rate (APR)** is the number of compounding periods per year times the rate of interest per compounding period:

$$APR = m \times i$$

In the example of the credit card balance, the interest is compounded monthly, or $m = 12$ times per year, and the interest rate for the compounding period is $i = 1.5\%$, so the APR is $12 \times 1.5\% = 18\%$. The APR is the rate that the Truth in Lending Act requires the lender to disclose to the borrower. *The APR is not the effective annual rate* (as we have already seen in the credit card example).

REVIEW VOCABULARY

Adjustable-rate mortgage (ARM) A loan whose interest rate can vary during the course of the loan. (p. 815)

Amortization payment formula The formula for installment loans that relates the principal P, the interest rate i per compounding period, the payment d at the end of each period, and the number of compounding periods n needed to pay off the loan:

$$d = P\left[\frac{i}{1 - (1 + i)^{-n}}\right], \ P = d\left[\frac{1 - (1 + i)^{-n}}{i}\right]. \quad \text{(p. 811)}$$

Amortize To repay in regular installments. (p. 809)

Annual percentage rate (APR) The number of compounding periods per year times the rate of interest per compounding period. (p. 808)

Effective annual rate (EAR) The effective rate per year. (p. 808)

Effective rate The actual percentage rate, taking into account compounding. (p. 808)

Equity The amount of principal of a loan that has been repaid. (p. 813)

Interest Money charged on a loan. (p. 805)

Life income annuity An annuity with regular payments for as long as you live. (p. 818)

Nominal rate A stated rate of interest for a specified length of time; a nominal rate does not take into account any compounding. (p. 808)

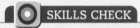

SKILLS CHECK

1. The interest charged on Federal Direct Stafford Loans is

(a) simple interest.
(b) compounded daily.
(c) compounded quarterly.

2. If you borrow $1000 at 5% interest per year, compounded quarterly, and pay back the principal and interest after four years, the amount that you pay back is _____.

13. The Truth in Lending Act requires that borrowers be told the

(a) APY of the loan.
(b) APR of the loan.
(c) effective annual rate of the loan.

14. Your credit union offers to finance a $6000 conventional loan at 4% to be repaid in four years of monthly payments. Your monthly payment is _____.

CHAPTER 22 EXERCISES
■ *Challenge* ▲ *Discussion*

22.1 Simple Interest

1. Suppose that you take out an unsubsidized Stafford loan on September 1 before your senior year for $7500 (the maximum allowed) and plan to begin paying it back on December 1 after graduation (so you will have had the loan for 15 months, including the six-month grace period after leaving school). The interest rate is 6.8%. How much will you owe then, and how much of that will be interest?

2. Assume the same situation as in Exercise 1, but you borrow $7500 on September 1 before your junior year and plan to begin paying it back on December 1 after graduation and grace period 27 months later. How much will you owe then, and how much of that will be interest?

3. Suppose that you borrow $5500 for your first year and $6500 for your second year (the maximum amounts), as unsubsidized Stafford loans. Suppose that each loan begins on September 1 of its year, that you finish college in four years, and that you begin repayment on December 1 after graduation. What is your total debt then, and how much of that is interest?

4. Assume the same situation in Exercise 3, but you also borrow $7500 for each of your third and fourth years (again, the maximum amounts), again on September 1. You finish college in four years, and you begin repayment on December 1 after graduation. What is your total debt then, and how much of that is interest?

22.2 Compound Interest

5. If you borrowed $15,000 to buy a new car at 4.9% interest per year, compounded annually, and paid back all the principal and interest at the end of 5 years, how much would you pay back?

6. Assume the same situation as in Exercise 5, but the interest is compounded monthly.

7. If you borrowed $200,000 to buy a house at 6% interest per year, compounded annually, and paid back the principal and interest at the end of 30 years, how much would you pay back?

8. Assume the same situation as in Exercise 7, but the interest is compounded monthly (this is the usual case).

9. A recent credit card bill of mine showed an APR of 17.24%.

(a) What is the corresponding daily interest rate (the bank uses a 365-day year for this purpose)?
(b) What is the effective annual rate?

10. I received an offer for a credit card with 0% fixed APR for the first 12 months, followed by one of several rates depending on credit history. The highest was a 22.74% APR (and the company reserves the right to change the APR "at any time for any reason").

(a) What is the corresponding daily interest rate for the 22.74% APR?
(b) What is the effective annual rate?

►W WRITING PROJECTS

1. Locate current advertised incentives for a car that you would consider buying and compare them in an essay of two to three pages. For each option, give the price, the interest rate, the term, and how much interest you would pay over the course of the loan.

2. A substantial proportion of new cars today are not sold but leased. Contact a local car dealer about a car that you are interested in and find out the details on leasing. Compare the cost of the lease and associated expenses with the cost of purchasing and owning the car. Include estimated maintenance, repair, and insurance costs for each option. Which seems like a better deal, and why? Consult the "Suggested Web Sites" section at the end of this chapter. Write two to three pages describing and comparing the two options.

3. Banks often offer choices of mortgages with various combinations of interest rates and "points." A point is 1% of the mortgage amount. Points are paid to "buy down" the interest rate for the mortgage; they are paid upfront to

the bank at the closing of the house sale. For example, you may have a choice between a mortgage at 6% with 2 points (2%) and a mortgage at 8% and no points. Which would you choose, and why? Does it make a difference how long you are planning to own the home? Or how expensive the home is? Write a page justifying your decision.

4. One of the advantages of buying a home with a fixed-rate mortgage is that your payment stays the same but your earnings and the value of your home are likely to go up with inflation. You are paying back the loan with dollars of lesser value.

Consider the following scenario. Suppose that you buy a "starter" two-bedroom home for $105,000 under a special program for first-time home-buyers that requires a down payment of only $5000. You have a 30-year fixed-rate mortgage for $100,000 at 7%, on which the monthly payment is $665.30. You also have a $2000 one-time expense in closing costs and annual costs of $200 for insurance and $2000 for property taxes.

You live in the home for five years and spend $10,000 on maintenance, upkeep, and improvements. You then sell the home for $125,000, pay a realtor $9000 to sell it, and pay closing costs of $500 (for title insurance and other costs). Finally, it costs $3000 to move.

(a) Make out a balance sheet of revenue and expenses. How did you make out on owning the home?

(b) Remember that you also got to live in the home without paying rent. Translate the cost of owning the home into an equivalent monthly rent.

5. Explore actual costs of homes in your area, mortgages with local banks (including closing costs), and property taxes and insurance. Come up with data on a particular mortgage, and the costs and benefits of refinancing, and make out a corresponding balance sheet for five-year ownership.

Suggested Readings

KASTING, MARTHA. *Concepts of Math for Business: The Mathematics of Finance* (UMAP Modules in Undergraduate Mathematics and Its Applications: Module 370–372), COMAP, Inc., Arlington, MA, 1980.

MILLER, CHARLES D., VERN E. HEEREN, and JOHN HORNSBY. Consumer mathematics. In *Mathematical Ideas*, 11th ed., Pearson Education/Addison Wesley, Reading, MA, 2008.

YAREMA, CONNIE H., and JOHN H. SAMPSON. Just say "Charge it!" *Mathematics Teacher 94* (7) (October 2001), 558–564. Shows how to apply the savings formula and the amortization formula and graph the results on the TI-83 calculator. Notes that the 78% of undergraduates in the United States who have credit cards carry an average debt of more than $2700, with 10% owing more than $7000.

Suggested Web Sites

www.lendingtree.com/stmrc/calculators1.asp Java applet calculators (for any platform) to calculate payments and amortization schedules for conventional loans, adjustable-rate mortgages, auto loan vs. home-equity loan, and credit-card payoff. (Note: Lending Tree, Inc., is a loan broker; the mention here of calculators at its Web site does not imply endorsement of its other services by this book's authors, editors, or publisher.)

www.edmunds.com/calculators/ Commercial site offering a calculator to compare rebate vs. interest-rate offers for car purchase. (*Note:* Edmunds is a loan broker; mention here of calculators at its Web site does not imply endorsement of its other services by this book's authors, editors, or publisher.)

practice it 2.7   Post-Reading

Choose one of the Writing Projects ideas listed at the end of "Borrowing Models." Try it. When you have finished, write at least one paragraph reflecting on the writing project you chose. Include in your reflection some comment on the following: How realistic is this project for college math students to do? What would a student learn from doing it? Would it help a student understand the math covered in the chapter? Why or why not?

COMPREHENSION QUESTIONS

1. What is the difference between simple and compound interest? Which one would you rather pay and why?

2. How does an unsubsidized loan differ from a subsidized loan?

3. Why would the government have abolished the guaranteed student loan program?

4. What is APR?

DISCUSSION QUESTIONS

1. Why is it important to understand how interest works?

2. How do interest rates on credit cards affect the cost of purchases?

3. Based on the information in this textbook excerpt, would you consider taking out (or continuing to take out) a student loan? Why or why not?

4. Do you expect coverage of financial literacy in a math textbook? Why or why not? Is the coverage here adequate? Explain your answer.

5. What is the purpose of the Suggested Readings and Suggested Web Sites at the end of the chapter review? Under what circumstances would you use this information?

CHART   **model reading strategy**   Asking Questions

▶ For more about asking questions while annotating, see pages 15–16 in Chapter 1, Reading and Responding to College Texts. For more about making inferences, see page 138 in Chapter 5, Active Reading Strategies.

You will read many different types of texts in college, including textbooks, scholarly articles, Web sites, and magazine articles, as well as documents like the chart on page 47 that are primarily visual. Charts, such as this one from the U.S. Bureau of Labor Statistics, convey much helpful information if you know how to interpret them. Published annually, this chart shows the relationship between how much education a person has and his or her median salary and likelihood of unemployment.

The chart has been annotated to show two levels of questions you can ask while reading. The bubbles in orange show comprehension questions you can ask of the text, and the bubbles in blue show how you can make inferences—draw conclusions—from the text.

practice it 2.8   Pre-Reading

In order to "read" the chart, spend some time looking at its title, the numbers it presents, its structure, and the degree categories it lists. Try looking at it from top to bottom as well as from left to right.

BUREAU OF LABOR STATISTICS

Education Pays

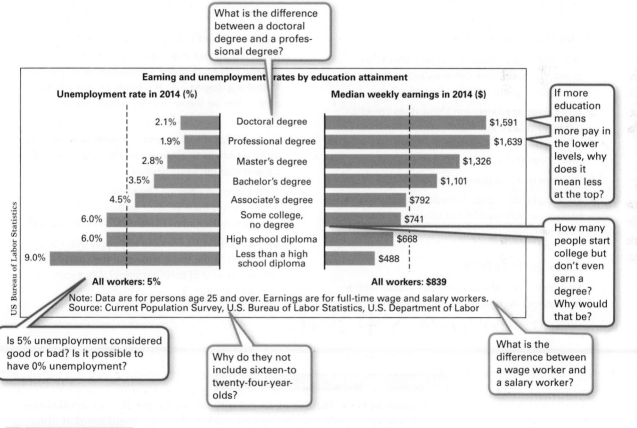

US Bureau of Labor Statistics

What is the difference between a doctoral degree and a professional degree?

Earning and unemployment rates by education attainment

Unemployment rate in 2014 (%)

Median weekly earnings in 2014 ($)

	Unemployment rate		Median weekly earnings
Doctoral degree	2.1%		$1,591
Professional degree	1.9%		$1,639
Master's degree	2.8%		$1,326
Bachelor's degree	3.5%		$1,101
Associate's degree	4.5%		$792
Some college, no degree	6.0%		$741
High school diploma	6.0%		$668
Less than a high school diploma	9.0%		$488

All workers: 5%

All workers: $839

Note: Data are for persons age 25 and over. Earnings are for full-time wage and salary workers.
Source: Current Population Survey, U.S. Bureau of Labor Statistics, U.S. Department of Labor

If more education means more pay in the lower levels, why does it mean less at the top?

How many people start college but don't even earn a degree? Why would that be?

Is 5% unemployment considered good or bad? Is it possible to have 0% unemployment?

Why do they not include sixteen-to twenty-four-year-olds?

What is the difference between a wage worker and a salary worker?

practice it 2.9   Post-Reading

Many of us have a love-hate relationship with statistics: We find them compelling, but we know they can be taken out of context, misquoted, and abused by advertisers and others, so we don't always trust them.

- Find the chart we have titled "Education Pays" by entering its original title, "Earnings and Unemployment Rates by Educational

continued ❯

Attainment," in the Search bar on the Bureau of Labor Statistics Web site (www.bls.gov).

● Look at the Web page where the chart is located, and then click around a little to other parts of the site, taking notes as you go. What did you learn about the Bureau of Labor Statistics? Does what you learned make you more or less likely to think of the evidence as reliable and credible? Why? Would you use this site as a source in college papers? Why or why not? What parts of it would be most useful?

COMPREHENSION QUESTIONS

1. Where do these statistics come from? Who collected them? How can you find out more about the Bureau of Labor Statistics?

2. What does *median* mean? How does "median" differ from "average"? What is the significance of a "median" when considering information like that presented in the chart?

3. What is the main point of the chart?

4. What is the difference between a doctoral and professional degree? What careers would you have with each type of degree?

DISCUSSION QUESTIONS

1. How much would you make per month with a high school degree, assuming you earned the median amount indicated by the chart? How much would you make per month with some college and no degree? An associate's degree? A bachelor's degree? Do the math. Would you be able to live on those salaries where you live now?

2. Do you think the chart gives reliable evidence? In other words, is the information trustworthy and current enough to be useful?

3. Does the chart's design (as a horizontal bar graph, rather than another kind of chart) help convey the Bureau of Labor Statistics' message?

4. Can you think of examples of people you know who don't fit the trend shown in the chart? How certain are you of their earnings? What sorts of jobs do they have?

RESEARCH REPORT AND INFOGRAPHIC

The annual *Money Matters on Campus* report is the product of a collaboration between EverFi, Inc., an educational technology company that aims to prepare college students with life skills through online programs, and Higher One, a business that works with colleges and universities to improve students' financial knowledge and use of college funding sources. The 2015 report explains the findings of their survey of the financial values, knowledge, and behavior of 42,000 U.S. college students, at both the two-year and four-year levels. The full report is available online; the excerpt reprinted here includes the Results Brief, which presents the key findings of the survey, and an infographic that presents those findings visually. Learning to "read" visual texts is becoming an increasingly important skill for accessing new research, both online and in print sources. Look back at the reading strategy modeled on the "Education Pays" chart (p. 47) for examples of types of questions you can ask and features you might examine.

Some difficult words and phrases are noted in the margins. Look up the ones you don't know, and write their definitions in your own words in the space provided. The first one has been done for you.

practice it 2.10 Pre-Reading

While you preview an infographic very much the same way you preview any other text, in order to "read" it you need to understand how the information is laid out. Look at how the information is presented. Are there sections or headers that identify subtopics? Is the information presented vertically or horizontally? What kinds of graphs, charts, and data does the infographic include? Scan the infographic and note whether the graphics follow or precede the information about them.

HIGHER ONE AND EVERFI

Money Matters on Campus: How Students Behave Financially and Plan for the Future

Money Matters on Campus details the findings of a survey of 42,000 first-year college students from across the U.S. conducted by EverFi and sponsored by Higher One. Students were surveyed on a variety of pertinent topics around banking, savings, credit cards, and school loans. This report outlines the survey's key findings, examining the financial attitudes and behaviors of students to better understand what most significantly predicts positive and negative financial outcomes.

pertinent: relevant or significant

outcomes:

Results Brief

This investigation comparing data collected from 2012–2015 revealed several interesting trends in the responses of college students. Young adults reported increased experience in high school with credit cards, bank accounts and the expected acquisition of student loans. Even though respondents stated that they were anticipating borrowing more and more frequently, they had fewer plans for repaying those loans. In general, responsible planning behaviors decreased over time, but risky financial moves such as using payday lenders or taking out cash advances on credit cards, remained stable. Students from two-year institutions reported more experience with money management, less and smaller loans, and more responsible behaviors than their peers from four-year institutions.

In a continuation of efforts from previous years to determine which attitudinal perspectives are the strongest predictors of financial literacy and behavior, this study conducted a factor analysis of the questions that have remained consistent across the three years of this research endeavor. The larger factor structure remained intact over time, including: Cautious Financial Attitudes, Indulgence for Status and Social Gain, Utilitarian Financial Behavior, Debt as a Necessity, Possessions Providing Happiness, Spending Compulsion and Aversion to Debt. However, several items shifted between constructs, and another factor—Financial Contentment—emerged from the data this year. These financial attitude and behavior factors proved to be strong predictors of both responsible and risky fiscal outcomes. Attitudes varied with personal characteristics in a similar manner as previously found, and community college students had a more responsible perspective on financial literacy than students at four-year institutions.

Questions assessing financial knowledge proved to be quite difficult for the students in this year's sample, but the number of correct responses increased with an individual's personal experience with money management and financial literacy education. Students at private four-year institutions generally had more financial knowledge than their peers at four-year public schools. However, students from two-year institutions had the most correct answers on average when compared to other groups. Findings supported the independent influences of both financial experience with a checking account and financial literacy education, especially in students from two-year institutions—which provides a unique context for this growing, and historically under-studied, population.

This year's investigation also considered how the emotional and ⁵ mental impact of fiscal independence fits into the study's framework. Financial stress was found to be only weakly associated with fiscal

acquisition:

payday lenders:

attitudinal:

factor analysis:

endeavor:

utilitarian:

aversion:

constructs:

fiscal:

attitudes, education, experience or knowledge. The strongest predictor of increased financial stress was the total amount of student loan debt students expected upon completion of their program. However, students overwhelmingly reported that they were most bothered by finding a job after graduation and were less concerned with money management and loan repayment. Interestingly, two-year students not only experienced more financial stress than four-year students, but also were more concerned about tuition, cost of supplies, financial aid and how to pay for another year of school.

Finally, respondents were asked how prepared they felt to handle several of the challenges that students face, including keeping up with coursework, staying organized and managing time and money. Consistently, students reported feeling less prepared to manage their money than any other aspect of college life, though this was greatly improved by experience with a transactional bank account and experience with financial literacy education. Two-year students also reported feeling much more prepared to manage their money and all other aspects of higher education when compared to four-year students, who did not vary among school type. As might be expected, education and certain types of personal experience were highly related to levels of self-efficacy in this domain.

These results have implications for campus-based financial literacy education programs—suggesting that it is important for colleges and universities to be aware of the context surrounding the development of financial literacy among their student population. The findings also highlight the importance of attitudinal, behavioral, knowledge-based and stress-related components in the development of fiscal interventions for young adults.

transactional:

self-efficacy:

implications:

interventions:

continued ⟳

Money Matters
ON CAMPUS

How College Students Behave
Financially and Plan for the Future

For the past three years, EverFi and Higher One have conducted intensive research into the financial attitudes, knowledge and behaviors of college students, with representative samples averaging more than 50,000 students per year. This research has uncovered some startling trends with real implications for financial education practitioners.

STUDENTS ARE GETTING MORE
FINANCIAL EXPERIENCE,
BUT IT'S NOT TRANSLATING TO
MORE RESPONSIBLE BEHAVIOR.

Over the past three years, college students are reporting higher levels of financial experience.

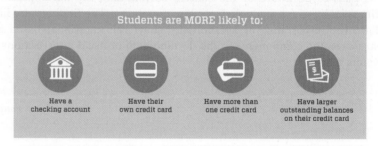

Students are MORE likely to:

Have a checking account

Have their own credit card

Have more than one credit card

Have larger outstanding balances on their credit card

HOWEVER, they are not reporting increased levels of responsible financial behavior.

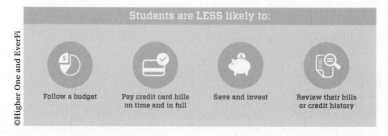

Students are LESS likely to:

Follow a budget

Pay credit card bills on time and in full

Save and invest

Review their bills or credit history

©Higher One and EverFi

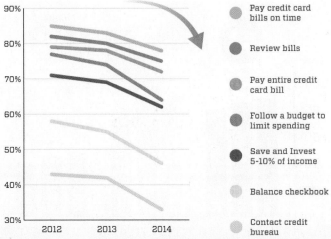

- Pay credit card bills on time
- Review bills
- Pay entire credit card bill
- Follow a budget to limit spending
- Save and Invest 5-10% of income
- Balance checkbook
- Contact credit bureau

STRESS OVER ANTICIPATED STUDENT DEBT CONTINUES TO GROW AS STUDENTS REMAIN UNDERPREPARED TO MANAGE IT.

Students report feeling less prepared to manage their money than any other challenge related to college life:

73%
were prepared to keep up with coursework

70%
were prepared to stay organized

67%
were prepared to find help and resources to succeed

58%
were prepared to manage money

The Power of High School Financial Education: Respondents who completed a high school course on personal finance management were 10% more likely to report being prepared to manage money.

Over the past three years, students have become MORE likely to take out student loans, and more likely to take out larger loans, but LESS likely to plan on:

continued ◗

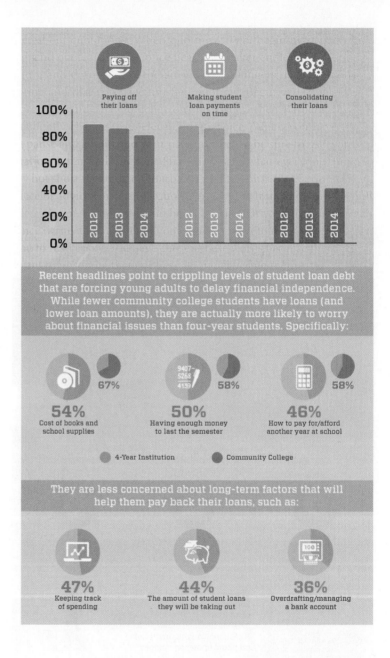

MEASURABLE PROGRESS,
BUT STILL A WAYS TO GO...

State standards for financial literacy are improving, and students are gaining more direct experience with money management, both of which are related to healthier fiscal knowledge, attitudes and behaviors. Nevertheless, risky behaviors are still pervasive among college students.

Only **62%** check their account balances

12% say they never check their balances because they are too nervous

16% live paycheck to paycheck, but only 3/4 stop spending when their resources are low

Shockingly, only **14%** have used a money management app or educational program

So now **what?**

In order to help young adults thrive in and beyond college, we must encourage and provide more opportunities for students to see themselves as active agents in their own financial development and responsible for their financial futures. Financial literacy education should focus on providing effective interventions that include personal experience and accountability, and incorporate more use of online and mobile technologies in teaching.

To learn more about this study:

www.moneymattersoncampus.org

EVERFI

Higher One
A shared course for success

---

practice it 2.11   Post-Reading

Infographics are a great way to visualize a lot of statistics, but you have to be able to make that information meaningful. Choose three statistics from the infographic and explain in your own words what point each statistic supports.

COMPREHENSION QUESTIONS

1. What are "payday lenders" (para. 2)?

2. According to the text, what was the "strongest predictor of increased financial stress" (para. 5)?

3. What is the overall point that the infographic is making?

4. What does it mean to have "financial independence" (p. 54)?

5. What are some examples of "healthier fiscal knowledge, attitudes and behaviors" (p. 55)?

DISCUSSION QUESTIONS

1. What are some possible reasons that the number of students taking out student loans and the loan amounts have increased?

2. What are the dangers of taking out student loans without having plans for paying them off?

3. In addition to having a checking account and one or more of their own credit cards, what other kinds of financial experiences might college students have? Do you think these kinds of financial experiences positively or negatively prepare students for financial independence? Explain.

4. How might financial literacy education programs on college campuses use the information from this report to help their students?

5. The "Results Brief" gives some context for the infographic. How helpful is the written information in this section? What does it provide that is not clear in the infographic? What are the advantages and disadvantages of the written form compared to the graphic format of the information?

TRADE PUBLICATION

Trade publications are newspapers, magazines, and journals that are written for an audience with a specific interest. As he describes in this article published in the *Chronicle of Higher Education* (a trade newspaper) in 2013, Ken Ilgunas was an English major at the University of Buffalo who graduated with a large student loan debt that he wanted to pay off quickly. He worked in Alaska to pay off that debt and then went to graduate school at Duke University, where he secretly lived in a van parked in a school parking lot so that he could avoid getting back into debt. After finishing his graduate education, he published a book about his experiences, *Walden on Wheels: On the Open Road from Debt to Freedom* (2013). Since then, he has launched a promising career as a writer across different platforms of online and print media and has continued to have adventures to fuel his writing.

Some difficult words and phrases are noted in the margins. Look up the ones you don't know, and write their definitions in your own words in the space provided. The first one has been done for you.

practice it 2.12 Pre-Reading

Do an Internet search for Coldfoot, Alaska. What can you learn about the town? What do you imagine it's like to live there year-round? Jot down thoughts in your notebook before tackling this reading selection.

KEN ILGUNAS

Out of Debt, on the Road

I thought of student debt like I thought of death: I didn't think of it at all. As a 21-year-old college student, I had a long life and bright future ahead of me. Why should I worry myself sick over gloomy inevitabilities? Best to shove worries of my $32,000 debt to the back of my mind alongside other yet-to-be-grown-up concerns, like paying a mortgage, finding good day care, and growing skin tags. I had little desire to leave college.

As a history and English student, I loved the thrill of a stimulating lecture, the long, caffeinated nights writing papers and outrageous columns for my campus newspaper, the pretty girls, and, above all, the feeling that I was "growing," which reassured me that, whether my degree was marketable or not, college was where I needed to be. I resented having to leave academe and toil in Career World while my fellow students would continue to thrive in graduate school.

Despite having been an editor at my college newspaper, all 25 of my applications to paid journalism internships were rejected. I began to feel desperate: It struck me that maybe I wasn't going to be able to pay off my debt after all. I'd heard of students who'd spent years, decades, lifetimes (!) paying off their student loans, and I'd heard of others who couldn't make their payments, afflicted with scary-sounding things like forbearance, deferment, and default.

Without a better idea, I wound up calling a friend, who hooked me up with a $9-an-hour job as a tour guide in Coldfoot, Alaska, 60 miles north of the Arctic Circle and 250 miles from the nearest stoplight. Coldfoot, the world's northernmost truck stop, has a winter population of 12 that triples during the summer, when buses drop off their cargo of tourists at Coldfoot's 52-room motel. I would be one of three guides who'd take the tourists on daylong tours in a 14-passenger van up the Dalton Highway or in a big blue raft down the sleepy Koyukuk River.

inevitabilities: things that are unavoidable

academe:

forbearance:

deferment:

default:

grueling:

pittance:

atrophying:

unfettered:

pedagogy:

compulsory:

frugally:

precarious:

carnie-like:

sinister:

surreptitiously:

The job was repetitive and the hours grueling, but I knew I wasn't the only   5
college graduate who'd had to sacrifice to pay bills. Plus, I was happy just to
have a job. Yet I'd never hated my debt more. I was working for a pittance, often
for as many as 70 hours a week. After work, I rarely had any energy to read or
write, and the mental muscles I'd worked so hard to strengthen in college were
atrophying from disuse.

Coldfoot offered free room and board, and I had no expenses to speak of,
but I was paying off my debt at a troublingly slow rate. I'd have to live like this
for years, I thought. For the foreseeable future, my life would be little more
than punch cards and jobs in places with prisonlike male-to-female ratios.
The debt was a ball and chain, restraining me from experiencing what I
wanted more than anything: unfettered freedom, which I hoped to use to go
to graduate school.

Toward the end of the season, I'd gotten the hang of guiding, and each night
I brought back to my dorm handfuls of tips, stashing the bills under my mat-
tress. By summer's end, I was sleeping on top of $3,000.

It was then that I began to realize that I was getting a very different education than I'd gotten in college. Jeffrey Williams, in his illuminating essay "The
Pedagogy of Debt," calls student debt a "mode of pedagogy." Williams says the
university experience teaches students that debt is not something to be avoided,
but normal and expected; it's how things are done. To buy something, we learn
to swipe our credit or college ID card and worry about the bill later. Policies like
compulsory campus housing and ridiculously priced dining plans force students to go deeply into debt. And, most tragically, the university experience
influences how we think about and handle money for the rest of our lives. College does not teach us to save, live frugally, or work our way through school. It
teaches us how to be debtors.

Now that I was on my own, in a precarious financial situation, far removed
from my old consumer-driven lifestyle, I was learning how to save, how to radi-
cally cut back on expenses, and that it didn't make sense to pay tens of thousands of dollars for something I couldn't afford—things I wished I'd known
before enrolling in college.

Over the course of the summer, between my tips and paycheck, I managed   10
to save $8,000. Not eager to give up my steady wage, I decided to spend the rest
of the year in Coldfoot, now as a line cook at the truckers' cafe. The winter
work crew was largely made up of desperate, carnie-like drifters, who brought
to mind a mostly fun-loving, sometimes sinister, and always sketchy gang of
thieves. Among them were a schizophrenic dishwasher, a compulsive liar, a
"cutter," a pair of alcoholic carpenters, and a trio of grunts, who, when on
some undisclosed narcotic, found satisfaction in surreptitiously defecating on
the roofs of co-workers' cars.

Gone were the days of lectures and seminars, of leafy campus lawns and elbow-patched professors. I was now daily exposed to alcoholism and drug addiction, beer-bellied truckers, and steel-toe boots in 30-below weather.

One night a week, I got to lead an "aurora tour," on which I'd drive Japanese guests up the road to a spot where we could get a clean view of the northern lights. With the tourists, I'd stand beneath a sky lit up with spumes of reds, pinks, and greens that swooped, twisted, and curled into each other, a glowing, throbbing curtain of color.

When gazing into the aurora, or standing alone on a mountaintop, or even working alongside my deranged, possibly homicidal coworkers, I'd feel the jolt of a direct, raw encounter with the world—a wild richness of being—and I was happy I wasn't embalmed in some stuffy Ph.D. program somewhere. The embarrassment of being a burger-flipper with a college degree at a far-flung truck stop turned into, well, pride. And I began to think that striving for a degree, a career, or a big wage ought to be secondary to striving for something as simple as a story to tell.

I left Coldfoot in the spring, having paid off more than half my debt. From there, I hitchhiked more than 8,000 miles across the country, taking jobs wherever the wind blew me. I worked on an AmeriCorps trail crew in Mississippi, delivered packages alongside a homophobic UPS truck driver in Denver, and moved back up to Coldfoot to work as a backcountry ranger for the Park Service, where, after two and a half years of work, I finally paid off my debt.

Over the course of my journey, I realized that it was only half an education 15 to have the university without the universe—or the universe without the university. And while I'd at first resented having to leave school to work, I came to believe that a true student would greet any situation as a discipline worthy of study, and that, whether in the classroom or on the open road, as Seneca said, "there is only one really liberal study—that which gives a man his liberty."

spumes:

aurora:

deranged:

embalmed:

AmeriCorps:

liberal:

practice it 2.13   Post-Reading

Look over your annotations and see where you noted you had a positive or negative reaction to specific aspects of Ilgunas's story. (If you didn't record those reactions on your first reading, read through the article again.) Choose three quotations from the article that you feel negatively or positively about. Copy out each quotation and then write a paragraph about your reaction to it.

COMPREHENSION QUESTIONS

1. In paragraph 8, Ilgunas summarizes an article by Jeffrey Williams called "The Pedagogy of Debt." What is the main point of the essay, and how does it fit into Ilgunas's essay?

2. What is an "aurora tour" (para. 12), and why would tourists go on one?

3. What does Ilgunas mean when he writes that "it was only half an education to have the university without the universe—or the universe without the university" (para. 15)?

4. Ilgunas ends with a quotation from the philosopher Seneca about liberal study. What does this quotation mean? (Do a quick Internet search on Seneca if needed.)

DISCUSSION QUESTIONS

1. Paragraphs 1–3 provide information about the writer. What can you infer from his description of his thoughts and feelings? What details lead you to make these inferences?

2. Do you agree with Ilgunas's views on education?

3. Ilgunas's essay fits into a long history of American writers who go to rustic places to discover truths about themselves. Can you think of other examples of this type of story? What similarities and differences do they share?

4. Is Ilgunas unfairly judgmental or accurately depicting his coworkers? How would you know? Do any details or the tone give you evidence for your viewpoint?

MAGAZINE

Magazine articles are enjoyable because they blend real-life examples with facts and statistics and appeal to emotion as well as logic. This helps them reach a large, general audience. Olivia Mellan does this in her article "Men, Women, and Money," from the January 1999 issue of *Psychology Today*, a magazine covering psychology for a general audience. Mellan gets her expertise from her own practice as a psychotherapist and money coach, and she draws on that experience to describe common problems that people have communicating about money. The most recent of her five books—*Money Harmony: A Road Map for Individuals and Couples*, second edition (2014), by Olivia Mellan and Sherry Christie— expands on concepts expressed in this article. For more about Mellan's work, see her Web site www.moneyharmony.com.

Some difficult words and phrases are noted in the margins. Look up the ones you don't know and write their definitions in your own words in the space provided. The first one has been done for you.

practice it 2.14 Pre-Reading

Take stock of what you already know about the topic by recalling real-life examples of couples' money disagreements you have had or witnessed. Then preview the article:

- What do you predict the article will be about?
- Look at how the article is structured. Does the structure help you understand the material?

- Look at the length of the article. How much time do you think you will need to read it?
- What do you want to know about the topic based on your preview of the article?

OLIVIA MELLAN

Men, Women, and Money

For most people, money is never just money, a tool to accomplish some of life's goals. It is love, power, happiness, security, control, dependency, independence, freedom, and more. Money is so loaded a symbol that to unload it—and I believe it must be unloaded to live in a fully rational and balanced relationship to money—reaches deep into the human psyche. Usually, when the button of money is pressed, deeper issues emerge that have long been neglected. As a result, money matters are a perfect vehicle for awareness and growth.

    Most people relate to money much as they relate to a person—in an ongoing and complex way that taps deep-seated emotions. When two individuals form an enduring relationship with each other, money is always a partner, too. In these liberated times, couples discuss many things before marriage, but the meaning of money is not one of them. Money is still a taboo topic. Often, the silence is a shield for the shame, guilt, and anxiety people feel about their own ways with money. I, for one, would not want to tell a date that I'm an overspender.

    Many individuals have a troubled relationship with money. Then, when they get into a couple relationship, money matters get explosive. Other people may have no problem with money individually; the trouble starts after they're in the relationship.

    In two decades as a psychotherapist specializing in resolving money conflicts, I have observed that couples usually polarize around money. Partners tend to assume defense styles, or personalities, in relation to money that are direct opposites to each other. I call it Mellan's Law: If opposites don't attract right off the bat, then they will create each other eventually.

    Commonly, a hoarder marries a spender. The United States is in fact a nation   5 of overspenders. We live in a market economy and we are led to believe that we are good citizens to the degree that we go out and spend. Because of our community breakdown and spiritual alienation, many people feel a core emptiness that they try to fill up with things. If we're not overspending, we're typically worrying about money or compulsively hoarding it.

loaded: filled with meanings

rational:

psyche:

vehicle:

enduring:

liberated:

taboo:

psychotherapist:

polarize:

hoarder:

market economy:

alienation:

We grow up in families where nobody talks about money. Most people will immediately protest: "Not true. My family talked about money all the time." When I ask, "How did you talk?" they reply, "My father worried about not having enough, and he yelled at my mother for spending too much."

The fact remains that people do not grow up with educational or philosophic conversations about what money is and isn't, what it can and can't do. We don't examine the societal messages telling us that **gratification** lies in spending or that keeping up with the Joneses is important. Information-based money discussions are so taboo that we usually reach adulthood without a realistic sense of our family's finances.

I once met a man who had no idea that he grew up in a wealthy family. He said, "We had a family restaurant and my mother was always worrying about how we were at the edge of doom. As a child I developed a **stammer** from all that money anxiety. As an adolescent, I worked day and night to keep the restaurant afloat. Years later, my mother was talking about the good old days when we were making so much money in the restaurant business. I started screaming at her about all the money anxiety I carried. I was outraged that it wasn't even based on a real threat. When I stopped screaming, I noticed that my stammer was gone."

And it never returned. That's a therapist's dream story: one **catharsis**, no symptom. But it does show how money carries a huge emotional load.

gratification:

stammer:

catharsis:

Doing What Doesn't Come Naturally

Growth, creativity, intimacy, and flexibility come from doing what is not automatic. For a hoarder, spending money on one's self or a loved one for immediate pleasure changes the pattern. For a spender, it's saving or investing money, or going on a slow, choreographed binge. Breaking habits doesn't happen all at once; it's a slow process. For example, I can't say, "Don't worry!" to a worrier. But I can say, "Pick one hour to worry, write down your worries for that time, and give up worrying for the rest of the day."

Partners can begin to change their ingrained habits by taking the following steps:

- Do what doesn't come naturally once a week. Eventually you and your partner will have moved enough toward some middle ground that you are not locked into your roles.
- While practicing a new behavior, write down how it feels in order to monitor your progress.
- Reward yourself for that new behavior.

As a result of the money taboo, I grew up as most kids do: imitating my   10
parents' way of handling money without being aware of it. My father, affected
by the Depression, worried out loud about money. My mother was a shopaholic, expressing love by buying me and herself clothes. She'd hide the
purchases behind a living room chair until my father was in a good mood. As
an adult, whenever I felt either depressed or particularly happy, I too would go
out and shop. And even if I bought everything at a thrift store, I'd hide all the
items behind a chair until my husband was in a good mood. Actually, I
alternated between shopping and worrying about money.

Some people do the opposite. They typically say, "My father was a hoarder and
a worrier. I hated the way he made me account for every penny of my allowance.
I made a vow to myself that I'd never be like that." Such people, however, are
anything but free of the parental attitude; their behavior is still defined by it.

In addition to irrational attitudes and beliefs about money that we   **irrational:**
internalize from our families of origin, we carry our own emotionally charged
memories of money from childhood. I remember being in a barbershop with   **internalize:**
my father when I was six, and some kid asked his father for a quarter. The
father said no. The kid started to sob uncontrollably. I remember being so   **families of origin:**
gripped by the child's sense of deprivation, I made a vow right then that I was
never going to feel deprived like that. If you tell yourself at six that you're
never going to feel deprived, you have the makings of a chronic overspender.   **gripped by:**

Couples polarized over money engage in a balancing dance of opposites.
Two spenders who come together will fight each other for the superspender
role; the other, as a defense, will learn to hoard because someone has to set
limits. When it comes to defense styles, there's always a pursuer (or clinger)
and a withdrawer. With two withdrawers, one will become the super-
withdrawer. The other will become a pursuer, because if they both withdrew
there would be no connection at all.

An equally common polarity is the worrier and avoider. Avoiders don't
focus on the details of their money life, such as whether they have enough
money or how much interest they're paying on their credit cards; they just
spend. A worrier will turn a mate into an avoider just as a way of escaping the
avalanche of worry. And an avoider will turn a mate into a worrier. Two
partners couldn't both avoid forever; somebody will eventually get concerned
and take on the worrier role. Doubling the trouble, hoarders are usually
worriers and spenders are usually avoiders.

As with all polar personality styles, hoarders and spenders live in different   15
universes marked by opposing beliefs. What feels good to one feels horrible to
the other. When not spending, a hoarder feels virtuous, in control. A spender   **virtuous:**
when not spending feels anxious and deprived. Indeed, spenders can't tolerate
the word "budget"; financial planners have to draw up a "spending plan."

Conversing with Cash

How do you turn your consciousness to an area that's usually in the dark? When a couple comes in fighting about money, I first have them clarify their own personal history and private relationship with money before turning to the dynamic between them.

I want people to see what money symbolizes to them. Then they can "unload" the symbol.

As an exercise at home, I ask each to engage in a dialogue with their money, and not share the conversation until they come back. The goal is to see what money symbolizes for each person, and to recognize that money is just a tool to accomplish certain of life's goals.

In the dialogue, imagine your money is being interviewed on *Oprah*. Ask how it thinks the relationship between you two is going, how it feels about the way you treat it.

Perhaps Money will reply, "You know, you're squeezing me so tight, I can't breathe. You need to let go a little." Or, "You throw me around, but you don't treat me with respect. You need to pay more attention to me." Either speak into a tape recorder or write the conversation down on paper.

After this dialogue, draw on at least three voices in your head—mother, father, and any other figure and have them comment on what has transpired. Finally, consider what God, a Higher Power, or inner wisdom might say.

Either Money or God, or both, will help you see the direction you need to move in to achieve money harmony.

Occasionally, a couple is unable to have a dialogue with Money. I then ask them to write down all their childhood memories and associations relating to money and start there.

---

visionaries:

amassers:

Other money personalities include planners, who are detail-oriented, and dreamers, who are global visionaries. In addition, there are money *monks*, often ex-hippies, political activists, or spiritual souls, who feel that money corrupts and it's better to not have too much. Sometimes they marry money amassers, who believe that the guy with the most money wins. Amassers are not hoarders; they don't simply save, they invest to make their money grow. They save, spend, and invest.

What makes each of the personality types is the operation of internal belief systems, what I call money myths—all the money messages, vows, and emotional memories acquired from the family of origin, the peer group, the culture at large and filtered through a person's intrinsic temperament. Many spenders, for example, don't give away just money; they are effusive with feelings, words, everything. Hoarders are typically taciturn and withholding. Even in therapy, they have to be encouraged to open up.

intrinsic:

effusive:

taciturn:

Here is the ironic part. The longer couples are married, the more they lock into polarized roles. Then they attack each other for their differences, projecting onto the other attitudes about every other spender or hoarder they have encountered in their life. They fail to acknowledge the positive aspects of their partner's personality type and of the balancing dance itself.

The failure of people to explore their money personalities leads to deep misunderstanding and hurt. Take the case of a man who views money as security. He does not believe in spending a great deal on gifts; he believes in saving. He's married to a woman who believes that money is both love and happiness; she's a spender. They are about to celebrate a major anniversary. He spends days in record stores searching for the song they danced to when they were dating in the '60s, "their song." When she gets his gift, she thinks he's chintzy and is insulted. He's inconsolably hurt. She, meanwhile, has bought him an expensive gift.

chintzy:

inconsolably:

Money issues rarely manifest themselves openly in relationships. Instead,   20 couples fight over what money represents. And while money issues can rear their head anytime, there are specific transition periods in relationships that force them to the surface: tax time, starting a family, and buying a house. Couples may complain, "We can't agree on where we want to live." Or, "He wants to go on vacation and I want to save our money for retirement." Or, "She keeps indulging the children, getting them everything they want, and I don't think that's good for the kids."

manifest:

rear:

In addition to money personalities, there are male-female differences in approaches to money that haunt many relationships. It could be said that some differences reflect men as hunters and women as gatherers. In his theater piece *Defending the Caveman*, Rob Becker describes men: They go out and buy a shirt, wear it until it dies, then go out and kill another shirt. Women, in contrast, gather. They shop for this for next Christmas for their niece and for that for their son-in-law.

Other pervasive money differences exist between the genders. First, men and women have differences of personal boundaries because they are both raised largely by women. Men have to psychologically separate more rigidly from women because of the sex difference; women do not have to separate so rigidly, and therefore can afford less distinct boundaries.

Second, men are raised to see the world as hierarchical and competitive. There's always a one-up and one-down position, a winner and a loser. Women

hierarchical:

vulnerable:

see the world as cooperative and democratic; they share. In addition, they are allowed—even encouraged—to be needy and vulnerable, while men are discouraged from such display.

The boundary and hierarchical differences between men and women lead to clashes around money decision making. Men think nothing of going out alone and buying a big-screen TV, or even the family car or computer, then coming home and saying, "Hi honey I have a new car." She says, "Why didn't you consult me? I thought we were a team." And he says, "Are you my mother? Do I have to ask your permission?"

intimacy:

Because of their more rigid boundaries, men think of themselves as islands   25
and withdraw when facing difficulties of intimacy. They don't see themselves as part of a team. And, of course, men and women are raised to believe different things about the way they should actually handle money. Despite many social changes, men are still bred to believe they will be good at dealing with money—although nobody tells them how to do it. In that way, money is like sex; they're just supposed to know. Women are raised to believe they won't be good at it and, if they're lucky, some man will take care of the details of money and investing.

canvassed:

One of the major financial houses recently canvassed high school students and asked how good they were about math and money. The boys said, "We're pretty good." The girls said, "We're not very good." In fact, they both knew the same amount about money; but their confidence levels were vastly different.

Moreover, when men make money in the stock market, they credit their own cleverness. When they lose money, they blame the incompetence of their advisers or bad luck. When women make money in the market, they credit the cleverness of their advisers, good luck, or even the stars. When they lose money, they blame themselves.

literally:

This explanatory style is literally and figuratively depressing. In addition, women are still paid three-quarters of what men are paid for the same job.

figuratively:

These events conspire to reduce women's confidence and inspire "bag-lady" nightmares. Because of the forced dependency on men to make decisions about money, women fear being out on the street with nothing.

conspire:

When men make more money than their spouse, they believe their superior earnings entitle them to greater power in decision making. By contrast, women who make more than their mates almost always desire democratic decision making.

As a woman and a therapist, I have a definite bias towards shared decision   30
making and shared power. It is the only arrangement that works. I prefer to

entitlement:

think of men's sense of money not as an entitlement but as a defense against the terrible provider burden they carry.

Men are trained to believe that money equals power and that power is the path to respect. However, power and control are not compatible with intimacy.

8 Tips to Talking about Money

Never try to negotiate about money before airing your feelings; otherwise, negotiations will always break down.

1. Find a nonstressful time when money is not a loaded issue (not tax season, please) and when the kids are not around. Agree on some ground rules: no interrupting each other; no long tirades; after one person shares a difficult piece of information, the partner will try to mirror it back before responding.
2. Take turns sharing your childhood messages about money. How did your parents save it, spend it, talk about it? How did they deal with allowances? What specific money messages did you get and how might they be affecting you today?
3. Share your old hurts, resentments and fears about money.
4. Mention your concerns and fears about your partner's money style. Then acknowledge what you admire about their methods and what you secretly envy. Hoarders secretly admire spenders' capacity to enjoy life in the present, while spenders secretly envy hoarders' ability to set limits, to budget and delay gratification. But typically they won't tell each other because they're afraid it confers license to continue in that style. In reality, positive statements help to make partners feel safe enough to give up the negative aspects of their behavior.
5. Talk about your goals for the future, short and long term.
6. Share your hopes and dreams.
7. Consider making a shared budget or a spending plan together by merging the hopes and the goals that have come up on your list more than once.
8. Set a time to have the next money talk. Aim for weekly conversations in the beginning, then monthly ones.

Relationships succeed only when both partners are willing to display their vulnerabilities to each other. It's important for men to know that failing to share power cheats them of the intimacy and love they want.

Another important difference between men and women concerns their interests in merging their money. Typically, men want to merge all the couple's money—while maintaining primary decision-making power. Women want to keep at least some money separate.

merge:

The fight goes like this:

HE: "Why do you want separate money? You must not trust me. Are you planning to file for a divorce?"

SHE: "Why do you want to merge all of our money? It must be that you want to control me." 35

There may be truth in both positions. Still, experience has led me to see a very positive, and probably unconscious, longing in both views, and it has to do with the challenge of intimacy. Merging, getting connected and staying connected, is more difficult for men. At the first sign of conflict, it's easy for them to withdraw.

I believe that men's desire to merge the family money is a loving expression of the desire for intimacy and connection. Perhaps it is even a safeguard against their withdrawing. I have come to see that women want separate money as a loving expression of their need for healthy autonomy. Their biggest challenge in relationships is not losing themselves; it's holding on to their own sense of self.

Neither his demand for merged money nor her desire for separate funds is a position taken up against the spouse—although that is how partners tend to see it. When couples understand this, their new perspective has the power to transform their entire relationship.

American culture, I believe, makes a big mistake in pressuring married couples to merge all their money. It is in fact unwise for couples to merge money right away. Since couples don't talk about money before they marry, you don't know if you're tying yourself to an overspender in debt or a worrier who could drive you crazy.

averts:

Couples can merge some of their common assets for joint expenses, savings, 40 and investing and keep the rest separate. That definitely averts some kinds of conflicts. Your partner doesn't get to comment on how you spend your money. I've always kept a portion of money apart because I knew I was an overspender and I didn't want to mess up the family finances or credit rating.

symmetrical:

Alternatively, couples could merge some money and only the woman could have separate funds. Solutions do not have to be symmetrical to work well. They just have to appeal to the deeper needs of both partners. The difficulty is in making clear to the other what your own needs are.

Money issues are different from other problems in relationships. They're harder to talk about and harder to resolve because of our extensive cultural conditioning. The most important thing in couples communication is empathy, or putting yourself in your partner's place. It is almost always more important to be heard and understood than to have a partner agree with what you say.

empathy:

Spouses who start talking genuinely about what they like about each other's money style create an atmosphere of safety and nondefensiveness. Once such a way of talking about money is established and once couples understand the positive intent of the partner, they can then work out a solution to almost any problem, a solution that best fits their own unique needs.

practice it 2.15 Post-Reading

To spark your thinking and deepen your participation in class discussion, pick a few quotes that you really liked and copy them out in a chart like the one below. Add rows to the chart as needed.

Quotation You Find Meaningful (page no.)	Why Quotation Is Meaningful
"... couples usually polarize around money. Partners tend to assume defense styles, or personalities, in relation to money that are direct opposites to each other." (59)	I see this in my own parents, and I have seen how feeling like they are on different teams with money makes them argue.

It will be helpful to return to these quotes later when you begin to do essay writing. For now, reflect on them in writing or share them in class discussion.

COMPREHENSION QUESTIONS

1. Who is the audience, and what is the purpose of this article? How do you know?

2. What is "Mellan's Law"? Give one or two examples from the article and/or your experience to illustrate Mellan's Law.

3. What is "keeping up with the Joneses"? How does this idea relate to the article?

4. What are the characteristics of hoarders and spenders? Planners and dreamers? Money monks and amassers?

5. How do traditional male and female gender roles contribute to our money personalities, according to the author?

DISCUSSION QUESTIONS

1. Do you agree that money is a "taboo" subject for most dating couples (para. 2)?

2. Do you think that same-sex couples have the same issues with money as opposite-sex couples?

3. What do you think of Mellan's advice for couples on how to talk about money? How do her professional background and experience influence her perspective on this topic?

4. What do you think is the most important thing couples can do to prevent (or at least reduce) arguments about money?

5. How might a couple's money problems affect their children's financial attitudes?

6. Are Mellan's examples and evidence fair and useful? Why or why not?

Working with Multiple Sources

When you grapple with many authors' ideas and try to figure out your own position, make time to pause and collect your thoughts. Such mental organization is time well spent. Often, when you step back and review your thoughts, you clarify your ideas, or new ideas emerge. You can begin by answering questions that bring out some of the central themes of this unit as a whole.

DISCUSSION QUESTIONS

1. What is financial literacy, and why is it important? What might happen if more Americans were financially literate?
2. Now that you have read these texts, what do you believe is the relationship between money and personal happiness?
3. How do you determine where the line is between "enough" and "too much" money? Where do you fall on the spectrum between keeping up with the Joneses and living completely outside of social financial norms?
4. How is it that we talk openly about the economy but are very private about our personal finances in America? What are the effects of the taboo on discussing money with family and friends?
5. Given the complicated nature of personal finance, what does an individual need to know to become financially literate? What does an individual need to do to put that financial literacy into practice?
6. What key terms did the readings introduce to you for understanding financial literacy? What important themes do these key terms suggest? Compare your list to your classmates' lists, if possible.
7. What connections, if any, do you see between general literacy and financial literacy?

CHARTING TO ORGANIZE IDEAS

One effective and efficient tool used by many successful students is a chart to synthesize ideas about a particular subtopic. To synthesize is to make connections among texts, or between new information and prior knowledge, drawing new conclusions from the combination. Synthesis shows that you have reached a sophisticated level of learning, that you understand and can make new meaning from the information presented to you. Your instructors will want to see that you don't just repeat given information, but that you have synthesized it and made it your own.

Synthesis is a skill that you will develop with practice. For now, focus on gathering ideas from your annotations on the readings in this chapter and your class notes. Then transfer some of your best observations into one well-organized chart; this will help you draw some conclusions about the articles and how they relate to one another. Think of the chart as a tool, not a test: You won't write the same amount in every box, and you might end up leaving some of them blank. That's fine.

The following steps will help you create a chart in your notebook:

> **STEP 1:** At the top of your paper, write down one focused topic related to the overall theme of money and wealth. This could be the assigned topic given by your instructor or one you generate yourself by looking at the main ideas in the readings. Make sure you choose a focused topic that relates to more than one of the readings. For instance, you might choose "money and status," which could relate to several of the articles, rather than just "money personalities," which is too narrow.

> **STEP 2:** Draw a table on the paper, putting the title of each article that you read in the far left column. In the bottom row of that column, write "MY IDEAS."

FOCUSED TOPIC: MONEY AND STATUS

Source	Key ideas and vocabulary	What authors would say to each other and my reactions
Holder and Meeks, "Teach Your Children the Building Blocks of Finance"	financial literacy financial empowerment important to start young so children learn how to build real wealth (and not just pursue empty status)	might disagree with Mellan—they don't think it's as hard to talk about money as she seems to think would agree with their point about the importance of financial literacy, but I think they make it look too easy
Ilgunas, "Out of Debt, on the Road"	freedom people who chase status don't really appreciate life deeply doesn't care about status much personally, though he sees how important it is to others	probably didn't have the kind of childhood that Holder/Meeks suggest, but still was able to change and gain some serious financial empowerment his non-status, off-the-grid lifestyle— just another type of status?
Mellan, "Men, Women, and Money"		
Higher One and EverFi, "Money Matters on Campus"		
My Ideas		

> **STEP 3:** In the center column, record key ideas and important vocabulary terms from the readings that relate to your focused topic. Look over your annotations for ideas. List the page numbers of specific information you quote or paraphrase.

> **STEP 4:** In the right-hand column, write what the authors might say to one another about each topic.

> **STEP 5:** Finally, jot your ideas down in the boxes in the bottom row. What ideas do you have about the topic and/or the authors' perspectives on it? What do you think about the readings? With whom do you most agree? Why?

▶ For more about
synthesis charts, see
pages 238–41 in Chapter
10, Pre-Writing.

Charts like this one serve many purposes, and as you move through your college classes, you will likely adapt chart making to various writing and studying situations. Sometimes, when you make such a chart, you begin to realize what the focus of your paper will be. Other times, making a chart helps you predict essay-exam questions or otherwise study for a test. Essentially, charts prepare you to synthesize texts, which is a very advanced type of thinking. Keep adding to your chart as you get ready to begin the essay-writing process.

Additional Online and Media Sources

The readings in this chapter may spark your thinking and leave you wanting more information, and possibly even a little personal financial help. You might want to consult the following online and media sources.

WEB RESOURCES

- **Bureau of Labor Statistics** (www.bls.gov): This site provides current data on the U.S. labor market. The Occupational Outlook Handbook portion of the site presents data on employment and salaries in various professions.
- **Council for Economic Education** (www.councilforeconed.org/): This comprehensive site about economic education includes reports, video presentations, games, and other materials. These resources will definitely be interesting to students who are also parents.
- **EconEdLink** (www.econedlink.org/): Produced by the Council for Economic Education, this site offers lesson plans on financial literacy for various K–12 grade levels. Although directed at teachers, it provides a glimpse of how financial education is taught in the schools.
- **Federal Student Aid** (http://studentaid.ed.gov/): This U.S. Department of Education Web site provides information on student aid.
- **FinAid! The SmartStudent™ Guide to Financial Aid** (www.finaid .org/): This site gives substantial information about resources to help pay for college and counsels students to beware of financial aid scams.
- **Jump$tart Coalition®** (www.jumpstart.org/): This site offers information about financial literacy for children and has a thorough handout on the K–12 standards for a financial literacy program.
- *Planet Money*, **blogs and podcasts** (www.npr.org/blogs/money/): This podcast explains the global economy in everyday language.

- **TED Talk: "Paradox of Choice"** (www.ted.com/talks/barry_schwartz _on_the_paradox_of_choice?language=en): Sociologist Barry Schwartz talks about how too much choice makes us miserable.
- **U.S. Census** (www.census.gov): The U.S. Census provides well-respected data on people's lives.

RADIO & TELEVISION

- *Frontline* (www.pbs.org/wgbh/pages/frontline/): *Frontline* episodes dealing with economics include "The Card Game," "Inside the Meltdown," "The Secret History of the Credit Card," and "Is Wal-Mart Good for America?"
- *This American Life*, **episode 355, "The Giant Pool of Money" (May 9, 2008)** (www.thisamericanlife.org/radio-archives/episode/355/the-giant -pool-of-money): This radio program on the Great Recession of 2008 explains how the mortgage industry crisis developed. It focuses on real people, including a man who went from being a bartender to being a mortgage broker of shoddy loans.

chapter review

In the following chart, begin by filling in the second column to record in your own words the important skills included in this chapter. Then assess yourself and determine whether you are still developing the skill or believe you have mastered it. If you are still developing the skill, make some notes about what you need to work on to master it in the future. If you believe you have mastered it, explain why.

Skills and concepts covered in this chapter	Explanation in your own words	I'm developing this skill and need to work on . . .	I believe I have mastered this skill because . . .
Reading with and against the grain			
Understanding charts and infographics			
Pre-reading effectively			

Skills and concepts covered in this chapter	Explanation in your own words	I'm developing this skill and need to work on . . .	I believe I have mastered this skill because . . .
Annotating effectively			
Using post-reading strategies to understand difficult texts			
Creating a synthesis chart			

3

Putting Ideas into Writing

©robodread/Shutterstock

Visit **LaunchPad Solo for Readers and Writers** for extra practice in the skills covered in this chapter.

What Is an Essay, and How Do You Write One?

There are many names and labels for the different types of writing a student does in college. Depending on the classes you take, you might be asked to write paragraphs, essays, journals, summaries, research papers, or lab reports. These types of writing have one thing in common: Each is an attempt to connect to the reader, to share ideas. Good writing communicates ideas, makes a connection with the reader, and has a clear purpose. By carefully reading your assignment (also known as a "prompt") and listening and participating in class, you should have a good idea about the type of writing you have been assigned.

Your assignment should also get you thinking about two key issues you need to consider for any piece of writing: your audience and your purpose. In most college writing assignments, the assumed audience is "college-level readers," people who can read and understand a sophisticated essay but may not be experts in the particular topic and may not have read the books or articles referred to in the paper. The purpose of most college writing is to argue a point, to persuade the reader to adopt the writer's viewpoint.

THE ESSAY

▶ To learn more about audience and purpose, see Chapter 7, Audience, Purpose, and Topic.

The most common assignment you will be asked to write and read in college is the essay. The word *essay* itself can mean lots of different things. Generally, people use the term to mean a piece of nonfiction writing that focuses on a specific topic. Essays can be short or long. They can be personal and fun to read, or factual and dry. They may include a list of sources or not, be serious or not, be formal or not. For each college writing assignment you get, determine which type of essay is required and figure out the instructor's expectations. Instructors also give writing assignments that help you figure out your essay thesis, like lists, ideas, and short answers to questions. Just as pre-reading helps you comprehend readings, pre-writing activities prepare you for writing by generating ideas and getting you into the mind-set to write the assigned essay. So don't forget about all those smaller in-class and homework assignments your instructors may ask you to do. Look for the ways they are connected to the larger essay.

What does a college essay look like? This varies from course to course; for instance, sociology, biology, and English instructors have different expectations about what a paper should be. Your instructor will tell you about specific rules and expectations for writing in a specific discipline. In general, though, most college essays follow the guidelines on the next page.

General Characteristics of College Essays

- They have an introduction, body, and conclusion. This means they usually have at least three paragraphs, but often they are longer, especially when they involve research.
- They have a thesis statement or main idea, which is often an argument.
- They have one or more body paragraphs that focus on and develop a single idea or point.
- They require thought, planning, and revision.
- They require you to give credit when you use someone else's ideas.

THE WRITING PROCESS

So how do you write an essay? Although there is no magic formula, there is something called "the writing process," and real writers do it every day when faced with a writing task. What is this thing called the writing process? First, let's talk about what it's not. It's not the stay-up-late-and-write-the-whole-paper-the-night-before-and-then-run-into-the-computer-lab-to-print-it-out-five-minutes-before-class method. Sorry. While that method may have worked for you before, it certainly never helped you produce your best work, and it definitely won't work in college, where the paper assignments get far more challenging. Think of it this way: Even if you are able to pull off the "write it the night before" approach with a short, three-page paper, that won't work when you have to write ten- and twenty-page papers later in your college career or papers that require more complex use of outside sources. Our advice? Learn and practice good reading and writing process skills now, so that you will know how to do it when your paper assignments get longer.

The writing process requires time and effort, but it works like a charm. It looks like this:

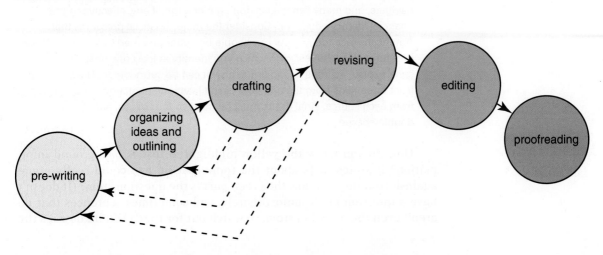

You'll have plenty of practice in these stages throughout your course and college.

How to Read an Essay Assignment

Writing the college essay begins with understanding the assignment. Generally, essay prompts have three types of information:

1. **Background information about the topic,** including specifics on what you have read or studied
2. **The question stem,** which is the main part of the assignment prompt that tells exactly what you should write
3. **Hints, guidelines, and expectations** about length, number of sources, and other things your instructor wants you to include

These three elements won't always appear exactly in this order, so take your time and read the assignment carefully to sort them out. Sometimes the instructor gives a written assignment with just the question stem and then explains the background information and hints, guidelines, and expectations during class. Write down oral instructions so that you can refer to them later.

Since argument writing is the core of most college subjects, let's look at a typical argument essay assignment. While some writing prompts will not require you to respond to outside readings, as this one does, all assignments require you to understand a question stem, background information, and guidelines or expectations.

In the following example, the background information is yellow; the question stem is green; and hints, guidelines, and expectations are blue.

> Personal finances have become more complicated than they were half a century ago when the majority of people had simple checking, savings, and pensions. Today, there are endless financial products and services to navigate, and many Americans don't get enough, if any, effective formal financial literacy education. Consider the major financial pressures that Americans face today. How can people be better prepared to surmount these pressures? Write an essay in which you identify at least one financial pressure, explain its impact, and argue how it can be surmounted. Draw from at least three texts from the unit, and use at least one quotation or paraphrase from each source. Final drafts must be three to four pages, typed and double-spaced.

How do you know the yellow-highlighted text is background information? It states facts about the topic that no one could really argue against. How do you know the green part is the question stem? (It doesn't have a question mark, unfortunately, and sometimes sentences that do aren't even the question stem, so watch out for that!) You'll know it's the question stem because it outlines the specific task that the essay requires you to do. In this case, there are three tasks:

1. Identify one financial pressure.
2. Explain the impact of that financial pressure.
3. Argue how people can surmount that financial pressure.

The blue-shaded section, which offers hints, guidelines, and expectations, reminds you to use quotations or paraphrases as evidence. The second sentence shaded in blue explains length expectations.

Take a look at those main tasks again. Words like *identify*, *explain*, and *argue* each require a specific type of response, so you need to do all three. The chart that follows provides a list of words commonly used in writing assignments.

WORDS TO LOOK FOR IN WRITING ASSIGNMENTS

Word	Means in plain English . . .
analyze; interpret	explain what you think is going on and why
anecdote	a little story used to support or explain a point
argue; make an argument	take a stance and defend it, giving evidence to support your opinion; also note counterarguments
compare	describe the similarities
compare and contrast	describe the similarities and differences
contrast	describe the differences
counterargument	the opposite or other side of an argument
describe in detail	use vivid language and lots of specific examples so the reader can picture what you are saying
evidence	quotes and paraphrases, usually from course readings, that help your reader understand why you believe what you do
explain	give the meaning of something, usually answering some "why" question
narrative	a story
paraphrase	ideas or facts from a source that you put in your own words and also cite properly
quotation	exact words taken directly from a source and properly cited

Word	Means in plain English . . .
summarize	give an overview of an event or text but do not comment on it
support your ideas	provide quotes, paraphrases, and/or other evidence to explain why you believe what you believe
thesis	the main point or claim of your essay

practice it 3.1   Analyze Your Essay Assignment

Step 1: Take a few minutes to analyze the assignment you have selected or your instructor has assigned. Label or use different-colored highlighters to mark the background information, the question stem, and any hints, guidelines, or expectations. Make a note of anything you don't understand so you can ask for clarification.

Step 2: What exactly are you being asked to do? Rewrite the question stem in your own words, breaking it down into parts if necessary as in the list following the highlighted example (pp. 79–80). Note the specific "question words" included in the prompt.

Step 3: Make a quick list of the requirements of the essay. For example, how long should it be? Should it include support from readings? If so, how many readings? Is there a rough draft due first? Add all essay-related due dates to your calendar.

Time Management for Writing an Essay

Once you understand writing as a process, you will realize that creating a good workflow and schedule is part of a writer's job. Organizing a big project—whether it's an essay or term paper for a college course or a project at work—requires you to get a sense of all the steps involved, how long each step will take, and the most logical order for the steps. Not budgeting enough time to do your best at each step in the writing process can lead to extra stress, "writer's block," difficulty coming up with enough to say, and poor proofreading. However, when you plan your time wisely so that you have the right amount of time to complete each step, you will find the writing process much more enjoyable.

A time-management chart like the one that follows will help you plan and manage the essay-drafting process. Keep track of the amount of

TIME-MANAGEMENT CHART FOR DRAFTING AN ESSAY

Task	Estimated time to complete	Actual time to complete
Reading and annotating the articles in Chapter 2	4 hours	6 hours
Organizing thoughts about the articles in Chapter 2		
Reading and understanding the essay prompt		
Pre-writing		
Thesis development		
Outlining		
Generating support and evidence		
Writing topic sentences		
Writing rough, rough draft		
Adding an introduction and conclusion		

▶ For a time-management chart for revising an essay, see page 105 in Chapter 4, Revising, Editing, and Proofreading.

time you spend on each part of the writing process. Consult your calendar to schedule when you will do each part of the process and estimate how much time you think each step will take.

practice it 3.2   Time Management for Drafting an Essay

Copy the time-management chart for drafting an essay into your notebook. Right now, fill in the time you estimate it will take to complete each task. If your assignment does not require you to respond to readings, start with the fourth row down, pre-writing. After you finish drafting your essay, return to this chart and record your actual times in the last column. Recording how much time you spent on each task and a few reflections on your process helps you accurately estimate the time needed for the next essay.

Pre-Writing for Your Essay

Pre-writing is a broad term that applies to all the thinking, doodling, sketching, writing, and discussing that you do before you actually sit down to write the first rough draft. Some people prefer the term *brainstorming* for this kind of work. Many writers enjoy the pre-writing stage because it allows them to explore various creative ideas without having to worry about being perfect. Pre-writing may be fun, but it's also a serious and helpful stage of the writing process. Students in a hurry who think they can skip pre-writing usually end up wasting lots of time later on, because they didn't prepare well enough to start writing. If you spend too much time staring at a blank piece of paper or blank screen, or believe you suffer from "writer's block," or feel you can never meet the length requirement for assignments, then the problem is most likely that you don't do enough pre-writing.

Often, you have read about your topic already, before you start your writing assignment. Remember that the reading and writing activities you did while reading in Chapters 1 and 2 are also a sort of pre-writing. They prepared you to formulate your own ideas about the topic. It is important to make those thoughts conscious, to put them on paper through pre-writing.

▶ For demonstrations of many pre-writing techniques, see Chapter 10, Pre-Writing.

Literally hundreds of pre-writing techniques and warm-up exercises exist. Some writers pre-write by talking into a recorder as they kick around ideas. Others draw extensive diagrams and charts. Some writers talk about their topic with friends and experts and then sit down, and their ideas just flow. For now, we'll focus on two strategies: freewriting and listing.

FREEWRITING

Freewriting is exactly what it sounds like: writing freely. It's easy to do as long as you don't think of it as having to be perfect. Begin by writing anything that comes to mind about your topic. Start writing, and write for at least five minutes without stopping. Do not tell yourself that an idea isn't interesting enough or clear enough to write down. Just write it anyway. Freewriting can include examples, bits of evidence, points you want to make, or even questions you have.

Here's a sample of a piece of freewriting by a college student named Emma, who is responding to the prompt on page 79.

> Having enough money is a financial pressure and paying bills, rent, tuition, books. Finding a job that can pay me enough while giving me a flexible schedule for classes is a pressure. Also, theres pressure to find a career that is something I want to do for a long time—and pays enough!! It seems like just making enough money these days is a big pressure. I also don't really understand all the fees my credit card charges, so it's hard to budget because

I don't even really know what my credit card payment will be each month! a lot of people face financial pressure when it comes to buying a house or paying off their house—so many people are getting foreclosed on. That would be incredibly stressful and sad. That's one thing I don't have to worry about since I rent, but some day I'd like to own a home. I have no idea how I might be able to do that though. I have no idea how to come up with a down payment or what that even would include. will probably have to take out a student loan when I transfer to a four-year school and I hadn't really thought about what it will take to pay it back or how much I will need to borrow, etc. There should be a class or something that you can take to figure out how to pay for college—what all your options are. I don't want to be in debt the rest of my life, but I know that it will be easier for me to concentrate on my classes if I don't have to work full-time esp since I have to take full load of classes too get through. It's like if you don't go to college, you probably will only make minimum wage your whole life, but if you do go to college you'll probably make a good salary, but you might have huge student loans for many years to come. I still think getting the degree will be more benefit in the long run though.

As you can see, this piece of freewriting reflects Emma's personal reactions to the material. Also, she didn't worry about spelling, punctuation, or grammar. She just wrote her ideas down as quickly as they came to her. It can take a while to get started, but once you relax and let yourself just write, the ideas usually flow. Give it at least five minutes, and if you can't think of anything to say, write anything you know about the topic, even if it seems really obvious. Getting the "obvious" ideas down on paper often leads you to your more original ideas. (Plus, what's "obvious" to you is often quite interesting and not at all obvious to others—you just don't realize it.)

Once you finish freewriting, reread your work, and locate one or two gems. A gem does not have to be a completed thought. Usually, it's a theme or the start of an idea that you recognize as worth developing. In the previous freewrite, the student has a couple of good examples, but the point about education that she ends with seems most relevant. Now she can take that idea and do another, more focused five-minute freewrite on it and see where it leads. Often, repeating these freewriting steps two or three times puts into words the focus of your essay. That's pretty good for fifteen to twenty minutes of work!

LISTING

Listing is just that: making a list of all the ideas, thoughts, and examples that come to mind about your topic. It's different from freewriting because rather than writing sentences or a paragraph, you just jot down a few words or phrases for your ideas. Listing after you have already done some freewriting helps you focus the ideas you are generating and begin to shape, in a rough form, your essay structure.

After doing her freewriting, Emma determined that the Bureau of Labor Statistics' "Education Pays" chart, the *Money Matters on Campus* excerpt and infographic, and Holder and Meeks's "Teach Your Children the Building Blocks of Finance" were most relevant to how she wanted to approach the essay assignment. She made a list that looked like this:

Debt

Credit cards

Student loan debt vs. student loan help

Understanding fees for credit cards and loans

Ask for help

Take a class/workshop on taking out loans

Research part-time jobs that pay a lot

Stress from working

Stress from not having money for tuition/books/etc.

College degree vs. no college degree

Learning to budget

Then she paged through her annotations of the articles, her pre-reading and post-reading writing about the articles, and her class notes from the days the articles were discussed. As she did that, she listed the points that seemed most relevant to her essay topic, like this:

"Education Pays"

A bachelor's degree will get you a higher paying job than just a h.s. diploma or A.A. degree.

Getting a master's degree would be even better!

The difference between unemployment rates for B.A. vs. no college is pretty big— it's pretty clear that the higher your level of education the higher pay you will get.

"Money Matters on Campus"

More college students have credit cards, and more than one credit card, than in past years.

More credit cards mean you are more likely to use them a lot and owe a lot of money on them which means you pay high interest.

I didn't even know you were supposed to pay your credit card in full every month! The costs of having a credit card are hidden from most college students.

Credit card companies prey on students bc they know that they'll use them a lot and have to pay a lot of interest.

Only 58% of college students are prepared to handle their own money, but I bet almost all of them have credit cards. A lot of students aren't really prepared to handle their own finances.

Money is one of those things that doesn't really get talked about much, so how will you know how to handle it?

"Teach Your Children the Building Blocks of Finance"

Have family meetings about money.

Show kids how to pay bills.

Teach kids early how to save by having a savings piggy bank and a spending piggy bank.

Encourage kids to have a side job like a lemonade stand or babysitting so they can make their own money.

Don't stress your kids out though, when it comes to paying bills. Only show them what they can handle.

Teaching kids early how to pay bills will help them when they are on their own.

Maybe show them how credit cards work so when they have their own, they won't make mistakes and ruin their credit.

Once you've created a list like Emma's, take a short break and then examine your list. You might want to share it with a friend for some brief comments. If you're satisfied you have enough ideas, move on to the next step in the writing process: developing a thesis.

practice it 3.3 Pre-Writing

If you did the activities in Chapter 2, have your notes handy. Feel free to look through them at any point in the process.

Step 1: Do a five-minute freewrite on your essay assignment. Then stop and read what you have written. Is there one gem or good idea? Underline it or summarize it in a new sentence. If your essay prompt has more than one part, try doing a separate freewrite for each part.

Step 2: Reread your essay prompt and then reread that good idea from your first freewrite. Write that idea at the top of another blank page. Now freewrite for five more minutes, this time making more of an effort to stay focused on the prompt and your gem or good idea.

Step 3: Next, try listing. Make a quick list of ideas you think you want to include in your essay. Then skim through the articles and your annotations on them, making lists of important terms, ideas, or quotes to include in your paper. If you include a quote, write down the page number so you don't have to waste time tracking it down again later.

continued ❯

Step 4: Now, return to your essay prompt. Reread it, with your freewrite and list on your desk. Are you developing some good ideas to begin the assignment? If so, great! Move on to the next section on thesis statements. If not, spend more time pre-writing, either by yourself or in consultation with classmates or your instructor.

Thesis Statements

Developing your own point of view, argument, or thesis for the essay grows out of your pre-writing activities. Most writers significantly revise their thesis statement several times throughout the writing process, so don't get stuck in your writing if you can't get your thesis statement perfect early in the process. Write a good "working" thesis, and know that you will revise it as you go.

What, exactly, is a thesis statement? The thesis is the central claim of your essay. It's the overall point you want to make. The thesis statement is the *answer* to the *question* posed by the assignment. This is why properly reading the prompt and identifying the question stem helps so much in writing a good thesis. For instance, suppose this is the question stem:

How would you describe a financially stable middle-class standard of living where you live? What kind of lifestyle and assets does a person who is considered "financially stable" usually have?

The answer, in its most rough form, might be something like this:

A financially stable middle-class standard of living in [name of your city] includes _____ and _____, and middle-class people usually are able to _____.

Of course, the details are missing at this point, but formulating such a statement helps you get a handle on what you're trying to say. Then you'll refine and improve your statement as you write the essay drafts. The thesis is usually one sentence long in early college papers, though as you take on longer and more complicated writing projects, your thesis statements may grow too.

General Features of Good Thesis Statements

In general, good thesis statements:

- Respond directly to the assignment.
- Make claims about the topic, and are not merely restatements of the topic.

General Features of Good Thesis Statements (*continued*)

- Develop a complete idea about what the writer believes about the topic as well as why he or she believes it.
- Are written as statements, not questions.
- Are clearly worded.
- Are not too broad or too narrow.
- Do not include words like "I," "we," or "this essay will . . ."

Let's look again at Emma's assignment to see how she begins to write her thesis. Here's the prompt. (To see the different parts of the assignment identified, return to p. 79.)

Personal finances have become more complicated than they were half a century ago when the majority of people had simple checking, savings, and pensions. Today, there are endless financial products and services to navigate, and many Americans don't get enough, if any, effective formal financial literacy education. Consider the major financial pressures that Americans face today. How can people be better prepared to surmount these pressures? Write an essay in which you identify at least one financial pressure, explain its impact, and argue how it can be surmounted. Draw from at least three texts from the unit, and use at least one quotation or paraphrase from each source. Final drafts must be three to four pages, typed and double-spaced.

Emma's first attempt at a thesis, based on her previous brainstorming, began by breaking down the question stem:

What is one financial pressure that Americans face today?

Economy

Low-paying jobs

Credit card debt/fees

Student loans

Not knowing how to manage money / not being financially literate

Paying bills, rent, etc.

Explain the impact

Getting far into debt

Ruining your credit—making it harder to get other kinds of credit or loans later in life

Paying much more for things you buy b/c of interest

Paying interest fees and other charges

Living beyond your means

Stress, embarrassment

How can this pressure be surmounted?

Pay attention to credit card statements and due dates.

Really think about whether you can afford what you are buying to avoid spending beyond your means.

Learn about interest, cc fees.

Learn how to make and stick to a budget and save money.

Make sure your kids learn the value of money and how to manage it early on.

Show kids how to spend responsibly.

Don't give kids everything they want bc they'll get in the habit of spending all their money when they have it.

Take a financial literacy class in school or at a community center.

Pay off credit cards or switch to lower interest rate card.

Limit the number of cc's you have.

Check your credit report.

Based on this thought process, the first draft of Emma's thesis might look something like this:

> Credit card debt is a big financial pressure Americans face and it can cause a lot of problems with your finances. These problems can be solved by paying off your credit cards and cutting them up.

This is a good start. However, the thesis should clarify what kinds of problems credit card debt can cause, so this needs to be added to the thesis.

Let's review the general impact Emma came up with:

- Ruin credit
- Pay more (in interest, fees, and the illusion you can afford things you can't)
- Debt

Good, now Emma can add that into her thesis.

> Credit card debt is a big financial pressure Americans face and it can cost you a lot, in money and credit ratings. The solution is to make a plan to pay off your credit cards and cut them up.

Again, Emma will probably continue to revise this thesis throughout the writing process, but this working thesis provides a solid enough foundation to begin outlining the body of the essay.

practice it 3.4 Brainstorm to Create Your Thesis

An effective way to begin putting a thesis together is to simply answer the questions of the assignment. Try these steps in your notebook:

Step 1: Write down the question stem, either in your own words or as it appears in your prompt.

Step 2: Break the stem down into its specific parts and transform them into questions.

Step 3: Answer each question in one sentence.

Step 4: Look over your answers and decide which direction you would most like to go with the essay. Write the idea up in one or two complete sentences. That's your working thesis.

▶ **For more help developing a thesis, see Chapter 11, Thesis and Main Idea.**

practice it 3.5 Evaluate Working Thesis Statements

Evaluate the following three working thesis statements for the essay assignment on page 87. Think about what works, what is missing or unclear, and how the thesis can be revised. Finally, rewrite each thesis statement as necessary until it clearly states a main point that responds to the assignment.

1. This essay will explain how the pressure to save for retirement is wrecking people at the start of their careers.

2. I think that if you made good decisions about money, your only pressure is the unknown.

3. Is debt the biggest pressure Americans face today?

Outlining Your Ideas

Once you have a working thesis, you can begin to organize your ideas. Writers organize their ideas in many different ways.

Sketch out a rough outline to clarify and develop your ideas as you organize them. The method seems simple at first, but it requires pretty intense thinking, so be prepared to spend some time on it. Here are the steps:

STEP 1: **Jot down ideas.**   Looking over your pre-writing, jot down a list of all the ideas you think you will cover in your essay. Do not worry about

TIP

In the early stages of writing, formal outlines with Roman numerals and capital letters are difficult to create because you won't know all the points and examples of your essay until you do more prep work. So start with a rough outline: At this stage of the writing process, messy is best.

the order of ideas now. Just make a list of phrases about the ideas you believe you want to include. It might look like this:

> Learn about interest
> Anyone can get multiple cards
> Paying more for items due to interest
> Not being able to pay off cards and getting bad credit

STEP 2: **Now, examine that list.**   What does each item really mean? Have you explained your meaning clearly and specifically enough? Which points are related? Clarify each point, adding details, combining ideas if necessary, or breaking one idea into two or more if necessary. This is the part that takes significant time and thought, so don't rush. By the time you finish, your rough list might look like this:

> Getting into credit card debt is easy
> Credit card debt ends up costing more money
> Debt hurts your credit score
> Learn how to avoid the problems of credit cards

▶ For more on outlining, see Chapter 14, Essay Organization and Outlining.

STEP 3: **Order your points.**   Now, put the ideas in order. The order of your ideas depends on your overall thesis. Sometimes it makes sense to begin with background or context and then move on to ideas that explain and prove your thesis. Other times, you might begin with the simpler points and then move on to more complex ones. The assignment itself might also suggest a logical order: Your prompt may ask for a cause-and-effect essay, or one that moves from problem to solution, or from past to present. The main rule of thumb is that your points should be in whatever order makes the most sense to support your thesis.

practice it 3.6   Group Activity to Organize Ideas

Sometimes two, or three, or four heads are better than one. In the case of organizing ideas, additional minds (and eyes) can help you see possible patterns of organization. For this activity, you need several index cards or small pieces of paper.

Step 1: Have each group member write his or her thesis on one card and label it "thesis."

Step 2: Then each group member writes each point of his or her rough outline on a separate card. Spread one person's cards out on the desk. Discuss different ways to put the cards in order, moving them around as you do. If you decide that a new idea needs to be added, or that two ideas should be combined, make new cards that show this. (If some cards have evidence instead of ideas, note that and put them aside. The author of the cards should keep those ideas handy for a later stage of the writing process: generating support for the thesis.)

Step 3: When the group arrives at an order of points that works well, the author of the cards writes the points down in that order on his or her paper.

Step 4: Repeat with the other group members.

Generating Evidence to Support Your Thesis

Now that you have a working thesis and some idea of the points you intend to include in your paper, you need examples and evidence to support your thesis and points. Review your earlier pre-writing, gather quotes and paraphrases from the readings, and consider new ideas that no doubt emerged while you were writing your working thesis and sketching out a rough order for your points. As you search for evidence, bear in mind your audience. For instance, if you write to a college-level audience, your readers may be more convinced by facts and figures, whereas if you write to a general audience or a younger audience, your readers might find personal anecdotes more compelling. A mixture of types of evidence often appeals most to readers. Your instructors will likely be impressed if you handle various types of sources in an essay, as long as you do enough analysis of the evidence you present.

practice it 3.7 Finding Evidence and Connecting It to Claims

Look back at the "Education Pays" chart (p. 47). This chart offers many pieces of evidence, but you have to interpret the chart to find the evidence. Pull three statistics out of the chart and paraphrase them so that they can be included in an essay. Then write down the point that each of these paraphrases might support.

practice it 3.8 Gathering Quotations and Paraphrases

It's best to complete this activity on a computer so you won't have to recopy quotations and paraphrases. If you haven't already done so, type up the outline you created in the previous stage of the writing process.

continued ❯

Gather your notes and books, and give yourself plenty of time and space for this task. Slowly work your way through the articles you have read, your pre-writing, and any other notes. Each time you find a piece of evidence that interests you—a quotation, paraphrase, fact, example, observation, or anecdote—ask yourself why it is interesting, to whom it might be convincing, and where you could put it in your paper. If you think you might use it in your essay, type up the information under the relevant point in your outline, being sure to include the source and page number so that you don't have to find it again later. For now, just insert the author's last name and the page number in parentheses, like this: (Mellan 00). When you are finished, print the document out and review all the material you have so far.

Topic Sentences

Each paragraph should develop one idea or make one clear point in support of the thesis. This idea or clear point is stated by the paragraph's topic sentence. You can think of a topic sentence like a mini-thesis; it is usually a claim that tells the reader what to expect of the paragraph. Topic sentences are important because they help guide the reader through your essay.

A topic sentence states two things:

1. The topic of the paragraph
2. The point the paragraph will make about the topic in support of the thesis

▶ **For more on topic sentences, see Chapter 13, Topic Sentences and Paragraphs.**

In academic writing, topic sentences are generally the first sentence of each paragraph so that they indicate to the reader what point the paragraph will make. In professional writing (articles, stories, essays), topic sentences may be located at the beginning, in the middle, or even at the end of the paragraph. In professional writing, the topic sentence sometimes isn't even in the paragraph at all—it's implied. For college writing, however, the topic sentence should usually start the paragraph.

FINDING TOPIC SENTENCES

Because the topic sentences in a piece of writing are usually clear statements of the major claims of that writing, they help you understand the reading. By practicing finding and evaluating topic sentences you also improve your writing skills: By seeing examples of various ways to write topic sentences you learn through experience what makes a good, clear topic sentence.

practice it 3.9   Finding Topic Sentences

Take a look at the following excerpt from Andrea Chang's "The Kardashians: Cashing in with a Capital K" (pp. 522–26). The original article was broken down into many short paragraphs. It was published that way because it was a newspaper article. Here all the paragraph breaks are removed. Your task is to find the topic sentences and re-paragraph this portion of the text as you would if you were writing a college paper instead of a news article. Hint: You are likely to find at least three topic sentences. Remember that topic sentences are often, but not always, the first sentence in the paragraph.

Step 1: Read the excerpted text, underlining main points / topic sentences.

Step 2: Insert the paragraph symbol (¶) where you would add a paragraph break.

Step 3: Evaluate the topic sentences you have identified:

    a. Do they cover the material from the entire paragraph?
    b. Are they clearly written?

    Feel free to change your underlining if you find a sentence that works better as the topic sentence.

Step 4: Reread just the topic sentences you have identified, skipping the rest of the sentences in the paragraph. Do they make sense? Do the topic sentences present a coherent map of the ideas in the excerpt?

Excerpt

Having conquered reality television, the Kardashians are fashioning a celebrity retail powerhouse. Beyond the glittery red carpets and steamy tabloid fodder, the famous family has transformed itself into a branding machine, quickly leveraging the hype into a retail empire worth tens of millions of dollars. Unlike other reality-stars-turned-entrepreneurs such as Snooki of Jersey Shore fame or Lauren Conrad of The Hills, the Kardashians are in a class by themselves and unfazed by skeptics who doubt they can keep it up for the long haul. There are Kardashian boutiques, fragrances, jewelry, apparel, bikinis, self-tanner, skin-care products, candles—even bottled water, if you're willing to shell out $10 for it. Whether it's business

continued ❯

savvy or shameless self-promotion, it's paid off: Kardashian Inc. raked in an estimated $65 million last year, according to the Hollywood Reporter, a trade publication. And with the family signing on to a slew of new projects, it's poised to make even more in 2011. This year alone, sisters Kourtney, Kim and Khloe released their own "glam pack" of Silly Bandz, the wildly popular rubber-band shapes that kids trade and wear as bracelets. They're also opening Kardashian Khaos, a celebrity retail store at the Mirage in Las Vegas. Kim has been promoting her jewelry line Belle Noel and touting Midori liqueur as a company spokeswoman; she and mother Kris are also the new faces of Skechers Shape-Ups sneakers. Khloe and Laker husband Lamar Odom, who are starring in their own spin-off series on E!, recently released a unisex fragrance called Unbreakable. The sisters' biggest project this year is the launch of the Kardashian Kollection, an ambitious "shop-within-a-shop" concept that will launch at Sears stores in late August and in international markets. The global lifestyle brand is Sears' biggest celebrity deal ever. The line will span categories including dresses, outerwear, T-shirts, denim, footwear, jewelry, handbags and lingerie, and will reflect the sisters' individual styles: classic red-carpet glamour for Kim, bohemian chic for Kourtney and edgy rocker for Khloe. "It's new and exciting and different, and they're going to be a big part of that change," said John Goodman, executive vice president of apparel and home for parent company Sears Holdings Corp. "In order to evolve and move forward, you're going to have to step out of the comfort zone." Not everything the Kardashians have lent their name to has been a success. In November, the sisters were forced to pull their prepaid debit card, called the Kardashian Kard, amid slow sales and an outcry about high fees. After releasing "JAM (Turn It Up)," a dance-pop-infused single last month, Kim was criticized as having an uneven voice and talking her way through the song. But for the most part, strong sales have followed their many pursuits. Kim's eponymous perfume was Sephora's No. 1-selling fragrance last year and the sisters' exclusive Bebe collection was a huge success, a company spokeswoman said. Their memoir and style guide, Kardashian Konfidential, debuted at No. 4 on the New York Times bestseller list in December. Unbreakable, available exclusively at Perfumania, has sold out twice since its February launch. In recent interviews with The Times, the Kardashians said they're just getting started. "There's some days we definitely go crazy," Khloe said during a recent appearance at the Beverly Center, where hundreds of hysterical fans lined up for photos and autographs. Added Kourtney: "There's no way I could do this alone. . . . We all kind of pick up the pieces for each other." The Kardashians became household names in 2007 with the debut of Keeping Up with the Kardashians on the E! channel, which was conceived of by Kris as a modern-day Brady Bunch–esque reality show. At the time, Kim Kardashian, still the most well-known of the brood, had already made a name for herself as Paris Hilton's sidekick and fellow socialite. And like Hilton, Kim was also facing notoriety over the release of a sex tape made with her then-boyfriend. The family's less-than-wholesome reputation has earned the Kardashians a fair amount of criticism that retail experts say could hinder the family's long-term viability as a brand. "The Kardashians are a great example of, in my mind, talentless celebrities or celebrity for celebrity's sake who took advantage of their looks, a sex tape, a lot of pretty raw and low-level stuff that titillated and fascinated the American public," said Eli Portnoy, a marketing and branding expert in Los Angeles. Led by Kris, who describes herself as the family's "momager," the Kardashian brood includes Kourtney, 32, Kim, 30, Khloe, 26, and Rob, 24, her children with her first husband, former O. J. Simpson lawyer Robert Kardashian, who died of esophageal cancer in 2003.

WRITING TOPIC SENTENCES

Now it's time to write your own topic sentences for your essay. Take your outline, which lists the topic of each paragraph and some evidence under each bullet point. Make each topic into a complete thought by asking yourself: What point do I want to make about that topic? Answer in just one sentence. Check that the point you made supports the thesis and matches the evidence you have collected so far. Each sentence will then serve as the topic sentence of one paragraph of your essay.

Sounds simple, right? To be honest, it's easier said than done. Sometimes, when you try to write up your sentences, they come out easily and you feel confident about your work. Other times, you struggle and have to go back to the brainstorming stages to figure out exactly what you are trying to say. That's fine. It happens to all writers. Don't forget to adopt the growth mind-set. If you expect struggles to be part of the learning process, you are less likely to give up when you encounter difficulties.

A few hints will help you get through this tricky stage of the writing process. First, think about the key terms of your essay, which may even be words from the assignment. Try to use those key terms in your topic sentences. For instance, if the prompt asks about financial pressures and how they can be surmounted, the terms *pressure*, *finance* or *financial*, and *overcome* or *surmount* will likely show up in one or more of your topic sentences.

Here's Emma's thinking process in getting from a list to topic sentences. She started with this list of topics for the body paragraphs:

Getting into credit card debt is easy.
Credit card debt ends up costing more money.
Debt hurts your credit score.
Learn how to avoid the problems of credit cards.

Then she wrote up a rough topic sentence for each point:

> Credit cards are easy to get, and many teens and young adults have more than one (*Money Matters on Campus* infographic).
> People live beyond their means with debt (Ilgunas).
> People rack up huge debt on several cards and can't pay it off.
> Late payments and even big balances on cards lead to a bad credit score, and that makes future borrowing a problem.
> Learning about credit cards should start before you get them, in school or from parents.
> Paying off your cards will help you reduce your debt and improve your credit score. It will also help you avoid late fees and interest fees.

These topic sentences are not set in stone, but they are a good start. Emma can continue to revise them as she moves through the writing process.

Drafting a Rough Essay

You spent a serious chunk of time pre-writing; you have a focused topic, a working thesis, and some decent topic sentences; and you feel good enough about your outline to start writing. How do you write that first draft? One. Word. At. A. Time. Seriously, the drafting stage is the most overrated stage of the writing process. Most people think of that first draft as the most important part of writing, when really it's probably the least important part. So don't sweat it; just get writing. You'll be impressed with what you have, once you start putting it all together.

TIP

Write out or print out your thesis and tape it to the top of your computer screen so you have it clearly in view as you write. This little reminder will help you stay focused as you draft the body paragraphs.

practice it 3.10   The Quick Draft

Gather your working thesis, topic sentences, and notes about what support you plan to use. Also, print out all your notes and put them on the desk beside you so you can easily look at them while you write.

Start writing the beginning of the essay. Don't worry about an introduction; just start with your first point. Keep writing, sticking to your outline as much as possible. Don't worry about making every sentence perfect yet. Don't worry about spelling or other things that might make you stop writing. Just keep putting sentences down. If you get stuck, feel free to put in a placeholder note to yourself like:

> Say more here about how being financially inexperienced is a problem

or:

> Need a good example for this idea

Jot down a note to yourself about what you still need in this part of your essay and keep writing. You can come back to it later.

When you think you are finished, give yourself a pat on the back! Then save your document (in more than one place and with a sensible name, like "Money Essay 1") and print it out. If you are writing by hand, now is a good time to type up your draft; then save and print the document.

Read what you have written. Does it really feel like a complete rough draft? Have you answered all parts of the prompt (even in a rough form)? Add any information that needs to be added. Don't cut too much yet. You can always cut later. If you do delete large amounts, put the deleted material into a "junk" file that has the same document name (for example, "Money Essay 1 Junk"), just in case you need it later.

▶ For additional drafting strategies, see Chapter 15, Drafting.

Introductions and Conclusions

Introductions set the tone for your essay right away, and conclusions leave a lasting impression. Strong writers spend considerable time thinking about an essay's introduction and conclusion. Possibly you wrote a decent introduction and conclusion when you did the quick rough draft, but if you're like most college students, you didn't know quite what to include in the introduction, and so you left it rather short, and perhaps you didn't write a conclusion at all yet.

For now, think of the introduction as the place to draw in the reader, explain the topic, give readers the background information they need, and state the thesis. For instance, if you are writing about two articles, the introduction should provide the full titles of the articles, the authors' full names, a one- to two-sentence summary of each article, and perhaps some information about where and when they were published. In short, the introduction should include the following things:

▶ For more about writing introductions and conclusions, see Chapter 16, Introductions and Conclusions.

Parts of a Good Introduction

- One or two sentences that "hook" your reader and get him or her interested in your topic. The hook could be a fact or quote that really stands out or gets to the heart of the issue.
- A statement about the focused topic of the essay
- Background information on your topic so your reader knows a bit about the context of your essay
- Your thesis statement

Here's a sample introduction for the paper our student writer, Emma, is drafting. Key components of the paragraph are coded as follows: The hook is green; background information is yellow; the topic is blue; the thesis is orange.

It seems that at least once a week an offer for a credit card comes in the mail. At first this seems great and exciting, a new credit card with zero or a super low interest rate! But if you don't read the fine print, those zero or "low" interest rate cards could soon have very high interest if you are late or miss even one payment. They convince you with promises of great rates, but they count on the fact that most people will not know how to manage their credit cards and end up with the very high interest rate, and that's how credit cards make so much money off of us. Most Americans have one or more credit cards, but do they really know how to use them responsibly? Credit card debt is a big financial pressure Americans face, and it can cause a lot of problems with your finances. These problems can be solved by paying off your credit cards and cutting them up.

Emma's introduction provides adequate background information and states the topic, but she will probably decide later to revise the hook and thesis.

The conclusion, usually one paragraph long, should sum up the paper and leave the reader with some last thoughts. First think of the main points you covered in your body paragraphs, and then sum up each one along with your thesis. When offering your final thoughts on the essay, think about whether you learned something, want to make a recommendation, or have a prediction or suggestion for your reader. Conclusions can refer back to an idea sparked in the introduction, particularly if the introduction was especially creative in getting the reader's attention. Here is Emma's sample, with parts that sum up the main points noted in blue and those that offer final thoughts highlighted in green:

Paying off your credit cards will help you reduce your debt and improve your credit score. It will also help you avoid late fees and interest fees. With all the stress and pressure that being in debt causes Americans, getting a handle on these fees should be everyone's priority. More credit cards don't mean you actually have more money, but it can feel that way. There are lots of Web sites that can help you learn how to budget your money so you don't live beyond your means.

Like many first draft conclusions, Emma's is very rough. She will certainly revise it later.

Evaluating a text's introductory and concluding paragraphs serves as a useful strategy for reading comprehension because those paragraphs usually state and restate the thesis, or main point, of the reading. Looking at how an author introduces and concludes a reading also provides an example of how to write an introduction and conclusion. These examples can serve as models for you in creating your own introductions and conclusions.

| practice it 3.11 | Group Activity: Evaluating the Introduction and Conclusion |

Reread the introductory paragraph and the two concluding paragraphs in Olivia Mellan's article "Men, Women, and Money," which are reprinted here. With a group, follow the steps below to evaluate the paragraphs.

Step 1: Read over the introduction and conclusion two or three times.

Step 2: Find and label each of the major parts of the introduction:

- The hook/attention grabber
- The statement of the article's topic
- The background information a reader might need to know to read the article
- The thesis or main point

Step 3: Find and label in the conclusion the sentences that do each of the following:

- Sum up the main ideas of the article
- Give readers some final thoughts to consider or something they can do with the information that has been presented

Step 4: Evaluate the effectiveness of the introduction. Does it make you want to read the article? Why or why not? Discuss.

Step 5: Evaluate the effectiveness of the conclusion. Does it make the article feel finished, complete, and meaningful? Why or why not? Discuss.

Mellan's Introductory Paragraph

For most people, money is never just money, a tool to accomplish some of life's goals. It is love, power, happiness, security, control, dependency, independence, freedom, and more. Money is so loaded a symbol that to unload it—and I believe it must be unloaded to live in a fully rational and balanced relationship to money—reaches deep into the human psyche. Usually, when the button of money is pressed, deeper issues emerge that have long been neglected. As a result, money matters are a perfect vehicle for awareness and growth.

continued ❯

TIP

Note how paragraph length is related to genre. Mellan's article was originally published in a magazine, where paragraphs are typically short so readers' eyes can follow along with the long, thin text columns. What might have been one longer concluding paragraph in a book or essay is therefore broken into two shorter paragraphs for the magazine. Both paragraphs are shown here, since together they serve as the conclusion.

Mellan's Concluding Paragraphs

Money issues are different from other problems in relationships. They're harder to talk about and harder to resolve because of our extensive cultural conditioning. The most important thing in couples communication is empathy, or putting yourself in your partner's place. It is almost always more important to be heard and understood than to have a partner agree with what you say.

Spouses who start talking genuinely about what they like about each other's money style create an atmosphere of safety and nondefensiveness. Once such a way of talking about money is established and once couples understand the positive intent of the partner, they can then work out a solution to almost any problem, a solution that best fits their own unique needs.

Finishing the Rough Draft

You have come a long way from the beginning of this chapter, and you probably have a solid rough draft of your essay. Read it over a few more times, make any changes you need to, and print it out. As you move into the revision stages, you will make significant changes to it, but hopefully you budgeted your time well so that you can take a short break. A few days or even hours away from the essay can give you some perspective.

At this point, if you haven't already done so, go back to the Time-Management Chart for Drafting an Essay that you made for the Practice It 3.2 activity on page 81 and fill in the last column. What might you do to tweak your time management next time around? Make a note of that before you move on to Chapter 4, Revising, Editing, and Proofreading.

Essay Assignments for Unit on Money, Wealth, and Financial Literacy

To give you an idea of the kinds of assignments you might see in college, the following prompts show some possible essay questions that might be asked in response to the readings on financial literacy in Chapter 2.

Definition Assignment

Financially literate behavior encompasses many things, from personal attitudes about money in relationships to understanding financial terms and saving for retirement. Write an essay that defines good financial behavior as you see it.

Narration Assignment

Write an essay that explains your money history and your level of financial literacy. To answer this prompt, think about the following questions: Did you grow up with an allowance? Do you remember having money worries? Was money discussed openly in your family, or was it a taboo topic? Did you witness arguments about money in your family? What were your family's values about money, and how were they passed on to you or not passed on to you? Refer to at least two of the texts from the unit on Money, Wealth, and Financial Literacy as you write your essay.

Process Analysis Assignment

What can individuals or families do to become more financially stable in America today? Write an essay that explains what you believe are the most important steps to take in the process of becoming financially stable. You may use yourself or your family as an example or create a hypothetical family, but make sure you give some details about who is in the family, what their educational levels are, and what goals they have.

Compare/Contrast Assignment

Choose two people you know who are in an important relationship (your parents, you and your significant other, two friends) and compare and contrast their money personalities, using the psychological types outlined in Olivia Mellan's article "Men, Women, and Money." Make sure you give details from real life that show why they fit the personality type that you believe they fit. In the concluding paragraph, show how their different money personalities affect their relationship.

Analysis/Argument Paper

As the readings in this unit demonstrate, many people need to learn more of the mathematics necessary to manage their finances. However, the readings also point to incredibly important psychological aspects to the financial illiteracy problem. Write an essay in which you identify one important psychological quality or characteristic that people need to have a healthy relationship to money. Explain why it is important and how it will help them in their personal relationship to money. Refer to at least two texts from the unit, using at least one quotation or paraphrase from each. Final drafts must be three to four pages, typed and double-spaced.

Take a Position/Argument Paper

Ken Ilgunas writes about how he took out student loans for his undergraduate education and then worked extremely hard to pay them back. Later, he lived out of a van to avoid any student loan debt for graduate school. In contrast, the "Education Pays" chart demonstrates that the increased earning power of a higher education would make some student loan debt economically justified. Consider the costs and benefits of higher education that are reflected in the readings and in your own experiences. Given these costs and benefits, do you think it is worthwhile for college students to take out loans to attain a higher education? Under what circumstances? Write an essay in which you state your position about the advisability of student loan debt.

Problem/Solution Paper

According to the survey data found in the *Money Matters on Campus* infographic, "Students report feeling less prepared to manage their money than any other challenge related to college life" (52), despite the rise in financial literacy programs and the wide availability of financial literacy information online. In the conclusion of the infographic, the authors note that "to help young adults thrive in and beyond college, we must encourage and provide more opportunities for students to see themselves as active agents in their own financial development and responsible for their financial futures" (53). What are some of the reasons the majority of college students might not be responsible for or feel like they can meaningfully participate in their own financial lives? What could help them feel that they have more control over their financial lives? Write an essay in which you explain why many young adults feel they don't have control, and outline at least one possible solution that would help them develop this sense of agency in their financial lives.

Research Assignment

What are your life goals? Where do you hope to see yourself in fifteen years? Freewrite on your future life, brainstorming specifics about where you wish to live, what kind of career and family you hope to have, how you plan to give to children or others, and how you plan to retire. Next, research that dream life, using your school's career center, the online resources listed in Chapter 2, and Web sites that will give you information about salaries and housing costs. Would the salary of your dream career support the lifestyle you hope to have? What do you need to do to achieve success in your chosen career? Write an essay that explains the path you will need to take to achieve your dream life. If you discover that your dream life needs to be revised, write an essay about what you need to change and how you will decide to rearrange your priorities.

chapter review

In the following chart, fill in the second column to record in your own words the important skills included in this chapter. Then assess yourself to determine whether you are still developing the skill or feel you have mastered it. If you are still developing the skill, make some notes about what you need to work on to master it in the future. If you believe you have already mastered it, explain why.

Skills and concepts covered in this chapter	Explanation in your own words	I'm developing this skill and need to work on . . .	I believe I have mastered this skill because . . .
Understanding essay assignments			
Understanding the writing process			
Managing time for essay writing			
Pre-writing, including freewriting and listing			
Drafting a thesis statement			
Outlining			
Generating evidence			
Finding and writing topic sentences			
Writing a rough draft			
Drafting an introduction and conclusion			

4

Revising, Editing, and Proofreading

Once you have a complete rough draft, the most serious work of writing begins. Writing the first draft of an essay is a major accomplishment, but good writing comes from rewriting, which includes revising for major changes, editing to make your sentences clear, and proofreading to polish your final product. In the real world, writers go through this process every day. It takes work, but the good news is that you do not have to do it alone. In fact, revising is most productive when done in consultation with others; we call this peer review.

In Chapter 3, you filled out a time-management chart for drafting an essay to give yourself an idea of how long each step in the drafting process takes. The chart that follows includes the steps in the revising process. You can copy this chart into your notebook and estimate how long the revising, editing, and proofreading steps will take you. By the time you complete this chapter, you will have an accurate idea of how long it takes you to write a complete essay, from reading and brainstorming to editing and proofreading.

TIME-MANAGEMENT CHART FOR REVISING AN ESSAY

Task	Estimated time to complete	Actual time to complete
Peer review		
Making a plan of action for big-picture and sentence-level concerns		
Revising thesis		
Organizing from one paragraph to the next		
Organizing inside paragraphs		
Revising for clear transitions		
Developing paragraphs		
Integrating quotations and paraphrases		
Editing for sentence errors		
Proofreading for minor errors and format		

Revising as Re-Seeing Your Work

The revising stage of the writing process requires that you switch hats: You have been working on your essay as a writer; now it's time to review your essay as a critical reader. It's important to be able to identify which parts of your essay are strong and which parts need more attention and work. In fact, revising is perhaps the most important step in the writing process. Revising can make a garbled mess of ideas into a decent paper, and it makes a decent rough draft into a very good second draft. Successful writers always revise their work many times before considering it "done." The American writer Ernest Hemingway had an intense revision process; he told one interviewer that he often rewrote the first chapter of a book forty or fifty times! We don't expect you to rewrite or revise that many times, but a successful college writer must be open to making major changes to a draft.

What exactly is revising? Revising is the process of working out the thesis and structural support of your essay. Revising requires you to think about big-picture concerns and analyze your focus, points, support, and/or organization. Frequently, your first rough draft will have an unfocused thesis, insufficient support, or major organizational problems. You may need to cut out paragraphs, rearrange your essay entirely, or add substantial amounts of new information. Occasionally, writers figure out their thesis only at the end of the first draft, and they have to shift the paper around completely to make the thesis clear and focused. As you can see, being open to revision means being open-minded about your writing.

Many students confuse revision with editing and proofreading, which are separate stages of the writing process. Editing, the stage that follows major revision, focuses on making your sentences clear. During the proofreading stage, the last stage in the writing process, you correct spelling and other minor errors. Make sure you complete your revisions before you attempt to edit or proofread. After all, there is really no point in struggling to find the perfect word if you may end up cutting the entire paragraph.

When working with a rough draft, work on big-picture issues first so you can make clear what it is you are trying to say. Once your thesis, ideas, logic, and organization are solid, you can work on concerns at the sentence level, fine-tuning your words and proofreading for errors. Think of it like building a house: Once the structure is complete (a solid foundation, framing, walls, and roof), you can add details, paint, and decorate. Similarly, when writing, you need a solid foundation for your essay (the thesis, audience, purpose, organization, topic sentences, and support) before you can polish it by finding the just-right word or perfecting your punctuation.

Big-Picture Issues

Audience, Topic & Purpose

Chapter 7

Thesis

Chapters 11 & 12

Organization

Chapters 8 & 14

Paragraph Development & Coherence

Chapters 10, 13, 24, 25, & 26

Introduction & Conclusion

Chapter 16

Sentence-Level Issues

Grammar

Chapters 31, 32, 33, 34, 36, 37, 38, & 39

Word Choice & Vocabulary

Chapters 9 & 39

Punctuation

Chapters 35 & 40

Spelling

Chapter 41

Citation Format

Chapters 17, 22 & 23

---

practice it 4.1 Finding Big-Picture and Sentence-Level Concerns

Look over the following student essay and read the comments. What big-picture issues should this student focus on in revision? What are the sentence-level concerns? What would you suggest this student focus on while revising? How would you prioritize the instructor's comments? Be specific about how this student should proceed with a revision.

Emma, don't forget to add your last name with page numbers. You want to make a good first impression!

Can you think of a good title that helps to focus your topic for the reader?

I like the idea for your hook. Can you revise so it's more descriptive and draws us in a little more? Make us "see" it.

Sometimes you use a comma correctly with a coordinating conjunction and sometimes you leave it out. Make sure you edit carefully for this throughout the paper. See Ch. 35 for help.

I think you actually discuss more things in the paper than are clearly stated in the thesis. Reread your paper and revise the thesis.

Can you add more evidence from the texts to develop this paragraph? Right now, it's not giving your readers much new information.

Are you talking about teens / young people or all people in general? The last paragraph focused on young people, and here you have various examples. Think about your focus, and make sure that's clear in your thesis and topic sentences. If you want to have one paragraph just on young people, that's fine, but connect it to the thesis better.

Emma Poole

Prof. Lawlor

English 95

February 12, 2016

It seems that at least once a week an offer for a credit card comes in the mail. At first this seems great and exciting, a new credit card with zero or a super low interest rate! But if you don't read the fine print, those zero or "low" interest rate cards could soon have very high interest if you are late or miss even one payment. They lure you in with promises of great rates, but they count on the fact that most people will not know how to manage their credit cards and end up with the very high interest rate, and that's how credit cards make so much money off of us. Most Americans have one or more credit cards, but do they really know how to use them responsibly? Credit card debt is a big financial pressure Americans face and it can cause a lot of problems with your finances. These problems can be solved by paying off your credit cards and cutting them up!

Credit cards are easy to get and many teens and young adults have more than one and carry big balances on them. Credit card companies prey on college students by setting up tables on campus where students can apply for a card and get a free water bottle or small gift in exchange for just applying. Just about every clothing store asks you if you want to sign up for their credit card to save an extra 15 percent on your purchase. Just about everywhere you go, there is an offer for a credit card. If you shop online, you are just as likely as in a store to be offered a chance to get a credit card to complete your purchase for a big discount. With so many credit card offers, it's no wonder it's a big problem.

People live beyond their means with debt and can't pay it off. In his article "Out of Debt, on the Road," Ken Ilgunas says "I thought of student debt like I thought of death: I didn't think of it at all" (55). As a student, paying off debt like student loans or credit cards seems like something so far in the future that it isn't necessary to pay attention to, but this thinking can lead to spending money that you don't have. Living beyond our means is something that most Americans can relate to. Whether it's a new car or that "have to have it" latest phone or computer, we often feel the impulse to buy buy buy. According to Olivia Mellan in "Men, Women, and Money" "The United States is in fact a nation of overspenders. We live in a market economy and we are led to believe that we are good citizens to the degree that we go out and spend" (61). This means that many Americans do not practice good financial behavior or don't know how to control their spending. If their spending gets out of control then they won't be able to pay it off. This is especially true if they carry large balances on several credit cards or in student loans or any other kind of loan. "[M]any people feel a core emptiness that they try to fill up with things. If we're not overspending, we're typically worrying about money . . . " says Mellan. People might think that buying something new will make them happy, but can they really afford it? If not, it will more than likely lead to stress rather than happiness.

  Not being in control of your spending can lead to late payments and even big balances on credit cards which could result in a bad credit score, and that makes future borrowing a problem. Having a good credit score will make a big difference in whether you can take out a loan later in life when you might really need it. It will also affect how much interest you will have to pay when you do have a loan. The higher your credit score, the lower the interest you will be charged. So, to make your future-self happy, be sure to keep your credit score high by not making any late payments on your bills and not carrying too high of a balance on your credit cards.

  Learning about credit cards should start before you get them, in school or from parents. Although more and more teens have experience with credit cards than ever before, they haven't necessarily improved their spending habits regarding credit cards

Don't forget a comma before the quotation. You make that mistake other places too. Proofread carefully on the last draft.

Good explanation!

Page number?

Using questions can be effective, but don't use questions in place of developing your idea. Can you make a statement here?

You might need to explain the graphic in a little more detail.

Good point! ———————

(Money Matters Infographic). According to Sherie Holder and Kenneth Meeks in "Teach Your Children the Building Blocks of Finance," "The learning process should start when you're a child. Parents have to teach children the value of money and guide them in their spending, encourage them to save, explore entrepreneurship opportunities, and expose them to solid financial planning (35). Parents set the tone for how a child thinks about money, so they should begin with learning the value of a dollar and saving. If kids get a good understanding of how to save and budget their allowance or any money they earned, they will probably be more careful with how they spend their money as they get older. Of course, they should also learn how to calculate interest and understand all the fees that come with having a credit card, so they will know how much that pair of shoes really cost them—tax, interest, fees and all. Finding this out the hard way, after you have racked up a lot of debt, may be too late.

Paying off your credit cards will help you reduce your debt and improve your credit score. It will also help you avoid late fees and interest fees. With all the stress and pressure that being in debt causes Americans, getting a handle on these fees should be everyone's priority. More credit cards don't mean you actually have more money, but it can feel that way. There are lots of Web sites that can help you learn how to budget your money so you don't live beyond your means.

Emma, you have clearly done a lot of work here, and I appreciate that. You can shape this into a very strong essay. Think about how you want to focus your thesis and topic sentences. Do you notice how some of your paragraphs are very developed and some aren't? That's a sign that the overall argument isn't clear yet. I've underlined your topic sentences. Go back and read them together. Do they flow? How could you reorganize them? Look at Chapter 14 for help with reorganizing using the reverse outlining technique. Good start!.

Practicing Peer Review

▶ **For more detailed information about peer review, see Chapter 18, Giving and Receiving Feedback.**

Peer review, which is also sometimes called "workshopping," is when a group of writers read and offer constructive criticism about one another's work. Peer review has two distinct purposes: It provides you with feedback on your draft during the revision process, and it helps you become a better reader and evaluator of good writing. As you get feed-back on your essay, you evaluate other essays and hone your critical reading skills by analyzing the strength of a thesis, the organizational logic, and the thoroughness of evidence and support. It's certainly valu-able to get feedback from your peers, but by giving others feedback, you strengthen your ability to recognize what needs work, and this helps you when writing and evaluating your own essays.

Your peers can offer you feedback on your ideas and organization. They can also point out parts of the essay that just don't seem quite right, which can be immensely helpful. For students, peer review works best when comments focus on big-picture issues.

Guidelines for Peer Review

- **Make your rough draft as complete as possible.** Your reviewers can't give you feedback on what isn't there, so the more complete your draft is, the more thorough the feedback you'll receive.

- **Ask for feedback on specific trouble spots.** If you have been struggling with an aspect of your essay such as your topic sentences or your introduction, ask your reviewers to pay particular attention to that area.

- **When you respond to a peer's work, always begin by saying something positive but offer constructive criticism as well.** The purpose of peer review is to suggest ways to improve a piece of writing.

practice it 4.2   Asking for Specific Feedback on Your Draft

Whether you have a formal peer review in your class or not, seek out a classmate, friend, or tutor to give you feedback on some specific areas of the rough draft that you'd like the most help on. Ask your reviewer for feedback on how well you address both the big-picture and the sentence-level issues. This activity will help you figure out what parts need the most work, so you can prioritize these problem areas of your essay. You should end up with a list of the big-picture and sentence-level concerns that need the most attention.

Revision Strategies

To begin revising, reread the assignment prompt. Keep it on your desk as you reread your essay a few times. Read critically, and determine the strengths and weaknesses of your work. Make a list of what things you do well and what needs improvement. Once you have identified your areas of weakness, choose revision strategies that will help you focus on those areas. The strategies presented in this section focus on improving six aspects of an essay:

- making your audience and purpose clear
- focusing your topic or strengthening your thesis
- reorganizing a paragraph
- developing your paragraphs
- integrating quotations and paraphrases
- reorganizing your essay

Use as many of these strategies as you need to improve your essay. You might not be able to address all the areas of weakness with your second draft, so prioritize your efforts and do more drafts if necessary.

STRATEGY 1: MAKE YOUR AUDIENCE AND PURPOSE CLEAR

▶ For more help with audience and purpose, see Chapter 7, Audience, Purpose, and Topic.

Reread the prompt. Are you being asked to write to a particular audience? If you are not being asked to write to a particular audience, do you have an audience in mind? Your classmates? Your campus community? Residents of your city? Young people? People with children? Once you determine your audience, look over your introductory paragraph. The introduction sets the tone for the essay and introduces your topic and thesis as well as any background information. All of these parts of your introduction should be written with your audience in mind. How much background information you include about your topic depends on how well-informed your audience is about it. If your audience is young people, for example, you need to consider whether your topic is something young people are likely to know much about. If necessary, revise to add enough background information for your audience. This focuses your essay by establishing a clear audience right from the beginning.

Your writing assignment probably makes your purpose clear: For instance, you may be asked to explain the difference between two plans for educating young people about the complicated issues of money, wealth, and financial literacy. If your writing prompt allows for a range of possible purposes, use your thesis to state the goal or purpose of your essay. Sometimes instructors provide broad prompts so that you can narrow the focus and purpose to something specific that interests you.

STRATEGY 2: FOCUS YOUR TOPIC OR STRENGTHEN YOUR THESIS

▶ For more help on strengthing your thesis, see Chapter 11, Thesis and Main Idea.

When you preview a text as part of pre-reading, you try to anticipate the scope of what an article will cover. In a well-structured essay, you should also get the gist of the whole essay just by reading the thesis statement and the topic sentences. Because these key parts of the essay direct the focus of the information, you want to make sure there is coherence from one topic sentence to the next.

In Chapter 3, you wrote a "working thesis" that gave you a focus for the draft as you wrote it. Now that you have a completed rough draft, it's time to revise the thesis and your essay to make a stronger point.

practice it **4.3**   Preview to Revise the Thesis

Copy your thesis out and then list your topic sentences. Taken together, the thesis and topic sentences should read like an overview of your entire paper. Ask someone who has not read your essay to read the thesis and topic sentences and then determine if the points made in the topic sentences logically flow from and support the thesis. The reader should answer these questions:

1. Based on the thesis, what do you anticipate the essay will be about?
2. After reading the topic sentences, can you understand the flow of the ideas? Do they progress naturally and logically from one idea to the next?
3. Is the essay focused? Do the topic sentences relate back to and support the thesis? Are there any topic sentences that seem out of place? (If so, strategy 3 below discusses getting them back in place.)
4. Are these topic sentences enough to support the thesis? Are there other points the writer needs to add?

Look over the feedback. What did your reviewer expect the essay to say based on your thesis? Is this how you see your essay? If not, then reconsider what your thesis promises. It could be that your thesis is exactly what you want to say, but the body paragraphs veer off topic or are missing supporting topics. If this is the case, you have two options: Revise the thesis to fit the body paragraphs, or revise the body paragraphs to fit the thesis.

STRATEGY 3: REORGANIZE A PARAGRAPH

Sometimes your essay is generally well organized, but you need to revise one particular paragraph's structure. When you add new information as you write, you may end up with paragraphs that include more than one topic. Revising for this problem can get messy, but it's also a very valuable strategy to practice, and the result will be a much clearer essay. Determine the main point of the paragraph and whether or not you have a clear topic sentence for this main point. Then evaluate the support. Quite frequently, student writers have good topic sentences and decent supporting evidence, but the evidence doesn't truly fit the point it is supposed to support. Next, check to see if the paragraph includes enough analysis of the evidence it presents. Is it clear how and why the evidence supports the point? Finally, review the transitions: Are there adequate transitions from idea to idea, or does the paragraph jump around?

▶ **For more information on paragraph structure, see Chapter 13, Topic Sentences and Paragraphs. For more on transitions, see pages 306–10 of Chapter 14, Essay Organization and Outlining.**

Reading your work against the grain and thinking critically about paragraph coherence helps you to improve the paragraph.

practice it 4.4   Organization within a Paragraph

Look over the following paragraph. Based on the point made in the topic sentence, what single topic/point will the paragraph cover? Does the paragraph stray off topic by addressing or introducing additional ideas not suggested by the topic sentence? Underline sentences that make this paragraph disorganized by addressing other topics. How can this paragraph be fixed? Suggest possible strategies for removing off-topic material or relating off-topic material to the topic sentence.

Learning financial literacy at a young age gives someone the best chance to gain financial stability. A big problem with many people is that they never learned financial literacy. This prevents them from knowing how to budget their money and can lead to overspending or debt. Not everyone can rely on an inheritance for their future stability. In fact, not everyone has family resources or support to help them if they get in a financial jam or want to try to buy a house and need help with the down payment. If you don't get an inheritance and you haven't gone to college, you might consider going back to school to get your A.A. degree or your B.A. According to the "Education Pays" chart, people with only a high school education are almost twice as likely to be unemployed as people with a bachelor's degree. Also, having a bachelor's degree will likely give you a higher paycheck than just having a high school diploma or an associate's degree. Teaching kids to save early in life will ensure that they are able to save money for unexpected problems that may come up later, or will help them to buy a home one day.

STRATEGY 4: DEVELOP YOUR PARAGRAPHS

▶ **For help with paragraph development, see Chapter 13, Topic Sentences and Paragraphs.**

The body paragraphs have a very specific job: They explain and support the claim of the thesis. Each body paragraph should cover one point and should begin with a topic sentence that states that point or idea and provides information and explanations. After the topic sentence, paragraphs should be made up of information, examples, details, and explanations to help prove the paragraph's main point. Generally, college essays use some information from one or more readings or from research, so all those great annotations you did when reading and those notes you took during class discussion will be very useful when building up your paragraphs. Problems with paragraph development usually emerge from an unclear topic sentence, a lack of supporting details, or not enough explanation or elaboration. Take note of the following common indicators of a lack of development in body paragraphs:

- Paragraphs that begin with evidence (such as a quotation) instead of a topic sentence / point in your own words
- Paragraphs that contain very little supporting evidence
- Paragraphs that end with evidence (such as a quotation) instead of some explanation of how that evidence supports your point

STRATEGY 5: INTEGRATE QUOTATIONS AND PARAPHRASES

Develop your paragraphs by adding more evidence—in the form of well-chosen quotations or paraphrases—to prove your point. A quotation is the *exact words* of a writer, surrounded with quotation marks. A paraphrase is a restatement of an author's words or ideas in your own words.

    Use either quotations or paraphrases to support your point, but be careful not to just drop a quotation or paraphrase into your essay. You need to provide a framework so that the reader understands where it comes from and how it helps you make your point. Integrating quotations and paraphrases well makes for a more coherent paragraph. Whenever you use a quotation or paraphrase, it should be part of a "sandwich." Here's how to make a quotation or paraphrase sandwich:

▶ **For more information about quotation and paraphrase, see Chapter 17, Quotation and Paraphrase.**

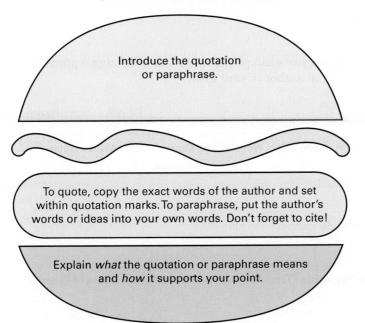

Introduce the quotation or paraphrase.

To quote, copy the exact words of the author and set within quotation marks. To paraphrase, put the author's words or ideas into your own words. Don't forget to cite!

Explain *what* the quotation or paraphrase means and *how* it supports your point.

▶ For detailed information
on citing sources,
see Chapter 22, MLA
Documentation, or
Chapter 23, APA
Documentation.

Introducing and explaining the quotation are ways to smoothly integrate it into your essay. Be aware that when you quote (or paraphrase), you must always let the reader know where you got the information.

Introduce a Quotation.   Someone once suggested that a quotation is like a dinner guest; you would never think of inviting a guest over and then not introducing him or her to everyone else. In the same way, you should never just drop a quotation into your paper without a proper introduction. Dropping a quotation into an essay without introducing it is generally abrupt and doesn't provide enough transition between your ideas and those of the author you are citing. The same is especially true of a paraphrase because the reader may not even realize that you are citing information from someone else.

Introduce a quotation or paraphrase using a signal phrase, or introductory word(s), to let the reader know its source. Most of the time, the best way to do this is to use the full name of the author and the title of his or her work the first time you mention them. You can refer to the author by last name after that, but don't ever refer to an author by first name.

Common Signal-Phrase Words

argues	illustrates	says
claims	makes the point that	suggests
explains	reveals	writes

The following two examples show how to use a signal phrase for the first mention of an author in your essay:

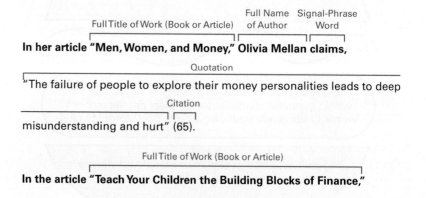

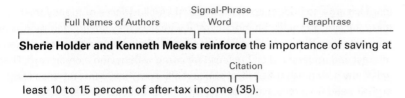

Sherie Holder and Kenneth Meeks reinforce the importance of saving at least 10 to 15 percent of after-tax income (35).

If you fully introduced the author earlier in the essay, you can use a shortened signal phrase:

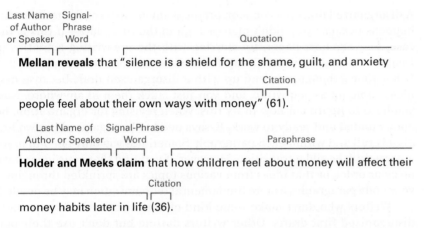

Explain What the Quotation Means and How It Supports Your Point. Often, students assume that the reader understands what the quotation means or that it explains itself. This is rarely the case. Different readers can interpret a quotation differently. Remember, you have carefully read and annotated the text, probably several times, and possibly even discussed it in class or elsewhere. Assume your reader is seeing it for the first time, so be sure to explain what you think the author means in your own words.

Again, a quotation does not speak for itself. You introduced it into the essay—now explain why. Let's look back at Emma's essay, which appeared earlier in this chapter. In the following paragraph from a later, revised draft, we can see how a quotation sandwich might look in a paragraph:

> Learning about credit cards should start before you get them. According to Sherie Holder and Kenneth Meeks in "Teach Your Children the Building Blocks of Finance," "The learning process should start when you're a child. Parents have to teach children the value of money and guide them in their spending, encourage them to save, explore entrepreneurship opportunities, and expose them to solid financial planning" (35). Holder and Meeks wisely advise parents to set the tone for how a child thinks about money. If kids

learn saving and budgeting methods for their allowances or money they earn, they will probably be more careful with how they spend their money as they get older. Similarly, parents should teach their children how to calculate interest and understand all the fees that come with having a credit card. They will know how much that pair of shoes really cost them—tax, interest, fees, and all—and hopefully avoid racking up a lot of debt in the first place.

STRATEGY 6: REORGANIZE YOUR ESSAY

A disorganized draft is a common problem among writers. Sometimes this happens because you didn't plan enough in the first place—if this is the case, for your next paper, try starting with the pre-writing activities in Chapter 3, especially the Group Activity to Organize Ideas (pp. 90–91). Other times, though, you end up with a disorganized draft because new ideas came up as you wrote, and you just stuck them in anywhere. Now you have to figure out how to fix this. When revising for organization, be open-minded and ready to work. Essays need to be organized on two levels: overall and within each paragraph. Sometimes you only need to move a paragraph or add a transition. However, if you find that your ideas have no clear order, or that ideas from various topics are sprinkled throughout your body paragraphs, a more fundamental reorganization may be needed.

Writers who don't make some kind of outline often have extremely disorganized first drafts. Other writers outline but don't use their outlines, ignoring important work they have already done. Either way, if your entire essay needs an organization overhaul, start by determining what you have already written and where exactly your organization went off course. Follow these steps:

STEP 1: **Make a list of your paragraph topics or points.**

STEP 2: **Gather a handful of colored pens, pencils, crayons, or highlighters.**   You need as many colors as you have paragraph topics. Assign each topic a color.

STEP 3: **Print out your essay.**   Go through the essay with one colored pen or pencil at a time, and underline sentences that directly support or relate to that color's assigned topic. Read carefully through all the body paragraphs. If a sentence fits more than one topic, underline it in both colors; later you can decide where it ultimately should go.

STEP 4: **After you color-code all the sentences, look over your paper.**   Does it resemble rainbow sprinkles on an ice cream cone, with a little of each color everywhere? Or maybe you have mostly one color per paragraph with only a few odd colors stuck in here and there? The idea is to put all the sentences underlined in the same color together in a paragraph. You should end up with all the pink sentences in one paragraph and all the blue sentences in another, for example.

STEP 5: **Evaluate the "leftovers."**   Are there some sentences that you didn't underline in any color? Evaluate them one at a time. Possibly they don't fit at all and should just be deleted. However, if you think they are important, maybe you need to add a new point to your paper and put those sentences in a new paragraph.

STEP 6: **Return to the document on your computer.**   Save it as a new document. Using your word-processing program, cut and paste the sentences into the correct paragraphs, based on the color-coding steps. Print it and read it out loud, paying attention to transitions that may need to be changed in the new organizational structure.

---

practice it 4.5   Revising to Make Major Changes

Read your essay once or twice, bearing in mind the following list of questions. As you read, annotate the parts of your paper that need more time and attention.

Audience and Purpose
- Who is the audience for your paper?
- How are you communicating to this particular audience?
- Why are you writing? To persuade? To inform? To argue? To describe? To compare? Is your purpose clear in your paper?

Topic and Thesis
- Does your essay respond to the prompt? Does it fit the topic?
- Do you have a clear, strong thesis that states a claim?
- Does the thesis address all parts of the question stem?

Paragraph Development and Coherence
- Does each body paragraph have a clear topic sentence that states the point that the paragraph will make?
- Do all the sentences in a paragraph focus on the same topic?
- Do the evidence and examples appropriately support the main point of the paragraphs?
- Are quotations and paraphrases integrated well?
- Does each body paragraph feel complete and finished?

Organization
- Are the major sections in a logical order?
- Are the transitions from one paragraph to the next logical and clear? Are the transitions from sentence to sentence within the paragraphs clear?

Introduction and Conclusion
- Does the introduction hook the reader and provide some good, general background about the topic?
- Does the conclusion sum up the ideas and offer final thoughts?

continued ❯

Finally, review what you marked on your essay and make a plan for your revision. What big-picture issues do you need to focus on? List your specific "next steps" for your essay and consult the following relevant sections for help.

Editing Strategies

As you can see, revising takes time, effort, and focus. It is difficult, if not impossible, to edit sentences at the same time you make major changes to content and organization. If you find yourself hitting the delete key far more than you are typing words, you probably need to loosen up, stop censoring everything you write, and remember that there will be a time for editing after all your ideas are in place.

▶ **For more help with editing, see the chapters in Part 4, How Do I Make My Sentences Say What I Mean?**

Now that you are at that editing stage, there are specific techniques that you can use to improve your word choice and grammar and to check for minor errors. Give each a try and see which ones you like best. Ideally, you will have more than one strategy that works well for you.

Guidelines for Editing

- Always edit from a printed copy; never edit from the computer screen.
- Make corrections by hand on your paper and enter them into your computer. Then go back and compare your handwritten marks to the new printout to make sure you didn't miss anything. Then read the paper again.
- Editing requires that you read the paper several times. Reading it over once is not enough.
- Give yourself adequate time to edit. You might spend fifteen minutes or more on each page of text that you have to edit.
- Try not to edit immediately after you finish writing something. Give yourself a break between revising and editing; editing requires a fresh mind and clear focus.
- Take a three-minute break every twenty minutes.
- Never skip editing.

EDITING STRATEGY 1: READ YOUR ESSAY OUT LOUD

Reading your work out loud is one of the most effective ways to edit. Sure, it may be embarrassing to do this in your local coffee shop or, even worse, in class. You'll get over the embarrassment pretty quickly, though, once you have tried it a few times. Most student writers find five or more errors per page when they use this technique. Here's how it works:

STEP 1: **Print a copy of your paper and grab a pencil or pen.**

STEP 2: **Read your paper out loud.**   Read slowly, clearly, and carefully, as if you are a newscaster reading the evening news. As you read, underline the places that sound wrong or bad. Do *not* stop to fix them as you are reading. This will break the rhythm. Just read and underline the mistakes.

STEP 3: **When you finish reading the whole document, go back and focus on those underlined parts.**   Make corrections.

STEP 4: **Edit your document on the computer.**   Print it.

STEP 5: **Repeat steps 1–4 until your paper sounds great.**

If you can't bear to read your own writing, or if English is not your first language, enlist a friend, classmate, or relative to help. In that case, print two copies of your paper. Give your friend a copy and keep a copy for yourself. Have your friend read it while you listen, watch, and underline the bad parts. (Seriously, keep your eyes open: Your friend's face will show it when he or she gets confused by something that isn't clear.) Then make the changes yourself.

EDITING STRATEGY 2: READ BACKWARDS

Reading your essay backwards may sound funny, but it is a highly effective editing technique. If you can get the answers right when you take multiple-choice tests and do grammar exercises, but still can't figure out how to find and fix your own errors, this may be the best editing technique for you. When editing, you look for lots of different kinds of things: grammar errors, punctuation, and word choice. You need several read-throughs to adequately search for each kind of issue. This takes some time, especially at the beginning, but it is worth it. Here's how you edit by reading backwards:

STEP 1: **Choose your most serious sentence-level error.**   Review your instructor's comments from past assignments.

STEP 2: **Print your essay and also find a blank piece of paper.**

STEP 3: **Turn to the last page of your essay.**   Use the blank piece of paper to cover up everything except the last sentence.

STEP 4: **Read that last sentence.**   Does it include the error you're looking for? If it doesn't, move on to the second-to-last sentence in the essay. If it does, try to fix the error. Check the relevant chapter of this book and if you can't fix it on your own, see your instructor or a tutor for advice and for help learning the grammar rule.

STEP 5: **Continue on throughout the essay, one sentence at a time, back to front.**   Remember to look for only one error at a time.

STEP 6: **Take a break between passes so you are always looking at your essay fresh.**   For example, if you know you have trouble with sentence fragments and commas, read your essay backwards for sentence fragments, and then start over and read it backwards again for comma errors. You are much more likely to find errors when you focus your search.

STEP 7: **Repeat the steps with your next-most-serious error and then the next.**   Do this until you have covered all the errors you commonly make.

If you're not sure what kinds of errors you tend to make, look over older writing assignments to see what errors your instructors marked, or go to Chapter 27, How to Learn the Rules and Apply Them to Your Own Writing, to begin keeping a personalized Grammar Log of your frequent errors. Knowing what kinds of errors you are most likely to make is valuable information!

Proofreading

You are nearly finished! You have brainstormed, organized, drafted, revised, and edited your essay. It's time to put the final polish on it by carefully proofreading and correcting any minor errors you may have missed. After you have the major ideas in place and have made changes to your sentences by using one or more editing techniques, double-check your work by proofreading. Careful proofreading of your document will catch errors that you make, such as when you make a change in one paragraph but forget to follow through with the change in the next. The proofreading stage is also a good time to catch your own commonly made spelling or word-choice errors, such as if you always mix up *there/their/they're*. Finally, if you haven't already done so, now is the time to double-check that your typed document includes your name, the course number, and other necessary information and is properly formatted with the correct margin size, line spacing, and font. If your instructor hasn't stated a preference for font size, 12-point Times New Roman is a good bet.

practice it 4.6 Proofreading for Errors and Format

Print a copy of your essay and proofread for typographical errors. Then compare it to the sample MLA-formatted essay on pages 402–4. (If your instructor requires APA style instead, then consult the sample paper on pages 418–23.) Make sure you include the correct information in your header and that your margins and font size are correct. Remember to delete extra spaces between paragraphs—they just look like "filler."

chapter review

In the following chart, fill in the second column to record in your own words the important skills included in this chapter. Then assess yourself to determine whether you are still developing the skill or feel you have mastered it. If you are still developing the skill, make some notes about what you need to work on to master it in the future. If you believe you have already mastered it, explain why.

Skills and concepts covered in this chapter	Explanation in your own words	I'm developing this skill and need to work on . . .	I believe I have mastered this skill because . . .
REVISING			
Identifying big-picture and sentence-level concerns			
Participating in peer review			
Making audience and purpose clear			
Focusing the topic or strengthening the thesis			

continued ❯

Skills and concepts covered in this chapter	Explanation in your own words	I'm developing this skill and need to work on . . .	I believe I have mastered this skill because . . .
Reorganizing a paragraph			
Developing a paragraph			
Integrating quotations and paraphrases			
Reorganizing an essay			
EDITING			
Reading out loud			
Reading backwards			
PROOFREADING			

Designed to emphasize specific reading or writing skills for further practice and in-depth study, these chapters will help you refine your skills or learn new ones.

How Do I Do That? Reading and Writing Workshops

5
Active Reading Strategies

in this chapter

- How Do You Read Nonfiction Texts?
- How Do You Read Visual Texts?
- How Do You Read Fiction Texts?

Because we learn to read as children, we often take this skill for granted. You might ask why you need to learn reading strategies. You already know how to read! While this is true, there is always room to improve your reading skills. Reading is not like riding a bike, where there is only one set of basic skills (balancing, steering, and pedaling) to master. Reading involves a more complex set of skills that continue to grow and improve the more you practice and develop them. As you progress in your academic career, reading tasks become more challenging and require stronger comprehension and analysis skills.

Strong readers do more than just understand and recall what they read; they also have a growth mind-set about the challenges of reading. All college students face difficult readings at times, but one main difference between strong readers and struggling readers is that strong readers can evaluate the challenges in a reading and can draw from an arsenal of reading strategies to meet them. Throughout this chapter you will be introduced to strategies for reading nonfiction, fiction, and visual texts like charts, photographs, and film or video. Add these strategies to your toolbox so you can use them as needed and confidently approach any kind of text.

▶ For more on "growth mind-set," see Carol S. Dweck's article "The Perils and Promises of Praise" in Chapter 1 (pp. 6–13).

Reading Nonfiction

There are many reading strategies; some are very similar to one another, but each has a slightly different purpose. The more reading strategies you know, the easier it will be to pick the right one to help you tackle a challenging reading task. Think of it this way: If you are a chef but you only know how to sauté, what happens when you are faced with ingredients that don't sauté well? Lots of foods are delicious sautéed, but that cooking strategy won't work for everything. Knowing several reading strategies makes you a more flexible reader.

Following are four important strategies to help you prepare to read and understand nonfiction texts. Some strategies can be used throughout the reading process, while others apply only to certain stages.

STRATEGIES FOR READING NONFICTION

Strategy	Reading stage
SQ3R	pre-reading and during reading
KWL+	pre-reading, during reading, and post-reading
Mapping	post-reading
Outlining	post-reading

▶ For more on pre-reading, see pages 3–5 in Chapter 1, Reading and Responding to College Texts.

SQ3R

SQ3R stands for Scan, Question, Read, Recite, Review. This reading strategy will help you get ready to read a short work like an article, essay, or book chapter.

Scan.   This step is about previewing the text by scanning it.

- **Look at the title of the reading, the headings, the length, and any pictures or graphs.** What do you already know about the topic? What does the title tell you about the topic?
- **Read the introductory paragraphs.** How does this information relate to the title? What connections can you make?
- **Read the last paragraph and any questions at the end of the essay or chapter.** How do these parts relate to the introduction and the title? What connections can you make between them?
- **Read the topic sentences or the first sentence of each paragraph.** What can you figure out about the different points the essay will cover? Even if you can't identify all the main points, this step will help you with the next step.
- **Notice any words that are highlighted, italicized, or in bold type.** These are probably key words or new vocabulary words to learn.

Question.   Turn the headings, subheadings, and topic sentences into questions so you can anticipate questions that the article, essay, or chapter might answer. Write all the questions down in your notebook or a computer file, leaving space between each section or paragraph so you can fill in the answers later. What information or points do you think you will learn? Write questions for all the pictures, graphs, and charts as well. What do you anticipate they will help you learn? Start with the journalist's six questions: who, what, where, when, why, how?

Read.   Read the whole work, but not all at once. If the reading is divided into sections, read one section at a time while actively looking for answers to your questions. As you find answers, write them down under each question. Don't forget to "read" the pictures, graphs, and charts. If the reading is not divided into sections, read each paragraph separately while looking for answers. If the paragraphs are very short, group related paragraphs together and treat these like a section. Also write main points or significant examples in the margins and in your notes.

Recite.   This step is the fun one. After reading a section, look away or cover the reading and recite out loud or in your head the answers to the questions you wrote. Summarize the points you learned in this section. Reciting is important because it builds a mental link to the information. Write down your answers, including any helpful or important examples. After you do this, move on to the next section and repeat the QRR.

Review.   After reading the whole text by questioning, reading, and recit-ing, you are ready to review. You will be amazed at how much you learned. Go back to the start of the reading and, looking at the title, try to remem-ber what the first section was about. Summarize it out loud or at least in your head. If you can remember the points from the first section, move on to the next section and repeat the review. If you have trouble with any section, go back and do the QRR for that section again. The notes you create while doing SQ3R are a perfect study guide for a reading. Review them occasionally, especially before a quiz or exam.

KWL +

A second reading strategy for nonfiction is called KWL+. KWL+ is an acronym—a phrase created from the first letter of a series of words. The acronym KWL+ stands for:

K = What do I **Know** about the topic?
W = What do I **Want**/expect to learn?
L = What have I **Learned**?
+ What questions do I still have about the topic?

KWL+ is a strategy that helps you prepare to read and engage actively with the text to improve comprehension.

STEP 1: **Create a chart with four columns.** Label the first column "K," the second column "W," and so on.

STEP 2: **In the first column, under "K," write down what you already know about the topic.** You haven't done the reading yet, so you may not think you know much about the topic, but fortunately we don't learn everything new, from scratch, every day. We have some prior knowledge about almost everything. What words or phrases are associated with the topic? It's fine if you don't know a lot about a topic, but what do you know? Write it down in this column.

STEP 3: **Preview the reading, taking note of the title, any headers or topic sentences, images, graphs, and questions.** Based on your preview, write what you want to learn or expect you will learn from this reading in the second, "W," column. When filling in the "W" column, make a list of things that you think might be important to know about your textbook or your chapter.

STEP 4: **Read, annotating as you go.** Identify main points and support, and make note of the places in the text where your questions are answered or your knowledge on the topic is expanded.

STEP 5: **After reading, fill the "L" column up with information about what you learned in the reading.** This is a good time to look back at the "K" column to see if there is anything you thought about the topic that needs correcting or clarifying. In the "L" column, correct any misinformation that you might have had before reading. For example, if there is an idea you had about the reading that now seems incomplete or perhaps

KWL+ CHART

K What do I Know about the topic?	W What do I Want/expect to learn about the topic?	L What did I Learn about the topic?	+ What more do I want to know about the topic?

inaccurate, you might write something like, "So _____ is not what I thought it was before I read the article," in order to clarify what you now know. Be sure to include main points and concepts from the reading in the "L" column as well as anything you found interesting.

STEP 6: **Look over the "W" column to see if you learned everything you expected to learn about this topic.** If there is anything that the reading did not address, write down any remaining questions you have or what you still want to know about the topic in the "+" column. This is also a place to write down any questions you have about the reading itself.

---

practice it 5.1   Using KWL+ on "Long Live the Mammoth"

Try your hand at KWL+ with the article "Long Live the Mammoth" (pp. 131–35), using the preceding steps. Copy the following chart into your notebook. Fill out the "K" and "W" columns before reading the article. An example is shown below. Once you complete the reading, fill out the last two columns.

KWL+ CHART FOR "LONG LIVE THE MAMMOTH"

K What do I <u>K</u>now about the topic?	W What do I <u>W</u>ant/expect to learn about the topic?	L What did I <u>L</u>earn about the topic?	+ What more do I want to know about the topic?
• The mammoth was a huge elephant that became extinct. • There are lots of endangered animals in the world, like the polar bear, panda bear, and Bengal tiger. • In "Jurassic Park" scientists brought back dinosaurs.	• Why did the mammoth become extinct? • How is it possible to make an animal un-extinct? • Is this the same as cloning an animal? • What would happen if mammoths came back? • Will this help save endangered species as well? • Is it possible to bring back dinosaurs like in "Jurassic Park?!"		

BETH SHAPIRO

Long Live the Mammoth

The first use of the word "de-extinction" was, as far as I can tell, in science fiction. In his 1979 book *The Source of Magic*, Piers Anthony describes an explorer who suddenly finds himself in the presence of cats, which, until that moment, he had believed to be an extinct species. Anthony writes, "[The explorer] just stood there and stared at this abrupt de-extinction, unable to formulate a durable opinion." I imagine this is precisely how many of us might react to our first encounter with a living version of something we thought was extinct.

The idea that de-extinction may actually be possible—that science could advance to the point where extinction is no longer forever—is both exhilarating and terrifying, even to me. I am a biologist. I teach classes and run a research laboratory at the University of California at Santa Cruz. My lab specializes in a field of biology called ancient DNA. We and other scientists working in this field develop tools to isolate DNA sequences from bones, teeth, hair, seeds, and other tissues of organisms that used to be alive. We then use those sequences to study ancient populations. The DNA we extract from these remains is largely in terrible condition, which is not surprising given that it can be as old as 700,000 years.

During my career, I have studied DNA from an assortment of extinct animals, including dodos, giant bears, steppe bison, North American camels, and saber-toothed cats. By piecing together the DNA sequences that make up these genomes, we can learn nearly everything about an individual animal's evolutionary history: how and when the species to which it belonged first evolved, how the population in which it lived fared as the climate changed during the ice ages, and how the physical appearance and behaviors that defined it were shaped by the environment in which it lived. I am fascinated and often amazed by what we can learn about the past simply by grinding up a piece of bone and extracting DNA from it. Yet, regardless of how excited I feel about our latest results, the most common question about them I receive is, "Does this mean that we can clone a mammoth?"

Always the mammoth.

The problem with this question is that it assumes that, because we can learn 5 the DNA sequence of an extinct species, we can use that sequence to create an identical clone. Unfortunately, this is far from true.

To clone Dolly the sheep in 1996, scientists at the Roslin Institute, which is part of the University of Edinburgh in Scotland, removed a small piece of mammary tissue that contained living cells from an adult ewe. They used the DNA in these cells to create an identical copy of the ewe. This process is called somatic cell nuclear transfer, or, more simply, nuclear transfer. For species that have been extinct for a long time, however—the passenger pigeon, the dodo, the mammoth—cloning by nuclear transfer [is] not a viable option. It requires intact cells. No such cells have ever been found in the remains of extinct species recovered from the frozen tundra.

Degradation of cellular DNA begins immediately after death. Plant and animal cells contain enzymes whose job it is to break down DNA. These enzymes, called nucleases, are found in cells, tears, saliva, sweat, and even on the tips of our fingers. Nucleases are essential while we're alive. They destroy invading pathogens before they can do any damage. They remove damaged DNA so that our cells can fix what's broken. And, after our cells die, they break down the DNA in those dead cells so that our bodies can more efficiently get rid of them. In the lab, we stop nucleases from degrading away the DNA we're trying to isolate, either by dropping a fresh sample into a solution of chemical inhibitors or by subjecting it to rapid freezing. The Arctic is a cold place, but it can't freeze something as large as a woolly mammoth quickly enough to protect its DNA from decay.

Besides nuclear transfer, the other path to creating a living organism is eerily reminiscent of the movie *Jurassic Park*. As is likely to be true in real-life de-extinction projects, *Jurassic Park* scientists were able to recover only parts of the dinosaur genome—in their case, from mosquito blood preserved in amber. When they came across gaps in the dinosaur genome, they used frog DNA to complete the sequence. Unfortunately, they couldn't know beforehand which bits of DNA would help make a dinosaur look and act like a dinosaur and which bits were junk. We can assume these fictional scientists were hoping that the holes they were filling were mostly in the junk-containing regions. But, of course, they were wrong, and some of that frog DNA let the unextinct dinos switch sexes miraculously, leading to disaster and $1 billion in global box-office earnings.

In real-life de-extinction science, the plan is to determine which parts of the genome are important in making the extinct species look and act the way it did. We would then find the corresponding parts of the genome of a close living relative, cut out key sequences, and replace them with versions from the extinct species.

That's easier said than done.

10

• • •

The common ancestor of mammoths, Asian elephants, and African elephants lived about six million years ago. This means the mammoth spent many millions of years evolving separately. Some of the hardest parts of the mammoth's genome to assemble will be those that changed in mammoths since they diverged from elephants. For the purposes of de-extinction, these sequences will likely be the most critical to get right.

Fortunately, we don't have to clone a mammoth to resurrect mammoth traits or behaviors. We could, for example, learn the DNA sequence that codes for mammoth-like hairiness and then change the genome of a living elephant to make a hairier one. Obviously, resurrecting a mammoth trait is not the same thing as resurrecting a mammoth, but it is a step in that direction.

Scientists know much more today than they did even a decade ago about how to manipulate cells, sequence the genomes of extinct species, and engineer the genomes of living ones. These three technologies pave the way for the most likely de-extinction scenario, or at least the first phase: the creation of a healthy individual.

Here's how that might work. First we find a well-preserved bone from which we can sequence the complete genome of an extinct species, such as a woolly mammoth. Then we study that genome, comparing it with those of living relatives. The mammoth's closest living relative is the Asian elephant, so that is where we will start. We identify differences between the elephant's genome and the mammoth's, and we design experiments to tweak the elephant genome, changing a few DNA bases at a time, until it looks more mammoth-like. Then we take a cell that contains one of these new, mammoth-like genomes and allow it to develop into an embryo. Finally, we implant this embryo into a female elephant, and about two years later, that elephant gives birth to a baby mammoth.

Scientists have already sequenced most of the mammoth genome, which   15
was pieced together from fragments of DNA extracted from mammoth bones. Researchers in George Church's lab at Harvard University have also taken the next step. They used a new genome-editing tool to splice the DNA that codes for 14 mammoth characteristics—among them, denser hair, thicker layers of fat, and blood cells that could transport oxygen more efficiently at cold temperatures—into an elephant genome. It is not yet possible to grow these cells into a whole organism, but the Harvard team is working to develop that technology as well. If successful, the embryo, whose genome contains some very tiny portion of mammoth DNA, could eventually develop into a living, breathing animal.

But what would be the end product of this experiment? Is making an elephant whose genome contains a few mammoth parts the same thing as making a mammoth? After all, an animal is more than a simple string of As, Cs, Gs, and Ts—the letters that represent the nucleotide bases that make up DNA. Today, we don't fully understand the complexities of how we get from simply stringing those letters together in the correct order to making an organism that looks and acts like the real thing. That will involve much more than merely finding a well-preserved bone and using it to sequence a genome.

• • •

When I imagine a successful de-extinction, I don't imagine an Asian elephant giving birth to a slightly hairier elephant under the close scrutiny of veterinarians and excited scientists. I don't imagine the spectacle of this exotic creature in a zoo enclosure, on display for the gawking eyes of children who'd prefer to see a *T. rex* or *Archaeopteryx* anyway.

What I do imagine is the perfect arctic scene, where mammoth (or mammoth-like) families graze the steppe tundra, sharing the frozen landscape with herds of caribou, horses, and reindeer—a landscape in which mammoths are free to roam, rut, and reproduce without the need for human intervention and without fear of re-extinction. This constitutes the second phase of de-extinction, which builds on the successful creation of an individual to produce and eventually release an entire population into the wild. In my mind, de-extinction cannot be successful without this second phase.

That idyllic arctic scene might be in our future. But first, science has some catching up to do with the movies. Though we have sequenced nearly the entire mammoth genome, that work is not yet complete. We are also a long way from understanding precisely which bits of that sequence are important to making a mammoth look and act like one. This makes it hard to know where to begin and nearly impossible to guess how much work might be in store for us.

Another problem is that some major differences between species or individuals, such as when a particular gene is turned on during development, are inherited epigenetically. That means that the instructions for these differences are not coded into the DNA but are determined by the environment in which the animal lives. What if that environment is a captive breeding facility? Baby mammoths, like baby elephants, ate their mother's feces to establish a microbial community capable of breaking down the food they consumed. Will it be necessary to reconstruct mammoth gut microbes? A baby mammoth will eventually need a large, open space where it can roam freely but also be safe from poaching and other dangers. This will likely require a new form of international cooperation and coordination. 20

My goal is not to argue that de-extinction will not and should never happen. In fact, I'm nearly certain that someone will claim to have achieved de-extinction within the next several years. I will argue, however, for a high standard by which to accept this claim. Should de-extinction be declared a success if a single mammoth gene is inserted into a developing elephant embryo and that developing elephant survives to become an adult? Purists may say no, but I would want to know how inserting that mammoth DNA changed the elephant. What if a somewhat hirsute elephant is born with a cold-temperature tolerance exceeding that of every living elephant? And what if that elephant not only looks more like a mammoth but is also capable of reproducing and sustaining a population where mammoths once lived?

While others will undoubtedly have different thresholds for declaring de-extinction a success, I argue that this—the birth of an animal that is capable, thanks to resurrected mammoth DNA, of living where a mammoth once lived and acting, within that environment, like a mammoth would have acted—is a successful de-extinction, even if the genome of this animal is decidedly more elephant-like.

De-extinction is a process that allows us to actively create a future that is better than today, not just one that is less bad than we anticipate. It is not important that we cannot bring back a creature that is 100 percent mammoth or 100 percent passenger pigeon. What matters is that—today—we can tweak an elephant cell so that it expresses a mammoth gene. In a few years, those mammoth genes may be making proteins in living elephants, and the elephants made up of those cells might, as a consequence, no longer be isolated to pockets of declining habitat in Africa and Asia. Instead, they will be free to wander the open spaces of Siberia, Alaska, and Northern Europe, restoring to these places all the benefits of a large dynamic herbivore that have been missing for around 8,000 years. Large herbivores knock down trees and trample bushes, for example, and transport seeds and nutrients over long distances. By removing snow, mammoths—or rather, cold-tolerant Asian elephants—may also expose the permafrost to the bitter cold of Siberian winters. This would lower the temperature of the soil and slow the release of greenhouse gases trapped within it.

De-extinction is a markedly different approach to planning for and coping with future environmental change than any other strategy that we, as a society, have devised. It will reframe our possibilities.

practice it 5.2   Using KWL+ on Assigned Readings

All reading strategies require practice to be able to use them well. Try KWL+ on an assigned reading for a class. Be sure to take the time to fill out every column. When you finish, assess how well the strategy worked for you. When would you use this strategy?

MAPPING

The third reading strategy for nonfiction, mapping, involves using visual cues to navigate long or difficult texts. There are many ways to map a reading selection. You can use words and graphics, such as circles, arrows, and underlining, or draw images that suggest the literal content of the reading.

Mapping is often used as a post-reading strategy. The first task is to read, always making sure to carefully annotate and determine the main points. Once you do this, you can start mapping the reading. Here are the

▶ For more help finding the main points, see Chapter 11, Thesis and Main Idea.

steps to follow, using "Long Live the Mammoth" by Beth Shapiro (pp. 131–35) as the reading.

STEP 1: After you complete the reading, in the center of a large, blank piece of paper, draw a circle or box and write the topic in it. Be as specific about the topic as you can. In this case, the reading is not really about mammoths, although it might seem so at first glance. It is really an article about de-extinction.

STEP 2: Draw lines out from the central topic and write the main points about the topic in a circle or box at the end of the lines. You can leave these as words on a line or make a box around the words.

STEP 3: Beneath each main point, draw lines on which to write the main point's supporting details. Be careful not to overdo it with too many examples or details; identify only the significant supporting details and examples.

Here's one example of what your map might look like after following the preceding steps:

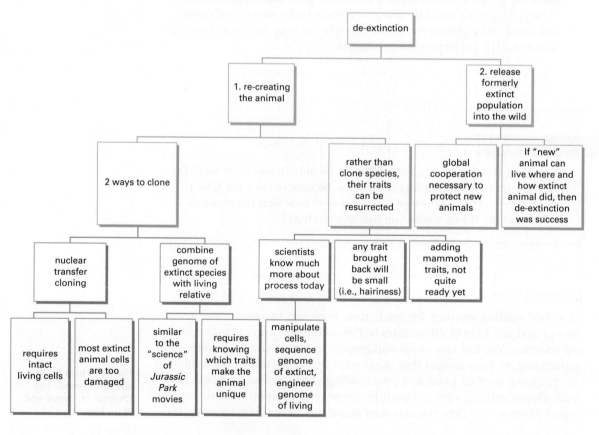

There are many ways to organize information, so no two maps will look exactly the same. Mapping a reading helps you understand the concepts in the reading and how these concepts connect; there's no one "right" way to map.

▶ See mapping in action as a model reading strategy with Jake Halpern's "The Desire to Belong" in Chapter 26, pages 551–61.

OUTLINING

Another way to determine the structure of a reading is to make a traditional outline. In contrast to maps, which organize information from a reading spatially to show connections among ideas, outlines reveal the linear structure of a reading—that is, they put the information in the order that it appears. Following is an outline of "Long Live the Mammoth" that includes the same information as the map on the mammoth article but organizes it in a way that indicates the hierarchy of main points and supporting details or examples.

▶ For more on outlining, see Chapter 14, Essay Organization and Outlining.

De-extinction
    A. Re-creating the animal
        1. two ways to clone
           a) nuclear transfer cloning
                (1) requires intact living cells
                (2) most extinct animal cells are too damaged
           b) combine genome of extinct species with living relative
                (1) similar to the "science" of *Jurassic Park* movies
                (2) requires knowing which traits make the animal unique
        2. rather than clone species, their traits can be resurrected
           a) scientists know much more about process today
                (1) manipulate cells
                (2) sequence genome of extinct
                (3) engineer genome of living
           b) any trait brought back will be small (e.g., hairiness)
           c) adding mammoth traits, not quite ready yet
    B. Release formerly extinct population into the wild
        1. global cooperation necessary to protect new animals
        2. if "new" animal can live where and how extinct animal did, then de-extinction was successful

> **practice it 5.3**   Mapping or Outlining a Reading
>
> Create a map or outline of any article you have been assigned to read for this course. Preview the text before you read and annotate. Use any headers or topic sentences to help guide you to the main and supporting points. Compare your map or outline with those of your peers.

Reading Visual Texts

Throughout college, and beyond, you will likely encounter many texts that include charts, graphs, diagrams, or photographs to convey information. Or you may read extended visual texts; for example, an infographic uses a combination of visual texts. But unlike written documents, visual texts are not necessarily organized from top to bottom or meant to be read from left to right, and if your visual text is a documentary film or video, you may not even be aware that you are "reading" it. Photographs usually draw the eye to what is visually dominant. Advertisements use the many skills of graphic design to direct your attention to specific parts of the image. Although the specific organization of the visuals might differ, all of them can be "read."

Keeping in mind that these visuals are intended to help you process information, begin by looking to see what kind of information the visual text includes. Reading the title or caption will be your first clue to help you understand its meaning. Like titles of books or articles, the title of a visual text may give away its scope or purpose. When you are reading a visual text, you are likely doing one or more of the following:

- Comprehending—understanding so you can explain the meaning
- Analyzing—looking at all the various parts as a way to understand the significance of the whole
- Inferring—drawing conclusions based on the information provided

Remember, in most of your college classes, except perhaps those in the art department, the visual texts you will encounter are generally meant to augment, or add to, your understanding of the written word, so it is important to understand not only the purpose and meaning of the visual but also its relationship to the surrounding text.

Here is a chart of the most common visual texts you will come across and the general purpose of each one.

Kind of visual	Where you are likely to find it	How it is used
Bar graph	textbooks, reports, scholarly articles, popular magazines	compares data
Pie chart	textbooks, reports, scholarly articles, magazines, news reports	shows breakdown of how a whole is divided into parts or classified
Line graph	textbooks, reports, scholarly articles	compares or shows data over time
Illustration or diagram	textbooks, magazines, scholarly articles	shows a concept visually
Map	textbooks, reports, scholarly articles, popular magazines	represents data geographically, shows relationships between bits of information
Infographic	Web sites, newspapers, reports	combines various visual texts to provide a more comprehensive picture of the subject matter
Photograph	all kinds of readings, advertisements in magazines and online	conveys a concept or idea, appeals to emotions or desires
Film or video	TV, Internet	conveys information through images, dialogue, and storytelling

▶ **Illustrations are not covered in this chapter, but an example is shown on page 163 in Chapter 6, Strategies for Reading Textbooks.**

TIP

Look for this information with visuals:

- Title
- Note explaining the purpose, source, or context
- Key to interpret the values

BAR GRAPHS

A bar graph is one of the most common graphs used to compare data because it shows the relationship between the different categories or points of comparison quickly. It is also especially useful for comparing multiple kinds of data. The bar graph is composed of a horizontal axis (the line across the bottom) and a vertical axis (the line up the side). One axis shows the range of values, and the other shows the categories or points of comparison. In the following chart, the horizontal axis shows the various age groups of adults reporting at least twenty to thirty

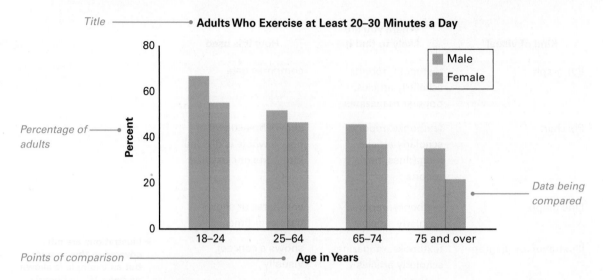

Title ———————→ **Adults Who Exercise at Least 20–30 Minutes a Day**

Percentage of ——→
adults

Data being
compared

Points of comparison ——————→ **Age in Years**

Based on a graph from Kathleen Stassen Berger, *Invitation to the Life Span*, 2nd ed. (Worth Publishers, 2014).

minutes of exercise a day. The values are on the vertical axis, in this case percentages of adults. The vertical axis shows the percentage of each age group reporting that amount of daily exercise.

practice it 5.4 Test Your Understanding

1. According to the graph, which age group reported the most people exercising daily?
2. What percentage of females age seventy-five and over exercised daily?
3. Which age group reported about 50 percent of its members exercising daily?
4. Looking at all the data together, what inferences can you make about daily exercise and gender? About daily exercise and age?

▶ **For more about making inferences, see page 263 in Chapter 12, Argument.**

PIE CHARTS

A pie chart indicates parts of a whole. In this kind of chart, the numbers must add up to a whole (100 percent). The following pie chart identifies what percentage of commuters uses the following transportation methods: driving alone, carpooling, taxi, bicycle or motorcycle, walking, or other modes. Note that the chart also takes into consideration the percentage of people who work from home and do not commute.

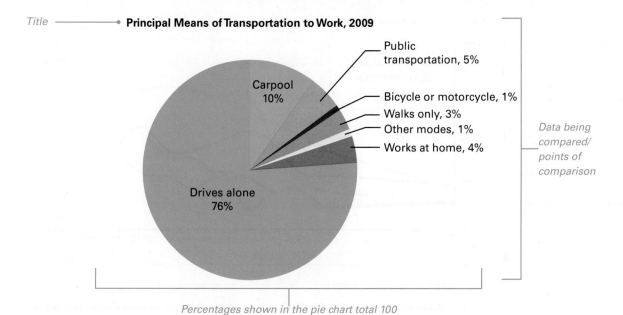

Title ————————• **Principal Means of Transportation to Work, 2009**

Public transportation, 5%

Carpool 10%

Bicycle or motorcycle, 1%

Walks only, 3%

Other modes, 1%

Works at home, 4%

Drives alone 76%

Data being compared/ points of comparison

Percentages shown in the pie chart total 100

Data From National Transportation Library.

practice it 5.5   Test Your Understanding

1. What percentage of people carpooled?
2. What percentage of people used a commuting method other than car or taxi?
3. What method of commuting was used the least? What method of commuting was used the most?
4. What inferences can you make about commuters and transportation based on this pie chart?
5. How might this chart be used by city planners?

LINE GRAPHS

A line graph is a useful way to show trends or changes over time for one or more elements. In these graphs, the vertical axis usually indicates a measurement of quantity, which could be a percentage or whole numbers. It's important to know what values this axis represents. Do the numbers represent tens, hundreds, thousands, hundreds of thousands? Line graphs also have a horizontal axis that usually indicates a measurement of time, which could be hours in a day, number of days, weeks, months, or years.

The following line graph shows how the number of people commuting by bicycle in four cities has changed over a period of twelve years.

Title

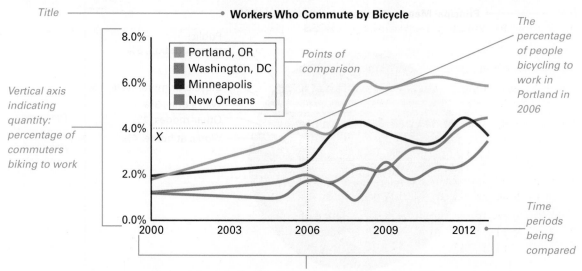

Workers Who Commute by Bicycle

Points of comparison

The percentage of people bicycling to work in Portland in 2006

Vertical axis indicating quantity: percentage of commuters biking to work

- Portland, OR
- Washington, DC
- Minneapolis
- New Orleans

X

Time periods being compared

Horizontal axis indicating the time period being measured: years

Based on a graph by BikePortland with data from Census American Community Survey.

Note that the change has not always been an increase; line graphs are particularly well suited to show both upward and downward trends.

practice it 5.6   Test Your Understanding

1. Between the years 2007 and 2008, how much did commuting by bicycle increase in Portland?
2. Which city had the greatest overall increase in commuting by bicycle? Which city had the smallest increase?
3. Which city had the greatest dip in bicycle commuting between the years 2006 and 2009?
4. What can you infer about commuting by bicycle in the Pacific Northwest? What can you infer about commuting by bicycle nationwide?

MAPS

Maps convey spatial data or information that is categorized geographically. For example, data arranged across cities or states on a U.S. map can clarify where something occurs more than elsewhere. When reading a map, you begin, as always, with the title, which should indicate what kind of data the map is representing. Look also for a legend or key that will identify what the various colors or shadings on the map mean.

OBESITY PREVALENCE IN 2014 VARIED ACROSS STATES AND TERRITORIES. ●——————————— *Title*

- No state had a prevalence of obesity less than 20%.
- 5 states and the District of Columbia had a prevalence of obesity between 20% and <25%.
- 23 states, Guam, and Puerto Rico had a prevalence of obesity between 25% and <30%.
- 19 states had a prevalence of obesity between 30% and <35%.
- 3 states (Arkansas, Mississippi, and West Virginia) had a prevalence of obesity of 35% or greater.
- The Midwest had the highest prevalence of obesity (30.7%), followed by the South (30.6%), the Northeast (27.3%), and the West (25.7%).

Highlights of data

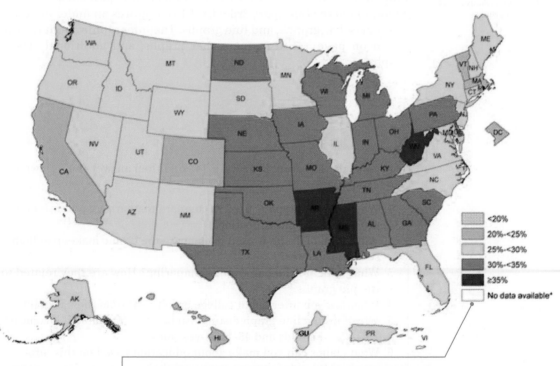

Legend identifying data being compared (prevalence of obesity)

Prevalence of Self-Reported Obesity among U.S. Adults by State and Territory, 2014
Source: Behavioral Risk Factor Surveillance System, CDC.

*Sample size <50 or the relative standard error (dividing the standard error by the prevalence) ≤ 30%.

Centers for Disease Prevention and Control

practice it 5.7   Test Your Understanding

1. What region of the United States had the lowest rate of obesity in 2014? Which region had the highest?
2. This map shows the prevalence of obesity in each state by percentage. Is that an effective way to measure obesity rates? Why or why not?
3. What was the lowest reported prevalence of obesity in the United States, according to this map?
4. What can you infer about obesity in America based on the information on this map?

INFOGRAPHICS

▶ For another example of an infographic, see *Money Matters on Campus*, pages 52–55 in Chapter 2, Active and Critical Reading.

Infographics are often used to tell a story or draw a conclusion based on several kinds of data, so you must navigate different kinds of charts or graphs to get the complete picture. For example, the following infographic on education, from the developmental psychology textbook *Invitation to the Life Span*, 3rd ed. (2016), requires an understanding of pie charts, bar graphs, and line graphs. The infographic about transportation on page 146 uses maps, bar graphs, and additional types of graphs.

practice it 5.8   Test Your Understanding

Look at the infographic on page 145 and then answer the following questions.

1. What kind of graph is used to compare the earning potential for different levels of education?
2. What kind of graph is used to compare the ethnic makeup of high school graduates?
3. What data are the bar graphs comparing? How are they related to the pie graphs?
4. What can you infer about college enrollment from the bar graphs?
5. Why does the line graph distinguish between the annual income of 25- to 34-year-olds and 45- to 54-year-olds?
6. What claims can you make about education based on this infographic? What inferences can you make?

EDUCATION IN THE UNITED STATES

10-year-olds in school (98.5%)	High school graduates (85%)	Enrolled in college (66%)	BA or BS earned (30%)

- European American males
- European American females
- African American males
- African American females
- Hispanic American males
- Hispanic American females
- Asian American males
- Asian American females

DATA FROM U.S. CENSUS BUREAU, 2012, EDUCATION WEEK, 2013, AND KENA ET AL., 2015.

AMONG ALL ADULTS

The percentage of U.S. residents with high school and college diplomas is increasing as more of the oldest cohort (often without degrees) dies and the youngest cohorts aim for college. However, many people are insufficiently educated and less likely to find good jobs. It is not surprising that in the current recession, college enrollment is increasing. These data can be seen as encouraging or disappointing. The encouraging perspective is that rates are rising for everyone, with the only exception being associate's degrees for Asian Americans, and the reason for that is itself encouraging—more of them are earning bachelor's degrees. The discouraging perspective is that almost two-thirds of all adults and more than four-fifths of all Hispanic Americans have no college degrees. International data find that many European and East Asian nations have higher rates of degree holders than the United States.

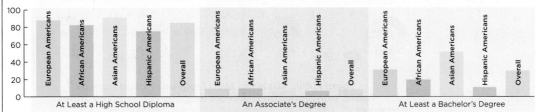

DATA FROM KENA ET AL., 2015 AND U.S. CENSUS BUREAU, 2013 AMERICAN COMMUNITY SURVEY.

INCOME IMPACT

Over an average of 40 years of employment, someone who completes a master's degree earns $500,000 more than someone who leaves school in eleventh grade. That translates into about $90,000 for each year of education from twelfth grade to a master's. The earnings gap is even wider than those numbers indicate because this chart includes only adults who have jobs, yet finding work is more difficult for those with less education.

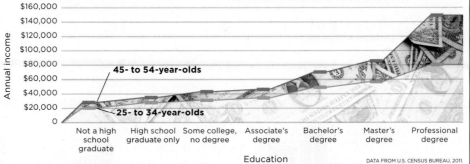

DATA FROM U.S. CENSUS BUREAU, 2011.

Transportation Alternatives by Census Region

2013 American Housing Survey

New questions about household public transportation use were added to the 2013 American Housing Survey to determine how many households have used public transportation for any reason, what type, how often, and how close transit was to their homes. Biking and walking data were also collected in order to determine the convenience of neighborhood amenities and services.

 West

 Midwest

 South

 Northeast

Although There Are More Households in the South...

= 10 million units

West	Midwest	South	Northeast
25,879,000	25,912,000	42,951,000	21,110,000

The Northeast Leads the Nation in Public Transportation Use and Expense

Percentage of households using public transportation and median monthly public transportation cost

West	Midwest	South	Northeast
23% $25	12% $30	9% $30	32% $75

Local Public Bus is the Most Frequently Used Type of Public Transportation in All Four Regions of the United States

Use public transportation

Use at least once a week

Percentage of households using public transportation by type*

Local public bus: West 76% | Midwest 72% | South 69% | Northeast 67%

Subway, elevated train, street car, light rail, or trolley: West 35% | Midwest 25% | South 32% | Northeast 51%

Commuter or inter-city train: West 8% | Midwest 14% | South 4% | Northeast 19%

Commuter or shuttle van: West 6% | Midwest 6% | South 8% | Northeast 7%

*May not add to 100 percent because respondents can select more than one mode of travel.

The West Leads the Nation in Walking and Biking Accessibility

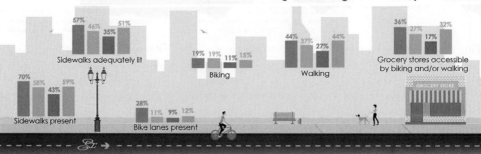

Sidewalks adequately lit: 57% 46% 35% 51%

Biking: 19% 19% 11% 15%

Walking: 44% 37% 27% 44%

Grocery stores accessible by biking and/or walking: 36% 27% 17% 32%

Sidewalks present: 70% 58% 43% 59%

Bike lanes present: 28% 11% 9% 12%

US Census Bureau

practice it 5.9   Reading an Infographic on Transportation

Using the information about reading charts and graphs on pages 139–44, read the infographic pictured on page 146 and then answer the following questions.

1. What is the overall message about transportation?
2. Which region of the United States has the highest median public transportation costs, and what form of public transportation is most frequently used in that region?
3. In what U.S. region is public transportation use the highest?
4. What form of transportation is the least used in any region?
5. What data suggest that the West is the most biking-friendly region?

PHOTOGRAPHS

When you look at a picture, you move your eye around the image without even realizing it. You are drawn to certain aspects of the image, and you take in information in ways that the artists or graphic designers who created the image manipulated you to do, sometimes without realizing it themselves. We call this composition, and when artists make an image, they are composing it, just like you compose an essay or a songwriter composes a song. If you understand a few key design principles, you will learn how to "read" the images that artists and designers have created.

One principle of composition is the rule of thirds, which applies especially to square and rectangular images. Imagine a picture frame, divided into threes like this:

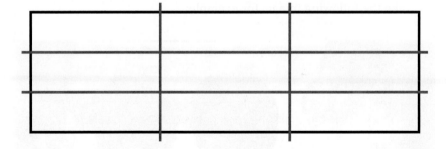

The rule of thirds in visual composition means that the image can be divided into left, center, and right as well as into top, middle, and bottom. The goal of the image is to make sure your eye moves around the boxes in a particular order, not missing any important information. But we don't "read" an image from left to right, as we read a book. Instead, we rely on the compositional balance of the image to tell us (usually unconsciously) how to "read" it: what to look at first, then second, and so on. This happens so quickly and automatically we are not even aware of it.

Your job, then, in analyzing a photograph, is to discover which elements of the image seem to have a lot of visual impact, and from there to determine how your eye moves around the page. Look for the following elements:

1. **Forms or shapes**, which can be large or small compared to other shapes in the image and can be layered on top of one another in a way that indicates importance
2. **Positive and negative space**, which is formed by the interplay between the foreground, what's in "front" of the image, and the background, what's in the "back" of the image
3. **Colors or shades of gray**, which influence the strength of an object when compared to other objects; for example, red and yellow tend to stand out, which is why we use them for fire trucks, but a pale turquoise object against a mostly black background can also stand out quite well—color is all relative to what it's surrounded by
4. **Lines**, which can be thick or thin, dotted or solid, jagged, curving or straight, light or dark, and so on; lines can frame an object or cut through objects or space
5. **Graphics**, such as letters, numbers, and other symbols, which have meaning by themselves but can also be used merely as shapes

As you look at a particular photograph, if you take time to see each element separately, you will notice how the image "works" much better. After you have identified and described the elements in an image, you will determine which ones have the most impact and what symbolic meaning they convey. Put it all together, and you're making an analysis of the image! In other words, how do the various visual elements that make up the photograph convey a message or meaning?

Take the following image, for example:

OJO Image/iStock/Getty Images

1. Where does the composition of this photo draw your attention?
2. What do the shapes and colors in this photo emphasize?
3. What can you infer about the children in this photo? What elements of the image help you make those inferences?

---

practice it 5.10   Image Analysis

Working alone or in groups, find an image in this textbook (look for the chapter openers for the thematic reading chapters on pages 434, 478, and 520) and analyze the overall composition and the use of the elements of design in the image. Remember to use descriptive vocabulary for any important elements. For instance, describe the type of line, its color, its width, and so on.

FILM AND VIDEO

When analyzing film or video, your first consideration is whether the video is fiction (primarily based on imagination) or nonfiction (based in fact). For fictional films, you will consider many of the same aspects you would for fictional written texts: characters, setting, plot, conflict, symbols, theme, and so on (see pages 150–55 in this chapter). For nonfiction videos, ask questions about any possible perspective or bias of the filmmaker, considering the arguments and counterarguments being made. Essentially, "read with and against the grain" as you would for a print text. (See pages 30–32 in Chapter 2, Active and Critical Reading.) This can be difficult when you get caught up in the interesting information being presented, but you must remain a critical viewer. It helps to watch the video several times, taking careful notes after your first viewing.

Most nonfiction videos still have a written text, which can be a combination of voice-over narration and the words of the people onscreen. You can often get a copy of the text of a video online by searching the title and the word "transcript." Reading the transcript after you have watched the video can be helpful if you need to find a particular piece of information or want to check facts. If you are going to quote a video, write down the exact wording from the video or the transcript. Do not just write down the quotation from memory. Hold information from videos to the same high standards of credibility as you have for written texts. Just as when a writer quotes an expert in an article, a filmmaker is quoting an expert when he or she films the expert speaking.

Try to pay attention to the way sound and image are layered. Is there an authoritative voice telling you what to think about the images on

▶ **For more about taking notes during film and video screenings, see page 382 in Chapter 20, Note Taking.**

screen? Often viewers unconsciously trust such a voice-over narrator more than they might if it were a "talking head," a person onscreen being interviewed. Is music being used to manipulate your reaction to a particular image or sequence? If so, how? Try watching a short bit of the film without sound or with sound turned down low to see if you have a different reaction to it.

Editing has perhaps the most profound effect on how we respond to video. Videos are a series of choices made by the filmmaker about what to show and not show, what to add and what to take away. For example, if a video cuts from an image of a man smiling to another image of a cute dog, we will have a positive response, assuming that the man is smiling because of the cute dog. In other words, we construct a meaningful connection between the shots, even if no other information is presented to make us do that. We put the man and the dog in the same space just because the images were edited together. The man must be smiling at the dog. (We know that viewers do this because if we take the exact same image of the smiling man and replace the cute dog with an image of a car crash, the audience will now say the man is a psychopath.) Essentially, the editing takes on even more meaning than any particular shot. Today's filmmakers use this editing effect all the time to make a meaningful text.

---

practice it 5.11   Critically Reading Film and Video

Choose an important short segment of a video text you are studying. Aim for about three to five minutes in length. Watch it through once, normally, making notes about anything that stands out. Then turn the sound off and watch it again. Add notes to your list. What else did you "see" once you couldn't hear it? Then play it again, this time only listening and not watching. What did you notice this time? Compare your lists with classmates.

Reading Fiction

Reading fiction requires slightly different strategies, since fictional texts are not organized in the same ways as most nonfiction texts you will read in college. When it comes to fiction, readers use a different set of analytical tools, though they still annotate, reflect on what they read, and question the text.

There are many genres of fiction: literary fiction, science fiction, fantasy, historical fiction, mysteries and thrillers, graphic novels, romance, and young adult, to name a few. Some nonfiction—such as histories, biographies, memoirs, autobiographies, and true crime—feels a lot like fiction, and you can use most of the techniques for fiction reading on those types of nonfiction. For instance, biographies often have compelling characters and settings and plots like fiction does.

ELEMENTS OF FICTION

When reading fiction, look for and analyze the following basic elements of a short story or novel.

Characters.   These people populate the story. Most short stories have at least one or two main characters; a novel might have more. Often, there are also minor characters who appear less frequently in the story.

Setting.   The setting is both the location where the story takes place and the time period (era) in which it is set. The same location one hundred years apart is not the same setting: For example, one story that takes place in New York City in the 1960s and another that takes place in New York City in 2060 do not have the same setting.

Plot.   The plot is, essentially, what happens during the story. It's what makes us want to turn the page to see what happens next. Some people refer to the plot as the story arc.

Conflict.   The conflict is the main problem that the characters are trying to deal with. A short story generally has one central conflict; a longer work might have one central and several other smaller conflicts.

Symbols.   A symbol is something that stands for something else. We use symbols all the time in our daily lives. We give the "thumbs up" symbol to mean that everything is good, or okay, and we use hearts to symbolize love.

Theme.   The theme is a central topic or subject of the story.

STRATEGIES FOR READING FICTION

Strategy	Reading stage
Annotating	pre-reading, during reading, and post-reading
Taking notes	pre-reading, during reading, and post-reading
Concept wheel	post-reading
Picture map	post-reading

ANNOTATING FICTION

Should you really write in the margins of your novel or short story? Absolutely! Annotating fiction is one of the best reading and study activities you can practice. Because works of fiction are not thesis driven or evidence based, it might not seem clear what you should annotate while you read. Really, though, you are annotating many of the same kinds of things that you would for an essay or article: interesting or significant passages, unfamiliar words, and questions or confusing sections. In addition, make notes in the margins when a new character is introduced or when a character behaves atypically—both might become something to discuss in class or in an essay. Underline important passages. Also annotate any symbols that seem important, themes that you recognize, and places where the plot "thickens."

TAKING NOTES ON FICTION

Taking notes requires discipline, but it does not have to take the fun out of reading. It should help you better appreciate the way the author writes. And it will definitely help you write a better paper. Take several different types of notes as you read.

Plot notes. In your notes, write down what happens in the novel as you finish reading each chapter or section. It's great if you can also write down page numbers so you can find things more easily. We always think we'll remember what happened where, but we often don't. This is especially true in a novel that does not follow a chronological time line. Does it begin at the beginning and then end at the end? Does the story begin at the end and then go backwards in time through memory or flashbacks? Nutshell summaries of each chapter's plot help you keep track of a novel's structure.

▶ **For more on nutshell summaries, see Chapter 1, Reading and Responding to College Texts.**

Thematic notes. As you read, you start to notice themes that keep emerging. A theme is a central topic or subject of a story or book. These themes vary from story to story or novel to novel. For instance, in Shakespeare's *Romeo and Juliet*, themes include love, family, coming of age, sexuality, and rebelliousness. Usually a novel or short story has a few major themes and several minor ones. Once you identify a theme, keep a running list of page numbers where it is mentioned. By the time you finish the book, you will have a chart with various themes and lists of page numbers under them. The inside of the book's back cover or a blank page at the end is a great place to keep your list. This list makes essay writing much easier; you just have to look back at those passages, figure out how they all relate, and develop your thesis from the material.

Character notes. Keep a chart, family tree, or list of all the characters. Write down the page number where they are first introduced. This is usually where they are described in most detail. Depending on the novel, you might find it useful to make a list of the major scenes with each major character.

CONCEPT WHEEL

A post-reading strategy for reading fiction is the concept wheel graphic organizer, which can help you see the "big picture" of the story and prepare you to write about it. After reading a short story or novel, think about what you will be focusing on for your paper. A specific character? A specific theme? The setting? Draw a circle and put that character, theme, or setting in the center. Then fill in the sections of the concept wheel with the specific fictional elements that relate to your paper focus.

For example, if you are writing about a character, usually the main character or protagonist, ask yourself: Who or what influences this character? Decide on three or four of the most important influences, and then put each in one sector of the concept wheel. If you were writing about Romeo, you might list Juliet in one part of the concept wheel, family expectations in another, his youthful immaturity in another, and his friends in the last. Next, skim through your annotations of the text, and list specific ideas, actions, or even quotations (probably just the page number and the start of the quotation) that are relevant. Once you have the chart mostly filled in, try to state in your own words what motivates your character to be who he or she is.

Here's an example, with the story of Pandora (see Chapter 24, pp. 437–39):

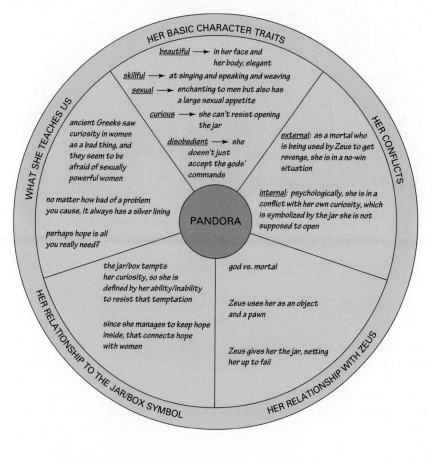

Another way to use the concept wheel graphic organizer is to put a theme at the center. In this case, choose an abstract term that you think the story is about, and add the different characters, the setting, symbols, or other elements of fiction that help you think through the theme. Then, in the outermost circle, make notes about the connection between those elements and the theme. The outer circle is also a place to note quotes from the text that show the connection between the theme and the element of fiction.

Here's an example of a concept wheel based on the theme of curiosity with Pandora:

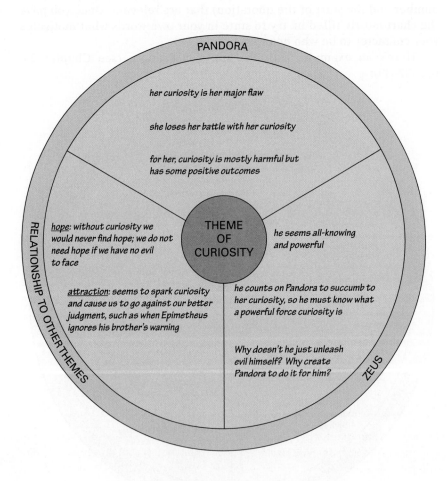

PANDORA

her curiosity is her major flaw

she loses her battle with her curiosity

for her, curiosity is mostly harmful but has some positive outcomes

THEME OF CURIOSITY

he seems all-knowing and powerful

hope: without curiosity we would never find hope; we do not need hope if we have no evil to face

he counts on Pandora to succumb to her curiosity, so he must know what a powerful force curiosity is

attraction: seems to spark curiosity and cause us to go against our better judgment, such as when Epimetheus ignores his brother's warning

Why doesn't he just unleash evil himself? Why create Pandora to do it for him?

RELATIONSHIP TO OTHER THEMES

ZEUS

PICTURE MAP

The strategy of mapping or outlining an article or book can be applied to fiction as well to better comprehend a story. Because fiction writing doesn't have a thesis or paragraph points the way nonfiction writing does, mapping a story is a useful way to visualize a plot or the relationship between characters. Here is an example of a picture map of the main characters and plot points of the story of Amaterasu from Chapter 24 (pp. 444–48). Note that simple symbols or images, even stick figures, can help clarify a plot and keep characters straight.

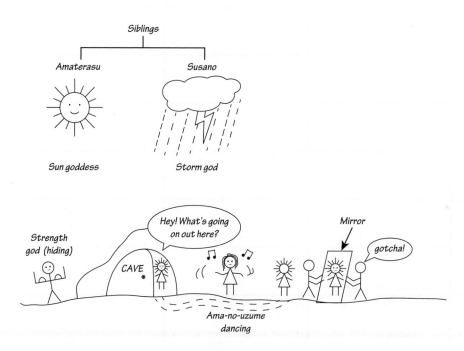

chapter review

In the following chart, fill in the second column to record in your own words the important skills included in this chapter. Then assess yourself to determine whether you are still developing the skill or feel you have mastered it. If you are still developing the skill, make some notes about what you need to work on to master it in the future. If you believe you have already mastered it, explain why.

Skills and concepts covered in this chapter	Explanation in your own words	I'm developing this skill and need to work on . . .	I believe I have mastered this skill because . . .
Using SQ3R			
Using KWL+			
Mapping			
Outlining			
Reading visuals			
Critically reading film and video			
Annotating fiction			
Taking notes on fiction			
Generating a concept wheel			
Creating a picture map			

6
Strategies for Reading Textbooks

Reading from a textbook might seem like a straightforward task; after all, you've probably been reading from textbooks for most of your time in school. Textbooks, however, present unique reading challenges for several reasons: They have many features (such as boxes, graphs, and diagrams) that pack in a tremendous amount of information. Unless you know how to use the various features that are unique to these books and practice some good textbook-reading strategies, you are likely to be overwhelmed by much of the information and not read efficiently. Because much of your reading in college will be from textbooks, it's important to be well-versed in strategies that will help you get the most out of your reading.

Of course, the reading strategies you learned in previous chapters (Chapters 1, 2, and 5, for example) will also be useful in reading college textbooks. So when reading your textbooks, use all the strategies that you have learned so far:

- Pre-reading to get a sense of what you know about the topic and a sense of the structure, audience, purpose, and design.

- Annotating to record your reactions and questions about the reading and to find main points and support. (You'll find more about annotating textbooks on page 159 in this chapter.)

- Summarizing the text to check your comprehension.

- Applying SQ3R, which stands for Scan, Question, Read, Recite, Review. Look back at the discussion of this strategy on pages 127–28 in Chapter 5. SQ3R is equally effective when reading textbooks; it helps you increase your comprehension as well as your reading speed.

▶ **For more about these and other active reading strategies, see Chapters 1, 2, and 5.**

This chapter first discusses how to pre-read a textbook and then takes you through the various features that make textbooks unique.

How to Pre-Read a Whole Textbook

STEP 1: Read the book title and the table of contents.   What does the title suggest about the book's purpose and content? Based on the table of contents, what topics does this book cover? How is the material organized? What kinds of topics are addressed in each part of the book? What can you learn about the audience and purpose from reading the table of contents? Does the table of contents reflect the title of the book? In what ways? How does this book compare to other textbooks you have used?

STEP 2: Skim the section headings and features for each chapter.   Pay particular attention to any charts, boxes, and tables that call out key aspects of the chapter's topic. What kind of material is covered in the chapters?

STEP 3: Look for chapter-opening and chapter-ending reviews, outlines, questions, and activities.   This will help you anticipate what important points might be covered.

STEP 4: Think about the intended purpose and audience (in this case, students). What do the authors think students should learn? What can you expect to learn by the time you are finished using this textbook?

Pre-reading an entire textbook is a good way to begin the semester because it gives you an idea of what material the course will cover, but it's also a great strategy to help prepare for comprehensive exams like midterms and finals. Other times you will want to preview a single chapter at a time. This strategy is useful when you begin a new unit in a class or are assigned a new chapter to read. It's also a great way to study for quizzes or shorter exams that cover a single chapter or one or two chapters.

practice it 6.1   Pre-Reading a Textbook Chapter

Textbooks often have features that show you how the information is organized. You can practice using these features in a chapter from this or another textbook that you haven't yet read. Read the chapter title, the list of chapter contents, and the headings that break up the information into manageable sections. Then look at the end of the chapter for a chapter review or for chapter questions. These can also give you a clue as to the main ideas and concepts the author wants you to understand. Often textbooks list these at the beginning of the chapter; they're sometimes called "objectives."

Annotating Textbooks

The most common textbook-reading strategy students use is probably underlining. But although underlining sounds easy, the tricky part is recognizing which main points and important concepts you need to underline. Without this information, underlining is random (not helpful) or so extensive that too much of the page is underlined (also not helpful). Not only that, but underlining doesn't assist you in understanding or remembering new information. Because of this, underlining by itself is not the most helpful textbook-reading strategy.

Because understanding the reading requires reading actively and reflecting thoughtfully on the information presented, annotating is still one of the most valuable strategies for reading anything, textbooks included. As with an article or book chapter, when you annotate a textbook, you add brief notes and explanations for what you have learned in the margins. These annotations are an excellent study tool for preparing for tests and quizzes. Annotating is a highly valuable reading strategy because it requires you to process the information as you read it so that you understand it and remember it. Another important part of annotating is asking questions in the margin for concepts or information that you don't understand. If you put a big question mark in the margin or, even better, write out a question in the margin to ask your instructor, you will be prepared to get clarification in class. Instructors expect you to have questions about the reading, but if you don't write down your question, chances are slim that you'll remember everything you wanted to ask.

▶ For a review of annotating techniques, see Chapter 1, Reading and Responding to College Texts.

Using Textbook Features

In addition to pre-reading and annotating, you will also want to use special textbook features to learn the material. Textbooks have many different design features, some unique to their discipline and some pretty standard across the board, all of which are intended to help you comprehend and recall the material more easily. Knowing how to use the various features will jump-start any reading you do. The following paragraphs discuss some of the most common features you find in textbooks.

TABLE OF CONTENTS

Most textbooks have both a **brief table of contents** and a **detailed table of contents** at the front of the book. Why both? The *brief table of contents* gives you a quick overview of the major contents of the whole book, usually just listing the major parts of the book and the chapter titles on one or two pages. Because the detailed table of contents provides a lot more information about each chapter and can take up many pages, the brief table of contents is useful

TIP
When you get your syllabus at the beginning of the semester, write down the dates each chapter needs to be read by on the brief table of contents so you always have that information handy even if you don't have your syllabus with you.

if you want to quickly see the big picture: how the book is organized and what chapters it includes. This is the feature you might use to see in what order the topics of the book are discussed or to quickly locate a chapter. The brief table of contents is also a good place to make notes (annotate) about chapters you have finished reading, need to review, or won't be covering in class.

The *detailed table of contents* is useful to get an idea of what, specifically, each chapter will cover. Because it goes into so much more detail than the brief table of contents, often taking up several pages, it does not quickly give a whole picture of the book; however, it's a great study tool when you are ready to prep for a test. It usually lists the main topics or headings in each chapter, and you can use this list to test yourself on your knowledge of the section. The detailed table of contents is also perfect for the first step in previewing a chapter. By reading the list of chapter contents prior to reading the chapter, you will have a head start on understanding the information and how the various sections of the chapter fit together.

CHAPTER OUTLINES OR OPENERS

Chapter outlines or openers provide a peek into the scope of the chapter, which allows you to prepare for reading it. Knowing, ahead of reading, what material you will be covering helps you understand the context of what you are reading (how it relates to what came before and what is coming next) as well as make more efficient annotations. For an example of a chapter opener, look on page 2 from the first chapter of this textbook. In this case, the chapter opener has a list of questions under the heading "in this chapter." Although you probably won't be able to fully answer each question before you read the chapter, the questions provide a clear idea of the main topics and important concepts that will be covered. Knowing those before you read allows you to identify them as you read, so you can be sure to understand them or ask questions in the margin if you don't.

KEY WORDS OR GLOSSARY

Textbooks usually identify important words in each chapter by bolding or highlighting them. They might also provide definitions of those words in the margins or in a glossary at the back of the book. Each discipline has its own lexicon (the vocabulary specifically related to that subject), and instructors will expect you to learn these terms in order to fully grasp the concepts of the reading. Making use of any glossary or vocabulary feature will help you learn key words more easily, which in turn will help you understand the material and do well on assignments.

To best make use of the words identified as key terms, write the meaning of each key word in the margin if it isn't already defined. If there is a definition in the margin, write an example of the key word either from the material or your observations next to the definition. You can see how this is done for the following page from a reading on volcanoes.

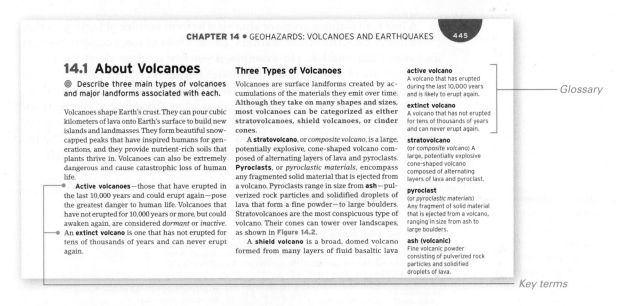

14.1 About Volcanoes

◉ Describe three main types of volcanoes and major landforms associated with each.

Volcanoes shape Earth's crust. They can pour cubic kilometers of lava onto Earth's surface to build new islands and landmasses. They form beautiful snow-capped peaks that have inspired humans for generations, and they provide nutrient-rich soils that plants thrive in. Volcanoes can also be extremely dangerous and cause catastrophic loss of human life.

Active volcanoes—those that have erupted in the last 10,000 years and could erupt again—pose the greatest danger to human life. Volcanoes that have not erupted for 10,000 years or more, but could awaken again, are considered *dormant* or *inactive*. An **extinct volcano** is one that has not erupted for tens of thousands of years and can never erupt again.

Three Types of Volcanoes

Volcanoes are surface landforms created by accumulations of the materials they emit over time. Although they take on many shapes and sizes, most volcanoes can be categorized as either stratovolcanoes, shield volcanoes, or cinder cones.

A **stratovolcano**, or *composite volcano*, is a large, potentially explosive, cone-shaped volcano composed of alternating layers of lava and pyroclasts. **Pyroclasts**, or *pyroclastic materials*, encompass any fragmented solid material that is ejected from a volcano. Pyroclasts range in size from **ash**—pulverized rock particles and solidified droplets of lava that form a fine powder—to large boulders. Stratovolcanoes are the most conspicuous type of volcano. Their cones can tower over landscapes, as shown in **Figure 14.2**.

A **shield volcano** is a broad, domed volcano formed from many layers of fluid basaltic lava

active volcano
A volcano that has erupted during the last 10,000 years and is likely to erupt again.

extinct volcano
A volcano that has not erupted for tens of thousands of years and can never erupt again.

stratovolcano
(or *composite volcano*) A large, potentially explosive cone-shaped volcano composed of alternating layers of lava and pyroclast.

pyroclast
(or *pyroclastic materials*) Any fragment of solid material that is ejected from a volcano, ranging in size from ash to large boulders.

ash (volcanic)
Fine volcanic powder consisting of pulverized rock particles and solidified droplets of lava.

Glossary

Key terms

SECTION HEADINGS

Part of previewing a textbook chapter is reading all the section headings and subheadings (also called *headers* and *subheaders*) so you can get a sense of how the information is organized and how it will be covered. Because textbooks are so full of information, they are usually broken down into sections with headings to make the information easier to digest. These headings also provide an outline of the chapter, which can be a fantastic study guide. To create the outline as a study guide, copy down the chapter title with all of the headers listed beneath the title. Leave some space to write between each header, and when you are ready to quiz yourself, write down an explanation of the material covered in each section. See also the related strategy of muscle reading on page 181.

BOXES AND CHARTS

Inset boxes are one of the features that distinguish textbooks from other kinds of books. These boxes may appear anywhere on the page, and they generally contain information the author wants to convey separately from the text in the form of a chart, graph, or image. The boxes might also be used to make a side note about related information, provide a hint, or show an example of something explained in the text. For instance, the boxes in the math textbook chapter "Borrowing Models" (pp. 40–45) give extended examples of the concepts the author discusses in the chapter. Whatever is in a box is worth paying attention to. Inset boxes are designed to make information stand out and get noticed, so be sure to look at these for clues to understanding the content better.

A box containing a graph or chart is a helpful feature of textbooks that particularly benefits visual learners. These kinds of tools convert the text into visual information. For example, if you are reading about the unemployment rate of recent college graduates between 2007 and 2011, the text will likely include statistics on the rate of change over this period of time, but it's difficult for most people to grasp what that "looks" like without seeing a visual representation of it. Enter the graph! The graph can convey this information in a way that simply reading the numbers cannot. The following extract from a passage on unemployment features a bar graph.

This bar graph makes it clear that the unemployment rate of recent college grads increased after 2007 but improved somewhat after 2009. It also shows how much higher the rate was for recent grads than for those over the age of twenty-five.

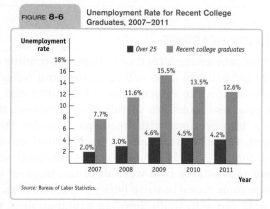

ECONOMICS ▶ in Action

Failure to Launch

In March 2010, when the U.S. job situation was near its worst, the *Harvard Law Record* published a brief note titled "Unemployed law student will work for $160K plus benefits." In a self-mocking tone, the author admitted to having graduated from Harvard Law School the previous year but not landing a job offer. "What mark on our résumé is so bad that it outweighs the crimson H?" the note asked.

The answer, of course, is that it wasn't about the résumé—it was about the economy. Times of high unemployment are especially hard on new graduates, who often find it hard to get any kind of full-time job.

How bad was it around the time that note was written? Figure 8-6 shows unemployment rates for two kinds of college graduates—all graduates 25 and older, and recent graduates in their 20s—for each year from 2007 to 2011. Even at its peak, in October 2009, the unemployment rate among older graduates was less than 5 percent. Among recent graduates, however, the rate peaked at 15.5 percent, and it was still well into double digits in late 2011. The U.S. labor market had a

FIGURE **8-6**   Unemployment Rate for Recent College Graduates, 2007–2011

Source: Bureau of Labor Statistics.

Note that although boxes often highlight especially important information or give an extended example of a concept, sometimes they are merely put in to make the page appear less boring. While boxes can help deepen your understanding of the material, don't let them distract you from the important points in the paragraphs.

IMAGES

Textbooks, like many newspaper or magazine articles, use images to help convey information. Images might be photographs, diagrams, illustrations, or maps. Often images are provided to help you understand and interpret information in the text or to give you greater context for the information. When reading your textbooks, be sure to "read" all the images as well as the text. Look carefully at each image to see if you can recognize the information it is representing from the text or the idea it is trying to convey. Each one was

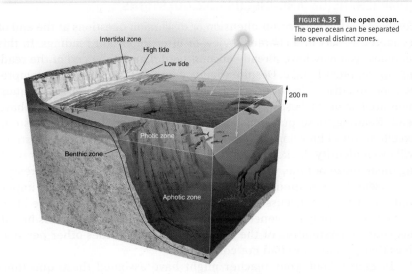

FIGURE 4.35 **The open ocean.**
The open ocean can be separated into several distinct zones.

Intertidal zone
High tide
Low tide
200 m
Photic zone
Benthic zone
Aphotic zone

---

problem: without the corals, the entire coral reef biome is endangered.

The Open Ocean

Away from the shoreline in deeper water, sunlight can no longer reach the ocean bottom. The exact depth of penetration by sunlight depends on a number of factors, including the amounts of sediment and algae suspended in the water, but it generally does not exceed 200 m (approximately 650 feet).

Like a pond or lake, the ocean can be divided into zones. These zones are shown in FIGURE 4.35. The upper layer of water that receives enough sunlight to allow photosynthesis is the **photic zone,** and the deeper layer of water that lacks sufficient sunlight for photosynthesis is the **aphotic zone.** The ocean floor is called the *benthic zone.*

them feed in the dark waters. These organisms include several species of crustaceans, jellyfish, squid, and fish.

The patterns that emerge as we study the terrestrial and aquatic biomes highlight the fact that regional variations in global climate have a major effect on the types of organisms that can live in different parts of the world. Among the terrestrial biomes, temperature and precipitation affect the rate of decomposition of dead organisms and the productivity of the soil. Understanding these patterns helps us understand how humans have come to use the land in different ways: growing crops in regions with enough water and a sufficient growing season, grazing domesticated animals in drier areas, and harvesting lumber from forests. Among the aquatic biomes, differences in water flow, depth, and salinity help us understand why different species of producers and consumers, including commercially important species of fish and shellfish, live in different

Example of an image from an environmental science textbook

> **TIP**
>
> Next to images in your textbook, make a note in the margin about the purpose of the image or what information is being illustrated.

---

specifically chosen to help clarify the information. In the following example, an environmental science textbook uses an image of a cross-section of ocean to illustrate the concept of a photic zone versus an aphotic zone.

▶ For more about reading visuals, see pages 138–50 in Chapter 5, Active Reading Strategies.

BULLETED OR NUMBERED LISTS

If there are bulleted or numbered lists of points in the text, you can be sure that the authors want to draw your attention to that information. So be sure to make note of the list in your annotations and how it might be useful to you. If it is a list of instructions, when would you use them? If it is a list of components of something, what is important about it? What will you be expected to do with that information? Explain it? Memorize it? Use it to explain something else? If you aren't sure, put a question about the list in the margin and ask your instructor in class.

COMPREHENSION AND DISCUSSION QUESTIONS

Textbooks often have comprehension or discussion questions at the end of a chapter as part of a chapter review or after important readings. In this textbook, you may have already encountered them at the end of the readings in Chapters 1 and 2. Despite what you might think, answering comprehension and discussion questions is not "busywork." Comprehension questions are one of the best ways to test your understanding of what you have read. Reading these questions as part of previewing the text is also an excellent way of knowing what to expect from the reading. These questions will often identify the key points or concepts from the reading, so by reading them ahead of time, you'll know exactly what to look for as you read.

Discussion questions have a slightly different, but equally important, function. The discussion questions ask you to think about the ideas of the text or apply the concepts with your classmates. Doing this broadens your understanding of the information and provides other perspectives that perhaps you had not considered.

In high school, your teacher might have assigned these questions and had your peers correct them in class. In college, instructors often just assume you are doing them and checking them on your own if the answers are in the back of the book. Even if they are not assigned, think or write out answers to the comprehension and discussion questions as a way to test your understanding of the material. Here is the Skills Check section of a reading you encountered in Chapter 2.

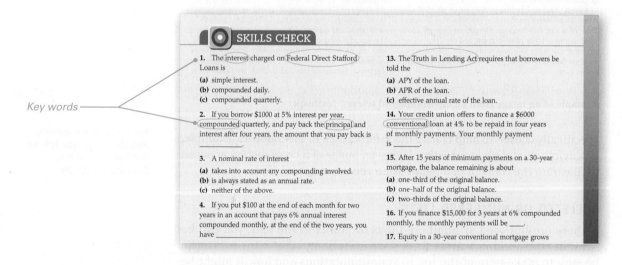

Key words

SKILLS CHECK

1. The interest charged on Federal Direct Stafford Loans is

(a) simple interest.
(b) compounded daily.
(c) compounded quarterly.

2. If you borrow $1000 at 5% interest per year, compounded quarterly, and pay back the principal and interest after four years, the amount that you pay back is _____.

3. A nominal rate of interest

(a) takes into account any compounding involved.
(b) is always stated as an annual rate.
(c) neither of the above.

4. If you put $100 at the end of each month for two years in an account that pays 6% annual interest compounded monthly, at the end of the two years, you have _____.

13. The Truth in Lending Act requires that borrowers be told the

(a) APY of the loan.
(b) APR of the loan.
(c) effective annual rate of the loan.

14. Your credit union offers to finance a $6000 conventional loan at 4% to be repaid in four years of monthly payments. Your monthly payment is _____.

15. After 15 years of minimum payments on a 30-year mortgage, the balance remaining is about

(a) one-third of the original balance.
(b) one-half of the original balance.
(c) two-thirds of the original balance.

16. If you finance $15,000 for 3 years at 6% compounded monthly, the monthly payments will be ____.

17. Equity in a 30-year conventional mortgage grows

PRACTICES, QUIZZES, AND EXERCISES

Many textbooks have exercises, practice tests, or quizzes to test your knowledge of the subject matter. These usually appear at the end of each chapter or at the end of a unit. Some textbooks come with separate work-books of exercises. If your textbook has this feature, be sure to make use of it! Testing yourself on what you have learned in the reading is one of the surest ways to commit the information to memory and makes study-ing for larger exams much easier. If your textbook does not have practice quizzes or tests, you can make your own quizzes based on the key words, section headers, and comprehension and discussion questions. However, if your textbook does have practice quizzes or tests, do the first set of practice exercises and check your answers either with the material in the chapter or with the answers provided. Some textbooks have answers to quizzes in the back for just these purposes. If only the odd answers are in the back, then try your hand at answering the odd questions first and then check them. If you are getting most of the answers right, then pro-ceed to answer the evens. Then move on to the next set. If, however, you are far off base, getting few or none of the practice exercises correct, then you should reread the relevant section of the chapter. If you are still stuck, see your instructor or a tutor for the course.

CHAPTER OR SECTION REVIEWS

Most textbooks have some kind of chapter review feature that will help you assess how well you have learned the important concepts of the chapter. Chapter reviews come in many different forms. Some of them list key terms or concepts for you to review, while others take the form of a practice quiz or another activity. However it is designed, the chapter review only works if you actually make use of it! As part of previewing the text, you should read through the chapter review before you read the chapter so you know what the chapter will cover and what you will be expected to learn from the reading. Then after reading the chapter, doing the activities of the chapter review will help you determine if you learned them or not. Chapter reviews are also excellent study tools prior to a quiz or test. To make the best use of them, review your annotations throughout the chapter, and then quiz yourself by doing the chapter review as a pretest study aid. The chapter review also works well to keep study groups or study partners on track.

---

practice it 6.2   Find the Features in Your Textbook

In this or another textbook, bookmark each of the features just discussed. Write down the function of each feature either in the margin of your textbook or in your notebook. Which ones do you already use? Which ones haven't you made use of yet? How will these features help you read your textbook? Write down your responses in your notebook.

Outlining or Mapping Textbooks

▶ For more about mapping and outlining, see pages 135–38 in Chapter 5, Active Reading Strategies.

Several other techniques discussed in Chapter 5 are also useful in reading textbooks. Creating an outline or map of a textbook chapter is a fantastic reading strategy that doubles as a study guide. Both outlining and mapping help you understand and identify the organization of the chapter material as well as how that information is categorized. Textbook chapters hold a ton of information, but outlining or mapping breaks it down to a clear structure, from broader concepts to specific examples and terms.

STEP 1: First, preview the chapter.   If you create an outline, list the section headings on a piece of paper with space between them to fill in later with specifics from each section. If you create a map, write the chapter title in a circle in the middle of the page. Draw circles or boxes in each corner for each heading (or spaced around the edge of the paper, depending on how many headings there are).

STEP 2: Read one section at a time and try to identify the major point of each section.   You might get extra clues from bold or highlighted words or section subheadings. Write the main idea or point under the section heading. If a specific example or person is connected with that idea, write down that information as well. Don't forget to read graphs, charts, and images too. These can provide clues to the important concepts or terms that the author wants to reinforce.

STEP 3: Continue to read each section, adding major points and significant examples to your outline or map.

STEP 4: When you complete the outline or map, congratulate yourself.   Then read through the whole chapter from start to finish with your outline or map in hand, referring back to it as you read. If you find anything additional that you left out the first time through, add it now.

STEP 5: Periodically review your outline or map, particularly before a quiz or exam.   You have now created a perfect chapter study guide!

Here's one example: a map of Chapter 10, Intelligence, from the textbook *Psychology*, by David G. Myers (11th ed., 2016). You can read an excerpt from the chapter on pages 169–80 that includes the first two main sections, "What Is Intelligence?" and "Assessing Intelligence." Note that our map follows the structure of the main headings of the chapter but is only partially complete.

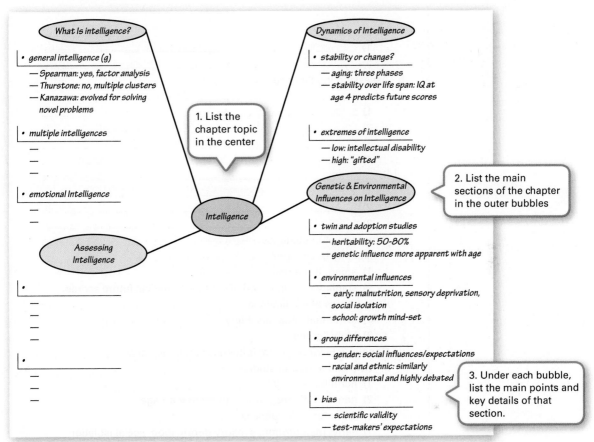

Map of Textbook Chapter

Below is another way to map the chapter following a more traditional outline structure. Note that this outline contains the same information as our sample map and is only partially complete.

1. Intelligence
   a. What Is Intelligence?
      i. general intelligence (*g*)
         1) Spearman: yes, factor analysis
         2) Thurstone: no, multiple clusters
         3) Kanazawa: evolved for solving novel problems
      ii. multiple intelligences
         1) _____
         2) _____
         3) _____

iii. _____
    1) _____
    2) _____
b. Assessing Intelligence
    i. _____
       1) _____
       2) _____
       3) _____
       4) _____
    ii. _____
       1) _____
       2) _____
       3) _____
c. Dynamics of Intelligence
    i. stability or change?
       1) aging: three phases
       2) stability over life span: IQ at age 4 predicts future scores
    ii. extremes of intelligence
       1) low: intellectual disability
       2) high: "gifted"
d. Genetic & Environmental Influences on Intelligence
    i. twin and adoption studies
       1) heritability: 50-80%
       2) genetic influence more apparent with age
    ii. environmental influences
       1) early: malnutrition, sensory deprivation, social isolation
       2) school: growth mind-set
    iii. group differences
       1) gender: social influences/expectations
       2) racial and ethnic: similarly environmental and highly debated
    iv. bias
       1) scientific validity
       2) test-makers' expectations

practice it 6.3 Map or Outline a Chapter

You probably noticed that both the sample map and the sample outline are only partially filled in. They are missing information about the sections of the chapter included in our excerpt on pages 169–80. To practice mapping or outlining, read the textbook excerpt on pages 169–80 and then fill in the rest of the key points on the map or outline for the sections "What Is Intelligence?" and "Assessing Intelligence."

CHAPTER 10

INTELLIGENCE

. . . .

Three huge controversies have sparked recent debate in and beyond psychology. First is the "memory war," over whether traumatic experiences are repressed and can later be recovered, with therapeutic benefit. The second great controversy is the "gender war," over the extent to which nature and nurture shape our behaviors as men and women. In this chapter, we meet the "intelligence war": Does each of us have an inborn general mental capacity (intelligence)? And can we quantify this capacity as a meaningful number?

School boards, courts, and scientists debate the use and fairness of tests that assess people's mental abilities and assign them a score. Is intelligence testing a constructive way to guide people toward suitable opportunities? Or is it a potent, discriminatory weapon camouflaged as science? First, some basic questions:

- What is intelligence?
- How can we best assess intelligence?
- How do heredity and experience together weave the intelligence fabric?
- What do test score differences among individuals and groups really mean? Should we use such differences to rank people? To admit them to colleges or universities? To hire them?

This chapter offers answers, by identifying a variety of mental gifts and concluding that the recipe for high achievement blends talent and grit.

What is Intelligence?

Assessing Intelligence

The Dynamics of Intelligence

Genetic and Environmental Influences on Intelligence

386   **CHAPTER 10:** INTELLIGENCE

Heiner Heine/© imagebroker/Alamy

Hands-on healing The socially constructed concept of intelligence varies from culture to culture. This natural healer in Cameroon displays intelligence in his knowledge about medicinal plants and his understanding of the needs of the people he is helping.

"*g* is one of the most reliable and valid measures in the behavioral domain . . . and it predicts important social outcomes such as educational and occupational levels far better than any other trait."

Behavior geneticist Robert Plomin (1999)

Jonathan Larsen/Diadem Images/Alamy

▉ What Is Intelligence?

10-1 How do psychologists define *intelligence,* and what are the arguments for *g*?

In many studies, *intelligence* has been defined as whatever *intelligence tests* measure, which has tended to be school smarts. But intelligence is not a quality like height or weight, which has the same meaning to everyone worldwide. People assign the term *intelligence* to the qualities that enable success in their own time and culture (Sternberg & Kaufman, 1998). In Cameroon's equatorial forest, *intelligence* may be understanding the medicinal qualities of local plants. In a North American high school, it may be mastering difficult concepts in tough courses. In both places, **intelligence** is the mental potential to learn from experience, solve problems, and use knowledge to adapt to new situations.

You probably know some people with talents in science, others who excel in the humanities, and still others gifted in athletics, art, music, or dance. You may also know a talented artist who is stumped by the simplest math problem, or a brilliant math student who struggles when discussing literature. Are all these people intelligent? Could you rate their intelligence on a single scale? Or would you need several different scales?

Spearman's General Intelligence Factor and Thurstone's Response

Charles Spearman (1863–1945) believed we have one **general intelligence** (often shortened to *g*) that is at the heart of all our intelligent behavior, from navigating the sea to excelling in school. He granted that people often have special, outstanding abilities. But he noted that those who score high in one area, such as verbal intelligence, typically score higher than average in other areas, such as spatial or reasoning ability. Spearman's belief stemmed in part from his work with *factor analysis*, a statistical procedure that identifies clusters of related items.

This idea of a general mental capacity expressed by a single intelligence score was controversial in Spearman's day, and so it remains. One of Spearman's early opponents was L. L. Thurstone (1887–1955). Thurstone gave 56 different tests to people and mathematically identified seven clusters of primary mental abilities (word fluency, verbal comprehension, spatial ability, perceptual speed, numerical ability, inductive reasoning, and memory). Thurstone did not rank people on a single scale of general aptitude. But when other investigators studied these profiles, they detected a persistent tendency: Those who excelled in one of the seven clusters generally scored well on the others. So, the investigators concluded, there was still some evidence of a *g* factor.

We might, then, liken mental abilities to physical abilities: The ability to run fast is distinct from the eye-hand coordination required to throw a ball on target. Yet there remains some tendency for good things to come packaged together—for running speed and throwing accuracy to correlate. So, too, with intelligence. Several distinct abilities tend to cluster together and to correlate enough to define a general intelligence factor. Distinct brain networks enable distinct abilities, with *g* explained by their coordinated activity (Hampshire et al., 2012).

Satoshi Kanazawa (2004, 2010) argues that general intelligence evolved as a form of intelligence that helps people solve *novel* (unfamiliar) problems—how to stop a fire from spreading, how to find food during a drought, how to reunite with one's tribe on the other side of a flooded river. More common problems—such as how to mate or how to read a stranger's face or how to find your way back to camp—require a different sort of intelligence. Kanazawa asserts that general intelligence scores *do* correlate with the ability to solve various novel problems (like those found in academic and many vocational situations) but do *not* correlate much with individuals' skills in *evolutionarily familiar* situations—such as marrying and parenting, forming close friendships, and navigating without maps.

Theories of Multiple Intelligences

10-2 How do Gardner's and Sternberg's theories of multiple intelligences differ, and what criticisms have they faced?

Other psychologists, particularly since the mid-1980s, have sought to extend the definition of *intelligence* beyond the idea of academic smarts.

Gardner's Multiple Intelligences

Howard Gardner has identified eight *relatively independent intelligences,* including the verbal and mathematical aptitudes assessed by standard tests (**FIGURE** 10.1). Thus, the computer programmer, the poet, the street-smart adolescent who becomes a crafty executive, and the basketball team's play-making point guard exhibit different kinds of intelligence (Gardner, 1998). Gardner (1999) has also proposed a ninth possible intelligence—*existential intelligence*—the ability "to ponder large questions about life, death, existence."

Gardner (1983, 2006; 2011; Davis et al., 2011) views these intelligence domains as multiple abilities that come in different packages. Brain damage, for example, may destroy one ability but leave others intact. And consider people with **savant syndrome.** Despite their island of brilliance, these people often score low on intelligence tests and may have limited or no language ability (Treffert & Wallace, 2002). Some can compute complicated calculations quickly and accurately, or identify the day of the week corresponding to any given historical date, or render incredible works of art or musical performance (Miller, 1999).

About 4 in 5 people with savant syndrome are males, and many also have *autism spectrum disorder (ASD),* a developmental disorder. The late memory whiz Kim Peek

intelligence the mental potential to learn from experience, solve problems, and use knowledge to adapt to new situations.

general intelligence (*g*) a general intelligence factor that, according to Spearman and others, underlies specific mental abilities and is therefore measured by every task on an intelligence test.

savant syndrome a condition in which a person otherwise limited in mental ability has an exceptional specific skill, such as in computation or drawing.

▼ FIGURE 10.1
Gardner's eight intelligences
Gardner has also proposed a ninth possible intelligence—existential intelligence—the ability to ponder deep questions about life.

Islands of genius: Savant syndrome After a brief helicopter ride over Singapore followed by five days of drawing, British savant artist Stephen Wiltshire accurately reproduced an aerial view of the city from memory.

(who did not have ASD) inspired the movie *Rain Man.* In 8 to 10 seconds, he could read and remember a page. During his lifetime, he memorized 9000 books, including Shakespeare's works and the Bible. He could provide GPS-like travel directions within any major U.S. city, yet he could not button his clothes. And he had little capacity for abstract concepts. Asked by his father at a restaurant to lower his voice, he slid lower in his chair to lower his voice box. Asked for Lincoln's Gettysburg Address, he responded, "227 North West Front Street. But he only stayed there one night—he gave the speech the next day" (Treffert & Christensen, 2005).

Sternberg's Three Intelligences

Robert Sternberg (1985, 2011) agrees with Gardner that there is more to success than traditional intelligence and that we have multiple intelligences. But his *triarchic theory* proposes three, not eight or nine, intelligences:

- *Analytical (academic problem-solving) intelligence* is assessed by intelligence tests, which present well-defined problems having a single right answer. Such tests predict school grades reasonably well and vocational success more modestly.

- *Creative intelligence* is demonstrated in innovative smarts: the ability to generate novel ideas.

- *Practical intelligence* is required for everyday tasks that are not well-defined, and that may have many possible solutions. Managerial success, for example, depends less on academic problem-solving skills than on a shrewd ability to manage oneself, one's tasks, and other people. Sternberg and Richard Wagner (1993, 1995; Wagner, 2011) offer a test of practical managerial intelligence that measures skill at writing effective memos, motivating people, delegating tasks and responsibilities, reading people, and promoting

"You have to be careful, if you're good at something, to make sure you don't think you're good at other things that you aren't necessarily so good at. . . . Because I've been very successful at [software development] people come in and expect that I have wisdom about topics that I don't."

Philanthropist Bill Gates (1998)

"You're wise, but you lack tree smarts."

one's own career. Business executives who score relatively high on this test tend to earn high salaries and receive high performance ratings.

With support from the U.S. College Board (which administers the widely used SAT Reasoning Test to U.S. college and university applicants), Sternberg (2006, 2007, 2010) and a team of collaborators have developed new measures of creativity (such as thinking up a caption for an untitled cartoon) and practical thinking (such as figuring out how to move a large bed up a winding staircase). These more comprehensive assessments improve prediction of American students' first-year college grades, and they do so with reduced ethnic-group differences.

Gardner and Sternberg differ on specific points, but they agree on two important points: Multiple abilities can contribute to life success, and differing varieties of giftedness add spice to life and challenges for education. Under their influence, many teachers have been trained to appreciate such variety and to apply multiple intelligence theories in their classrooms.

Street smarts This child selling candy on the streets of Manaus, Brazil, is developing practical intelligence at a very young age.

Criticisms of Multiple Intelligence Theories

Wouldn't it be nice if the world were so just that a weakness in one area would be compensated by genius in another? Alas, say critics, the world is not just (Ferguson, 2009; Scarr, 1989). Research using factor analysis confirms that there *is* a general intelligence factor (Johnson et al., 2008): *g* matters. It predicts performance on various complex tasks and in various jobs (Gottfredson, 2002a,b, 2003a,b; see also **FIGURE 10.2**). Much as jumping ability is not a predictor of jumping performance when the bar is set a foot off the ground—but becomes a predictor when the bar is set higher—so extremely high cognitive ability scores predict exceptional attainments, such as doctoral degrees and publications (Kuncel & Hezlett, 2010).

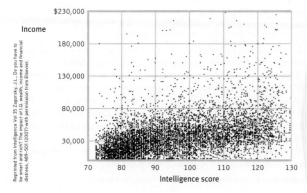

▼ FIGURE 10.2
Smart and rich? Jay Zagorsky (2007) tracked 7403 participants in the U.S. National Longitudinal Survey of Youth across 25 years. As shown in this scatterplot, their intelligence scores correlated +.30, a moderate positive correlation, with their later income. Each dot indicates a given youth's intelligence score and later adult income.

Reprinted from Intelligence Vol 35 Zagorsky, J.L., Do you have to be smart and rich? The impact of I.Q. wealth, income and financial distress, 489–501 (2007) with permission from Elsevier.

390   **CHAPTER 10:** INTELLIGENCE

Spatial intelligence genius In 1998, World Checkers Champion Ron "Suki" King of Barbados set a new record by simultaneously playing 385 players in 3 hours and 44 minutes. Thus, while his opponents often had hours to plot their game moves, King could only devote about 35 seconds to each game. Yet he still managed to win all 385 games!

Courtesy of Cameras on Wheels

Even so, "success" is not a one-ingredient recipe. High intelligence may help you get into a profession (via the schools and training programs that take you there), but it won't make you successful once there. Success is a combination of talent with *grit*: Those who become highly successful tend also to be conscientious, well-connected, and doggedly energetic. K. Anders Ericsson (2002, 2007; Ericsson et al., 2007) reports a *10-year rule*: A common ingredient of expert performance in chess, dancing, sports, computer programming, music, and medicine is "about 10 years of intense, daily practice" (Ericsson, 2002, 2007; Simon & Chase, 1973). Becoming a professional musician requires a certain cognitive ability. But it also requires practice—about 11,000 hours on average, and a *minimum* of 3000 hours (Campitelli & Gobet, 2011). The recipe for success is a gift of nature plus a whole lot of nurture.

For more on how self-disciplined grit feeds achievement, see Chapter 11.

━━━━━━━━━━━━ **RETRIEVAL PRACTICE** ━━━━━━━━━━━━

• How does the existence of savant syndrome support Gardner's theory of multiple intelligences?

ANSWER: People with savant syndrome have limited mental ability overall but possess one or more exceptional skills, which, according to Howard Gardner, suggests that our abilities come in separate packages rather than being fully expressed by one general intelligence that encompasses all of our talents.

Emotional Intelligence

10-3 What are the four components of emotional intelligence?

Is being in tune with yourself and others also a sign of intelligence, distinct from academic intelligence? Some researchers say *Yes*. They define *social intelligence* as the know-how involved in social situations and managing yourself successfully (Cantor & Kihlstrom, 1987). People with high social intelligence can read social situations the way a skilled soccer player reads the defense or a meterologist reads the weather. The concept was first proposed in 1920 by psychologist Edward Thorndike, who noted, "The best mechanic in a factory may fail as a foreman for lack of social intelligence" (Goleman, 2006, p. 83).

One line of research has explored a specific aspect of social intelligence called **emotional intelligence,** consisting of four abilities (Mayer et al., 2002, 2011, 2012):

emotional intelligence the ability to perceive, understand, manage, and use emotions.

• *Perceiving* emotions (recognizing them in faces, music, and stories)

• *Understanding* emotions (predicting them and how they may change and blend)

- *Managing* emotions (knowing how to express them in varied situations)
- *Using* emotions to enable adaptive or creative thinking

Emotionally intelligent people are both socially aware and self-aware. Those who score high on managing emotions enjoy higher-quality interactions with friends (Lopes et al., 2004). They avoid being hijacked by overwhelming depression, anxiety, or anger. They can read others' emotional cues and know what to say to soothe a grieving friend, encourage a workmate, and manage a conflict.

These emotional intelligence high scorers also perform modestly better on the job (O'Boyle et al., 2011). On and off the job, they can delay gratification in pursuit of long-range rewards, rather than being overtaken by immediate impulses. Simply said, they are emotionally smart. Thus, they often succeed in career, marriage, and parenting situations where academically smarter (but emotionally less intelligent) people might fail (Cherniss, 2010a,b; Ciarrochi et al., 2006).

Some scholars, however, are concerned that emotional intelligence stretches the intelligence concept too far (Visser et al., 2006). Howard Gardner (1999) includes interpersonal and intrapersonal intelligences as two of his eight forms of multiple intelligences. But let us also, he acknowledges, respect emotional sensitivity, creativity, and motivation as important but different. Stretch *intelligence* to include everything we prize and the word will lose its meaning.

The procrastinator's motto: "Hard works pays off later; laziness pays off now."

* * *

For a summary of these theories of intelligence, see **TABLE 10.1**.

▼ TABLE 10.1
Comparing Theories of Intelligence

Theory	Summary	Strengths	Other Considerations
Spearman's general intelligence (g)	A basic intelligence predicts our abilities in varied academic areas.	Different abilities, such as verbal and spatial, do have some tendency to correlate.	Human abilities are too diverse to be encapsulated by a single general intelligence factor.
Thurstone's primary mental abilities	Our intelligence may be broken down into seven factors: word fluency, verbal comprehension, spatial ability, perceptual speed, numerical ability, inductive reasoning, and memory.	A single *g* score is not as informative as scores for seven primary mental abilities.	Even Thurstone's seven mental abilities show a tendency to cluster, suggesting an underlying *g* factor.
Gardner's multiple intelligences	Our abilities are best classified into eight or nine independent intelligences, which include a broad range of skills beyond traditional school smarts.	Intelligence is more than just verbal and mathematical skills. Other abilities are equally important to our human adaptability.	Should all of our abilities be considered *intelligences*? Shouldn't some be called less vital *talents*?
Sternberg's triarchic theory	Our intelligence is best classified into three areas that predict real-world success: analytical, creative, and practical.	These three domains can be reliably measured.	1. These three domains may be less independent than Sternberg thought and may actually share an underlying *g* factor. 2. Additional testing is needed to determine whether these domains can reliably predict success.
Emotional intelligence	Social intelligence is an important indicator of life success. Emotional intelligence is a key aspect, consisting of perceiving, understanding, managing, and using emotions.	The four components that predict social success.	Does this stretch the concept of intelligence too far?

392   **CHAPTER 10:** INTELLIGENCE

REVIEW What Is Intelligence?

LEARNING OBJECTIVES

RETRIEVAL PRACTICE Take a moment to answer each of these Learning Objective Questions (repeated here from within this section). Then turn to Appendix C, Complete Chapter Reviews, to check your answers. Research suggests that trying to answer these questions on your own will improve your long-term retention (McDaniel et al., 2009).

10-1 How do psychologists define *intelligence,* and what are the arguments for *g*?

10-2 How do Gardner's and Sternberg's theories of multiple intelligences differ, and what criticisms have they faced?

10-3 What are the four components of emotional intelligence?

TERMS AND CONCEPTS TO REMEMBER

RETRIEVAL PRACTICE Test yourself on these terms by trying to write down the definition before flipping back to the page number referenced to check your answer.

intelligence, p. 387

general intelligence (*g*), p. 387

savant syndrome, p. 387

emotional intelligence, p. 390

Use 🔗 LearningCurve to create your personalized study plan, which will direct you to the resources that will help you most in 🔗 LaunchPad.

> intelligence test a method for assessing an individual's mental aptitudes and comparing them with those of others, using numerical scores.
>
> achievement test a test designed to assess what a person has learned.
>
> aptitude test a test designed to predict a person's future performance; *aptitude* is the capacity to learn.

■ Assessing Intelligence

10-4 What is an intelligence test, and what is the difference between achievement and aptitude tests?

An **intelligence test** assesses people's mental abilities and compares them with others, using numerical scores. How do we design such tests, and what makes them credible? Consider why psychologists created tests of mental abilities and how they have used them.

By this point in your life, you've faced dozens of ability tests: school tests of basic reading and math skills, course exams, intelligence tests, driver's license exams. Psychologists classify such tests as either **achievement tests,** intended to *reflect* what you have learned, or **aptitude tests,** intended to *predict* your ability to learn a new skill. Exams covering what you have learned in this course are achievement tests. A college entrance exam, which seeks to predict your ability to do college work, is an aptitude test—a "thinly disguised intelligence test," says Howard Gardner (1999). Indeed, report Meredith Frey and Douglas Detterman (2004), total scores on the U.S. SAT have correlated +.82 with general intelligence scores in a national sample of 14- to 21-year-olds (**FIGURE 10.3**).

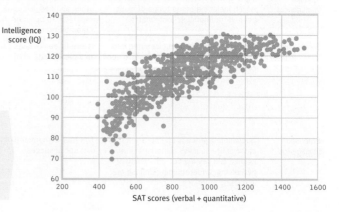

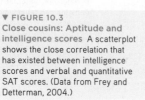
▼ FIGURE 10.3
Close cousins: Aptitude and intelligence scores A scatterplot shows the close correlation that has existed between intelligence scores and verbal and quantitative SAT scores. (Data from Frey and Detterman, 2004.)

Early and Modern Tests of Mental Abilities

10-5 When and why were intelligence tests created, and how do today's tests differ from early intelligence tests?

Some societies concern themselves with promoting the collective welfare of the family, community, and society. Other societies emphasize individual opportunity. Plato, a pioneer of the individualist tradition, wrote more than 2000 years ago in *The Republic* that "no two persons are born exactly alike; but each differs from the other in natural endowments, one being suited for one occupation and the other for another." As heirs to Plato's individualism, people in Western societies have pondered how and why individuals differ in mental ability.

Francis Galton: Belief in Hereditary Genius

Western attempts to assess such differences began in earnest with English scientist Francis Galton (1822–1911), who was fascinated with measuring human traits. When his cousin Charles Darwin proposed that nature selects successful traits through the survival of the fittest, Galton wondered if it might be possible to measure "natural ability" and to encourage those of high ability to mate with one another. At the 1884 London Health Exhibition, more than 10,000 visitors received his assessment of their "intellectual strengths" based on such things as reaction time, sensory acuity, muscular power, and body proportions. But alas, on these measures, well-regarded adults and students did not outscore others. Nor did the measures correlate with each other.

Although Galton's quest for a simple intelligence measure failed, he gave us some statistical techniques that we still use (as well as the phrase *nature and nurture*). And his persistent belief in the inheritance of genius—reflected in his book, *Hereditary Genius*—illustrates an important lesson from both the history of intelligence research and the history of science: Although science itself strives for objectivity, individual scientists are affected by their own assumptions and attitudes.

Alfred Binet: Predicting School Achievement

Modern intelligence testing traces its birth to early twentieth-century France, where a new law required all children to attend school. French officials knew that some children, including many newcomers to Paris, would struggle and need special classes. But how could the schools make fair judgments about children's learning potential? Teachers might assess children who had little prior education as slow learners. Or they might sort children into classes on the basis of their social backgrounds. To minimize such bias, France's minister of public education gave Alfred Binet and others, including Théodore Simon, the task of studying this problem.

In 1905, Binet and Simon first presented their work under the archaic title, "New Methods for Diagnosing the Idiot, the Imbecile, and the Moron" (Nicolas & Levine, 2012). They began by assuming that all children follow the same course of intellectual development but that some develop more rapidly. On tests, therefore, a "dull" child should score much like a typical younger child, and a "bright" child like a typical older child. Thus, their goal became measuring each child's **mental age**, the level of performance typically associated with a certain chronological age. The average 9-year-old, then, has a mental age of 9. Children with below-average mental ages, such as 9-year-olds who perform at the level of typical 7-year-olds, would struggle with age-appropriate schoolwork. A 9-year-old who performs at the level of typical 11-year-olds should find schoolwork easy.

To measure mental age, Binet and Simon theorized that mental aptitude, like athletic aptitude, is a general capacity that shows up in various ways. They tested a variety of reasoning and problem-solving questions on Binet's two daughters, and then on "bright" and "backward" Parisian schoolchildren. The items they developed eventually predicted how well French children would handle their schoolwork.

Alfred Binet (1857–1911) "Some recent philosophers have given their moral approval to the deplorable verdict that an individual's intelligence is a fixed quantity, one which cannot be augmented. We must protest and act against this brutal pessimism" (Binet, 1909, p. 141).

mental age a measure of intelligence test performance devised by Binet; the chronological age that most typically corresponds to a given level of performance. Thus, a child who does as well as an average 8-year-old is said to have a mental age of 8.

> "The IQ test was invented to predict academic performance, nothing else. If we wanted something that would predict life success, we'd have to invent another test completely."
>
> Social psychologist Robert Zajonc (1984b)

Binet and Simon made no assumptions concerning *why* a particular child was slow, average, or precocious. Binet personally leaned toward an environmental explanation. To raise the capacities of low-scoring children, he recommended "mental orthopedics" that would help develop their attention span and self-discipline. He believed his intelligence test did not measure inborn intelligence as a scale measures weight. Rather, it had a single practical purpose: to identify French schoolchildren needing special attention. Binet hoped his test would be used to improve children's education, but he also feared it would be used to label children and limit their opportunities (Gould, 1981).

RETRIEVAL PRACTICE

• What did Binet hope to achieve by establishing a child's *mental age*?

ANSWER: Binet hoped that the child's *mental age* (the age that typically corresponds to the child's level of performance), would help identify appropriate school placements of children.

Stanford-Binet the widely used American revision (by Terman at Stanford University) of Binet's original intelligence test.

intelligence quotient (IQ) defined originally as the ratio of mental age *(ma)* to chronological age *(ca)* multiplied by 100 (thus, IQ = *ma/ca* × 100). On contemporary intelligence tests, the average performance for a given age is assigned a score of 100.

Lewis Terman: The Innate IQ

Binet's fears were realized soon after his death in 1911, when others adapted his tests for use as a numerical measure of inherited intelligence. This began when Stanford University professor Lewis Terman (1877–1956) found that the Paris-developed questions and age norms worked poorly with California schoolchildren. Adapting some of Binet's original items, adding others, and establishing new age norms, Terman extended the upper end of the test's range from teenagers to "superior adults." He also gave his revision the name it retains today—the **Stanford-Binet.**

From such tests, German psychologist William Stern derived the famous **intelligence quotient,** or **IQ.** The IQ is simply a person's mental age divided by chronological age and multiplied by 100 to get rid of the decimal point:

$$IQ = \frac{\text{mental age}}{\text{chronological age}} \times 100$$

Thus, an average child, whose mental and chronological ages are the same, has an IQ of 100. But an 8-year-old who answers questions as would a typical 10-year-old has an IQ of 125.

The original IQ formula worked fairly well for children but not for adults. (Should a 40-year-old who does as well on the test as an average 20-year-old be assigned an IQ of only 50?) Most current intelligence tests, including the Stanford-Binet, no longer compute an IQ in this manner (though the term *IQ* still lingers as a shorthand expression for "intelligence test score"). Instead, they represent the test-taker's performance *relative to the average performance of others the same age.* This average performance is arbitrarily assigned a score of 100, and about two-thirds of all test-takers fall between 85 and 115.

Terman (1916, p. 4) promoted the widespread use of intelligence testing to "take account of the inequalities of children in original endowment" by assessing their "vocational fitness." In sympathy with Francis Galton's *eugenics*—the much-criticized nineteenth-century movement that proposed measuring human traits and using the results to encourage only smart and fit people to reproduce—Terman envisioned that the use of intelligence tests would "ultimately result in curtailing the reproduction of feeble-mindedness and in the elimination of an enormous amount of crime, pauperism, and industrial inefficiency" (p. 7).

With Terman's help, the U.S. government developed new tests to evaluate both newly arriving immigrants and World War I army recruits—the world's first mass administration of an intelligence test. To some psychologists, the results indicated the inferiority of people not sharing their Anglo-Saxon heritage. Such findings were part of the cultural climate that led to a 1924 immigration law that reduced Southern and Eastern European immigration quotas to less than a fifth of those for Northern and Western Europe.

Mrs. Randolph takes mother's pride too far.

Binet probably would have been horrified that his test had been adapted and used to draw such conclusions. Indeed, such sweeping judgments became an embarrassment to most of those who championed testing. Even Terman came to appreciate that test scores reflected not only people's innate mental abilities but also their education, native language, and familiarity with the culture assumed by the test. Abuses of the early intelligence tests serve to remind us that science can be value-laden. Behind a screen of scientific objectivity, ideology sometimes lurks.

> **Wechsler Adult Intelligence Scale (WAIS)** the WAIS and its companion versions for children are the most widely used intelligence tests; contain verbal and performance (nonverbal) subtests.

RETRIEVAL PRACTICE

• What is the IQ of a 4-year-old with a mental age of 5?

ANSWER: 125 (5 ÷ 4 × 100 = 125)

David Wechsler: Separate Scores for Separate Skills

Psychologist David Wechsler created what is now the most widely used individual intelligence test, the **Wechsler Adult Intelligence Scale (WAIS),** together with a version for school-age children (the *Wechsler Intelligence Scale for Children [WISC]*), and another for preschool children (Evers et al., 2012). The latest (2008) edition of the WAIS consists of 15 subtests, including these:

• *Similarities*—Reasoning the commonality of two objects or concepts, such as "In what way are wool and cotton alike?"

• *Vocabulary*—Naming pictured objects, or defining words ("What is a guitar?")

• *Block Design*—Visual abstract processing, such as "Using the four blocks, make one just like this."

• *Letter-Number Sequencing*—On hearing a series of numbers and letters, repeat the numbers in ascending order, and then the letters in alphabetical order: "R-2-C-1-M-3."

The WAIS yields not only an overall intelligence score, as does the Stanford-Binet, but also separate scores for verbal comprehension, perceptual organization, working memory, and processing speed. Striking differences among these scores can provide clues to cognitive strengths or weaknesses. For example, a low verbal comprehension score combined with high scores on other subtests could indicate a reading or language disability. Other comparisons can help a psychologist or psychiatrist establish a rehabilitation plan for a stroke patient. In such ways, these tests help realize Binet's aim: to identify opportunities for improvement and strengths that teachers and others can build upon. Such uses are possible, of course, only when we can trust the test results.

RETRIEVAL PRACTICE

• An employer with a pool of applicants for a single available position is interested in testing each applicant's potential. To help her decide whom she should hire, she should use an _____ (achievement/aptitude) test. That same employer wishing to test the effectiveness of a new, on-the-job training program would be wise to use an _____ (achievement/aptitude) test.

ANSWERS: aptitude; achievement

Principles of Test Construction

10-6 What is a normal curve, and what does it mean to say that a test has been standardized and is reliable and valid?

To be widely accepted, a psychological test must meet three criteria: It must be *standardized, reliable,* and *valid.* The Stanford-Binet and Wechsler tests meet these requirements. . . .

TEST YOUR-SELF INTELLIGENCE

Test yourself repeatedly throughout your studies. This will not only help you figure out what you know and don't know; the testing itself will help you learn and remember the information more effectively thanks to the testing effect.

What Is Intelligence?

1. Charles Spearman suggested we have one _____ _____ underlying success across a variety of intellectual abilities.

2. The existence of savant syndrome seems to support
   a. Sternberg's distinction among three types of intelligence.
   b. criticism of multiple intelligence theories.
   c. Gardner's theory of multiple intelligences.
   d. Thorndike's view of social intelligence.

3. Sternberg's three types of intelligence are _____ , _____ , and _____ .

4. Emotionally intelligent people tend to
   a. seek immediate gratification.
   b. understand their own emotions but not those of others.
   c. understand others' emotions but not their own.
   d. succeed in their careers.

Assessing Intelligence

5. The IQ of a 6-year-old with a measured mental age of 9 would be
   a. 67.
   b. 133.
   c. 86.
   d. 150.

6. The Wechsler Adult Intelligence Scale (WAIS) is best able to tell us
   a. what part of an individual's intelligence is determined by genetic inheritance.
   b. whether the test-taker will succeed in a job.
   c. how the test-taker compares with other adults in vocabulary and arithmetic reasoning.
   d. whether the test-taker has specific skills for music and the performing arts.

7. The Stanford-Binet, the Wechsler Adult Intelligence Scale, and the Wechsler Intelligence Scale for Children yield consistent results, for example on retesting. In other words, these tests have high _____ .

Muscle Reading

Muscle reading is another great strategy for both textbook reading and any dense reading packed with information.

STEP 1: Preview the chapter or reading.

STEP 2: Divide the chapter into sections. If the chapter has headings, follow them. If it doesn't, use a pencil to mark off sections based on paragraph topics. This doesn't have to be exact; you want to end up with manageable sections to work with.

STEP 3: Read the first section quickly. Don't stop to look up words you don't know, but do underline or circle them for later.

STEP 4: Go back and reread the first section, this time more carefully, trying to really understand the material. Annotate as you go. This read-through should be slower. Take the time to figure out words you don't know using context clues. Don't forget to note their meanings in the margin when you can figure them out. If you can't figure out the meaning of a word from context clues, look it up in a good dictionary. Remember to write the definition in your own words so that you know you understand the meaning fully.

STEP 5: Take a break. Stretch, stand up, or close your eyes for a minute.

STEP 6: Review your annotations on the first section.

STEP 7: Move on to the next section. Repeat the steps until you have worked your way through the entire chapter.

---

practice it 6.4 Try Your Hand at Muscle Reading

Select a chapter of *Read, Write, Connect* that your instructor has assigned and practice this strategy. Be sure to follow the steps thoroughly. When you have completed the activity, answer the following questions in your notebook: How did muscle reading improve your understanding of the material? Will you use this strategy again?

chapter review

In the following chart, fill in the second column to record in your own words the important skills included in this chapter. Then assess yourself to determine whether you are still developing the skill or feel you have mastered it. If you are still developing the skill, make some notes about what you need to work on to master it in the future. If you believe you have already mastered it, explain why.

Skills and concepts covered in this chapter	Explanation in your own words	I'm developing this skill and need to work on . . .	I believe I have mastered this skill because . . .
Previewing a textbook			
Annotating a textbook			
Using textbook features such as chapter outlines, key words, headings, boxes, and questions			
Outlining and mapping			
Muscle reading			

7

Audience, Purpose, and Topic

Imagine that you just started a new job and your boss invites you to attend a party. You know you have to go, but you don't know whether the party will be big or small, formal or casual, really about making friends or about impressing the higher-ups. You might be very nervous. When you arrive, you might need a few minutes to get your bearings and relax. Unfortunately, during those first few minutes, you are likely to be introduced to a lot of people, whose names you probably will promptly forget.

Now imagine that you are invited to the same party, but some nice coworker calls you beforehand to give you the lowdown: It's a suit-and-tie event, don't bring a date, and you're not there to have fun but to make connections and meet the upper-level executives, who are the people who decide how big your bonus will be that year. Now you might still be nervous—who wouldn't be?—but you would walk in with a clear sense of what to expect and be prepared to remember the names of all the people you met.

The major difference between these two scenarios is that in the second you know the audience and purpose of the event. Once you know who will be in the room and why they are there, you can get a lot more out of the event, right from the start.

Audience and Purpose

Knowing the audience and purpose is equally important while reading. When you start reading something, if you don't know the audience and purpose, you spend the first few minutes with your mind racing, trying to figure out what type of text you have in your hands. It's not that you aren't paying attention. In fact, your brain is very active. It's just that you

LaunchPad Solo
macmillan learning

Visit **LaunchPad Solo for Readers and Writers > Topic, Audience, and Purpose** for extra practice in the skills covered in this chapter.

are still trying to figure out *why* the author is writing the text, and *for whom*, and that makes you unable to focus on *what* the author is actually saying—just like at the party.

Figuring out the audience and purpose of a text *before* you start actually reading will help you understand the text much better. Once you know the audience and purpose, you will be better equipped to understand the vocabulary, point of view, voice, and tone of the reading. When you have a clear idea of the audience and purpose, you can also respond to the text more critically: You find yourself asking and answering questions as you read: "Is the author doing a good job choosing examples?" or "Why didn't the author talk about *X*?" Such questioning deepens your reading experience.

DETERMINING THE AUDIENCE AND PURPOSE IN A READING

▶ For more on pre-reading, see pages 3–5 in Chapter 1, Reading and Responding to College Texts.

So how do you figure out an author's audience and purpose? Before you begin to read something, quickly skim over the text to evaluate the following fundamentals:

- The title, subtitle, headings, and format of the article
- Any pictures or graphics
- Any "apparatus" surrounding the reading—the author's biography, glossed words, or questions/activities intended to guide the reader's response to the reading
- The context of the reading—when and where it was published

As you scan these features of the reading, look for clues about audience and purpose. For instance, if there are pictures, what types of pictures are they? Who might be their target audience? What might their purpose be?

Another way to learn about audience and purpose is to look at the type of publication in which the material was originally published. For instance, the purpose of the front page of a newspaper is to give news as objectively as possible. If you are looking at the editorial page, then the purpose is to give an opinion or news analysis. The audience is the same—newspaper readers, who are a diverse group—but the purpose is different.

Most successful college readers pre-read an article for the features listed here. They then read the opening lines and pause to ask themselves a few questions:

- **What kinds of words are being used in this reading?** Is this formal or informal writing? Is it full of jargon and technical terms or does it mostly use common words?
- **What's the point of view of this reading?** Objective or subjective? Third person or first person? How does the point of view relate to the author's purpose?
- **What does the language sound like?** What words best describe the tone, voice, and style of the writing? (For example, is it engaging? Dry? Sarcastic?)

READING FOR AUDIENCE AND PURPOSE

Imagine three different types of readings about the topic of drug addiction: a chapter from a college-level introductory psychology textbook; a scholarly journal article; and a personal memoir. Let's see how the features of the text provide clues to audience and purpose.

Textbook chapter.   Take a look at the excerpt on page 186 on drug addiction from the introductory college psychology textbook *Psychology*, 11th Ed., by David G. Myers.

The fact that the excerpt is from an introductory college textbook tells us that it is intended for an audience of college students, most of whom are fairly new to the material. The features highlighted in the excerpt reinforce this conclusion and suggest that the book's purpose is primarily informative, and the author's goal is to convey a lot of information as efficiently as possible. Textbooks often have a side column that might include points of importance and interest to the student reader: vocabulary, interesting facts, and even humor. The table creates an easy visual aid, and the use of bolded and colored subheadings helps the reader quickly determine the overall structure of the information.

Scholarly article.   Now take a look at the excerpt on page 187 from a scholarly journal article.

Again, knowing where the reading was published gives us information about the audience. The fact that this article was published in a scholarly journal suggests that the audience is scholars and experts— academics, researchers, and perhaps very advanced students. As the title, headings, and abstract indicate, its purpose is more narrow than that of the college textbook; the authors' goal is to tell this group of readers about a new scientific study on teenage use of ecstasy. The writing is full of specialists' jargon or terminology, and the highly detailed and technical charts in the middle of the article would likely be difficult for a nonexpert reader to interpret.

Personal memoir.   Now take a look at one final example: an excerpt from a blog-based memoir focused on drug addiction on pages 188–89. The author, Katie Allison Granju, is a regular blogger on parenting issues and has a large following, but before this entry, she had never before admitted to having a drug-addicted son. Since this blog is published online, you can assume the audience is a general one, made up of people who are curious to know what it's like to suffer from or recover from an addiction. In this case, as in many such memoirs, the author's purpose is to express her experience and to convey how painful and awful addiction is. How do the tone, voice, and use of examples in this blog differ from those in the other two sources? How does the use of first person influence your reading of the piece?

■ Drugs and Consciousness

LET'S IMAGINE A DAY IN the life of a legal drug user. It begins with a wake-up latte. By midday, several cigarettes have calmed frazzled nerves before an appointment at the plastic surgeon's office for wrinkle-smoothing Botox injections. A diet pill before dinner helps stem the appetite, and its stimulating effects can later be partially offset with a glass of wine or two Advil PMs. And if performance needs enhancing, there are beta blockers for onstage performers, Viagra for middle-aged men, hormone-delivering "libido patches" for middle-aged women, and Adderall for students hoping to focus their concentration.

Colored subheadings make information easy to find.

Tolerance and Addiction

3-12 What are substance use disorders, and what roles do tolerance, withdrawal, and addiction play in these disorders?

Most of us manage to use some nonprescription drugs in moderation and without disrupting our lives. But some of us develop a self-harming **substance use disorder (TABLE 3.3).** Such substances are **psychoactive drugs,** chemicals that change perceptions and moods. A drug's overall effect depends not only on its biological effects but also on the user's expectations, which vary with social and cultural contexts (Ward, 1994). If one culture assumes that a particular drug produces euphoria (or aggression or sexual arousal) and another does not, each culture may find its expectations fulfilled. We'll take a closer look at these interacting forces in the use and potential abuse of particular psychoactive drugs. But first, let's consider how our bodies react to the ongoing use of psychoactive drugs.

The odds of getting hooked after using various drugs:

Tobacco	32%
Heroin	23%
Alcohol	15%
Marijuana	9%

Source: National Academy of Science, Institute of Medicine (Brody, 2003).

Sources are cited in APA style.

Language is objective and informative but still readable.

▼ TABLE 3.3
When Is Drug Use a Disorder?

According to the American Psychiatric Association, a person may be diagnosed with *substance use disorder* when drug use continues despite significant life disruption. Resulting brain changes may persist after quitting use of the substance (thus leading to strong cravings when exposed to people and situations that trigger memories of drug use). The severity of substance use disorder varies from *mild* (two to three of these indicators) to *moderate* (four to five indicators) to *severe* (six or more indicators). (Source: American Psychiatric Association, 2013.)

Table breaks down important information.

Diminished Control

1. Uses more substance, or for longer, than intended.
2. Tries unsuccessfully to regulate use of substance.
3. Spends much time acquiring, using, or recovering from effects of substance.
4. Craves the substance.

Diminished Social Functioning

5. Use disrupts commitments at work, school, or home.
6. Continues use despite social problems.
7. Causes reduced social, recreational, and work activities.

Hazardous Use

8. Continues use despite hazards.
9. Continues use despite worsening physical or psychological problems.

Drug Action

10. Experiences tolerance (needing more substance for the desired effect).
11. Experiences withdrawal when attempting to end use.

Sample Textbook Page

Vocabulary words are defined as well as bolded in the text.

substance use disorder continued substance craving and use despite significant life disruption and/or physical risk.

psychoactive drug a chemical substance that alters perceptions and moods.

Drugs: education, prevention and policy,
October 2010; 17(5): 507–527

informa
healthcare

Article comes from a specialized academic journal

Factors associated with teenage ecstasy use

Title is plain and informative

PATRICK MCCRYSTAL & ANDREW PERCY

Institute of Child Care Research, School of Sociology Social Policy and Social Work, Queens University Belfast, 6 College Park, Belfast BT7 1LP, UK

Authors are academic researchers who are open to communication from other experts

Abstract

Article begins with an abstract

Aims: The aim of this article was to investigate the factors associated with ecstasy use in school-aged teenagers.
Methods: This was a longitudinal study of adolescent drug use, which was undertaken in three towns in Northern Ireland. A questionnaire was administered annually to participants. In this article ecstasy use patterns amongst a cohort of young people aged 14–16 years participating in the Belfast Youth Development Study (BYDS) was explored.
Findings: The percentage of those who had used ecstasy at least once increased from 7% when aged 14 years to 9% at 15 and 13% at 16 years. Female gender, delinquency, problem behaviours at school and the number of evenings spent out with friends each week were found to be significant variables predicting 'ever use' of ecstasy in all 3 years by logistic regression.
Conclusions: The findings suggest that ecstasy use patterns may be changing from their historical perception as a 'party' drug, as the demographic profile ecstasy of users in this study reflected the traditional profile of illicit drug use during adolescence, which raises challenges for addressing the problems associated with this drug.

Article is structured according to the scientific method (like high school lab reports)

Introduction

Despite being a relatively new drug (van Ours, 2005) ecstasy (3,4-methylene-dioxymethamphetamine, MDMA) has become widely used as a recreational drug by young people around the world (Christophersen, 2000), and for over a decade has been an established part of youth culture in some countries (WHO, 1996) and part of the acid house, rave and dance scene in the UK for 20 years now. It is labelled one of the 'party' or 'club' drugs with use highest amongst teenagers and young adults in social settings including bars, concerts and dance parties (Koesters, Greenberg, Pollack, & Dolezal, 2002). Early studies of ecstasy users

Correspondence: Patrick McCrystal, Institute of Child Care Research, School of Sociology, Social policy and Social Work, Queens University Belfast, 6 College Park, Belfast BT7 1LP. Tel: 00442890975991. Fax: 00442890975900. E-mail: P.McCrystal@qub.ac.uk

ISSN 0968–7637 print/ISSN 1465–3370 online © 2010 Informa UK Ltd.
DOI: 10.3109/09687630902810691

Sample Article Page

Mamapundit.com

Blog title shows it's about her life

First person, confessional article title

A Parenting Secret I Am No Longer Willing to Keep

Mamapundit / Katie Allison Granju

Opens with strong, emotional personal anecdote

I worried and fretted, when my eldest child was brought to the intensive care unit three days ago, that the nurses and doctors might treat him differently, maybe even give him substandard care once they knew why he was there. That's because he was admitted not after a car accident in which he was blameless. Not due to some mysterious, unknown fever. No, he was rushed to the hospital, nearly lifeless, after a massive drug overdose and a brutal physical assault related to his involvement with drugs. But I was wrong to worry about this; in the time since we began our bedside hospital vigil—could it really only have been three or four days ago?—every single medical professional on the staff here at the hospital has been wonderful—skilled, compassionate, and just plain amazing.

This wasn't the first time I've been concerned about what people would think if they found out. In fact, I've been worried about what would happen if our family's terrible secret "got out"—that my son suffers from a life threatening drug addiction—for several years now. I mean, some people DID know—the people closest to us. And as someone who has been writing essays and blogging about her family life for many years, I had alluded to the issue obliquely here and there since about 2008—so I am sure some readers had their suspicions. However, until this week, until H overdosed and ended up on life support in the ICU, I had never said it clearly, proactively, without obfuscation or minimizing.

But I am saying it now, out loud, in public, for the first time: I am the mother of a drug addict.

My beloved, firstborn child suffers from a terrible disease, addiction, and he has been struggling with it for several years. It started with early juvenile experimentation with marijuana at about age 14 and has progressed to where he is now, addicted to hard street drugs and as a result, lying in a critical care hospital bed, dealing with a horrific brain trauma along with various other physical injuries that are the direct result of that disease.

He has been to drug treatment (almost a year, inpatient), 12 step meetings, jail and on the streets. I have cried, begged, threatened, prayed, and beat myself up every way a mother can possibly beat herself up. I know I made mistakes in raising him. My first and biggest mistake—and one that I implore other parents reading this not to make themselves—was to minimize and rationalize my child's earliest drug use as the kind of "experimentation" that "lots of kids" try when they are adolescents. In fact, however, this "experimentation" was an early warning signal, a huge, blaring, shrieking, flashing early warning sign, and I chose not to see or hear it for what it really was. It was akin to early stage pediatric cancer and instead, I treated it like he had made a "D" on his report card or something similarly inconsequential.

When he was admitted to the hospital earlier this week, they warned us he might not make it. He has pulled through the critical first few days, and we are now looking at weeks and months of neurological and physical rehabilitation to bring our son back. I will fight like hell to get him where he needs to be, but then what? Then are we right back where we were at the beginning of this week, before the overdose? Back to a place where a beautiful, brilliant, sensitive, amazing, loved-beyond-all-reason teenage boy can't see past his next fix? Can't or won't stop careening down a one way path straight to hell?

I don't know. I don't know what our next steps will be. But I know this: I am no longer willing—or ABLE—to keep this secret. Maybe people will judge me. Maybe they will label me the bad mother I fear that I am to have ended up in this place. Maybe they will shun me, my son, my family. I don't know. But I do know that the disease has now declared itself to such a degree that it's no longer possible to keep it a secret, even if I wanted to.

By the end, the tone shifts—she seems to be taking a stand

practice it 7.1   Pre-Reading for Audience and Purpose

Look over the readings in Chapter 24, 25, or 26. Although each of the readings is about the same basic topic or theme, they vary in audience and purpose. Choose three readings, and evaluate their audience and purpose:

1. How can you make an educated guess about audience and purpose before you even start reading?
2. What specific features of each text did you use to determine the audience and purpose?

Topics

FINDING SOMETHING TO SAY AND CARING ABOUT IT

When deciding on a topic for a college writing assignment, student writers often face two common problems:

1. They were assigned a topic that just doesn't inspire them.
2. They choose a topic only because they think they will be able to write enough about it to meet the page requirement.

Good writing rarely results from either situation. The best writing comes from actually having something to say—from having a purpose and wanting to communicate to an audience.

As the old saying goes, "Write what you know." Whenever possible, choose a topic that truly interests you, and worry about the page limit later. If your instructor gives you three or four essay assignment options, don't rush to pick the first one or the one that seems easiest. Give it some thought. Which topic really interests you most? Which readings for the class did you like best, and how might you incorporate them into the assignment? Take the time to decide on your essay topic and to focus the topic in the way that is most interesting to you.

If you have an assigned topic that doesn't immediately thrill you, create a sense of excitement by connecting it to other things that *do* interest you and by molding the purpose and audience to suit the ideas you want to express. The big difference between a successful student and one who is just getting by is how the student approaches an assignment that doesn't immediately create a spark of interest.

So how do you motivate yourself to get interested in an assigned topic? There are as many approaches to the topic as there are students in the room. So make your essay interesting—maybe even fun—to write. Choose a particular focus that speaks to you. (Don't worry about limiting the topic too much—by focusing a topic more closely, you often actually make it easier to fill up the required pages.)

▶ **For more about freewriting, clustering, and listing, see Chapter 10, Pre-Writing.**

Convinced? Ready to get started? You probably already have the brainstorming skills you need. Start by reading over the essay assignment a couple of times. Highlight words or phrases that refer to the topic of the assignment. Then list these words at the top of a freewriting page, or put these words into cluster bubbles. Elsewhere on the page, make a list or cluster about something that you're currently very passionate about, even if it seems to have nothing in common with the assignment topic.

For example, let's say you just finished the readings on student loans in the unit on financial literacy. Your essay assignment looks like this:

> Write a thesis-driven argument essay about some aspect of student loans. You might consider the following topics: student loans for undocumented students, the relationship between student loans and the rising

costs of college, or the burdens of student loan debt on young college graduates.

Imagine that you couldn't care less about student loans because you don't need them to go to school, so you don't feel particularly inspired by this topic. However, you are really interested in running track. At first glance there seems to be no possible connection between running and student loans. When you think further about it, though, and brainstorm a little on both topics, you notice that the idea of giving up something to pursue a goal, which you do regularly for running track, has some similarities with the idea of getting into debt to pursue the goal of education. Use this connection, and your natural curiosity about things related to running, as springboards to a topic that matters to you.

For instance, in terms of running, you might be curious about the following questions:

- What types of sacrifices are worth it?
- When can sacrifices become too extreme or in some way bad for you?
- How does the coach influence when, how, and how much runners sacrifice? Who else urges runners to make sacrifices?

Now, think about how these questions might relate to student loans. You could substitute the phrase *financial debt* for *running track* and the word *counselor* for *coach*, and then ask essentially the same questions about the topic of student loans.

After trying brainstorming exercises like these, you may discover that the topic now intrigues you, or you may find that you still don't care about student loans. At the very least, though, this exercise gives you a better sense of how to focus your writing assignment and helps you get started.

practice it 7.2   Brainstorming to Find a Topic That Matters to You

Look at your essay assignment (or, if you aren't working on one currently, choose one of the sample prompts from Chapter 24, 25, or 26). What interests you about this essay prompt? What doesn't interest you? How can you spark some curiosity in yourself about this assignment? What can you connect it to that *does* really matter to you?

MAKING A BROAD TOPIC MORE SPECIFIC

Once you have arrived at a topic you like, if you are like most students, you still need to tweak it to make it specific enough. For example:

Unclear Topic   This paper will be about video games.

This topic is far too broad. What *about* video games? Ask yourself: Why did I think of the topic in the first place?

Clear Topic   Many people are concerned about children who sit at home and play video games alone every day after school. Should they be?

The second topic clearly states the *who* (children who play video games alone), *where* (at home), and *when* (every day after school). It also suggests a *what* (people's concern—is it warranted?). Now the topic is much more clear and specific.

Get input.   To figure out how specific you need to be, start by listening to your peers and friends. State your topic to them, and then sit quietly and take notes while they brainstorm a list of all the things they think you might be talking about. This method will give you a good idea of how clear and specific your topic is, because it will reveal their preconceived notions about the topic. Next, look at the list and use it to help focus your topic. Make your idea as specific as possible and write it up clearly in a complete sentence. Don't begin with "this paper is about" or "my topic is" or any other phrases that refer to yourself or the paper.

For example, tell your friends that your topic for your English class essay is money and how we manage it. Ask them what they think of when they hear the phrase "money management" and then sit back and see what they say. They are likely to brainstorm a list that looks something like this:

debt
credit cards
never having enough money to buy stuff
paying for college
student loans—good idea or not?
shopping and spending too much
running out of money
parents' money problems and fights about money
buying presents for boyfriend/girlfriend
college expenses—books, food, going out
paying bills
saving for vacations, cars, etc.

Take a close look at the list. It gives you a good idea about potential readers' expectations. The fact that this list is so wide-ranging demonstrates that you need to focus your topic. Maybe you are just talking about money management for college students, not everyone. Maybe you're just talking about avoiding credit card debt. In order to ensure that you are being clear and specific, carefully describe your topic so your reader knows exactly what you will discuss in your essay (and what you won't be covering).

Once you have a list like this, highlight the items on it that directly pertain to your topic and cross out those that don't. Then write a sentence that explains your topic, sticking to the words on the list. Here's an example:

> College students often struggle to pay their school expenses and have a hard time deciding whether student loans are a wise choice.

Ask questions.   Another way to become specific is to write a very basic topic idea and then revise it by asking questions. Often, you can take a vague or broad topic and make it more clear and specific by asking questions to get important details and then adding a few words.

STEP 1:   **In your notebook, write your topic as best you can.**

STEP 2:   **Now circle each word that could be made more specific.** Brainstorm more detail about each word.

STEP 3:   **Finally, take your best words and phrases and rewrite a more focused, specific topic.**

Let's look at an example:

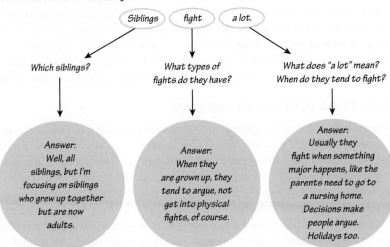

Now, take that information that you've added and rewrite the topic with more specifics:

> Adult siblings often argue during holidays or whenever major family decisions need to be made.

Much better! Incorporating the words and specific details from the question-and-answer process really helps focus the topic. Now your readers won't waste time wondering what exactly you mean, and they won't question why you're not discussing children's squabbles over toys.

> **practice it 7.3**   Identifying the Topic
>
> Reread the article "Men, Women, and Money" (see pp. 60–69). Underline or highlight the topic in the first few paragraphs of Mellan's essay. Can you clearly identify the topic? Do you understand it? How would you explain the topic to a friend who hadn't read the article? Write down your thoughts in the margins of the essay.

Crafting Your Paper's Audience, Purpose, and Tone

Once your curiosity is sparked and you have a clear, specific topic, you might be tempted to jump right in and start brainstorming all that you can on the topic. As part of your brainstorming, though, you must consider the audience and purpose of your writing. Remember, audience and purpose often shape the tone, word choice, style, content, and even the structure of a piece of writing, as we have seen in the three types of writing about drug use earlier in this chapter.

Audience and purpose also often determine what you put into a text and what you leave out. For instance, how much background information you include in an introductory paragraph depends entirely on who your intended audience is and what you expect your readers to already know about the topic. Your audience and purpose will influence the examples you choose to support your points, as well as provide the context for them.

WRITING FOR A PARTICULAR AUDIENCE

In most college writing assignments, the assumed audience is a "college-level reader." What exactly does this mean? Essays written for a "college-level reader" are generally academic in tone and style, and their purpose is usually to argue or persuade the reader about some aspect of the material. The audience for academic essays includes college students and college-educated general readers—people who read and understand sophisticated essays but who may not be experts in the particular topic under discussion and may not have read the books or articles referred to in the paper. (This is why you should briefly identify books and articles you discuss somewhere early in your paper, as well as identify experts to whom you refer, even if you know that your instructor knows who the expert is because he or she assigned the text.)

In most written and oral communication outside the college classroom, the audience you write to changes constantly, and your ability to adapt to these changes largely determines how successful your written and oral communication will be. For instance, an e-mail about your broken computer to your good friend who works in the IT department might be phrased very differently from a formal request to your boss justifying your need for an expensive replacement. A phone message left for a best friend differs significantly from one left for a potential employer.

If you are allowed to choose your audience for a college assignment, then use these basic demographic categories to determine your ideal reader.

Reader Demographics

- Age
- Gender
- Ethnicity
- Educational level
- Ability level
- Career/profession
- Role in society
- Other important and relevant factors (for example, if your topic is drug use, then it would be important to know if your audience had used drugs, had thought about using drugs, or had never used drugs)

Audiences are, after all, made up of people, and knowing something about the people you hope to reach with your writing will help you write better. Age, for instance, can be divided in many ways: babies, toddlers, preschoolers, grade schoolers, tweens, teens, young adults, thirty-somethings, middle-aged adults, empty nesters, and the elderly. You might group some of these together, depending on their shared experiences. An essay might speak to tweens and teens, or teens and young adults. As with topics, however, narrowing the focus of the audience sometimes makes it easier to generate ideas. In other words, the more you focus, the more you have to say.

For instance, if your instructor assigned a paper about the topic of fame and celebrity but allowed you to choose your audience and purpose, you might decide to focus on teen readers or parent readers, women or men, producers of media or consumers of media. How would an essay intended for teenagers who watch reality television differ from an essay intended for parents who want their young children to become stars? The purpose in both cases might be similar: to caution readers to be careful about valuing fame too much. However, the approach you would take—from the language used to the examples given—would probably be quite different because of the audience.

WRITING WITH A PURPOSE

Most writers determine the audience and purpose together, developing one alongside the other. For instance, if you want to write to teens who watch too much reality television, then you probably already know your purpose in choosing that specific audience: to convince them to turn off the television and do something else. Sometimes, though, you cannot quite articulate your purpose to the audience you have in mind or which has been assigned to you. If that's the case, ask yourself the following questions:

- What do I want to say to this audience?
- Why do I want to say this? What do I hope to accomplish?
- What can I say to this audience that might be original or unique, that they don't already know?
- Am I part of the group to whom I am speaking or not? In other words, am I speaking as an insider or an outsider? What advantages can I offer either way?

practice it 7.4   Brainstorming Audience and Purpose

Imagine that your instructor assigned a paper on the topic of public art but gave you complete freedom to choose the audience and purpose. Brainstorm a list of as many possible types of audiences as you can. Then, for each possible audience, brainstorm one or two possible purposes you might have in writing to that audience about that topic. (The process has been started on the following chart. Fill in the rest of the chart with your own ideas. You can copy the chart into your notebook if you need more space.)

Possible Audiences	Possible Purposes
Experienced professional artists	1. To showcase important new works of public art
Untrained artists and art students	
Homeowners	2. To share art techniques
Commercial property owners	3. To inform them of opportunities to promote their work
Taxpayers/citizens	
Educators	
Others?	

Once you select a specific audience and purpose, ask yourself these questions:

- What types of evidence will resonate most with this audience? Statistics? Facts? Expert testimony? Stories? Case studies? Personal experiences? Some combination?

- If I make an argument, what kinds of appeals will be most persuasive to this type of reader?
- How formal a tone should I take when writing to this audience? What kind of language should I use, or avoid using?
- Is humor appropriate for this audience? Why or why not?
- Should I use vivid sensory descriptions or stick to the facts?
- What comparisons or analogies are these readers most likely to find convincing and engaging?

Use these questions to spark your brainstorming about information to include in a paper with this topic and audience.

WRITING IN A PARTICULAR TONE

Tone is hard to define but easy to recognize—especially when someone uses an inappropriate tone. (Think of what provokes an irritated-looking mother to say to her teenage daughter, "Are you getting sassy with me, young lady?") "Tone of voice" refers to the way a person says something, which influences the meaning of the words. For instance, imagine people sitting down to a formal holiday dinner. One person says to another, "Please pass me the knife." The tone of that statement might be described as polite, ordinary, or untroubled. Imagine, however, that a hostage is trying to convince one of his captors to set him free while the other one is distracted. If the hostage says the same words—"Please, pass me the knife!"—the tone would be totally different.

Actors do a great job capturing the tone of voice of their characters. Writers, however, don't have the benefit of an actor, setting, costumes, props, or an action-packed scenario. All writers have to control tone are words, punctuation, and document format, so they have to use them extremely well.

Most academic writing has a fairly neutral tone, as you can see from the essays you have been reading. A neutral tone means that the writing doesn't use too much humor, doesn't reveal too much about the author, and doesn't sound like it's looking for a fight. Academic writers usually try to appear neutral and objective—or at least fair to opposing viewpoints. A neutral tone doesn't mean the writer doesn't have strong feelings; it just means that the writer is capable of putting his or her feelings aside in order to present the information clearly and logically and to examine an issue from all sides. (Since a neutral tone can be difficult to learn, some instructors discourage students from using "I" in all academic writing to ensure a neutral tone; others suggest using it sparingly.)

In addition, academic writers usually avoid slang because they do not wish to alienate or offend their readers. Slang words or phrases such as *crappy, for real, LOL*, and *u* when you mean "you" are very informal and are not considered Standard English. We often use informal language when talking with friends or when e-mailing or texting. But for the same reason that we talk differently with our friends than we do during a job interview, we use more formal language when writing for academic or job-related purposes than we do when e-mailing or texting friends.

SHARPENING YOUR TOPIC WITH A TITLE

Good titles are like doors cracked open: They make you want to open them wider and take a look around. One of Ernest Hemingway's novels is titled *The Sun Also Rises.* What if it had been called *The Sun Rises* instead? We might read it and shrug: "Of course the sun rises. So what?" When Hemingway puts the word "also" in the title, he implies its opposite: The sun sets. "Yes," we might think, "The sun sets, but it *also* rises. So there's light as well as darkness. Hmm . . . which way is this book going to go?" We might be intrigued enough to open the book to find out. The titles of the essays you write in college can also spark the reader's curiosity and hint at some of the subtle or metaphorical ideas in your piece of writing.

Few student writers think too much about their titles. In fact, here's a list of some of the phrases—hardly even titles—that appeared at the top of student papers for a class writing about the theme of money and wealth:

"Essay 1"
"Money and Wealth Paper"
"Money Essay"
"Wealth Essay"
"Does Money Buy Happiness?"

You get the picture. None of these titles inspire you to read the paper. The last one in the list is the best of the bunch, but when you realize that three students from the same class used the exact same title, it hardly seems original.

How do you create a focused title that reflects the ideas in your paper and piques the reader's curiosity? Group brainstorming for title ideas can be extremely helpful. In addition, try these strategies:

• **Reread your introduction and conclusion.** Are there any words or phrases that jump out at you that could be developed into an interesting title?

- **Reread your thesis statement.** What key words do you use there? Can they be made into a title?

- **Look at an important quotation or example that you used in your essay.** Can a word or phrase from it be the basis for a title?

- **Is there an image, analogy, metaphor, or symbol that you use in your paper or that you might be able to weave into your writing?** Perhaps you can use that as your title.

| practice it 7.5 | Brainstorming Titles |

Brainstorm three or four possible titles for an essay you are writing now. Run them by your peers, and ask them to put the titles in order from most to least interesting.

TITLES OF ACADEMIC ARTICLES

You may have noticed that many of the titles of the articles you read in college are rather dry, such as "Factors Associated with Teenage Ecstasy Use." Articles of this kind are meant to inform, not entertain, and their titles are as precise as possible to save their readers time. Many academic articles of this kind have a title and a subtitle, such as "Being a Celebrity: A Phenomenology of Fame." The reason for this is practical. Authors want you to be able to find their articles in searchable online databases, such as EBSCO and Gale databases, so they use the subtitle to include other words that may be search terms.

Titles do vary by discipline. The humanities allow authors more freedom than the sciences or social sciences in terms of writing titles that are metaphoric or otherwise creative. In college writing courses, unless your instructor tells you otherwise, determine whether a more creative or a more informative title best fits your essay's tone. In other courses, follow the expectations of the discipline; look at the titles of the course readings for clues to title tone, length, and style. (Ask your instructor for guidelines if you're unsure.)

| practice it 7.6 | Evaluating Titles |

Turn to the table of contents for this book, and look over the titles of the essays in Chapter 24, 25, or 26. Make a list of the titles that inspire you to read, and make another list of those that don't spark your curiosity. Compare your lists with those of your classmates.

chapter review

In the following chart, fill in the second column to record in your own words the important skills included in this chapter. Then assess yourself to determine whether you are still developing the skill or feel you have mastered it. If you are still developing the skill, make some notes about what you need to work on to master it in the future. If you believe you have already mastered it, explain why.

Skills and concepts covered in this chapter	Explanation in your own words	I'm developing this skill and need to work on . . .	I believe I have mastered this skill because . . .
Determining the audience			
Understanding the purpose			
Creating focused topics			
Relating tone to audience and purpose			
Crafting meaningful titles			

8

Rhetorical Patterns in Reading and Writing

in this chapter

- What Is a Rhetorical Pattern?
- How Can You Recognize a Particular Rhetorical Pattern?
- When and Why Do You Use the Rhetorical Patterns?
- How Can Rhetorical Patterns Help You Brainstorm Ideas?

What Is a Rhetorical Pattern?

Rhetorical patterns are ways of thinking, strategies that everyone uses on a daily basis, often unconsciously. Writers use these patterns consciously and thoughtfully to make their ideas strong. Take comparison and contrast as an example. On a daily basis, you often think in comparisons and contrasts. When you question whether you should eat at a fast-food restaurant for lunch or bring your own lunch, you weigh the similarities and differences, such as taste, convenience, cost, and healthiness, between the two options. Most people who live in a consumer society like America have highly developed comparison and contrast skills, since there are so many choices to be made each minute of the day.

It may seem odd to take a step back and think about how we think (we call this metacognition), but categorizing our ways of thinking can be very helpful. In doing so, you will become more aware of the rhetorical choices readers and writers make and will be better able to evaluate and control these choices.

First, rhetorical patterns often form the basis of essay structures, so being aware of these rhetorical strategies helps you understand readings. Imagine, for example, that you are reading an article that describes the current economic situation by comparing and contrasting it to the Great Depression. Why might that be effective, or ineffective, as a strategy? Which readers would find such an approach to the material useful? If you know nothing about the history of the Great Depression, how much can comparing and contrasting our present situation to it tell you? A lot?

LaunchPad Solo
macmillan learning

Visit **LaunchPad Solo for Readers and Writers > Patterns of Organization** for extra practice in the skills covered in this chapter.

▶ For organizational structures for specific rhetorical patterns, see pages 300–305 in Chapter 14, Essay Organization and Outlining.

A little? If the author extensively compares and contrasts the present with the past, how can a bit of quick research about that historical period improve your understanding of the article? If you as a reader take the time to think about why the author refers to the Great Depression, your reading comprehension will improve.

Second, we also become more critical readers when we question whether the author has chosen the most effective and appropriate rhetorical pattern. Perhaps within an essay the author overuses contrast and doesn't focus enough on comparisons between subjects. Perhaps the body paragraphs use only personal narrative as evidence, which might be interesting and emotionally compelling but not logically persuasive. As a reader, once you begin to recognize the rhetorical patterns the author uses, you will analyze the text in a more sophisticated way.

Third, when we write, we can do our best to choose the rhetorical strategy that fits our topic, audience, and purpose. For the student writer, this often means understanding the assignment. If your instructor asks you to compare and contrast two topics, but instead you describe them both but never get around to comparing and contrasting, then you won't earn a very strong grade.

Being aware of rhetorical patterns also helps deepen your thinking and your writing. Maybe you overuse narration and illustration to prove your points. You might be missing opportunities to expand your ideas by bringing some cause and effect thinking to the topic. Even taking the time to ask yourself, "Is what I'm writing about a cause or an effect?" can be helpful in generating your ideas.

▶ For more on reading essay assignments, see Chapter 3, Putting Ideas into Writing, and Chapter 19, Essay Exams.

A Detailed Look at the Patterns

There are many rhetorical patterns. In fact, even the idea of categorizing thought is itself a pattern: categorization or classification. Scientists classify every living thing into kingdom, phylum, class, order, family, genus, and species, so it's no wonder philosophers and writers want to classify the way we think, write, and speak into the various rhetorical patterns. Such metacognition is what distinguishes us from other mammals. Some of the more commonly used rhetorical patterns in college writing are:

- example/illustration
- definition
- classification/categorization
- narration
- description
- process analysis

- comparison and contrast
- cause and effect
- argument

Argument is such a rich and varied strategy that it merits an entire chapter in this book; see Chapter 12, Argument. Here's a detailed look at the other patterns.

EXAMPLE/ILLUSTRATION

We routinely use examples in writing and speech, and our choice of examples often says a lot about us. Does your best friend use a sports example to illustrate every new topic? Does your sister use examples from her workplace every time she's trying to give you advice? In college essay writing, you can sometimes draw examples from your own personal observation and experience, but usually you need to do reading and research to find additional examples. Nearly every piece of academic writing offers examples of one type or another, and your job as a critical reader is to evaluate these illustrations, reading them both with and against the grain to see if they support the author's points.

Take a look at an excerpt from the Los Angeles Police Department's policy statement about graffiti (pp. 511–13). Here, the LAPD explains what a "beautification project" is by giving various examples:

> Beautification projects such as trash cleanups, landscape enhancements, and gardens also serve as a focus for community organizing. Community groups working with law enforcement, public works, or parks and recreation staff clean up public areas and abandoned lots. The project may reclaim a public space for neighborhood use, establish new green space, or mark neighborhood boundaries.

Although the LAPD's policy statement about graffiti is intentionally brief, it takes time to list examples of beautification projects and goes into some detail about how they could be conducted. Notice how the examples of beautification projects will accomplish the same types of thing that gang graffiti often aims to do—"reclaim a public space . . . or mark neighborhood boundaries"—though in a more positive way. So even though this paragraph doesn't specifically mention the parallels between beautification projects and gang graffiti, the wording of the examples will hint at that for careful readers.

DEFINITION

When we think of definition, usually we think of simple meanings of specific words. Indeed, much of the work you do in college involves learning definitions of new terminology. The rhetorical mode, however, moves beyond simple dictionary definitions to include more extensive definitions such as historical definitions, cultural definitions, or definitions that argue for a particular interpretation of a word.

Notice how this paragraph from Koon-Hwee Kan's article "Adolescents and Graffiti" (pp. 505–10) begins with a simple definition (highlighted in purple) but then moves on to include a historical and cultural definition for *latrinalia* (highlighted in yellow):

> Another type of private graffiti is "latrinalia," the kind of graffiti found near toilets (Abel & Buckeley, 1970). In most civilizations throughout history, its creators were usually suppressed individuals in society, for example, slaves working in monumental construction or prisoners inside jail cells. In contemporary times, such creation is not the sole responsibility of adolescence; people of all ages are equally likely to perform such acts (Kan, 507).

The addition of the history of latrinalia deepens our understanding of it, for we see its social context. By showing that it's not just done by teenagers, the author challenges some of our assumptions about how latrinalia ought to be defined.

CLASSIFICATION/CATEGORIZATION

To classify means to put something into categories so that you can understand it better. Carol S. Dweck's (pp. 6–13) classification of students into two groups—growth mind-set and fixed mind-set—is one good example. As we already noted, much of scientific learning is about classifying and categorizing: the different systems of the body; the states of matter (solid, liquid, gas); the elements; the types of animals; and so on. In the following passage from Olivia Mellan's "Men, Women, and Money" (pp. 60–69), we see two of her major classifications of money personality types that present themselves in relationships. We've highlighted the key categories.

> An equally common polarity is the worrier and the avoider. Avoiders don't focus on the details of their money life, such as whether they have enough money or how much interest they're paying on their credit cards; they just spend. A worrier will turn a mate into an avoider just as a way of escaping the avalanche of worry. And an avoider will turn a mate into a worrier. Two partners couldn't both avoid forever; somebody will eventually get concerned and take on the worrier role.

Notice how Mellan starts the paragraph with a simple, straightforward topic sentence that identifies the two types (highlighted in yellow and blue). Then she elaborates on each type, giving each a sentence of further explanation. Then she offers the two ending sentences (highlighted in green) of the paragraph to describe how these two types of money personalities interact.

As you remember, worriers and avoiders aren't the only money personalities Mellan categorizes; the paragraphs before and after this one go into detail about the other money types. Her classification of these money types comes from her experience as a therapist, as she says earlier in the article. If you are going to use classification and categorization rhetorically, make sure your categories are valid and not overgeneralizations or stereotypes, particularly if you are describing different types of people. Whenever authors define categories or accept established ones, we should think about whether the categories they use are effective or not.

NARRATION

Narration tells a story, often but not always in a chronological way. While a full story has a beginning, middle, and end, often in writing an author will tell part of a story. This fragment is intended to spark the reader's interest, illustrate a concept, or give some background information about a topic. Readers gravitate toward narration, partly because it feels human and conveys "real life" topics, and partly because narrative writing usually uses strong description. Narration creates a tension, or suspense, that makes the reader want to keep reading to find out what happens next.

Certainly, narration is the primary rhetorical mode used in fiction, biography, autobiography, and memoir. Narrative can also be used effectively within expository (factual) or argument writing of all sorts. Writers often tell a brief story, sometimes called an anecdote, to illustrate a point. They then reflect on that story, exploring what it means and why it matters. For instance, Carlin Flora opens her article "Seeing by Starlight" (pp. 527–33) with the following anecdote. Narration is highlighted in yellow; reflection in blue.

> A couple of years ago, Britney Spears and her entourage swept through my boss's office. As she sashayed past, I blushed and stammered and leaned over my desk to shake her hand. She looked right into my eyes and smiled her pageant smile, and I confess, I felt dizzy. I immediately rang up friends to report my celebrity encounter, saying: "She had on a gorgeous, floor-length white fur coat! Her skin was blotchy!" I've never been much of a Britney fan, so why the contact high? Why should I care? For that matter, why should any of us?

The narration, while short, has a clear beginning, middle, and end: Britney arrived, Flora shook her hand, and then Flora called her friends. It leads up well to the questions and reflections, which express the central question the article tries to answer: Why are we so affected by fame? Narration works particularly well here to hook the reader, because the author is so honest. She's not telling a story that makes her look great;

rather, she's revealing something about herself that surprised her, something that she wants to invite her readers to explore. We are drawn in, both by the invitation and by the juicy tidbits that might follow.

DESCRIPTION

Good description is the key to telling a great story, and it is also useful in any writing where you want to offer a concrete, detailed example. Furthermore, descriptive writing serves as the basis for much nonfiction process analysis, definition, and illustration. Take this example from Ken Ilgunas's article "Out of Debt, on the Road" (pp. 56–60). Ilgunas uses strong, meaningful verbs as well as vivid imagery to help us see the tiny Alaskan town where he worked to pay off his student loan debt. Good descriptive words have been highlighted:

> Without a better idea, I wound up calling a friend, who hooked me up with a $9-an-hour job as a tour guide in Coldfoot, Alaska, 60 miles north of the Arctic Circle and 250 miles from the nearest stoplight. Coldfoot, the world's northernmost truck stop, has a winter population of 12 that triples during the summer, when buses drop off their cargo of tourists at Coldfoot's 52-room motel. I would be one of three guides who'd take the tourists on daylong tours in a 14-passenger van up the Dalton Highway or in a big blue raft down the sleepy Koyukuk River.

In this passage, the writer conveys not just the facts of where Coldfoot is ("60 miles north of the Arctic Circle" and the "northernmost truck stop") but the quality of its isolation ("250 miles from the nearest stoplight"). The buses don't just drop off the tourists. They drop off "their cargo" of tourists, which makes the people into objects. By pointing out that the raft was big and blue, Ilgunas points to a certain absurdity in the whole scene.

How do you write descriptively? Think about the who, what, where, when, and how questions. What details can you add to your description to make it more vivid for a reader? What details does the reader most need to know to grasp the larger point you are trying to make? Can you show these details, instead of telling them? In the Coldfoot example, the author aims to describe a place his readers have never seen, but he also wants us to feel the remoteness and small size of the town and experience how it triples its size with the tourist season.

Good descriptive writing often happens during the editing process, when the writer polishes the words until they shine. For starters, though, begin by choosing words that capture the senses. In Ilgunas's short passage, he uses words and phrases that capture the coarseness of his experience, such as "hooked me up" and "cargo of tourists." His language reflects the harsh environment of Coldfoot. Strong descriptive writing means that you must also choose good verbs, such as "wound up" in the

▶ For more about how to use strong verbs, see Chapter 39, Clear and Focused Language.

passage. If you find your paragraphs filled with words like *is, are, was, were, have, had,* and *seems,* then you have opportunities to rewrite and restructure the sentence around stronger verbs.

PROCESS ANALYSIS

Process analysis writing describes the steps of an activity, such as how a plant grows or how a volcano erupts. Read the following paragraphs from Daisy Yuhas's article "Curiosity Prepares the Brain for Better Learning" (pp. 469–71). Transitional words related to processes are highlighted.

> Neuroscientist Charan Ranganath and his fellow researchers asked 19 participants to review more than 100 questions, rating each in terms of how curious they were about the answer. Next, each subject revisited 112 of the questions—half of which strongly intrigued them whereas the rest they found uninteresting—while the researchers scanned their brain activity using functional magnetic resonance imaging (fMRI).
>
> During the scanning session participants would view a question and then wait 14 seconds and view a photograph of a face totally unrelated to the trivia before seeing the answer. Afterward the researchers tested participants to see how well they could recall and retain both the trivia answers and the faces they had seen.

These two paragraphs describe the experiment that was conducted. The passage is factual, clear, and easy to follow, largely because of the transitional expressions that indicate the various steps in the procedure.

COMPARISON AND CONTRAST

Comparison and contrast are two of the most common rhetorical patterns in school assignments. Perhaps on a history test you have been asked to compare and contrast World War II with the American Revolutionary War, or in a biology class you have been asked to compare the human brain to that of the dolphin. To compare means to describe the similarities; to contrast means to point out the differences.

Carol S. Dweck's article "The Perils and Promises of Praise" (pp. 6–13) relies extensively on comparison and contrast: She compares and contrasts the fixed-mind-set and the growth-mind-set students, the different types of praise, and the resulting educational outcomes. In this short passage, you can see how she encapsulates her argument. Comparison is highlighted in blue, while contrast is highlighted in yellow.

> It is not surprising, then, that when we have followed students over challenging school transitions or courses, we find that those with growth mind-sets outperform their classmates with fixed mind-sets—even when they entered with equal skills and knowledge.

Here the comparison goes last, and the contrast is listed first. Does this strategy emphasize the contrast or the comparison, or weigh them both equally?

CAUSE AND EFFECT

Cause and effect is one of the more common rhetorical patterns, and your ability to analyze and understand causes and effects is crucial to your success in college courses. Let's start with a fairly simple and straightforward example of the use of cause and effect from a section of the math textbook *For All Practical Purposes*, which describes student loans (pp. 40–45):

> Before July 1, 2010, another kind of student loan was available (and you may have one). That was a "federal guaranteed student loan," under which you got your loan not from the government but from a bank. If you failed to pay back the loan, the bank was paid by the federal government instead. (In other words, the bank charged an origination fee for the loan and then earned interest on it with no risk to the bank; because this arrangement did not seem fair, the Obama administration abolished this kind of loan.)

Here the words *if* and *because* are clues that the author is using cause and effect thinking in these two sentences. If you don't pay back a loan (cause), there will be a specific effect (the government will have to pay it). Because that process was unfair (cause), the president changed the law (effect).

While cause and effect seems simple enough on the surface, it is one of the most challenging rhetorical strategies. Often, writers assume that just because two things happened at the same time, one caused the other. Sometimes they jump to the conclusion that the simplest or most obvious "cause" of something is the actual or only cause, without investigating carefully hidden or underlying causes that may be more important. You will improve at this sort of thinking with time and practice, and as you gather more knowledge and research skills, your ability to think critically about the causes and effects of complex issues will develop quickly.

Let's look at an example of how complicated cause and effect can get. In the following paragraph from the article "Being a Celebrity" (pp. 534–50), authors Donna Rockwell and David C. Giles describe what they learned about the effects of becoming a celebrity:

> For the former child star at the age of ten, the experience of going from a "neighborhood kid" to a famous TV personality overnight was life-altering. Cast on a hit TV series, he recalls the reaction after the show's debut. "When I went outside the next day, my life was different. . . . And the first thing that I knew, 'Holy Toledo, I'm famous!'" The experience of being recognized comes with a person's celebritization. Celebrities become accustomed to looking into a crowd and seeing the adoration "in their eyes." "You know they know

who you are." The right to be anonymous is exchanged for all that fame has to offer. The famous person feels exposed, with very few places to experience privacy. There is a tendency to get "peopled out" when approached by those who engage the celebrity "24/7." There is a feeling that "I can't be left alone," with a lingering fear of tabloid paparazzi around any corner. It can be "a drag," and "a pain in the butt to have to worry about that." Moments of anonymity are relished, moments with family, "with good friends who I knew before I was famous." Privacy becomes a coveted luxury. If the celebrity is not feeling "100%" on a particular day, staying home may be preferable to facing the crowd. If "I'm not feeling all that sociable, I have to put that aside."

In this passage, we can see how cause and effect can build on one another and that things can be both causes and effects. For instance, becoming famous (cause) makes a person easily recognized (effect). Consequently, being recognized (cause) makes the star exhausted and fearful (effect). Experiencing this exhaustion and fear on a daily basis (cause) makes them desire privacy (effect), which, ironically, is the opposite of where they started when they were trying to become famous in the first place.

Notice that in this paragraph, the authors did not use many of the key words of cause and effect (*if*, *then*, *because*, *as a result*, and *consequently*). Rather, the logical pattern of cause and effect comes out in the ping-pong-like structure of the paragraph, where the sentences build back and forth, almost mimicking the feeling of contradiction and being pulled in two directions that the celebrity often feels.

practice it 8.1 Recognizing Rhetorical Patterns

Here are some paragraphs that use a particular rhetorical style to make a point. Read the paragraphs to determine the rhetorical strategy the author is using and compare your answers in groups or pairs. (These paragraphs are all from Olivia Mellan's article "Men, Women, and Money," which you can find in full on pp. 60–69.)

1. As a result of the money taboo, I grew up as most kids do: imitating my parents' way of handling money without being aware of it. My father, affected by the Depression, worried out loud about money. My mother was a shopaholic, expressing love by buying me and herself clothes. She'd hide the purchases behind a living room chair until my father was in a good mood. As an adult, whenever I felt either depressed or particularly happy, I too would go out and shop. And even if I bought everything at a thrift store, I'd hide all the items behind a chair until my husband was in a good mood. Actually, I alternated between shopping and worrying about money.

2. Other money personalities include planners, who are detail-oriented, and dreamers, who are global visionaries. In addition, there are money

monks, often ex-hippies, political activists, or spiritual souls, who feel that money corrupts and it's better to not have too much. Sometimes they marry money amassers, who believe that the guy with the most money wins. Amassers are not hoarders; they don't simply save, they invest to make their money grow. They save, spend and invest.

3. Moreover, when men make money in the stock market, they credit their own cleverness. When they lose money, they blame the incompetence of their advisers or bad luck. When women make money in the market, they credit the cleverness of their advisers, good luck, or even the stars. When they lose money, they blame themselves.

Rhetorical Patterns in Context

How do we actually use the rhetorical patterns in writing? How do they work together? Using the patterns to make your point is most likely not new to you, although you may not have been aware of using them before. If you ever used an example to illustrate your point or described the steps to accomplish something, you used a rhetorical pattern.

Let's look at the first few body paragraphs from Susan Engel's essay "The Case for Curiosity" (pp. 458–65). Engel uses a nice mix of rhetorical strategies in these paragraphs to establish a context for her argument:

Example/Illustration: The author offers one example from her and one based on personal experience.

Comparison and Contrast: We think one thing but do another.
Categorization: Two types of people.
Cause and Effect: One type of environment will cause curiosity while another won't.
Narration: The author's personal experience
Cause and Effect: Engel hints at possible outcomes.
Example and Process Analysis: Berlyne's research is an example, and it is described by explaining the process he went through to conduct the research.

Walk up to almost any teacher in the United States, ask her whether it's good for children to be curious, and what do you think she'll say? If you think that teacher will say yes, you're right. When my student Hilary Hackmann and I asked teachers to circle on a list the qualities they thought were most important for students to acquire in school, many circled curiosity. When asked on the fly, adults in our society say they value curiosity. Intuitively, people feel it's essential to learning.

But what we admire and what we deliberately cultivate aren't the same. When researchers dig deeper, they find that many adults think of curiosity as a trait possessed by some but not others. Or they think that as long as the environment isn't too repressive, children's natural sense of inquiry will surface (Engel, 2011). In fact, when Hilary and I asked teachers to list which qualities were most important without giving them a list to choose from, almost none mentioned curiosity. Many teachers endorse curiosity when they're asked about it, but it isn't uppermost on their minds—or shaping their teaching plans.

Why is this disturbing? Because research shows unequivocally that when people are curious about something, they learn more, and better. Daniel Berlyne (1954) first demonstrated this in the 1950s. He read people lists of facts, including some that were surprising to them, and led them to ask questions. Later, when asked to recall those lists, subjects remembered the times that had piqued their curiosity better than the others.

It's not just adults who benefit from having their curiosity piqued. When children want to know something, they're more likely to learn it and remember it. Babies play longer with toys in which they've shown a prior interest and explore those toys more; their interest allows them to learn more than they otherwise would. When older students are intrigued by unexpected or mysterious descriptions in their reading, they're more likely to remember the content later, and to more deeply understand what they read (Garner, Brown, Sanders, & Menke, 1992).

Comparison: Shows similarities between adults, babies, and older children.

Engel packs a variety of different rhetorical patterns into these paragraphs, yet it works as a piece of writing because of the very clear topic sentences that progress logically, as well as the consistent tone of the writing.

> ### practice it 8.2   Critical Reading for Rhetorical Patterns
>
> Turn to pages 458–65 and read the rest of Engel's article. As you read, annotate the article to make notes about the types of rhetorical strategies the author uses. Hint: She does not pack in quite so many different rhetorical strategies in one paragraph in the remainder of the article. Try to identify the predominant rhetorical pattern in each of her subpoints.

Using Rhetorical Patterns as a Brainstorming Strategy

So far in this chapter, we have been examining rhetorical patterns in texts written by others. However, we can also approach rhetorical patterns as a writing tool, especially when you are trying to generate more fresh and creative ideas.

RHETORICAL PATTERNS IN PRE-WRITING

Imagine, for example, that you are writing about a topic like career counseling. You can certainly begin your pre-writing with freewriting, listing, or clustering based on your reading, research, and personal experiences. Those are great strategies. You might then move on to the typical journalistic questions of *who, what, where, when, how,* and *why.* That works too. If you still need to push your ideas further, though, or if you feel particularly stuck on a topic, you might deepen the questioning, using the rhetorical patterns to help. Take a look at the following chart to see some examples of types of questions you might ask about this sample topic.

TOPIC: CAREER COUNSELING

Rhetorical pattern	Questions you could ask in this pattern	Your ideas
Example/ illustration	What are some examples of career counseling? In what examples did career counseling go well? In what examples did it go poorly?	—my high school gave us a career counseling test —my aunt had to see a career counselor to get unemployment —prof. said she used one when graduating college
Definition	How can career counseling be defined?	really any type of professional advice you get about careers—from a person directly, not just what you read online???
Classification/ categorization	What different types of career counseling exist? When do you use each type? Are the types related to the job seeker's life stages, his/her goals, or something else?	—required vs. optional —for students or older people —first job/career vs. career changers —paid or free?
Narration	What stories have I read or heard about career counseling? Did they tend to be positive or negative stories? Funny or serious? If you haven't heard any stories about this topic, why not?	—my aunt hated it and said it was stupid, but she tends to have a bad attitude about everything —we all used to laugh about what the tests told us we should be in school, but we didn't talk about it much —counselor at college tells stories about it all the time, how it helped her
Description	What descriptive words come to mind when I think about career counseling? What mood or tone do I associate with those words?	—depends on who you ask! I would say inspiring or dull
Process analysis	What is the process of career counseling? Is it always the same? What accounts for any differences?	
Compare and contrast	How does a job seeker who uses a career counselor compare and contrast with one who does not?	
Cause and effect	What causes someone to use or avoid career counseling services? What are the effects of using or avoiding career counseling services?	
Argument	What are the pros and cons of career counseling?	

After you have generated the list of questions in column 2, you will need to fill in the third column to jot down notes and ideas (or write notes on a separate piece of paper if you need more room). We have filled in some of the third column to give a sense of what it could look like, but there are no right or wrong ideas here.

With this brainstorming technique, you can often generate new ideas or deepen those you have already generated. A student writing about career counseling who took the time to brainstorm about all the above questions would certainly be able to generate enough ideas for a thesis on the topic. Even if the paper assignment requires a specific rhetorical approach—for example, a compare and contrast paper—you can still brainstorm a bit about the other patterns to help you develop areas of the paper. Perhaps your hook will emerge from your brainstorming about the narration or description questions. Remember, most writing uses a variety of rhetorical patterns.

▶ For more about the hook, see pages 319–22 in Chapter 16, Introductions and Conclusions.

practice it 8.3   Brainstorming Rhetorical Patterns

If you are working on a specific topic in class, draw a chart like the one on page 212 in your notebook, but put your topic in place of the career counseling topic. Generate the list of questions that you would ask about the topic for each rhetorical pattern. Next, swap your list of questions with a classmate and try to answer each other's questions. Compare your responses, and see which ideas you might want to incorporate into your next writing assignment.

RHETORICAL PATTERNS IN THE REVISION STAGE

Even if you have already drafted an essay, you can use the rhetorical patterns to try to revise a section of it. As writers, we can become creatures of habit. Perhaps you tend to use example after example, and your writing becomes a little monotonous. Maybe your go-to strategy is comparison and contrast, but you realize that it doesn't always work. One way to reframe an idea is to consider how it might change if you used a different way of thinking—a different rhetorical pattern—in that specific place. You might ask yourself, for instance, how your conclusion could work better if you introduced some cause and effect thinking into it, or how you could reinvent your hook to include some comparison and contrast. Using the rhetorical patterns to revise, even experimentally, might give you a fresh take on your work.

practice it 8.4   Experimenting with Rhetorical Patterns in Revision

Look at one of the texts you have read from Chapter 24, 25, or 26. Working in a group, find a paragraph in the text where the author clearly uses one of the rhetorical patterns to develop a main point. (Don't use one of the examples already described earlier in this chapter.) Discuss with your group what rhetorical pattern the author is using and whether or not you think it is effective. Then each group member should choose a different rhetorical pattern (make sure there are no duplicates) and rewrite the paragraph in that pattern. When finished, read your paragraphs out loud and compare the outcomes. What is lost and gained with each different rhetorical mode? Which one do you prefer? Why?

practice it 8.5   Changing Rhetorical Patterns

Look at an essay you are writing or one that you recently finished.
Find a passage in the essay that doesn't quite work well, that could be
more powerful. Analyze what you have already written in the passage.
What rhetorical pattern did you use? How might you make the same
point or convey the same information by using a different—perhaps
more interesting or persuasive—rhetorical pattern? Rewrite the
passage one or more times, using different approaches. Which do you
like best? Why? Gather opinions from peers, if possible, too.

chapter review

In the following chart, fill in the second column to record in your own words the
important skills included in this chapter. Then assess yourself to determine whether
you are still developing the skill or feel you have mastered it. If you are still developing the skill, make some notes about what you need to work on to master it in
the future. If you believe you have already mastered it, explain why.

Skills and concepts covered in this chapter	Explanation in your own words	I'm developing this skill and need to work on . . .	I believe I have mastered this skill because . . .
Understanding rhetorical patterns			
Example/illustration			
Definition			
Classification/ categorization			
Narration			
Description			
Process analysis			
Comparison and contrast			
Cause and effect			

9

Vocabulary Building

Building a bigger vocabulary makes you a more flexible writer because you have more words to choose from to express your point. It also allows you to tackle more difficult readings because you won't be hampered so often by unfamiliar words. Finally, having a broader vocabulary gives you confidence in speaking—which is critical, because the majority of our communication is still oral.

According to *The Oxford English Dictionary*, there are 171,476 words currently in use in the English language. We don't recommend that you try to learn all 171,476 of them (at least not in one semester!), but learning new words that you encounter in your readings is a good place to start. In many cases, to understand a reading fully, you must know how certain words are being used and what they mean. You definitely need to look up these words as part of your annotating process while reading.

Of course, learning new vocabulary is not confined to the books and articles you read for class. In addition to learning words from your readings, be on the lookout for words used frequently in class lectures and discussions. If you hear your instructor using a new term or if it appears on a list of words to learn for a test, then you should figure out the meaning and practice using the term.

Even outside of particular classes, your college experience is full of new terms and words that are important to know but may be unfamiliar, like *syllabus*, *prerequisite*, or *matriculation*. You also encounter unfamiliar words in everyday contexts—in conversations, in watching television or browsing Web sites, or in reading for pleasure. The dictionary is not the only way to find out the meanings of these words. You learn the meanings of some words in specialized sources like textbook glossaries; others you learn by asking people or by using context clues. It's extremely useful to keep a list of all these new words and their definitions in a dedicated notebook.

LaunchPad Solo
macmillan learning

Visit **LaunchPad Solo for Readers and Writers > Vocabulary** for extra practice in the skills covered in this chapter.

215

practice it 9.1   Learning College Vocabulary

Make a list of unfamiliar academic words you have heard or read as a student. You might draw from your syllabi and assignment sheets, registration material, student handbook, or other campus documents. Then join a few classmates and combine your lists.

Step 1: As a group, try to define as many words as possible on the list. In cases where you have differing opinions about the meaning of a word, write down more than one definition or explanation.

Step 2: Divide the words among the group members.

Step 3: Research your list of words. What can you deduce about what a word means from the context or from the information you gathered?

Step 4: At the next class meeting, update other group members with the results of your new word investigation. Add the meanings to your word list.

Step 5: Discuss how knowing these words will help you be more prepared as a student.

Strategies for Discovering the Meanings of Words

USING CONTEXT CLUES

Reading is the best way to build up your vocabulary. The more you read, the more words you encounter, and the more you practice learning vocabulary through context (the surrounding words or sentences). You won't always be able to figure out the meaning of a word from its context, but by using context clues, you have a good chance of understanding it.

Context clues are pieces of information in a sentence or sentences that help you decipher the meaning of a word you don't know. These might include a definition of the word, an example of the word, or an antonym that shows a contrasting meaning.

Did you notice the context clue for the word *antonym* in that last sentence? The phrase "that shows a contrasting meaning" is a context clue that gives a definition.

Deriving the meaning of a word in its "natural habitat"—that is, in a sentence or paragraph—is an effective way to learn its meaning. Often, when we look up a new word in the dictionary, the definition is not enough to show how the word is really used. Dictionaries that include example sentences do a better job of showing you the word in context, so keep an eye out for these. Using context clues also helps you keep a steadier reading pace because you don't stop to look up words as often.

When you come across context clues in a reading, mark both the new word and the context clue that helps you understand the word. Jotting down your understanding of the word in the margin is also a good practice that helps cement the meaning in your brain. In the following examples, the word being defined is underlined twice, and the context clues are underlined once.

▶ **See the use of context clues in action as a Model Reading Strategy with "Curious" by Ian Leslie (pp. 449–57).**

Common Types of Context Clues

Context Showing an Example

"In most civilizations throughout history, [latrinalia's] creators were usually suppressed individuals in the society, for example, slaves working in monumental construction or prisoners inside jail cells" (Kan 507).

"A hyperactive infant, Kanzi darted around the test room, jumping on his mother's head, pushing her hand away from the keyboard just as she was trying to hit a key, stealing the food she earned as a reward for good work" (Leslie 450).

"Public art can assume many forms. It is malleable, able to meet the needs of different communities and contribute to many types of projects, from city planning or a river cleanup to a memorial for a lost hero" (Becker 489).

Context Showing a Definition

"[M]en are raised to see the world as hierarchical and competitive. There's always a one-up and one-down position, a winner and a loser" (Mellan 65).

"Another type of private graffiti is 'latrinalia,' the kind of graffiti found near toilets" (Kan 507).

Context Showing a Synonym

"Couples polarized over money engage in a balancing dance of opposites" (Mellan 63).

Context Using Contrast

"Typically, men want to merge all the couple's money—while maintaining primary decision-making power. Women want to keep at least some money separate" (Mellan 67).

Because using context clues is not an infallible, airtight strategy for understanding a word's meaning, it's important to look up the new word in the dictionary to make sure you accurately understand it. If the definition is different from the one you derived from context clues, write the dictionary definition in your own words in the margin.

TIP
Fold a blank piece of paper in half and use it as a bookmark. While reading, when you come across a word you can't figure out from context clues, circle or underline it as part of your annotations, and then write it on the bookmark to look up later.

practice it 9.2 Finding Context Clues

In your reading for class, find one or two instances of each kind of context clue that help you figure out the meaning of an unfamiliar word in your reading. Circle or underline the unfamiliar word and underline the context clue. Write down your understanding of the definition in the margin, and then look up the word in the dictionary. If necessary, modify or correct the definition you wrote in the margin. Assess how well you were able to figure out the meaning using the context clues.

USING A DICTIONARY

Sometimes there won't be enough clues in the context to allow you to figure out the meaning of a word; in that case, you need to consult a dictionary. Your first impulse might be to look up unfamiliar words online. While this can work, you won't always have Internet access while reading, so we strongly recommend purchasing a paperback collegiate dictionary as a backup. Online searches yield highly variable results, so when you do look up a word online, be aware of the following guidelines.

First, don't just search for the word on Google or Yahoo or another Web browser. Go to an actual dictionary site like Dictionary.com or Merriam-Webster.com. Once you type in the word, what comes up should look similar to the entry in a print dictionary. Words are generally broken into syllables followed by the part(s) of speech of the word. Most words can appear as more than one part of speech, so look for the part of speech that matches the way it is being used in the reading. Because words often have more than one direct meaning, there will probably be numbered definitions listed. A good dictionary will have one or more examples of the word used in a sentence. Some online dictionaries allow you to hear a recording of the pronunciation.

Second, read through all the definitions of the word; don't assume the first one is the right meaning for your reading. If it's not immediately clear to you which definition the author intends, look again at the sentence in your reading. Use the various meanings of the word from the dictionary and the context of the sentence to think through which definition fits best.

pronunciation   *part of speech*

pen·ul·ti·mate \pi-nəl-tə-mət\ *adj* (1677) **1:** next to the last
<the ~ chapter of a book> **2:** of or relating to a penult ——*definitions*
<a~accent> – **pen·ul·ti·mate·ly** *adv*

Print Dictionary Entry

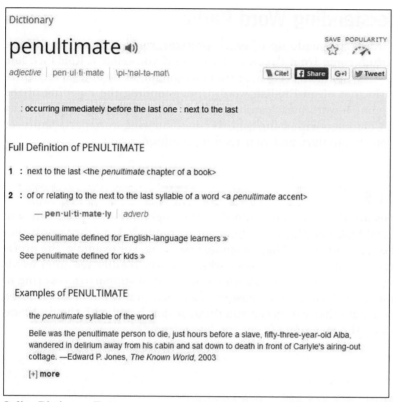

Dictionary

penultimate ◄))

SAVE POPULARITY
☆   ⟋⟋⟋

adjective | pen·ul·ti·mate | \pi-'nəl-tə-mət\

🗋 Cite!   ▩ Share   G+1   ▾ Tweet

: occurring immediately before the last one : next to the last

Full Definition of PENULTIMATE

1 : next to the last <the *penultimate* chapter of a book>

2 : of or relating to the next to the last syllable of a word <a *penultimate* accent>

— pen·ul·ti·mate·ly | *adverb*

See penultimate defined for English-language learners »

See penultimate defined for kids »

Examples of PENULTIMATE

the *penultimate* syllable of the word

Belle was the penultimate person to die, just hours before a slave, fifty-three-year-old Alba, wandered in delirium away from his cabin and sat down to death in front of Carlyle's airing-out cottage. —Edward P. Jones, *The Known World*, 2003

[+] **more**

Online Dictionary Entry

practice it 9.3   Evaluating Online Dictionaries

There are many online dictionaries, but not all are created equal. To evaluate an online dictionary, pick a word and look it up in three or four different dictionaries. (Use your Web browser to find several; search for "online dictionary.") Compare the results. Do the dictionaries provide all the basic information (word broken into syllables, part[s] of speech, pronunciation, examples of the word used in a sentence)? How do the actual definitions compare? Most online dictionaries include ads and other distractions; which one has the fewest? Identify the online dictionary that provides the best information presented in the clearest way and bookmark the site. Having a go-to dictionary helps you get the information you need more quickly.

Understanding Word Parts

Many words are made up of parts: prefixes, roots, and suffixes. These parts often come from Greek or Latin, so if you know a Romance language—like Spanish, French, or Italian—you might be able to recognize the Latin root of an English word. Understanding the meaning of the most common word parts can help you determine the meaning of many words. Combined with using context clues, knowing word parts improves both your vocabulary and your reading comprehension.

PREFIXES

Prefixes are the word parts added to the beginning of a word. Many of these will look familiar, and you might be reminded of other words that use the same prefix and have a similar meaning. For example, the prefix *ex-* means "out" or "away from," which we can readily see from words like *expel* (to force out), *exoskeleton* (an external supportive covering of an animal), *exile* (one who is cast out), and *exit* (a way out of an enclosed space). What other words can you think of that begin with the prefix *ex-* that share the meaning of "out" or "away from"?

COMMON PREFIXES AND THEIR MEANINGS

Prefix	Meaning	Prefix	Meaning
a-, an-	not, without	hetero-	mixed, unlike
ab-	away from	homo-	same
ad-	toward, addition	ideo-	idea
ante-	before	il-, im-, in-, ir-	not
anti-	opposite	mal-, mis-, ne-	bad
aud-, aur-	hear	pan-	all, every
ben-, bon-	good	poly-	many
co-, col-, con-, cor-	with	post-	after
de-, ex-	out, away from	pre-	before
di-	two, double	pro-	big, much
dis-	not, apart	re-	back, again
dys-	bad, abnormal	sub-	under, below

Using the preceding chart, think of at least three words that begin with each prefix, and write down the meaning of each word.

>   **Examples:**   *il-, im-, in-,* and *ir-*
>
>   illegitimate = not legitimate
>   improper = not proper
>   inconsistent = not consistent
>   irreplaceable = not replaceable

ROOTS

The root is the base of the word. Words can be customized based on the various combinations of prefixes (added to the beginning of the root) and suffixes (added to the end of the root). For example, the root *enn* means "year." Add the prefix *bi-*, meaning "two," and the suffix *-ial*, denoting a descriptive word, and you have the word *biennial*, which is an adjective describing something that happens every two years. However, change the prefix to *per-* (meaning "through") and you have *perennial*, an adjective describing something lasting through an indefinite number of years.

Not all words have prefixes *and* suffixes. Sometimes words have only a root and a suffix, in which case the root might look like a prefix, but it's not. Consider the words *audio, biological, captivate,* and *equal.* These words begin with a root and have a suffix attached at the end.

Look over the following roots and see how many you recognize. When you come across a word you don't know, check the following root list to figure out the meaning by understanding the word parts.

COMMON ROOTS AND THEIR MEANINGS

Root	Meaning	Root	Meaning
ann, enni	year	cred	believe
arch	chief, leader	demo	people
aud	sound	dox	belief
biblio	book	duc, duct	lead
bio	life	equ	equal
cap	take, seize	fac	make, go
ced	yield, go	frater	brother
chron	time	geo	earth
corp	body	grad, gress	step
crac, crat	rule, ruler	graph	writing, printing

(continued)

COMMON ROOTS AND THEIR MEANINGS (*continued*)

Root	Meaning	Root	Meaning
gyn	woman	sed, sess	sit
hem, hema, hemo	blood	sens, sent	to be aware, feel
hydro	water	sol	sun
man	hand	son	sound
mater	mother	soph	wisdom
met, meta	behind, between	spec, spic	look, see
mor, mort	death	stat	stay, position
morph	structure, form	tact, tang	touch
mut	change	temp	time
mym, onym	word, name	ten, tent	hold
ortho	straight, correct	terr	earth
pac	peace	theo	god, deity
pater	father	therm	heat
path	feeling, suffering	vac	empty
ped, pod	foot	ven, vent	come, go
phon, phono	sound	ver	truth
psych	soul, mind	vert	turn
sci	know	voc	call
sec, sect	cut		

practice it 9.5   Understanding Roots

For this activity, pick a root from the preceding list and, without looking at the meaning, think of other words with the same root to see if you can figure out the meaning.

Example: The root *temp* is recognizable from the words *temporary* and *contemporary*. It is probably related to time.

SUFFIXES

Suffixes are word parts attached to the ends of roots or words to add to or change the meaning. For example, the suffixes *-ist* and *-er* both indicate a person, as in *zoologist* or *treasurer*. Suffixes are often clues to the word's part of speech. For example, you may remember that adverbs often end in *-ly*. Words that end in *-ism* are generally nouns, while words that end in *-ical* are typically adjectives. (Keep in mind, however, that these are clues, not hard-and-fast rules.)

COMMON SUFFIXES AND THEIR MEANINGS

Suffix	Meaning	Suffix	Meaning
-able, -ible	capable of	-ette, -illo	little
-ac, -ic, -ical, -tic	having to do with	-ia, -y	act, state
-ate, -efy, -ify, -ise, -ize	make	-ism	belief in
-cede, -cess	yield, go	-ist	a person
-cide	kill	-ite	connected with
-cis	cut	-logy, -ology	study
-er, -orone	who takes part in	-ous	full of

practice it 9.6   Using Word Parts

Armed with the charts of word parts on the preceding pages, look over one of the readings you've been assigned from this text and find unfamiliar words. Can you use the word parts to figure out their meanings? Once you have a good idea of the meaning of a word, check a dictionary to see how accurate you are. Remember to write the definition in the margin of the reading in your own words.

The more practice you have using this strategy, the more accurate you will become.

practice it 9.7   Using Word Parts and Context Clues

Choose a paragraph in one of your assigned articles that has the most challenging vocabulary for you. Using roots, prefixes, suffixes, and context clues—but not the dictionary—define as many of the words as you can. Then look up the words in the dictionary to check your accuracy.

Committing New Words to Memory

It's easy to identify unfamiliar words in a reading. Looking them up takes a bit of effort, but committing them to memory so that you really learn them is more difficult. Most people have to use new words many times before really mastering them.

USING MNEMONICS

Mnemonics, or memory aids, are a good way to commit new words to memory. Did you ever learn "Please Excuse My Dear Aunt Sally" in a math class? It's a mnemonic device to help you remember *PEMDAS*, the order of operations (Parentheses, Exponents, Multiplication, Division, Addition, Subtraction). Mnemonics like this work because they are shorter and simpler than what they stand for, and they also give us the first letter of the words we're trying to remember. Forming a sentence from the letters also helps us remember the order of terms, because a sentence has a built-in order that most of us recognize and use without difficulty.

You should use all the mnemonics you can to learn new words and commit them to memory, including making rhymes with words and their definitions ("*syllabus*—what you expect of us"), using word associations ("*penultimate*—I use a pen second to last, before the eraser"), or creating graphic images that represent a word's meaning (runners jumping a hurdle, something they are required to get through, for *prerequisite*). Try a few of these methods to see which work best for your memory.

MAKING GRAPHIC FLASH CARDS

Flash cards are another good way to remember important words. Adding an image to the flash cards helps you visualize the meaning of a word, which is a great memory device. Here's how to do it.

STEP 1: Get a set of 3 x 5 inch note cards.

STEP 2: Identify vocabulary words and terms you are trying to learn from your annotations or elsewhere.

STEP 3: Write each word on one side of a note card.

STEP 4: On the other side of the note card, write:

a. A definition of the term in your own words.
b. A sentence (at least six words) using the word. If you are struggling with the sentence, go back to the reading where you found the word. Seeing the word in context might help.
c. The part of speech. If you aren't sure what part of speech the word is, you can find this information in the dictionary entry just after the word. Dictionaries use the following abbreviations for the parts of speech:

Noun = **n**
Verb = **v, vt** (transitive verb—a verb like *love* that takes an object), **vi** (intransitive verb—a verb like *appear* that does not take an object)
Adjective = **adj**
Adverb = **adv**

STEP 5: On the front of the card, below the word, draw a picture to help you remember the meaning. You don't need to be an artist or spend more than a few moments on the image for it to be effective. The image helps anchor the definition in your memory.

STEP 6: Practice with your flash cards. Making them is the first step, but to use them to help you improve your vocabulary, you have to practice with them.

Sample Graphic Flash Cards

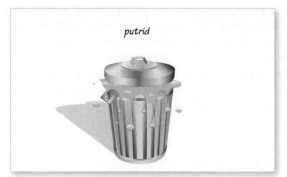

putrid

Front

Having a horrible smell from decomposing

The rotting garbage was putrid.

adj

Back

reminisce

Front

To think about past experiences

On his 15th wedding anniversary, he reminisces about his wedding day.

v

Back

---

practice it 9.8 Making Graphic Flash Cards

Make a list of the difficult vocabulary from a few of the readings you have been assigned and, following the preceding steps, make a graphic flash card for each new word. Once you have made your graphic flash cards, don't forget to use them to learn the new vocabulary.

Using a Thesaurus

All words have shades of meaning (or *connotations*), so even though two words might be *synonyms* (words sharing the same meaning), they may not both work in the same context. For example, when describing a sky darkened with storm clouds, you might refer to the sky as *frightening*. But perhaps you want to use a more sophisticated word, so you decide to try a thesaurus. You look up *frightening* in a thesaurus, and you see that *macabre* is listed as a synonym. Great, right? Not so fast. Although *macabre* is related to *frightening*, it doesn't mean quite the same thing: *macabre* more precisely means *horrifying* or *gruesome*. A Halloween haunted house might be macabre with its monsters and ghostly images, but storm clouds are not likely to be macabre, so describing a sky as *macabre* is likely to be more confusing than impressive.

What's the point here? A thesaurus is a good tool, but it needs to be used correctly. Once you find a synonym for the word you want to replace, you need to look up the new word in the dictionary to be sure that you use it correctly.

> **practice it 9.9**   Using the Right Word in Context
>
> Choose the best word to complete this sentence from the choices below.
>
> > If a person is not knowledgeable about finances, we might say that he or she is financially _____.
>
> a. ignorant
> b. unacquainted
> c. unfamiliar
> d. insensible
> e. oblivious
>
> Each of these words means "not having knowledge," but they wouldn't all work in this context. Look up each word in the dictionary to determine which word is the best fit for this context and explain why.

TIP
Challenge yourself to use a new word in conversation and/or in writing five times each day for a week.

Using New Vocabulary

Practice the strategies in this chapter when you identify new words, and you will build a robust vocabulary for yourself. Don't forget, however, that learning what the new word means is only the beginning of developing an *active* vocabulary; to really benefit from knowing the word, you have to use it, whether in writing or in speech.

Most people understand more words than they use regularly when they write. Have you noticed that you tend to use the same verbs repeatedly? Or that you often describe people as "nice" or "mean," places as "beautiful" or "boring"? You may know many words that could replace each of these words, but out of habit, you use the same ones repeatedly. Try to shake this habit and instead create a style and tone to fit your audience. Do you want to sound academic? Sophisticated? Familiar with current events? Replace *nice* or *mean* with words that reflect how you would like to sound.

As you experiment, try out new words from your readings. It's particularly useful to use new words from the readings when you write essays based on the readings or their topics, but keep an eye out for other opportunities: Post new words on social media, use them when writing e-mails, or weave them into conversations. Also, listen for instances when other people use any of the new words you are learning. You might hear them in lectures or conversations or on the news.

One useful strategy for fully understanding newly acquired vocabulary is finding and making connections between new words—even if they seem unrelated.

practice it 9.10   Making Connections between Words

Make a list of new words from a reading and divide them into two columns. Pick any two words (one from each column) and find a way to compare or connect the two words in a sentence that shows the meaning of both words. Continue making sentences with words from both columns until you use up all the words in both lists. Try different match-ups to practice using words in different contexts. It might be helpful to write down the definition in your own words to help you come up with a good sentence.

Example 1

Words	gratuitous	anecdote
Definitions	unnecessary	a short story
Sentence	A gratuitous anecdote in an essay is unnecessary and can make the essay too wordy.	

Example 2

Words	indict	plaintiff
Definitions	make a formal accusation	person who begins a lawsuit
Sentence	A plaintiff indicts someone by suing that person.	

Another way to improve your vocabulary and style in your writing is to look over your writing during the editing stage to identify words you use repeatedly and words that sound vague or bland, and replace them.

Check the signal phrases you use with quotations. Do you use the same verb to introduce your quotations every time? Vary the signal verbs. Also, look out for the passive voice ("The ball was thrown" rather than "The girl threw the ball") and replace passive verbs with active ones. If you find that you use the verb *to be* frequently, replace it in at least some instances with strong, active verbs.

practice it 9.11   Improving Style through Word Choice

In the following paragraph, vague, repetitive, or slang words are underlined, as are passive verbs. Find better replacements for these words to improve this paragraph's style.

Being famous is not all it's cracked up to be. Most people think they want fame, but they don't think of all the problems with fame. Being famous is isolating; it is thought that a famous person will always have lots of friends around, but it must be even harder to know who your real friends are and who is just a groupie. Being famous is also hard because you have no privacy. Imagine being photographed all the time, even when you go grocery shopping or wash your car. You can't ever have a bad hair day without it showing up in a magazine. Once you are famous, there are expectations that you will stay famous; it would be difficult to ever have a "normal" job after being famous. This shows that being famous is not all that.

practice it 9.12   Stretching Your Vocabulary

Reread a few pages of essays you have written. Circle words that you use repeatedly. Do you notice patterns? Are there particular words that you seem to overuse? Words that seem vague or bland? Circle those too. Then, without using a dictionary or thesaurus, replace the circled words with different words that you know. Think hard. Spend some time and really rack your brain, and come up with some alternatives.

Building your vocabulary doesn't end when class is over. Using the strategies in this chapter will help you not only increase your vocabulary but also use your new words well. Be diligent about looking up unfamiliar words or using context clues to determine their meaning, and then apply these new words to your own writing and experiences. As always, the best way to keep your vocabulary growing is to read, read, read!

chapter review

In the following chart, fill in the second column to record in your own words the important skills included in this chapter. Then assess yourself to determine whether you are still developing the skill or feel you have mastered it. If you are still developing the skill, make some notes about what you need to work on to master it in the future. If you believe you have already mastered it, explain why.

Skills and concepts covered in this chapter	Explanation in your own words	I'm developing this skill and need to work on . . .	I believe I have mastered this skill because . . .
Using context clues and a dictionary to understand unfamiliar words			
Using word parts (prefix, root, suffix) to learn new words			
Creating mnemonics and graphic flash cards to remember new words			
Understanding how to use a thesaurus			

10
Pre-Writing

Pre-writing is a key phase of the writing process; in pre-writing you move from reading and thinking about a topic to writing about it. If you are like many writers, you may find this phase the most fun because it captures the first thoughts or ideas about your topic, and unlike the rest of drafting, you don't need to worry about perfect grammar or organization or spelling. Instead, you focus on thinking creatively to generate ideas and make connections. You've probably already done some pre-writing earlier in this class or in other classes.

▶ For more on pre-writing basics, see Chapter 3, Putting Ideas into Writing.

In pre-writing you essentially get all your thoughts and ideas onto paper so you can see what you have and evaluate it. This chapter covers five popular pre-writing activities: freewriting, clustering, listing, questioning, and using synthesis charts. Practice them all so you have more than one strategy at your fingertips the next time you start a writing assignment. It's always good to have several techniques to choose from.

Freewriting

Freewriting is what it sounds like: writing freely. When you freewrite, you begin with a topic or question and write freely, without stopping, for five or ten minutes. You generally freewrite in sentence or paragraph form.

Freewriting sounds easy because it's informal writing that isn't graded, but students often find this technique a bit challenging at first. Since you're usually asked to produce writing for a grade or to be evaluated, it can be hard to get used to the idea that freewriting can be rough. Really rough. In fact, freewriting is supposed to be messy and disorganized and full of grammar or spelling errors, so you focus on your ideas and not on editing. As long as you can read it and understand it, it's good enough.

Freewriting is like free association. Don't stop to consider whether what you're writing is good enough: This should be nonstop writing. This instruction often produces a blank stare from students, who wonder, "Nonstop? What if I can't think of what to write?" Well, exactly. The idea of freewriting is to stop censoring your ideas. Stopping to think of what you should write or whether your ideas are any good actually gets in the way of the activity. If you can't think of what to write, just keep rewriting what you previously wrote, or write over and over: "I can't think of what to write. I can't think of what to write." Pretty soon, your brain will come up with something related to the topic, which will lead to another thought about the topic, and another, and so on. If you have ever meditated, the concept is similar. By trying not to direct your thinking, your mind will focus on what you need to.

Here's a student freewrite on the question "What is art?":

> What is art? Hmmmm. What is art? Well, art is pictures on the wall. It's also photographs and sculptures. Not all photos though—like, school photos from when you were a kid, those aren't art. unless an artist did something with those pictures like put them in a collage or something. that would be artistic. but by themselves, they are just embarrassing! I always seemed to have the worst haircuts in grade school. Blech. Ummmm, I don't really know what else art is. i guess computer graphics are art. but i don't consider video games playable art. I guess art is made with the idea that is going to be art. or it is things collected and put together like art. I used to love art day in school when I was little. My mom still has my ceramic hand print hanging on her wall. parents think almost anything their kids do is art. That makes me wonder if art has to be any good for it to be considered art. I guess not because I don't even like or get a lot of the art in museums. Everyone has different tastes when it comes to art.

Notice that this writer didn't correct grammar or worry about going off topic. In this case, going "off topic" about parents always loving kids' art was a good thing, because it led the writer to an important question about art: Does it have to be "good" to be considered art?

After freewriting, the next step is to reread the freewrite, underlining ideas you want to think about more or examples that seem useful. Here's an example of what this writer might have underlined:

> What is art? Hmmmm. What is art? Well, art is pictures on the wall. It's also photographs and sculptures. Not all photos though—like, school photos from when you were a kid, those aren't art. unless an artist did something with those pictures like put them in a collage or something. that would be artistic. but by themselves, they are just embarrassing! I always seemed to have the worst haircuts in grade school. Blech. Ummmm, I don't really know what else art is. i guess computer graphics are art. but i don't consider video games playable art. I guess art is made with the idea that is going to be art. or it is things collected

and put together like art. I used to love art day in school when I was little. My mom still has my ceramic hand print hanging on her wall. parents think almost anything their kids do is art. <u>That makes me wonder if art has to be any good for it to be considered art.</u> I guess not because I don't even like or get a lot of the art in museums. Everyone has different tastes when it comes to art.

Either of the underlined phrases could be the starter question for another freewrite to develop each idea more fully. In this way, freewriting has unlimited potential as an idea-generating activity.

practice it 10.1   Freewriting

Pick one of the following topics, or use a topic for an essay you are working on, and write freely for five minutes. Remember, don't try to direct your thinking or edit your writing. Write continuously for the full five minutes, and if you can't think of what to write, recopy what you just wrote or copy down "I can't think of what to write" until you can.

Hint: Set a timer for five minutes so you don't have to focus on the time.

- Do you wish you were famous?
- What makes a school good?
- What does it mean to be educated?
- Why is financial literacy important?
- What is art?
- What role does curiosity play in learning?

Clustering

Clustering is sometimes called mapping, webbing, or bubbling. A cluster is essentially a graphic organizer that you can make to help you generate ideas. Because it's a series of bubbles or boxes that you connect with lines, you can roughly organize your ideas while you create it.

STEP 1: Begin a cluster by putting your idea, topic, or thesis, if you have one, in a central circle in the middle of a blank piece of paper. Write down anything you think relates to that central idea or claim, and circle that. Draw lines from your circle in the center to the other circles, connecting them. At this point, don't worry about whether your ideas are organized or even whether they are any good; the main point of this activity is to get as many related ideas as possible down on paper. Here's what a cluster on the question "What is art?" might look like:

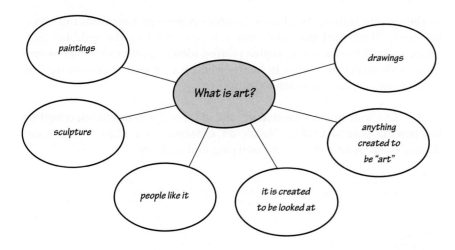

STEP 2: After you spend a few minutes mapping out your ideas, review your cluster.   See if there are more ideas you'd like to add or clarify or ask questions about. This additional step is just as important as step 1.

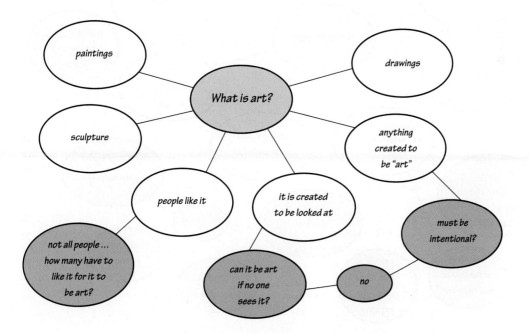

In the second figure, the shaded bubbles represent new thinking about the topic. Note that the additions are connected to the bubbles they relate to. In this way, you organize related ideas together as you generate them. This structure comes in handy when it's time to create an outline or to organize your ideas for writing.

STEP 3: Continue to clarify questions and ideas and add examples, repeating the process several times. Here's an example of a cluster that went through four or five stages of clarifying and addition:

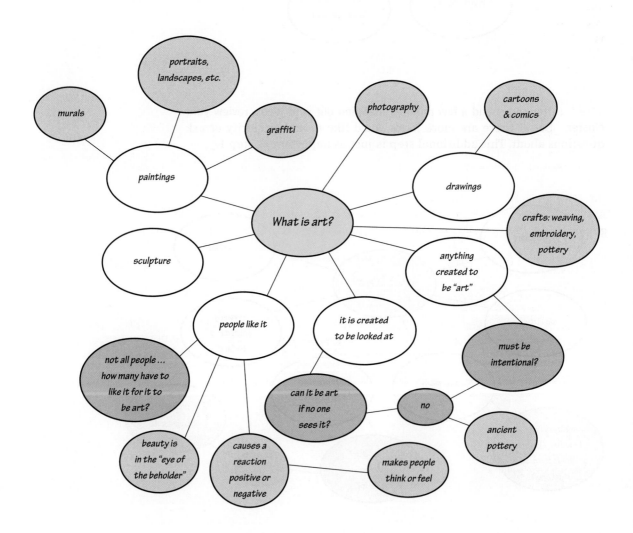

Listing   **235**

practice it 10.2 Clustering

After looking over the "What is art?" cluster, make your own cluster in response to a topic you are writing about. Add to and clarify ideas through several stages of clustering before you consider it done.

TIP
There are several good clustering computer programs that make it very easy to create pre-writing clusters. Ask if any are installed at your campus computer lab, or do a search online. Clustering software programs are sometimes referred to as "mind mapping" programs.

Listing

Listing is just that, making a list of everything you can think of that's related to your topic. Begin by writing your topic, thesis, or idea at the top of a piece of paper, and then beneath that, list as many related ideas as you can.

What is art?
paintings
sculpture
drawing
people like it
it's created to be looked at
anything created to be "art"

Note that in this list, the first things that come to mind are written down. As in clustering or freewriting, you should look over your list once you generate it and then take another pass at adding and clarifying.

What is art?
paintings
sculpture
drawing
people like it—not all people . . . how many have to like it for it to be "art"?
it's created to be looked at—can it be art if no one sees it?
anything created to be "art"—must it be intentional?
portraits
murals, graffiti
photography
cartoons, comics
can it be art if no one sees it? no . . .
crafts like weaving, embroidery, pottery
art has to cause a reaction—positive or negative
makes people think or feel
doesn't need to be intentional—think of ancient pottery—we consider it art today but
   it prob. wasn't when it was made

▶ For more on outlining, see Chapter 14, Essay Organization and Outlining.

Remember that a list is not the same as an outline. Your list is generated quickly and spontaneously, to help you get your ideas into writing, but it is not structured. Just because you brainstorm an idea first doesn't mean it should be the first point in your paper.

---

practice it 10.3   Listing

Make your own list in response to a topic you are writing about. Add to and clarify ideas through several stages of listing before you consider it done.

Questioning

When it comes to generating ideas for an essay, asking increasingly complex questions will help you develop a much richer selection of ideas on which to base your essay.

Not all questions are equal, however. Some questions result in straightforward, factual answers, which are good for starters but don't engage more complex thinking. To use the right kinds of questions for this pre-writing strategy, it's important to first understand what the different kinds of questions are. The following chart shows six different levels of questions, moving from the easiest to the most difficult. (This chart is based on the research of Benjamin Bloom, an educator who created this system of questions, known as Bloom's Taxonomy.)

Level	Kind of question and purpose	Examples
1	Knowledge: to get facts	What is the issue? Who is involved? Where does it take place? How long has it been going on?
2	Comprehension: to understand	How do you summarize the article, topic, or event? How can you explain the issue or topic? What is the main idea/purpose? Whom does this issue affect? How? Who might benefit from change? How?
3	Application: to show you can use information	How can you apply this information to a new situation? How is this used? How would changing this change the outcome? What are examples of this?

Level	Kind of question and purpose	Examples
4	Analysis: to explain the whole by understanding parts	What do you think about [a certain part]?
		How are [one part] and [another part] related?
		What evidence is there for this?
		How does this compare with other things?
		Why is this effective/not effective?
		What can you infer from this?
		What does this mean?
		What are the most important parts/reasons/issues, and why?
5	Synthesis: to make new meaning	How do the various sources relate?
		What is a different solution?
		What would you change or modify?
		How could this situation/issue be improved?
		What needs to change, and why?
6	Evaluation: to assess and judge information	What is your opinion on the issue?
		What works well? What doesn't work?
		What would you suggest or recommend?
		How valid are the various points of view?
		How would change benefit some people?
		How would change put people at a disadvantage?

Start with questions from level 1, and then move down the list to the more complex questions, to deepen your critical thinking.

In the following example, a student uses questioning to develop ideas for the essay "Is Graffiti Art?"

Level	Questions	Ideas
1. Knowledge	What is the issue?	Is graffiti art or vandalism?
	Who is involved?	Graffiti artists, art critics, anyone who likes art
	Where does it take place?	Graffiti is all over the place—urban centers and suburban as well.
	How long has it been going on?	Graffiti as a "scene" really started in the 1970s and 1980s, but it goes back much further.
2. Comprehension	How do you summarize the article, topic, or event?	A lot of people think of graffiti as vandalism and gang markings. But some think graffiti is art, especially the colorful and very complex "pieces" that are seen in cities mostly. Even museums have recognized graffiti as art. Some owners of buildings hire graffiti artists to paint elaborate "pieces" on their walls.

continued

Level	Questions	Ideas
3. Application	Whom does this issue affect?	Building owners and members of a community are affected by seeing graffiti in their neighborhood, perhaps even on their buildings. They might have to pay to have graffiti removed. Also, though, members of a community might be positively affected by the color and brightness that lots of graffiti adds to a community, especially a run-down neighborhood.
4. Analysis	How is graffiti/art/vandalism used?	Graffiti is used to express the personality of the "writers" as well as their design skills and use of color. It's also used to promote their names and to get attention or "street cred," particularly for pieces in hard-to-reach locations. Art is used to express personality and skill as well. Art is often sold, so it's used to make money for the artist as well as recognition. Vandalism is used to express anger or frustration or mark territory.
5. Synthesis	How would changing art and graffiti change the outcome?	Changing the definition of art to include graffiti would make graffiti officially art. It would also make this paper a lot easier. ☺ If graffiti was done only on approved surfaces (on art gallery walls, on buildings that allow it, etc.), it would probably change most people's view of it being art. But probably graffiti artists would be less interested in it and probably move on to do something else. They like being outside the art world.

You can see that by moving from easier to increasingly complex question levels, you are writing down much more specific and interesting ideas. After answering as many questions as you can, you have a lot of great material to then organize into an outline and topic sentences.

practice it 10.4   Asking Questions

With a small group of classmates, put your heads together to brainstorm or do the questioning activity to generate ideas. Either work independently for the first five to ten minutes and then compare and share your ideas, or work together from the beginning. Just remember, all group members should take their own notes during the group pre-writing so they have ideas to take home.

Using Synthesis Charts to Generate Ideas

In many pre-writing methods, the writer puts away all the books and articles he or she has been reading and sits with a piece of paper or a blank computer screen to generate ideas. Then the writer returns to the articles or books while working on the first draft. The advantage of this approach is that it frees up the writer to focus on his or her own ideas.

Some writers, however, like to take the opposite approach. They start with the readings they have been studying, looking over their notes, pulling out interesting quotations, and finding connections between the readings that they might not have noticed the first time around. This type of pre-writing can be very informal and messy, which is fine if it works for you. Many writers, particularly those who like (or need) more structure, prefer to use a chart to help them organize their thoughts during this process. One effective type of chart is called a synthesis chart. Synthesis charts come in many shapes and sizes. In fact, part of the beauty of the synthesis chart is that once you understand the basic concept, you can adapt it easily to a variety of reading and writing situations.

First, make a table that lists the texts you have read along the left-hand side. At the bottom of this list, include a row for "My Thoughts" so that you have space to record your own ideas. Then, along the top, fill in important topics related to the essay prompt. These might be topics you noticed while reading, but they probably include the topics that were discussed several times during class, so consult your class notes as well as annotations to choose the topics. Do not worry about whether these topics are all parallel or perfect. This is pre-writing, after all! Also, you might want to leave a blank category or label it "other ideas" for random ideas that pop up that might be meaningful to you.

Next, look back over your readings and annotations, and jot down notes, reflections, and sometimes even quotations (or page numbers for important quotations) in the relevant boxes of the chart. Not all the boxes will be filled in equally, and some of them won't be filled in at all. That's okay. This is pre-writing. There are no "right answers." Jot down your questions and partial thoughts too. The ideas need to make sense to you; this isn't meant for someone else, so don't worry too much about how you phrase your ideas. The point is to spark your thinking to help you see how the readings relate to one another, and hopefully to help you generate original ideas of your own in response to the connections you see across the texts.

After you have filled in the boxes about the readings, take a few minutes to look over what you have and synthesize the ideas. Look for comparisons and contrasts. See if you can put the ideas in conversation with one another. Would these authors agree? Disagree? Why? Fill in the "My Thoughts" column last, after you have had a chance to think about how the readings relate to one another.

Let's look at a sample student synthesis chart to see how it works. In the chart on page 240, a student studying the topic of public art wrote the titles of the texts she read along the left side, with "My Thoughts" added at the end of the list. Along the top, the student wrote several of the key themes and ideas found in the readings. In this case, the class was focusing on the question "What is art?" so the topics are all related to that question. Finally, she jotted down important material from the readings and her own thoughts in the boxes of the chart.

▶ **Another type of chart for pre-writing is based on rhetorical patterns. See pages 211–213 in Chapter 8, Rhetorical Patterns in Reading and Writing.**

> **STEP 1:** List the names of the texts you've read.

> **STEP 2:** Brainstorm topics related to your essay prompt.

> **STEP 3:** Review the readings and your annotations and fill in the blanks.

> **STEP 4:** Review what you have and add your ideas.

	Examples of "art" that they gave	Who gets to decide what's art?	Why care? What's at stake?	Other ideas
Becker, "Public Art"	big variety—memorials, monuments, tourist stuff, festivals—seems like pretty much anything that's in public	not entirely clear—seems like a lot of committees, jury??—really, the public, but he doesn't expect them all to agree	shared culture democratic **** SEE LIST on page 488!	"What would life be like without fireworks displays, puppet parades, sculpture parks..." (487)
Pfleger, "What Right Do Muralists Have ..."	murals	that's what she's asking! could be artists, building owners, or "the community"—she's leaning toward the artists and community, I think, but kind of assumes the community agrees with the artist—wonder if that's always true???	art the artist's reputation what else????	lots on VARA
Kan, "Adolescents and Graffiti"	tons of examples of graffiti—private (doodling, toilet) vs. public (gangs, tags, pieces)	teachers maybe? not sure here	what gets taught in school how adults view teens	
LAPD graffiti policy	none—they don't think graffiti is art at all	mostly public opinion—but not necessarily the exact people who live in a community—more like the mainstream society	control of the neighborhood	a community can use gardens and trash cleanup to come together and have a sense of identity—they don't need graffiti
My thoughts	seems like art can be anything	it's like it's a war between the people who have power and those who don't, and some people don't want it to be	keeps coming back to control	

▶ For more about synthesis charts, see pages 70–72 in Chapter 2, Active and Critical Reading.

In looking at the chart, for instance, you can see that the student writer has identified a theme of control that is woven throughout the readings. That would be an excellent idea to put with the question *"What is art?"* in order to move toward a thesis: *People try to define art in ways that will give them more control.*

practice it 10.5   Synthesis Chart

Using the basic synthesis chart structure just described, create a synthesis chart for an upcoming writing assignment in this class or another class.

Now that you have learned several good pre-writing strategies, practice them whenever you begin a writing project or whenever you have trouble coming up with something to say as you are writing. Many writers continue to brainstorm throughout the writing process, so feel free to revisit this chapter at any point.

chapter review

In the following chart, fill in the second column to record in your own words the important skills included in this chapter. Then assess yourself to determine whether you are still developing the skill or feel you have mastered it. If you are still developing the skill, make some notes about what you need to work on to master it in the future. If you believe you have already mastered it, explain why.

Skills and concepts covered in this chapter	Explanation in your own words	I'm developing this skill and need to work on . . .	I believe I have mastered this skill because . . .
Freewriting			
Clustering			
Listing			
Questioning			
Using synthesis charts			

11

Thesis and Main Idea

in this chapter

- What Does a Thesis Do?
- How Do You Find the Main Point in a Reading?
- How Do You Shape and Draft Your Thesis?
- How Do You Make Your Thesis Stronger?

The Purpose of a Thesis

LaunchPad Solo
macmillan learning

Visit **LaunchPad Solo for Readers and Writers > Thesis** for extra practice in the skills covered in this chapter.

The thesis statement is the central, controlling idea in a piece of writing; it states the writer's main point or purpose. As the central purpose or idea, the thesis is almost always a claim, meaning that it is the perspective or position of the author. Another way to think about the thesis is to distinguish it from the topic. The topic is what the author is writing about, and the thesis is what the author is saying about that topic.

Most articles or essays have many points, so the thesis is the central point, the umbrella point that all the other points help prove. All the paragraphs, examples, explanations, and evidence in an essay support the thesis. Without a thesis, an essay would be much harder for the writer to organize and much harder for the reader to follow.

Not all kinds of writing have a thesis statement, but all academic essays do, and much of what you read in college will have a central, controlling idea. For example, letters or e-mails may have a purpose, but they usually won't have a thesis. Short stories have messages and themes that drive them, but they won't have a thesis. Academic writing is driven by a thesis that aims to inform, analyze, or argue.

You may have been taught at some point to write a five-paragraph essay with a three-part (or tripartite) thesis that has three major supporting points. If you learned this kind of thesis, practice stretching your thinking beyond it, and think of the tripartite thesis as you would riding a bike with training wheels: Training wheels help you get comfortable with the general feeling of riding a bike, but eventually you take them off and ride that two-wheeler on your own. Similarly, the three-part thesis has limitations. It assumes you have three points to make, and only three. So when you use this format, you don't develop your thinking beyond three points, even if there are many more points to be made. Your writing assignments become longer and more complex as you move through college, and you need to know how to organize an essay around your arguments or ideas, which rarely come in threes.

THE EXPLICIT THESIS OR MAIN IDEA

In Chapter 3, Putting Ideas into Writing, you learned that a thesis statement should express a complete idea about what the writer believes about the topic as well as why he or she believes it. In your own writing, your thesis should appear toward the beginning of your essay and should be an arguable claim. For academic essays, assume your instructor wants to see an explicit (that is, directly and clearly stated) thesis statement.

THE IMPLIED THESIS OR MAIN IDEA

In essays and articles that you read, you won't always find the thesis at the beginning. Professional writers sometimes put a thesis in the conclusion. Other readings may not have an obvious thesis statement but instead have an implied thesis that you must figure out. The author has the central claim in mind when developing the essay; he or she has just decided to let the reader figure out the thesis rather than stating it. This kind of writing is trickier and requires much practice in both reading and writing.

SAMPLE THESIS STATEMENTS FROM DIFFERENT TYPES OF READINGS

Different kinds of writing require different kinds of thesis statements, but they all have some common features. Here are some examples of different kinds of thesis statements. Some may be familiar to you from readings you encountered in Chapter 2, Active and Critical Reading. Looking over this selection, you can see some of the breadth and variety of kinds of thesis statements.

> **Thesis from a Magazine Article, "Teach Your Children the Building Blocks of Finance" by Sherie Holder and Kenneth Meeks**
> Parents have to teach children the value of money and guide them in their spending, encourage them to save, explore entrepreneurship opportunities, and expose them to solid financial planning.

Thesis from a Student Literature Paper on Kate Chopin's "The Story of an Hour"
While Kate Chopin does allow her protagonist, Louise Mallard, to experience a moment of self-discovery, the fact that she dies shortly thereafter undermines the potentially feminist message.

Thesis from a Student Psychology Paper on Sigmund Freud's Theory of Defense Mechanisms
Defense mechanisms operate in every person all throughout their lives, and to help better understand ourselves, it is important to look at how defense mechanisms work for and against us.

Thesis from the Book *Curious* by Ian Leslie
If you allow yourself to become incurious, your life will be drained of color, interest, and pleasure. You will be less likely to achieve your potential at work or in your creative life. While barely noticing it, you'll become a little duller, a little dimmer. You may not think it could happen to you, but it can. It can happen to any of us. To stop it from happening, you need to understand what feeds curiosity and what starves it.

The next thesis example is from the "Education Pays" chart in Chapter 2. The chart has no explicit thesis; in fact, it has very little text at all, but it does make a clear point to its readers. In this case, it has an *implied thesis*, meaning that you can figure out the central argument from reading the whole chart.

Implied Thesis from the "Education Pays" Chart by the Bureau of Labor Statistics
The higher your level of education, the less likely you are to be unemployed and the more likely you are to earn a higher salary.

Note that in all these examples, the thesis does more than just state the topic of the work. The topic is *what* the reading is about, and the thesis is the central claim and overall point the author makes about the topic.

Finding the Main Point in a Reading

▶ For more on pre-reading strategies, see Chapter 1, Reading and Responding to College Texts, and Chapter 5, Active Reading Strategies.

Finding the thesis is an important part of reading comprehension and analysis. To find the thesis, begin by following these steps.

STEP 1: **Preview the text.** Previewing the text gives you an idea of what the overall purpose or point of the reading is, which is the first step in identifying the thesis. What is the topic of the reading? Write it down in the margin as part of your annotations or in your notebook. Then write down in one sentence the point you expect the author might make about that topic.

STEP 2: Read the introductory and the concluding paragraphs. Is there a broad claim that the author is making? If so, that might be the thesis. Make a note of it and move on to step 3. If there is more than one claim, check to see if one of them is a broader, more general claim that the other claims might serve. If you can't tell, make a note of the various claims and move on to step 3.

STEP 3: Read the entire article or essay. As you read, keep in mind the claim or claims you have found to see if they are developed and supported in the essay. If you haven't already found a claim, keep a lookout for the point the author seems to be making about the overall topic. If you have already read the article or essay, read through it again. Annotate any places where the author makes claims, particularly at the beginning of paragraphs (topic sentences).

STEP 4: At the end of the reading, go back to any claims you wrote down in steps 2 and 3 and evaluate whether any of them are the thesis. Consider the following:

- Do any of the claims seem too narrow? Do they only fit one paragraph or one section of the overall reading? If so, those claims are probably not the thesis.

- Does the essay support one claim throughout by proving it, developing examples of it, or discussing it in detail? If yes, then you probably have found the thesis. If you can answer yes about more than one claim, see if one of those claims can support the other (for instance, two different claims about specific threats of animal extinction might support a thesis about climate change). If so, the claim supported by the other is probably the broader claim. If the claims are equal, go to the next step.

STEP 5: If there is no stated claim, or if there are a few that seem equally important to the essay, the thesis may be implied rather than written into the essay. Cover the essay with a blank piece of paper and ask yourself, what was the main point of this essay? Write down the answer without thinking too much about it. If you have trouble answering this question, pretend that a classmate just asked you what the reading was about. What would you tell him or her? Be as specific as you can. Write the answer down, and then uncover the essay and look it over with this statement in mind. Does it fit the essay? Is it the main point the author is trying to make?

> **practice it 11.1** Finding the Thesis
>
> Choose an article or essay that your instructor has assigned and follow the preceding five steps to find the thesis. Check with a few class-mates or with your instructor to see if you have correctly identified the thesis. Remember, finding the thesis takes practice, so if you don't get it at first, keep reading and practicing. Soon it will become second nature to you.

Shaping Your Thesis

Shaping your own thesis is one of the most important steps in the writing process. It takes practice and usually several drafts to write a good the-sis, but that's because you have to figure out what you're really trying to say before you can write one. Remember, the thesis is the controlling, central idea or claim in the essay. It is the claim that all the body para-graphs and evidence will support, so your thesis should clearly reflect the point you want to make.

CHARACTERISTICS OF A THESIS

Your thesis should:

- **Be an arguable claim.** A claim is what you think about the topic. Not everyone would agree with your claim, which makes it arguable. Claims differ from opinions in that opinions aren't arguable. You are entitled to any opinion you happen to have, but a claim must be supported by evidence to be considered valid.

Opinion	I like soup.
Claim	Soup is often thought of as healthy, but cream-based soups are among the unhealthiest dishes you can eat.

- **Be a statement, *not* a question.** A question is a way to get someone to think about your topic and be interested in it. In fact, questions make great "hooks" for an introduction, but because a thesis is a claim, it can never be a question.

Question	What is the meaning of life?
Statement	Developing close relationships with family and friends is the meaning of life.

- **Address the question or task of the assignment.** Your thesis must respond directly to the essay prompt and fulfill all parts of the assignment.

Sample Assignment	Evaluate your city's public transit options and argue which is the best method of getting around town.
Sample Thesis	Chicago has taxis that are costly and buses that sometimes run late, so the best way to get around the city is the famed "L" rapid transit system with over a hundred miles of track and easy access.

In this case you are being asked to do two things: evaluate all the public transit options and make a claim that one of them is the best method of public transportation. If your thesis doesn't answer both parts of the prompt, your essay won't either.

- **Use "announcing" language.** You want your reader to know your specific topic, but don't use announcements like "this essay will discuss" or "in this essay, I will prove." Such statements may be appropriate in some disciplines, like the sciences, but they are not appropriate for general academic essay writing and are definitely not suitable for English papers.

- **Be significant.** Ask yourself "So what?" about your claim. Why does the point you're making matter? Why is your claim relevant? What difference should it make to your reader? If you can't answer these questions, your claim isn't strong enough to support an essay. See the section on revising your thesis (pp. 250–56) for more about this.

FIGURING OUT WHAT CLAIM YOU WANT TO MAKE

It's true that it takes practice and usually several drafts to write a good thesis, but that's because you have to figure out what you're trying to say before you can write a great thesis. Many writers—even professional writers—need to do an entire rough draft before they determine what they really want to say. Some people write a draft without a thesis and then go back and figure out what the thesis should be. Other writers won't start until they have what they believe is a perfectly crafted thesis. Beginning writers should probably take the middle road: Draft a thesis you think is good, but be open to changing it as your ideas evolve. Here's a definition of a thesis statement that might make the process easier:

A thesis statement is what you will argue is true about your topic.

In academic writing, the thesis usually begins with the essay assignment. What is your assignment? What are you being asked to do? Usually the thesis is an answer to the essay question or the prompt.

Let's say the essay assignment is to take a position on whether schools should stop selling soft drinks and other sugar-filled drinks like juices at school. (In fact, many school districts already have such a ban in

▶ **For more on essay assignments, see pages 78–81 in Chapter 3, Putting Ideas into Writing.**

place, and many others are debating whether to make this change.) Your topic is this:

> Banning sugary drinks at school

Your assignment is to take a position on this topic. Suppose you think the topic is a good idea. Your position would be:

Draft Thesis   Schools should ban the selling of sugary drinks.

▶ **For more on developing your ideas, see Chapter 10, Pre-Writing.**

That's a good start because it's a clear position on the issue, but it's not yet a strong thesis. To make this a stronger thesis, include the reason for your position, which will help focus your essay. Why should schools ban the selling of sugar-laden drinks? You will come up with a reason or two. (If you have trouble coming up with reasons, you haven't done enough brainstorming and probably aren't ready to write a thesis yet.) Here are the reasons you might generate:

- Sugary drinks are unhealthy (lots of calories, bad for teeth, no nutritional value).
- Kids don't make the best choices about what to eat or drink.
- Sugary drinks are partly to blame for high rates of childhood obesity.

In this case, you can combine the first two reasons into one:

> Not having sugary drinks at school will help students make healthier choices.

Great! Now you can add the reasons to the thesis:

Revised Thesis   Schools should ban the selling of sugary drinks <u>to help kids maintain a healthier diet and reduce childhood obesity.</u>

Much stronger! Next, let's look at an example taking the opposite position:

Draft Thesis   Schools should not ban soft drinks and juices.

This thesis has the same weakness as our first draft of the previous thesis: There are no reasons given. Why should schools not ban selling soft drinks and juices?

> It's not the school's job to tell kids what they can or can't drink. That's the parents' responsibility. Parents are responsible for teaching kids healthy habits.

Great! Now let's put that all together:

> Parents, not schools, are responsible for teaching kids to have a healthy diet.

Here's the much-improved thesis with the reasons added:

Revised Thesis	Schools should not ban selling soft drinks and juices because parents, not schools, are responsible for teaching kids to have a healthy diet.

Notice that each thesis in this case is a direct answer to the prompt. But what if your position isn't clearly for (pro) or against (con)? Remember that all thesis statements are claims, so even if your position is not clearly pro or con, you are still taking some sort of position. For example, if you write a paper on siblings and your topic is birth order, you wouldn't take a pro or con position on birth order—it's not the kind of topic one would be for or against. However, you can still make a *claim*, based on evidence, about the effect of birth order: For instance, do you think evidence indicates that birth order determines personality? Whether you answer yes or no, this position can be developed into your claim.

STEP-BY-STEP GUIDE TO A WORKING THESIS

STEP 1: Brainstorm the assignment.   Have your essay prompt in front of you and underline the question stem. Spend at least five minutes writing down your initial response to the prompt.

STEP 2: Read through the results of your brainstorming.   Underline places where you state your opinion about the topic that fits the assignment.

STEP 3: Draft the thesis.   A good way to begin putting a thesis together is to simply answer the questions of the prompt. You may have some of these answers already jotted down in your brainstorming material. If not, write out each part of the question stem and answer each part separately.

Here is an example for an essay on education.

Assignment	What are the problems with public education today? Are charter schools the answer?

In one sentence each, answer the following questions:

1. What are the problems with education?
2. What is good about charter schools?
3. What is not good about charter schools?
4. Can charter schools alleviate the problems of public education? Why or why not?

STEP 4: Look over your answers and think about which one you have the strongest claim for or which one you are most interested in writing about.   Your answers to questions 2 and 3 should help you come up with a good answer for question 4. Your answers for questions 1 and 4 should be your working thesis. Remember, it's a *working thesis* because you might revise it a few more times before the essay is finished, but it's a good start for building the rest of your paper.

Revising Your Thesis

Thesis statements are generally written and then revised many times. The first draft of your thesis is really a working thesis, which means it is good enough to work from but will probably still need development. Let's look at an example of a working thesis about siblings:

> **Working Thesis**   Adult siblings often argue whenever major family decisions need to be made.

This is a good start, but it needs to be more of an argument. To make your thesis better, try to make it more arguable and more specific. Your thesis might answer one or more of the following questions:

- **Why is this true?**
- **What impact will this have on other people or things?**
- **Who should care about this?**

Here are some possible thesis statements that "answer" those questions:

> **Why?**
> Adult siblings often argue when major family decisions need to be made because stress makes them go back to the ways they acted as children.

> **What impact?**
> When adult siblings argue during a family crisis, the next generation of cousins may have difficulty becoming close friends.

> **Who cares?**
> Elderly parents continue to get upset by their children's arguments, especially when those fights are about the parents' care.

Each of these thesis statements is deeper than the earlier draft of the thesis, though each takes the paper in different directions. Extensive pre-writing helps you generate a variety of options for how to focus your essay's thesis, so you can choose the direction you wish to go instead of feeling that there is only one possible way to write the paper.

IMPROVING WEAK THESIS STATEMENTS

Part of the reason that thesis statements seem difficult to write is that they have so many possible variations. Although much college writing assigns you to take some kind of position, you may also be asked to write other kinds of essays. Following are examples of working thesis statements for specific kinds of assignments. Each one starts out weak but ends up strong. With practice, you'll accomplish the same thing.

Definition Thesis Statement.   The thesis of a definition essay should state your interpretation of the word in a way that shows your point of view. The following thesis misses the mark completely:

> **Poor Thesis**   The definition of *voting*, according to *Merriam-Webster's Dictionary*, is to "exercise political franchise."

In a definition paper, your instructor is not looking for the dictionary's meaning of a concept; he or she is looking for what the word means to you, to a specific group, or to people generally. With these things in mind, the student revises the thesis:

> **Better Thesis**   Voting means having a voice.

This revision is much closer to stating what voting means to the author. The thesis still needs work, though. What is meant by "having a voice"? How does that relate to voting, and why is it important?

> **Best Thesis**   Voting is much more than a quiet democratic exercise; it is about having a voice in important issues.

Now the thesis states what kind of voice (a voice in important issues), and it puts the definition in context by stating how voting may be thought of (a quiet democratic exercise). These big improvements make the thesis a much stronger claim.

Narration Thesis Statement.   Even though a piece of narrative writing tells a story rather than making an argument, it often has an explicit thesis that reveals the message or significance of the story. Imagine, for instance, reading a paper with the following thesis:

> **Poor Thesis**   I remember the first time I voted.

Most readers would not be moved or inspired by this thesis and would be unlikely to want to read the paper. There is no deeper meaning here; it is just a fact. What point does the author want to make about the first voting experience? What was significant about that experience? These considerations go into writing the revised thesis:

> **Better Thesis**   When I stood at the voting booth for the first time, I realized what an amazing right it is to vote.

This is a big improvement on the first thesis draft because the author has added the significance of the experience by including the claim that the right to vote is amazing. The thesis is still a bit generic, though—what is amazing about this new right? What caused the realization? These questions help the student revise the thesis again:

Best Thesis   Having the right to vote was not exactly the highlight of turning eighteen, but when I stood at the voting booth for the first time, I was struck by what an amazing privilege it is to vote, since women have had the right to vote for fewer than one hundred years.

This thesis does a much better job of showing how the experience of voting didn't hit the author until she actually voted and why the experience of voting was so meaningful (because women have had the right to vote for fewer than one hundred years). The addition of "Having the right to vote was not exactly the highlight of turning eighteen" emphasizes how much her thinking about voting shifted.

Process Analysis Thesis Statement. A process analysis paper describes how to do something, usually something fairly complex or abstract. The thesis of a process paper does not have to forecast every single step in the process. That would end up reading like a laundry list. However, the thesis should offer some claims about how best to go about doing the process. Take a look at this first attempt at a process thesis on democracy.

Poor Thesis   There are several steps to achieving democracy.

This thesis draft doesn't make a strong point other than saying there are steps involved in achieving democracy. What are these steps? Why are these steps important or significant?

Better Thesis   The steps to achieving real democracy begin with the critical thinking of voters.

This revision is an improvement: The addition of the word *real* tells us more about what the author thinks of the current state of democracy—that it's not a "true" or "real" democracy. It also includes some of the process required to achieve that—"the critical thinking of voters." The author could improve the thesis by clarifying what role "the critical thinking of voters" has in the process of achieving real democracy.

Best Thesis   The steps to achieving real democracy begin with critical thinking, which will lead voters to make informed choices at the voting booth.

This is a terrific thesis. It is much stronger because it is now clear how critical thinking can lead to "real democracy"—by helping voters make informed choices at the voting booth.

Compare-Contrast Thesis Statement. The thesis for a compare-contrast paper has multiple jobs to do. It has to identify the two (or more) things that are being compared and contrasted, and it has to make a clear claim about a significant point of comparison or contrast. The following thesis avoids making a claim:

> Poor Thesis Which are ultimately more important, local or national elections?

This thesis breaks one of the important standards of thesis writing: It is in the form of a question, not a statement. As a question, it's not taking a position about which kind of election is more important, so it is not a claim.

> Better Thesis National elections seem more important than local elections.

This is a definite improvement because the thesis is a claim and no longer a question. It's far from perfect, though, because it doesn't make a strong point. It says that one kind of election seems more important, but it doesn't say why or whether it actually is or not. This thesis still needs a stronger position and a reason for that position.

> Best Thesis National elections seem more important, but local elections have a bigger impact on your day-to-day life.

Much improved! The thesis now includes a specific, strong claim: Local elections have a bigger impact than national elections. After starting with a general assumption that national elections seem more important, this thesis immediately interests the reader by claiming the opposite.

Cause-Effect Thesis Statement. A cause and effect thesis will state both the cause (why something happened) and the effect (the result of something happening). In a cause and effect essay, you might be emphasizing the cause or the effect or discussing them equally, and your thesis should reflect that emphasis.

> Poor Thesis If more people voted, things would be really different.

This thesis doesn't make a specific claim. Because the wording is left vague ("things" and "different"), it's not clear what the focus of this essay will be. What things would be different? How would they be different?

> Better Thesis If more people voted, it would show that they have a stake in current issues.

This thesis is an improvement because now we know what would be different, but the significance is not specifically stated. Which people is the author referring to? Why is it important for them to show that they are interested and care about current issues?

> **Best Thesis**   If more young adults voted, they could dispel the myth that they're apathetic and show that they have a stake in current issues.

Excellent revisions! Now it's very clear what this essay is going to discuss. We now know whom the essay will be about (young adults) and some important context (young adults are often considered apathetic). It is also clear what effect an increase in voting would have (it would show that they are not apathetic but concerned about current issues).

Problem-Solution Thesis Statement.   A problem-solution essay identifies a problem and makes a claim about a solution to that problem. The thesis should make a claim about what the problem is and the recommended solution.

> **Poor Thesis**   If you are unhappy, the solution is to vote.

There are a couple of problems with this thesis. First, although the solution is clear (voting is the solution), the problem is so generic as to be meaningless. There are many reasons people might be unhappy that have nothing to do with politics or elections, so voting is not logically a solution to general unhappiness. It was probably clear in the writer's mind that he meant unhappy with elections or politics, but if it's not clear on the paper, the reader won't know what the connection is. Second, the writer directly addresses the reader in the second person by writing "you." In academic writing, you should avoid using "you." The standard is to write in third person ("people are unhappy"), or sometimes in first person, but generally not in second person.

> **Better Thesis**   If people are unhappy with society, the solution is to vote.

Here the writer has made a good change by replacing "you" with the third-person perspective ("people"). It's a little clearer now what people are unhappy about, but the writer could clarify more. How would voting make people happy with society? What about society are people unhappy with? *Society* is one of those broad words that get seriously overused in essays. Be careful when using it. Unless you really are referring to all of society, it's a generic word that is hard to live up to.

> **Best Thesis**   If young adults are generally unhappy with the decisions of elected officials, the solution is to vote and campaign.

Wow, a big improvement here. This thesis has gone from very unclear to very clear and specific. The vague word *society* has been replaced with more concrete, specific words and ideas. The problem is that young people are unhappy with the decisions of elected officials, and the solution is for them to vote and campaign. This writer decided to add more clarity to the solution as well.

Argument Thesis Statement. An argument essay makes a clear claim stating the author's position on an issue and offering one or more reasons for that position.

> Poor Thesis   This essay will explain why the voting age should not be lowered to sixteen.

Although there is a clear position (voting age should not be lowered to sixteen), this thesis doesn't explain why the author takes this position. Another problem is that it announces that the reasons will be provided in the essay. Don't include a discussion of what you are going to discuss. In an academic argument essay, a thesis should state a clear position and one or more reasons for that position.

> Better Thesis   The voting age should not be lowered to sixteen because teenagers are not ready for that.

The writer has greatly improved this thesis by getting rid of the announcement "this essay will explain." And the writer has started to indicate the reason behind this position, which is good. It could still be improved by clarifying the reason. Why are teens not ready? What does it mean to be ready to be a voter? Are there any other significant reasons why age sixteen is too young for voting?

> Best Thesis   At age sixteen, teenagers are still learning how to be responsible, which is often trial and error, but because voting is a big responsibility, the voting age should remain eighteen.

This thesis is now a winner. It states the author's position clearly (voting age should not change), and it gives a solid reason: Voting is a big responsibility and sixteen-year-olds are still learning responsibility.

practice it 11.2   Improving Weak Thesis Statements

Evaluate the following four working thesis statements about fame and celebrity. What works and what needs more work for each thesis statement? Analyze each one based on these criteria:

- Is it an arguable claim? (Would some people disagree with it? Can it be supported by evidence?)
- Is it clearly and specifically phrased?
- Does it address the question or task of the assignment?
- Is it a statement (*not* a question)?

1. The question is, what is fame?
2. This essay will explore the downsides of celebrity and why we still want it despite the negatives.

continued ❯

3. Casually following celebrities' lives can be inspirational for many who relate to the struggles some celebrities have overcome, but celebrity obsession can cause a person to lose his or her identity and live in a fantasy world far from reality.

4. Michael Jordan is not just the world's most famous athlete; he is a role model.

After you have analyzed each statement, revise it to improve its weaknesses. Then, after practicing with these sample thesis statements, evaluate and revise your own working thesis, using the same criteria.

It takes time and practice to learn how to write a strong thesis. The strategy of brainstorming will give you the foundation for a strong working thesis and can also save you some time. Remember, it can also be very helpful to consult with your instructor, a tutor, or a classmate or two to get feedback on your thesis.

chapter review

In the following chart, fill in the second column to record in your own words the important skills included in this chapter. Then assess yourself to determine whether you are still developing the skill or feel you have mastered it. If you are still developing the skill, make some notes about what you need to work on to master it in the future. If you believe you have already mastered it, explain why.

Skills and concepts covered in this chapter	Explanation in your own words	I'm developing this skill and need to work on . . .	I believe I have mastered this skill because . . .
Finding the main point in a reading			
Drafting a working thesis			
Revising the working thesis			

12

Argument

What Is an Argument?

When you hear the word *argument*, what comes to mind? Two people in a heated disagreement? This may be the most obvious kind of argument, but in most kinds of academic writing you are asked to make a claim about something. That claim is, in fact, a statement of opinion that then must be *argued*. In argument essays, your thesis states a clear position or claim, and the body of the essay provides ample support to convince your reader of your position.

Taking a stand and making an argument are skills we have honed since childhood, such as when we made a case for staying up past our bedtime or negotiated for an extra dessert after dinner. In fact, if you spend any time around kids, you will recognize in their behavior the early development of some of the strategies that college writers use: making a claim, sizing up the audience, offering reasons and evidence for support, and sometimes concluding with a tantrum (college writers should avoid this last strategy).

Let's begin by looking at the parts of an argument. A solid argument has four major components:

- position
- evidence and reasons
- counterargument
- rebuttal

Visit **LaunchPad Solo for Readers and Writers > Argument** for extra practice in the skills covered in this chapter.

Taking a Position

Your position is your claim about an issue or stand on an issue, and it will be stated in your thesis. It is more than a simple opinion; it must be an arguable claim. For example, suppose you make the following assertion:

Graffiti is my favorite form of art.

This statement is an opinion. It is not arguable because it is a matter of personal taste, and therefore it couldn't be your position in an argument paper.

However, suppose you make this assertion:

Graffiti is one of the most controversial art forms.

This statement is both your opinion and an arguable position to take. It is arguable because another person could argue that graffiti is not art at all. A different person might take the position that graffiti isn't all that controversial. Your position would need to be supported by reasons and evidence. If your assignment asks you to argue for or against something, your position will be one or the other. If you argue for a compromise or third option, then that will be your position. The position must be stated clearly in the thesis at the beginning of the essay, and the body of the essay must prove and support it.

▶ **For more about figuring out what claim to make, see Chapter 11, Thesis and Main Idea.**

Before you decide on the position you wish to take on an issue, prewrite to figure out and evaluate all the possibilities. Begin by working out what you think about an issue and evaluating the reasons and support for the various positions you can take. For example, if you are asked to write an essay arguing whether graffiti is art or vandalism, you might begin by sketching out the following brainstorm:

Graffiti is art.
- Most graffiti is made up of big "pieces" that are colorful and very stylistic.
- "Tagging" is usually considered different from graffiti and that's more vandalism.
- Graffiti "pieces" or murals are often requested from building owners to add to their building walls.
- Many graffiti images are very artistic and can even be murals.
- Although some graffiti is done without permission, it's often done on abandoned building walls or public walls like overpasses, and walls of freeways or subways.

Graffiti is vandalism.
- Graffiti created without the authorization of the building owner is vandalism and often costs small business owners a lot of money to cover up, not to mention time.
- Graffiti pops up on public property like schools, parks, subways, freeway walls, buses, overpasses, and signs. It's vandalism b/c it messes up the space and requires public funds to clean up or cover.
- When graffiti covers freeway or street signs, it's a hazard for the public who can't read the information on the signs. This could cause people to miss a freeway exit or even get lost.

- Even graffiti that is unauthorized can really beautify a neighborhood, esp. when neighborhood is falling apart.
- Graffiti can be artistic with lots of colors and images.
- Not all "art" through the ages was necessarily popular or accepted as art when it was made.
- Not all art is authorized—just because it is illegal or might vandalize a building doesn't make it not artistic, and therefore it is art.

- Just because some might find graffiti to be cool or even beautiful doesn't mean it's everyone's taste. It's still vandalism.

Based on the brainstorm, which position would you take? Explain why.

> **practice it 12.1** Choosing a Position
>
> If your assignment is to write an argument paper based on what you have read, pick a side or a position by first going over your reading notes and annotations and then listing or brainstorming all the reasons why you chose that position. If you are still unsure which position to take, do this for both sides or more than one position to see which one you have more support for or interest in.

Evidence and Reasons

The evidence in your argument provides the support for your reasons and claim. Evidence is made up of facts, statistics, observations, quotations, and paraphrases. Your reasons are what led you to your position. Strong and logical reasons provide the rationale for your position. The reasons answer the question "why?" about your position. For example, suppose you take the following position:

> Graffiti is one of the most controversial art forms.

You can then ask yourself a few questions: Why is graffiti considered art? What makes graffiti controversial? Your answers would be your reasons. You should have several reasons to support any position, and your reasons usually become your topic sentences.

Position	Graffiti is one of the most controversial art forms.

Reasons

- Much of the graffiti in urban areas is painted illegally and is expensive to clean up.
- Major museums, such as the Museum of Contemporary Art, Los Angeles have had street art exhibits that include graffiti.
- Some people find that the artistic quality of graffiti beautifies a community.

KINDS OF EVIDENCE

Evidence includes facts, statistics, anecdotes, observations, quotations, and paraphrases that come from your readings, experience, and observations. Not all evidence is equally useful or convincing. When crafting an argument, you must consider your audience to determine how much and what kind of evidence will support your position. If you write to a well-informed group, you need less background information or detail. If you write to an audience that already agrees with some of your points, you can choose evidence suited to what they already know or believe. If you write to an audience that disagrees with your point of view, then you need to carefully select the most convincing evidence and be sure to address counterarguments thoroughly.

▶ **For more information and practice understanding audience, see Chapter 7, Audience, Purpose, and Topic.**

Just as you learned to critically evaluate the credibility of an author or source, you should apply the same scrutiny to your own evidence to test its strength. If you gathered facts, statistics, anecdotes, and observations from several readings and the information is well documented and/or comes from a reputable source, you should consider your information to be strong. Here are some examples of evidence to support the argument that graffiti is vandalism:

Reason	It is costly to remove graffiti.
Fact as Evidence	The four main methods of removing graffiti all cost money for supplies and labor: paint-overs, chemicals, replacing or removing structure that has graffiti on it, and cleaning with sandblasting or other methods. (This fact comes from a U.S. Department of Justice guide for police; government documents are widely considered to be credible sources.)
Statistic as Evidence	The city of Seattle, Washington, spent over $1 million on graffiti cleanup and prevention in 2009. (This fact comes from a well-known national newspaper; newspapers are expected to research what they publish to verify that it is true.)
Reason	Graffiti can be hazardous when it covers freeway or street signs.
Anecdote as Evidence	I was almost hit by a car that didn't stop because a stop sign was covered up by graffiti.
Observation as Evidence	Freeway signs on overpasses are sometimes covered up by graffiti tags, which make it difficult or impossible to read names of exits.

practice it 12.2 Reasons and Evidence

Underline the reasons and evidence in the following sample paragraph supporting the position that graffiti is art:

> Graffiti may not be everyone's cup of tea, but graffiti can definitely be considered art because of its use of color, its stylistic design, and the pride graffiti artists take in their work. Most urban graffiti is made up of big "pieces," short for masterpieces, that use lots of color. In many poor urban neighborhoods, these bright bursts of color that pop up on walls of abandoned buildings or freeway underpasses are usually the only colorful spots. Most graffiti artists take pride in their creations and are very thoughtful and creative in their designs. According to Deborah Lamm Weisel in her publication *Graffiti*, "Some tagger graffiti may involve creative expression, providing a source of great pride in the creation of complex works of art" (8). The complexity of the designs and the pride that the "tagger" takes in his or her work make the graffiti artistic rather than pure vandalism. Although many graffiti pieces are considered vandalism because they are not painted with permission, vandalism includes the intent to deface property. These creative, stylistic, freestyle masterpieces may be painted without permission, but they are not painted with the intention to deface. On the contrary, they are painted with the purpose of beautifying.

After you identify the reasons and evidence in the paragraph, evaluate how convincing they are. Is this paragraph well supported? Why or why not? Would you add anything? If so, discuss what you would add and why.

EXPERT OPINION AS EVIDENCE

One particularly tricky kind of evidence is expert opinion. Most people choose a position on an issue because they have an opinion about it. Opinions are often based on several things: values, beliefs, reasons, evidence, experience, and others' beliefs. We all have opinions on just about everything, and this is good because opinions, in part, shape who we are and what we like and don't like. When crafting support for an argument, opinions are essential, but it's important to clearly understand the difference between opinions and evidence.

Evidence is made up of facts and information as well as expert opinion, which is supported by knowledge of the facts and not by simple belief. We often need to rely on the expert opinion of others because it's impossible to research every fact personally. For instance, in choosing a new computer to buy, we might call on the expert opinion of a friend who works in the technology industry and follows computer trends. Or we might rely on the expert opinion of a publication like *Consumer Reports* that reviews products and their reliability. Either of these choices is reasonable because the source in both cases is someone more informed than us, and his or her opinion is based on research and knowledge of the product. Opinions not based on evidence cannot support an academic argument.

However, if an opinion is based less on evidence and mostly on belief, you should not use it as support for an argument. For example, imagine that a strong swimmer refuses to swim in the ocean because he or she fears sharks. Now, admittedly, sharks are the kinds of creatures you want to avoid when swimming, but this person is a terrific swimmer, loves to swim, and otherwise would be happy swimming in the ocean if not for fear of a shark attack. Where does the belief that swimming in the ocean is dangerous because of sharks come from? Is it based on recent reports of shark attacks or sightings? Is it based on movies like *Jaws* or *Deep Blue Sea* or *Mega Shark versus Giant Octopus*? All oceans have sharks, and, unfortunately, people have been attacked by them, but it's also true, according to the department of ichthyology at the Florida Museum of Natural History, that the chances of being the victim of a fatal shark attack are smaller than the chances of being killed by falling into a sand hole on the beach. Does the frightened swimmer see only the negatives and ignore the rest? Now, there might be many valid reasons why someone would not want to swim in the ocean (for instance, not being a strong swimmer), but without more evidence about the danger of potential shark attacks, this opinion that the ocean is too dangerous for swimming is not well supported.

---

practice it 12.3 Taking a Side

Working with a classmate or friend, select one of the following issues, and have each person take a different position. (Put aside your personal beliefs for the moment if you need to argue a side opposite to your own views.) Sketch out a quick brainstorm to gather evidence and reasons to support the position you have selected, and then compare the reasons and evidence with your partner.

- Children should get an allowance.
- Schools should have metal detectors.
- Dogs should always be on leashes.
- Colleges should be tuition-free.
- Fame is overrated.
- You should always maintain contact with your siblings.

---

practice it 12.4 Building an Argument

Now that you have learned how to craft a good argument, take time to work on your own argument. First, list reasons that support your position, and then list the evidence. If you take evidence from a reading, be sure to include the author, title, and page number, whether you paraphrase or quote directly.

MAKING INFERENCES FROM EVIDENCE

An inference is an educated guess based on available evidence and information. We make inferences all the time in everyday life, in what we read, and in making arguments. For example, let's say Brian is waiting for a bus. It's later than he usually leaves work, and no one else is waiting at the bus stop. He knows that during rush hour the bus stops here every fifteen minutes, but he's been waiting over thirty minutes. He can infer two things from the available information:

1. The bus runs less frequently after rush hour. Instead of every fifteen minutes, perhaps the bus runs only once an hour at this point in the day.
2. The bus no longer services this stop after rush hour.

Brian has no way of knowing which of these, if either, is the case, but based on the available information, either of these scenarios is a reasonable inference.

Reading critically requires making inferences, as does building a well-reasoned argument. To fully support your argument, make sure you draw a logical and reasonable conclusion based on your evidence. If you support your argument with the right evidence, your readers will probably believe your conclusion.

When reading, making inferences is like "reading between the lines." We tend to automatically make inferences as we read, but to really understand and build your own argument, write your inferences in the margins as you read so you can easily refer back to them later.

Making Inferences

Practice reading between the lines of the following blog post from the *New York Times*. Read the post and then answer the questions that follow it.

NewYorkTimes.com

Disney Limits Junk-Food Ads

KJ Dell'Antonia, *MotherLode: Adventures in Parenting blog*

Finally, an entity powerful enough to challenge food manufacturing conglomerates takes affirmative action against advertising food to children that we don't, as a society, actually want them to eat. The Food and Drug Administration? No, not them. The Federal Communications Commission? Not them, either.   1

What we need, it turns out, in order to find someone willing to stand up and put some limit on exactly what kinds of products we will put millions of dollars into encouraging children to eat, is someone that's able to be largely independent of those millions of dollars. Maybe it takes a powerful corporation to take on powerful corporations.   2

Disney announced today that all products advertised on its child-focused television channels, radio stations and Web sites must comply with a strict new set of nutritional standards. Many products that already advertise on Disney, like Capri-Sun and Kraft Lunchables meals, won't make the cut as they currently stand. Disney will also "reduce the amount of sodium by 25 percent in the 12 million children's meals served annually at its theme parks, and create what it calls fun public service announcements promoting child exercise and healthy eating."   3

Will it help? It can't hurt. It could be argued by the cynical that most large businesses involved in selling food to consumers, including children, have an incentive (if not an active duty) to encourage consumers to eat as much as possible. If they don't create products that are unique to them and encourage us to eat them, their business won't prosper—and if we as a society don't recognize the power (and the origin) of that incentive, all of our efforts at change will go nowhere.   4

Disney is the rare company with a huge marketing and media reach to children whose revenues aren't dependent on food products or closely tied to their advertising, and its initiative fits in well with the national conversation. Like Walmart, it's powerful enough (and profitable enough) to take a stand. Does Disney think that stand will ultimately benefit its bottom line? Of course. Disney, as a company, needs consumers' love more than it needs their tastebuds. But just because Disney   5 sees encouraging good health as an area in which it can profit doesn't mean it can't help promote positive change. On the contrary—that financial incentive may be the only thing that will work.

Answer these questions about the reading:

1. What is the specific topic of the article?
2. What position does this author take? Underline the evidence and reasons that lead you to that conclusion.
3. In paragraph 2, the author states, "What we need, it turns out, in order to find someone willing to stand up and put some limit on exactly what kinds of products we will put millions of dollars into encouraging children to eat, is someone that's able to be largely independent of those millions of dollars." What can you infer is the reason for this claim?
4. In paragraph 3, what inference can you draw from Disney's announcement that "all products advertised on its child-focused television channels, radio stations and Web sites must comply with a strict new set of nutritional standards"?
5. In paragraph 4, what can be inferred about the role of large food corporations in our national diet?
6. In paragraph 5, what can you infer the "national conversation" means here?

Counterarguments and Rebuttals

Imagine that a skeptical reader is reading an essay; the *counterarguments* are the ideas that he or she would use to counter, or argue against, the text. A counterargument is an opposing position to the one you take in your paper. A *rebuttal* is your response to the counterargument.

Why would you include an argument opposing your central claim in your paper? A good writer knows there is more than one side to every story, and it's important to acknowledge the other positions and evidence. Including counterarguments intelligently in your writing accomplishes two things. First, it shows that you are well-informed about the issue. Second, rebutting or accommodating counterarguments addresses concerns that readers might have. Once you have crafted your position and brainstormed some solid evidence to support it, you can make your writing more convincing by imagining the reasonable counterarguments to your position. Think about how a skeptical reading would counter, or argue against, your ideas. You can think of the counterarguments as the "reading against the grain" ideas. Effective argument writers not only brainstorm those counterarguments, but also include and address them in their essays, often using a specific rebuttal to refute the counterargument.

Consider the following situation: Francesca wants to get a group of friends together to take a vacation in Hawaii, but Anthony has another vacation destination in mind. See how Anthony uses counterargument and rebuttal to address concerns about Francesca's proposition.

> **Francesca:** Hawaii has great beaches, sun, and tropical sunsets. Pack your bags, and let's go!

What's wrong with this position? It only acknowledges one side of the issue. Are there any reasons *not* to go to Hawaii that ought to be considered?

> **Anthony:** While Hawaii is a beautiful tropical destination with great beaches and warm water for snorkeling, which makes it a popular vacation spot, these "benefits" also make it a very crowded place to visit, and it's a long plane flight away and can be very expensive. Camping at a nearby lake can provide warm days and plenty of swimming on less crowded beaches, at one-fifth of the cost of a trip to Hawaii.

In the preceding example, the counterargument is highlighted in blue, and the rebuttal to the counterargument is in yellow.

Anthony's counterargument and rebuttal may not convince Francesca to give up her dream of a Hawaiian vacation, but the counterargument that such a vacation is expensive, is crowded, and requires a lot of travel time identifies the weaknesses in the argument. Addressing counterarguments is important so you don't look like you are ignoring the obvious or, worse, are ignorant of it.

When reading, look for places in the text where the author considers the evidence for other sides of the argument and rebuts that evidence or offers alternatives or a solution. This indicates that the author is aware of the complexity of the issue and shows respect for his or her readers by acknowledging the potential questions or weaknesses represented by counterarguments.

practice it 12.6   Find the Parts of the Argument

The following paragraphs are taken from Donna Rockwell and David C. Giles's article "Being a Celebrity" (pp. 534–50). Rockwell and Giles spend much of their article interviewing celebrities about the problems associated with fame. Armed with that information, find the counterargument and any rebuttal they might offer. Underline the counterargument and put brackets around the rebuttal.

> The data collected in this study have given us insight into the experience of fame through the eyes of celebrities themselves. The set of textural themes indicates that although fame is experienced as providing wealth, access to a privileged world, gratification and symbolic immortality, it also robs the celebrity of privacy; leads to isolation; engenders mistrust of others; introduces temptations; can lead to creating a character-split between the "celebrity entity" and the "private self"; and heightens concern about risks to other family members.
>
> Perhaps some findings of this study could have the unintended effect of encouraging fame-seekers. All research participants claimed that despite its negative elements, fame is worth it after all and they would not trade it back. The material rewards of fame confirm the celebrity's being-in-the-world such that neither character-splitting, isolation, mistrust, nor fame's impact on family members, led to celebrity regret over becoming famous. At the heart of the fame experience lies an intrinsic affirmation of individual uniqueness and "specialness" that spurs those who seek celebrity status. Participants distinguished the self-affirmative trajectory of fame from the aspirations to make a difference and leave a mark on history that benefits others, goals often cited by famous people like actor Paul Newman and rock star, Bono, who have used their celebrity for philanthropic or altruistic ends. However, inasmuch as fame itself makes possible such impressive altruism, self-expansion and serving others are ambiguously intertwined in the consequent symbolic immortality.

CONCESSION WORDS

Concession words are words that show you acknowledge or accept a point or position. Because the most important part of a counterargument is to accept or concede a point for another position, concession words are an important tool to help you do that. Concession words are especially useful for counterarguments because they allow you to acknowledge the merits of an opposing point of view while still giving more emphasis to your position. Consider the following example:

Arguing to Prevent New Freeway Construction
Although *traffic levels have reached a tipping point*, adding another freeway will be costly and won't provide immediate relief.

Arguing to Construct a New Freeway
Although *adding another freeway will be costly and won't provide immediate relief*, traffic levels have reached a tipping point.

Notice how each sentence uses essentially the same words, but the concession word *although* gives less emphasis to the part of the sentence that the word is attached to (in italics), which can shift the meaning of the sentence.

Here are two more examples:

Although the restaurant only got two out of five stars in an online review, my neighbor recommends it highly.

Although my neighbor recommends it highly, the restaurant only got two out of five stars in an online review.

Which sentence suggests the speaker wants to try the new restaurant? Which sentence implies the speaker doesn't think the new restaurant is worth trying?

Common Concession Words

although
even though
though
whereas
while

▶ For more about using concession words and dependent clauses, see "Subordinating Conjunctions," page 589 in Chapter 28, Parts of Speech.

The key to using these words is to remember that the part of the sentence the concession word is attached to gets less emphasis. When using a concession word to join two sentences, the sentence the concession word is attached to becomes a dependent clause and can no longer stand on its own. Join the dependent clause to the second sentence with a comma. See the example below:

Original idea with two statements.
Vanilla is often thought of as a boring ice cream flavor. It's the best ice cream to pair with a really good hot fudge or caramel sauce.

Use a concession word to emphasize that vanilla is a boring flavor.
<u>Even though</u> + it's the best ice cream to pair with a really good hot fudge or caramel sauce, vanilla is often thought of as a boring ice cream flavor.

Use a concession word to emphasize that vanilla is the best flavor for toppings.
<u>Even though</u> + vanilla is often thought of as a boring ice cream flavor, it's the best ice cream to pair with a really good hot fudge or caramel sauce.

practice it 12.7   Concession Words

Use concession words to combine the following sentence pairs:

1. Dogs are not allowed off leashes. The park is empty.
   - Combine to emphasize that dogs are not allowed off leashes.
   - Combine to emphasize that the park is empty.
2. Fame is something many people secretly yearn for. It comes with many problems, such as lack of privacy and unrealistic expectations.
   - Combine to emphasize that people want fame.
   - Combine to emphasize that fame is problematic.

Using concession words to add emphasis to your point while acknowledging other positions or information is an excellent way to show more sophistication in your writing and is especially useful in argumentative writing. Practice using these words when you can, and keep an eye out as you read for writers using them in articles and books.

practice it 12.8   Understanding an Argument

Read the following opinion piece from the editorial board of the *Los Angeles Times*, September 2015. The writers are responding to a series of events in which firefighters had to halt airdrops of fire retardant on wildfires in California, Oregon, and Washington because of hobby drones. As you read, remember to:

- Identify the author's claim.
- Read with and against the grain.
- Identify types of reasons and evidence.
- Evaluate the quality of the evidence.
- Identify any counterarguments.
- Make inferences—what conclusions can you draw from this article?

continued ◑

▶ **For more on reading with and against the grain, see pages 30–32 in Chapter 2, Active and Critical Reading.**

LOS ANGELES TIMES EDITORIAL BOARD

How Can We, How Should We, Regulate Hobby Drones?

Not too long ago, unmanned aircraft systems—better known as drones—were seen primarily as a tool the military used to spy on bad guys in combat zones and, in some cases, to bomb them, preferably without civilian casualties.

But now, anyone can walk into a Fry's Electronics or Samy's Camera store and buy a quadcopter with a camera for less than $100 and have it zipping through the sky in minutes. No instruction, no registration and no requirement to know the rules governing airspace. And, often, no clear understanding of the havoc one plastic toy can cause.

The litany of drone mishaps in recent months has underscored the free-wheeling nature of this new technology, which recalls the early days of automobiles, when there were few rules and many accidents. In the latest incident—but surely not the last one—an 11-month-old girl was hit with debris when a man crashed his drone near the Pasadena Civic Center last week.

A few drone accidents wouldn't themselves be cause for concern. But increasingly, recreational or hobby drones are interfering with firefighting operations, helping smugglers move drugs and causing near-misses with airplanes. With the popularity of drones growing exponentially—analysts estimate that more than 1 million have been sold in the U.S. since 2013—state and federal officials have a responsibility to address promptly the expanding public threat with appropriate rules and regulations.

Industry experts and the Federal Aviation Administration—the agency   5 that regulates aircraft safety and the use of airspace—recognize the need to regulate drones operating in U.S. skies. But so far the focus has been on commercial drones, which aren't allowed in the air at all except with special permission. The FAA has proposed to change that, allowing commercial drones to operate under strict rules. The rules are expected to be finalized in the next few months.

Hobby drones, meanwhile, are barely regulated by the FAA, which considers them model aircraft and mostly out of its purview. It's wholly inadequate to lump this sophisticated technology—which can practically fly itself, carry cameras or weapons and soar thousands of feet—with old-fashioned radio-controlled hobby aircraft that take expertise and training to operate.

The only rules for drone operators are these: Don't fly within five miles of an airport or in no-flight areas; don't interfere with manned aircraft; and keep the drone in sight. Those who break the rules or hurt people face criminal and civil penalties. If the authorities can find them, that is.

Holding reckless drone operators accountable has become a real problem for authorities. To that end, FAA officials are discussing whether to require registration for all drones, as it does for manned aircraft. Registration, which could be done by the states, could solve many of the headaches caused by private drone operators who don't know the rules of the air and are simply looking for a great photo of a fire or parade. It could also help officials communicate important information to drone users, such as temporary flight restrictions. The FAA has launched a phone app to keep drone users informed of such restrictions, but it still must rely on getting the word out to news outlets and on social media for events such as the pope's visit to the U.S. this week. It's exhausting for the FAA and not a long-term solution for communicating crucial no-fly information.

Other regulatory solutions being discussed include mandating "geofencing," or using software to create virtual barriers to flying (though this would only work for expensive drones with GPS); requiring drone pilots to pass a certification test on airspace rules similar to the road rules test for motorists; and expanding education for recreational users. All are worthy of consideration.

California Department of Forestry and Fire Protection officials don't have 10 a particular prescription but say that something must be done. This summer, the occasional nuisance became a serious problem. After a high-flying drone stopped planes from dropping water on the Lake fire in June, the agency launched the "If you fly, we can't" campaign. That hasn't done much to stop drones from flying over fires, however. Cal Fire reports about a dozen drone incursions since then, compared with just a few the year before.

This is where states can step in. The federal government may control airspace, but states have long made laws about what people do on the ground, such as launching or landing aircraft, and how aircraft affect the people and property below. The National Conference of State Legislatures is trying to help states negotiate this new gray area by developing guiding principles for state lawmakers hoping to protect the public without inhibiting the emerging drone industry.

What states must not do is overreach and try to regulate federal airspace. That's one of the main reasons the drone industry opposed a bill (SB 142) that would have allowed property owners to file trespassing lawsuits when drones flew less than 350 feet above their land. Gov. Jerry Brown vetoed the bill this month, saying it exposed drone users to "burdensome litigation."

Another bill (SB 168), by state Sen. Ted Gaines (R-Roseville) and Assemblyman Mike Gatto (D-Glendale), is an example of legislation that focuses on a drone's effect on the ground—in this case, on fires. It would allow firefighters to

continued ❯

knock drones out of the sky in a fire zone while imposing stiffer penalties on violators. The governor should sign it and encourage more discussion about how to regulate recreational drone use.

Drone makers also have a stake in encouraging hobbyists to use their products responsibly. They would be wise to include in the boxes of recreational drones warnings about unsafe flying and specific instructions for checking flight restrictions.

Like the initial airplanes or cars, drones are part of a huge technological shift 15 and not a fad that might fade in a few years. It's essential that we start figuring out how to incorporate them safely and responsibly into the landscape.

chapter review

In the following chart, fill in the second column to record in your own words the important skills included in this chapter. Then assess yourself to determine whether you are still developing the skill or feel you have mastered it. If you are still developing the skill, make some notes about what you need to work on to master it in the future. If you believe you have already mastered it, explain why.

Skills and concepts covered in this chapter	Explanation in your own words	I'm developing this skill and need to work on . . .	I believe I have mastered this skill because . . .
Taking a position			
Identifying evidence and opinion			
Making inferences			
Identifying counter-arguments and rebuttals			

13

Topic Sentences and Paragraphs

in this chapter

- What Makes a Good Topic Sentence?
- What Makes a Good Paragraph?
- What Is PIE Paragraph Structure?
- How Do You Improve Your Paragraphs?

Writing coherent, clear, well-organized, and well-developed paragraphs will help you throughout your life, as we are often asked to write a one-paragraph response to a question posed by a teacher or co-worker. In addition, strong body paragraphs are the core of a well-written essay, so the more you understand how paragraphs work, the better college reader and writer you will be.

LaunchPad Solo
macmillan learning

Visit **LaunchPad Solo for Readers and Writers > Topic Sentences and Supporting Details** for extra practice in the skills covered in this chapter.

Topic Sentences

A topic sentence is the sentence that states the main point of a paragraph. You've already read about topic sentences in Chapters 1–4; this chapter will help you both recognize and write topic sentences.

Good topic sentences:

- Make one point that the paragraph will cover
- Are the most general sentence of the paragraph
- Are appropriately focused—not too broad or too narrow

In addition, if your paragraphs are body paragraphs of an essay, they should:

- Have a direct relationship to the thesis
- Use key words (or synonyms of key words) from the thesis
- Progress logically

IDENTIFYING TOPIC SENTENCES

In some types of writing, especially college textbooks, the topic sentence is often the first sentence of the paragraph. But what if it is buried

▶ **For more practice identifying topic sentences, see pages 291–96 in Chapter 14, Essay Organization and Outlining.**

further within the paragraph or is a question or a statement of fact? Read the whole paragraph, paying careful attention to the point being made. If this doesn't lead you to the topic sentence, look for the most general sentence of the paragraph: Because the topic sentence is the broadest point made in the paragraph, it should be the most general sentence. Or look for examples or quotes in the paragraph and ask yourself: What point does that evidence support? Then try to find a sentence that answers that question. In most cases, you will find the topic sentence using one of these critical reading strategies.

Topic sentences that are the first sentence in a paragraph are the easiest to find. Take this example from Jake Halpern's "The Desire to Belong: Why Everyone Wants to Have Dinner with Paris Hilton and 50 Cent" (pp. 551–61).

> <u>The social lives of cheerleaders and celebrities are strikingly similar.</u> Both groups consist of and are defined by two types of people: the "stars," who appear talented, glamorous, and popular; and the "acolytes," who strive to endear themselves to the stars. The question is: What exactly motivates the acolytes? To a certain extent, Belongingness Theory explains why so many of us yearn to belong to groups in general, but not why we prefer these highly prestigious groups above all others, or why we toil to ingratiate ourselves with the leaders of these groups.

Do you notice how the main point of the paragraph is clearly identified in the first sentence, and all the other sentences of the paragraph support that point?

Here are some examples of trickier paragraphs where the topic sentence is in the middle or at the end of the paragraph. In his essay "Public Art: An Essential Component of Creating Communities" (pp. 486–95), Jack Becker begins this paragraph by drawing the reader in and then providing the main point.

> Imagine, if you can, a world devoid of public art: no Statue of Liberty, no Eiffel Tower, no Vietnam Veterans Memorial, no Tribute in Light. No murals, memorials, or monuments. What would life be like without fireworks displays, puppet parades, sculpture parks, and visionary roadside folk art? <u>These landmarks and special events enhance our experience of a place and our quality of life.</u> They engender a sense of pride and community identity. They reach audiences outside museums, galleries, and theaters, and they add to the beauty of everyday life. They declare the worth of a place and a time in our shared culture.

This paragraph from the middle of Donna Rockwell and David C. Giles's article "Being a Celebrity" (pp. 534–50) follows from one of their earlier points.

> In order to put fame in its proper place, Richard has decided to use his fame and wealth for "good works" and community-based causes, creating

something that will live on beyond him. In the small town where he and his family live, Richard has paid for the building of high school sports stadiums that are "premiere facilities." These fields exist "because I'm famous," he says. He also supports a local music school. "We can . . . leave the place better than we found it. . . . It's a great use of the fame. It's like turning a negative into a positive, I guess." <u>Turning the negative of fame into a positive allows Richard to tolerate the loss of privacy and isolation he faces as a result of being a celebrity.</u>

Notice how the author's placement of the topic sentence at the end of the paragraph makes it sound stronger and more emphatic.

practice it 13.1   Identifying Topic Sentences

Find and underline the thesis and topic sentences in the following short article on social media, published on Econtentmag.com in 2014. If you cannot find an *explicit thesis* (written out in the article), see if you can come up with the author's *implied thesis* and write it out. After identifying the thesis and the topic sentence of each body paragraph, read only the thesis and the topic sentences together to get a sense of the overall structure of the article. Does each topic sentence make a point? Is each the most general sentence in the paragraph? How does each topic sentence connect back to the thesis?

▶ **For more about the difference between an explicit thesis and an implied thesis, see page 243 in Chapter 11, Thesis and Main Idea.**

Econtentmag.com

Would You Quit Social Media If You Could?
Theresa Cramer

On the average weekday, I spend hours sorting through my social media feeds—mostly Facebook and Twitter. I fire up HootSuite to make this task a little easier and dutifully retweet, share, and schedule posts. For many of us, managing social media has gone from a way to kill time to an integral part of our jobs. But by Friday night, I'm ready to hang up my social media hat (except for Pinterest because I need it to make new, exciting meals). On Saturday and Sunday, I need a break from the endless streams of news, opinions, and baby pictures—but giving up social networks all together seems unfeasible.

1

Social media has fundamentally changed from being something college kids used to cyberstalk their crushes to big business. Lately,

2

continued ❯

though, I've been hearing from people with large social media followings—and professional reputations built largely on their social skills—who would love to just throw in the towel and walk away. All you have to do is tune into *Jimmy Kimmel Live* on a night when he is featuring "Mean Tweets"—where he has celebrities read harsh tweets about themselves on camera—to understand why some people might want to escape the trappings of Twitter. The open, accessible nature of Twitter that made it so popular for connecting with fans (of a celebrity or a brand) has also turned it into a cesspool of insults and bile. Meanwhile, every time we turn around we hear how teens are leaving Facebook in droves, making it the domain of people too old and tired to bother moving their profiles or learn how to use a new app.

I don't quite believe the hysteria over the supposed exodus of teens   3
from Facebook. Snapchat may be new and exciting, but it is also fundamentally different from Facebook, which has become a content destination as much as a social network. Facebook—along with Pinterest, Twitter, and Instagram—has become an integral part of most publishers' content strategy (as well as a must-use channel for marketers). Many of those publishers would happily go back to the days when their websites were the destination, but that's as unlikely as me deleting my Facebook account—or even my Google+ account.

As anyone who has watched as a friend deactivated a social media   4
account—and, sometimes, reactivated it later—knows, social media fatigue is certainly real. According to a 2013 study from Pew Research Center's Pew Internet & American Life Project, "61% of current Facebook users say that at one time or another in the past they have voluntarily taken a break from using Facebook for a period of several weeks or more."

Going a step beyond that, the same study found that "20% of the   5
online adults who do not currently use Facebook say they once used the site but no longer do so." The reasons that 61% of people gave were varied—from a lack of time to engage to "too much drama." But whatever the reason your potential audience is shunning social media—even temporarily—this is something you have to consider when you're planning your strategy. You don't want to become part of the problem.

The good news is that a relatively small number of people (4%)   6
blame ads and spam for their disillusionment. Still, every time someone decides to take a break from any social network—no matter the reason— that means there is one less set of eyeballs for you to reach. If you have a well-rounded, multichannel marketing plan, a few fatigued Facebook users shouldn't be too big of a deal. That doesn't mean there isn't an impact, though, and having a plan for reaching those valuable users outside the realm of social media should be a priority.

As Angie Picardo puts it on Gartner, Inc.'s blog, "People who are getting weary of social media still remain social through the human network. What online marketing often lacks is a sense of authenticity and trust, a contributing reason for social media fatigue. Algorithms cannot compensate for a good local buzz surrounding a new restaurant, or personal testimony from a local celebrity about a specialty hardware store. Spread awareness of your business through traditional means by exalting great customer service and waiting for the trickle down process to bring customers in."   7

Can you imagine a world where you didn't check in with Facebook and Twitter a few times a day? If you even slightly long for the days when social media wasn't part of your job, then it's time to realize that you aren't the only one.   8

THE TOPIC SENTENCE AND THE THESIS

Once you identify the topic sentences, you can see how they work together to support the thesis of an essay (in other words, how the topic sentence links the thesis and the paragraph information). The topic sentence states the point the paragraph will make and must clearly relate back to the thesis. The body paragraph explains, develops, or supports the topic sentence, and in so doing, supports the thesis. One helpful metaphor is that of a wooden plank bridge. Each topic sentence is like one plank of wood in the bridge. If you put them all together, they add up to the thesis, the bridge itself, across which you will lead your readers.

A visual example of the relationship between the topic sentences and the thesis will help. Look at the following first page of a student essay on murals. The annotations and highlighting show how the topic sentences in blue relate back to the thesis (in yellow).

Murals are not only a way to decorate neighborhoods and public buildings; they also are a way to honor people who have contributed to society and to help pass on lessons about a culture. One such mural is painted on the side of a drugstore and it's called *Mission Celebration*. This mural takes up about half of the wall of the building. It is painted with vibrant, bright colors and includes scenes of Latino culture, and it has a very large image of Cesar Chavez. This mural is hard to miss. The mural *Mission Celebration* is a piece of art created with the purpose of motivating the general public to celebrate and learn about Cesar Chavez and Mexican folklore.

By prominently portraying Cesar Chavez, the mural encourages the community to know about this Mexican American leader. Many people are already aware of who Cesar Chavez was, but if someone didn't know, this mural would make him or her want to know. The image of Cesar Chavez in

The thesis claims the purpose of the mural is to inform the public about Cesar Chavez and Mexican folklore.

Topic sentence 1 relates back to the thesis and helps develop it by discussing one aspect of the thesis: encouraging community to learn about Cesar Chavez.

this mural is positioned in such a way as to suggest he is someone important. His portrait is just of his head, and it's by far the largest image in the
mural. Anyone driving or walking by would wonder who this man is and
what he might mean to the community. The muralist used size to show him
as an important figure.

*Topic sentence 2 relates
back to thesis and helps develop it further by showing
how learning about Cesar
Chavez is inspiring.*

   Mission Celebration, by depicting Cesar Chavez's legacy, is an inspiration for other political and social leaders. The community is shown celebrating Cesar Chavez in the mural by depicting him surrounded by other things
that are important to the community. This is inspiring to others who want to
make a difference in their community, because they can see how honored
someone like Cesar Chavez is and aim to be like him. In this way, the mural
serves as a positive inspiration to all.

practice it 13.2   Connecting Topic Sentences to the Thesis

One common problem in student writing is that while the topic
sentences might be interesting, they don't always relate back to the
thesis. Take a look at two examples from student essays. How well does
each topic sentence connect to the thesis? Ask yourself the following
questions to help you evaluate the examples:

1. Looking at the topic sentences, what point will the paragraph
   make? Underline that point.
2. Does the topic sentence relate back to the thesis?
3. If the topic sentence does not relate back to the thesis, what is
   missing?
4. Which topic sentence is a better fit with the stated thesis? Why?

Example 1

Thesis	**The mural *Revive* conveys the message that the wildlife of Golden Gate Park could be restored with the help of the San Francisco community.**
Topic Sentence A	The red-tailed hawk symbolizes creation on the top of the mural because it is part of nature and one of the original inhabitants of the San Francisco Bay Area.
Topic Sentence B	The possibility of the park being restored can be seen in the images of the volunteers and the growth of new plants in the mural.

Example 2

Thesis	**The mural *A Past That Still Lives* shows the struggle the people from El Salvador have had healing from their civil war.**

| Topic Sentence A | The colors of the mural—bright yellows, oranges, reds, and greens—make the mural vibrant. |
| Topic Sentence B | The shadow images of past events painted throughout the mural show that what happened during the civil war still haunts people. |

WRITING TOPIC SENTENCES

To draft good topic sentences, you have to know what points you want to make in the body of your essay. Because each body paragraph focuses on one point in support of the thesis, a good place to start is to look at your working thesis and any brainstorming you have already come up with. Generally speaking, topic sentences are written after the thesis to ensure that they fully support and develop the thesis's central claim.

Begin by listing all the points you want to make in support of your thesis. If you already have a list like this from your pre-writing, you can use that. Write down your points with plenty of room between each one so you have room to work on topic sentences. For each point, create a sentence that can be developed into a paragraph. Check the topic sentence criteria at the start of the chapter (p. 273) to see if these sentences work as topic sentences. If they don't, revise until they fit.

If you aren't sure what points to make in support of your thesis, begin with the broader topics or evidence you have selected during the pre-writing stage. If you have done the post-reading practice activities in this book, you probably already know some quotations or examples from the class readings that might support your thesis. Make a list of either the topics or the evidence you have gathered, and then, one by one, ask yourself what you want to say about each topic or piece of evidence and write it out in a sentence.

Here's an example of a college student named Kiyoung going through the process of writing topic sentences. He starts with a working thesis.

Kiyoung's Working Thesis
Murals are often painted by artists who are either untrained or are not part of the established art world, and because the majority of murals are located on the streets rather than in galleries or museums, they are sometimes not considered "real" art.

After writing his thesis, Kiyoung generates a list of topics and ideas that can support it. From this list, he picks the topics that will provide the strongest support for the thesis and that can be developed into paragraphs. Remember, not everything you come up with in your brainstorm will necessarily support your thesis. Don't be afraid to weed out the topics that don't quite fit. In the following list, Kiyoung has bolded the topics he wants to develop into paragraphs.

Ideas to Support the Thesis

types of art
murals are painted by everyone
murals are everywhere
murals are colorful and often tell a story or have a message
murals can represent the people of the community or important leaders
    like Martin Luther King Jr. or Cesar Chavez or Gandhi
painting murals can bring community together
people don't see murals as art
museum art isn't only art
murals are free to see
art vs. art world
murals aren't for sale
you don't have to be trained as an artist to be considered an artist
not all artists go to art school
I like mural art even better than most of the art I've seen in museums

Next, Kiyoung takes the bolded topics and puts them into rough topic sentences without worrying too much about getting the perfect wording just yet. He begins with the topic and then asks himself: What point do I want to make about this topic? The answer to that question is generally the rough topic sentence.

Rough Topic Sentences

Topic: murals are painted by everyone
What point do I want to make about this?
TS: Who paints murals?
Topic: museum art isn't only art
What point do I want to make about this?
TS: Mona Caron is a good enough artist to be in a museum.
Topic: people don't see murals as art
What point do I want to make about this?
TS: People just walk right by murals all the time.
Topic: art vs. art world
What point do I want to make about this?
TS: Art doesn't need approval to be enjoyed or considered art.
Topic: not all artists go to art school
What point do I want to make about this?
TS: Many muralists create stunning visual works but don't follow the
    "rules" of art.

Great! Now that Kiyoung has several rough topic sentences, he checks them against the topic sentence criteria at the start of the chapter to see if these sentences will work as topic sentences. If they don't, he'll have to revise them. Let's look at each one:

Topic Sentence   Who paints murals?

Problem: This sentence is a question, not a point (claim), so it will need to be revised. The solution? Answer the question.

Revision   Murals are painted not only by artists but also by home-owners, schoolchildren, teens, and community groups.

Topic Sentence   Mona Caron is a good enough artist to be in a museum.

Problem: This is too specific a detail and doesn't relate directly enough to the thesis. The solution? Connect the point being made about Mona Caron to the thesis.

Revision   Many muralists create great visual works but don't create the kind of art that goes in museums.

Topic Sentence   People just walk right by murals all the time.

Problem: Too vague. What is the point being made here?

Revision   Because they are out in public and not in museums, people walk by murals all the time without thinking of them as art.

Topic Sentence   Art doesn't need approval to be enjoyed or considered art.

Problem: Topic sentence could be stronger and more connected to the thesis. The solution? Add key word from the thesis.

Revision   Murals don't have to be part of the established art world to be enjoyed or considered "real" art.

Notice that each topic sentence was a good start but needed a bit of revision. Just like thesis statements, topic sentences often need revision to make sure they make a clear point that connects to the thesis. Now Kiyoung can experiment with how he wants to arrange these topic sentences in his paper. He will probably want to type his thesis at the top of the page so he can see how they all work together.

practice it 13.3   From Topics to Topic Sentences

Make a rough list of your topics that support your thesis. The next step is to turn each of these phrases into a complete, grammatically correct sentence that states the point the paragraph will make about that

continued ❯

topic. This way, you will know *what* you plan to say about each of these ideas. For example, if the topic is financial literacy, you can ask yourself what point you want to make *about* financial literacy. Put the answer into a complete sentence, such as "Financial literacy leads to a better understanding of one's financial situation and good decision making about money." This sentence certainly gives you a clearer sense of where you're going with the paragraph. As you start to generate your topic sentences, you might discover that you delete, combine, focus, or expand some of your topics. That's fine! Your ideas will certainly evolve as you do this topic sentence writing activity.

Paragraphs

The function of the body paragraphs is to develop the information that supports the topic sentence and the thesis. Body paragraphs are the muscle behind the thesis: They do all the heavy lifting to prove the claim that your thesis makes. That's a lot of work. To convince the reader that the thesis is valid, body paragraphs begin with their own point, the topic sentence. Each body paragraph must also have sufficient evidence to fully support its topic sentence.

UNDERSTAND PIE PARAGRAPH STRUCTURE

By now you are familiar with the role of the topic sentence; it states the point of the paragraph, and in academic writing it is the first sentence of the paragraph. So, what does the rest of the paragraph do? The rest of the paragraph works to support that point in a clear, logically ordered way. Paragraphs are not written haphazardly; rather, the sentences follow a logical progression so the reader can easily follow the ideas. All the sentences in a paragraph relate directly to the topic sentence so that the whole paragraph is unified around one point. Strong paragraphs also are well developed. They begin with a point and "prove" that point by providing facts, examples, details, observations, and quotations or paraphrases from relevant sources and explaining them. A paragraph in an essay often ends with a transition to the next paragraph point.

A well-built paragraph has several important features:

- **Purpose**—a clear point is stated in the topic sentence.
- **Unity**—all the sentences relate to and address the point of the paragraph.
- **Development**—the paragraph provides enough information and explanation to make the point that the topic sentences promise and also to help support the thesis.

An easy way to understand how an expository paragraph works is to remember the acronym *PIE*: Point, Information, and Explanation/Elaboration, the three main parts of a body paragraph in academic writing. The PIE paragraph structure serves two main purposes: (1) to help you analyze your paragraph to see if your information and explanation are well balanced, and (2) to help you develop your paragraph if your topic sentence is not well supported.

PIE PARAGRAPH STRUCTURE

Point = your topic sentence	Topic Sentence
Information = observations, facts, statistics, examples, anecdotes, quotes, and other types of evidence	Evidence
Explanation/elaboration = your reasons why the information supports and explains the point of the paragraph or thesis; your discussion of what the information means, and how it is relevant	Analysis

Each body paragraph (not the introduction or conclusion) should have P, I, and E. Although you will only have one P per paragraph, you should have several I and E sentences, and they don't necessarily have to be in that order. Let's look at a student's sample body paragraph in which the P, I, and E are highlighted in different colors. The P (point) is highlighted in yellow, the I (information) is highlighted in blue, and the E (explanation/elaboration) is highlighted in green.

Ruben's Paragraph

Financial know-how is necessary for individuals to become debt-free and **P**
learn to grow their wealth. Financial knowledge includes learning how to **I**
save and keep a budget. In the article "Teach Your Children the Building **I**
Blocks of Finance," Sherie Holder and Kenneth Meeks reinforce the importance of the practice of saving at least 10 to 15 percent of after-tax income
(35). Getting into the practice of automatically saving a certain amount **E**
every month will help you grow your wealth. Another part of financial **E**
know-how is learning how to manage money, which includes knowing how
to avoid getting into debt in the first place. By knowing how to budget your **I**
money, you can learn how much money you actually have, which can help **E**
you spend within your means. When you spend within your means, you are **E**
able to avoid having to use credit cards, which, in turn, will prevent you
from having to pay costly interest fees and prevent you from getting further
into debt.

You can see that the pattern for this paragraph is P/I/I/E/E/I/E/E. It has a good balance of both information and explanation/elaboration.

practice it 13.4   Identifying Information and Explanation

Look over these two student sample paragraphs and label each
sentence with P, I, or E. Does each paragraph have a good balance of
information and explanation/elaboration? Does either paragraph need
development in one or both of these areas?

Lisa's Paragraph

Many parents who have their children enrolled in some sort of financial
education are happy with the results. The students are more confident in
their approach to spending, and more inclined to save or wait instead of
having an immediate gratification. Parents then feel more at ease when
they are getting ready to send their children to school or on an outing
instead of worrying that their children will spend frivolously. More
importantly, the pupils will be ready to go on to a job or higher education
with the skills and knowledge to succeed financially. Their financial literacy
will ensure that they are capable of managing bills and student loans
instead of going into severe debt. They will be able to understand the
importance of saving and of postponing gratification for a later time when
they might be more stable in their finances.

Holly's Paragraph

Parents who are unintentionally sending their children down the path of
financial illiteracy may not even fully understand the results of their
actions. Parents who send mixed messages about money by telling their
children to do one thing while they demonstrate another are making one
of the most common mistakes that can be made. Unless they are personally setting the right example themselves, their children will not be willing
to follow their advice. If their parents are not doing it, then why should
they? It must not be that important, right? Parents who show their children
that it is possible to borrow money when you cannot afford to, hinder their
children's decision-making process, in turn teaching them to take shortcuts
to get what they want, instead of working hard. Using credit cards as a

means to supplement the difference between one's income and one's spending is also a nasty shortcut that children have been known to pick up on. This will lead them to believe that living beyond their means is a normal and acceptable way of life. Children will then use this mentality to easily talk themselves into getting or buying whatever they desire, whether they can afford it or not. Also, parents who refuse to ever say no to their children's every wish will set them up for failure. In the end, these tactics can make children unable to say no to things that they do not need, ultimately teaching them that spending is fun! This will lead children to believe that money equals happiness.

Evaluate Your Paragraphs

A paragraph without a clear topic sentence and sufficient evidence won't convince your reader of your point. Labeling the sentences in your body paragraphs with P, I, or E identifies your paragraph's strengths and weaknesses. It shows whether or not your paragraph is balanced with both information and explanation, and what you need more of. If you find you are missing the P (topic sentence), think about what point that paragraph is trying to make. Sometimes you can figure that out by looking at the I in the paragraph and asking yourself: Okay, why did I include that information/example/quotation? What point does it support? Often this will help you focus on the point of the paragraph. If your paragraph is low on I, remedy the situation by adding more examples, facts, observations, or other forms of information. Just make sure the new information you add to the paragraph fits the point you are making. The most common piece of PIE missing from body paragraphs is usually E. If your paragraph lacks enough explanation or elaboration, now is the time to add it. You need to explain how all the information in your paragraph supports your overall point.

Each paragraph is a unit of writing that focuses on supporting one point, the topic sentence. Strengthening the I and E of your PIE paragraph structure adds texture and sophistication to your writing.

practice it 13.5 Balancing Body Paragraphs

In the essay you are writing, review your body paragraphs one at a time and label each sentence with P, I, or E. Determine if your paragraphs have a good balance of information and explanation or if they need development in one or both of these areas.

DEVELOP YOUR POINT (P)

If you can't find the sentence that states the point your paragraph will make, you may be missing a topic sentence in that paragraph. Take a step back and read over the whole paragraph, and then ask yourself what single point the paragraph makes. Write that point in the form of a sentence, and then check the topic sentence criteria on page 273 of this chapter. If you find the paragraph makes more than one point, you will probably want to develop each point into its own paragraph. Review the section in this chapter on writing topic sentences (see pp. 279–82) for more help.

STRENGTHEN THE INFORMATION (I)

Sometimes strengthening the information in a paragraph is simply a matter of adding more. If you are missing the I in the paragraph, go back to your annotated articles and pre-writing to see what evidence, examples, quotes, or anecdotes you found interesting but have not yet included. Would anything there help provide support for your point in this paragraph? List all the possible pieces of information you might use to support your topic sentence, and then choose the best ones. Peer or instructor feedback can be useful at this point in the writing process.

Another way to improve your information is to use a variety of examples, facts, anecdotes, quotations, personal experiences, reasons, and statistics. You may have lots of sentences of information, but if they aren't varied enough the paragraph will be weak. Begin building your paragraph with an idea; then you can often find many kinds of evidence to make your point. If you begin with a quote or example, you might have a harder time seeing how other sources or kinds of information can be used.

For example, look at Martha's paragraph from an essay about celebrity and fame. The paragraph is adequate, but the entire paragraph is focused only on support from "Seeing by Starlight" by Carlin Flora. Read the paragraph, and then brainstorm additional kinds of support that this author could have used to make a stronger paragraph.

Martha's Paragraph

We are drawn to celebrities not only because they are beautiful people, but because they seem to be living the lives most of us can only dream of. Carlin Flora writes about our fascination with celebrities in her article "Seeing by Starlight." The huge salaries and lavish homes of stars keep us interested because "our lives seem woefully dull by comparison" (Flora 528). They are elegant walking the red carpet in couture fashion and dripping with real jewels, perfect hair, and makeup. Flora also argues, however, that some of the beauty we attach to stars is based more on how often we see images of them than their actual beauty. "The more we see a certain face, the more our brain likes it, whether or not it's actually beautiful," writes Flora (531). It helps, too, that they have access to the best skin and hair professionals in the business. Whether it is because of their looks or their lavish lives, we can't stop looking at stars.

This writer misses an opportunity to use quotations from additional sources about celebrity attraction. She could also use anecdotes from the personal experiences of people who are drawn to the glamour of celebrities. This kind of personal perspective could add variety and broader support to the paragraph.

▶ **For more help on developing support, see the Quotation or Paraphrase Sandwich activity, page 349 in Chapter 17, Quotation and Paraphrase.**

STRENGTHEN THE EXPLANATION OR ELABORATION (E)

Once you have sufficient and varied information to support your topic sentence, make sure you elaborate on or explain it. In journalistic writing, many paragraphs simply end with a quotation, but in college writing, you are expected to say something about the information in your paragraphs. Start by reviewing every piece of information in the paragraph and ask yourself, how does this support my point? Ask yourself why you picked that information to include in your paragraph. The answer is your E. Often we think it's obvious how the information in our paragraphs proves the point, but what's obvious to you is not always obvious to your reader.

Here is a body paragraph from a student paper on curiosity. The author, William, is making a claim about how curiosity and creativity are related. He offers some interesting examples from his personal experience as well as from the readings. However, he does not elaborate enough upon this information, so his readers might not see how the information he gives supports his claim. Read through the paragraph and see where he could develop the paragraph further by adding more explanation.

William's Paragraph

Curiosity and creativity are flip sides of the same coin. For example, my **P** sister is curious about everything. When we go on a trip, she's always the **I** one who wants to stop and talk with strangers about where they live, or the **I** one who wants to go into a grocery store to buy foods we don't have back home. It's no surprise my sister is also an artist. In her article "The Case **I** for Curiosity," researcher Susan Engel describes one behavior her research **I** team looked for when they were trying to measure how much curiosity students showed. She explains that they looked for "[t]imes when a **I** student physically investigated something (such as opening up the back of a cassette machine)" (459).

William's examples make sense to him, but they aren't entirely clear to a reader. How do the examples relate to the main point, and to each other? He needs to add more elaboration. Here's how he revised:

William's Revised Paragraph

Curiosity and creativity are flip sides of the same coin. For example, my   **P**
sister is curious about everything. When we go on a trip, she's always the   **I**
one who wants to stop and talk with strangers about where they live, or the   **I**
one who wants to go into a grocery store to buy foods we don't have back
home. It's no surprise my sister is also an artist. She takes all the interest- **I**
ing facts and ideas that she learns by being so curious about the world and   **E**
develops those ideas in her art. This process can also happen inside the   **E**
classroom, and in the very best types of schools, it's an everyday occur-
rence. In her article "The Case for Curiosity," researcher Susan Engel   **I**
describes one behavior her research team looked for when they were trying
to measure how much curiosity students showed. She explains that they   **I**
looked for "[t]imes when a student physically investigated something (such
as opening up the back of a cassette machine)" (459). Taking something   **E**
apart and putting it back together is the sort of creativity that sparks new
inventions and new discoveries. Engel obviously knows that curiosity and   **E**
creativity go together in students, which is why she looked for creative
actions when she was trying to measure curiosity.

TURN YOUR TOPIC SENTENCE INTO A QUESTION

Another way to check whether your body paragraphs are well developed, unified, and coherent is to turn the topic sentences into questions. When you do this, you essentially take on the role of a reader. Based on the question, what do you expect the paragraph to cover? Try a few different questions to see which one best fits the purpose of the paragraph; then scan the paragraph to see if it adequately answers the question. If it doesn't, there's a good chance you need more evidence. What part(s) of the question does it not answer? What additional evidence and explanation would help the paragraph answer the question?

Let's practice with a body paragraph from a student essay on the importance of financial literacy. Here is Jabal's paragraph:

Jabal's Paragraph

Having financial literacy also helps you become stable in your personal finances. Having financial literacy will help you be stable financially. A big reason people in the United States are having trouble with money is that they don't know how to use it wisely. But the thing is that nobody teaches you how to manage your personal finances. From my experience, there is no class in school that teaches you how to budget. So people go on to graduate high school and go into the real world without having any financial literacy. When those people get jobs, they end up using their paychecks on all the wrong things and might end up losing all their hard-earned money.

If we turn the topic sentence into questions, they might look like this:

1. When does having financial literacy help you become stable in your personal finances?

2. Why does having financial literacy help you become stable in your personal finances?

3. How does having financial literacy help you become stable in your personal finances?

After reading the paragraph, we can determine that the topic sentence seems to be trying to answer the third question, *How does having financial literacy help you become stable in your personal finances?* The paragraph does not give examples about when or why financial literacy leads to stability. Instead, it focuses on the result of not budgeting or not knowing how to spend money.

Now, write down the question the topic sentence is trying to answer, and then reread the paragraph looking for answers to the question. When you find an answer to the question, jot it down. Here's how that might look for Jabal's paragraph:

> How *does* having financial literacy help you become stable in your personal finances?
> - Not knowing how to use money leads to trouble with money.
> - Not budgeting can cause you to lose your money or spend it on unnecessary things.

Hmm. Jabal's paragraph doesn't really have much evidence to show how financial literacy makes you stable in your personal finances. Instead, it spends more time discussing how *not* having financial literacy makes you *not* stable. This tells us that the paragraph needs to be revised.

Fortunately, there is a lot of room for development in Jabal's paragraph because there are several claims that can each be developed into a full paragraph:

- Having financial literacy also helps you become stable in your personal finances.

- A big reason people in the United States are having trouble with money is that they don't know how to use it wisely.

- But the thing is that nobody teaches you how to manage your personal finances.

To improve his essay, Jabal needs to develop each of these claims into a full paragraph, providing support (information and explanation) for each point. Not only will this method help him develop the paragraph, but it will help him develop a couple of pages for his essay.

practice it 13.6   Asking Questions to Improve Paragraph Unity and Coherence

Practice the preceding strategy on your own essay, turning your topic sentences into questions. Then take on the role of a critical reader to see if your paragraphs have appropriate evidence and elaboration. If they don't, add information and explanation to fill in the gaps in support. If you find that you have more than one claim, develop each claim into a new paragraph.

chapter review

In the following chart, begin by filling in the second column to record in your own words the important skills included in this chapter. Then assess yourself to determine whether you are still developing the skill or feel you have mastered it. If you are still developing the skill, make some notes about what you need to work on to master it in the future. If you believe you have mastered it, explain why.

Skills and concepts covered in this chapter	Explanation in your own words	I'm developing this skill and need to work on . . .	I feel I have mastered this skill because . . .
Identifying topic sentences			
Writing topic sentences			
Identifying PIE paragraph structure			
Evaluating your para-graphs to develop or strengthen them			

14

Essay Organization and Outlining

Sometimes we talk about being organized as a person—knowing where we put our keys, paying bills on time, meeting deadlines, that sort of thing. But in writing, the word *organization* can mean a few different things. With texts, we talk about organization within each paragraph as well as among the paragraphs of an essay, and *organization* refers to the order of information, from sentence to sentence and then paragraph to paragraph, as well as the transitions from one idea to the next. Paying attention to the organization, or structure, as we read helps us work through difficult readings and see deeper meanings in the text. Paying attention to organization as we write saves us time and frustration by decreasing the likelihood that we will have to do major structural revisions.

There is no one right way to organize a piece of writing. The order of information and the types of transitions used will vary depending on the author's purpose, audience, and style. Some types of texts, such as lab reports or scholarly journal articles, have an expected order of information. Other texts are organized more organically, with authors making choices based on what they wish to express and how they wish to express it. If a piece of writing is organized well, the content and ideas of the writing shine. In contrast, poor organization results in a text that is confusing and hard to follow.

Outlining as a Reader

One effective critical reading strategy is to make an outline as you read or reread a text. Essentially, this involves locating the topic sentences and highlighting them or inferring the main points or ideas. (You did this in

Chapter 1 when you wrote "nutshell summaries" of main points as you annotated your readings.) Recognizing the topic sentences as you read and writing down a list of main points help you see the underlying structure of a text and thus gain a deeper understanding of the reading. When you complete the process, you have created an informal outline of the reading, one the author might have used while writing it. Informal outlines help us think through the structure of a piece of writing. They are also known as "working outlines" and so are different from formal outlines, which are generally much more detailed and can serve as study guides for a chapter or article.

Making informal outlines as you read also helps you identify places where you don't understand the main point the author is trying to convey. If you can't sum it up in a few words, then you probably didn't catch it, and you may need to reread a few times or backtrack to figure out from the context what the author is saying. Outlining is an especially helpful technique when you work with a particularly long or difficult text. In addition, outlining is an excellent study tool for reviewing material before a test or as part of pre-writing for an assignment.

Let's try the technique first on a short article to see how it works. Here's an annotated version of the article "Income Inequality within Families Is Emerging as a Major Issue" by Janna Malamud Smith, published in 2013 in the online periodical *The Daily Beast*. The annotations identify the thesis and topic sentences to help you figure out how the text is structured.

---

thedailybeast.com

Income Inequality within Families Is Emerging as a Major Issue
Janna Malamud Smith

Income inequality isn't just bad for our economic health. It's bad for our   1
mental health. Working for decades as a psychotherapist has accustomed me to listening closely. And—in and outside the office—I've lately been hearing painful stories told about how families, friendship circles, and neighborhoods are being strained by ever greater wealth differences among their members. Yes, some folks have always earned more than others, and people have always had greater or lesser luck and success. The small town in Vermont where I grew up for a while had its local millionaire, and his children owned a trampoline and we didn't. But the

thesis   situation now is different. As the rich have gotten massively richer, the emotional climate has deteriorated for all of us. People now routinely tell me about the impact on them of wealth gaps so yawning they threaten the bonds of affection and blood.

Some examples? A woman who could easily afford to pay the college tuition for much less well off nieces and nephews, doesn't. She feels she's worked harder than the others, and resents being put in the position of seeming selfish. Meanwhile, the rest of the family resents her turning her back . . . A man sells the beloved family property because he's tired of maintaining it alone—though it breaks the hearts of his kin who cannot pay what would be their fair share, and who consequently have no say in the decision. A brother, guilty that he had better educational opportunities than his siblings, repeatedly pays off his sister's credit card debt—even as he dislikes the way she implies that he owes her. A businessman jets half a dozen neighbors to his home in a warm climate to give them a vacation they cannot afford; he feels beneficent. While grateful, they feel small and weird. Kind of like they've just received charity from a feudal lord.

2   no topic sentence

examples of problem defined in thesis

The evidence of stress is not just anecdotal. Research suggests that people indeed feel worse as disparity increases. An abstract in the *British Journal of Psychiatry* succinctly sums up a global overview: "Greater income inequality is associated with higher prevalence of mental illness and drug misuse in rich societies. There are threefold differences in the proportion of the population suffering from mental illness between more and less equal countries. This relationship is most likely mediated by the impact of inequality on the quality of social relationships and the scale of status differentiation in different societies."

3   topic sentence

In other words, people feel generally worse about themselves the more they feel they earn less and have lower social rank than those around them. The term "relative deprivation," used in other disparity studies, applies. We are acutely sensitive to slight differences of status, and the wider the income gap grows, the more people experience relative deprivation, even if by objective measures they have more than enough. Dissonance emerges between what people know (I have plenty) and what they feel (I don't have as much as he does). That breeds first envy or resentment, and then shame. And when many people feel relatively deprived, and a few feel on top of the heap, not only do real interests diverge, but interpersonal tensions increase. The sibling with children in private school, and the one who can't afford it, no longer have the same stake in passing the budget override to fund local public schools. And, at Thanksgiving dinner, that conversation about taxes can quickly go south.

4   topic sentence

Conversely, when people feel more equal, they feel happier and closer. For the past few years, I've been interviewing fishermen and their families on a Maine island, and over and over I've heard islanders utter more or less the same words. (I'm offering a composite here.) "We had little when we were growing up. But, you know, it didn't matter. We had a good

5   topic sentence

time." Why? I ask. Well, . . . really—I get told repeatedly—I think it was because everybody was in the same boat.

examples to support topic sentence of previous paragraph

Gradually I caught on. My interviewees knew that they could deal   6
with backbreaking work and the tough times because they felt they were in it together with everyone else. Or, as one woman observed, "We didn't know we were poor until I grew up and then I was like, 'Wow we were poor!'" No one earned much. Everyone pitched in to help when someone was slammed.

Meanwhile, in suburban and city worlds many people have siblings or friends who go into finance, or start a business, or join a lucrative law   7
firm. And even if other siblings do well and become firemen, plumbers, teachers or architects, or even pediatricians and public defenders, the income differences, decade by decade, just keep growing. And the

topic sentence

ones who don't make it into the top 1 percent, or 10 percent, just keep finding it harder not to feel one down, their labors subtly—or not so subtly—devalued.

topic sentence

We're unsure just how to traverse this new terrain. Years ago, visiting   8
Ghana, I heard stories about how, when families became more affluent, they added rooms to their houses for their relatives. But that seems not to be our way. Here owners of McMansions tend to favor empty rooms over poor kin. So, too, with friendship. True or not, our national myths suggest that the ambitious, like Jay Gatsby, know to leave old ties behind as they jump aboard the passing yacht and begin their journeys toward "crazy" rich.

examples to support topic sentence of previous paragraph

Meanwhile, I hear stories of friends who stop traveling together   9
because the luxury one pair takes for granted is out of reach of the others. Or of dinners where the wealthiest friend picks up the check while everyone else looks at his/her sneakers. Or of extended families whose Christmas celebrations seem modest to some and like a nightmare of materialist extravagance to others. Or of kids' birthday parties when the mom who bakes cupcakes and makes a piñata feels like a chump beside her children's friends' parents who hire caterers and entertainers. Meanwhile, she implies that "homemade" is morally superior.

counterargument

In part, I'm just describing the normal discomfort that constitutes   10
adulthood. But the wealth gap has stretched us so far apart that the

summary of main point / restatement of thesis

disparities heighten negative feelings among people who would otherwise feel closer and more at ease. On the one side, there is envy, shame, inadequacy, longing, deprivation, and a sense of being left out. On the other, superiority, disdain, guilt, and a fear of being befriended or loved for all the wrong reasons. I don't know what will happen next. Some people may simply find ways to sever their awkward ties that chafe.

> But the experiences of the Maine fishermen suggest that *reducing* extremes of rich and poor would be the better way for us to go; even, perhaps, worth its weight in gold.

As you can see from the annotations, the reader has underlined some of the topic sentences and has made marginal notes about the examples. Annotations also show that some of the paragraphs support the same point. Look back at just the underlined topic sentences and the annotations. Taking a step back to look at the overall structure of the article, we might then group the paragraphs or "chunks" of text as shown in the graphic that follows, indicating the main points of paragraphs without a topic sentence.

Paragraph 1   Thesis: "As the rich have gotten massively richer, the emotional climate has deteriorated for all of us. People now routinely tell me about the impact on them of wealth gaps so yawning they threaten the bonds of affection and blood."

Paragraph 2   No clear topic sentence; this paragraph gives examples of the thesis.

Paragraph 3   "Research suggests that people indeed feel worse as disparity increases."

Paragraph 4   "In other words, people feel generally worse about themselves the more they feel they earn less and have lower social rank than those around them."

Paragraph 5   "Conversely, when people feel more equal, they feel happier and closer."

Paragraph 6   No clear topic sentence; more examples to support the point in paragraph 5.

> The author describes the problems in these paragraphs.

Paragraph 7   "[T]he income differences, decade by decade, just keep growing. And the ones who don't make it into the top 1 percent, or 10 percent, just keep finding it harder not to feel one down, their labors subtly—or not so subtly—devalued."

Paragraph 8   "We're unsure just how to traverse this new terrain."

Paragraph 9   No clear topic sentence; the implied point is that relationships break down because we don't talk openly about our differences in wealth.

> The author explores the problem more deeply in these paragraphs.

Paragraph 10   Counterargument and conclusion: It's hard when your siblings or friends make very different amounts of money.

> The author concludes and suggests how we might approach the problem.

Once we see the structure, we realize that the article follows a fairly common essay structure in which an author explains the cause(s) of a complex problem. Here, understanding the reasons for the problem—the breakdown in social relationships—is the author's primary goal. She reports on what her patients and others have told her recently and tries to work out the root cause of the problem. She is not writing a problem-solution paper; she doesn't outline a complete solution, but her final line, which includes the words "reducing extremes of rich and poor would be . . . worth its weight in gold," hints at her preference. Still, she does not explain how we might go about that difficult task, since that is not her focus.

Once we see Smith's overall structure, we can evaluate the choices she makes as a writer. Are the Maine fishing communities a good example? Do you think she should have suggested more solutions to this problem? How do the expertise and experience she brings to the subject affect the focus she chooses for this article? Does she offer enough evidence and examples to prove her points? Why does she only bring up the counterargument in the end, and then only briefly? How would you approach this topic if you were writing about it? Questions like these emerge when we take a step back and look at a reading's organizational structure. These sorts of critical-thinking questions will deepen your understanding of the material. The more you outline as a reader, the better you get at seeing the possibilities for organizing your own thoughts in writing.

practice it 14.1 Outlining as a Reader

Choose an article you have been assigned to read and, working independently or in groups, make an informal outline of it.

Step 1: Find the topic sentence of each paragraph, or figure out the main point and summarize it briefly in the margin.

Step 2: In your notes, translate your annotations into a list of the main points in the order they appear in the reading.

Step 3: Review the list to see how the author builds his or her discussion. What do you notice about the overall structure of the essay or article? Can some main points be grouped together? In other words, are some paragraphs subtopics of other paragraphs? Does the author repeat the same point with a new example? Group together any similar points and subdivide any points, as necessary.

Step 4: Make your list into a bullet-point outline to reveal the text's organizational structure.

Outlining as a Writer

For you as a writer, outlining is one of the best ways to organize your thoughts before you start writing a draft of an essay. Generally, outlining comes after you do a fair amount of pre-writing and already have a good idea about what you want to say. Most writers start with informal outlines and then, if necessary, make the informal outline into a formal one. Since you are probably familiar with formal outlines, we will begin with a review of those.

FORMAL OUTLINES

Here is a formal outline for a researched argument essay on siblings:

I. Introduction

II. Overview of Research on Advantages and Disadvantages of Siblings
   A. Advantages
      1. Sharing Resources
      2. Learning Collaboration and Competition
      3. Sharing Burden of Parents' Care When Older
   B. Disadvantages
      1. Fewer Resources per Child
         a. Parents' Time and Attention
         b. Money
      2. Sibling Rivalry

III. Overview of Research on Advantages and Disadvantages of Only Children
   A. Advantages
      1. Only Children Often Successful
      2. Only Children More Individualistic
   B. Disadvantages
      1. Possible Lack of Peer Interaction
      2. Child Behaves More Like Adult

IV. Arguments in Favor of Raising an Only Child
   A. More Attention and Financial Support
   B. Can Find Other Ways to Socialize and Collaborate
   C. Myths of Only Children Not Proven Scientifically

V. Conclusion

Another example of a formal outline would be the table of contents for this book. Flip to the front and take a look at both the brief and the full tables of contents. Though the table of contents evolved as we wrote this book, it was a constant guide to help us stay organized and on track. We kept a printed version of the full table of contents on our desks as we worked.

As you compare the student outline on siblings and the table of contents, what features do you see that they have in common?

- They include a clear plan of what will be covered in what order.
- They are neat and precise in terms of format.
- They are generally parallel—care was taken so that each point and subpoint is the same form.

Formal outlines are especially useful for longer writing projects and collaborative writing projects, where you need to clearly communicate the structure of what you are writing as you write it. Outlines like this often guide writers and give them confidence that they have enough material to flesh out their ideas.

INFORMAL OUTLINES

▶ For more on rough or informal outlines, see Chapter 3, Putting Ideas into Writing.

Despite the advantages of a nice, clear formal outline, the reality is that few writers can successfully create a formal outline while they are in the early planning stages of writing. Early in the writing process, an informal outline is much more useful. You can polish it later into a formal outline, if your audience requires one—for instance, if your instructor wants to see the fully developed structure of your intended essay or if you need to turn a research paper into a slide presentation. Indeed, the outlines that many writers use in thinking through the structure of a piece of writing are very messy. (You should see all the notes that were scribbled on our table of contents at various points!) We call these working outlines rough or informal outlines.

Outlines often start out as a bullet-point list and then are fleshed out in more detail. When you're not worrying about making points parallel, you feel more free to move them around, juggle things, and experiment with different options. This informal outlining is one of the most creative—and difficult—parts of the writing process. If you're having trouble with organization, you may want to sit down with a tutor or instructor to talk through ideas. It helps to have someone ask questions like "What would happen if you moved this here?" or "Don't you need to explain X before you make an argument about Y?" As you become a more experienced writer, you can ask these questions of yourself more and more, but even professional writers work with a fellow writer or editor during this process.

So how do you do this type of informal outlining? If you were given an essay assignment, how would you proceed?

STEP 1: **Figure out what you need or want to include in your essay.** Write down a quick bullet-point list of these ideas, referring to the essay prompt to make sure you fulfill the purpose of the assignment.

STEP 2: Think about each point on the list.   Should any points be combined or divided? Are they clear? How many paragraphs will it take to cover each point? If you think it will take more than one paragraph, can you rewrite the list so that each point corresponds to one paragraph? You will probably need to rewrite one or more of the points during this step.

STEP 3: Decide the order of your rewritten list of points.   Too often, writers tend to use the idea they brainstormed first as the first point in their paper, and that is not always the best choice. What principles, then, should guide you as you decide on an order for your points? While there is never only one "correct" way to write, the order of paragraphs in an essay is often based in part on your essay's audience and purpose. Usually, we put ideas in order in one of these ways:

Ways to Order Ideas

- From the simplest to the most complex
- From the ones your readers will agree with most easily to the ones they will need to be persuaded to accept
- From the most obvious or least interesting to the most original or most interesting
- From the ones you talk about the least to the ones you talk about the most
- In chronological order (the order in which they happen or happened), if applicable

---

Depending on your audience and purpose, you may want to begin with simple information and then build toward complex evidence and ideas. This works well with an audience that is unfamiliar with your topic. If your purpose is to persuade, you might begin with paragraphs that readers are most likely to agree with before hitting them with controversial points.

Now, let's create a sample informal outline. Imagine you are planning to write an essay about how financial literacy can lead to financial stability and your audience is young adults. You have brainstormed the points in the following list, and you plan to write one full paragraph on each idea:

- How to become financially literate
- The costs of not being financially literate
- The importance of financial literacy and how it can lead to financial stability
- What does *financial literacy* mean?

In what order would you put these ideas for this audience and purpose? It would make the most sense to define *financial literacy* first, wouldn't it? In order to understand the *importance* of financial literacy or the costs of *not* being financially literate, your reader needs to first understand *what* financial literacy is. Since your overall point is to show how financial literacy can lead to financial stability and your audience is young adults who may not have much experience with either financial literacy or its potential benefits, you might organize like this:

1. What does *financial literacy* mean?
2. The importance of financial literacy and how it can lead to financial stability
3. The costs of not being financially literate
4. How to become financially literate

What other ways are there to reorganize these topics? Would you reorganize them differently if you were arguing why schools should teach financial literacy? Why or why not? Considering the organization of your ideas is an important way to strengthen their logic and make your point really hit home.

> ### practice it 14.2   Outlining as a Writer
>
> Go through the preceding steps to make an informal outline for your next essay assignment. As you try to decide on the order of the information, outline it in two different ways. Show both options to a peer or your instructor, and talk them through the pros and cons of each possible organizational structure.

Two Commonly Assigned Essay Structures

▶ **For more on common essay structures, see Chapter 8, Rhetorical Patterns in Reading and Writing. For more on structuring an argument paper, see Chapter 12, Argument.**

Sometimes, especially on timed essays and final exams, the assignment is to write an entire essay in one rhetorical mode or with a set structure. When instructors give these sorts of assignments, they expect you to use certain organizational structures. For instance, in a problem-solution paper, you are usually expected to outline various solutions, argue why yours is the best solution, and explain what's wrong with other people's solutions. Although some assignments might be flexible, there is wisdom in the idea that you need to know the "rules" before you break them. So let's take a look at some common essay structures that can help you organize your writing.

COMPARE AND CONTRAST ESSAYS

The compare and contrast essay is a classic college assignment, and there are a few different ways you can structure such a paper, based on the type of information you plan to include. Each structure begins with an introduction and ends with a conclusion, but the content in the body paragraphs differs.

Point-by-Point Structure.   If you are comparing and contrasting two very similar things, use a point-by-point structure because you can then do the comparing and contrasting right there in each body paragraph. For instance, if you compare and contrast regular college classes with online college classes in order, ultimately, to argue which one is better, you might structure your paper according to key features of education, which you would evaluate. The following sample outline is for a student essay that focuses on the classroom activities, the student-class fit, the data on student performance, and the potential for collaboration in each type of class:

---

1. Introduction

2. What types of activities can be offered in each type of class?
   A. Details about regular class
   B. Details about online class
   C. Discuss the similarities and differences

3. Which types of students do well in each type of class?
   A. Details about regular class
   B. Details about online class
   C. Discuss the similarities and differences

4. How well does each type of class increase individual student performance?
   A. Details about regular class
   B. Details about online class
   C. Discuss the similarities and differences

5. How well does each type of class foster collaborative learning?
   A. Details about regular class
   B. Details about online class
   C. Discuss the similarities and differences

6. Conclusion

This outline clearly follows a formula, and we encourage you to use it only as a starting point in your writing. The format works well for this topic because, generally, you have the same kinds of things to say, and the same kinds of questions to ask, about online classes as you do about regular classes. The benefit of this structure is that you do the comparing and contrasting right in each body paragraph, so you are certain to do it.

Similarities and Differences Structure.   If you are writing about more of an "apples and oranges" topic, comparing and contrasting two very different things, the point-by-point structure outlined previously probably won't work. For instance, imagine you are writing an essay comparing and contrasting taking a class in the summer and getting a summer job. These two options have different features, advantages, and disadvantages, and trying to force them into the preceding structure might not work. Your first step is, of course, to brainstorm your ideas about each option. Then you have a couple of different ways to structure the essay.

The first possible structure is the similarities and differences approach. Your essay will look something like this if you want to emphasize the differences between the two options:

1. Introduction
2. Similarities between the two options
3. Differences between the two options
4. Conclusion, often where you take a position on which option is best

The same type of essay will look like this if you want to emphasize the similarities:

1. Introduction
2. Differences between the two options
3. Similarities between the two options
4. Conclusion, often where you take a position on which option is best

As you might expect, the information that comes later in the essay carries more weight, so if you want to emphasize similarities, put those last; if you want to emphasize differences, put those last. Either structure could work well for an essay four paragraphs or longer. It's fine to have one paragraph on similarities and two or three on differences: Allow the number of genuine ideas you have to dictate the length. It's comforting, though, to be familiar with some of the more basic structures when you write under pressure, as in a timed essay situation or a final exam.

Subject-by-Subject Structure.   Another type of compare-contrast structure, one that is the most difficult to do well, is the subject-by-subject
method. Let's take the same essay topic from the previous example: writing an essay comparing and contrasting taking a class in the summer and
getting a summer job. You might structure your essay like this:

1. Introduction
2. Working during the summer
3. Taking classes during the summer
4. Conclusion

This may seem like the easiest way to structure a compare and contrast essay, but what often happens is that you describe one topic, then
describe another topic, and you never really compare and contrast
them. In this essay structure, you must do significant writing in the
conclusion to discuss the similarities and differences thoroughly. Such
a conclusion will often become longer than the body paragraphs themselves. Whenever possible, choose one of the other options, even
though this structure appears to be easier. Remember, looks can
be deceiving!

▶ For more on compare
and contrast, see
Chapter 8, Rhetorical
Patterns in Reading and
Writing.

CAUSE AND EFFECT ESSAYS

If you're the type of person who always wonders why things happen the
way they do, you will enjoy writing cause and effect essays in college.
Such assignments ask you to dig deep and figure out why things have
happened or evaluate the effects of various possible scenarios. Cause
and effect thinking is the core of problem solving, so, like the problem-
solution paper, this type of essay helps you develop key critical-thinking
skills that you will need on the job and in the world.

While brainstorming for causes and brainstorming for effects tend
to go hand in hand, often the essays you produce based on that brainstorming emphasize cause more than effect—or vice versa. A history professor, for example, might ask you to write an essay in which you identify
and describe the *effect* of the Boston Tea Party of 1773, in which case you
would talk about the Tea Party's role in the American Revolution. However, the professor might ask you to write an essay about the *cause* of the
Boston Tea Party; here, you would talk about the fact that the British
government passed the Tea Act, which unfairly taxed the American colo-
nists. In either essay, you would need to be sure that you did not merely
cover the most obvious causes or effects, but also did your research and
discovered any hidden causes or effects.

In structuring an essay about the *effects* of something, you might use
the format on page 304 as a starting place.

1. Introduction
2. Describe the event or topic in detail
3. Explain effect 1, including what the effect was, why it happened, and its significance
4. Explain effect 2, including what the effect was, why it happened, and its significance (Repeat as necessary for as many effects as you have)
5. Conclusion

Generally, in listing the effects, you would put them in some logical order. You might list them chronologically, or in order of most obvious effect to least obvious effect. You might also list them in order of least significant to most significant. Think of it this way: Save your best ideas for last, so your reader isn't disappointed. If you reveal your most interesting or original effect first, then the other paragraphs will be a disappointment for your reader.

In structuring an essay about the *causes* of something, you might use a similar format:

1. Introduction
2. Describe the event or topic in detail
3. Explain reason 1 (cause 1), for why the event happened the way it did
4. Explain reason 2 (cause 2), for why the event happened the way it did (Repeat as necessary for as many reasons as you have)
5. Conclusion

Again, especially with causes, you should give significant thought to the deeper or hidden causes and order your points well. Do not assume that just because two things happen at the same time, one caused the other. Nor can you assume that the most obvious reason for something is the most important.

For instance, if you try to work out why your best friend is always broke, you might jump to the obvious conclusion that he's always broke because he doesn't have a job. Sure, that's an important reason, but push your thinking further: Why doesn't he have a job? Maybe it's because the economy is bad and he couldn't find one despite lots of work on his résumé and interview skills. Or maybe it's because he doesn't want a job and hasn't tried to find one because he believes his parents should still provide for him. While the obvious cause—not having a job—is the immediate reason he's broke, if you want to help him change the situation, address the deeper, hidden cause: that his values and beliefs don't line up with getting a job.

▶ **For more on cause and effect, see Chapter 8, Rhetorical Patterns in Reading and Writing.**

practice it 14.3   Sample Structures for Problem-Solution Papers

One common type of paper you may be asked to write in college is the problem-solution paper. You might focus more on the problem, more on the solution(s), or equally on both problem and solution. Using the sample structures for the compare and contrast and cause and effect papers as examples, make sample generic outlines for problem-solution papers. Try to come up with as many possible structures as you can, and then evaluate them.

Outlining Your Own Rough Draft

Despite our best intentions, sometimes our rough drafts suffer from serious organizational problems. Fortunately, the strategy for outlining a reading that you learned at the beginning of this chapter can also be applied to your own rough draft! If your draft is disorganized, stepping back from it and doing your own "reverse outline" reveals ways to make substantial revisions to the essay's structure. Go through the essay, paragraph by paragraph, asking yourself, what does this paragraph accomplish? Don't ask yourself, what did I intend for this paragraph to accomplish? Stick to the facts. What did you actually accomplish? Write nutshell summaries in the margins as you go, and then type up the points in a list. Play around with the list, reordering the information in a way that makes sense. Then return to your draft, and copy and paste the old material into a new document in the new order. You may be surprised that a complete restructuring of the essay isn't as time-consuming as it sounds and can produce huge rewards in terms of the overall quality of your work.

practice it 14.4   Reverse Outlines

Make a reverse outline of a rough draft of a paper you are working on or have recently finished. You can do this on a computer by inserting comment boxes, but most people prefer to work by hand. Remember as you create the reverse outline that your paragraphs might not be unified—which could be one of your problems. So don't just assume every paragraph only covers one topic. Perhaps one paragraph includes topics A and B; another paragraph includes topics B, C, and D; and a third paragraph includes material related to topics A and C. In such a case—not uncommon in a rough draft—a major reorganization greatly improves the paper without much significant new material being added.

Transitions

Good writing flows. This means that the reader can easily follow the organization of the piece as the author transitions from one idea or point to the next. Well-placed transitions not only give your essay a good flow, but also help you make your point by indicating how one idea relates to another. You should pay attention to transitions while you draft, of course. However, most writers also make extensive improvements to their transitions during the revision and editing stages. In other words, don't feel you have to make your transitions perfect the first time. Writing, after all, is all about revision.

TRANSITIONAL WORDS AND EXPRESSIONS

Within your paragraph, use transition words or phrases to show how your information is connected. You can also begin a paragraph with a transition word to reveal how that paragraph's ideas or points grew out of the previous paragraph. Transition words can show contrast between ideas, cause and effect, or compare and contrast. Within a paragraph, they are useful to introduce examples, to indicate meaning, or to outline a sequence of events or a time line. Here's an example of a paragraph you just read with the transitional expressions highlighted:

> Good writing flows. This means that the reader can easily follow the organization of the piece as the author transitions from one idea or point to the next. Well-placed transitions not only give your essay a good flow, but also help you make your point by indicating how one idea relates to another. You should pay attention to transitions while you draft, of course. However, most writers also make extensive improvements to their transitions during the revision and editing stages. In other words, don't feel you have to make your transitions perfect the first time. Writing, after all, is all about revision.

COMMON TRANSITION WORDS

To show contrast	To show cause-effect	To give examples
but	as a result	for example
however	because	to illustrate
on the contrary	consequently	for instance
on the other hand	due to	specifically
still	since	
yet	therefore	

To compare	To show meaning	To concede a point
despite	of course	although
like	in other words	even though
nevertheless	that is	though
similarly	therefore	whereas
still		while

To show additional meaning	To show sequence
in addition	after
furthermore	before
this too	finally
	now
	then
	first
	next

practice it 14.5 Transition Words

In the excerpt from *Curious* (Chapter 24), Ian Leslie begins his paragraphs with transitions, showing the reader how one paragraph or idea relates to another. Scan the first four paragraphs of the text on pages 449–50 and circle the transition words. Which types of transition words does he use? How do they help the reader follow his points and interpret the information?

TRANSITIONS FROM PARAGRAPH TO PARAGRAPH

Sometimes transitional words and phrases don't provide enough information to show how you are getting from one idea to the next. Be careful not to overuse transition words instead of thinking through the connections between ideas more thoroughly. If a word or phrase like *in addition*, *for example*, or *on the one hand* appears at the start of every single sentence in a paragraph, you are probably overusing transitional words and phrases, expecting them to do more than they are capable of doing to guide the reader through your ideas.

Instead of just throwing in a transitional word here and there, use more substantive transitions, up to a sentence or two long. Such transitional sentences—or even, in a very long work, a short transitional paragraph—use repeated words or synonyms to connect for the reader one idea to the next. In this way, they show the reader the connections between two ideas. Take a look at this excerpt from "Teach Your Children the Building Blocks of Finance" by Sherie Holder and Kenneth Meeks:

> **Plant the seeds of entrepreneurship.** Not all children receive weekly allowances. When Angelina and Marvin Lipford, of Hampton, Virginia, were married twenty years ago, they entered into their marriage carting around $15,000 to $20,000 worth of credit card and student loan debt. They spent the first five years of their marriage paying off the debt along with the accompanying high interest rates. The couple was determined to keep their three children from falling into the same trap.
>
> Knowing the financial sacrifices they had to make early in their marriage, the Lipfords are making sure their three children keep a tight rein on their finances and avoid the same pitfalls. They have an eighteen-year-old daughter, Jasmine, who is attending Howard University on a basketball scholarship; a fifteen-year-old son, Marvin Jr., who is a sophomore in high school; and a nine-year-old, Nehemiah. A natural progression in teaching their children the building blocks of finances was to encourage their children to either work, as Jasmine had done before going to college, or to start their own business. Instead of giving their children allowances, the Lipfords encouraged them to earn their own money by doing chores around the house. It was on a pay-per-work arrangement. And if the children asked their parents for additional money, they were required to pay their parents back with interest.
>
> This arrangement encouraged Marvin Jr. to earn money on his own. In 2002, he took the financial and entrepreneurial lessons he learned from attending a weeklong financial camp to cut grass during the summer months using his father's lawn mower. This past summer, he charged $20 a yard and earned $1,000, which he put into his savings account.

Transition from poor financial management to teaching their children successful financial management

Refers back to the arrangement described in paragraph 2

The repetition of ideas forms a bridge from one paragraph to another, so we see that the decision Angelina and Marvin made in how to raise Jasmine, Marvin Jr., and Nehemiah grew out of the couple's experience early in their marriage and then came full circle when Marvin Jr. made different financial choices from his parents. The repetition encourages us to see the cause-effect connections, in this case, without even using words like *cause* and *effect*. Such repetition of key ideas, concepts, and even words and phrases makes logical connections for your readers: problem to solution, comparison to contrast, or cause to effect, to name a few.

SEQUENCING TRANSITIONS

When you describe events that take place over a period of time, transitions need to be especially clear so that the reader can follow the ideas. For instance, process writing, such as step-by-step instructions, uses sequencing transitions because the reader needs to keep track of where he or she is in the process. Words like *first*, *next*, and *finally* serve well, but most readers will need additional transitions. Authors of process writing, in fact, use a significant number of transitional expressions, as you can see in this excerpt from the article "Influence of Licensed Characters on Children's Taste and Snack Preferences," published in 2010 in *Pediatrics*, a journal for pediatricians. This passage describes an experiment in which the investigators, Christina Roberto et al., tried to determine if children would choose snack foods in packages with licensed cartoon characters (such as Scooby-Doo, Dora the Explorer, and Shrek) over other foods. Transitional words and phrases are highlighted.

> Each participant sat at a table across from the investigator, who began by saying "I am going to give you 2 foods to taste." The child was then presented with 2 samples of 1 of 3 food products. The 3 different food items were presented to each child in a randomized order, and the 3 licensed characters and 3 foods were paired randomly for each child. Therefore, participants were exposed to all 3 food conditions and all 3 characters but not in the same order or combination. Throughout the procedure, children could view only the food item they were currently evaluating.
>
> The investigator placed the 2 food items on paper plates in front of the child and said, "I'd like you to take a bit of this food," pointing to one side of the table. The side of the table that was pointed to first was alternated, as was the side for the licensed-character sample. Next, the investigator pointed to the other sample on the table and said, "Now take a bite of this food." After the child finished tasting the 2 samples, the investigator asked the child, "Tell me if they taste the same to you, or point to the food that tastes the best to you." After recording the child's response, the investigator placed a smiley-face Likert scale, as a secondary measure of taste preference, in front of the child and asked, while pointing to one side of the tray, "How much do you like the way this food tastes? Do you love it, like it, it's OK, you don't like it, or you hate it?" After the child gave an answer, the investigator asked him or her to rate the taste of the other food sample by using the Likert scale. Next, the investigator asked, "If you had to pick one of these 2 foods for a snack, which one would you pick?" After the child's responses were recorded, the investigator repeated the procedure for the remaining food pairs. At the end of the study, the investigator presented the child with images of Scooby-Doo, Dora, and Shrek and asked the child to identify the characters and to rate how much he or she liked each character, by using the smiley-face Likert scale.

You can see that the writers use some transitional expressions—like *next* and *then*—but more often, the transitions are longer and convey some real information. One action happened after another action. This helps the reader visualize what happened during the experiment, as if he or she were there. Remember, transitions don't just flow magically from your pen as you write the first draft. Transitions need a lot of attention during revising and editing, as they are usually some of the roughest spots in a draft.

practice it 14.6 Identifying Transitions

Take out an essay you are currently drafting or a finished piece. Highlight all the transitional words and phrases you find. What did you discover? Did you use adequate transitions? Did you repeat the same words? What could you do to improve? If you are currently revising the essay, work on all the transitions to make them clearer.

chapter review

In the following chart, begin by filling in the second column to record in your own words the important skills included in this chapter. Then assess yourself to determine whether you are still developing the skill or feel you have mastered it. If you are still developing the skill, make some notes about what you need to work on to master it in the future. If you believe you have mastered it, explain why.

Skills and concepts covered in this chapter	Explanation in your own words	I'm developing this skill and need to work on . . .	I feel I have mastered this skill because . . .
Outlining			
Using formal versus informal outlines			
Structuring a compare and contrast essay			
Structuring a cause and effect essay			
Making a reverse outline			
Creating effective transitions			

15
Drafting

in this chapter

- What Is a Rough Draft?
- How Do You Write a Rough Draft?
- What Is the Public First Draft?

Sitting in front of a blank computer screen or a blank piece of paper trying to write a perfect first draft would make anyone unhappy. That's why writers don't do it much, if at all. Successful writers—and college students in a writer's mind-set—do loads of reading and pre-writing to get the ideas flowing. By the time a writer gets to the drafting stage, he or she has already written pages of notes, ideas, freewrites, outlines, and perhaps even a thesis and topic sentences. The rough draft is just an extension of all that thinking.

You'll get the best results if you think of the rough draft as taking at least two stages: First, you write a very rough draft, just to get something on the page. Then you revise that first draft, asking yourself important questions, such as whether your draft responds to the assignment given and whether your thesis is clear. That revised first draft will be your public first draft, the one you show your first readers.

There are going to be times when you're having difficulty, and some concrete strategies for getting started writing can be very helpful. This chapter gives you strategies for getting those first sentences on paper and then shaping them into something you might be willing to share as a rough draft.

LaunchPad Solo
macmillan learning

Visit **LaunchPad Solo for Readers and Writers > Drafting** for extra practice in the skills covered in this chapter.

▶ **For more on pre-writing, see pages 190–93 in Chapter 7, Audience, Purpose, and Topic, and Chapter 10, Pre-Writing. You can't start writing without some ideas to write about.**

Writing the Very Rough Draft

Writer Anne Lamott has a quote that writers love: "For me and most of the other writers I know, writing is not rapturous. In fact, the only way I can get anything written at all is to write really, really shitty first drafts." We should all listen to Anne Lamott. Getting rid of the idea that the rough draft should be perfect is crucial to writing. While you write that first rough, rough draft, don't erase or delete anything. Don't censor yourself. Too often, student writers judge themselves too harshly, think every word they write is wrong, and spend more time erasing than thinking about what they want to say. If you are stuck on the rough draft, sitting in front of a blank piece of paper with a mind that feels even more blank, try one of the following strategies so you can just get started.

EXPLORATORY DRAFTS

Some people work best when they take away all the pressure of having to write a perfect first draft. If that's you, then give yourself permission to write an exploratory or idea draft and be willing to throw much of it away. Here's how.

STEP 1: Open a new document or get a blank piece of paper.

STEP 2: Read over your outline, your notes, and your working thesis.   If you have a thesis already, put that at the top of the page. If not, put your best idea at the top, or choose one quote or idea from the readings that really speaks to you.

STEP 3: Put your notes away and write a "quick, throwaway draft."   Don't make corrections or stop to make anything perfect. Think of this draft as almost freewriting, but try to stay focused on your topic and thesis. Get all your ideas down on paper as quickly as you can. Don't spend more than a half hour on this draft. (If you spend more time, you won't be willing to throw it away.)

STEP 4: Take a short break.

STEP 5: Go back and read what you have written.   Compare it to your outline. What's usable? Can you cut and paste some paragraphs into the points on your outline? Save what's good and use it to build your confidence to start the first public rough draft in a more careful way. Chances are good that you will find you do have something to say.

EVIDENCE DRAFTS

Other people work best when they start with the source material, support, and examples. If this strategy sounds like it might work for you, begin by writing up your sources or examples and write your way around them. Here's how to start.

STEP 1: Type up your outline.

STEP 2: Find all the quotes or examples that you want to use in the paper and type them up under the relevant point in the outline. Don't forget to include the source information and page number (if there is one).

STEP 3: Now, write a sentence or two after each quote or example to explain how it supports that particular point.

STEP 4: Save, print, and read what you've written. (If you write by hand, type up what you have written so far. Double-check that you are accurately typing all quotations.) Reread all you have accomplished so far. You have probably written half the draft just by typing up your examples and supporting points.

STEP 5: Go back to the beginning of the document and fill in the gaps until you have fleshed-out body paragraphs. Review the strategies in Chapter 13, Topic Sentences and Paragraphs, for help here.

STEP 6: Finally, add an introduction and conclusion. Write down what interested you in the topic, and begin with that as your hook. Then think about the final thoughts you want to leave your reader with, and include these in your conclusion.

CONVERSATION DRAFTS

Some writers know what they want to say and just need to get their ideas down on paper without worrying about how their ideas fit with sources. If that's you, then think of the rough draft as a conversation you are having and write down all the things you want to say in the draft. Here's how.

STEP 1: Imagine you are explaining your ideas to a friend. Imagine your friend is asking you questions about your topic and you are answering them. (If you have a friend who is willing to help you, ask him or her to take notes on what you say as you speak your way through the following steps.)

STEP 2: Write down all the questions your friend would ask. Don't worry about the exact wording, since you're going to be changing it later anyway.

STEP 3: Under each question, fill in your answers. Write just like you would talk. Don't worry about making it sound like a college paper right now.

STEP 4: Type up this conversation. As you type, you might discover that you are rewriting as you go, making it sound more like an essay and

TIP

Some writers actually start off by recording themselves talking out their ideas. Then they play back the recording and type it up. Check your smartphone or computer to see if it has a voice recorder you can use for this purpose.

less like people talking. Or you might just type it up as is; that's fine too.

STEP 5: Read what you have written.   Think about the strengths and weaknesses of the ideas and the organization; don't worry yet about sentence-level concerns.

STEP 6: Make an outline based on what you have on the paper, leaving room to add or subtract major points, if necessary.

STEP 7: Read over all the other notes that you made for the paper earlier in the writing process, and reread the essay assignment to make sure you're on track.

STEP 8: Write your very rough draft based on the conversation notes, your outline, and your other notes.   Make it as complete and clear as possible, but do not worry about how it sounds, since you will revise it later.

---

practice it 15.1   Writing a Rough Draft

Choose one of the three strategies just outlined and write a very rough draft of your current essay project. Then let it sit for a day or two—or at least a couple of hours. Then reread it, and identify three or four things you did well. Forget about the weaknesses for the moment. Concentrate on your strengths. Hopefully, you'll be ready to work on making that very rough draft into something you might, possibly, be eager to show your peer group or your instructor.

Writing the Public First Draft

What do you need to do to your rough draft to make it suitable for that first round of peer review? Most writers ask themselves the following questions to make a solid public first draft.

After answering these questions and scribbling notes on your rough, rough draft, rewrite it into the first public draft. Read it over a few times, make the changes you need to, and get ready for peer review. At this point in the writing process, you will probably have some specific questions about your paper, such as "Does my thesis make sense?" or "Is it okay to use that example in paragraph four?" Go ahead and jot down the questions you have so that you can remember to ask your peer reviewers or your instructor.

rough draft checklist

☐ **Have I finished the draft?** Are all the points and examples that you can think of right now actually in the draft somewhere? Check your outline to see if you included all your points. If not, make a list directly on the paper where you wish to include more ideas.

☐ **Does the draft change its topic, focus, or thesis?** If the draft shifts topic, focus, or thesis, think about in what direction you want to take the draft, and adjust the draft so that it is coherent—in other words, change the thesis, points, or evidence as necessary so that the paper sticks to the same topic, focus, and thesis. (This happens more often than you might expect; we think we want to write about one topic, but as we write without censoring ourselves, another, more interesting topic or thesis emerges. Go with it!)

☐ **Does the essay as it is fit the assignment and address all parts of the prompt?** Are there some expectations in the assignment (about source material, type of writing, or anything else) that you need to meet? Reread the essay prompt and adjust the paper to fit it if necessary.

☐ **Have I included a complete introduction and conclusion?** Many writers write their introduction after the body, which is fine so long as you remember to do it. Write a conclusion too, even though it may be difficult at this early stage in your essay. No one will hold you to it.

☐ **Is the essay divided into paragraphs in a sensible way?** If you forgot to break it up into paragraphs, do so as you make the rough, rough draft into a public first draft.

chapter review

In the following chart, fill in the second column to record in your own words the important skills included in this chapter. Then assess yourself to determine whether you are still developing the skill or feel you have mastered it. If you are still developing the skill, make some notes about what you need to work on to master it in the future. If you believe you have already mastered it, explain why.

Skills and concepts covered in this chapter	Explanation in your own words	I'm developing this skill and need to work on . . .	I believe I have mastered this skill because . . .
Writing exploratory drafts			
Writing evidence drafts			
Writing conversation drafts			
Writing a public first draft			

16

Introductions and Conclusions

Introductions and conclusions are like the bookends around your essay. They give the first and last impressions, and they get and keep your reader interested in what you have to say. In the simplest terms, the purpose of the introduction is to set the scene for your main points, and the purpose of the conclusion is to reinforce why your ideas are relevant or important. It's usually easiest to write the introduction and conclusion if you think about what motivated you to choose the topic or focus of the paper. Even if your instructor assigned a particular topic, your paper differs from everyone else's, right? Think about what most interests you, whether it is a particular anecdote, a burning question you have, or simply a statistic that amazes you. Then share that interesting idea to introduce your ideas to your reader, and build on that idea to conclude the paper.

You may know people who like to write their introductions last. These are usually experienced writers or people who write many, many drafts of a paper and are very open to revising their ideas. This can lead to wonderful essays, but it usually takes more time. Beginning writers or writers with a deadline usually do better with a little more structure to the writing process. Try writing an introduction paragraph as you write the rough draft. You can always change it later.

Introductions

Introductions are as important in writing as they are in life. Readers pick up an article or book, read the first couple of lines or paragraphs, and then decide whether or not they want to continue. To make your

▶ If you have a thesis but aren't confident about it, see Chapter 11, Thesis and Main Idea.

readers care about your writing, you have to grab their attention and keep it. In an essay, the introduction is the place to get their attention. The good news is that you probably already have what you need to write a good introduction. You know what you're talking about—your topic and thesis. If you don't have a good sense of your topic and some idea about a thesis, you're not ready to write your introduction or conclusion. Thesis development is a major part of the pre-writing process, so look back at Chapter 3, Putting Ideas into Writing.

There are four elements to an introduction.

Elements of an Introduction

1. The hook grabs the reader's attention.
2. The topic is what the paper is about.
3. Background information gives the reader context for the topic.
4. The thesis states your position or main idea about the topic.

Let's look at an example of an introduction for a student paper about young people and voting:

> As many studies have proven, only about one-third of American youth aged eighteen to twenty-two usually vote in presidential elections. Voter apathy among young Americans is a problem in America today. Issues such as college funding, abortion laws, military recruitment, and even taxes and global warming affect young people. Voting rates among young people have not always been so low. Young people give a variety of reasons for why they don't care about politics, ranging from lack of education about the issues to not knowing how to register to vote. Martin P. Wattenberg discusses some of these reasons in his book *Is Voting for Young People? With a Postscript on Citizen Engagement* (2007). He explains why young people don't vote and how it is undermining our democracy. Young people need to take the responsibility to educate themselves about the issues and to vote, or else they will have to live with the laws that older people make for them.

This introduction is a good-sized paragraph that gives real information: It's not just a couple of sentences stuck on at the beginning of an essay to please the instructor. It sets up the paper so the writer can say something meaningful. This paragraph has a clear hook, a clear topic, background information, and a strong thesis. They are color-coded below so you can identify them and see how they fit together.

Hook

As many studies have proven, only about one-third of American youth aged eighteen to twenty-two usually vote in presidential elections. Voter apathy among young Americans is a problem in America today. Issues such as college funding, abortion laws, military recruitment, and even taxes and global warming affect young people. Voting rates among young people have not always been so low. Young people give a variety of reasons for why they don't care about politics, ranging from lack of education about the issues to not knowing how to register to vote. Martin P. Wattenberg discusses some of these reasons in his book *Is Voting for Young People? With a Postscript on Citizen Engagement* (2007). He explains why young people don't vote and how it is undermining our democracy. Young people need to take the responsibility to educate themselves about the issues and to vote, or else they will have to live with the laws that older people make for them.

Statement of topic

Background information

Thesis

If you have trouble seeing the difference between the parts, ask your instructor for help. With practice, you will get better at identifying the parts—and therefore making sure your own introductions are complete.

---

practice it 16. 1   Evaluating Introductions

Look at the essays by professional writers that you have read so far, and determine where their introduction begins and ends. (In a short college paper, the introduction is usually one paragraph, but in longer pieces, the introduction is often more than one paragraph.) What sorts of strategies do they use to gain your interest? Choose the introduction you like best and list the reasons you like it. Next, choose the one you like least and list the reasons you don't like it. What can you learn from these examples to improve your own introductions?

THE HOOK

The hook is what interests the reader in your writing, whether that reader is your instructor, with a stack of thirty papers in front of her; a scholarship or job application committee; or someone just curious about what you have to say. Hooks are one of the most fun things to write because you get to be a little creative. You can think like an advertising executive or a storyteller, even in the most formal research paper.

Also called an "attention grabber" or "dramatic opening," the hook can take many forms. It can be a short sentence or several sentences. The hook can be emotional (provoking laughs, tears, or shock in readers), or it can appeal to readers' logic and reason or their ethics, their sense of right and wrong. To get started, think about what made you interested in the topic in the first place. If you were assigned the topic, why did you choose this particular approach to it? What about the topic sparks your curiosity? Most likely, you can develop a well-written hook based on

TIP

Sometimes you are assigned to write on a topic that doesn't interest you. Instead of focusing on the fact that you don't like the subject, find a way to get curious about it. Ask good questions. Get your brain going. Successful writers can make any topic interesting and can see the significance of topics where it might not be obvious.

whatever drew you into the topic. What quote from the course readings jumped out at you? What question did you find yourself asking? What story from your personal experience illustrates the topic well? Trust your own instincts. Good writing comes from having something to say. To write an effective hook, you can use one of the following strategies.

Ways to Write an Effective Hook

- Give a statistic or fact to capture the reader's interest
- Ask a question
- Tell an anecdote, a brief interesting story
- Give a quote
- Dramatize a key idea
- Offer a provocative or unexpected comment
- Do some combination of the above

Whichever approach you take, the hook should grab your readers, fire their interest, and make them want to continue reading.

Let's look at some examples. Here's a hook that uses an interesting statistic to draw the reader into a paper on wealth:

> According to the *Money Matters on Campus* 2015 report, only "62% [of college students] check their account balances" and a small portion, 12%, "say they never check their balances because they are too nervous" (55). When they fail to do the most basic financial steps, whether through carelessness or fear, many college students are setting themselves up for financial failure while in college.

What's good about this hook is that it's not just a shocking fact about the number of college students who don't check their accounts. It also shows the reason behind the statistic and makes the reader start to ask questions, such as, "Why wouldn't they check their balances, especially when so many college students report stress over finances? Are those who don't check most likely to become overdrawn on their accounts? Are some of these students being supported by parents who will cover any overdrafts? If so, when will their parents expect them to take over the finances?" Also, this hook gives the source for the statistic through the signal phrase. This is important because you want your reader to know where you got your information and that your information is valid.

Here's another example. This time, the writer uses an anecdote (or brief story) to hook the reader into reading a paper about college student success.

When Paula Mason wanted to go to college, her parents told her to go to the mall and get a job. When her brother wanted to go to college, they paid his way to a four-year university. He dropped out and got a job as a truck driver. She worked her way through community college at night and is now a branch manager for a bank.

This hook tells a brief story related to the topic of college student success. It also prompts the reader to reflect on some "big life questions" and to wonder what happened in the rest of the story. A reader might think, "Wow! That's amazing—not what I would expect. I wonder what made Paula so successful. Maybe making your own way in life is more meaningful? Still, it must have been hard. What makes some people successful in upper-level careers and others unsuccessful? Why didn't Paula's parents expect her to go to college?" The hook did its job. It made the reader curious. The rest of the introductory paragraph will provide the paper's topic, some background information, and the thesis.

practice it 16.2   Finding the Hook

Look at the following three hooks. Read each one over a couple of times, jotting annotations on them. Then answer the following questions for each hook:

- What kind of hook is it?
- Why do you like the hook? Why is it effective?
- When could you use this sort of hook in your own writing?

From Engel's "The Case for Curiosity"
Einstein was wrong. I'm not referring to anything he said or wrote about physics but to his famous comment, "Curiosity is a delicate little plant which, aside from stimulation, stands mainly in need of freedom."

From Yuhas's "Curiosity Prepares the Brain for Better Learning"
Do we live in a holographic universe? How green is your coffee? And could drinking too much water actually kill you?

From Cramer's "Would You Quit Social Media If You Could?"
On the average weekday, I spend hours sorting through my social media feeds—mostly Facebook and Twitter. I fire up HootSuite to make this task a little easier and dutifully retweet, share, and schedule posts.

<hr>

practice it 16.3   Revising the Hook

What "hooked" you about your current writing project? List as many ideas for hooks as you can. Remember to note the source if you're taking information (like a statistic) from someone else. If you have already drafted an introduction to your paper, take a look at its hook. Are any of your new ideas better than what you already have? Rewrite your hook to make it more interesting and meaningful. You may also want to get a second or third opinion from a classmate or friend.

<hr>

THE TOPIC

▶ For help generating topics, see Chapter 7, Audience, Purpose, and Topic.

The introduction is your chance to establish your topic so that the reader doesn't assume you're trying to cover everything related to that subject. Take the topic of video games, for example. If you just write "Video games are a big part of American culture" as your topic, that's too broad. Your reader might assume you're going to discuss all types of video games—the games for children or for adults, online gaming, console gaming, handheld gaming, playing games on company time, maybe even arcade games. You know you won't include all of these, but your reader doesn't. In your introduction, be specific and clear about your topic. Remember, the topic (subject) is not the same as the thesis (your position on the topic). Your reader needs to know exactly what your topic is before he or she will be ready to read your thesis.

BACKGROUND INFORMATION

Once you've hooked the reader and stated a clear topic, you then need to provide background information. Ask yourself: What does my reader need to know about my topic? For college papers that focus on a particular book, article, or film, your background information should always include:

- the full author's name
- the full title
- the year published, if available
- a short summary of the text

Here is an example:

> Beth Kobliner's 2009 book *Get a Financial Life: Personal Finance in Your Twenties and Thirties* provides basic financial planning advice on budgeting, paying off debt, and making good long-term financial decisions.

Sometimes the necessary background information comes from a text you are reading in class, as in the preceding example. Other times, it's more generally about the concept or historical period you have been studying. In papers about a concept or historical period that is not well-known or is often misunderstood, explain it as clearly and succinctly as you can in your own words. For example, if you're writing about graffiti, you might say:

> Many people think that the word *graffiti* just refers to illegal tagging done by gangs in cities, but graffiti is created by all different types of people and is found in the suburbs and on farms as well as in cities. Actually, modern graffiti in America started in the railroad cars during the Depression and later was used by American soldiers and airmen.

This background information helps the reader who might have some sense of what *graffiti* means but might need some clarification. Since you will be going into more detail in the body of the paper, this is enough for now.

Let's look at what happens when a student doesn't provide sufficient background information in the introduction, as in the following example:

Twenty Dollars?!
Micah Yu

After many attempts to perfect an NBA game, Visual Concepts may have finally created an avid basketball fan's fantasy. The ESPN NBA series has been among the best of its kind since it entered the basketball gaming scene in 1999. Now, after battling its rival NBA Live for six consecutive years, ESPN is offering the new 2K5 at a bargain price of twenty dollars. Does this game have the features of a twenty-dollar game, or is it a gem at an amazingly low price?

Read Micah Yu's paragraph again. This time, circle all the words or phrases that you don't understand. Make a list of questions in the margins. Here's a list of some of the questions the typical reader who does not play video games might have:

What is Visual Concepts?
I know what ESPN is, but I don't get how it's a rival for NBA Live. Is that a
    show or a network?
What is the 2K5?

Imagine how confused the reader would be if he or she didn't know the answer to these questions. Here's how Micah could rewrite the paragraph, sprinkling background information in here and there so that his reader would understand the context of his topic. Added information is highlighted in yellow.

Twenty Dollars?! [Revised Introduction]

After many attempts to perfect an NBA video game based on the National Basketball Association (NBA), video game developer Visual Concepts may have finally created an avid basketball fan's fantasy. Its ESPN NBA game series has been among the best of its kind since it entered the basketball

> gaming scene in 1999. Now, after battling its rival Electronic Arts (EA) Sports' NBA Live for six consecutive years, ESPN Visual Concepts is offering the new ESPN NBA 2K5 game at a bargain price of twenty dollars. Does this game have the features of a twenty-dollar game, or is it a gem at an amazingly low price?

You may have figured out by now that background information is related to audience. A reader who knows the sports video game industry wouldn't need this information, but a general reader would.

practice it 16.4   What Background Does Your Reader Need?

What background information is needed to understand your paper? Remember to think about the audience you are trying to reach. Do you need to give them information about a reading, explain what you mean by a certain term or concept, or provide any historical, cultural, or other information? Jot down ideas in your notebook. Then take these notes and draft a sentence or two of background information that you want to add to your introduction.

practice it 16.5   Evaluating Background Information

Look at the following introduction written by a student. Does it confuse you because it does not offer sufficient background information? Does it provide too much background information? Annotate it to indicate where you think the author needs to add or cut background information. Make sure you say what the writer needs to add or why the writer needs to cut. Write down your thoughts in your notebook or in the margins.

> In our world today, having a proper education can be a make-or-break factor when considering our financial futures. It's very common to see a college graduate's salary substantially higher than that of those who have discontinued their education after high school. However, being properly educated is not the only asset that will pave your way to a more comfortable, financially stable life. Having resources and financial assistance from family or close friends can make a world of difference. Sadly, not all of us have these options and the racial wealth gap is blatant evidence. Along with helpful financial resources, financial know-how is a key necessity for being financially stable and avoiding the stress of poverty.

THE THESIS

As the central idea or claim of your essay, the thesis lets the reader know what point your essay will make. For this reason, the thesis belongs in the introduction for academic essay writing. You want readers to know exactly what you intend to discuss before you begin discussing it. If you don't have a thesis yet or you don't feel confident enough in your ideas to write one at this point, remember that thesis development is a major part of the pre-writing process, so look back at Chapter 3, Putting Ideas into Writing, or Chapter 11, Thesis and Main Idea.

The thesis differs from the topic in that the topic is the subject and the thesis is what you believe about your topic (specifically). It's important to first introduce your reader to the general topic before stating your claim about it.

Here are some thesis examples:

Elderly parents continue to get upset by their children's arguments, especially when these fights are about the parents' care.

When adult siblings argue during a family crisis, it can make it hard for the next generation of cousins to become close friends.

Adult siblings often argue when major family decisions need to be made, because stress makes them go back to the ways they acted as children.

Let's take a thesis and see how it looks at the end of a complete introduction paragraph:

The image of the huge happy family is all over television, especially during all those holiday specials. As everyone knows, most real-life families do not look like the ones on television, though. In reality, adult siblings often argue during holidays or whenever important family decisions need to be made. They fight about stupid things like who is going to make the Thanksgiving turkey, or they fight about major things like whether or not to put Grandma in a nursing home. This happens in most families, especially in families where there is not a set of cultural "rules" about who does what. But what the adults do not realize is that it's not all about them. When adult siblings argue at family get-togethers or during a family crisis, this can make it hard for the next generation of cousins to become close friends.

practice it 16.6 Finding the Parts of the Introduction

Identify the four parts of the introduction in the preceding sample introduction paragraph. Label them in the margins of your book.

> **practice it 16.7** Moving from Topic to Thesis
>
> If you don't have a thesis but think you are ready to write one now, practice moving from topic to thesis. Select an essay topic that you are writing about in your English class. Rewrite your topic in your notebook. Then draft a list of questions you could ask about the topic. Next, decide which direction you most wish to go with your paper. Finally, take some time to draft (or revise) your thesis.

If you have followed along with all the Practice It activities, you practically have an introduction already. Look at your work and put your sentences together. Feel free to tweak things, and revise as you rewrite so that transitions are smooth. You'll probably want to do this in your notebook or on your computer.

Conclusions

Once you feel confident about how you revised your introduction, review your draft conclusion. Reading and revising the introduction and conclusion at the same time makes your essay more coherent as a whole. Conclusions are often completed in a hurry: You have a deadline looming, so you slap a quick summary paragraph onto the end of the paper and call it finished. For the reader, this feels like having a burnt cookie for dessert after a fantastic meal—it's a letdown. Taking the time to brainstorm, draft, and revise the conclusion makes your whole essay more interesting and powerful. Your reader will feel that the essay finished well and will engage with your ideas. A strong conclusion can even motivate the reader to change his or her way of thinking about a topic.

Essentially, an essay's conclusion should accomplish two things:

Elements of a Conclusion

- Sum up the essay's major points.
- Make the reader care about the information you presented in the paper by offering final thoughts.

Sometimes you have to bring in new information and ideas in the conclusion in order to make the reader care, but your job as a writer is to do that without adding so much new information that it reads like a body paragraph or the beginning of another essay. You will learn to strike the right balance with practice and a little help from your peers.

SUMMING UP YOUR ESSAY

Let's start with summarizing your essay's main points, which is one of the two major purposes of the conclusion. Don't just copy your thesis or main points word for word into your conclusion. Rephrase them in a way that shows how and why they are important. In other words, restate the thesis by including all the fantastic main ideas you have just presented.

Let's look at a few examples from one of our readings. Take a look at Carol S. Dweck's article "The Perils and Promises of Praise" (pp. 6–13). We've placed her thesis and her summary statement side by side:

Thesis (from the Introduction)	Summary Statement (from the Conclusion)
"Research shows us how to praise students in ways that yield motivation and resilience. In addition, specific interventions can reverse a student's slide into failure during the vulnerable period of adolescence" (7).	"Our research shows that educators cannot hand students confidence on a silver platter by praising their intelligence. Instead, we can help them gain the tools they need to maintain their confidence in learning by keeping them focused on the *process* of achievement" (12).

What similarities do you notice? What differences? By closely comparing and contrasting the language in these two statements, you can see how to shape a strong summary statement for the conclusions. Here we have highlighted some of the similarities in the two passages:

Thesis (from the Introduction)	Summary Statement (from the Conclusion)
"Research shows us how to praise students in ways that yield motivation and resilience. In addition, specific interventions can reverse a student's slide into failure during the vulnerable period of adolescence" (7).	"Our research shows that educators cannot hand students confidence on a silver platter by praising their intelligence. Instead, we can help them gain the tools they need to maintain their confidence in learning by keeping them focused on the *process* of achievement" (12).

In the green-highlighted areas, the language is almost identical, but these are the only words that match in these passages. Clearly, Dweck wants to emphasize that her ideas are research based, not just hunches or anecdotes. In the blue-highlighted areas, Dweck is conveying one of the main points: She wants to help students become more motivated, resilient, and confident. These qualities all relate to one another, but in the conclusion, she develops the point by including the word "tools." One major point of her article is that being good at learning is itself a learned behavior. Students can learn to use the tools of learning.

Now, let's look at some of the differences between the passages. Differences are highlighted in purple:

Thesis (from the Introduction)	Summary Statement (from the Conclusion)
"Research shows us how to praise students in ways that yield motivation and resilience. In addition, specific interventions can reverse a student's slide into failure during the vulnerable period of adolescence" (7).	"Our research shows that educators cannot hand students confidence on a silver platter by praising their intelligence. Instead, we can help them gain the tools they need to maintain their confidence in learning by keeping them focused on the *process* of achievement" (12).

In the thesis, Dweck mentions "specific interventions." Then, in the conclusion, she explains what kind of interventions these are: ones that help students "[focus] on the process of achievement." These are the types of interventions that she has spent the article describing, and this phrasing sums that up nicely.

As you can see, when Dweck summarizes the main point of her essay in her conclusion, she does more than just restate the thesis. She sums up the major ideas she has covered in the body of the essay as well. She does not list each intervention, but she does mention the factor they all have in common: All the interventions emphasize "the process of achievement."

So how do you summarize the main points for your own essay? First, don't be intimidated by Dweck. She's had years of experience with this. You might start by listing all the key words you used in your essay, so you know what to include in your summary statement. You should also reread your introduction, but don't copy the thesis exactly. Instead, imagine that you have to restate your whole essay in one or two clear sentences. One way to do this is to imagine that you are explaining your essay to a person who doesn't know anything about it. What would you say? Say that out loud to a friend and ask him or her to write down what you say. Then read it over and edit it until you like the way it sounds.

PROVIDING CONTEXT AND ADDING FINAL THOUGHTS

The second important job of a conclusion is to leave your readers with the feeling that the information they just read matters. The job of the conclusion is to wrap up all the great points you made in your body paragraphs and conclude something about them; show readers why your ideas matter and what it all means. Readers need to know why they should care about what they've read. At the back of their minds, questions often lurk: "So what?" "Why should I care?" "Why does this matter to me?" (We're pretty sure you've asked these questions yourself once or twice, even while reading this book.) You don't want readers to finish your paper, put it down, say "So what?" to themselves, and forget everything they just read.

You need to answer the lingering "So what?" question in their minds. Sometimes this answer can be direct: They should care about the information in your paper because it will directly influence their lives. More often, it's indirect: They should care about the information because in some way—sometimes in an abstract way—it will influence the society they live in, the world around them, or the future. Writers often use the conclusion to offer recommendations or make predictions about the issue. They have some idea about how their topic could change society or how it might affect people in the future. This shows the context of your essay: how the topic relates to people and why they should care.

For example, let's say you are writing a paper about financial literacy. This topic has a direct and clear influence on most of us, as we have to manage our money, keep a budget, and set financial goals. It's easy for readers to see how the information matters, and your job in the conclusion may be to inspire them to act, rather than to just convince them that the topic matters. Maybe you want to push your readers to communicate better about money with their own family members by making that recommendation in your conclusion.

Imagine, though, that your essay is about something more narrowly focused, like the budget of your college. Clearly, people who attend or work at your college would care about that topic, but others might not see themselves as stakeholders. So, if you want to reach a wide audience, show in the conclusion why the issue matters. You might, for instance, show that your college is typical of a general trend going on across the country, and then explain the implications of that trend for taxpayers in general or for education as a whole. You could even go a step further and make a prediction by discussing the long-term consequences of the issue as you describe it in your paper. Maybe you could talk about what will happen to the workforce in your state if the trend you describe continues. In other words, you need to demonstrate the significance of the ideas you express in your essay, answering any lingering "So what?" questions that your readers might have.

Let's look at an example. Here again is the beginning of a paper about young people and voting.

> As many studies have proven, only about one-third of American youth aged eighteen to twenty-two usually vote in presidential elections. Voter apathy among young Americans is a problem in America today. Issues such as college funding, abortion laws, military recruitment, and even taxes and

global warming affect young people. Voting rates among young people have not always been so low. Young people give a variety of reasons for why they don't care about politics, ranging from lack of education about the issues to not knowing how to register to vote. Martin P. Wattenberg discusses some of these reasons in his book *Is Voting for Young People? With a Postscript on Citizen Engagement* (2007). He explains why young people don't vote and how it is undermining our democracy. Young people need to take the responsibility to educate themselves about the issues and to vote, or else they will have to live with the laws that older people make for them.

Now, let's imagine that we wrote out the paper's conclusion:

Clearly, young people have shown at certain times that they can be educated and involved voters. Not everyone ignores his or her responsibility or thinks that someone else will take care of it. However, the percentage of young people who make it out to the polls is still shockingly low. What if young people had a habit of voting all the time? How might our country make decisions differently? Would America be better off or worse? Whether young Americans would vote intelligently or not is not clear, but politicians would definitely have to pay more attention to issues that affect young people. One thing is clear, though: The more they take the time to vote, the more likely they are to become more educated about voting, and the more involved they will be in our democracy later in life. So getting people involved in voting when they are young does not merely influence a current election. It makes the entire country move in a positive direction over the long term. That's definitely something we can all support.

Does this conclusion work? Does it leave you feeling satisfied and full of ideas? What might you change? Why?

---

practice it 16.8   Evaluating Conclusions

Look at the essays you have read so far for this course. Reread their conclusions. Remember that for a long essay, the conclusion could be more than one paragraph. For scholarly journal articles, the conclusion is often even labeled for you as "Conclusion" or "Discussion." As you skim through a few conclusions, choose the one you like best and make a list of the reasons you like it. Choose the one that you like least and list the reasons you don't like it. What can you learn about conclusions that you can apply to your own writing?

STRATEGIES FOR WRITING STRONG CONCLUSIONS

Remember how we said that the introduction and conclusion can function as bookends around your essay? If you are stuck on how to conclude your paper, you might return to the ideas expressed in the introduction, particularly the hook. The hook makes the reader want to read your paper, and it's usually the first thing in the introductory paragraph. This strategy works well if you wrote a hook based on what "hooked" you on the paper topic. If you did, then building on that for the conclusion will likely get right to what you consider the heart of the issue. Here are a few types of hooks with their corresponding conclusion strategy:

BOOKENDING YOUR CONCLUSION AND HOOK

Type of Hook	Example	Corresponding Strategy for Conclusion	Example
statistic or fact	As many studies have proven, only about one-third of American youth aged eighteen to twenty-two usually vote in presidential elections.	Refer back to the statistic and add another, more inspiring fact.	Although only about one-third of American youth now vote, the potential for big change is there. There are many young nonvoters in America. If even half of them started to vote, we could see more turnout in local and state elections, and then make an even bigger difference in the presidential election.
anecdote (real-life or hypothetical story)	My friend Paul turned eighteen six weeks before the last election. He never registered to vote. Six months later, budget cuts forced his college to raise tuition 12 percent. He's not sure he can pay for school this year.	Finish the story in a thought-provoking or inspiring way.	Paul is managing to get more loans for this semester, but he wonders if he can continue next year. Now that his education is on the line, he makes sure to vote in all local and state elections. He realizes now how important voting is to his future.
quotation	I once saw a bumper sticker that said: "The Vote: Use It or Lose It!"	Restate the quotation in your own words, and then add a new thought.	Maybe "Use it or lose it" is a little simplistic, but it's a good start. We need to remember that we didn't always have the rights we have now, and to keep them we need to participate in politics.
question	You would never let someone tell you what to wear every day, so why would you let someone else make even bigger life decisions for you?	Answer the question.	Obviously, young people want freedom. We want freedom to dress the way we want, listen to the music we want, and be who we want. We don't vote because we don't always see the connection between voting and freedom, but once we understand it, we begin to take part.

▶ For more on peer review, see Chapter 18, Giving and Receiving Feedback.

The technique of revisiting the hook works well so long as it doesn't become too predictable or boring. Good writing offers surprises. Good writing makes the reader want to read more. Have fun with the introduction and conclusion, and use these tips and techniques as a starting point for your own creativity. When in doubt, do what all writers do: Ask your peers, instructors, friends, and family to read your work and give you feedback.

chapter review

In the following chart, fill in the second column to record in your own words the important skills included in this chapter. Then assess yourself to determine whether you are still developing the skill or feel you have mastered it. If you are still developing the skill, make some notes about what you need to work on to master it in the future. If you believe you have already mastered it, explain why.

Skills and concepts covered in this chapter	Explanation in your own words	I'm developing this skill and need to work on . . .	I believe I have mastered this skill because . . .
Understanding how hooks function			
Grabbing the reader's attention in the introduction			
Finding and writing a focused topic			
Determining relevant background information			
Finding or stating a clear thesis in the introduction			
Restating main ideas in the conclusion			
Providing context and adding final thoughts in the conclusion			

17

Quotation and Paraphrase

When you make a claim in writing, it's not enough that you believe in your position; you need to provide the evidence to support it. Quotations and paraphrases provide evidence for your points. In academic writing, quotations and paraphrases usually make up the bulk of your support in a paragraph. This chapter will help you decide when to quote and when to paraphrase and will help you integrate source material into your own writing.

- **A *quotation* is a direct copy of words from another source.** Because you want to make it clear to your reader that these words are not your own, you use quotation marks (" ") at the start and end of the quotation.

- **A *paraphrase* is your own rewording of the ideas from another source.** Because the words are your own, quotation marks are not necessary, but citation (formal acknowledgment of the original source) is necessary.

- **A *summary* is a shorter version of someone else's writing in your own words.** When you summarize, you take a whole paragraph, essay, or longer work and reduce it to its most important points, entirely in your own words. Note that paraphrase should not be confused with summary, which is used for a different purpose. The key distinction between summary and paraphrase is that in a *summary*, you restate the overall point, whereas in a *paraphrase*, you rephrase more directly the meaning of a single sentence or short passage. Usually you summarize a text to provide background information about it, often in your introductory paragraph, or when you introduce a source if you plan to refer to it extensively in your paper.

▶ **For more on finding and evaluating sources, see Chapter 21, Research.**

Whether you decide to quote a piece of text or paraphrase it, you absolutely must do the following:

- evaluate the source for credibility
- make sure the quotation or paraphrase you choose is relevant
- cite the source material properly
- integrate the source material well using signal phrases and explanation

The following sections discuss the specific rules for quotations and for paraphrases that you need to master.

Evaluating Sources for Credibility

Quotations and paraphrases are only as good as the sources they come from, so be sure the sources you use are *credible*—that is, trustworthy or reliable. Credible source material tends to be written by experts or professional journalists, with some form of review provided by editors or fellow experts. As a result, the information these sources provide is accurate and unbiased.

Virtually all nationally distributed newspapers, magazines, journals, and books have the advantage of professional or expert authors and editors who help make sure the author has his or her facts straight, so the information in them tends to be credible.

Other sources need to be evaluated more carefully for credibility: Web sites in particular are like the Wild West when it comes to standards of credibility and accuracy. You have probably encountered this issue when you are surfing the Internet. Perhaps you are researching information about a soccer player and come across a Web site that says this player has been traded to another team, only to find out later that the trade was rumored to happen but never did. The truth is, you can post almost anything on the Internet—there is no Internet editorial board keeping information accurate and current.

So how can you tell if your source is reliable? For starters, consider the reputation and editorial procedures of the publication. Next, read any biographical information you can find about the author. Is this person an expert in his or her field? Let's say Michael Jones is a professor of biology at an accredited college and he's writing about biodiversity; you can assume he is an expert on this topic. As a professional, too, he has a reputation to maintain, which makes him less likely to publish inaccuracies.

If you cite from a newspaper, there are two general categories of writer: journalists and op-ed ("opposite the editorial page") writers. Journalists follow a code of ethics that requires them to maintain a standard of accuracy and objectivity. (Of course, journalists can make mistakes, and they don't always intend to show all sides of an issue, so don't assume what they write is absolutely true and unbiased.) Op-eds are written not by a newspaper's staff writers but by outside contributors who are generally well-informed on the topic but who are not necessarily bound by a code of journalistic ethics. You can often learn more about the author of an op-ed piece by reading the biographical information that the newspaper offers, which should help you judge whether the piece is likely to be credible.

Web sites are the trickiest sources to evaluate because often the information about the Web site and its author(s) is not available. Since just about anybody can publish a Web site, you don't always know who wrote the content. While a quick search on the Internet might seem like a researching shortcut, determining the reliability of Web sources often requires a lot more work. You may need to search for information about the author or even track down the original version of the article.

Making Sure Source Material Is Relevant

Once you have determined that a source is credible, check to be sure it is relevant to your point. Does the particular quotation or paraphrase that you have selected really fit the point you want to make, or is there a more appropriate piece of evidence that you could quote or paraphrase? Sometimes we are drawn to a quotation because it is very well written, or we find a statistic that we wish to paraphrase because it is so interesting. While it's great to be enthusiastic about your source material, make sure that you have considered several possible pieces of evidence before you select the best one to use.

Consider the following example from a student paragraph on the importance of public art:

Original Student Paragraph

Public art plays an important role in giving an identity to a city or community. We can see public art in many places, from libraries to city centers and public parks. Murals line the walls of schools, and parks are home to sculptures showcasing local artists or famous people from that city. Jack Becker, in his article "Public Art: An Essential Component of Creating Communities," states, "Imagine, if you can, a world devoid of public art: no *Statue of Liberty*, no *Eiffel Tower*, no *Vietnam Veterans Memorial*, no *Tribute in Light*" (487). In this quotation Becker shows how important public art is to creating a community's identity.

Does the quotation by Becker actually support the point the author of this paragraph is trying to make? Not really. The examples of public art that Becker mentions are good examples of art that give a community an identity, but the quotation from Becker doesn't directly state that point; it only indirectly states it through examples. The result is that the paragraph is weakened. The author of this paragraph was probably drawn to the references to important and famous works of public art in this quotation, but unfortunately, this selection of text from Becker doesn't strongly support the paragraph point.

So, what can the writer of this paragraph do to improve the relevance of her quotation to the point of the paragraph? The first thing to do is to reassess the point that paragraph is making. In this case, the point is that *public art is important in giving an identity to a city or community.* The next thing to do would be to review the reading to see what, if anything, the author says about this point. Because Becker has a subheading titled "Why Is Public Art Important?" that would be a good place to start reviewing, and, in fact, this is the same paragraph the original quotation came from.

Becker's Original Paragraph: Why Is Public Art Important?

Imagine, if you can, a world devoid of public art: no *Statue of Liberty*, no *Eiffel Tower*, no *Vietnam Veterans Memorial*, no *Tribute in Light*. No murals, memorials, or monuments. What would life be like without fireworks displays, puppet parades, sculpture parks, and visionary roadside folk art? These landmarks and special events enhance our experience of a place and our quality of life. They engender a sense of pride and community identity. They reach audiences outside museums, galleries, and theaters, and they add to the beauty of everyday life. They declare the worth of a place and a time in our shared culture.

Reviewing the text with the paragraph point clearly in mind helps to uncover a potentially better quotation. The highlighted selection is where Becker states what kind of role public art plays in a community. The only problem with this sentence is that if we take it out of context, it won't be clear what the word "they" refers to. In this paragraph, "they" refers to famous landmarks and events; we can add clarifying information in the quotation within brackets.

Revised Student Paragraph with New Quotation

Public art plays an important role in giving an identity to a city or community. We can see public art in many places, from libraries to city centers and public parks. Murals line the walls of schools, and parks are home to sculptures showcasing local artists or famous people from that city. Jack Becker, in his article "Public Art: An Essential Component of Creating Communities," states, "They [famous landmarks and events] engender a sense of pride and community identity" (487). In this quotation Becker shows how important public art is to creating a community's identity.

Avoid Plagiarism by Citing Source Material

It's crucial that you properly cite any quotations, paraphrases, and summaries you include in your writing. In college, original thoughts and ideas are highly valued, so when you use other people's ideas, you must give them credit. In fact, when you acknowledge your sources, your credibility increases because your reader will see you have done your research. Not properly giving credit—by acknowledging the source and including a proper citation—is considered plagiarism, and plagiarism is a very serious offense in academic writing. Most colleges and universities have codes of student conduct that spell out the penalties for students caught plagiarizing, which can range from a zero on the assignment to expulsion. You did all the hard work to find and evaluate the source material, but if you do not cite your sources, you lose the opportunity to be rewarded for that work. Good citations make you appear intelligent and responsible. Why would you choose to plagiarize instead?

▶ For a complete discussion of when and how to cite your sources, see Chapter 22, MLA Documentation or Chapter 23, APA Documentation.

DOES THIS SOUND LIKE YOU?

Have you ever found yourself procrastinating on a writing assignment, stressed out by a severe case of writer's block, or confused by so much reading online about your topic that you can no longer find where the ideas came from? Students rarely plan to plagiarize; it happens as a last resort when someone feels unprepared to complete an assignment. You might even plagiarize without realizing it if you don't take clear enough notes when researching online for more information or inspiration. If this sounds like you, take steps to avoid procrastinating. Make a schedule like the one on page 81 and ask someone to help you stick to it. Don't know how to get started? That's the perfect time to get help! See a tutor or your instructor well before the assignment is due. And be sure to take meticulous notes whenever you are reading up on your topic online so you can properly cite any good information you find. You might find yourself struggling as you work on more challenging assignments, but plagiarism is never the solution. This book can be a resource to help you out of any writing jam.

▶ For more about avoiding plagiarism when taking notes, see pages 384–88 in Chapter 20, Note Taking.

When and How to Use Quotations

In general, you use a quotation for one of two reasons. First, the source says it better than you could rephrase it. Here's an example:

> According to Koon-Hwee Kan in "Adolescents and Graffiti," "The 1980s were the Golden Age of graffiti art with the emergence of 'wild style,' an

intertwined and decorative lettering that mixes icons and images from popular culture to form a complex composition" (508).

In this case, the best way to say something was the Golden Age is to say it was the Golden Age. The language Kan uses to make her point is vivid, precise, and skillfully constructed, so it both conveys her message well and adds to her credibility as an academic expert.

Here's another example:

According to art education specialist Koon-Hwee Kan, for adolescents "[school] becomes a boring, frustrating, stressful, or anxious experience" (506).

Finding synonyms for "boring, frustrating, stressful, or anxious" so that you could paraphrase would be awkward and difficult.

The second reason to use a direct quotation is to draw specific attention to the language or the author's use of words. This situation often occurs when you are quoting literature. In this case, the purpose of the quotation is to highlight the author's particular use of language. For this reason, a quotation is preferred over a paraphrase. Here's an example:

In Shakespeare's *Hamlet*, Hamlet begins his famous soliloquy by questioning whether life is worth living by saying, "To be, or not to be: that is the question" (3.1.55).

Putting the quotation in your own words in this case simply wouldn't capture the spirit of Shakespeare.

HOW TO QUOTE CORRECTLY

When you have evaluated your source and have decided to quote from the source material, take care to quote correctly to avoid confusing the reader. Make sure that:

- **Quotations are enclosed correctly in quotation marks.**
- **Quotations work with the grammar of your sentence.** It is your responsibility to complete the sentence if the quotation is not already complete or to otherwise change the quotation, using very specific rules, to make it grammatically correct.

As with all material taken from an outside source, you must also remember the following:

- **Cite your sources.** At all times. No exceptions. None. Ever.
- **Introduce and explain your source material.** In other words, don't just drop a quotation into your writing and move on. It's your responsibility

to let your reader know why it's there and what it means. (We'll cover this in more detail on pp. 348–50.)

Use double quotation marks (" ") when quoting. The following example incorporates another quote from the article "Adolescents and Graffiti" by Koon-Hwee Kan (the full selection can be found on pp. 505–10):

> Artist and teacher Koon-Hwee Kan describes interviewing people who "felt personally connected to the graffiti-art style and deliberately copied and learned its forms" (000). Kan shows how influential graffiti is in the overall artistic production of adolescents, even those who are not out there writing in the streets.

The words from the source are in quotation marks, and the quotation is introduced and cited.

However, if the text you are quoting already has quotation marks in it, you can see that just putting quotes around the source material makes it hard to distinguish where Kan's quote begins and ends:

Incorrect   As artist and teacher Koon-Hwee Kan writes, "Living in multiple realities including the "daydream reality" is common among adolescents" (506). Kan connects teenagers' doodling to this "daydream reality."

To fix this problem, when you quote something that already contains quotation marks, replace the double quotation marks in the original with single quotation marks (the apostrophe key on a keyboard: ' '). Here's how it should look (see the highlighted word below):

Correct   As artist and teacher Koon-Hwee Kan writes, "Living in multiple realities including the 'daydream reality' is common among adolescents" (506). Kan connects teenagers' doodling to this "daydream reality."

Note, too, that the quotation is properly introduced, commented on, and cited, and it's placed as part of a complete, grammatically correct sentence.

practice it 17.1   Basic Quotations

Choose a basic quotation to incorporate into an essay you are writing. Copy the quotation out, inserting the quotation marks and citation correctly. Ask your instructor or a tutor to review your work to make sure you understand the basics of quotation marks.

HOW TO ALTER QUOTATIONS

Sometimes the quotation that you want to use doesn't quite fit because the verb tense or a pronoun doesn't work with the grammar of your sentence. In such cases, it's acceptable to make slight changes to the quotation. However, you need to indicate to your reader that you are making a change to the quotation, and there are specific rules about how to do so. Common reasons to make a change within a quotation include:

- To clarify a pronoun reference (for example, *he* becomes the name of the actual person)
- To change the part of speech (for example, *schooling* becomes *school*)
- To change the verb tense (for example, from past to present)
- To add necessary explanatory information (such as to spell out the name of an acronym or provide other information from nearby in the text)
- To omit irrelevant information (such as to make a quotation more concise)

If these reasons do not apply, you should always copy a quotation exactly as it is written in the original, punctuation and all. If you do change a quotation, you need to follow certain rules.

Omitting Words from a Quotation.   Sometimes you find a really great quotation, but it's rather long or part of it is unrelated to your point. In these cases, you can leave part of the quotation out, but you must not change the meaning of the original material. In other words, you can leave out part of the quotation as long as this doesn't change the author's intended meaning. Use an ellipsis, three little dots (. . .), to replace any part of the quotation you have removed. Here's an example with a sentence from Jim Whitehurst's article "How I Hire" on page 466.

> Jim Whitehurst describes how he knew that an interviewee had a passion for learning when he writes, "When I was interviewing candidates for Red Hat's executive vice president of Global Sales and Services position, we talked to several extremely talented candidates, but the conversations with Arun Oberoi . . . were different" (467).

The ellipsis (. . .) replaces the few words that were omitted, yet Whitehurst's meaning is maintained even with the omission.

Note: You will sometimes see writing using four dots at the end of a quotation, which is really an ellipsis plus a period. MLA bibliographic style requires the use of ellipses if you omit the end of a sentence.

Modifying a Quotation. If you need to add or change a word in a quotation, you must use square brackets [ ], not parentheses ( ), and you must change the text as little as possible to make the quotation work with the rest of your sentence.

Imagine, for example, that you want to quote the following passage from Olivia Mellan's essay "Men, Women, and Money" (see p. 61 for the entire selection):

Original Sentence
I call it Mellan's Law: If opposites don't attract right off the bat, then they will create each other eventually.

Say you want to introduce part of this quotation from a third-person perspective. To adjust the pronoun, you might write:

Quotation
Mellan has a name for the way couples become opposites about money. "[She] call[s] it Mellan's Law: If opposites don't attract right off the bat, then they will create each other eventually" (61).

Here, *I* is changed to *she* because that makes more sense in the sentence. Note that the verb also must be changed to match the subject that was replaced. *Call* becomes *calls*.

Similarly, you may need to change the capitalization of a word so that it fits the rules of capitalization for your sentence. For instance, if you want to quote the following sentence, you'll need to change the capitalization of the first letter:

Original Sentence
When not spending, a hoarder feels virtuous, in control.

Quotation
In describing the characteristics of one of the money personality types, Mellan says that "[w]hen not spending, a hoarder feels virtuous, in control" (63).

The letter "W" was capitalized in the original, but it shouldn't be capitalized here, so it has been changed to lowercase, as the square brackets indicate. This is done to make the quotation a part of the sentence. If, however, you just wanted to introduce the quotation (usually with words like "writes," "says,"), you would retain the capital "W":

In describing the characteristics of one of the money personality types, Mellan says, "When not spending, a hoarder feels virtuous, in control" (63).

A more substantial change may be needed to make your sentence grammatically correct. For example, here is one way you might change the verb tense in the following sentence from the myth of Amaterasu:

Original Sentence
Catching sight of her reflection, Amaterasu slowly came out of her refuge and approached the mirror.

Quotation
Amaterasu's downfall was when she "[caught] sight of her reflection" (Littleton 447).

Here the original *catching* is changed to *caught* because that fits the sentence's verb tense better. Note that the letter *C* was changed from a capital to lowercase as well. To add explanatory information, you might write:

Quotation
After she "[caught] sight of her reflection [in the mirror put there by the other gods to trick her], Amaterasu slowly came out of her refuge and approached the mirror" (Littleton 447).

Here the additional information—that the gods put the mirror there—refers directly to something in the previous paragraph of the reading. This is not information that you made up; it is an actual paraphrase of some of the text that needs to be clarified for your reader.

Square brackets and ellipses are extremely useful to help you manipulate a quotation so it fits smoothly into your own writing. However, if you need to make major changes to a quotation to make it fit your sentence, that's a good indication that you would be better off paraphrasing instead of quoting.

---

practice it 17.2   Altering Quotations

Choose a quotation from a source that you would like to incorporate into an essay you are writing. Alter the quotation to shorten it, modify its grammar, or otherwise make it fit into your sentence. Show your work to your instructor or a tutor to make sure you understand how to alter quotations.

Once you master the nuts and bolts of how to use quotations, you can also become a more critical reader, examining how the authors you read use quotations, and determining if they really choose their quotations well.

practice it 17.3 Examining Quotations in a Published Work

Almost all the reading you do in college will be the work and ideas of others. Reread a few previously assigned articles and find examples of quotations. What kinds of quotations did the author include? How did he or she introduce these quotations? How did the quotations help support his or her point? How did he or she cite sources? Does the text look like MLA style or another style? Does the source omit citations? How does that influence your assessment of the source's credibility?

When and How to Paraphrase

Why paraphrase? Essentially, you paraphrase for the same reasons you use a quotation: to add support to your point, to provide an example to discuss, or to show what others think about a topic. You paraphrase rather than quote when you don't need the exact sentence or paragraph from a source, just the ideas. Paraphrasing is also a good choice when the sentence or phrase you would quote is written in an awkward way or in a style or tone that doesn't fit your paper. There is one additional benefit of paraphrasing for students: Paraphrasing shows your instructor that you have a good grasp of the material, because you are putting it into your own words. For this reason, some instructors require all source material to be paraphrased.

How do you paraphrase? When you paraphrase, whether it's a sentence or a paragraph, you put the author's ideas into your own words. This does not mean just changing a few key words here or there. It means rewriting the sentence, using your own words to convey the author's information. However, it is essential that you maintain the *meaning* of the original sentence or paragraph. Here is another example from Koon-Hwee Kan's article "Adolescents and Graffiti" (the full selection can be found on p. 505).

Quotation   "Yet, latrinalia is common in school toilets and poses a major vandalism problem."

Paraphrase   Bathroom graffiti, which destroys school property, is a frequent and difficult challenge for administrators (Kan 507).

The highlighted words hold the key meaning in this sentence and need to be stated in a different way, while keeping their same point. If you match the colored highlighting in the quotation and the paraphrase, you can see how each key part of the original sentence was reworded in the second sentence. (A word like *graffiti* is okay to keep; since that's the topic of the sentence and not easily replaced, it can remain in the paraphrase.)

Here's another example, from the article "Teach Your Children the Building Blocks of Finance" by Sherie Holder and Kenneth Meeks (the full selection can be found on p. 35).

Quotation "By the time your child turns nine, talk to him or her about creating a small budget to keep track of income and expenses."

Paraphrase Parents should encourage kids before they're nine to track both their savings and their spending (Holder and Meeks 36).

Finally, here's one more example from Chapter 10 of David G. Myers's textbook *Psychology* (the excerpt can be found on p. 169).

Quotation "This idea of a general mental capacity expressed by a single intelligence score was controversial in Spearman's day, and so it remains."

Paraphrase Using an IQ score to represent a person's intellectual ability has been debated ever since Spearman introduced the concept (Myers 170).

Note that each of these paraphrases closely maintains the meaning of the original.

practice it 17.4 Paraphrasing Sentences

In each sentence, underline the key words that convey the meaning of the sentence. Then rewrite the sentence in your own words, making sure to keep the meaning of the underlined words.

1. From Carol S. Dweck's "The Perils and Promises of Praise":

   "Praise is intricately connected to how students view their intelligence" (7).

2. From *Money Matters on Campus*:

   "Recent headlines point to crippling levels of student loan debt that are forcing young adults to delay financial independence" (54).

3. From Olivia Mellan's "Men, Women, and Money":

   "Typically, men want to merge all the couple's money—while maintaining primary decision-making power. Women want to keep at least some money separate" (67).

4. From Carol S. Dweck's "The Perils and Promises of Praise":

   "Many educators have hoped to maximize students' confidence in their abilities, their enjoyment of learning, and their ability to thrive in school by praising their intelligence" (9).

Introducing a Quotation or Paraphrase

As you learned in Chapter 4, a signal phrase is the group of words that introduces a quotation or a paraphrase so that the reader knows where you got your information. The signal phrase also hints at the reasons you chose to include this particular information in your writing. For instance, you might give the author's credentials in your signal phrase, or you might provide some context for the information. At the most basic level, the signal phrase should work together with the citation to give your reader enough information to find the source if she or he so desires. Successful writers also skillfully use the signal phrase to help the reader take in the information presented in the quotation or paraphrase.

BASIC SIGNAL PHRASES

The simplest way to introduce a quotation or paraphrase is to use the full name of the author and the title of his or her work the first time you mention them. This information can go before or after the quotation or paraphrase. After you mention an author by his or her full name the first time, refer to him or her by last name only. (Never refer to an author by first name only.) Here's a general pattern, followed by some examples:

Full-Introduction Signal Phrase (for the First Mention of an Author in Your Essay)

Full name of author or speaker + full title of work (book or article) + signal-phrase word + quotation or paraphrase

With a Quotation	**In her article "Men, Women, and Money," Olivia Mellan claims**, "The failure of people to explore their money personalities leads to deep misunderstanding and hurt" (65).
With a Paraphrase	**Sherie Holder and Kenneth Meeks, in their article "Teach Your Children the Building Blocks of Finance," reinforce** the importance of the practice of saving at least 10–15 percent of after-tax income (35).

If you already introduced the author fully earlier in the essay, use a shortened signal phrase:

Shortened Signal Phrase (for Additional References to a Previously Introduced Author)

Last name of author or speaker + signal-phrase word + quotation or paraphrase

With a Quotation	**Mellan reveals that** "[o]ften, the silence is a shield for the shame, guilt, and anxiety people feel about their own ways with money" (61).

With a Paraphrase   **Holder and Meeks claim** that how children feel about money will affect their money habits later in life (36).

> **practice it 17.5** Locating and Evaluating Signal Phrases in Published Works
>
> Flip through any of the readings in this book and find places where the author uses signal phrases to introduce a quotation and where the author doesn't use signal phrases. Compare the articles that include signal phrases with those that don't. Which are clearer? Smoother? Easier to follow?

USE SIGNAL PHRASES TO ADD MEANING

Signal phrases can do more than simply identify the source: They can also make your point clearer by emphasizing the meaning of the author. For example, look at the differences between the following signal phrases:

Carol S. Dweck writes that "students in the fixed mind-set don't recover well from setbacks" (8).

Carol S. Dweck argues that "students in the fixed mind-set don't recover well from setbacks" (8).

Carol S. Dweck proposes that "students in the fixed mind-set don't recover well from setbacks" (8).

Each of these signal-phrase verbs makes a different statement. When you use *writes*, you merely state that this is what the author says. There is no hint of what the author thinks about the information you cite. However, when you use *argues* or *proposes*, you give the reader more information about the point the author makes. Sometimes it makes the most sense to use *says* or *writes*, but if the author is clearly making a claim or disputing an argument, use a signal phrase to show that. The right signal phrase adds meaning not only to your reader's understanding of the quotation, but to the overall point you are making.

Common Signal Words and Phrases

according to	illustrates	refutes
admits	implies	reveals
argues	informs	says
as stated by (or in)	maintains	states
claims	makes the point that	suggests
demonstrates	proposes	thinks
discusses	recalls	writes
explains		

practice it 17.6   Using Different Signal Phrases

Find a place in one of your readings where the author uses a quotation. Rewrite the quotation with different signal-phrase verbs to introduce the quotation. Which signal phrases best fit the meaning of the quotation?

USE MORE SOPHISTICATED SIGNAL PHRASES

You can use other types of signal phrases to eliminate repetition of information or to de-emphasize the source author and title. If you have already established the author and title, and it's clear you are referring to them, repeating the same information over and over will get boring. Or perhaps the author and title are not the most important factor that you wish to emphasize in your signal phrase; this is often the case with news articles, scholarly studies, and even some video materials. In these cases, you might use a different type of signal phrase, taking care to include a complete citation in the parenthetical reference.

To generate more sophisticated signal phrases, ask yourself again the questions: What will best set up this quotation or paraphrase for my readers? What context is most important for readers to see the quoted or paraphrased information the way I want them to see it? Again, once you clearly establish the source, you can highlight other important information about the reading.

For example, you might decide to use the date of the information, as with this example that quotes the report *Money Matters on Campus*:

> A 2015 report on the financial attitudes and behaviors of college students found that "[i]n general, responsible planning behaviors decreased over time, but risky financial moves such as using payday lenders or taking out cash advances on credit cards, remained stable" (Higher One and EverFi 50).

You might want the signal phrase to emphasize some other important context for the information, such as how it fits into the history of the topic you are discussing, as in this example that quotes Daisy Yuhas's article "Curiosity Prepares the Brain for Better Learning":

> History is filled with warnings against curiosity in the form of myths like Pandora or sayings like "curiosity killed the cat," but recent scientific research reveals that "curiosity could prepare the brain for learning and long-term memory more broadly" (Yuhas 470).

The signal phrase can also indicate how the quoted or paraphrased information fits into the argument you are outlining, as in the next example that paraphrases Koon-Hwee Kan's article "Adolescents and Graffiti."

One counterargument to the common belief that graffiti is purely vandalism is the argument that graffiti is a way for teenagers to rebel against the consumer culture of their lives (Kan 507).

With works of fiction or memoir, once you've established the title and author, you may want to use the signal phrase to let readers know when in the story the action you are describing occurs, as in this example that quotes the opening soundtrack of Banksy's film *Exit through the Gift Shop*, a documentary about street art:

The film opens with a montage of graffiti artists while a song plays with the refrain "tonight, the streets are ours" (*Exit through the Gift Shop*).

As you gain more experience with signal phrases, you will see how much heavy lifting they can do for you in your writing.

Explaining a Quotation or Paraphrase

Even when you write good signal phrases and quote or paraphrase properly, you need to explain the quotation or paraphrase in order for it to be fully integrated into your paragraph. You can think of it as a "sandwich": Your words are the pieces of bread that come before and after the filling (the quoted or paraphrased information).

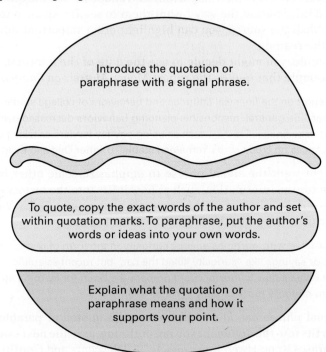

Introduce the quotation or paraphrase with a signal phrase.

To quote, copy the exact words of the author and set within quotation marks. To paraphrase, put the author's words or ideas into your own words.

Explain what the quotation or paraphrase means and how it supports your point.

The introduction is the signal phrase, and the quotation or paraphrase itself comes next. What follows determines how useful the quotation is in your writing: Quotations and paraphrases are evidence, and you need to explain exactly how that evidence supports the point you want to make.

Explain what the quotation or paraphrase means as objectively as you can so that you are true to the original meaning of the information. In some cases, the meaning will be easy for most people to understand, but think carefully about the material before assuming that is the case. Depending on both your audience and the context of the quotation or paraphrase in the original source, its meaning might need some explaining.

Once you're sure you've made the meaning of the quotation or paraphrase clear, show the reader how it supports your point. Again, don't assume the reader sees the connection between your information and your overall point. You picked the source material for a reason, so explain to the reader how it provides insight or support for the point that you are making.

practice it 17.7   Make Yourself a Quotation or Paraphrase Sandwich

Make a list of the quotations or paraphrases you plan to use in your essay and write up a complete quotation or paraphrase sandwich for each one. Begin by writing an appropriate signal phrase for each one and then copy down the quotation or paraphrase accurately followed by the proper in-text citation. Follow up each one with a sentence or two clearly explaining what the quotation or paraphrase means and how it supports your point.

The following paragraph by student writer Ariel is a great example of the use of the quotation sandwich. In the paragraph, the signal phrases and citations are highlighted in yellow, the quotations are highlighted in blue, and the explanations of the significance of the quotations are highlighted in green. Ariel is writing about Carlin Flora's "Seeing by Starlight," which she has summarized in prior paragraphs of her essay.

We constantly see celebrities flaunt their lifestyles, and we become jealous of them. We read and constantly watch celebrities put their lives on display for the world to see, and we become envious of what they have. In the article "Seeing by Starlight," Carlin Flora quotes Francisco Gil-White when he explains that we start to follow the celebrities' clothes and fashion by stating, "Humans naturally copy techniques from high-status individuals" (530). Gil-White means that with the constant reminder of what celebrities have, we become so attracted to the material things these celebrities have that we go out and copy their style. When we go out and buy these clothes, shoes, cars, and so on, we feel as though we are one step closer to becoming like these celebrities and having this lifestyle we look up to. When we are jealous, we often feel as though we can pass judgment on celebrities as well. Flora states, "[W]e're quick to judge when stars behave too outrageously or live too extravagantly" (530). As observers, we constantly pass judgment on celebrities whether it's wearing an ugly outfit on the red carpet or how much weight they have gained or lost. By judging celebrities, we make ourselves feel good because we constantly compare ourselves to them and when they do something wrong we feel like it's our need to pass judgment on them so we can feel confident about ourselves.

Note that the signal phrase for the first quotation explains that Flora is quoting someone else in her article. It's important to let your reader know whose words are being quoted. The words of Gil-White quoted in Flora's article are followed by an explanation of the quoted material, highlighted in green, where Ariel explains what it means to "copy techniques from high-status individuals." The meaning of the quoted material "we're quick to judge when stars behave too outrageously or live too extravagantly" becomes clear when Ariel writes, "As observers, we constantly pass judgment on celebrities whether it's wearing an ugly outfit on the red carpet or how much weight they have gained or lost. By judging celebrities, we make ourselves feel good because we constantly compare ourselves to them and when they do something wrong we feel like it's our need to pass judgment on them so we can feel confident about ourselves."

| practice it 17.8 | Identifying the Parts of the Quotation Sandwich |

For the following two paragraphs from student essays, identify the parts of the quotation sandwich. Label or highlight the parts of the quotation sandwich: signal phrase, quotation, and explanation. How well did each author use the elements of the quotation sandwich? How effective is the quotation sandwich in helping the reader understand the use of the quotations? What advice would you give these authors for revision?

1. From Julie's essay "Marketing to Children":

The effects of marketing vary with age. As stated in *Pediatrics*, "Among

U.S. preschool-aged children (2–5 years of age), obesity rates have more

than doubled since the 1970s; among 6- to 11-year-old children, rates have more than tripled" (Roberto et al. 89). Young children are easily persuaded and manipulated with popular cartoon characters and fancy labeling on junk food. As a mother of a two-year-old, I realize my son can easily identify popular cartoon characters and prefers junk food that is packaged with their images. This must come to a stop; if it doesn't, our children can develop any of the many disorders that come from eating unhealthy food.

2. From Karla's essay on teen spending:

Overspending has been a huge problem throughout America, especially among young teens. Parents are not aware of ways to inform teens about smart purchasing habits. "Advertising is a pervasive influence on children and adolescents" (Committee on Communications 2563). "This targeting occurs because advertising is a $250 billion/year industry with 900,000 brands to sell" (Committee on Communication 2563). Young teens are spending $155 billion a year and those younger are spending $25 billion. The teens living on the West Coast prefer to purchase clothes from brands like American Eagle, Forever 21, and Hollister. Specifically among brands ranked by young women, Hollister took the "most preferred" position (Committee on Communication 2563), while West Coast brands continued to be a favorite among young men. Men and women today are choosing these top brands because they're the brands that are being worn here in California and among teens.

chapter review

In the following chart, fill in the second column to record in your own words the important skills included in this chapter. Then assess yourself to determine whether you are still developing the skill or feel you have mastered it. If you are still developing the skill, make some notes about what you need to work on to master it in the future. If you believe you have already mastered it, explain why.

Skills and concepts covered in this chapter	Explanation in your own words	I'm developing this skill and need to work on . . .	I believe I have mastered this skill because . . .
Evaluating the credibility of sources			
Making sure source material is relevant			
Avoiding plagiarism			
Quoting correctly			
Altering a quotation			
Paraphrasing			
Introducing quotations or paraphrases with signal phrases			
Explaining a quotation or paraphrase (making a quotation or paraphrase sandwich)			

18

Giving and Receiving Feedback

Before you were able to purchase this book, approximately sixty people read drafts of it, made suggestions, and offered their advice and opinions about everything from the title to the content to the size of the margins. Surprised? Many people who see writing as a solitary process—a tortured artist sitting in a cold, damp room—are shocked to find out how collaborative it really is. Even writers who do work alone typically have a small group of writer friends, as well as editors and other people, they go to for advice. Your English class will help you begin to see yourself as a writer by offering opportunities for your classmates to provide feedback on your writing.

Feedback Is Essential

So why do writers so often ask for feedback from others? What do they do with that feedback? Writers seek feedback for many reasons, including these:

- to check whether something they are trying to do "works"
- to answer that nagging "I know what I mean to say, but am I really saying it?" question
- to get ideas for how to expand and develop a piece of writing
- to identify strengths and weaknesses in a piece of writing

Do writers always follow the advice they get? Definitely not. Sometimes readers have a difference of opinion about a piece of writing, but if three out of four peer reviewers all agree that your introduction isn't clear, you should probably listen to them. You might not change it the way they would like you to, but you should consider revising it.

The other important key to peer review may also surprise you: You learn just as much—if not more—by giving feedback as you do by receiving it. Why is that? Think for a moment about a time when you had to teach someone something. Maybe you had to teach your little sister how to make a foul shot, or your cousin how to balance his checkbook. Sure, you know how to do it, but explaining it is another matter. You have to understand something far more deeply to teach it than you do to just do it. This is true of everything—writing included. So, if you are in a peer-review writing group with classmates and one of the writers doesn't have a strong enough thesis, being able to recognize the problem and then explain why the thesis is not strong will help you develop a deeper knowledge of thesis statements, the assignment prompt, and the content of your own paper.

Peer review can be a scary thing. Even though you ask for honest, constructive criticism, hearing negative comments can be tough, especially when you worked hard on something. Still, the rewards far, far outweigh these difficulties. While peer review may never be a totally comfortable process, as you practice it, you will probably find that you enjoy working on your writing with your classmates and friends. By the end of the course, you will probably discover that your peer-review skills have improved significantly and that you revise and edit your essay more confidently because of the experience.

Guidelines for Peer Review

Many models for peer review exist, and your instructor will choose one that best suits your class. Most frequently, peer review in college English classrooms happens in a writing workshop, where students working in small groups exchange drafts, read and comment on them, and then discuss ways the authors can improve them. Another model is a written peer response, usually accompanied by a set of specific written questions. One student reads another student's draft and fills out a questionnaire about the paper, often as homework. Then the students collect one or more responses to their work and interpret these responses on their own. Sometimes your instructor will ask for a volunteer to have his or her paper "workshopped" by the entire class. This is a fantastic opportunity to get feedback on your writing from the instructor as well as your classmates; try to volunteer if asked, even if you are nervous.

Whatever method of peer review your instructor chooses, adhering to some basic principles of peer review will make the entire experience more worthwhile and pleasant.

- **Always say something positive first.** This is the cardinal rule of peer review among writers. People learn from what they did right, not just from having what they did wrong pointed out to them repeatedly.

- **Refer to the assignment.** Have the essay assignment and any notes about the assignment that your instructor gave you out on your desk, and refer to them as you do peer review.

- **Consult the sources.** As much as possible, return to the books and articles referred to in your classmate's paper as you work with it.

- **Make your criticism constructive.** If you find a weak point, offer a couple of possible suggestions for improvement.

- **Be specific and detailed in your feedback.** Just saying "It's good" doesn't help anyone. Instead, say something specific, such as "Your hook really makes me want to read the paper." If you find a weakness, be specific in that too. Saying "This paragraph doesn't work" might be somewhat helpful, but it would be more helpful if you said, "This paragraph doesn't work because the example you give doesn't really fit with the point you're trying to make."

- **Follow the directions that your instructor gave.** Perhaps in this round of review, your instructor only wants you to focus on the thesis statement because you're going to work on the rest of the essay next week. If he or she gave handouts or wrote lists of items to discuss on the board, use them.

- **Have an open mind, have fun, and stay focused.** Peer review is the place where you can admit mistakes, figure out better ways to do things, and have a little fun. Peer review works best, though, when you stay on track, so be disciplined about it.

- **Make a real effort.** There's nothing worse than being in a peer group with a bunch of writers who don't really try to give feedback. For the process to work, everyone needs to participate. For shy students, that means speaking up. For talkative students, that means giving others the chance to speak, sometimes by asking for their opinions. Make sure no one person dominates the conversation.

- **Establish a time frame and appoint a timekeeper.** Often, peer groups run out of time, which isn't fair to the last person. Divide the amount of time you have equally among the participants, and set an alarm or appoint a timekeeper to make sure you stay more or less on schedule.

Interpreting and Applying Instructors' Comments and Corrections

Wouldn't it be wonderful to get a paper back from your instructor with just the words "You're Brilliant!" written at the top and a big fat A grade? Of course we all want that, but even if it did happen, it wouldn't be great for you. Instructor comments, like the comments you receive from peers in writing groups, are a way to teach and learn, and a paper with no comments means a lost opportunity for you to learn. Usually instructors provide you with positive as well as negative feedback, but even if the comments you get are mostly about ways to improve, you can use that information positively for your next paper if you follow these guidelines:

- **Understand the difference between a correction and a comment.** Instructors often make corrections by circling errors or actually correcting errors on your papers. Typically, these are errors in document format or sentence-level issues, and usually when an instructor circles or fixes a problem, there is one right way to fix it—for instance, you spelled a word wrong, had the wrong margins, made a mistake in subject-verb agreement, or left off a citation.

  Comments, on the other hand, are like annotations. Comments address larger issues (often called higher-order concerns), like your ideas, support, or writing style. For example, an instructor might comment that your evidence doesn't fit your point, or that you misunderstood the tone of the text you are discussing. Being able to distinguish between a correction and a comment helps you prioritize your revisions. When in doubt about what your most pressing writing problems are, ask your instructor.

▶ To learn how to create a Grammar Log, see page 575 in Chapter 27, How to Learn the Rules and Apply Them to Your Own Writing.

- **Do your best to fix your errors.** Instructors often wish that students would look at their corrections, figure out how to fix the errors, and never make those errors again. This is a big wish, and they know it doesn't really happen like that, but they do expect you to try your best. Start in the right direction by keeping track of your common mistakes and recognizing the ones you make most often. The Grammar Log described in Chapter 27 is a useful tool for learning to edit your writing. You need to track your errors and edit specifically for those errors you tend to make so that you will eventually, with lots of practice, stop making these same mistakes.

- **Really *think* about the comments.** Instructors expect you to read their comments, especially the comments they write at the end of the paper, and really think about them. Instructors who write substantial comments see them as the beginning of a conversation about your work. They expect you to think carefully about their comments, and they hope to see some of that thought process reflected in your revisions or in your next papers.

  For instance, if your instructor writes on your paper that you often seem to have trouble with conclusions, but you do not have another chance to revise that paper, you should make a special effort on your conclusion in the next paper. If you need help figuring out how to apply the comment to your next paper, ask your instructor or see a tutor if one is available.

- **Study the course or assignment rubric (if there is one).** A *rubric* is a document that divides up the writing task into different skills so they can be evaluated one by one. For example, a rubric might have sections for content, organization, use of evidence, and editing. If your instructor grades with a rubric, he or she may show it to you before the assignment is due so that you understand the grading standards better and, hopefully, produce better work.

As you look over the rubric, take time to distinguish between big-picture concerns and sentence-level concerns. Sometimes the sentence-level concerns are listed in greater detail on the rubric because this format allows the instructor to check off boxes and save time, but that does not mean he or she sees those items as more important than big-picture concerns—in fact, the opposite is almost always true.

- **Spend time reviewing your efforts.** If you really worked hard on an assignment and got a lower grade than expected, reread the assignment, your work, and the instructor's comments. Then, if you are still confused, set up an appointment to speak privately with the instructor. Make sure you ask the instructor what you can do better next time.

Comparing your grade to another student's grade can be tempting, but try to avoid it. Two papers both earning C grades might have different problems and strengths, and instructors often have to weigh the quality of the ideas against the actual writing of the paper to arrive at a fair grade.

CORRECTIONS

The following chart explains some common marks or correction symbols instructors write on papers. Many instructors hand out their own personalized editing chart at the beginning of the semester. When in doubt about what a correction means—or when you can't read the handwriting—make sure you ask for clarification.

Correction	What it might mean	Related chapters in this book; other places to go for help
frag **fragment** **incomplete sentence**	You do not have a complete sentence. You are making a sentence fragment.	Chapter 32, Fragments
run-on **RO** **fused sentence** **cs** **comma splice**	You have two (or more) complete sentences joined together improperly, either with or without a comma.	Chapter 33, Run-Ons: Fused Sentences and Comma Splices
verb **s/v agr** **tense** **tense shift** **verb form**	You have a problem with your verbs in this sentence.	Chapter 31, Finding and Fixing the Major Verb Errors

(*continued*)

Correction	What it might mean	Related chapters in this book; other places to go for help
(,)	Either you have a comma that shouldn't be there or you need a comma.	Chapter 35, Commas
pro agr pro ag pro ref pronoun ref pronoun circled pronoun with "?" next to it	Either you used the wrong pronoun or the reader cannot tell what noun your pronoun is replacing.	Chapter 34, Pronouns
awk awkward unclear mixed sentence predication error	Your sentence is hard to follow. It needs a total rewrite. (Don't worry; we've all been there.)	Chapter 37, Mixed Constructions; Chapter 38, Misplaced and Dangling Modifiers
// parallel faulty parallel	You have a sentence with a series of items, but the items in the series do not match up grammatically.	Chapter 36, Parallelism
wordy	You used too many words to say something. You need to be more clear and succinct.	Chapter 39, Clear and Focused Language
word choice wc ww	You used a word that doesn't quite mean what you intended. This error is often caused by an overreliance on a thesaurus.	Look the word up in a dictionary; then figure out a better word for what you meant to say by looking at synonyms. See also Chapter 9, Vocabulary Building.
sp	You spelled a word incorrectly.	Use a dictionary. See also Chapter 41, Spelling and Capitalization.
cap C (or three lines drawn under a letter)	You have a capitalization error.	Chapter 41, Spelling and Capitalization
proof! proofreading edit!	You have many mistakes. If your instructor uses exclamation points, chances are good he or she thinks you are being sloppy and knows you can do better.	Chapter 4, Revising, Editing, and Proofreading; Chapter 27, How to Learn the Rules and Apply Them to Your Own Writing

COMMENTS

The following chart lists some shorthand terms for the comments instructors make on papers. Remember, a correction addresses a problem—usually small or sentence level—that has a right or wrong answer. In contrast, a comment targets ideas, organization, purpose, audience, and other big-picture areas of writing, where there is no one "right" way to revise.

Comment	What it might mean	Related chapters in this book; other places to go for help
plus sign (+) check mark (√)	A plus sign usually means you made a strong point. A check mark probably means you made a good point or did something the instructor wanted you to accomplish. It could also mean you made a mistake.	Do yourself and your classmates a favor by politely asking what a check mark on your paper means, if your instructor forgets to explain it when handing back the first stack of papers.
Underlining	Underlining probably means you wrote something particularly good, but it could mean something else.	Ask your instructor what underlining means.
good! great!	Congratulate yourself—you did well! Now take the time to figure out what was so good. We learn from what we do right, not just from what we do wrong.	If your instructor neglected to put any positive feedback on your paper, set up a private time to go over the paper and ask what strengths he or she sees in your writing.
TS?	You may not have a topic sentence, or your topic sentence may not fit your paragraph.	Chapter 13, Topic Sentences and Paragraphs
organization? structure? org prob	Perhaps you have a paragraph where all the information does not fit under the topic sentence, or a paragraph that does not fit with the rest of the essay. Check to see if the instructor drew arrows or brackets to suggest how you might change the order of information or the paragraph breaks.	Chapter 14, Essay Organization and Outlining

(continued)

Comment	What it might mean	Related chapters in this book; other places to go for help
¶	You may need to break up your paragraph into two paragraphs, which will probably require some revising to smooth over the transition and make sure both paragraphs are complete.	Chapter 13, Topic Sentences and Paragraphs
thesis?	Clarify or strengthen your thesis, or do another revision.	Chapter 11, Thesis and Main Idea
confusing clarity ?	You expressed your idea unclearly. This may require editing, but you probably need to think more about your content.	Reread what you wrote, and try to identify what is unclear. Then choose the chapter that applies. When in doubt, ask your instructor.
more support expand say more	You began to make a good point, but you need more evidence or examples to support your idea well.	Chapter 10, Pre-Writing; Chapter 12, Argument
focus off-topic	You drifted away from the main point you were making or the assigned paper topic generally.	Chapter 11, Thesis and Main Idea; Chapter 14, Essay Organization and Outlining
relate to thesis connection? How does this relate?	You may offer a good example or other piece of evidence, but you don't explain how it supports your point or thesis.	Chapter 13, Topic Sentences and Paragraphs

Eventually, you will learn to interpret your instructor's corrections and comments. To speed this process along, ask questions if you do not understand what your instructor has written.

practice it 18.1 Reviewing Comments and Corrections

Find an essay your instructor has graded and marked, even one from a previous class. Examine the different corrections and comments that were made. Which corrections or comments did you find most helpful? Why? Which corrections or comments do you still not fully understand? How might those corrections or comments still apply to your writing? Make notes, if applicable, on your Grammar Log of any sentence-level issues.

How to Use a Rubric

As we mentioned earlier, some instructors grade with a rubric—an assessment tool that lists the categories on which you are graded, such as content, organization, mechanics, and citations. Rubrics can be simple or very detailed. Sometimes all the instructors who teach a specific course use the same rubric, whereas other times an instructor will personalize rubrics, perhaps for every assignment. A couple of examples follow.

This rubric is point-based, which means it lists specific values for each area:

POINT-BASED RUBRIC

Area	Possible Points	Your Points
Thesis and supporting points	5	
Evidence: amount and quality of quotes, paraphrases, and examples	5	
Organization: paragraphing, order of ideas, transitions	5	
Grammar and mechanics	3	
Proper use of bibliographic style (MLA or APA)	2	
TOTAL	20	

The next rubric is holistic, which means it records strengths and weaknesses in an overall way:

HOLISTIC RUBRIC

	Excellent	Good	Average	Poor	Failing
Content/ quality of argument/ development and support of thesis	Clear thesis; detailed examples; excellent analysis	Same qualities as for excellent, but some examples need more detail or analysis	Insufficient examples to support thesis; examples lack detail; insufficient analysis	Lacks a thesis and/or supporting examples; provides partial argument	Lacks thesis and supporting examples; examples are off-topic; thesis inappropriate for assignment

(continued)

	Excellent	Good	Average	Poor	Failing
Use of source material	Appropriate source material supports argument; introduces all quotes and paraphrases; summarizes well; uses citation correctly	Appropriate source material supports argument; generally introduces quotes and paraphrases; 1–2 minor errors in citation	Uses source material but does not clearly tie it to argument; 3 or more errors in citation	Lacks appropriate source material; multiple errors in citation	Plagiarism (intentional or inadvertent); lacks appropriate source material; multiple errors in citation
Organization/ structure	Clear and logical structure for introduction, body, and conclusion; uses effective transition sentences; has a coherent paragraph structure	Same qualities as for excellent, but may have 1–2 problems with organization, such as ineffective order of information, missing transition, or misplaced paragraph break	Organization is solid and predictable; may have 3–4 problems with some aspect of organization, but these problems do not substantially undermine the argument	Problematic organization, structure, and coherence get in the way of understanding the argument	Essay is disorganized and hard to follow; introduction does not include basic background information; paper lacks a conclusion
Grammar, mechanics, and style	Readable, clear prose; free of major errors	Generally readable prose; 1–2 recurring errors, but they do not impede meaning	Generally readable prose; 3–4 recurring errors, but they do not impede meaning	More than 4 recurring errors or errors that are significant enough to impede meaning	Sufficient major errors that essay is frequently unreadable
MLA style	Follows all aspects of MLA style	Minor errors in MLA style	Several or more serious errors in MLA style	Fundamental problems with MLA style	Fundamental problems with MLA style; may include inadvertent plagiarism

practice it 18.2   Using a Rubric

Score one of your previous essays or several essays from your classmates according to the preceding holistic rubric. Identify specific examples from the essay(s) to justify your scoring. Give the essay an overall grade. Compare your scoring with that of your peers.

Whatever type of rubric your instructor uses, refer to the rubric to understand the grade you earned, and prepare to do better on the next essay. The best way to use a rubric, though, is to keep it on hand during the rough draft and revision stages and refer to it as a checklist to guide your revisions. The clearer the instructor's expectations, the better you will be at following them.

practice it 18.3   Making Your Own Rubric

Make a rubric of your own. Imagine that you are the instructor and are creating a grading rubric for a major assignment in one of your college classes. Looking at the assignment instructions, design a rubric for the assignment. Show it to your instructor for that class and ask his or her opinion. Did you correctly predict the evaluation criteria?

Meeting with an Instructor or Tutor

When you were in high school, being asked to stay after class to meet with your teacher usually meant trouble. College, however, is the complete opposite. In college, students often meet with the instructor outside of class to discuss their work, even when their work is pretty good already. In fact, most full-time instructors are required to have a certain number of regularly scheduled office hours so that students can see them privately to discuss the course material. (Part-time or adjunct faculty members often do not have office hours, but they should have other ways to touch base with you, so ask.)

Meeting with your instructor should be a part of your college mindset. When you need help, knock on his or her door, send an e-mail, or stay after class to ask a question. (If it's a basic question—like the date for a test—then ask a classmate or consult the course schedule, of course.) Generally, your instructors are happy to help you with anything related to the course, and they can even help guide you to appropriate resources on campus if you have other problems that affect your work—such as difficulty adjusting to college life. Getting to know at least one instructor, especially one in a field of study that you are considering pursuing, will benefit you because he or she can offer advice about your educational and career path and often write you letters of recommendation later.

Sometimes you may be advised by your instructor to visit a tutor on campus. Again, this may require a mental shift for you. Seeing a tutor does not mean you are "dumb" or "don't get it." In fact, once you get to the tutoring center, you discover that the one thing the students there have in common is their motivation to improve, a hallmark of successful students. Sometimes students who need to review basic skills seek tutoring, but just as often, the most advanced students pull up a chair with a tutor to improve their work.

Whatever you do, don't wait until it's too late to seek help. Coming to your instructor for help fifteen minutes before an essay is due won't accomplish much—except maybe irritate your instructor. However, students who show a solid track record of seeking help and try their best are generally treated with fairness and respect by instructors, especially when an emergency arises.

So, once you decide to see your instructor or a tutor, how can you make the most of the visit? Come prepared by bringing:

- a copy of your paper, outline, or notes for wherever you are in the writing process
- the sources (books, articles, and printouts of Web pages) you are planning to use in the essay
- a specific list of questions you have or a specific problem to work on

When you sit down with a tutor, he or she will probably start by asking what kind of help you need. The more specific you are, the better. If you just show a tutor your draft, he or she may focus on grammar errors, when you really need more help with the thesis of a very rough draft. Remember, tutors are not taking the class with you and aren't familiar with the readings or assignment, but they can still tell whether a piece of writing makes sense or not. In fact, they serve as good outside readers exactly for this reason. Be clear about the type of help you want at this stage of the process, and both you and the tutor will find the meeting more useful and enjoyable.

chapter review

In the following chart, fill in the second column to record in your own words the important skills included in this chapter. Then assess yourself to determine whether you are still developing the skill or feel you have mastered it. If you are still developing the skill, make some notes about what you need to work on to master it in the future. If you believe you have already mastered it, explain why.

Skills and concepts covered in this chapter	Explanation in your own words	I'm developing this skill and need to work on . . .	I believe I have mastered this skill because . . .
Participating in peer review			

Skills and concepts covered in this chapter	Explanation in your own words	I'm developing this skill and need to work on . . .	I believe I have mastered this skill because . . .
Understanding instructors' corrections			
Interpreting and applying instructors' comments			
Using a rubric			
Having effective meetings with instructors and tutors			

19
Essay Exams

Believe it or not, instructors don't give essay tests to be mean. Rather, they need to find out how well you can prepare and write an essay in a limited amount of time without getting feedback from others or writing multiple drafts. They may also be checking your grammar when you write under pressure. It's a challenge to write an essay in a limited time, but learning a few simple strategies for essay-test preparation can help you write a better essay and earn a higher grade on your exam.

Preparing Mentally and Physically for an Essay Exam

Preparing effectively for an essay exam helps reduce your test anxiety. Test anxiety is that nervous feeling you get when you are going to take a test. Your palms get sweaty, you feel butterflies in your stomach, or—worst of all—your mind goes blank. Test anxiety affects most people to some extent. Many of us feel a little nervous before a test, even when we are well prepared. Some people, however, have severe test anxiety: They may hyperventilate, feel like they will be sick, or be utterly unable to perform. If you have this type of debilitating anxiety, certainly you should look into test anxiety counseling resources at your school.

If your problem is the run-of-the-mill test anxiety that most people face, what are the best coping strategies? Right before and during the test, you can practice the same helpful strategies you use for any stressful life situation:

- Make sure you're well rested and have had a good breakfast.
- Take some deep breaths.

- Tense and then relax each of your major muscle groups.
- Do whatever you might normally do to get "psyched up" for something like a big game, a big date, or a job interview.

What *shouldn't* you do? Don't sit out in the hall cramming right before the test—this won't help, and it could hurt. Also, don't talk about how nervous you are. You'll only make the feeling worse. Definitely avoid any friends who are complaining about the test or going on about how nervous they are. Anxiety can be contagious, and you don't need more of it.

These do's and don'ts for coping with test anxiety really do help. But over the years, we have found that the very best way to reduce test anxiety is to *prepare well for the test*. Many students seem to think that they can't prepare for essay exams, that they have to just "wing it," but really there is a lot you can do to make sure you're prepared. So let's look at some key strategies for essay-test preparation.

Understanding the Expectations for the Essay Exam

To prepare well for tests, you need to understand your instructors' expectations for essay exams in general and for the specific tests you are taking. Let's start with the expectations for essay exams in general.

ESSAY EXAMS IN GENERAL

When instructors give essay exams, they want students to engage in higher-level thinking. Multiple-choice and fill-in-the-blank questions are useful for assessing students' understanding and memorization of facts. This is often important in college, especially in introductory classes. But you will eventually be required to do more than just show that you understood and retained information: You will be expected to apply, analyze, synthesize, and evaluate complex ideas. And that's where essay tests come in.

A good way to understand what's involved is to look at something called "Bloom's Taxonomy." This taxonomy, or classification system, divides knowing and thinking into six levels—a sort of pyramid with each level built on the previous ones. As you move up the pyramid, you find more complex thinking tasks. Let's take a quick tour of the levels in Bloom's Taxonomy, starting at the bottom (see figure on p. 368).

Knowledge is the basic level. Questions at this level merely ask, "What do you already know about the topic?" They test your ability to recall facts.

EVALUATE
Assess and
judge

SYNTHESIZE
Put ideas, concepts, or parts
together as a new whole

ANALYZE
Break a concept, event, or text into parts

APPLY
Use what you have learned in a new context or situation

COMPREHEND
Show your understanding of what you have learned

KNOW
Recall facts

Pyramid Based on Bloom's Taxonomy

Questions at the *comprehension* level ask, "Do you understand what you have recently learned?" That is, can you explain in your own words what you read for class or heard in a lecture? Both knowledge and comprehension are necessary for higher-level thinking.

Higher-level thinking begins with *application*. Questions at this level ask, "Can you apply what you have learned to a new context or situation?" If, for instance, you learned a formula for solving one math problem, can you apply that formula to solve another, similar math problem?

Analysis has many specific forms. But, essentially, an analysis question asks you to take a complex thing—for example, an article or a poem or a historical event—and break it down into parts so that you can better understand the whole. For instance, can you analyze the way an author structures an article so you see his or her main points in a better (deeper and more sophisticated) way?

Synthesis questions ask you to put things together into a new whole. Think about a musical synthesizer: It takes a bunch of different sounds and puts them all together to make a song. A synthesis question might ask you to take various articles on a topic and put them together, and then to use the result to come up with new ideas about that topic. Often you synthesize other people's ideas to propose the best solution to a complicated problem.

Finally, we have the highest level of thinking: *evaluation*. An evaluation question might ask you to take a position and defend it with evidence from what you read.

Instructors often write questions that ask for a combination of these types of thinking, as you will see when we look at sample questions.

THE SPECIFIC EXAM

A week or two before a test, make time to gather information about the test: What will the format be? What content will it cover? How will your instructor be grading it? That is, what does he or she expect from you? For most English composition classes, essay exams cover the readings you have been doing for the class, and the format will be a long essay, but be sure to confirm this and to get details. There are several possible sources for this information.

- **The course syllabus.** Reread the part of the syllabus that refers to this test, looking for details such as how it might be structured, what it will cover, and how many points it is worth. You might also look at the course learning objectives, as these are generally good guidelines of the instructor's expectations.

- **The rubric.** A rubric is an assessment tool that lists the categories on which you are graded. If your instructor has given you a rubric for the exam, this is the best guide to his or her expectations. By reviewing the rubric beforehand, you gain a clear sense of what you need to accomplish in the exam. Alternatively, you might look at the rubrics for previous out-of-class essays or the comments that he or she wrote on your papers. While the expectations for in-class exams and out-of-class essays are usually not identical, looking at these rubrics and comments gives you a useful review of the instructor's expectations as well as your strengths and weaknesses.

▶ **For more on rubrics, see Chapter 18, Giving and Receiving Feedback.**

- **Your notes.** Over the semester, instructors usually give a few hints about the test questions. And if they refer to certain topics again and again, you can assume these topics will show up on the test.

- **Your instructor.** If you feel these sources don't give you enough information, ask the instructor, either in class—your classmates will thank you for it—or privately during office hours or via e-mail. Be polite, and ask far enough in advance. Instructors really hate to hear the question "Is this gonna be on the test?" because it implies that students don't care at all about the topic being discussed and only care about their grades. However, instructors love to hear things like "I'm trying to do my best, but I'm a little overwhelmed by the material. Can you give me some guidance on the test format and content?" Some instructors make previous exam questions or study guides available to students, while others expect students to make the study guides themselves.

Studying for an Essay Exam

Once you have gathered information about the content and format, you are ready to *study*. Many students feel they can't study the content for an essay exam, but that's not true. In fact, essay exams usually assume that you have deep familiarity with a topic, the kind of familiarity you can best get by reviewing and thinking through the material beforehand. So how do you do that?

STARTING WITH AN OVERVIEW

Hopefully, you have been taking good notes on class lectures and discussions, and have been annotating in your books all along. This helps tremendously. Gather your materials and find a big table or workspace free of distractions. (Those study tables in the library are ideal.) Take a few minutes to read through your notes and annotations just to refresh your memory about the major topics covered in class. Go back and read through the weekly schedule. Sometimes this really helps you get the big-picture view.

For instance, let's say you are taking a midterm in your English class. You've read seven or eight articles at this point. You can barely remember the titles or authors, much less see the big picture of how they all fit together. An hour spent reviewing them may reveal the common threads or themes or issues that you couldn't see when you read the articles one at a time. It's likely the essay exam will ask you to synthesize this information, so you have to be able to see the connections between the readings. Rereading the questions that accompany each reading is also extremely useful.

practice it 19.1 Brainstorming Sample Questions

Take some time—either by yourself or with some classmates—to try to guess what the upcoming exam questions will be for your English course. Write up sample questions as if you were the instructor. Compare your questions to those of your classmates. Which questions seem most likely to be asked? Why?

CHARTING

Another way to review the materials is to make a chart that covers all the readings, similar to the one on page 71 in Chapter 2, Active and Critical Reading.

Typically, you would use an article-by-article chart to prepare for an essay exam in an English composition class. As you can see from the example, each article has its own row, with columns to list the main points, key details (including, possibly, quotes), and your notes and ideas.

ARTICLE title and author(s)	Main points	Key details	My notes and ideas

Filling out a chart like this one helps you to review the material, see the big picture, and identify connections between the readings—all of which, in turn, make it easier for you to come up with a thesis for your essay exam.

Charts can be created in a variety of ways, depending on what you have read and what you hope to accomplish. A chart about one long book might have each chapter listed in the column on the left, with different themes or topics across the top. A chart about a film or novel might list each character across the top and down the left, and then you would write the characters' interactions with one another in the boxes. In fact, just thinking about the best way to create the chart is a critical-thinking activity, since it requires you to reflect on what you've read, choose how you will organize your thoughts, and then do the hard work of interpreting the texts along those lines. Visual learners especially like to make charts. If your instructor allows you to bring a page of notes into the exam, your chart would be a great thing to have on that page.

---

practice it 19.2   Designing a Chart

Choose a class for which you have an upcoming exam. Look at the course syllabus to find out the structure of the exam and to review the readings you have completed for the course. Then design a chart that would help you study for that exam. Be prepared to explain why you designed it the way you did.

Dissecting the Question

▶ For more about how to read an essay assignment, see pp. 78–80 in Chapter 3, Putting Ideas into Writing.

If you have prepared well in advance, you will be eager to get started on your essay on the day of the test. However, when the instructor passes out the question on test day, take time to read the entire test carefully and make sure you understand what you are being asked to do. The important point to know and keep in mind is that essay-exam questions are like the essay prompts you've seen throughout the semester. So, to read and understand exam questions, use the process you learned for reading essay prompts in Chapter 3, Putting Ideas into Writing. Really pay attention to what types of thinking you are being asked to do. Often, students write excellent essays but do not earn high grades because they write the wrong type of essay. If the question asks you about cause and effect and you discuss comparisons and contrasts, then your essay will miss the mark. Similarly, if you do not push your thinking high enough on Bloom's Taxonomy, you might get into trouble. Some instructors really do just want you to demonstrate comprehension, which you would do by writing a summary of the ideas that were presented in class. However, if the question asks you to evaluate and all you do is summarize, you will not succeed on that exam.

Take, for example, the following prompt:

> Summarize and make an argument about whether you agree with Ian Leslie's argument in his book *Curious*. Answers must be a (complete essay) and must (use quotations) from the article (be sure to cite page numbers).

Start by looking at the question stem, which is underlined. (Remember, the question stem is the main question or task that the exam is asking you to do.) In this case, the question specifically asks for two things. First, you have to "summarize" ideas—this would be comprehension in Bloom's Taxonomy. Second, you have to "make an argument" about these ideas—this would be evaluation. So you will defend your position with evidence from the text.

Next, look for expectations, which are circled. "Answers must be a complete essay"—this means your answer must have an introduction with a thesis, a body, and a conclusion. Also, the prompt says that you "must use quotations" from Leslie's text.

Finally, look for hints from the instructor. You are reminded to cite page numbers for any quotations you use. Good reminder!

---

practice it 19.3   Understanding Essay-Exam Questions

Choose an article that you have read recently in your English class. Write a sample essay-exam question that requires evaluation, one that requires summary and evaluation, and another that requires summary and application. Remember to include a clear question stem and some hints and parameters.

Making and Sticking to a Plan of Action

Once you have analyzed the essay prompt, the next step is to organize your time and make an action plan. The most common mistakes students make in taking essay exams are the related mistakes of not budgeting time well and not following the steps of the writing process—brainstorming, outlining, drafting, editing, and proofreading. Budget your time so that you can accomplish all these steps during the essay exam. To understand why this is important and to learn how to do it, consider what's involved when you write an essay.

When writing an essay out of class, we break up the many tasks of the writing process and do them separately. But when faced with writing an essay exam, students often try to complete all the steps together at the same time. With their focus stretched too thinly over too many tasks, all of which require focus and attention, there's a good chance they won't do any of them very well.

Make a plan of action that allows you to focus on each part of the writing process separately. Of course, to go through the entire writing process in the test's time frame, you need to budget your time wisely. For a two-hour exam, typically you should budget your time something like this:

Analyzing the question, brainstorming ideas, and generating a working thesis	10–15 minutes
Outlining your ideas	10 minutes
Drafting the essay	70 minutes
Revising the draft for larger changes and additions to content	20 minutes
Editing and proofreading the draft	10–15 minutes
TOTAL TIME	120 minutes

If your class period is only one hour, then you should shorten the time periods for each task something like this:

Analyzing the question, brainstorming ideas, and generating a working thesis	10 minutes
Outlining your ideas	5 minutes

(*continued*)

Drafting the essay	25–30 minutes
Revising the draft for larger changes and additions to content	10 minutes
Editing and proofreading the draft	5–10 minutes
TOTAL TIME	60 minutes

You are probably thinking that these plans don't give you enough time for the drafting part. Keep in mind, however, that much of what slows a writer down when writing is trying to come up with ideas and keep them organized, all while trying to craft strong sentences and remember spelling, grammar, words, and ideas. Anytime you try to do too many things at once, it slows you down. If you separate out each of the steps of the writing process, you won't need as much time for the drafting part of the exam.

You will, of course, customize this time budget to your strengths and weaknesses as a writer. For example, if organization is particularly challenging for you, then budget a little more time for that step and cut back in one of your areas of strength. Consult your previous essay exams to help determine where to expand and contract these sample time lines.

---

practice it 19.4 Customizing Your Essay-Exam Time Budget

▶ For more on time management, see Chapter 3, Putting Ideas into Writing.

Determine the time allowed for your upcoming essay exam. Then review your strengths and weaknesses as a writer by looking over your past essay feedback. Finally, write up your own time budget based on the samples just given.

Step-by-Step Guide to the Essay-Exam Writing Process

STEP 1: **Analyzing the question, brainstorming, and generating a working thesis.** Begin by reading the question carefully several times and underlining the question stem. Then do some brainstorming. Choose whichever method you prefer—freewriting, listing, clustering, questioning, whatever—but do spend a few minutes coming up with ideas. If you were allowed to bring in a chart or any notes, read them over for information that will help with your essay. You might be surprised at how effective a five-minute freewrite can be.

Draft a tentative thesis as part of your brainstorming. Start by using the question stem and turning it into a statement. Don't worry if it sounds a little clunky: You can always make it sound better in revising, but it's helpful to make sure you stick to the question and do what is asked of you. Remember that your thesis should be a direct response to the prompt.

STEP 2: Outlining your ideas.   With a workable thesis and a few key ideas, move to outlining. Jot down a quick bullet-point outline of what you plan to cover. Many students do this on a piece of scrap paper and keep it beside them as they write to help them stay on track. Your outline won't be fancy or perfect, but it should give you enough structure to feel confident enough to start drafting. Some students like to write out the complete topic sentences at this stage.

STEP 3: Drafting the essay.   Now, write the first draft, making sure to check the time after each paragraph to stay within your time budget. Remember to consult your outline periodically so you don't forget any good ideas. If you don't know how to spell a word or can't think of exactly the right phrasing, do not spend too much time on it while drafting. Underline the words you are struggling with so that you remember to fix them later.

STEP 4: Revising the draft for larger changes and additions to content. When you finish the first draft, you might be tired, or you might be excited that you got it done within the time limit, but those are not good reasons to say you are finished. Don't just get up and leave, even if other students have done so. In revising, look for *big* things: Did you break the paragraphs in good places? Did you use good supporting points or examples? Did you explain the support clearly? Are there places where you should add transitions? Do you have a strong introduction and conclusion? Make any necessary changes by neatly inserting them with a caret (∧). Then go back and reread the essay-exam question carefully to make sure you didn't misunderstand or omit anything important.

STEP 5: Editing and proofreading the draft.   Now read through your essay as many times as you can to work on the sentence-level issues. Try to recall the errors your instructor pointed out on previous writing. Make sure each sentence is clear and your vocabulary is appropriate. Fix all the errors you find, but don't recopy your exam. If you have time left, keep proofreading your essay until the exam period is finished.

Finished? Hooray! One down, dozens more to go. Taking essay exams will just keep getting easier as you continue to practice these steps.

chapter review

In the following chart, fill in the second column to record in your own words the important skills included in this chapter. Then assess yourself to determine whether you are still developing the skill or feel you have mastered it. If you are still developing the skill, make some notes about what you need to work on to master it in the future. If you believe you have already mastered it, explain why.

Skills and concepts covered in this chapter	Explanation in your own words	I'm developing this skill and need to work on . . .	I believe I have mastered this skill because . . .
Reducing test anxiety			
Understanding expectations for an essay exam			
Studying for essay exams			
Analyzing essay prompts			
Making an action plan			
Working through the steps of the writing process			

20
Note Taking

in this chapter

- Why Is Note Taking Important?
- What Is the Cornell Method?
- How Do You Avoid Plagiarism When Taking Notes?
- How Do You Create Good Note-Taking Systems?

Taking good notes requires discipline, but it pays off immensely. When you translate what you see and hear in class through your own hand into your own words and pictures, you understand it more fully and are able to recall it more easily. Studying your notes later makes the learning even deeper, but the very action of taking the notes increases learning more than you probably realize.

Taking notes is similar to the reading and writing processes in many ways. To take useful notes:

- **Prepare** your mind to receive the information *before* you take notes
- **Process** the information *during* note taking
- **Synthesize** the information *after* receiving it

Just before class, for instance, you might jot down in your notes a few thoughts about the topic, answering questions such as these:

Preparation Questions

- What do you already know about the topic?
- What have you learned so far in this class? In other classes?
- What key terms or vocabulary applies to the topic for the day?
- Why is the instructor spending time on this topic now? How does it fit into the course as a whole?

Once the presentation begins—whether it is a formal lecture or a class discussion—take notes on the main points, taking time to write down your responses to that information as much as possible. Finally, at the end of the lecture or class, or later that day if necessary, add some comments about what you learned, write down questions about things you still do not understand, and generally organize your thoughts on the topic.

Notes are rarely complete sentences; capture the ideas you've heard accurately but quickly, since instruction continues while you're taking notes. Abbreviations will help you do this. Efficient note takers also develop their own shorthand, leaving out letters. You may already have developed your own system, but here are some common abbreviations and symbols you can use if you haven't:

Common Abbreviations and Symbols

@ = at	govt = government
b/c = because	w/ = with
btwn = between	←→ = relates to
dif = different or difference	+ = positive, pro, or good point
esp = especially	− = negative, con, or bad point
ex = example	~ = approximately or about

The Cornell Method of Note Taking

You will eventually develop your own style for taking notes, but a good place to begin is with the Cornell method, developed at Cornell University. This method gives you space to write down what the instructor says and to record your thoughts, reactions, questions, and connections to the material. In essence, the Cornell note method allows you to record notes on the material and then annotate your notes, just as if you were reading a text. This level of thought (called *metacognition*) means you process the material more deeply than if you just listen.

Here's how it works:

STEP 1: **Take notes.**   Divide your page into two columns; the right column should be wider than the left. On the right side of your page, take notes as you read or listen to a lecture or class discussion, summarizing the main ideas and points and jotting down examples.

STEP 2: **Annotate with your ideas and questions.**   On the left side of the page, you take notes on your notes. While you take notes—or, if you feel pressured for time, shortly afterwards—write down your responses, key terms, and any questions you have. For example, if the lecture you're taking notes on is about the wealth gap, you might write, "What is the wealth gap?" in the left column. Then, when you study the notes, fold the paper to cover the right side (the "answer") and quiz yourself using the questions you wrote about the material. Try to write *how* and *why* questions as well as *who, what, where,* and *when* questions.

You can also use the left column for your reflections about the material, especially ideas that come up as you are reviewing the material after class. In classes that are more about critical thinking than memorization of information, the left column becomes a space for you to generate your ideas about the course material.

STEP 3: Summarize.   After class, spend a short time briefly summarizing the information. Your summary can go at the bottom of the page of notes. You can also use this space to reflect more deeply on the material—for example, by connecting the ideas to a previous day's information or even another course you have taken.

STEP 4: Review and recite.   On a daily or weekly basis, reread, recite, and rethink your notes, questions, and summaries. Actually reciting the information—saying it out loud—can be effective for people who learn best by listening and speaking. Waiting until the day before the test to read your notes is not as effective as reviewing them more frequently.

Here's a sample of what your notebook page would look like in the Cornell notes system:

LIST THE COURSE NAME, TOPIC, AND DATE HERE:

Your Annotations on Your Notes	Your Notes on the Lecture or Discussion
List key terms, specific questions that will help you recall the material, and anything you don't understand. In a content-heavy class, like biology, use this section to write down questions to use while quizzing yourself later.	List, in your own words, the main points from the presentation, lecture, or class discussion. Don't try to copy down everything. Focus on the main points. Make drawings or diagrams to help you remember the key points. If you think you missed something, draw a line and remember to ask a classmate or your instructor after class about what you missed.

Your Summary of the Lecture or Discussion

Review all your notes from both columns. Write a summary of the entire lecture or discussion, and make comments about how this information fits in with the other information from the course.

> **practice it 20.1** The Cornell Method
>
> Make a Cornell notes page in your notebook. Then take notes on your next class lecture, discussion, or reading using the Cornell notes method. Afterward, reflect on how well the method worked for you. Were you able to study the information more or less effectively than with your current note-taking method? Why? Did you stay more engaged with the material when you forced yourself to take notes on it? Remember, you will need practice if the method is new to you.

Note Taking in Other Situations

The Cornell notes method described in the preceding section was designed for students to use during lectures, where the instructor presents large amounts of information and expects students to record it accurately in their notes. You can adapt the Cornell method in your own ways to many situations, but sometimes you need additional techniques, such as for classroom discussions, small-group activities, film viewings, and interviews.

CLASS DISCUSSIONS

It's easy to neglect to take notes on classroom discussions, either because you get so wrapped up in the conversation that you forget or because you—erroneously—believe that you should only take notes on material the instructor presents. Remember, any classroom discussions or small-group activities your instructor has you do are part of the planned coursework. Class discussion provides additional perspectives on a reading or topic. The instructor expects you to take new knowledge or skills away from the experience, and recording notes about what you heard, observed, or said is the best way to ensure that you will recall the information later.

When you take notes on a classroom discussion, it is not necessary to write down each student's name with his or her comments (though if you can, that's great). Rather, you might put people's comments into categories or groups based on the content of what they say. For instance, if you have a class debate, you might create two columns in your notes, one for "comments from people who are for X" and another for "comments from people who are against X." You might even add a third column for miscellaneous comments and your own ideas.

On the next page you will find an example from a student's notes on a class discussion about whether financial literacy should be taught in the school system or at home.

Taught at school	Taught at home	Other ideas
parents don't know enough to teach kids—just look at the mess the older gen. has already created—we need schools to do it	different cultural values—money is personal—I don't want someone else teaching my kid those kinds of values	why can't you do both? first @ home then @ school?
it's a basic life skill—we teach home ec, why not how to balance a check-book or pick the best credit card?	kids need to focus on reading, writing, and math, not "extras" like finance	
	if it's supposed to start early, then it has to start in the home b/c kids don't go to school until age 5	

Taking notes in this way helps you see the different sides of the debate—and the holes in each side's thinking. Remember, you don't have to end up in the same place you started. Maybe after listing all the ideas that come out of class discussion, you will decide to change your own position a little or a lot.

SMALL-GROUP ACTIVITIES

Small-group activities are another situation in which students often don't take good notes. Too often, when an instructor assigns students to a small group to complete a specific task, the students agree to let one person—usually the one with the neatest handwriting—take all the notes. This causes trouble for a few reasons. First, what happens if that person misses the next class period? The notes are usually gone. Second, note taking has really nothing to do with handwriting, so there's no rea-son why the person with the best handwriting would be the best note taker. Third, and most important, the very process of taking notes is a learning experience. By writing down your thoughts and other people's ideas, you are processing and learning the information. Sure, it's work, but it's very worthwhile work—hardly the busywork that many people believe it to be. So make sure you take your own notes, even if a group note taker has been appointed, so you have the information to study and for future assignments.

TIP

Sharing notes electronically is a good way to keep everyone involved; this way if someone is out sick, the group does not fall behind.

FILM AND VIDEO SCREENINGS

▶ For more about
analyzing film and
video, see pages 149–50
in Chapter 5, Active
Reading Strategies.

Taking notes during a film is an art developed by film reviewers decades ago, before videos and DVDs allowed multiple viewings. While you may have the opportunity to watch a film a second time, this won't always be the case. Taking good notes the first time around saves time and helps you remember the film's contents. Here are a few tips:

- **Predict what the film will be about before it starts.** Use the title of the film to make a prediction, and consider all the ways you might want to refer to the film in your upcoming writing assignments. Determine why the instructor chose to show this film at this time. What do you expect to get out of it?

- **Jot down the title, director, date (if known), and company that made the film at the top of your notes.** This information is usually in the credit sequence. If you miss it, consult an online database, like the Internet Movie Database, to fill in details.

- **For fiction films, make note of important details.** While watching, make note of characters' names, music, repeated lines, frequently used colors, repeated shots, significance of clothing, symbolism in props, and anything else that seems important, even if you don't know why it is important yet. If you have a particular reaction to the film—like you laugh or get scared while watching it—note when in the film this happened.

- **For documentary films, make notes on the arguments presented.** Just as you would annotate an article that tries to inform or persuade, write notes about the evidence used to support the arguments in the film. Note down the types of experts used—and their names, if you can catch them—and if any "ordinary" people's opinions are included. Write down facts that you might want to look up in more detail later. If the documentary presents an argument, you might divide your notes into two columns marked "argument" and "counterargument."

- **After the film, take ten to fifteen minutes to summarize it.** Record your thoughts while they are fresh in your mind.

- **Remember to take notes on anything your instructor mentions about the film,** as well as on any class discussion of it afterward.

While you are usually not expected to catch entire quotes from films, make your best attempt to include accurate information in your essays. Good notes help you earn credibility.

INTERVIEWS

One of the most difficult note-taking situations that you are likely to encounter in college is when you have to interview someone. Interviewing requires several sophisticated tasks: asking good questions, listening, interpreting someone's tone, being open and pleasant even if you're nervous or confused, and thinking on the spot. Add to that the need to take absolutely accurate notes on what your interview subject says, and you understand why most reporters actually study formal shorthand, a very rapid system for writing. Ask your subject in advance for permission to record the interview: If he or she agrees, this will be very helpful. Either way, however, preparation is key to successful interviews. These steps will help you prepare for an interview:

STEP 1: Brainstorm a list of questions you hope to ask. Open-ended questions (those without a yes-or-no answer) work best. For instance, "What was it like to major in engineering?" is an open-ended question. If you ask "Did you like majoring in engineering?" you will likely get a simple "yes" or "no" answer.

STEP 2: Review your list of questions. Group items into categories, starting at basic information and moving to deeper and/or more personal questions. Always end on one or two positive questions. Don't try to cover more than ten deeper questions during an interview. Usually, you only have time to ask five or six intensive questions during a short interview with a talkative person.

STEP 3: Type up a note-taking page. Include spaces for all the basic information you need to gather, followed by your questions with spaces below to jot down notes.

STEP 4: Highlight the questions that are your top priorities. You can skip other questions if you are running out of time.

Here's a sample of what a note-taking page might look like for a student interviewing another student on his or her attitudes about money.

My interview with: _____

Date: _____

Interview conducted at _____

Sex: M/F   Age: _____ Live with parents? Yes/No

Major: _____

Career goals: _____

Paying for school yourself? Yes/No

Credit cards? Yes/No   How many? _____

What kinds of early experiences do you remember having with money as a kid?

(continued)

How does money influence your career goals? _____

_____

What, in your view, is the relationship between money and
happiness? _____

_____

How much control do you feel you have over your finances?

_____

What is your biggest strength in terms of money? _____

_____

Thank you for your time.

Coming to the interview prepared with a sheet like this saves you from
having to write down the basics, giving you more time to make eye contact and create a rapport with the interview subject.

Avoiding Plagiarism When Taking Research Notes

▶ **For more on avoiding
plagiarism, see Chapter 17,
Quotation and Paraphrase.
For more on evaluating
sources, see Chapter 21,
Research.**

You have probably heard of plagiarism and know it is bad, but if you are
like most college students, you may not fully understand it or know how
to avoid it. Plagiarism means that you improperly take credit for someone else's work, whether intentionally or unintentionally. Intentional or
not, it's wrong, and it will get you into all sorts of trouble—not to mention that you'll never learn much if you let other people do your thinking
for you. Unintentional plagiarism often comes about as a result of
improper note taking, so avoiding plagiarism is one more important
reason to develop strong note-taking skills.

Develop good note-taking and study habits now so that you do not
get into crisis mode or even inadvertently plagiarize. It is best to develop
these good habits when paper assignments are relatively short, instead
of waiting until you have a massive paper with multiple sources to juggle. To develop good organizational habits while doing research, begin
with consistently using an organized system for note taking. Three
options are a note card system, a notebook system, or an electronic
system.

THE NOTE CARD SYSTEM

In a note card system, you write all the bibliographic information for
each source on a separate note card and assign each card a number: 1, 2,

3, and so on. These are called the bibliography cards. Then you take notes from your sources, writing one piece of information (one quotation or paraphrase) on each card. These are called the note cards. Write the source number and page number (if there is one) on the note card as well. Be extremely careful to add the quotation marks around the exact words you take from a source so that you do not get confused later on, think those are your words, and unintentionally plagiarize. Making the quotation marks extremely large can help. Some students write quotes in one color pen and their own words in another color to make clear which words are theirs.

When you are planning your essay, you can move the note cards around to help you visualize how the essay might be organized. Then, when typing up the draft, add in the appropriate citations for each note, which you find by looking at the corresponding bibliography card. Make sure you include the parenthetical documentation when you write the sentence, or else you will waste time later looking it up again.

THE NOTEBOOK SYSTEM

To use a handwritten notebook system, make sure you use a clean page of your notebook for each source so that you are clear about which piece of information came from which source. At the top of the page, write the full bibliographic citation in MLA style (or in another style recommended by your instructor, such as APA style). (Writing it up in proper style now helps you avoid the problem of leaving out information you didn't know you needed, information that might take you precious time to track down again.) Then take notes from that source—and that source only—on that page. List the page numbers directly next to each note, and copy quotations carefully. If you run onto a second page, immediately staple the pages together, or recopy the citation at the top of the page so that you don't lose the source if the pages get separated later.

▶ For more on citing sources properly, see Chapter 22, MLA Documentation, and Chapter 23, APA Documentation.

ELECTRONIC NOTE-TAKING SYSTEMS

Note cards and notebooks work perfectly well, but many students become frustrated quickly with the time it takes to copy out citations and quotations, and then type them up. Since the majority of your information is accessed in an online form, you may decide to take all your notes for a project on a computer. If you have established a good system for online document management, with folders for each college course, use it to stay organized and avoid accidental plagiarism. The image on page 386 shows what one student's online folders for her English course look like.

My Drive > **English 100 Fall 2016** ▾		
Name ↑	Owner	Last modified
📁 Dweck Paper	me	2:28 pm
📁 Money and Wealth Essay	me	2:23 pm
📁 My Homework Assignments	me	2:23 pm
📁 Readings from Class	me	2:23 pm
📁 Syllabus and Other Course Handouts	me	2:23 pm

Many commercial note-taking software products are available, and they may be useful as you continue your college career. Essentially, these programs allow you to create a personal database of all the notes you have from your classes. For example, suppose you are writing an essay on twins for your English class. You would add notes on all your sources directly into the database. Then, two semesters later, when you are in a psychology class and are asked to write a research paper on twins, you can easily access those potentially useful English class notes. For students who plan to major in medical fields, this can be especially helpful, as you can track all the studies you have read and can access your notes on them later, when you start your career. If you plan to purchase note-taking software, sign up for a free trial first to make sure you like it. Also, check for educational software discounts online or at your school bookstore if you decide to purchase.

Alternatively, here's an easy system for taking research notes within your word-processing program. While it may not provide a comprehensive searchable database of notes, if you organize all your course notes into folders, you will be able to access the information years later.

STEP 1: Create a folder on your computer, flash drive, or online documents storage for each class. Label folders and subfolders clearly and consistently. For example, you might have a folder called "English 100 Fall 2016" and within that folder, subfolders for each major essay you are writing. You might have separate folders for homework, readings, and course handouts.

STEP 2: Save the articles you find, giving them clear document titles. Since it's so easy to save PDFs or other electronic versions of articles, save them while researching even if you're not sure you'll use them. Give them titles that will help you remember what they're about. In the image

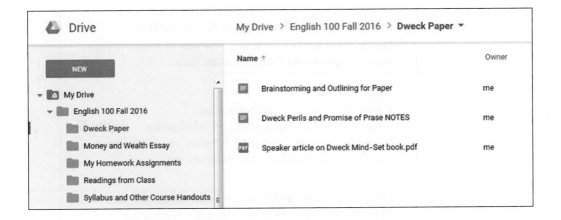

shown above the student has named one PDF file "Speaker article on Dweck Mind-Set book."

STEP 3: For each source that you consult, create a new note-taking document and save it in the appropriate folder.   Name the document with the author's last name and a shortened version of the title of the article or book so that you will recognize it easily. For example, for the article by Carol S. Dweck called "The Perils and Promises of Praise" in Chapter 1, you might label the document "Dweck Perils and Promises of Praise NOTES" (as in the sample document on page 388) or "Dweck NOTES."

STEP 4: At the top of the note-taking document, type out the full citation.   Do this now, at the beginning, and use the bibliographic style your instructor recommends—probably MLA style in an English class. Then, when it comes time to write your paper, you can copy and paste the citation into your Works Cited list and you will not be rushed. You will also know what to put into the parenthetical citations in the text of your paper. The References tool in MS Word can help you create citations.

STEP 5: After you write up the full citation, type up your notes from that source.   If you copy and paste material from an online source, be especially careful to add quotation marks around it so you do not later think those are your own words and unintentionally plagiarize. Record page and paragraph numbers for all information from your sources, whether a quote or something you put in your own words. If you take notes from a Web site, include the date you looked at the material (called the "access date"). As you take notes, write up all the relevant information, using questioning: Who? What? Where? When? Why? How? If you mention a person, make sure you note that person's credentials and/or area of expertise. Also be sure to spell first and last names correctly.

Dweck Perils and Promises of Praise NOTES

Dweck, Carol S. "The Perils and Promises of Praise." *Educational Leadership* 65.2 (2007): 34–39. Print.

MAIN POINTS:
- fixed mind-set vs. growth mind-set
- teachers should praise effort, not intelligence
- growth mind-set is better b/c it makes you more open to learning, not afraid to make mistakes, etc.

QUOTES:
"Most of those praised for intelligence wanted the easy task, whereas most of those praised for effort wanted the challenging task and the opportunity to learn" (37).
"Finally, when asked to report their scores (anonymously), almost 40 percent of the intelligence-praised students lied. Apparently, their egos were so wrapped up in their performance that they couldn't admit mistakes" (37).

STEP 6: **When you finish gathering notes and are ready to begin planning your paper, print out all your notes, looking for patterns and ideas.** As you read and arrange the notes, use different-colored highlighters to mark different subtopics. Once you complete your outline, keep your highlighted notes on the table as you write. That way, you can copy and paste quotes and paraphrases into your paper, making sure to include the correct parenthetical citation as you do. Having the hard copy on your desk can really help you keep your thoughts organized, and you can check off information as you put it into your draft so that you do not reuse the same example or forget a point. This will save you time and ensure that you do not accidentally leave out a source, mistype a quote, or get confused about which source you are using.

practice it 20.2 Taking Notes

Check your syllabus to see the next reading assignment you have for this course. Create a note-taking document for the source and begin to take notes on it. Remember to give the document a title you'll be able to find in your computer files.

chapter review

In the following chart, fill in the second column to record in your own words the important skills included in this chapter. Then assess yourself to determine whether you are still developing the skill or feel you have mastered it. If you are still developing the skill, make some notes about what you need to work on to master it in the future. If you believe you have already mastered it, explain why.

Skills and concepts covered in this chapter	Explanation in your own words	I'm developing this skill and need to work on . . .	I believe I have mastered this skill because . . .
Taking notes with the Cornell method			
Taking notes during class discussions			
Taking notes during collaborative activities			
Taking notes with films and videos			
Taking notes during interviews			
Avoiding plagiarism			
Using an organized system for note taking			

21
Research

in this chapter

- What Should You Look for in Source Materials?
- What Resources Can a College Library Provide?
- What Is the Role of the Internet in Academic Research?
- How Do You Work with Sources?

With the digital culture in which we live, information is easily accessible and in many cases free. However, more access to information doesn't necessarily make researching easier. In fact, sifting through vast amounts of information—online or in a library database—can prove challenging and require finely tuned skills. Information literacy—the ability to find, evaluate, and organize information from a wide variety of sources—will play a growing role in your educational and professional lives. Acquiring excellent research skills begins with understanding the fundamentals of good sources, the different avenues you can use to find them, and the best way to present them in your own work.

What to Look for in Source Materials

If you are reading this chapter, either you have been assigned to write an essay that requires research or you have decided on your own to seek out extra information to flesh out the ideas in your paper. Remember that your instructor has already selected your course materials, so be sure to rely on your instructor-provided course content first, before you tackle research. Then, if there are gaps in your knowledge, or you are curious to find out more about an issue covered in your course materials, use research to supplement your evidence. As you do research, bear in mind certain key factors about the information you find: its source, credibility, relevance, and currency.

SOURCE

The *source* of information means simply that: Where does it come from, and who wrote it or said it? With the expansion of the Internet, it can be difficult to figure out where a piece of information originated. Some sites simply plagiarize from other sources, often badly misrepresenting the information in the process. Many sites pick up information from other places and present it with an acknowledgment of where it originally appeared. In other cases, an article that is published in a scholarly journal, like *Pediatrics*, might get rewritten for a more general audience in a magazine like *Psychology Today*. Your best bet when researching information is to find the place where that information comes from, its original publication. It's sort of like that old game of telephone; when information is repeated several times, the facts become distorted.

CREDIBILITY

Credibility is the cornerstone of good research: As you look for sources, you always need to judge whether the author and publication should be trusted. Ask yourself, "What qualifications does this author have to write about this topic?" and "What kind of reputation does the publication have? Why did it publish this work?" Ideally, you will find sources where the author's background is clearly indicated, either at the start or the end of the article. If you cannot find the author's credentials, search for that person on a biographical database or the Internet. Figuring out the quality of a particular publication can be trickier. How does the *New York Times* compare to the *Toledo Blade*? An Internet search can also help here, to some extent. Research librarians and your instructor can help, too. You will also learn through experience, which you will accumulate much more quickly if you ask for help from instructors and librarians.

▶ **For more about evaluating sources for credibility, see pages 334–35 in Chapter 17, Quotation and Paraphrase.**

RELEVANCE

In research, *relevance* refers to how appropriate the information is for your project. With so much information available at our fingertips, sometimes we get fascinated by a statistic or example and want to include it, even when it might not be directly relevant to the point we are trying to support. One common problem with doing open-ended Google searches is that the search results are based on popularity; or companies pay to have their results listed first, and the top-listed search results don't always fit your topic. You have to sort through pages and pages of links to find something relevant. Learning to focus your search strategies can help solve that problem, and library databases are a great place to start.

CURRENCY

Finally, note the currency of a piece of researched information. *Currency* refers to how current, or recent, a source is. Your writing topic is important in determining currency. For instance, if you are writing about computer technology, a source that is three years old will probably be so outdated as to be completely useless, but if you are writing about the Civil War, a well-written ten-year-old book about the war might be just fine.

▶ For more on reading critically, see Chapter 2, Active and Critical Reading.

In the digital age, you need fairly sophisticated skills in reading and interpreting a wide variety of sources, from books to Web sites and everything in between. As you research, annotate sources to determine their usefulness and quality, just as you would with a book or article. Use the same critical-reading strategies in choosing sources that you use in reading the texts that your instructor has selected for you.

Your College Library

Your research should begin with your college library's resources, whether these are in the physical library or online. College and university libraries—also known as academic libraries—operate somewhat differently from public libraries. In your college life, you will mostly use your school's library, but you may need to supplement your research with books and articles from your public library or other academic libraries.

---

practice it 21.1   Web Resources

Visit the following important Web sites and bookmark them for quick reference.

Your college library

Your public library or libraries

Nearby academic libraries, especially those that have an exchange with your campus

WorldCat: www.worldcat.org (WorldCat allows you to search worldwide library catalogs simultaneously.)

Take a library tour, if one is available, whether your instructor requires it or not. It's best to take your tour early in the semester, before you are in a big rush to finish a major project. Take the time to get familiar with the layout of the place and you will feel far more comfortable doing research there. Many libraries offer research orientations online or in person, so ask about this while you visit the library. Also, freshen up your knowledge of your library from time to time. Information databases are always changing, and as you progress in your education, you will be required to consult more and more specialized resources. So, in the beginning of your college career, you will use some of the more general materials, such as the ProQuest or EBSCO periodical databases, but as you move into your field of study, you need to learn more about the specialized resources the library offers.

The college library offers many resources for research:

- **Books** are usually available on open library shelves, but special or rare books might be held in special collections, which you can access by permission. Some colleges have e-books that you can electronically check out to download or read on e-readers. Most colleges offer Interlibrary Loan to get books you need from other libraries, though there may be a fee for this service. If you need a book that your college does not have, it is usually best to also check your local public library or other area academic libraries for it first. You can use WorldCat to do that.

- **Media**, including movies, television shows, taped lectures, music, and sometimes even art works or other artifacts, are often available for checkout. Find out whether you have to check separate catalogs to find these materials.

- **Periodicals** include newspapers, magazines, and scholarly journals. Increasingly, most of these materials are accessed in an online format through a periodical database. ProQuest, EBSCOhost, SIRS, JSTOR, and Project MUSE are examples of databases to which your school might subscribe. What this means is that the college pays a fee so that students can quickly and easily locate and access articles that were published in many different newspapers, magazines, or journals. Specialized databases in specific disciplines—like ProQuest Nursing & Allied Health Source, PsycARTICLES, or Literature Resource Center—will be important as you do more advanced research in your field of study. Take time to visit your library, or go online to see which databases your school provides and how to access them. You will probably need to log in with a student ID or library card to gain access. Your school may offer an orientation to the databases or an online tutorial.

- **A learning environment** such as a library is a great place to study, work on group projects with other students, use a computer on campus, or get reserve materials: books, articles, or other course materials, such as videos, sample tests, and class notes, that your instructor has provided. Usually you can check these out for a specified period, from an hour to a day or two. This system allows many students to share the materials fairly. Ask your instructors if they have put any materials on reserve for your classes.

practice it 21.2   Tour Your College Library

Many people are nervous about going to new places. Your college library might seem huge, and you might worry that you'll have trouble finding what you need in it. Find a map of your library, either at the

continued ❯

library or on its Web site. Scan the map to get a general sense of where the different sections of the library are located. Once you have an idea of where things are, visit the library for a half hour or so. Make sure that during your visit you learn how to check out a book, find course reserves, and get access to articles.

The Role of the Internet in Academic Research

The best thing about the Internet is that it offers so much free information. The worst thing about the Internet is that it offers so much free information. Anyone can create a Web site, but relatively few sites are worthwhile. Often, a Google search of the open Web (that is, the nonsubscription, freely accessible portions of the Internet) returns too many sites to sort through efficiently, so inexperienced researchers end up just following the top few results, which do not necessarily provide credible or relevant information.

When you have a question that requires research, it's tempting to turn on your computer or smartphone or tablet, type a phrase into Google, and consider your research done. The truth is, all of us—and certainly the authors of this book—use this research strategy for some purposes every day, and that's okay. An expert researcher, though, knows when a quick search is adequate—like when you can't remember particular dates from the U.S. Civil War—and when it isn't. For any academic project that requires research, you'll need to hunt for and evaluate a variety of relevant sources before considering your research complete.

Your best tools as a college researcher are the online periodical databases to which your college library subscribes, like ProQuest, EBSCO, Gale, JSTOR, and Opposing Viewpoints. Learning to use these databases well saves you time and gives you access to a wider array of credible resources than you can find through a Google search. Online periodical databases comb through millions of articles—many of which are not freely accessible through an Internet search—and organize them in a clear, easily searchable way. They also eliminate most of the questionable sources that pop up in a random online search. Think of it this way: If a group of experts were willing to search all the source material on the Internet and present you with the best sources, wouldn't you be happy to let them?

Evaluating Web Sources

When you do go to the open Web for information, take particular care in examining the information's quality and credibility. First, look at the site's title, sponsor, and URL. For many Web sites, the extension (the last three letters of the URL) gives clues about the type of organization or person that created the site as the examples on the next page show.

.com = commercial, for-profit organization, which refers to a profit-making business (such as adweek.com or amazon.com)

.edu = educational organization (such as your college)

.gov = government organization (such as census.gov, the Web site for the U.S. Census)

.org = charitable or nonprofit organization (such as www.lls.org, for the Leukemia and Lymphoma Society)

.net = network (such as an Internet service provider)

.mil = military organization (such as the U.S. Army)

Web sites with any of these extensions might be good sources in the right context, but be aware of any political or profit motive behind a Web site. Information from a government or nonprofit organization might be more objective than that from a commercial Web site, particularly about topics such as product safety. Information on Web sites ending in .edu may be credible information from academic professionals, but students can sometimes have Web sites with .edu URLs, and teachers sometimes post student projects and assignments on their class Web pages. Elementary and high schools also generally have an .edu extension, so it doesn't necessarily indicate a college or university. Follow the usual process of evaluating the information, even with an .edu URL.

In addition to a site's URL, look for other clues about credibility. Ask the same questions about Web sources as you would about any sources: Is the author some sort of expert? Does he or she provide a list of sources and references (a bibliography)? Is the information on the site confirmed by other sources? Are there any obvious errors on the site? What sorts of biases might the Web site or author have? College instructors usually prefer to see sources from reputable nonprofit organizations, like the American Academy of Pediatrics or the U.S. Department of Energy, rather than commercial sites, like BabyCenter or Solar Power USA.

Another part of evaluating sources is evaluating their currency. Find out how recently the Web site has been updated. Page or site updates are often listed at the bottom of a Web site; article dates tend to be under the article title. If no dates are given on the Web site or the article within the Web site, the absence of a date should make you suspicious.

Sometimes you find online information that appears useful, but you can't find enough background knowledge to determine whether it's credible. There are a few strategies, though, to help you figure this out:

• **Ask whether the site was recommended to you by an expert.** Did your instructor or textbook refer to it? Was it listed as a resource in another reputable source? (Chapters 2 and 24–26 list several of the

TIP

Be particularly careful if you're thinking of citing a blog. Blogs can look professional and might be hosted by a newspaper or magazine site, but they are not always checked by editors or other experts to verify facts or review claims. If you want to cite a blog post, do some research on the post's author first. It's also a good idea to search for a source that confirms the information in a database like EBSCOhost.

best Web sites on the topics covered in those chapters; those sites would be good places to start.)

- **Look carefully at the area of the Web site that lists information about the sponsoring organization**—usually in a tab labeled "About Us" or a link through the name of the organization. Is the organization endorsed by other reputable groups? Is it for profit or not? What is its purpose in providing this information?

- **Ask the reference librarian in your college library to look at the Web site if you are really stuck.** Some libraries even have an online chat feature, or a twenty-four-hour "ask a librarian" service, so you can send a librarian the link, explain your topic, and ask if the site is a good one. If it isn't a good source, he or she may even have time to point you to better ones.

Let's look at a sample from the Web site of the Administration for Children and Families, a division of the U.S. Department of Health and Human Services:

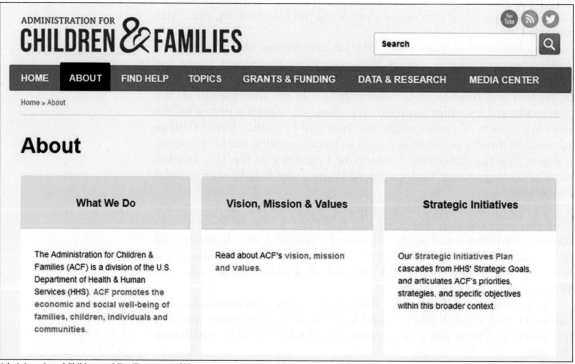

Administration of Children and Families, www.acf.hhs.gov

For most credible Web sites such as this one, you will find an "About" section that will describe the organization's purpose and scope. Check both the top tabs and the bottom of the home page to find the section about the organization. Read this information to determine the perspective or biases of the sponsoring organization, which in turn can help you make better decisions about how you will use the information you find on the Web site.

---

practice it 21.3   Evaluating Web Sites for Bias

Look at the following Web sites:

www.adweek.com

www.pbs.org/wgbh/pages/frontline/view

www.councilforeconed.org

www.monacaron.com

www.nea.org

What kinds of biases, or perspectives, might each of these sites have? How might you acknowledge the perspective of the source if you were to use a quotation or paraphrase from it in an essay? Where might you find other articles that would balance the perspective?

Working with Sources

Once you locate sources that are credible, relevant, and current, you need to be organized when taking notes so that you do not accidentally plagiarize and do not waste precious minutes of your life tracking down a source that you had in your hand or on your computer screen a week ago. Whether you use a note card system, a notebook, or an electronic style of organization, be consistent. Good research-organization habits save you hours of time in the long run and prepare you well for any future profession.

▶ For details on the various methods of note taking, consult Chapter 20, Note Taking.

Good writers adapt their views based on the research they find, but they do not lose their own sense of style, perspective, or voice. Make sure your sources do not "take over" your paper. Avoid long blocks of quotations unless they are absolutely necessary, and be sure to integrate source material effectively and to quote document source material correctly. Research, when done well, can be one of the most fun parts of writing. Enjoy all the resources at your fingertips!

▶ For more on using quotations, see Chapter 17, Quotation and Paraphrase. For more on documenting sources, see Chapter 22, MLA Documentation, and Chapter 23, APA Documentation.

chapter review

In the following chart, fill in the second column to record in your own words the important skills included in this chapter. Then assess yourself to determine whether you are still developing the skill or feel you have mastered it. If you are still developing the skill, make some notes about what you need to work on to master it in the future. If you believe you have already mastered it, explain why.

Skills and concepts covered in this chapter	Explanation in your own words	I'm developing this skill and need to work on . . .	I believe I have mastered this skill because . . .
Evaluating sources for credibility			
Making sure sources are relevant			
Evaluating sources for currency			
Evaluating Web sources			
Working with sources			

22

MLA Documentation

*M*LA stands for the Modern Language Association, an organization made up of professors, writers, and graduate students working in English, foreign languages, and the humanities. This association has developed a standard style, known as MLA style, for formatting research papers and documenting sources. Usually, students in English classes learn to document sources in MLA style because it is one of the simplest and most common systems. You may use other documentation methods, such as APA (American Psychological Association) style, in a health sciences or social science class down the road. Always check with your instructor to make sure you use the documentation style required.

Why, you might wonder, do you need to use a standard style of documentation? For the same reasons that we use standards in anything. When a recipe calls for a cup of sugar, we all know how much sugar that means. If ten different recipes each meant something different by "one cup," then coming up with edible results would be much harder. Similarly, standard rules for formatting a document and including references to sources help the writer and the reader communicate effectively and efficiently. This is especially necessary because so many sources are online, and merely listing the author and title of an article won't give the reader enough information to find the correct version of it.

Your main goal in using any system of documentation (MLA, APA, or any other) is to show your readers exactly where you got any information from outside sources that you include in your paper. Proper documentation provides readers with all they need to find the articles, books, Web sites, or other materials you refer to in your paper. Not providing such

▶ **For more about APA style, which is used in psychology and the social sciences, see Chapter 23, APA Documentation.**

TIP

The *MLA Handbook* is in its eighth edition, published in 2016. It is periodically reviewed and updated as standards in the field and types of sources change. For updates, visit style.mla .org.

information makes it look like you are plagiarizing, or trying to pass off other people's ideas as your own.

This chapter explains the basics of MLA style as simply as possible. As you move on in college, you might need other, more detailed guides to MLA style, but this chapter will get you on the right track.

Citation and Credibility

Once you master the nuts and bolts of MLA style—or any style you are assigned to use—you will come to appreciate how it helps increase your credibility as a writer. Credibility means believability—essentially, if you are a credible writer, your reader believes that you are fairly and accurately representing the ideas of others. Using sources well demonstrates that you have done your homework on the topic, and it builds your reader's trust. Shoddy or sloppy use of MLA style can leave readers wondering, "What else did this person get wrong? If this author can't even remember to put down the source's page number, should I trust that this person got the information right?"

At worst, making an error or leaving something out of a citation leaves you open to the charge of plagiarism, which means that you have unfairly copied someone else's ideas and presented them as your own. Plagiarism is a serious offense, and you can earn a zero or "failing grade" on an assignment or, in severe cases, be expelled from college for plagiarizing. Mastering the rules of MLA style allows you to integrate material from outside sources correctly and confidently into your writing.

A NOTE ABOUT PLAGIARISM

Clearly, intentionally copying and taking credit for someone else's work or buying a paper off the Internet is plagiarism, and it's wrong. Why, then, do good students sometimes do wrong things? Sometimes students experience anxiety about their ability to do well in a course and think someone else's work will be better than their own. Other times, students—not you, of course!—procrastinate on an assignment and then search the Web for "ideas" and end up taking information from a Web site without properly documenting it or worse, without documenting at all. Other students may have seen cheating in high schools—or in the "real" world around them—and figure that "everyone else is doing it."

Here's a news flash, though: Most colleges and universities have much stricter policies about plagiarism than high schools. Consequences for plagiarizing might be earning a failing grade or receiving no credit on an assignment or failing an entire course. So be ethical, do the right thing, and realize that plagiarism in college has serious repercussions. You can do well in college based on your own work if you give yourself a chance. Good study skills and time-management techniques should reduce your anxiety about doing well and give you a buffer against any crisis that life throws your way, and learning proper MLA documentation will enable you to use additional material credibly. Still, there might be a time when you feel that your only option is to cheat. It's not. Go to your instructor, explain your situation without trying to make excuses for yourself, and ask for a reasonable extension with a reasonable penalty. If your instructor won't make accommodations—and he or she does not have to do so—then chalk it up to a life lesson learned. Plagiarizing will haunt you far more than one bad grade on an assignment, and it could cost you your college career.

Components of an MLA Research Paper

MLA style has two major components: the Works Cited page and in-text (parenthetical) citation. Document format is also important for creating research papers that look professional. Let's take a quick look at each part:

1. **Document format** refers to the design and layout of your document. This includes margins, spacing, page numbers, and headings.
2. The **Works Cited page** lists all the sources you referred to in the paper, with all the information readers would need to find your sources. Note that this list does not include all the sources you might have casually looked at while writing the paper; it includes just the ones you actually quoted, paraphrased, or summarized in the paper.
3. **In-text (parenthetical) citation** refers to the source information you add, in parentheses, following material that you've found in an outside source. This information leads your reader to one of your Works Cited entries, and to the particular page (if available) where you found the material.

The sample paper on pages 402–4 shows these components.

Put your last name
and the page number
in the upper right.
Use the "insert page
number" and "header"
functions in your
word-processing
program.

This information
goes on the first
page only.

Center your title.
Capitalize the first
word in your title (and
subtitle, if you have
one) as well as all
major words. Do not
bold, italicize,
underline, or put
quotation marks
around your own title.

The entire text is
double-spaced. Use
Times New Roman.

Indent new para-
graphs five spaces
or ½ inch.

Provide necessary
information in the
parenthetical citation.
Here, the writer gives
the author's last names
because they do not
appear earlier in the
sentence.

Include the page
number for a print
source that has page
numbers.

Smith 1

Sally Smith

Professor Green

English 100

20 April 2016

When Siblings Grow Up

Hollywood loves siblings who fight. In *Brothers*, Captain Sam
Cahill (Tobey Maguire) and his brother, Tommy (Jake Gyllenhaal),
both are in love with Sam's wife. In *Rachel Getting Married*,
recovering drug addict Kym (Anne Hathaway) seems to want to
wreck the wedding of her sister, Rachel (Rosemarie DeWitt).
Movies about siblings almost always have the obligatory scene of
the two brothers duking it out or the two sisters hurling insults
and ending up in tears. Watching such dramatic scenes, one
wonders if all adult siblings are doomed to bad relationships, and
if all pairs of siblings end up as opposites. While stormy sibling
relationships make for great movie drama, many siblings have
successful relationships as adults. How do they do it? Siblings can
have strong adult relationships if they start off well in childhood
and continue to nurture their relationship as they grow older.

Most people envision that the path to family harmony is to
minimize arguments when children are little. Good intentions
might actually undermine the sibling relationship, though. Ironically, young siblings who barely fight may not be on the path to a
happy adult relationship. Researchers who study sibling interaction have observed that playing and fighting make siblings
friends as adults, and that young "siblings who simply ignored
each other had less fighting, but their relationship stayed cold and
distant long term" (Bronson and Merryman 122). So while all the
arguments about whose turn it is or who got more might drive
parents crazy at times, siblings who take the time to argue it out as
children often end up with more positive communication as adults.

Smith 2

As siblings grow into adults, one of the major hurdles they face has to do with the roles they had as children and their ability to relate outside those roles. As Jane Mersky Leder writes, "Our siblings push buttons that cast us in roles we felt sure we had let go of long ago—the baby, the peacekeeper, the caretaker, the avoider" (2). Even if we as adults have outgrown those roles, when we step into the house we grew up in, we are seen and even sometimes act in ways that we did as children. Our siblings, who usually outlive our parents, have a huge impact on our sense of self: "Our brothers and sisters bring us face to face with our former selves and remind us how intricately bound up we are in each other's lives" (Leder 2). Sometimes that former self is not someone we want to know anymore—as was the case of Kym, the recovering drug addict in *Rachel Getting Married*, who wanted so badly to move beyond her addiction but would always be seen with a certain amount of suspicion by her family.

Family harmony is possible, once you realize that "harmony" doesn't mean the absence of all arguments. Getting conflicts out in the open and working them through is important. We learn how to do that as children, if our parents don't step in to solve our problems for us. However, we need to keep practicing it as adults, and we need to allow our siblings to change and grow. Good sibling relationships might not make their way into a movie script, but most of us would probably prefer them to the storminess of the popular images.

Here the author's name is in the signal phrase, so it does not need to be repeated in the parentheses. Only the page number needs to go in the parentheses.

Include the film in the Works Cited. No parenthetical citation is needed when you refer to the complete work and name it in the sentence.

Smith 3

Works Cited

Bronson, Po, and Ashley Merryman. *NurtureShock: New Thinking about Children*. Hachette Book Group, 2009.

Brothers. Directed by Jim Sheridan, performances by Jake Gyllenhaal, Natalie Portman, and Tobey Maguire, Lionsgate, 2009.

Leder, Jane Mersky. *Brothers and Sisters: How They Shape Our Lives*. Ballantine Books, 1991.

Rachel Getting Married. Directed by Jonathan Demme, performances by Anne Hathaway, Rosemarie DeWitt, and Debra Winger, Sony, 2008.

The Works Cited page starts on a new page, with the title "Works Cited" centered.

List all the sources you quote, paraphrase, or summarize. Readers use this list to locate your sources.

DOCUMENT FORMAT

Computers are wonderful things, and, if you use yours wisely, you only have to set up your document format for MLA papers once in your entire college life. If you are unfamiliar with word-processing basics, like how to set the margins on a document and insert a page number, you should go to the computer lab with this book and have a lab assistant help you set up a template.

Create a document in your computer files that you title "MLA Template." Set this up as a blank sample paper, and then every time you need to write an essay for your English class, you will open up the document, use it to type your essay, and re-save it under a different name. That way, your template will always be there, and you never have to worry about setting the margins or font again. If your instructor does not provide specific instructions for how to format your paper, follow these steps, in this order:

STEP 1: Open a new document.

STEP 2: Change the document line spacing to 2 to double-space the entire document.

STEP 3: Set the margins at 1 inch on top, bottom, left, and right.

STEP 4: Change the font to 12-point Times New Roman. You should not use different or fancy fonts to try to make your work unique. Times New Roman translates universally among computer programs with no problems. Stick to it.

STEP 5: Create a header for the document that has your last name, a space, and then the page number. If you don't know how to do automatic page numbering in your word-processing program, ask someone or use the Help function. Do not type the number "1" on the first page; if you do, "1" will appear as the number on all the pages.

STEP 6: On the top left of the first page only, type the following:

> Your name
> Instructor's name
> Course title
> Date

STEP 7: On the next line, type the words "Title Goes Here" centered, and then hit "enter" or "return" once. Do not use bold, underlining, or quotation marks for your title.

STEP 8: Set up a tab to indent paragraphs ½ inch.

STEP 9: Hit "enter" or "return" a few times.

STEP 10: Insert a page break.

STEP 11: Type the words "Works Cited" centered at the top of the page. Do not use bold, underlining, or quotation marks for these words.

STEP 12: Set up your ruler or tabs for the Works Cited page so that the first line of each new paragraph starts at the left margin and all following lines indent ½ inch. (Called a "hanging indent," this is the exact reverse of a normal paragraph.) To set the ruler, you need to see it. Generally, find the "View" drop-down menu and select "Print Layout." Another way to set a hanging indent in MS Word is to use the paragraph menu.

STEP 13: Save the document as "MLA Template."

STEP 14: Whenever you write a paper, open this template, and begin to write your paper in the new file, typing in your current instructor's name and your current class number. Make sure you "save as" a different title so that you do not save over your MLA template.

The final product should look like the sample on pages 402–4, so check yours against that example to see if you did everything correctly.

Done correctly and used regularly, the template should make your work look professional instead of sloppy. Once the document format is out of the way, you can focus on the more important task of citing your outside sources properly.

> ### practice it 22.1   Creating a Template for an MLA Paper
>
> Set up an online template for an MLA paper, and save it in an appropriate folder on your computer or online file management system.

THE WORKS CITED PAGE

Most people think that the Works Cited page should be completed last because it always appears as the last page of the paper. Wrong! Creating your Works Cited page as you gather information, and before you even start to write your rough draft, saves you lots of time in the end. We have seen thousands of students over the years waste precious minutes, hours, and sometimes even days of their lives trying to track down the correct information for a source that they once had in their hands. We have also seen students struggle to figure out in-text parenthetical documentation, when it's relatively simple if you do your Works Cited page first. Countless students turn in sloppy work, which destroys their credibility, because they rush to do the Works Cited page at the last minute.

Understanding the Elements of the Works Cited Page.   What do you put on the Works Cited page, and what does it look like? Let's take a closer look at the Works Cited page of our short example paper from page 404:

Use the ruler toolbar to adjust the indentation or set a hanging indent using the paragraph settings in MS Word.

List each source only once, even if you use it more than once.

Citations differ, but they all have the same type of information, like titles and publication dates.

Smith 3

Works Cited

Bronson, Po, and Ashley Merryman. *NurtureShock: New Thinking about Children.* Hachette Book Group, 2009.

Brothers. Directed by Jim Sheridan, performances by Jake Gyllenhaal, Natalie Portman, and Tobey Maguire, Lionsgate, 2009.

Leder, Jane Mersky. *Brothers and Sisters: How They Shape Our Lives.* Ballantine Books, 1991.

Rachel Getting Married. Directed by Jonathan Demme, performances by Anne Hathaway, Rosemarie DeWitt, and Debra Winger, Sony, 2008.

Creating Your Own Works Cited Page.   Ready to give it a try with your sources? Follow the steps below.

STEP 1: Gather the sources you think you will use in your paper. (If you create a citation for a source and end up not using it, that's good practice. Just delete it from the final version of your paper.)

STEP 2: Open up your MLA template document and save it under the name of your new essay, such as "Fame Essay 1" or "Curiosity Essay" or whatever your title or topic might be. (If you did not already create a template, see pages 404–5.)

STEP 3: Go to the Works Cited page within your template. The margins, spacing, and indents should already be set up properly.

STEP 4: Type up the citation for each of your sources, following the sample formats below.

STEP 5: Put your citations in alphabetical order after you are sure you have the format for each citation correct.

SAMPLE FORMATS FOR WORKS CITED CITATIONS

Works Cited citations can be broken down into several categories:

- books
- newspaper, journal, and magazine articles
- web sources
- articles and other materials that you get from a database, like ProQuest, EBSCOhost, ERIC, or SIRS from your college library
- media sources
- other sources (for example, interviews, drawings, and performances)

Examples of some of the most common types of citations appear on the following pages.

Print Books and Articles.   The following examples show how to cite a book or article in a physical form.

BOOK

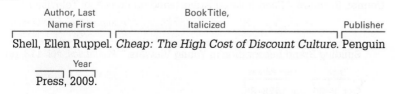

Author, Last Name First · Book Title, Italicized · Publisher
Shell, Ellen Ruppel. *Cheap: The High Cost of Discount Culture.* Penguin

Year
Press, 2009.

TIP

Pay attention to punctuation when citing sources. In most MLA citations, a period follows the author, the title, and the whole entry. Commas separate other elements within the entry.

SELECTION IN AN ANTHOLOGY OR TEXTBOOK

Author of Selection,
Last Name First   Title of Selection,
in Quotation Marks

Becker, Jack. "Public Art: An Essential Component of Creating

Title of Book, Italicized

Communities." *Read, Write, Connect: A Guide to College Reading and*

Editor(s) of Book, Name(s)
in Normal Order   Edition

Writing, edited by Kathleen Green and Amy Lawlor, 2nd ed.,

Publisher   Year   Page Range
of Selection

Bedford/St. Martin's, 2017, pp. 486–95.

NEWSPAPER ARTICLE

Author, Last
Name First   Second Author,
in Normal Order   Article Title,
in Quotation Marks

Braudy, Leo, and Michael Cieply. "Hollywood's High-Powered Image

Newspaper Title,
Italicized   Date: Day +
Month + Year   Page
Range

Machine." *Los Angeles Times*, 10 July 1988, p. 10A.

MAGAZINE ARTICLE

If an article has page numbers that are not consecutive—for example, pp. 29–30 and p. 45—list the first page number with a plus sign.

Author, Last
Name First   Article Title,
in Quotation Marks

Palmer, Kimberly. "Talking to Gen Y about the New Culture of Thrift:

Companies Fumble as They Try to Appeal to 20-Something Consumers."

Magazine Title,
Italicized   Date: Day +
Month + Year   Page
Range

U.S. News & World Report, 1 Mar. 2010, pp. 29+.

SCHOLARLY JOURNAL ARTICLE

Author, Last
Name First   Article Title,
in Quotation Marks

Connor, Susan M. "Food-Related Advertising on Preschool Television:

Journal Title,
Italicized   Volume,
Issue

Building Brand Recognition in Young Viewers." *Pediatrics*, vol. 118, no. 4,

Date   Page Range

Oct. 2006, pp. 1478–85.

Online Books and Articles.   Citations for online sources differ depending on how you accessed the material—through a Web browser, a paid subscription database, or another digital platform.

E-BOOK

Author, Last Name First	Book Title, Italicized	Publisher	Year	Digital Platform

Doerr, Anthony. *All the Light We Cannot See.* Scribner, 2014. Nook.

E-BOOK FROM A WEB SITE

Author, Last Name First	Book Title, Italicized	Other Contributor (if any)

Piketty, Thomas. *Capital in the Twenty-First Century.* Translated by Arthur

	Publisher	Year	Name of Site, Italicized	URL

Goldhammer, Harvard UP, 2014. *Google Books,* books.google.com/

books?isbn=0674369556.

NEWSPAPER ARTICLE ON THE NEWSPAPER'S WEB SITE

Author, Last Name First	Article Title, in Quotation Marks	Title of Online Newspaper, Italicized	Date of Publication, Inverted

Banks, Sandy. "Where Poor Students Soar." *LATimes.com,* 5 Nov. 2011,

URL

articles.latimes.com/2011/nov/05/local/la-me-banks-20111105.

MAGAZINE ARTICLE FROM THE PUBLISHER'S WEB SITE

Author, Last Name First	Article Title, in Quotation Marks	Title of Magazine, Italicized

Yuhas, Daisy. "Curiosity Prepares the Brain for Better Learning." *Scientific*

	Date of Publication, Inverted	URL

American, 2 Oct. 2014, www.scientificamerican.com/article/

curiosity-prepares-the-brain-for-better-learning.

MAGAZINE ARTICLE FROM A DATABASE

Author, Last Name First	Article Title, in Quotation Marks	Magazine Title, Italicized	Date of Publication

Sharp, Kathleen. "The Rescue Mission." *Smithsonian,* Nov. 2015,

Page Range	Name of Database, Italicized	URL

pp. 40–49. *OmniFile Full Text Select,* web.b.ebscohost.com.ezproxy.bpl.org/.

SCHOLARLY JOURNAL ARTICLE FROM A DATABASE

DOI stands for "digital object identifier." Some publishers assign DOIs to articles so that they have a stable link even when URLs change. If the article you use has a DOI, list it in your citation. If not, list the URL.

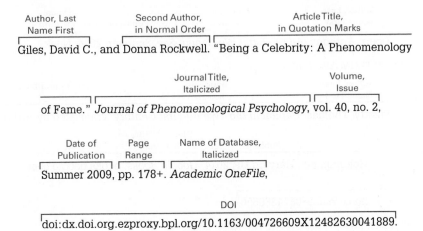

TIP

In citations for works from a database, a period goes after the page numbers and information about the database follows.

Author, Last Name First   Second Author, in Normal Order   Article Title, in Quotation Marks

Giles, David C., and Donna Rockwell. "Being a Celebrity: A Phenomenology

Journal Title, Italicized   Volume, Issue

of Fame." *Journal of Phenomenological Psychology*, vol. 40, no. 2,

Date of Publication   Page Range   Name of Database, Italicized

Summer 2009, pp. 178+. *Academic OneFile*,

DOI

doi:dx.doi.org.ezproxy.bpl.org/10.1163/004726609X12482630041889.

Web Sites.   Short works on Web sites are sometimes updated, so they can have more than one publication date. Cite the date that is most relevant to the way you use the source in your paper. If no date of publication is available for a Web site, include the date you accessed the site at the end of the entry.

title of Web site

title of page

author

date

SHORT WORK FROM A WEB SITE

Author, Last
Name First   Title of Page,
                        in Quotation Marks

Mares, Chad. "Understanding the Debt Ceiling Debate and the Budget

                        Date of
            Title of Web   Publication,
            Site, Italicized   Inverted

Control Act of 2011." *EconEdLink*, 3 Dec. 2012,

                        URL

www.econedlink.org/teacher-lesson/1041/

Understanding-Debt-Ceiling-Debate-Budget-Control-Act-2011.

WEB SITE WITH AN ORGANIZATION AS AUTHOR

            Organization Name   Title of Web Site

United States Department of Commerce. *United States Census Bureau*.

        URL   Date of Access, Inverted

www.census.gov/. Accessed 28 Mar. 2016.

Other Sources

FILM

Film Title,
Italicized   Director   Major Performers

Brothers. Directed by Jim Sheridan, performances by Jake Gyllenhaal,

                                                Distributor

Tobey Maguire, Natalie Portman, and Mare Winningham, Lionsgate,

Release Year

2009.

If you focus on the director more than the movie itself in your paper, list
the director first.

Director, Last   Film Title,
Name First   Italicized   Major Performers

Sheridan, Jim, director. *Brothers*. Performances by Jake Gyllenhaal, Tobey

                                        Release
                            Distributor   Year

Maguire, Natalie Portman, and Mare Winningham, Lionsgate, 2009.

VIDEO ACCESSED ONLINE

Creator, Last   Title of Video,   Name of Site,
Name First.   in Quotation Marks   Italicized

Nayar, Vineet. "Employees First, Customers Second." *YouTube*,

Date of Publication,
Inverted   URL

9 June 2015, www.youtube.com/watch?v=cCdu67s_C5E.

RADIO SHOW ACCESSED ONLINE

For radio and television shows, the narrator, writer, director, producer, or star is often significant. Include this key additional information as shown in the examples below.

Episode Title, in Quotation Marks | Title of Program or Series, Italicized | Key Additional Information | Network or Station

"Bad Bank." *This American Life*, narrated by Ira Glass, Public Radio

Date of Broadcast | URL

International, 27 Feb. 2009, www.thisamericanlife.org/

radio-archives/episode/375/bad-bank.

TELEVISION SHOW ACCESSED ONLINE

Episode Title, in Quotation Marks | Title of Program or Series, Italicized | Key Additional Information | Network or Station

"Merchants of Cool." *Frontline*, produced by Douglas Rushkoff, PBS,

Date of Broadcast | URL

27 Feb. 2001, www.pbs.org/wgbh/pages/frontline/shows/cool/view/.

INTERVIEW YOU CONDUCTED PERSONALLY

Subject of Interview, Last Name First | Type of Interview | Date of Interview

Shepherd, Trixie. Personal interview. 15 Sept. 2013.

This list of sample citations is hardly complete. The official *MLA Handbook*, 8th ed. (2016) includes additional guidelines, and at some point in your college career you will probably need to refer to it or some other handbook. MLA style may seem overwhelming, but remember, no one expects you to memorize the exact details of Works Cited formatting. Understand the core concepts, and each time you do a citation, look up the finer details.

Formatting Titles

When you are learning to cite sources in MLA style, formatting titles correctly can sometimes be challenging. Here are some tips:

- Big things are italicized. Little things go in quotation marks. So a book title is italicized, and the title of a chapter from a book—which is smaller than a book—goes in quotation marks. A CD title is italicized; a song title goes in quotation marks.

- If you italicize a title in your Works Cited list, then you should italicize it everywhere in the paper, any time you mention it, even in parenthetical documentation. The same goes for titles that are in quotation marks.

- Whether the document or book in front of you capitalizes all the letters in a title, capitalizes none of them, or makes the letters out of elbow macaroni, you should use what are called "title caps" for all titles all the time. This means that you capitalize the first word and all the big words in a title, and you capitalize the first word and all the big words in a subtitle.

- Just type the title of your own paper in regular 12-point Times New Roman with title caps. Don't use a fancy font, a bigger font, bold, underlining, or italics.

- Errors with titles drive most instructors batty for some reason. Take time to do titles correctly, and your instructors will look kindly on you.

practice it 22.2   Creating a Sample Works Cited Page

Practice doing a sample Works Cited citation for two or three of the sources you think you might use in your essay. Handwrite or type them clearly, with proper margins and spacing. Ask your instructor or a tutor to check them for accuracy.

IN-TEXT (PARENTHETICAL) CITATION

The other component of MLA style, in-text (parenthetical) citation, is truly the most important from a writing perspective because the information you put into the parentheses at the end of your sentences communicates the most to the reader. The basic concept of MLA style is that when a reader reaches a passage in an essay that includes information (a quotation, paraphrase, or summary) that the writer found in another source, the writer will at this point let the reader know where the information comes from. To do this, the writer puts the information in parentheses.

For example, here's an original passage taken from the article "The Perils and Promises of Praise" by Carol S. Dweck:

> We often hear these days that we've produced a generation of young people who can't get through the day without an award. They expect success because they're special, not because they've worked hard.
>
> Is this true? Have we inadvertently done something to hold back our students? I think educators commonly hold two beliefs that do just that. Many believe that (1) praising students' intelligence builds their confidence and motivation to learn, and (2) students' inherent intelligence is the major cause of their achievement in school. Our research has shown that the first belief is false and that the second can be harmful—even for the most competent students.

This article is one of many in an anthology, in this case your textbook, which has page numbers. This article has an author and a title, and the book has an edition number. The citation in the Works Cited page would look like this:

> Dweck, Carol S. "The Perils and Promises of Praise." *Read, Write, Connect: A Guide to College Reading and Writing*, edited by Kathleen Green and Amy Lawlor, 2nd ed., Bedford/St. Martin's, 2017, pp. 6–13.

Now, let's say we want to include a quotation from the article in an essay. The sentence might look like this if we want to emphasize the idea that Dweck is the author of the article being quoted:

> Educational psychologist Carol S. Dweck's research shows that many teachers are wrong when they think that "praising students' intelligence builds their confidence and motivation to learn" (6).

Or the sentence could look like this if we don't want to emphasize Dweck herself, but care more about the date that the study was originally done:

> A groundbreaking study published in 2007 suggests that teachers do more harm than good by "praising students' intelligence" (Dweck 6).

What do you notice? In both examples, we use Dweck's name and the page number. The only difference is that in the first example, we include Dweck's name in the sentence, so we don't need to repeat it in the parentheses. In the second example, we don't include Dweck's name in the sentence, but we include it in the parentheses, so that the reader can locate the source on the Works Cited page. We don't include any other publication information, nor do we use "page" or "p." or "pg." Simple, right?

Remember, the key to MLA style is that when the reader notices the source name, he or she can flip back to the Works Cited page (which is conveniently alphabetized and designed to make finding the names easy) for more information about the source. Either in your sentence or in your parentheses—or some combination—you need to provide your reader with the first word in the Works Cited list. If the source has a page number, that has to go into parentheses. Never introduce a quote by saying "On page 3 of her article, . . ." The fact that the quote is on page 3 does not add useful information to the meaning of your sentence, so you always keep the page number in the parentheses.

To review again, in the second example, why did we choose to put "Dweck" in the parentheses? Why not the title of the article? Or the title of the book in which it was published? The answer is simple, and it is the basic rule of MLA style:

In your sentence or parenthetical reference, you need to include the first word(s) from the Works Cited citation.

Usually, the first word is an author's last name, but sometimes it's the first word(s) in the title, if the article has no author. That's why you should create the Works Cited page first: so you know what you need to put in the parentheses as you write, and you can do it correctly the first time.

Students who skip listing their citations as they research and say to themselves "I'll put all the sources in later" are wasting their time and almost always make mistakes. Not only do they often forget to do the citations, but when they do remember, they spend more time on this task, because they have to find the quotes and paraphrased text all over again. Why not just create the citations first and spare yourself the effort? The quicker you develop this mind-set, the less time you'll spend on the details of MLA style, and the more time you'll have to think about what you want to say in your writing.

chapter review

In the following chart, fill in the second column to record in your own words the important skills included in this chapter. Then assess yourself to determine whether you are still developing the skill or feel you have mastered it. If you are still developing the skill, make some notes about what you need to work on to master it in the future. If you believe you have already mastered it, explain why.

Skills and concepts covered in this chapter	Explanation in your own words	I'm developing this skill and need to work on . . .	I believe I have mastered this skill because . . .
Using in-text citations accurately			
Building credibility			
Avoiding plagiarism			
Creating an MLA Works Cited page			

23

APA Documentation

TIP

The *Publication Manual of the American Psychological Association* is in its sixth edition, published in 2010. It is periodically reviewed and updated as standards in the field and types of sources change. For updates, visit apastyle.org.

▶ **For more about MLA style, which is used in English, foreign languages, and the humanities, see Chapter 22, MLA Documentation. For more about avoiding plagiarism, see Chapter 17, Quotation and Paraphrase, and Chapter 20, Note Taking.**

*A*PA, which stands for the American Psychological Association, is the preferred style for formatting papers and citing sources in the social and behavioral sciences. You will likely encounter APA style in many of your readings, and when writing papers in your social science classes, you will be expected to use it.

Why use a style guide like APA? In order to clearly and efficiently convey information, it is important to cite research and data in a uniform way. The APA style was created by social scientists to provide a clear guide to uniformity in their field. For experts in the social and behavioral sciences, it is extremely important that research is current—generally, the more recent the source the better, though there are some exceptions. Therefore, APA style emphasizes the year a source was published (you will notice that the date follows right after the author's name in citations).

Many disciplines have adopted APA style, but many others have their own style guides. In your college classes, your instructors might ask you to format your papers and document your sources in APA style, MLA style, or another style. The good news is that no one expects you to memorize these style guides or know them by heart. Knowing how to navigate them and apply them when needed is enough. Regardless of which style of documentation you use, the most important point is that you give credit where credit is due. Documenting your sources properly helps you avoid plagiarizing.

Components of APA Style

APA style has three major components: document format, the References page, and in-text (parenthetical) citation. Let's take a quick look at each part.

1. **Document format** refers to the design and layout of your document. This includes margins, spacing, page numbers, and headings, as well as required sections of the paper like the title page and abstract.

2. The **References page** lists all the sources you referred to in the paper, with all the information readers would need to find your sources. Note that this list does not include all the sources you might have casually looked at while writing the paper; it includes just the ones you actually quoted, paraphrased, or summarized in the paper.

3. **In-text (parenthetical) citation** refers to the source information you add, in parentheses, following material that you've found in an outside source. This information leads your reader to one of your References page entries and to the particular page or paragraph (if available) where you found the material.

DOCUMENT FORMAT

APA document format defines the rules for the different kinds of pages you will have in your paper. For papers following APA style, there are four kinds of pages to include.

Four Sections of an APA Paper

- title page
- abstract page
- text pages
- references page

Take a look at the sample APA-style paper on pages 418–23 to get a sense of how these sections look.

Because any documentation style (APA or MLA) will have very specific and highly detailed rules to follow, it's a good idea to create a document template with the proper margins, header, and spacing, among other details. Then anytime you need to write a paper following this style guide, you have a document already set up and properly formatted in which you can type your new paper. To create a template, open a new document file and name it "APA Template." Then follow the steps below.

STEP 1: Double-space the entire document, including the header.

STEP 2: Set the margins at 1 inch on top, bottom, left, and right.

STEP 3: Set the font to Times New Roman. APA requires a serif font, and Times New Roman is a good choice because it's used so widely. The exception to this rule is titles of any figures or charts you include. These titles should be in a sans-serif font like Arial.

TIP

Each time you begin to type up a paper using your APA template, be sure to save it as a file with a different name so that your template document will always be there. You might want to even make a copy of the APA Template file by saving it as "APA Template COPY" so that you don't accidentally save over it.

(Continued on page 423.)

Begin page numbers on the title page, and place them in the upper right of each page.

The running head is a shortened version of the title; it is typed in all capital letters in the upper left of the page. On the first page only, insert "Running head:" before the title.

Title is centered. Capitalize the first word in your title (and subtitle, if you have one) as well as all major words. Do not bold, italicize, underline, or put quotation marks around your own title.

Double-space, and then center your name below the title.

Double-space, and then center your school below your name (called an affiliation).

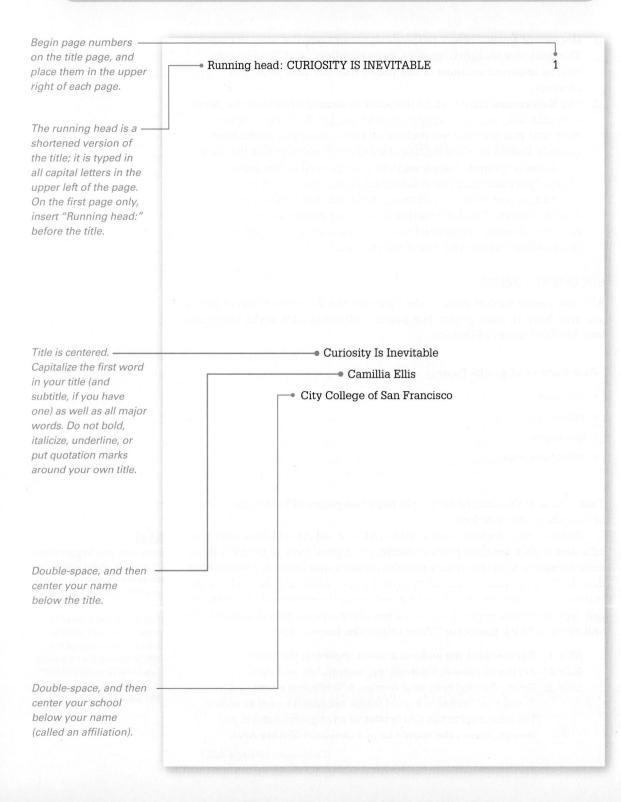

Running head: CURIOSITY IS INEVITABLE   1

Curiosity Is Inevitable

Camillia Ellis

City College of San Francisco

CURIOSITY IS INEVITABLE   2

Abstract

This paper describes the development of human curiosity and argues that the American public education system currently fails to foster curiosity in students. Suggestions to help improve secondary education are discussed.

   Keywords: curiosity, public education, fixed mind-set, growth mind-set

After the first page, running heads have only the title in all caps (do not include the words "Running head:").

Center the heading "Abstract" at top of the second page.

The abstract is a brief summary of your paper, double-spaced. Do not indent the first line.

Keywords are indented ½ inch.

CURIOSITY IS INEVITABLE   3

Curiosity Is Inevitable

   If curiosity is something that comes naturally at birth, why is it something that's being discouraged in our educational system? Curiosity is a quality that gives people a strong desire to know or want to learn something. Having a curious mind is necessary during a child's early development. However, the public school system in America does not implement it in a way that they should in order to encourage students to utilize this quality. The American Public Education system primarily discourages human curiosity through its set curriculum and is shown to create a pattern that leads to fixed-minded students (Dweck, 2007/2017). The good news is that it is never too late to make a difference.

   The human brain is stimulated by curiosity and wanting to know more about what piques your interests. In the article "Curiosity Prepares the Brain for Better Learning," Daisy Yuhas (2014/2017) describes neuroscientist Charan Ranganath's experiment of asking questions to determine how the brain retains information in the most efficient way (p. 469). In this procedure,

Title is centered at top of the third page.

Text is double-spaced throughout; paragraphs are indented ½ inch.

Publication years are placed after the first reference to an author.

Page number in parentheses follows the quotation.

CURIOSITY IS INEVITABLE   4

he and his colleagues tested hundreds of people on how curious they were about the answers to questions the researchers asked. Later, after running various tests, Ranganath's team found that "brain activity ramped up in . . . the ventral tegmental area and nucleus accumbens. These regions transmit the molecules dopamine, which help regulate the sensation of pleasure and reward" (p. 470). With this in mind, the researchers concluded that curiosity is important to one's desire to learn more. Also, Yuhas cites a study from the University of California, Davis, that has demonstrated that "when our curiosity is piqued, changes in the brain ready us to learn not only about the subject at hand, but incidental information, too" (p. 469). Meaning, the more curious one is, the more engaged they will be in taking in information.

Humans are born naturally with curious minds. As babies, from the first time we lay hands on an object, we are curious about what it is and what it does. Schools seem to embrace children's curiosity by encouraging various hands on exercises and by answering the various questions children may have. Susan Engel (2013/2017), lecturer and expert in psychology and technology, informs us in her article "The Case for Curiosity" that "Curiosity is essential to learning, but in scarce supply in most schools" (p. 458). During adolescence, middle and high school students tend to be discouraged from asking questions in the class as schools promote more one-way learning. Much like in a college lecture class, the teacher's main goal is to release information to the students with very minimal to no question asking. Engel observes a teacher tell a student "'Zoe, no questions now, please; it's time for learning'" (p. 461). This statement is a contradiction to the human learning process that most teachers seem to have the wrong idea

In this paraphrase, the author is named in the sentence and the years of publication immediately follow the author's name. Two years are given: the original publication year and the year of the book in which the writer found the article.

When referencing the same source more than once in a paragraph, it is not necessary to include the years of publication in the second mention, as long as the author is named in the sentence and it is clear which source you mean.

CURIOSITY IS INEVITABLE 5

about. How is learning possible if asking questions isn't allowed? How are students able to get the clarification they need? Lastly and most importantly, how will students be able to satisfy their curious minds? The answer is, they will not! Asking questions is a part of life's learning process, and it is something that should be uplifted in classrooms in order to keep students engaged in wanting to learn.

The majority of teachers across the country do not encourage questioning, and it is only hurting the education system; however, the teachers aren't the only ones to blame in this. Engel (2013/2017) states, "Teachers are faced with umpteen goals and many obstacles that get in the way of meeting them. . . . Teachers are less likely to encourage questions, tinkering, or deviations from the script when they feel pressure to accomplish goals that might not leave time for questions" (pp.461–462). The administration provides time constraints that the teacher is ordered to follow, thus ensuring that there may not be enough time to answer everyone's question. This pressure from higher authority can be intimidating and stressful, and can result in there not being enough time to answer questions. Therefore, the administration contributes greatly to the impairing of curiosity.

Question asking in the classroom is crucial to student development and creates a pattern throughout their academic careers in preparation for adulthood. As long as the discouragement of curiosity is present in our educational system, students are less likely to retain information and want to know more about what they're learning. This type of "shutdown" is a pattern that is related to people who are fixed-minded, a mind-set that is fixed on thinking that what they already know is all they really need to know and are uninterested in growing and learning more (Dweck, 2007/2017, p. 7).

In this paraphrase, the author is not named in the sentence, so the author's name appears with the years of publication and the page number in parentheses. A page number is not always required for paraphrases, but you should include it if possible.

Students with this mind-set tend to direct their focus on maintaining a grade needed to pass the class rather than developing a desire and interest to learn information in the curriculum—which is a contrast between one with a fixed mind-set and one with a growth mind-set. Having a fixed mind-set can be a crucial factor coming into adulthood. Jim Whitehurst (2013/2017), President and CEO at Red Hat, discusses in his article "How I Hire" what his ideal candidate is: "I'm looking for people who are thoughtful and eager to learn new things. . . . I want to know if they're curious about the business and industry they work in. . . . I find that people who are curious, and who care about their companies and industries, can grow their roles [and] become company leaders. I want those people" (p. 467). During his hiring process, he looks for candidates that are similar to him in that they are curious about what they do and interested to learn more. He also looks for people who are different from him in that they inhibit the ability to think beyond their main focus at the job and are able to be a diverse asset to the company in bringing new ideas to the table.

All in all, curiosity is essential in our lives. It's a part of our growth as humans; therefore, we need to do whatever it takes to fulfill our curiosity in order to continue to move up in life. In order to correct this hitch, we need to develop different techniques and teaching methods that will make the student more engaged in wanting to learn and ask questions. This can be accomplished through various ways. One way to start off is by hiring more curious teachers who'll spread the importance of curiosity. If we follow a path to encourage curiosity in the American Public Education system instead of discouraging it, we will see improvement in the lives of young adults, who will exhibit a growth mind-set ready to take on new challenges.

CURIOSITY IS INEVITABLE   7

References

Dweck, C. (2017). The perils and promises of praise. In K. Green &
    A. Lawlor (Eds.), *Read, write, connect* (2nd ed., pp. 6–13).
    Boston, MA: Bedford/St. Martin's. (Original work published
    2007)

Engel, S. (2017). The case for curiosity. In K. Green & A. Lawlor
    (Eds.), *Read, write, connect* (2nd ed., pp. 458–464). Boston,
    MA: Bedford/St. Martin's. (Original work published 2013)

Whitehurst, J. (2017). How I hire: Intellectual curiosity required. In
    K. Green & A. Lawlor (Eds.), *Read, write, connect* (2nd ed.,
    pp. 466–468). Boston, MA: Bedford/St. Martin's. (Original work
    published 2013)

Yuhas, D. (2017). Curiosity prepares the brain for better learning.
    In K. Green & A. Lawlor (Eds.), *Read, write, connect* (2nd ed.,
    pp. 469–471). Boston, MA: Bedford/St. Martin's. (Original work
    published 2014)

The References page starts on a new page, with the heading centered.

The References list includes all the sources quoted, paraphrased, or summarized in your paper. Readers will use this list to locate your sources.

(APA template steps continued from page 417.)

STEP 4: Set the margins to align left, leaving the right-hand margin "ragged."

STEP 5: This first page of the template will be your **title page**. Create a
         "running head" on this page that will appear on every page of
         your document by opening the header of your document and
         typing "Running head: SHORTENED VERSION OF PAPER TITLE
         GOES HERE" (title in all caps). When you write your first paper,
         keep the words "Running head:" on the first page only and replace
         the "SHORTENED VERSION OF PAPER TITLE GOES HERE" with a
         shortened version of the title of your paper on every page.

STEP 6: On the same line as the running head, on the right margin, set up
         your page numbers beginning with "1" for the title page and
         continuing to the end of the document.

STEP 7: Centered, on the upper half of the title page, type "Title Goes Here." When you type your actual title, do not use underlining, boldface, or italics, but do capitalize the first word and all major words in the title. Beneath the title, on the next double-spaced line, type your name. On the next line, type the name of your school.

STEP 8: Insert a page break so the template moves on to the next page, which is the **abstract page**. Center the word "Abstract" at the top of the page, on the line beneath the running head.

STEP 9: On the next line, aligned left, type "Abstract goes here." This is where you will write a brief summary of the paper. Keep the abstract to one paragraph, and be sure to use the specific vocabulary that is important in your paper.

STEP 10: On the next line, indent ½ inch and type "Keywords" in italics followed by a colon. This is where you will list the major keywords of your paper.

STEP 11: Insert a page break and type the words "Title Goes Here" centered on the page. The text of your paper will begin on the next line.

STEP 12: Format headings throughout the paper by centering them and using boldface.

STEP 13: Set up a tab to indent paragraphs ½ inch.

STEP 14: Insert a page break and type the word "References" centered at the top of the page. For detailed instructions on how to format your various references, see the next section.

TIP

Most newer word-processing programs and many research databases, such as EBSCO and Gale databases, will format citations for you once you enter basic source information, but the result is often incorrect. Software commonly makes errors, such as not properly capitalizing titles or not giving enough information. Make sure the program is based on the most recent version of the APA manual. Remember, you are responsible for the accuracy of your citations; you can't blame the computer for getting it wrong.

practice it 23.1 Creating a Template for an APA Paper

Follow the steps just outlined to create your own template. Be sure to save it as "APA Template," and re-save it as a new file when you use it to write a paper with APA format.

THE REFERENCES PAGE

The References page lists all of the sources that were cited in the body of the paper so that your readers can find those sources. It is the last page of the document and begins on a new page, separate from the text of the paper. Many students tend to wait until the last minute to create their References page, but you will find that getting into the habit of building the APA References page as you write the paper, or even before you start the rough draft, will save you time and frustration in the end. Let's take a closer look at the References page from our sample paper from page 423.

CURIOSITY IS INEVITABLE 7

References

Dweck, C. (2017). The perils and promises of praise. In K. Green & A. Lawlor (Eds.), *Read, write, connect* (2nd ed., pp. 6–13). Boston, MA: Bedford/St. Martin's. (Original work published 2007)

Engel, S. (2017). The case for curiosity. In K. Green & A. Lawlor (Eds.), *Read, write, connect* (2nd ed., pp. 458–464). Boston, MA: Bedford/St. Martin's. (Original work published 2013)

Whitehurst, J. (2017). How I hire: Intellectual curiosity required. In K. Green & A. Lawlor (Eds.), *Read, write, connect* (2nd ed., pp. 466–468). Boston, MA: Bedford/St. Martin's. (Original work published 2013)

Yuhas, D. (2017). Curiosity prepares the brain for better learning. In K. Green & A. Lawlor (Eds.), *Read, write, connect* (2nd ed., pp. 469–471). Boston, MA: Bedford/St. Martin's. (Original work published 2014)

The References page starts on a new page, with the heading centered.

The References list is alphabetized by author. Readers will use this list to locate your sources.

The first line of each reference begins at the left, and each subsequent line is indented ½ inch.

Each reference is formatted according to the type of source it is (see pp. 427–431). These examples follow the format for articles reprinted in an anthology.

Creating Your Own References Page.   Following these basic rules will help you avoid common errors in creating the References page:

STEP 1: List all of the references cited in your paper alphabetically by the author's last name.

STEP 2: If you have more than one source by the same author, list the one with the earlier publication date first.

STEP 3: Begin the first line of each reference at the left margin, and indent all additional lines ½ inch.

STEP 4: Double-space all lines.

STEP 5: Italicize titles of books. Titles of articles receive no special treatment (do not italicize them, underline them, bold them, or put them in quotation marks).

STEP 6: Capitalize only the first word in the title and subtitle (plus any proper nouns) for titles on your References page (though in the body of your paper, use regular title caps).

Ready to give it a try with your sources? Gather the sources you are using in your paper. For each source, first assess what type of source it is, and then follow the appropriate models in the following pages. If you are struggling to determine what type of source you have—which is not unusual, given how quickly online sources are changing—ask your instructor or a reference librarian at your college library. Many libraries have reference librarians who can answer such questions over the phone or via e-mail. Check out your library Web site to see if your school offers this service. As you gain more experience, you will begin to recognize the titles of journals, newspapers, and magazines, but when you are just starting out in college-level research, this is one area where you might need some guidance. Whatever type of source you have, you will start by listing the author. Then you will give the year in parentheses, and from there you need to look at the relevant examples listed in this chapter to see how to finish off the citation, depending on whether you have an article, a book, or an online source.

How to List the Author(s) on the References Page

In general, on the References page, you use an author's complete last name and only the initial of his or her first and middle name. So John K. Smith would be listed as Smith, J. K., and Sally Perez would be Perez, S. There are some odd cases, though, that you may run into as you find sources. Here are a few of the common exceptions to this general rule:

Two to Seven Authors: Put them in the order in which their names appear on the publication, and use the ampersand sign (&) before the last one.

Phillips, M., Cave, T., Ramirez, T., & Agegian, A.

More than Seven Authors: List the first six, then use an ellipses, and then list the last.

>   Perez, V., Lucas, T., Smith, J. R., Algonquin, P., Perez, H., Gingham, L., . . .
>   Slick, G.

Government Author: Go from larger part of the government to smaller.

>   U.S. Department of Labor, Bureau of Labor Statistics, Occupational Outlook
>   Handbook.

Editor(s) but No Author(s): Include the abbreviation "Ed." or "Eds." (for more than one) after the name(s).

>   Harrison, L. K. (Ed.).

>   Madison, D., & Washington, M. (Eds.).

If the source has no author, in most cases, just skip it and begin with the title of the source, though sometimes an article that seems to have no author is actually authored by an organization or department.

Print Books and Articles.   When you refer to books or articles in their original paper sources (such as in a newspaper or journal), these are considered *print* sources, and you use the following reference formats.

BOOK (PRINT)

Author Last — Year in — Title, Italicized, First Word
Name, Initials — Parentheses — of Title and Subtitle Capitalized

Engel, S. (2015). *The hungry mind: The origins of curiosity in childhood.*

City and State
of Publication — Publisher

Cambridge, MA: Harvard University Press.

BOOK CHAPTER (PRINT)

Author of — Year in — Title of Chapter, First Word
Chapter — Parentheses — of Title and Subtitle Capitalized

Fodor, J. A. (2000). The language of thought: First approximations.

Editors of Book, — Title of Book, Italicized, First Word
Initials First, Preceded by "In" — of Title and Subtitle Capitalized

In R. Cummins & D. D. Cummins (Eds.), *Minds, brains, and computers:*

Page Range

The foundations of cognitive science, an anthology (pp. 51– 68).

City and State
of Publication — Publisher

Malden, MA: Blackwell Publishers.

NEWSPAPER ARTICLE (PRINT)

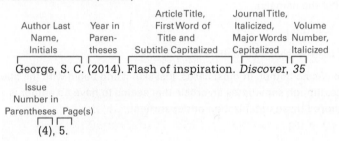

Author
Last Name,
Initials

Year, Month,
and Day
in Parentheses

Article Title,
First Word of Title and
Subtitle Capitalized

Bryant, A. (2014, July 13). If you're curious, you hold the keys.

Newspaper Title,
Italicized, Major
Words Capitalized   Page

New York Times. p. 2.

MAGAZINE ARTICLE (PRINT)

Author Last
Name,
Initials

Year in
Paren-
theses

Article Title,
First Word of
Title and
Subtitle Capitalized

Journal Title,
Italicized,
Major Words
Capitalized

Volume
Number,
Italicized

George, S. C. (2014). Flash of inspiration. *Discover, 35*

Issue
Number in
Parentheses   Page(s)

(4), 5.

ARTICLE REPRINTED IN AN ANTHOLOGY

If you are citing an article that was originally published in a magazine, newspaper, or journal but you found it published in a collection of articles in book form (an anthology), cite the date of the book in parentheses after the author's name and include the article's original year of publication at the end of your citation, as shown here.

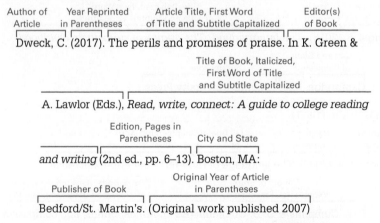

Author of
Article

Year Reprinted
in Parentheses

Article Title, First Word
of Title and Subtitle Capitalized

Editor(s)
of Book

Dweck, C. (2017). The perils and promises of praise. In K. Green &

Title of Book, Italicized,
First Word of Title
and Subtitle Capitalized

A. Lawlor (Eds.), *Read, write, connect: A guide to college reading*

Edition, Pages in
Parentheses   City and State

and writing (2nd ed., pp. 6–13). Boston, MA:

Publisher of Book

Original Year of Article
in Parentheses

Bedford/St. Martin's. (Original work published 2007)

Online Books and Articles.   The wide variety of online sources are sometimes difficult to cite because you have to sleuth around a bit to find the relevant information that you must include in a citation. Also remember that not everything you find while at a computer counts as an online source. Articles from databases, one of the most frequently used types of sources in student papers, are cited differently (see the section on articles above).

As a general rule, to cite an online source, you list the author's name, the date, the title, a comment in square brackets that explains the type of source, and then the "Retrieved from . . ." information.

BOOK (ONLINE VERSION OF PRINT BOOK)

Author Last Name, Initials	Year in Parentheses	Title, Italicized, First Word of Title and Subtitle Capitalized

Engel, S. (2015). *The hungry mind: The origins of curiosity in childhood*

Version in Brackets	"Retrieved from" and URL, No End Period

[Kindle version]. Retrieved from http://www.amazon.com

NEWSPAPER ARTICLE (ONLINE)

Author Last Name, Initials	Year, Month, and Day in Parentheses	Article Title, First Word of Title and Subtitle Capitalized (and Proper Nouns)

Miller, D. (2015, April 27). 2015 Milken Institute: Bob Iger, Brian Grazer

Newspaper Title, Italicized Major Words Capitalized	"Retrieved from" and URL, No End Period

discuss curiosity. *Los Angeles Times*. Retrieved from http://www

.latimes.com

MAGAZINE ARTICLE (ONLINE)

Author Last Name, Initials	Year, Month, and Day in Parentheses	Article Title, First Word of Title and Subtitle Capitalized

Main, D. (2015, July 9). There may be infinite universes—and infinite

Magazine Title, Italicized, Major Words Capitalized	"Retrieved from" and URL, No End Period

versions of you. *Newsweek*. Retrieved from http://www.newsweek.com

JOURNAL ARTICLE WITH A DOI (ONLINE)

Author Last Name, Initials	Year in Parentheses	Article Title, First Word of Title and Subtitle Capitalized	Journal Title, Italicized, Major Words Capitalized	Volume Number, Italicized

Phillips, R. (2014). Space for curiosity. *Progress in Human Geography*, *38*

Issue Number in Parentheses	Page Range	DOI

(4), 493–512. doi:10.1177/0309132513506271

A note about online articles: These days, articles are published many times in many forms, and they are often published simultaneously in more than one way. The DOI, or *digital object identifier*, can be extremely useful in such cases. If an article has a DOI, then all you need to do is include that at the end of the citation. Usually you will find the DOI at the end of the article, or sometimes at the beginning. If an article does not have a DOI, then you need to add the URL or the Web site where you found the article, and if that is unstable (as in a newspaper Web site that changes daily), then include the home page for the online publication.

JOURNAL ARTICLE WITHOUT A DOI (ONLINE)

Author Last Name, Initials	Year in Parentheses	Article Title, First Word of Title and Subtitle Capitalized

Workman, J. L. (2015). Parental influence on exploratory students' college

	Journal Title, Italicized, Major Words Capitalized	Volume Number, Italicized

choice, major, and career decision making. *College Student Journal, 49*

Issue Number in Parentheses	Page Range	"Retrieved from" and URL, No End Period

(1), 23–30. Retrieved from http://www.projectinnovation.com/college

-student-journal.html

WEB SITE ARTICLE

Author Last Name, Initials	Year, Month, and Day in Parentheses	Title, First Word of Title and Subtitle Capitalized

Yong, E. (2015, October 15). Caffeine makes for busy bees, not productive ones

Type of Source in Brackets	"Retrieved from" and URL, No End Period

[Online article]. Retrieved from http://phenomena.nationalgeographic

.com/2015/10/15/how-plants-manipulate-bees-with-caffeine/

BLOG

Author Last Name, Initials	Year, Month, and Day in Parentheses	Title, First Word of Title and Subtitle Capitalized

Price-Mitchell, M. (2015, February 17). Curiosity: The force within a hungry mind

Type of Source in Brackets	"Retrieved from" and URL, No End Period

[Web log post]. Retrieved from www.edutopia.org/blog/8-pathways

-curiosity-hungry-mind-marilyn-price-mitchell

IN-TEXT (PARENTHETICAL) CITATIONS

The third key component of APA style has to do with how you cite—or give the source for—the information you got from others. The basic concept of in-text citations is that when a reader reaches a passage in an essay that includes information (a quotation, paraphrase, or summary)

that the writer found in another source, the writer will at this point let the reader know where the information comes from. To do this, the writer puts the information in parentheses.

Look back at the text pages of the sample paper on pages 419–22. Notice that each time some material from an outside source is referred to, the source is listed.

APA in-text citations require three things to accompany quotations:

- the author's last name
- the year(s) of publication
- the page number (or paragraph number if page numbers are not available)

In-text citations for paraphrased material must include the author's last name and the date or dates of publication. If a source, such as a film, does not have a page number, then simply omit this part of the citation.

Sample Formats for In-Text Citations

QUOTATION WHEN THE AUTHOR IS NAMED IN THE SENTENCE

Put the year(s) of publication in parentheses after the author's name and the page or paragraph number in parentheses at the end of the quotation.

> In her article Daisy Yuhas (2014/2017) states that "researchers found that curious minds showed increased activity in the hippocampus, which is involved in the creation of memories" (p. 470).

In this case, the years directly follow the author's name (Daisy Yuhas), and the page number is listed in the parentheses at the end of the sentence. Note that in this example, the work being cited was reprinted in this textbook, so we include both the original publication year (2014) and the date of publication of the book we are citing (2017). If we were citing page numbers from an original publication, we would include only the year of that publication, as in the next example.

> In his book *Curious: The Desire to Know and Why Your Future Depends on It*, Ian Leslie (2014) observes that "the great unlocking of curiosity translated into a cascade of prosperity for the nations that precipitated it" (p. xv).

Here, Ian Leslie is named in the signal phrase, and because this is a direct quotation, the page number is included in parentheses at the end of the sentence.

QUOTATION WHEN THE AUTHOR IS NOT NAMED IN THE SENTENCE

Put the author's name, date(s) of publication, and page or paragraph number in parentheses at the end of the sentence.

> Being curious can actually increase your memory according to "researchers [who] found that curious minds showed increased activity in the hippocampus, which is involved in the creation of memories" (Yuhas, 2014/2017, p. 470).

TIP

In APA style, unlike MLA style, if you need to make the first letter of a quote either uppercase or lowercase to fit your sentence, you do not need to acknowledge this change by enclosing the letter in brackets.

TIP

Note that APA style requires "p." or "pp." or "para." to indicate page or paragraph number in in-text citations, whereas MLA style does not (see Chapter 22).

PARAPHRASE WHEN THE AUTHOR IS NAMED IN THE SENTENCE

Include the year(s), but do not include the page or paragraph number.

> According to Daisy Yuhas (2014/2017), researchers have learned that curiosity can stimulate brain activity related to memory.

PARAPHRASE WHEN THE AUTHOR IS NOT NAMED IN THE SENTENCE

Include the author's last name and the year(s) of publication in parentheses at the end of the sentence.

> Researchers have learned that curiosity can stimulate brain activity related to memory (Yuhas, 2014/2017).

Students who skip listing their citations as they research and say to themselves, "I'll put all the sources in later" are wasting their time and almost always make mistakes. Not only do they often forget to do the citations, but when they do remember, they spend more time on this task because they have to find the quotes and paraphrased text all over again. Why not just create the citations first and spare yourself the effort? The quicker you develop this mind-set, the less time you'll spend on the details of APA style, and the more time you'll have to think about what you want to say in your writing.

chapter review

In the following chart, fill in the second column to record in your own words the important skills included in this chapter. Then assess yourself to determine whether you are still developing the skill or feel you have mastered it. If you are still developing the skill, make some notes about what you need to work on to master it in the future. If you believe you have already mastered it, explain why.

Skills and concepts covered in this chapter	Explanation in your own words	I'm developing this skill and need to work on . . .	I believe I have mastered this skill because . . .
Creating an APA document in correct format			
Creating an APA References page			
Citing sources in the text of an APA paper			

Each chapter in Part 3 includes a variety of readings from different disciplines in conversation on a particular theme. Every reading is accompanied by pre- and post-reading activities as well as comprehension and discussion questions. At the end of each chapter, you'll find help for synthesizing the readings and writing an essay.

part three

Food for Thought: Thematic Readings and Sources

24
Curiosity

NASA/JPL–Caltech/MSSS

NASA's Mars Rover *Curiosity*

Theme Overview

To be human to be curious. From the small children who constantly ask "why?" to the elderly people who continue to be vibrant and connected with the world, we are a curious species. Curious people are alive, engaged with the world and with others. They are outwardly directed, wanting to know how things work, why people believe or feel or think as they do. Their curiosity drives them to innovate, to discover, to make mistakes and create new knowledge.

In 1952 the great Albert Einstein wrote in a letter to his friend and biographer, the writer Carl Seelig: "I have no special talents. I am only passionately curious." Einstein's belief that curiosity is the greatest driver of creative thought is shared by many people now, although, in ancient times, curiosity was often described as something to be feared or quashed. Indeed, myths and tales across cultures include characters whose curiosity brings mostly trouble.

Today, few people would outwardly argue against Einstein's modern view of curiosity as a positive character trait that keeps people young in mind and spirit. However, as the readings in this unit show, we do not always cultivate curiosity in ourselves or our societies. Sometimes parents tire of hearing "why" and subtly or not-so-subtly shut down the inquisitive toddler. Sometimes teachers don't have the time to allow students to follow their curiosity—too many tests to take, too much content to cover. Sometimes people in power value cleanliness, order, and predictability over the messiness and mistakes that inevitably come when people follow the path of curiosity. Sometimes we even stifle our own curiosity, out of fear of being different; think of the teenagers who believe it is only acceptable to be curious about some topics (like music or sports or sex) and not about others (like science or math or anything academic). And sometimes our lives are too chaotic, or our mental health too fragile, to sustain a curious self.

Lack of curiosity is contagious too. When we surround ourselves with people who lack curiosity, we become less and less curious, content with a few hobbies or passions, but not fully engaged with the world around us. When our curiosity diminishes, we stop asking questions, and we accept things as they are, assuming that they have always been that way and always will. Social progress stalls in such conditions. So does innovation.

Some of the writers in this unit believe we are at a cultural low point in curiosity, one that the next generation of young people will, hopefully, send upward. As you read these texts, decide whether or not you agree, and think about what can be done to increase or sustain your curiosity. The readings in this unit range from mythology to education to business to science. You will examine this question of curiosity in a variety of ways. Perhaps your own curiosity will be sparked!

practice it 24.1 Taking Stock of What You Already Know

What is your experience with curiosity in your own life? Think about the following questions, and then freewrite for five minutes on at least two of them:

- Who do you know well that you would describe as a curious person? How do they act, think, or talk? In other words, what details about them make them curious?

- Who do you know well that you would describe as lacking curiosity? How do they act, think, or talk? In other words, what details about them make them lack curiosity?

- Think about the old saying "Curiosity killed the cat." What does this saying mean? In what types of situations do people typically use it?

- Think about the cartoon character Curious George. What happens in most Curious George stories? Is George's curiosity positive, negative, or somewhere in between? What brings you to this conclusion?

- Have you ever seen a curio cabinet or a curiosity cabinet (also known as a cabinet of wonders)? What do you know about such cabinets? Who kept them? What did they put in them? Why? If you had such a cabinet, what would you put in it?

- Why did NASA give the name *Curiosity* to its latest robot exploring the planet Mars? Is it inspiring?

- Think about the fairy tales or classic stories you can remember from childhood. Which had curious main characters? What happened because of the characters' curiosity?

- How frequently does your curiosity get sparked throughout the day? What do you do when you are curious?

- Do you think greater access to the Internet has increased or decreased our curiosity? Why?

Amy T. Peterson has studied history as well as educational technology and currently works in online curriculum development for higher education. David J. Dunworth is an author and entrepreneur who has worked in a wide variety of fields, including advertising. Together they wrote the reference book *Mythology in Our Midst: A Guide to Cultural References* (2004), which is used in both high school and college courses on mythology and history. The book is composed of encyclopedia-like entries on aspects of mythology that students will often encounter in their studies. The entry on Pandora, reproduced here, provides a succinct overview of the goddess and her importance in Greek myths. *Some difficult words have been identified in the margins. Look up those you do not know, and write the definition in your own words in the margins either before or as you read. The first one has been done for you.*

practice it 24.2 Pre-Reading Activity

Having some knowledge of major figures in Greek mythology will help you understand this reading. Look up the Greek gods online, and try to identify the main characteristics and relationships among the following: Prometheus, Zeus, Hephaestus, Athena, and Aphrodite. Draw a family tree or other diagram that shows their connections.

Amy T. Peterson and David J. Dunworth

PANDORA

Although the Greek myth of Pandora is a relatively simple one, it explains the origin of women as well as the evils in the world. According to the myth, Zeus created the first woman, Pandora. His motivation for creating Pandora was not altruistic, but to get revenge against Prometheus and man. Prometheus had offended Zeus by giving man the fire that he stole from the gods; man's crime was accepting the gift.

Zeus' revenge involved destroying mankind's ideal existence of leisure, health, and goodness. He swore that he would plague mankind with evil and his plan centered on the creation of a mortal woman. By pooling the resources of his fellow gods, he was able to create an enchanting creature. Hephaestus began the process by using earth and water to craft Pandora's

altruistic: unselfish caring for the well-being of others

leisure:

plague:

mortal:

pooling:

likeness:

melodious:
deceitful:

insatiable:

ravage:

idyllic:

pithos:

succumbed:

seductive figure and bewitching face in the likeness of the most beautiful goddesses. Athena dressed her and taught her skills like weaving. Aphrodite's contribution was Pandora's elegance and sexual appetite. Her melodious voice was a gift from Hermes, who gave her a persuasive and deceitful nature as well. Her name means "all-gifted" and is a reflection of the collaborative effort of the gods.

Once his seductive gift was complete, Zeus offered Pandora to Epimetheus, Prometheus' brother. Knowing that Zeus was up to no good, Prometheus (whose name means "foresight") warned his brother against accepting the gift. Epimetheus (whose name means "hindsight") ignored his brother's advice, welcomed Pandora into his home, and by some accounts, married her.

Initially, Pandora's existence on earth went well, but her insatiable curiosity about a covered jar soon got the better of her and changed mankind. Some versions of the myth describe the jar as another gift from Zeus to Epimetheus, while others depict Pandora as its owner. Regardless, Pandora was not supposed to open the jar, but she could not resist. Upon her opening of the jar, the evils of mankind escaped and began to ravage mortal life. Illnesses, work, envy, revenge, death, and insanity transformed man's formerly idyllic existence. Realizing her error, Pandora scrambled to replace the lid, but only "hope" was left inside.

When this myth is related today, people refer to the container 5 of evils as "Pandora's box." Hesiod's (eighth century B.C.) account, one of the earliest and most cited versions of the story, describes the container as a pithos, which is a storage jar. When an influential sixteenth-century humanist named Erasmus confused the word "pithos" with the word "pyxis," he transformed the jar of evils into Pandora's box. Today, we use Pandora's box to describe something that holds unknown or uncontrollable misfortunes or difficulties.

The story of Pandora's creation and role in humanity bears a strong resemblance to the story of Eve in Hebrew myth. Both Pandora and Eve were the first mortal women in their cultures and both of them succumbed to curiosity, which led to the suffering and mortality of humans. Although these stories do not reflect these first women in a positive light, Pandora's story offered the ancient Greeks the prospect of hope.

practice it 24.3 Post-Reading Activity

Analyze the underlying meaning of the Pandora story and draft a rough thesis that completes the following: *The myth of Pandora suggests that curiosity is. . . .* If you have read "Sun and Moon in a Box" (p. 440) or the myth of Amaterasu (p. 444), compare your analysis of that story to this one.

COMPREHENSION QUESTIONS

1. Prometheus is a Titan (one of the earliest of Greek gods), and according to Greek mythology, he created man. Why was Zeus angry at Prometheus, and what did Zeus do to get revenge?

2. Who helped Zeus create Pandora? What was she like?

3. What was life like for man before and after Zeus introduced Pandora?

4. What is Pandora's box, and why should it probably be called Pandora's jar?

5. What are the similarities and differences between Pandora and Eve?

DISCUSSION QUESTIONS

1. Why is it significant that Pandora was created collaboratively by the gods and goddesses?

2. Why do you think hope remained inside Pandora's box?

3. All cultures have origin stories that explain how the world as we know it came to be. Usually such origin stories reflect deeply held beliefs about aspects of the culture. What beliefs about women and curiosity might be reflected in the Pandora story?

4. Pandora and her box are often referred to in American popular culture today, such as with the online music streaming service. What other references to Pandora have you heard? For each reference, try to decide why the artist or writer used it and whether you think it is an effective use of the myth.

BOOK

The following Native American Zuni myth is a creation (or origin) story that explains how the sun and moon came to be in the sky. Editors Richard Erdoes and Alfonso Ortiz included this story in their collection *American Indian Trickster Tales* (1998). Erdoes, an illustrator and writer, fled Nazi Germany after Hitler's rise to power and eventually ended up in New York, where he wrote for *Life* magazine. He became active in the Native American civil rights movement and wrote several books about Native Americans, including *Lakota Woman*, which he wrote with Mary Crow Dog. Ortiz was a professor of cultural anthropology at the University of New Mexico and served as president of the Association on American Indian Affairs for fifteen years. A member of the San Juan Pueblo himself, Ortiz studied and wrote extensively about Native American culture and mythology. Most Native American myths have been passed down orally for many generations. *American Indian Trickster Tales* encompasses many of those stories from across dozens of tribal oral histories. In the scope of Native American mythology, there are many different trickster characters and Coyote is one of the more common ones. In mythology, a trickster is a character that breaks the rules or creates disorder. *Some difficult words have been identified in the margins. Look up those you do not know, and write the definition in your own words in the margins either before or as you read. The first one has been done for you.*

practice 24.4 Pre-Reading Activity

Most children grow up hearing a variety of stories, from family memories to ghost stories and urban legends, to myths and folk tales. Think about a specific story you were told as a child. What was it? Did it have a clear moral or purpose? Would you tell that story to children in the next generation of your family? Why or why not? Freewrite on any or all of these questions as you prepare to read "Sun and Moon in a Box." Then, as you read, think about the structures and details of the stories from your childhood and see if you notice any similarities.

Richard Erdoes and Alfonso Ortiz, eds.

SUN AND MOON IN A BOX

Coyote and Eagle were hunting. Eagle caught rabbits. Coyote caught nothing but grasshoppers. Coyote said: "Friend Eagle, my chief, we make a great hunting pair."

"Good, let us stay together," said Eagle.

They went toward the west. They came to a deep canyon. "Let us fly over it," said Eagle.

"My chief, I cannot fly," said Coyote. "You must carry me across."

"Yes, I see that I have to," said Eagle. He took Coyote on his back 5 and flew across the canyon. They came to a river. "Well," said Eagle, "you cannot fly, but you certainly can swim. This time I do not have to carry you."

Eagle flew over the stream, and Coyote swam across. He was a bad swimmer. He almost drowned. He coughed up a lot of water. "My chief," he said, "when we come to another river, you must carry me." Eagle regretted to have Coyote for a companion.

They came to <u>Kachina</u> Pueblo. The Kachinas were dancing. Now, at this time, the earth was still soft and new. There was as yet no sun and no moon. Eagle and Coyote sat down and watched the dance. They saw that the Kachinas had a square box. In it they kept the sun and the moon. Whenever they wanted light they opened the lid and let the sun peek out. Then it was day. When they wanted less light, they opened the box just a little for the moon to look out.

"This is something wonderful," Coyote whispered to Eagle.

"This must be the sun and the moon they are keeping in that box," said Eagle. "I have heard about these two wonderful beings."

"Let us steal the box," said Coyote. 10

"No, that would be wrong," said Eagle. "Let us just borrow it."

When the Kachinas were not looking, Eagle grabbed the box and flew off. Coyote ran after him on the ground. After a while Coyote called Eagle: "My chief, let me have the box. I am ashamed to let you do all the carrying."

"No," said Eagle, "you are not reliable. You might be curious and open the box and then we could lose the wonderful things we borrowed."

For some time they went on as before—Eagle flying above with the box, Coyote running below, trying to keep up. Then once again Coyote called Eagle: "My chief, I am ashamed to let you carry the box. I should do this for you. People will talk badly about me, letting you carry this burden."

"No, I don't trust you," Eagle repeated. "You won't be able to 15 refrain from opening the box. Curiosity will get the better of you."

"No," cried Coyote, "do not fear, my chief, I won't even think of opening the box." Still, Eagle would not give it to him, continuing to fly above, holding the box in his <u>talons</u>. But Coyote went on pestering Eagle: "My chief, I am really embarrassed. People will say: 'That lazy, disrespectful Coyote lets his chief do all the carrying.'"

Kachina: A Pueblo Indian spirit often represented by dancers in masks or as dolls for children.

talons:

"No, I won't give this box to you," Eagle objected. "It is too precious to entrust to somebody like you."

They continued as before, Eagle flying, Coyote running. Then Coyote
begged for the fourth time: "My chief, let me carry the box for a while.
My wife will scold me, and my children will no longer respect me,
when they find out that I did not help you carry this load."

Then Eagle relented, saying: "Will you promise not to drop the box
and under no circumstances to open it?"

"I promise, my chief, I promise," cried Coyote. "You can rely upon   20
me. I shall not betray your trust."

Then Eagle allowed Coyote to carry the box. They went on as
before, Eagle flying, Coyote running, carrying the box in his mouth.
They came to a wooded area, full of trees and bushes. Coyote pre-
tended to lag behind, hiding himself behind some bushes where Eagle
could not see him. He could not curb his curiosity. Quickly he sat down
and opened the box. In a flash, Sun came out of the box and flew away,
to the very edge of the sky, and at once the world grew cold, the leaves
fell from the tree branches, the grass turned brown, and icy winds
made all living things shiver.

Then, before Coyote could put the lid back on the box, Moon
jumped out and flew away to the outer rim of the sky, and at once snow
fell down from heaven and covered the plains and the mountains.

Eagle said: "I should have known better. I should not have let you
persuade me. I knew what kind of low, <u>cunning</u>, stupid creature you
are. I should have remembered that you never keep a promise. Now we
have winter. If you had not opened the box, then we could have kept
Sun and Moon always close to us. Then there would be no winter. Then
we would have summer all the time."

cunning:

practice 24.5   Post-Reading Activity

Analyze the underlying meaning of "Sun and Moon in a Box" and draft a
rough thesis that completes the following: *The tale of "Sun and Moon in a Box"
suggests that curiosity is. . . .* If you have read "Pandora" (p. 437) or the myth of
Amaterasu (p. 444), compare your analysis of those stories to this one.

COMPREHENSION QUESTIONS

1. In Native American myths, the eagle is often portrayed as having healing and hunting powers or as a chief. Compare Coyote to Eagle in this story. How would you describe each character?

2. How does Coyote convince Eagle to give him the box?

3. What happens as a result of Coyote's curiosity? How is the world affected?

DISCUSSION QUESTIONS

1. What is the significance of the roles of Eagle and Coyote in the story?

2. What does the story suggest about trust?

3. As a trickster, Coyote causes trouble or disorder through his curiosity. Are there any benefits to his curiosity, or are the effects all negative?

4. If you have read the story of Amaterasu (p. 444), compare and contrast it with "Sun and Moon in a Box." What similarities and differences do you find?

TEXTBOOK

This myth of Amaterasu is one of the most important stories in Japanese mythology. The version here, written by C. Scott Littleton, is from the textbook *World Mythology: The Illustrated Guide* (2006), edited by scholar Roy Willis. The late C. Scott Littleton was a professor of anthropology at Occidental College in Los Angeles, California, for many years and authored numerous books on Japanese culture and mythology as well as books on Arthurian legends. *Some difficult words have been identified in the margins. Look up those you do not know, and write the definition in your own words in the margins either before or as you read. The first one has been done for you.*

practice it 24.6   Pre-Reading Activity

Do an Internet search for Amaterasu and jot down some notes about what you find out before reading. Finding out who she is and what her importance is in Japanese culture and in the Shinto religion will help your comprehension as you read this myth.

C. Scott Littleton

AMATERASU

The Contest of the Sibling Deities

banished: *forced to leave as punishment*

usurp:

quivers:

deities:

vindicated:

When the Storm God Susano was <u>banished</u> by his father, Izanagi, he announced his intention to take leave of his sister, the Sun Goddess, Amaterasu. The goddess suspected her brother of wanting to <u>usurp</u> her lands and prepared herself for battle, arranging her long hair in bunches and arming herself with a bow and two <u>quivers</u> of arrows. She shook her bow furiously and stamped and kicked the earth beneath her feet while she waited for him. Susano assured her he had no evil intentions. He suggested that they could prove which of them was mightier by having a contest of reproduction: whichever of them bore male <u>deities</u> would be <u>vindicated</u>.

The contest began with the Sun Goddess asking for her brother's sword. She broke this into three pieces which she chewed up and then spat out as three graceful goddesses. Next, Susano took the long strings of *magatama*, or fertility beads, which Amaterasu wore around her hair-bunches, hairband and arms. From these he produced five male gods and proclaimed himself the victor. Amaterasu pointed out that her brother's male offspring had come from her possessions and that in fact *she* had won

The Sun Goddess

The Sun Goddess Amaterasu, the elder daughter of Izanagi, is one of the greatest deities in Japanese myth. She was born out of her father's left eye as he washed after returning from Yomi, the underworld. Amaterasu is worshipped both as a spiritual divinity and as a sacred ancestor of the imperial family. She was once worshipped in the imperial palace itself, until it became politically expedient to put the authority of the emperor beyond the power of the priestesses and erect a shrine to her elsewhere. The main shrine to Amaterasu is at Ise, in Mie Prefecture. This is the most important Shinto shrine in Japan. The main building is a thatched, unpainted hut of cypress, constructed in ancient Japanese style. It is regularly rebuilt in wood in exactly the same form: from the seventh century to the seventeenth century it was rebuilt every twenty years; since the seventeenth century it has been rebuilt every twenty-one years.

divinity:

imperial family:

expedient:

Shinto:

the contest. Susano refused to concede and celebrated his victory by breaking down the ridges of the divine rice paddies and covering up the irrigation ditches. Then he defecated and strewed his excrement in the hall where it was customary to taste the first fruits of the harvest. Finally, Susano skinned a "heavenly" dappled pony (probably a reference to the stars) and hurled it down through the thatched roof of the sacred weaving hall, where Amaterasu and her maidens were weaving. One of the maidens was so alarmed by this that she banged her genitals against the shuttle of the loom and died. Amaterasu fled in terror. The *Nihonshoki* includes a version of this story in which Amaterasu herself was the victim of her brother's violent prank, although she was merely injured, not killed.

defecated:

excrement:

The Divine Crisis: Amaterasu's Removal of the Sun

The Sun Goddess Amaterasu was badly frightened when her brother Susano hurled a skinned horse through the roof of the sacred weaving hall. Her decision to withdraw into what the *Kojiki* calls the "Heavenly Rock Cave" (or Ama-no-iwato) produced a divine crisis analogous to the crises found in almost every ancient mythology, such as the Egyptian account of the temporary triumph of the evil god Seth and the Greek myth of the abduction of Persephone, both of which caused all manner of disasters to befall the world. Some scholars interpret her withdrawal as a symbolic death and entombment; however, it may equally be a metaphor for a total

analogous:

The Sacred Weaving Hall

Neither the *Kojiki* nor the *Nihonshoki* is precise as to the purpose of the sacred weaving hall, or what indeed Amaterasu and her maidens were weaving. However, several possibilities have been suggested.

Amaterasu was a priestess-queen, responsible for weaving the clothes of the gods, and the weaving hall may have been her workroom. Some authorities suggest that she and her female attendants were making garments to be worn by priestesses officiating at ceremonies connected with the sun cult. A more profound possibility is the notion that they were weaving the fabric of the still incomplete universe. Susano's actions can perhaps be seen as a chaotic assault upon the cosmos or universal order. The sacred weaving hall, as a scene of creation, would be a fitting arena for the confrontation between the divine embodiments of cosmos (Amaterasu) and chaos (Susano).

chaotic:

cosmos:

universal order:

embodiments:

precipitated:

eclipse of the sun, precipitated by the event that the Sun Goddess had just witnessed.

Amaterasu's self-imposed retirement plunged both the High Plains of Heaven and the Central Land of the Reed Plain (that is, the mortal realm) into total darkness. As a result, the rice paddies lay fallow, and various calamities ensued. In desperation, the "eight-hundred myriad" gods came together in solemn assembly by the heavenly river to discuss ways of coaxing Amaterasu from her hiding place. (In this context, the Japanese number eight, or *ya*, is a sacred number, implying many or an entire contingent rather than a specific total.)

fallow:

calamities:

solemn:

Omori-kane-no-kami, the wise son of Takamimusubi, was directed to come up with a solution. After the sounds of certain "long-crying birds" (probably roosters) failed to produce the desired result, Omori-kane and his fellow divinities conceived an elaborate stratagem. First, they constructed a magical mirror which they suspended from the branches of a sacred sakaki tree uprooted from a mountain forest. Then, while several divinities held magical objects and performed a solemn liturgy, a beautiful young goddess called Ama-no-uzume (in this context seemingly a dawn goddess, like the Roman Aurora, the Greek Eos or the Vedic Indian Ushas, although none of the ancient sources actually characterize her in this way) climbed on top of an overturned tub and performed an erotic dance.

strategem:

liturgy:

5

This nineteenth-century woodblock print by Utagawa Kunisada shows Amaterasu emerging from her cave.

The Dawn Goddess

In her capacity as a <u>prototype</u> of the female <u>shaman</u>, or *miko*, who regularly engaged in ecstatic dancing, Ama-no-uzume, the dawn goddess, appears again later in the story as told by the *Nihon-shoki*. On this occasion she displays her charms in order to distract a local solar deity called Sarutahiko, or the "Monkey Prince," who had attempted to block the descent from heaven of Amaterasu's grandson, Honinigi. She and Sarutahiko eventually married, and from their union is said to have sprung an historically attested clan of female Heian court dancers called the Sarume.

Ama-no-uzume's aim was to trick the sun into re-emerging, by employing methods consistent with those of the ancient *miko*, or female shaman. When she exposed her breasts and pushed her skirt down to her genitals, the assembled gods laughed so <u>uproariously</u> that the High Plains of Heaven shook as if struck by an earthquake. The sound even penetrated to where Amaterasu was hiding. Her curiosity aroused by the commotion, she opened the door of the rock-cave by just a crack and called out: "Why is Ama-no-uzume singing and dancing, and all the eight-hundred myriad deities laughing?" The young goddess replied for them all: "We are rejoicing because here is a deity superior to you." While she was speaking, two gods aimed the mirror in the direction of the partially open door and another god, whose name includes the word for strength (*chikana*), concealed himself nearby.

Catching sight of her reflection, Amaterasu slowly came out of her refuge and approached the mirror. As she gazed intently at herself, the god who was in hiding nearby suddenly grabbed her by the hand and pulled

prototype:

shaman:

uproariously:

her all the way out. Another divinity stretched a magic rope (*shiru-kume*) across the doorway, saying: "This is as far as you may go!" Things rapidly returned to normal after this, and the sunlight returned to both heaven and earth. The divine crisis had been resolved.

The eight-hundred myriad deities then reassembled to deliberate over the fate of the one who had caused the crisis, the willful and destructive Susano. The punishment imposed on him was severe: the gods fined him "a thousand tables of <u>restitutive</u> gifts," cut off his beard and the nails of his hands and feet, and finally expelled him from heaven, forcing him to descend once more to the Land of the Reed Plain.

restitutive:

practice it 24.7   Post-Reading Activity

Draw a simple picture of the various characters in the myth of Amaterasu and label each one with his or her role, or create a table with the various characters and their roles. What part does each play in the effort to get Amaterasu out of hiding?

COMPREHENSION QUESTIONS

1. What is a divine crisis, and why is the divine crisis a feature "found in almost every ancient mythology" (para. 6)?

2. What happens to the earthly world when Amaterasu decides to withdraw into the rock cave?

3. What is Amaterasu curious about that makes her come out of the cave?

4. Why do the gods use a mirror in their plan to get Amaterasu out of the cave?

DISCUSSION QUESTIONS

1. Is Amaterasu's curiosity positive, negative, or neutral?

2. In a way, Amaterasu's curiosity was used against her by the other gods, but the myth does end happily (for the people) because light is restored to the world. How does this myth compare and contrast with other stories about curiosity being a benefit or a problem? (If you have read the Pandora story on p. 437, you might specifically consider the similarities and differences between those two goddesses in terms of curiosity.)

3. As Littleton says, some people interpret this myth as a fertility ritual, and others interpret it as a way to explain a total solar eclipse. What evidence in the story can you find for each interpretation? Which interpretation is most convincing to you?

| BOOK | **model reading strategy:**   Using Context Clues |

Ian Leslie studies and writes about modern culture in his books, blogs, and journalism. He is also a producer of modern culture through his work in advertising and his role as a television commentator. Before writing *Curious: The Desire to Know and Why Your Future Depends on It* (2014), Leslie took on another vital aspect of human psychology with his book *Born Liars: Why We Can't Live without Deceit* (2011). He blogs and tweets regularly about modern life, politics, and people. The reading selection below is excerpted from the introduction to his book *Curious*, and it provides an overview of topics that he examines in greater depth in the book.

The highlighting on this reading models how you can use context clues to figure out the meaning of unfamiliar words. The four colors represent the four different types of context clues described in Chapter 9:

| example | definition | synonym | contrast |

As you read, try to use the highlighted clues to help you understand the difficult vocabulary. You might notice other words that are unfamiliar to you and find additional clues to help you understand them. When not enough clues are available, you can look up words in the dictionary and write their definitions in the margins.

▶ **For more about context clues, see pages 216–18 in Chapter 9, Vocabulary Building.**

| practice it 24.8 | Pre-Reading Activity |

Make a cluster diagram with yourself at the center. Add circles to show the topics that you are curious about. If you have done anything to pursue that curiosity, add a circle to that topic explaining how you have followed your curiosity. (For more on creating a cluster diagram, see pp. 232–35.)

Ian Leslie

CURIOUS: THE DESIRE TO KNOW AND WHY YOUR FUTURE DEPENDS ON IT

Introduction: The Fourth Drive

The researchers first realized that Kanzi was an unusually talented ape when they discovered that he had taught himself language. Sue Savage-Rumbaugh and her colleagues at the Language Research Center near

lexigrams:

eluded:

hyperactive:

Atlanta, Georgia, had devoted months of painstaking effort to teaching Kanzi's adoptive mother, Matata, how to communicate using symbols. They worked with a keyboard that had lexigrams corresponding to things and actions in the real world; there was a key for "apple," another one for "play."

Despite being exceptionally intelligent, Matata made slow progress. She understood that the keyboard could be used to communicate, but the idea that specific symbols had specific significance eluded her. She would take Savage-Rumbaugh's hand and lead her to the keyboard, intent on sharing what was on her mind. Then Matata would press any key and look up expectantly, as if Savage-Rumbaugh would surely know what she meant. She might press "juice" when what she really wanted was a banana, or "groom" when she wanted to go outdoors.

While the researchers were working with Matata, Kanzi was usually in the room, entertaining himself. It had been a condition of Kanzi's transfer to the Language Center at six months old that he be allowed to remain with his mother while she participated in language studies. A hyperactive infant, Kanzi darted around the test room, jumping on his mother's head, pushing her hand away from the keyboard just as she was trying to hit a key, stealing the food she earned as a reward for good work.

The researchers had noticed that Kanzi also liked to play with the keyboard when it was free, but they thought little of it. Then one day, when he was two years old, Kanzi went up to the keyboard and very deliberately selected the "chase" key. He looked at Savage-Rumbaugh to see if she had seen what he'd done. When she nodded and smiled, he ran off, looking behind him as he did so, a big, cheeky grin on his face.

That day, Kanzi used the keyboard 120 times, making requests 5
for specific foods or games, or announcing what he was about to do. To the astonishment of Savage-Rumbaugh and her colleagues, it became clear that he had mastered the symbolic keyboard, despite having never been trained on it, or even seeming to have paid attention to his mother's lessons. Over the following months and years, the researchers turned their full attention to this ape prodigy. Kanzi went on to demonstrate linguistic aptitude of such sophistication that he changed the way cognitive psychologists thought about human learning and language.

The difference between an ape and a human being is less than you might think. Kanzi learned a vocabulary of more than two hundred words. When he was given tests of reading and communications skills, he matched, and in some respects exceeded, a child of two and a half years. He made up and follows his own rules of grammar, indicating a creative capacity. He understands spoken language and can follow spoken instructions—when Savage-Rumbaugh told him to throw something in the river, he picked up a rock and hurled it in. He can use symbols to ask for treats or for help opening a door. He loves to play, and he loves to learn.

The story of Kanzi shows just how much we have in common with apes, which ought not to be a surprise, given that we share nearly all of their DNA. Yet it also suggests there is something that isn't shared—something very important.

What Kanzi never did, and never does, is ask *why*. He never furrows his brow, leans over the keyboard, and bashes out a sentence like, "Why are you asking me all these questions?" or "What *exactly* are you trying to discover?" He doesn't ask about what lies beyond the confines of his home at the research center. He can go to the refrigerator, but he has no interest in how the refrigerator works. Although he spends time with human beings who are clearly interested in what it is like to be an ape, Kanzi shows no curiosity about what it's like to be a human. For that matter, he shows little curiosity in what it means to be an ape. He has never asked, "Who am I?"

• • •

Our oldest stories about curiosity are warnings: Adam and Eve and the apple of knowledge, Icarus and the sun, Pandora's box. Early Christian theologians railed against curiosity: Saint Augustine claimed that "God fashioned hell for the inquisitive." Even humanist philosopher Erasmus suggested that curiosity was greed by a different name. For most of Western history, it has been regarded as at best a distraction, at worst a poison, corrosive to the soul and to society.

There's a reason for this. Curiosity is unruly. It doesn't like rules, 10   unruly:
or at least, it assumes that all rules are provisional, subject to the laceration of a smart question nobody has yet thought to ask. It disdains the approved pathways, preferring diversions, unplanned excursions, impulsive left turns. In short, curiosity is deviant. Pursuing it is liable to bring you into conflict with authority at some point, as everyone from Galileo to Charles Darwin to Steve Jobs could have attested.

A society that values order above all else will seek to suppress curiosity. But a society that believes in progress, innovation, and creativity will cultivate it, recognizing that the inquiring minds of its people constitute its most valuable asset. In medieval Europe, the inquiring mind—especially if it inquired too closely into the edicts of church or state—was stigmatized. During the Renaissance and Reformation, received wisdoms began to be interrogated, and by the time of the Enlightenment, European societies started to see that their future lay with the curious and encouraged probing questions rather than stamping on them. The result was the biggest explosion of new ideas and scientific advances in history.

The great unlocking of curiosity translated into a cascade of prosperity for the nations that precipitated it. Today, we cannot know for sure if we are in the middle of this golden period or at the end of it. But we are, at the very least, in a lull. With the important exception of the Internet, the innovations that catapulted Western societies ahead of the global pack are thin on the ground, while the rapid growth of Asian and South American economies has not yet been accompanied by a comparable run of indigenous innovation. Tyler Cowen, a professor of economics at George Mason University in Virginia, has termed the current period the Great Stagnation.

Cowen says that the rich world is struggling to cope with the consequences of its own success; it now finds it much harder to raise the educational levels of its populaces. Rather than just getting more people to school and university, therefore, the new challenge is to find ways of making more people hungry to learn, question, and create. Meanwhile, the leaders of Asian societies, such as those of China and Singapore, are wondering how to instill a culture of inquiry and critical thinking into their educational systems, aware that people who defer too much to the authority of their elders' ideas are less likely to transcend them. The world is in need of more curious learners.

Edmund Phelps, the Nobel Prize–winning economist, believes that the grassroots spirit of enterprise that fueled the Industrial Revolution is being suffocated by the dead weight of state and corporate bureaucracy. During a roundtable discussion of Phelps's work, a senior executive at the international bank BNY Mellon told Phelps: "So much of what you've talked about is what we struggle with daily as a large global financial corporation. . . . [A]s our regulators and societies want us to be more controlled, we want to create a culture that is more collaborative, is more creative and more competitive. We need our staff to be active, inquiring, imaginative, and full of ideas and curiosity in order to create innovation."

The truly curious will be increasingly in demand. Employers are looking for people who can do more than follow procedures competently or respond to requests, who have a strong, intrinsic desire to learn, solve problems, and ask penetrating questions. They may be difficult to manage at times, these individuals, for their interests and enthusiasms can take them along unpredictable paths, and they don't respond well to being told what to think. But for the most part, they will be worth the difficulty. 15

Curious learners go deep, and they go wide. They are the people best equipped for the kind of knowledge-rich, cognitively challenging work required in industries such as finance or software engineering. They are also the ones most likely to make creative connections *between* different fields, of the kind that lead to new ideas and the ones best suited to working in multidisciplinary teams. Consequently, they are the ones whose jobs are least likely to be taken by intelligent machines; in a world where technology is rapidly replacing humans even in white-collar jobs, it's no longer enough to be merely smart. Computers are smart. But no computer, however sophisticated, can yet be said to be curious.

Another way of putting this is that there is a rising premium on people with a high "need for cognition." Need for cognition, or NFC, is a scientific measure of intellectual curiosity. The drive to make sense of the world is a universal characteristic of human beings, but the world is divided into those who always seek out shortcuts and those who prefer to take the scenic route. Psychologists use a scale of NFC to distinguish between individuals who like their mental life to be as straightforward as possible and those who derive satisfaction and pleasure from intellectual challenges.

I'm going to assume that if you're reading this book, you have a reasonably high NFC, but here is a simple way to assess yourself, based on a questionnaire invented by the psychologists who first formulated the concept. Answer each question "true" or "false," choosing the answer that most often applies to you (truthfully!):

1. I would prefer complex to simple problems.
2. I like to have the responsibility of handling a situation that requires a lot of thinking.
3. Thinking is not my idea of fun.
4. I would rather do something that requires little thought than something that is sure to challenge my thinking abilities.
5. I try to anticipate and avoid situations where there is a likely chance I will have to think in depth about something.
6. I find satisfaction in deliberating hard and for long hours.
7. I only think as hard as I have to.
8. I prefer to think about small, daily projects than long-term ones.
9. I like tasks that require little thought once I've learned them.
10. The idea of relying on thought to make my way to the top appeals to me.
11. I really enjoy a task that involves coming up with new solutions to problems.
12. Learning new ways to think doesn't excite me very much.
13. I prefer my life to be filled with puzzles that I can't solve.
14. The notion of thinking abstractly is appealing to me.
15. I would prefer a task that is intellectual, difficult, and important to one that is somewhat important but does not require much thought.
16. I feel relief rather than satisfaction after completing a task that required a lot of mental effort.

17. It's enough for me that something gets the job done. I don't care how or why it works.
18. I usually end up deliberating about issues even when they do not affect me personally.

If you answered "true" to most of the questions 1, 2, 6, 10, 11, 13, 14, 15, and 18, and "false" to most of the others, then the chances are you are higher in NFC than the average person.

People who are low in NFC are more likely to rely on others to   20
explain things, or to fall back on cognitive heuristics, like agreeing with what everyone else seems to be saying. If you are high in NFC, you are more likely to actively seek out experiences and information that make you think, challenge your assumptions, and pose puzzles. You have a restless, inquiring mind, and you are constantly on the lookout for new intellectual journeys. Low NFC people are "cognitive misers" who seek to expend as little mental effort as they can get away with, whereas high NFC people positively enjoy "effortful cognitive activity"—they are the ones who tingle with anticipation at the prospect of learning about a new idea.

That word "effortful" is important—digital technologies are severing the link between effort and mental exploration. By making it easier for us to find answers, the Web threatens habits of deeper inquiry— habits that require patience and focused application. When you're confident that you can find out anything you want on your smartphone, you may be less likely to make the effort to learn the kind of knowledge that might lead you to query the answer that comes at the top of a Google search. As we'll see, there are those who argue that by releasing us from the need to use our memories, the Internet is allowing us to be more creative. But such claims fly in the face of everything scientists have learned about how the mind works.

Effort and pleasure can go together, of course. If you are high in NFC, you are probably good at solving problems for your employer, because you're really solving them for yourself. Social scientists who study group

social loafing:

behavior have observed a phenomenon they call "social loafing"—the widespread tendency of individuals to decrease their own effort when they start working collaboratively. When confident that others are working on the same problem, most people cut themselves some slack. But individuals who are high in need for cognition seem to form an exception to this rule; when given a cognitively challenging task to do in a group, they generate just as many different ideas as when working alone. They're having fun.

If you scored high on the test, congratulations. Don't let it go to your head, though. Just because you have a high NFC now doesn't mean you'll always have one. It's true that some people are more disposed to be cognitively demanding of themselves than others. But the scientific literature on curiosity, while it disagrees on many things, agrees on this: a person's curiosity is more state than trait. That is, our curiosity is highly responsive to the situation or environment we're in. It follows that we can arrange our lives to stoke our curiosity or quash it.

Curiosity is vulnerable to benign neglect. As we grow older, we tend to become less active explorers of our mental environment, relying on what we've learned so far to see us through the rest of the journey. We can also become too preoccupied with the daily skirmishes of existence to take the time to pursue our interests. If you allow yourself to become incurious, your life will be drained of color, interest, and pleasure. You will be less likely to achieve your potential at work or in your creative life. While barely noticing it, you'll become a little duller, a little dimmer. You may not think it could happen to you, but it can. It can happen to any of us. To stop it from happening, you need to understand what feeds curiosity and what starves it.

• • •

Sometime in the early 1480s, Leonardo da Vinci made a doodle in his note- 25 book. He seems to have bought a new pen and was trying it out, absentmindedly. What he wrote was a wandering riff on the phrase *Dimmi* ("Tell me"). "Tell me . . . tell me whether . . . tell me how things are . . ."

Curiosity starts with the itch to explore. From a very early age, we display a yearning to conquer the unknown. A 1964 study found that babies as young as two months old, when presented with different patterns, will show a marked preference for the unfamiliar ones. Every parent knows about a child's compulsion to stick tiny fingers where they are not supposed to go, to run out of the open door, to eat dirt. This attraction to everything novel is what the scientists who study it call diversive curiosity.

diversive curiosity:

In adults diversive curiosity manifests itself as a restless desire for the new and the next. The modern world seems designed to stimulate our diversive curiosity. Every tweet, headline, ad, blog post, and app at once promises and denies a satisfaction for which we are ever more impatient. Our popular entertainments are expertly crafted to hook our attention and keep it, by moving fast; the average shot in an American movie today is about 2 seconds, compared with 27.9 seconds in 1953.

Diversive curiosity is essential to an exploring mind; it opens our eyes to the new and undiscovered, encouraging us to seek out new experiences and meet new people. But unless it's allowed to deepen and mature, it can become a futile waste of energy and time, dragging us from one object of attention to another without reaping insight from any. Unfettered curiosity is wonderful; unchanneled curiosity is not. When diversive curiosity is

futile:

entrained:

entrained—when it is transformed into a quest for knowledge and under-standing—it nourishes us. This deeper, more disciplined, and effortful type of curiosity is called *epistemic* curiosity.*

For individuals, epistemic curiosity can be a font of satisfaction and delight that provides sustenance for the soul. For organizations and nations, it can supercharge creative talent and ignite innovation, turning the base metal of diversive curiosity into gold. To get a probe to Mars, you need a powerful desire to explore a distant planet, but you will need to combine this with an enduring appetite for problem solving if you are to figure out how to get a camera up there.

Diversive curiosity has always been with us, and so has epistemic curi- 30 osity, but the latter has flourished on a widespread scale only in the mod-ern era, since the invention of the printing press allowed people to read, share, and combine ideas from all over the world and since the Industrial Revolution created more time for more people to think and experiment. The Internet ought to be giving epistemic curiosity another epochal boost, because it is making knowledge more widely available than ever before. But its amazing potential is undermined by our tendency to use it merely to stimulate diversive curiosity.

empathic curiosity:

A secondary subject of this book is empathic curiosity: curiosity about the thoughts and feelings of other people. Empathic curiosity is distinct from gossip or prurience, which we can think of as diversive curiosity about the superficial detail of others' lives. You practice empathic curiosity when you genuinely try to put yourself in the shoes—and the mind—of the per-son you're talking to, to see things from their perspective. Diversive curios-ity might make you wonder what a person does for a living; empathic curi-osity makes you wonder *why* they do it. I'll be arguing that empathic curiosity became a common cognitive habit at around the same point in history as epistemic curiosity.

It is no coincidence that the two are tied to each other; curiosity is a deeply social quality. Almost from the beginning of life, we wonder what it is that other people know that we don't; a baby's way of saying "tell me" is to point to an object while looking at her mother. Whether our curiosity grows or shrinks is also dependent on others. If the baby's mother answers his wordless question, he'll point to something else. If she ignores his gesture, he'll stop pointing. It's a dynamic that works its way through our lives, from home to school to the office. Curiosity is contagious. So is incuriosity.

———

*Curiosity is often discussed in relation to scientific discovery. Science and scientists cer-tainly play major roles in this book. But I'll be placing curiosity in a wider context, one that accommodates curiosity about the structure of a Beethoven symphony or the life of Martin Luther King. Epistemic curiosity, in these pages, refers to a wide-ranging desire for intel-lectual and cultural exploration.

practice it 24.9 Post-Reading Activity

A helpful post-reading strategy for complex readings like this one is to review the reading's structure. One way to see the structure of a text is to break it into sections based on the topics covered. In the margins of your book, directly on the reading, make a topic map of the main topics Leslie discusses. (For a sample topic map, see the Model Reading Strategy on Jake Halpern's "The Desire to Belong," pp. 551–561 in Chapter 26, Fame and Celebrity.) Compare your map with that of your classmates.

COMPREHENSION QUESTIONS

1. What is the significance of the story of Kanzi? Why does Leslie begin his introductory chapter with this story? Is this an effective beginning?

2. In paragraph 12, Leslie argues that we are in a prosperity "lull." What reasons does he give or infer for this "lull"?

3. In characterizing curious people, Leslie says, "Curious learners go deep, and they go wide" (para. 16). Explain what he means by this.

4. Does Leslie make the claim that curiosity is an intrinsic trait or something that can shift throughout our lifetime, or both? Explain his position.

5. What is "diversive curiosity" according to Leslie? What are examples of how this kind of curiosity is manifested in our society?

DISCUSSION QUESTIONS

1. In paragraph 9, Leslie argues that "[f]or most of Western history, [curiosity] has been regarded as at best a distraction, at worst a poison, corrosive to the soul and to society." In the very next paragraph, however, he explains this attitude about curiosity and clearly sides with those who are curious, even though they might be "deviant" according to conventional values. Where do you stand in this? Is curiosity "deviant"? Is it "corrosive"? If so, is that a positive or a negative?

2. Leslie writes that "[a] society that values order above all else will seek to suppress curiosity. But a society that believes in progress, innovation, and creativity will cultivate it, recognizing that the inquiring minds of its people constitute its most valuable asset" (para. 11). Based on this claim, how would you characterize your community and America as a whole?

3. Did you take the self-assessment about your curiosity level? How did you score? How accurately does this reflect your own view of yourself? Will taking the quiz make you rethink any of your decisions? Why or why not?

4. Some researchers claim that our easy access to the Internet helps to feed our curiosity by giving us the satisfaction of seeking answers, but Leslie worries about ways that the Internet can have a negative impact on developing an inquiring mind. What role do you think the Internet plays in fostering or hindering our curiosity?

SCHOLARLY ARTICLE

Susan Engel is a senior lecturer at Williams College in the psychology department and the director of the Program in Teaching at the college. She is the author of many articles on education published in scholarly journals, popular magazines, and the *New York Times*, as well as of several books on the education of children and curiosity. Her most recent book, *The Hungry Mind: The Origins of Curiosity in Childhood* (2015), delves deeply into where curiosity comes from and how it can be developed and fostered in school. The following article, from the journal *Educational Leadership* (February 2013), addresses these same questions. *Some difficult words have been identified in the margins. Look up those you do not know, and write the definition in your own words in the margins either before or as you read. The first one has been done for you.*

practice it 24.10   Pre-Reading Activity

Think back to your earliest memories of school. Try to think of a time you were encouraged to be curious about a topic. What was the topic? How were you encouraged? What did you do? Freewrite on this event, including as many specific details as you can recall.

SUSAN ENGEL

The Case for Curiosity

Curiosity is essential to learning, but in scarce supply in most schools.

Einstein was wrong. I'm not referring to anything he said or wrote about physics but to his famous comment, "Curiosity is a delicate little plant which, aside from stimulation, stands mainly in need of freedom." Curiosity needs more than stimulation and freedom. For children to develop and satisfy their urge to know, they need role models, opportunities to practice, and guidance.

Walk up to almost any teacher in the United States, ask her whether it's good for children to be curious, and what do you think she'll say? If you think that teacher will say yes, you're right. When my student Hilary Hackmann and I asked teachers to circle on a list the qualities they thought were most important for students to acquire in school, many circled curiosity. When asked on the fly, adults in our society say they value curiosity. Intuitively, people feel it's essential to learning.

But what we admire and what we deliberately cultivate aren't the same. When researchers dig deeper, they find that many adults think of curiosity as a trait possessed by some but not others. Or they think that as long as the environment isn't too repressive, children's natural sense of inquiry will surface (Engel, 2011). In fact, when Hilary and I asked teachers to list which qualities were most important without giving them a list to choose from, almost none mentioned curiosity. Many teachers endorse curiosity when they're asked about it, but it isn't uppermost on their minds—or shaping their teaching plans.

cultivate: *to make grow*

repressive:

inquiry:

Why is this disturbing? Because research shows unequivocally that when people are curious about something, they learn more, and better. Daniel Berlyne (1954) first demonstrated this in the 1950s. He read people lists of facts, including some that were surprising to them, and led them to ask questions. Later, when asked to recall those lists, subjects remembered the items that had piqued their curiosity better than the others.

unequivocally:

piqued:

It's not just adults who benefit from having their curiosity piqued. When children want to know something, they're more likely to learn it and remember it. Babies play longer with toys in which they've shown a prior interest and explore these toys more; their interest allows them to learn more than they otherwise would. When older students are intrigued by unexpected or mysterious descriptions in their reading, they're more likely to remember that content later, and to more deeply understand what they read (Garner, Brown, Sanders, & Menke, 1992).

5

Given that curiosity has such a positive impact on learning, you might assume that teachers are doing everything they can to encourage it. But that's not the case.

Where Have All the Questions Gone?

When my students and I observed suburban elementary classrooms in 2006, looking for signs of students' curiosity, we found a surprising absence of it. To gauge curiosity, we looked for

gauge:

- The number and types of questions students asked (anything from "Where is the Sudan?" to "When is recess?").
- Stretches of time that students spent gazing at something (for instance, standing in front of an aquarium observing fish).
- Times when a student physically investigated something (such as opening up the back of a cassette machine).

For the most part, kindergartners asked very few questions and spent little time investigating the environment. In any given two-hour stretch, we'd see anywhere from two to five questions or explorations. What students were doing instead was often engaging to them, or educationally productive—learning about the sounds of letters, discussing the day's weather, detecting visual patterns on worksheets, and the like. But students weren't coming up with questions about what they wanted to know, spending time learning how to answer those questions, or exploring the physical world.

In the liveliest classrooms, kids did lots of hands-on activities—acting out scenarios, building with blocks, following instructions to do an experiment, and so on. But in virtually all these activities, students followed adult instructions, and, in most of the more **experiential** activities, the teacher had a very clear idea of what students should get out of the activity.

When our transcripts noted questions, they were most often asked by the teacher: "What do you think this is?" or "What makes bears different from birds?" In some cases, when a student piped up with a question that might lead the discussion in another direction, the teacher kindly but firmly put that question aside to get back to the lesson's focus.

In 5th grade classrooms, the situation was even more striking. A typical two-hour stretch of time often didn't yield even one student question. That means 11-year-olds often go for hours at a time in school without indicating anything they want to know about.

The irony is that children are born with an overpowering need to know. They want to know what every object feels and looks like and what will happen when they attempt to do different things with that object. They want to know why people behave the way they do. This **voracious** appetite for knowledge defines us as a species. And it doesn't evaporate when babies become toddlers. Every preschool teacher knows that children between the ages of 18 months and 5 years are **insatiable** for information. Their curiosity drives much of their learning—through asking questions, watching what others do, listening to what adults say, and tinkering with the world around them. But somehow the incessant curiosity that leads to so much knowledge during the first five years of life dwindles as children go to school.

Encouragement: A Key Ingredient

What might explain the gap between the intense curiosity of young children and the apparent lack of curiosity among older children? I think many adults **implicitly** believe that children naturally get less

10

experiential:

voracious:

insatiable:

implicitly:

curious over time. This belief isn't totally unreasonable. Data do suggest that curiosity becomes less robust over time (Coie, 1974). And if curiosity is, as psychologists say, the urge to explain the unexpected, then as more of everyday life becomes familiar, a child might encounter fewer unexpected objects and events. Perhaps the reduced curiosity of the 7-year-old is simply a by-product of that child's increased knowledge.

by-product:

However, adult influence may also be a factor. When researchers invite children into a room containing a novel object, they find that children are very attuned to the feedback of adults. When the experimenter makes encouraging faces or comments, children are more likely to explore the interesting object. Experiments I've done show that children show much more interest in materials when an adult visibly shows how curious *he or she* is about the materials. In other words, children's curiosity can be fostered or squelched by the people they spend time with.

novel:

fostered:

squelched:

Although it's hard to discourage the investigations of a 2-year-old, 15 it's all too easy to discourage those of 7-, 11-, or 15-year-olds. In one classroom I observed, a 9th grader raised her hand to ask if there were any places in the world where no one made art. The teacher stopped her midsentence with, "Zoe, no questions now, please; it's time for learning."

Often the ways in which teachers unwittingly discourage curiosity are much subtler. By the same token, teachers can also encourage curiosity in subtle ways. One teacher I've observed often begins sentences to her students with the phrase, "Let's see what happens." She's showing them the value of finding things out.

What Can Educators Do?

If you consider both the idea that curiosity is a powerful elixir for learning and the idea that as children age their curiosity requires more nurturing, it's clear teachers should pay serious attention to helping students acquire or retain a thirst to find out about the world.

elixir:

Easy to say; harder to do. Teachers are faced with umpteen goals and many obstacles that get in the way of meeting them. We want students to read, learn algebra, master scientific concepts, understand fundamentals of their nation's history, work things out with peers, become motivated to do well on unappealing tasks, and much more. Society expects teachers to do all that with students who have widely varying levels of skill and motivation. It's understandable that taking time to foster something as amorphous as students' eagerness to explore the unexpected would fall off the to-do list.

umpteen:

amorphous:

deviations:

Further, teachers are less likely to encourage questions, tinkering, or <u>deviations</u> from the script when they feel pressure to accomplish goals that might not leave time for questions, tinkering, or deviations from the script. In my lab, I found that when teachers were subtly instructed to help children learn about science, they were more likely to encourage children's questions and unexpected manipulations of materials. When teachers were instead subtly encouraged to help students finish a worksheet, they were more likely to discourage children's investigations.

Given curiosity's central role, it's essential to figure out what   20
educators can do to help students become more—rather than less—curious over time. An equally important question is, How can we help children gain expertise in satisfying their curiosity? Here are four suggestions.

1. Hire Curious Teachers

Schools should hire teachers who've demonstrated that they're curious. It is hard to fan the flames of a drive you yourself rarely experience. Many principals hire teachers who seem smart, who like children, and who have the kind of drive that supports academic achievement. They know that teachers who possess these qualities will foster the same in their students. But why not put curiosity at the top of the list of criteria for good teachers?

How do we judge whether someone is truly curious? A teacher's thirst for finding out should be evident in what he or she has done or in how he or she behaves. Sometimes a teacher with plenty of curiosity has done scientific research or spent years studying some topic of personal interest (such as butterflies or architecture). Sometimes their curiosity is expressed as an urge to know more about their students. Often teachers of young children excel because of their unending interest in early development. Either way, the teacher who knows what the itch to find out feels like is in a better position to foster that itch in students.

2. Count Classroom Questions

Teachers should record lessons or conversations in their classrooms and then count and categorize the questions their students ask. In his groundbreaking book *Better*, physician Atul Gawande (2007) encourages people in the medical profession to "count something." He means that causal intuitions about what's happening in one's workplace can be misleading. Even the most thoughtful reflection at the end of the day does not provide the same information as actual recordings.

This observation is as true of schools as it is of hospitals. Few teachers readily see that they're discouraging students' questions, just as few parents readily see that they're short-tempered with their children. Precise and <u>methodical</u> data collection enables us to learn things that are counterintuitive. Teachers who watch video recordings of themselves and count the number of questions students ask will see how much inquiry is being expressed in their classroom—and they'll learn how they respond to students' inquiries.

methodical:

Moreover, simply by counting questions, teachers will begin to be   25 more aware of them, which will thereby encourage more questioning. Other riches lie in store for them. Teachers can also discover what kinds of things individual students are curious about, who asks lots of questions, and who never asks one. By attending to the quality of their students' questions, they can get ideas about how to help their students develop better questions. What better cues are there for thinking up new activities or topics to discuss?

3. Make Questioning a Goal

Think of question asking as the goal of an educational activity, rather than a happy by-product. Develop activities that invite or require students to figure out what they want to know and then seek answers.

One easy starting place is urging students to use the Internet to ask any question that occurs to them—or arises in class discussion or work. Google can be a curious person's best friend. For instance, today I used Google to answer the following unexpected questions: Which of Henry VIII's wives came after Anne Boleyn, what kind of milk is Mozzarella made of, and what does the city Hyderabad look like? The ease with which we can look things up online is <u>exhilarating</u>—and it makes the urge to know feel good more often.

exhilarating:

Of course, a class that invited students to ask questions without helping them seek accurate answers or acquire a robust body of knowledge would leave the educational task half done. The child who's genuinely curious doesn't rest until he or she has satisfied the urge to know. So to cultivate students' curiosity, we must give them both time to seek answers and guidance about various routes to getting answers, such as looking things up in reliable sources or testing <u>hypotheses</u>.

hypotheses:

Teachers should encourage students to think about whether their original question has been answered to their satisfaction. These techniques are the bread and butter of the <u>autodidact</u>. Students who learn to teach themselves something new are better prepared for lifelong learning than those who simply learn well from others.

autodidact:

4. Measure Curiosity

It doesn't mean much to value a quality like curiosity in children if   30
you never assess whether it's present. What we measure is what we'll
teach. In classrooms where teachers are deliberately cultivating
curiosity, they should see more of it in May than in September—and
they should see their own responses becoming more encouraging.

Video recording is a great tool for this work. Teachers should
regularly videotape activities in their classrooms and score one
another's students (to increase objectivity and accuracy) on things
like individual students' level of interest, the number of exploratory
gestures students use when encountering materials or objects, and
the duration of each student's engagement with one activity.

Teachers who keep journals of their daily work with students
might go through them at the end of the year to see how many
occasions they created for students to figure out what they wanted
to know—and pursue answers.

Actually, Einstein was partly right. Curiosity is delicate, and it does
need freedom and stimulation. But that's not enough. It needs to be
fostered and guided by teachers who feel curious themselves, and who
value curiosity. Curiosity isn't the icing on the cake; it's the cake itself.

References

Berlyne, D. (1954). A theory of human curiosity. *British Journal of Psychology, 45,*
180–191.

Coie, J. (1974). An evaluation of the cross-situational stability of children's
curiosity. *Journal of Personality, 42,* 93–116.

Engel, S. (2011). Children's need to know: Curiosity in school. *Harvard Educational Review, 81*(4), 625–645.

Garner, R., Brown, R., Sanders, S., & Menke, D. J. (1992). "Seductive details" and
learning from text. In K. A. Renninger, S. Hidi, & A. Krapp (Eds.), *The role of
interest in learning and development* (pp. 239–254). Hillsdale, NJ: Erlbaum.

Gawande, A. (2007). *Better: A surgeon's notes on performance.* New York: Metro-
politan Books.

practice it 24.11   Post-Reading Activity

Reread paragraphs 19 and 20 with and against the grain. What parts do
you agree with or find reasonable and why? What parts do you disagree
with or find unreasonable and why? (For more about reading with and
against the grain, see pp. 30–32 in Chapter 2.)

COMPREHENSION QUESTIONS

1. Explain what Engel means when she says "what we admire and what we deliberately cultivate aren't the same" (para. 3). Come up with one or two examples from your observations about what people admire but don't necessarily cultivate to support her view.

2. What kinds of learning activities do Engel and her students observe in the kindergarten classroom?

3. What did Engel and her students notice about the rate of questioning from kindergarten to fifth grade in the classes they observed?

4. According to Engel, how might adults inadvertently be "fostering" or "squelching" children's curiosity?

5. In her recommendation for what teachers can do to help foster curiosity, Engel says to "count questions" (para. 23). What does she mean by this, and how might this help foster curiosity?

DISCUSSION QUESTIONS

1. Engel observes a reduction in student questions between kindergarten and fifth grade. What does she infer are the causes of students' not asking more questions? What are other reasons why young students would not ask questions in class?

2. In her examination of curiosity, Engel focuses largely on the classroom. What other aspects of children's lives might affect their curiosity level?

3. Engel provides four suggestions for how educators can encourage curiosity in the classroom. As a student, you have a great perspective on the classroom experience. Do you think these suggestions would be effective? Why or why not?

4. What are ways that you could foster curiosity in your own educational experience?

BLOG POST

As CEO and president of Red Hat, an innovative technology company, Jim Whitehurst writes about the qualities he looks for when hiring, especially intellectual curiosity. Whitehurst has a background in business development, finance, and global operations and previously held several positions at Delta Airlines, including that of chief operating officer. He was also named CEO of the Year in 2015 by the *Triangle Business Journal* in North Carolina. In addition to contributing business articles like this September 2013 post to LinkedIn's news blog, Whitehurst is the author of *The Open Organization* (2015), a book on the principles of open management. *Some difficult words have been identified in the margins. Look up those you do not know, and write the definition in your own words in the margins either before or as you read. The first one has been done for you.*

---

practice it 24.12 Pre-Reading Activity

Make a list of the questions you would ask if you owned your own company and were interviewing for a new manager. What qualities would you look for in a candidate, and how would you design interview questions to reveal those qualities?

LinkedIn

How I Hire: Intellectual Curiosity Required
Jim Whitehurst

tedious: *tiring because it is lengthy or dull*

daunting:

vetted:

The hiring process can be both tedious and daunting. The "war for talent" is no secret, and particularly among tech companies where competition is fierce, hiring and retaining the best and brightest is a top priority.

When I'm speaking to a candidate, chances are they've already been extensively vetted. They likely have the skills and experience required for the position, and they fit our work culture. As a result, there is not much to be gained by having me test them on these areas.

Instead, after years of interviewing candidates for a wide variety of positions, I focus my time with them on determining two things:

1. Do they possess the characteristic I value the most on my teams: intellectual curiosity, and

2. Are they different from me?

First off, I'm looking for people who are thoughtful and eager to learn new things. I want to hire people who can achieve and think beyond the role they're interviewing for, and understand how that role fits into the bigger company picture. For instance, if I'm talking to someone who is being considered for a finance position and also currently coming from finance, I'll ask questions about their current company but on areas totally unrelated to their current job. I want to know if they're curious about the business and industry they work in, or if they are simply there to perform their designated role without genuinely understanding what their company does.

I like to think that intellectual curiosity has helped in my own career.   5
When I stepped into my first role at Delta as the company's treasurer, I was fascinated with how the airline industry worked. I wanted to understand how passengers and customers flowed through the company's processes, and I spent nights and weekends poring over data to help me   **poring:**
learn this. I built relationships with people sitting in other departments beyond finance.

I wanted to know how our network worked and I actively asked questions in hopes of figuring it out. I built a reputation for my obsession with Delta's network, operations, and business flow. So when bigger jobs opened up, I was a logical choice.

My genuine curiosity for how our business worked and drive to find answers and solutions resulted in a large stepping stone in my career.

How do I determine if candidates have this intellectual curiosity? When I interview candidates today, I find myself asking questions to help me determine if they understood their previous company's challenges. If not, why not? I find that people who are curious, and who care about their companies and industries, can grow their roles [and] become company leaders. I want those people.

Unsurprisingly, I've found that you can talk to intellectually curious individuals for hours. When I was interviewing candidates for Red Hat's executive vice president of Global Sales and Services position, we talked to several extremely talented candidates, but the conversations with Arun Oberoi (who got the job and serves in that role today) were different. Yes, Arun had the experience and skills we were looking for, but what struck me most after our initial conversation was his thoughtfulness and clear eagerness to learn. I could see his passion and I remember thinking that I could have talked to him for two more hours. Those are the type of people I want in my company: People who can and want to grow.

complement:

vice versa:

hashes:

Second, I've found that, in hiring, many people look for others with   10
the same skills and similar backgrounds, and those who approach issues
from the same perspective. I'd encourage those people to rethink their
hiring strategies. You should hire people who <u>complement</u> your strengths
and weaknesses, and <u>vice versa</u>. You don't need another "you" at the
table. You need people who bring different things. You should strive to
build a balanced team that is equipped to handle any challenge they may
face. I strongly believe that diversity of personality, perspective and
background leads to a stronger team. Those differences should cause a
team to disagree, to argue, and yell, but a well-functioning team <u>hashes</u>
through those issues and ultimately delivers better results.

My ultimate target is having intellectually curious people with diverse
strengths and perspectives on my team. It all starts with hiring the right
people, but it doesn't end there. Building a team is an ongoing process . . .
but it's a lot easier when you start with the right people.

practice it 24.13 Post-Reading Activity

Look back at your list of interview questions from the Pre-Reading
Activity and rewrite it as if you were going to follow all of Whitehurst's
advice about how to hire new employees. How would you change your
questions, and what qualities would the new questions be addressing?

COMPREHENSION QUESTIONS

1. What does Whitehurst mean when he says that
   by the time he speaks with candidates "they've
   already been extensively vetted" (para. 2)?

2. Why does Whitehurst believe that being intellectually curious led to his own career success?

3. How can Whitehurst tell if a candidate is a
   curious person?

DISCUSSION QUESTIONS

1. As stated in the headnote, Whitehurst is the CEO
   of a very innovative technology company. Do you
   think technology companies are more likely to
   seek curious employees than more traditional
   companies? Why or why not?

2. If you were interviewed by someone like Whitehurst, what would they learn about your level of
   curiosity at your current or former job?

3. Why does Whitehurst think curiosity in an
   employee is important? Do you agree? Why or
   why not?

4. Are there any potentially negative outcomes to
   curiosity in the workplace? Explain.

ONLINE ARTICLE

Daisy Yuhas is a young science journalist who combined her English major with a love of science. After graduating from Swarthmore College, she took a series of internships around the world, studying birds, soil, electric cars, and physics, among other topics. These internships helped her to build up her experience in science as well as her writing portfolio. She is now an associate editor of and regular contributor to *Scientific American Mind* and has written articles and blogs on a diverse set of scientific topics, with a particular focus on birds. *Some difficult words have been identified in the margins. Look up those you do not know, and write the definition in your own words in the margins either before or as you read. The first one has been done for you.*

practice it 24.14   Pre-Reading Activity

Recall your prior knowledge about the nervous system, specifically the different parts of the brain, the function of the hippocampus, and the difference between short- and long-term memory. If you have not learned about these parts of the brain or don't remember them, do a brief search online to familiarize yourself with their functions.

---

scientificamerican.com

Curiosity Prepares the Brain for Better Learning

Daisy Yuhas

Do we live in a holographic universe? How green is your coffee? And could drinking too much water actually kill you?

    Before you [look up those ideas] you might consider how your knowledge-hungry brain is preparing for the answers. A new study from the University of California, Davis, suggests that when our curiosity is piqued, changes in the brain ready us to learn not only about the subject at hand, but incidental information, too.

    Neuroscientist Charan Ranganath and his fellow researchers asked 19 participants to review more than 100 questions, rating each in terms of how curious they were about the answer. Next, each subject revisited 112 of the questions—half of which strongly intrigued them whereas the rest they found uninteresting—while the researchers scanned their brain activity using functional magnetic resonance imaging (fMRI).

    During the scanning session participants would view a question then wait 14 seconds and view a photograph of a face totally unrelated to the

holographic universe: in physics, the idea that the universe might actually be a creation of human imagination

green:

piqued:

incidental:

intrigued:

functional magnetic resonance imaging:

trivia:

colleagues:

preceded:

reminiscent:

neuroscientist:

arousal:

bolster:

imaging:

midbrain:

nucleus accumbens:

dopamine:

cognitive:

hippocampus:

manifold:

replicate:

trivia before seeing the answer. Afterward the researchers tested participants to see how well they could recall and retain both the trivia answers
and the faces they had seen.

Ranganath and his colleagues discovered that greater interest in a   5
question would predict not only better memory for the answer but also
for the unrelated face that had preceded it. A follow-up test one day later
found the same results—people could better remember a face if it had
been preceded by an intriguing question. Somehow curiosity could
prepare the brain for learning and long-term memory more broadly.

The findings are somewhat reminiscent of the work of U.C. Irvine
neuroscientist James McGaugh, who has found that emotional arousal
can bolster certain memories. But, as the researchers reveal in the
October 2 *Neuron*, curiosity involves very different pathways.

To understand what exactly had occurred in the brain the researchers
turned to their imaging data. They discovered that brain activity during
the waiting period before an answer appeared could predict later memory
performance. Several changes occurred during this time.

First, brain activity ramped up in two regions in the midbrain, the
ventral tegmental area and nucleus accumbens. These regions transmit
the molecule dopamine, which helps regulate the sensation of pleasure
and reward. This suggests that before the answer had appeared the
brain's eager interest was already engaging the reward system. "This
anticipation was really important," says Ranganath's co-author, U.C. Davis
cognitive neuroscientist Matthias Gruber. The more curious a subject was,
the more his or her brain engaged this anticipatory network.

In addition, the researchers found that curious minds showed
increased activity in the hippocampus, which is involved in the creation of
memories. In fact, the degree to which the hippocampus and reward
pathways interacted could predict an individual's ability to remember the
incidentally introduced faces. The brain's reward system seemed to
prepare the hippocampus for learning.

The implications are manifold. For one, Ranganath suspects the   10
findings could help explain memory and learning deficits in people with
conditions that involve low dopamine, such as Parkinson's disease.

Piquing curiosity could also help educators, advertisers and storytell-
ers find ways to help students or audiences better retain messages. "This
research advances our understanding of the brain structures that are
involved in learning processes," says Goldsmiths, University of London
psychologist Sophie von Stumm, unconnected to the study. She hopes
other researchers will replicate the work with variations that can clarify
the kinds of information curious people can retain and whether results

differ for subjects who have broad "trait" curiosity as opposed to a temporarily induced specific interest.

Ranganath's findings also hint at the nature of curiosity itself. Neuroscientist Marieke Jepma at the University of Colorado Boulder, who also did not participate in this study, has previously found that curiosity can be an unpleasant experience, and the brain's reward <u>circuitry</u> might not kick in until there is resolution. She suspects, however, that her findings and Ranganath's results are two sides of the same coin. To explain this, she refers to the experience of reading a detective novel. "Being uncertain about the identity of the murderer may be a pleasant reward-anticipating feeling when you know this will be revealed," she says. "But this will turn into frustration if the last chapter is missing."

Ranganath agrees that the hunger for knowledge is not always an agreeable experience. "It's like an itch that you have to scratch," he says. "It's not really pleasant."

circuitry:

practice it 24.15 Post-Reading Activity

Looking back at the article when needed, draw a picture of the brain and label its parts. Then annotate your drawing, representing all the main points that Yuhas covers.

COMPREHENSION QUESTIONS

1. Summarize in your own words the experiment conducted by neuroscientist Charan Ranganath and what the experiment concluded about curiosity and memory.

2. What is dopamine? What is the connection between curiosity and dopamine?

3. What are the implications of curiosity research for student learning?

DISCUSSION QUESTIONS

1. The article suggests that curiosity can be both pleasant and unpleasant. What examples from everyday life can you think of where you have experienced curiosity pleasantly? Unpleasantly? What trends do you notice in your list of pleasantly curious experiences versus your list of unpleasantly curious experiences?

2. If increasing curiosity can help students remember information, what could students do to increase their level of curiosity in a specific subject they are studying? How can students increase their level of curiosity in general?

3. How do advertisers pique our curiosity to make us remember products? Give an example of a recent or memorable advertisement that tried to make viewers curious. (Note that sometimes they make us curious about something other than the product they are selling.)

Synthesizing the Readings as Pre-Writing for Your Own Essay

Now that you have read a wide variety of texts on the topic of curiosity, you have enough schema, or background information, to begin to synthesize the material and build arguments of your own. It's helpful, though, to pause and discuss how the various readings "converse" with one another before you jump right into a writing assignment. You can use a variety of techniques and activities—alone or with peers—to help your thoughts take shape. Whichever method you choose, it's helpful to have the readings out in front of you so that you can review your annotations. Look for connections across articles as you review. Quite often, you don't see the bigger picture until you take the time to step back and review the material.

DISCUSS TO SYNTHESIZE IDEAS

Talk through the following questions with peers to reveal the connections among readings.

1. What causes a lack of curiosity in a person? What causes a person to have high levels of curiosity? How do mental health, personality, and environment factor into a person's curiosity levels?
2. What connections do you see among curiosity, creativity, and learning?
3. How have attitudes about curiosity changed over the centuries?
4. How does age influence a person's curiosity levels? Are there general trends in our curiosity development as we age, or is it completely individualized?
5. How do different American social institutions—such as education, the business sector, or the medical establishment—value or devalue curiosity, in your experience? What are the implications of that for creating a country of curious and innovative thinkers? Overall, would you say curiosity is valued in American culture? Why or why not?
6. What messages does your culture send about gender and curiosity?
7. Many people in America seem to value being cool or hip, which often means you have to be curious about the "right" things and not curious about the "wrong" things. How is acting curious about something related to social status?
8. How can we cultivate curiosity in students, workers, and citizens?

▶ For more about creating synthesis charts, see pages 70–72 in Chapter 2, Active and Critical Reading, and pages 238–41 in Chapter 10, Pre-Writing.

CHART TO SYNTHESIZE IDEAS

For many writers, organizing ideas graphically is a vital part of the reading/writing process. Using the method you learned in Chapter 2, make a synthesis chart on one focused topic related to the theme of curiosity. Remember to include space on the chart for your own ideas.

Look through your annotations on the texts you have read before filling in the chart.

IDENTIFY SUBTOPICS TO SYNTHESIZE IDEAS

If you're still struggling to settle on a specific focus for your essay after the discussion questions and synthesis charting, you can generate a list of possible subtopics that could be the focus of an essay. Here are a few sample subtopics to spark your thinking:

Curiosity Topics

Costs and benefits of curiosity

Definitions of curiosity

Curiosity with specific types of people, such as _____

How to become or stay curious

Curiosity and creativity

Take a few minutes to add to this list of subtopics, using the following questions to help you generate topics.

1. Which reading did you find most interesting? Why?
2. Which reading did you find most informative? What did you learn?
3. In which reading did you find the most to disagree with? What specific things did you disagree about?
4. In which reading did you find the most to agree with? What specific things did you agree about?
5. Which reading had good examples? List a few of the examples. What are they examples of?

Writing Your Essay

Once you have done some synthesis thinking, you can begin to write your essay. The following steps review how to get into the mind-set to write. These steps are outlined in greater detail in Chapters 2, 3, and 4.

STEP 1: What type of essay are you assigned to write about curiosity? Look over the question or your instructor's prompt, and write it in your own words.

STEP 2: Which readings from this chapter do you think you will include? List them in your notes, including any quotations that you think you might use. (Don't forget to include the author and page number when you write down the quotation or paraphrase so that you don't have to find it again later.)

STEP 3: What ideas from class discussion or your own experience and observations would you like to include? Look over your notes, and add those thoughts to your brainstorming for this assignment.

STEP 4: Take a few more minutes to brainstorm in your favorite method: listing, freewriting, clustering, questioning, synthesis charts, or group discussion.

STEP 5: Look back at the assignment prompt, and write up a tentative thesis or main idea based on your work so far. Remember, one way to think of the thesis is as the answer to the question posed in the assignment prompt. Don't worry that your thesis has to be perfect or set in stone right now. It's a working thesis that you will probably revise as you make decisions about what you want to say.

STEP 6: Make a bullet-point outline for your essay. Remember to first put the ideas down and then reorganize them into a logical order.

STEP 7: Copy or type up the relevant quotations and examples under each appropriate bullet point.

STEP 8: Pat yourself on the back! You have a lot of material so far.

STEP 9: Write the rough, rough draft, remembering that you'll be revising it.

STEP 10: Reread the assignment sheet one more time, and then make big-picture revisions to your focus, content, and organization. Peer review may help.

STEP 11: Once you are generally satisfied that your work is focused, complete, and organized, edit for sentence-level issues. Remember to use the editing techniques of reading your work out loud, reading "backward," and isolating your common errors. Refer to your Grammar Log frequently during this process. Edit and print your paper again and again until you are satisfied with the way each sentence sounds.

▶ To learn how to use the Grammar Log, see page 575 in Chapter 27, How to Learn the Rules and Apply Them to Your Own Writing.

STEP 12: Take a break.

STEP 13: Proofread your essay one or two more times to correct any minor errors and to make sure your document format is correct for this assignment.

Writing Assignments

DEFINITION ASSIGNMENT

Sometimes we can define a word better by understanding its relationship to another word. What word best helps you define the term *curiosity*? Choose one other major concept word (such as *creativity*, *innovation*, *learning*, or *questioning*) and explain why that word is important to developing a full understanding of the concept of curiosity.

NARRATION ASSIGNMENT

Are you a curious person? What are the key moments in your life that have helped your curiosity grow or shrink? Write your own curiosity narrative in which you tell the story of the development of your own curiosity. Use detailed examples from your own personal life to help your reader understand your story.

DESCRIPTION ASSIGNMENT

What would a workplace filled with curious people look like? Imagine a place you have worked, or a place you would like to work. Now imagine that it has been perfectly designed to cultivate curiosity. Write an essay in which you describe the workplace setting, the behavior of the workers, and the outcomes of this curiosity-filled workplace. Use specific details and descriptive writing to make your readers visualize the scene.

PROCESS ANALYSIS ASSIGNMENT

In your view, how does someone who has lost his or her curiosity begin to gain it again? Write an essay in which you explain the steps someone should take to cultivate his or her curiosity. If you wish, feel free to write about a specific subset of people—say, bored teenagers, or retirees in a slump. Refer to at least one reading to support each step that you discuss.

COMPARISON AND CONTRAST ASSIGNMENT

Compare and contrast the myths of "Pandora," "Sun and Moon in a Box," and "Amaterasu." In terms of the theme of curiosity, what do the stories have in common, and how are they different? Be sure to discuss the message of each myth as well as the details of the stories.

ARGUMENT ASSIGNMENT

Does the American public education system primarily foster or primarily discourage curiosity? If you think it fosters curiosity, give examples to support your points. If you think it discourages curiosity, explain how it should change. Make sure you refer to Susan Engel's article "The Case for Curiosity" in making your case, either as support or as a counterargument to your views.

Additional Online and Media Sources

The readings in this chapter may spark your thinking and leave you wanting more information for further study or personal reflection. Here are some additional resources you might wish to consult:

WEB RESOURCES

Cirque du Soleil, "Kurios" (www.cirquedusoleil.com/kurios): Interactive Web site for the famous performance art troupe's show on curiosity.

The Exploratorium (www.exploratorium.edu/explore): Not just a science museum, the Exploratorium is a hands-on museum exploring science, art, and human perception. In addition to the actual museum, the Web site has hundreds of online, curiosity-feeding ways to explore.

"How Curiosity Works" (http://science.howstuffworks.com/life/evolution/curiosity.htm): From a popular site that demystifies how the world works, this article attempts to explain curiosity in humans in a straightforward way.

"The Hungry Mind: The Origins of Curiosity" (https://www.youtube.com/watch?v=Wh4WAdw-oq8): Susan Engel gave this twenty-minute talk about her research on curiosity and learning at Williams College on August 18, 2011.

"Ian Leslie on Why We Must Continue to Learn and Be Curious" (https://www.youtube.com/watch?v=1JT_40wlxYY): Author Ian Leslie speaks on the topic of curiosity in this nineteen-minute video from a June 5, 2014, event sponsored by RSA, a nonprofit organization in London. In this talk, Leslie provides an overview of the main points of the book from which the excerpt on page 449 is taken.

Indra Nooyi, "Dig Deep" (www.makers.com/moments/dig-deep): Chairwoman and CEO of PepsiCo briefly talks about curiosity for the PBS *Makers* documentary series.

NASA's *Curiosity* Mars Rover's Facebook Page (https://www.facebook.com/MarsCuriosity): Follow the *Curiosity* Rover through posts from NASA scientists.

"**Understanding the Science of Curiosity**" (ieet.org/index.php/IEET
/more/curiosity20150214): University of Rochester researchers
present their scholarly work on the brain science of curiosity in an
accessible video format.

FILMS & TELEVISION

Elementary. Performances by Jonny Lee Miller and Lucy Liu, CBS,
2012–.

Hugo. Directed by Martin Scorsese, performances by Ben Kingsley
and Asa Butterfield, Paramount Pictures, 2011.

Mythbusters. Performances by Jamie Hyneman, Adam Savage, and
Robert Lee, Discovery Channel, 2003–.

Sherlock. Performances by Benedict Cumberbatch and Martin Freeman, Hartswood Films, BBC Wales, and Masterpiece Theatre,
2010–.

25
Public Art

Photo by Amy Lawlor.

Peace + love mural by Francisco Aquino and Banksy, San Francisco. Note how the dragons' mirror positions form a heart. The Chinese symbol in the orb means "peace."

Theme Overview

We as a species have always wanted to represent ourselves—our emotions, hopes, dreams, and fears—in a visual way. Art began as a public expression of personal or social ideas. As our cultures developed, the field of art became more professional, and as it did so, experts arose and were given the power to define and evaluate art. Art museums became the place where we "put" art. And for some, art museums became a way of defining what is art and what is not art. (If it's not museum quality, it's not art, some people think.) Public art, however, has never been held to the same standards as private art. As art intended for public view, public art is often more durable and more massive in scale than works that collectors or museums can accommodate. Public art includes both sanctioned and unsanctioned works, such as sculpture, installation art, fountains, murals, graffiti, tile art, and art built into the structure of public walkways, railings, or walls.

The readings in this chapter invite you to study a variety of human expressions in order to investigate this human motivation to make a mark on the world in a very public way. The readings address a range of different types of public art, from the commissioned public mural by the famous artist to the unsanctioned street art and graffiti of youth. Along the way, you will investigate some related questions: What is art? Who decides what art is good? What separates the private world from the public world? Who owns street art? And, finally, what rights does owning a piece of property give you?

---

practice it 25.1   Taking Stock of What You Already Know

What do you know about the following types of creative expression? How would you compare and contrast the types listed? Answer the questions, taking stock of your beliefs about how we define and value art.

- **Art:** What is art? What are the differences between public and private art? What kinds of public art exist in your community? Is art an individual interest or a community experience?

- **Graffiti:** What do you think of graffiti? Who is affected by it? Is it in your community? Have you ever made graffiti? If so, why?

- **Murals:** Does your community have any mural art? If so, where are the murals located? How are murals and graffiti similar? How are they different? Have you ever helped make a mural?

readings on
Public Art

Prebles' Artforms is a well-regarded visual arts textbook that covers, among many other topics, public art and street art. As a textbook selection, this reading provides a peek into the design and coverage common in many college-level textbooks. The excerpt here explains public art and street art. Author Patrick Frank is an art historian who writes general art history texts as well as specialized books on Latin American art history. *Some difficult words have been identified in the margins. Look up those you do not know, and write the definitions in your own words either before or as you read. The first one has been done for you.*

practice it 25.2 Pre-Reading Activity

Preview the text by looking carefully at the images and headings. What can you predict the reading will be about? What do you expect to learn from this text? Write your pre-reading notes directly on the text.

Patrick Frank

PUBLIC ART AND STREET ART

Public Art

Public art is art that you might encounter without intending to; it exists in a public place, accessible to everyone. The idea of public art originated in ancient times, as government and religious leaders commissioned artists to create works for public spaces. In our time, artists still make public art that responds to the needs and hopes of broad masses of people.

The *Vietnam Veterans Memorial,* located on the Mall in Washington, D.C., is probably America's best-known public art piece. The 250-foot-long, V-shaped black granite wall bears the names of the nearly sixty thousand American servicemen and women who died or are missing in Southeast Asia. The nonprofit Vietnam Veterans Memorial Fund, Inc., was formed in 1979 by a group of Vietnam veterans who

© Ron Sachs/dpa/Corbis

Maya Lin. *Vietnam Veterans Memorial*. The Mall, Washington, D.C. 1980–1982. Black granite. Each wall 10'1" × 246'9".

believed that a public monument to the war would help speed the process of national reconciliation and healing after the conflict.

After examining 1,421 entries, the jury selected the design of twenty-one-year-old Maya Lin of Athens, Ohio, then a student at Yale University. Lin had visited the site and created a design that would work with the land rather than dominate it. "I had an impulse to cut open the earth . . . an initial violence that in time would heal. The grass would grow back, but the cut would remain, a pure, flat surface, like a geode when you cut it open and polish the edge. . . . I chose black granite to make the surface reflective and peaceful."

entries: submissions for a
contest

Lin's bold, eloquently simple design creates a memorial park within a larger park. It shows the influence of Minimalism and site works of the 1960s and 1970s. The polished black surface reflects the surrounding trees and lawn, and the tapering segments point to the Washington Monument in one direction and the Lincoln Memorial in the other. Names are inscribed in chronological order by date of death, each name given a place in history. As visitors walk toward the center, the wall becomes higher and the names pile up inexorably. The monument's thousands of visitors seem to testify to the monument's power to console and heal.

When the Museum of Modern Art in New York expanded in 2004, 5 the neighbors in high-rise buildings complained about having to look down onto new ugly roof structures. The museum responded by turning to landscape architect Ken Smith, who said, "Let's camouflage it!" He

Minimalism:

inscribed:

inexorably:

console:

made the humorous *MOMA Roof Garden* out of colored gravel, asphalt, and plastic bushes. The composition is a camouflage pattern, the better to "hide" the building. This piece of public art is not visible from inside the museum and, more important, requires no maintenance. When the neighbors complained yet again that the garden was completely fake, Smith responded that it was about as fake as nearby Central Park, which had been carefully planted on a stripped and leveled field. The tongue-in-cheek humor of this piece and its witty quotation of camouflage patterns make this work a rare example of postmodern landscape architecture.

Ken Smith. *MOMA Roof Garden* (*Museum of Modern Art Roof Garden*). 2005. Outdoor garden at the Museum of Modern Art, New York. © 2013 Alex S. MacLean/Landsides

A great deal of public art in the United States is created under a mandate that one-half of one percent of the cost of public buildings be spent on art to embellish them. Sometimes the results can turn out unsatisfactorily, as the case of Richard Serra's *Tilted Arc* shows. But when a community-minded artist works with the local people, the results can be much more successful, as in the following case.

Seattle-based Buster Simpson specializes in public art, and one of his recent commissions embodies the environmental concerns of an eastern Washington agricultural community. *Instrument Implement: Walla Walla Campanile* begins with a core of metal farmers' disks arranged in a repeating bell-shape pattern. Sensors track environmental conditions in nearby Mill Creek: water temperature, flow level, and amount of dissolved gases. All three of these measures are critical for the annual salmon migration, which has been diminishing in recent years. The data are processed by a computer that encodes them into musical notes. Hammers on the piece then strike the proper disks to ring a chime, which becomes an hourly auditory update on the condition of the river. The health of the

camouflage:

tongue-in-cheek:

postmodern:

mandate:

embellish:

embodies:

encodes:

Buster Simpson. *Instrument Implement: Walla Walla Campanile.* 2008. William A. Grant Water & Environmental Center, Walla Walla Community College, Walla Walla, WA. Height 25'6". Photo by Starr Sutherland; permission by artist, Buster Simpson.

salmon is a "canary in the coal mine," an early warning of other environmental problems. Simpson included a yellow effigy of a salmon as an indicator of this. The entire piece is powered by an attached solar collector. *Instrument Implement* is located at Walla Walla Community College, within sight and earshot of hundreds of people each day.

effigy:

Street Art

In the late 1990s, many galleries in various cities began to exhibit work by artists who had previously made illegal graffiti. Many of these "street artists" were based in the culture of skateboards and punk music, and they used materials bought at the hardware store rather than the art supply house. Their creations were only rarely related to gang-oriented graffiti, which usually mark out territories of influence. Nor were they mere tags with names or initials. Rather, the street artists made much broader statements about themselves and the world in a language that was widely understandable. The ancestors of the movement in the 1980s were Keith Haring and Jean-Michel Basquiat, both of whom worked illegally for years before exhibiting in galleries. By the turn of the twenty-first century, street art was a recognized movement, and most of its main practitioners work both indoors and out. All of our artists here create under pseudonyms. While sometimes illegal, the boldness and personal risk-taking that street artists engage in inspires many in a society with strong corporate and government power.

Faile is a collaborative of two Brooklyn-based artists. They create imagery that seems as though it were lifted from magazines and advertisements, but it is their own work in silkscreen, stencil, and paint. They layer these images and then rip through them to leave a worn surface like a decaying urban wall. Some of their work at first seems self-promotional, such as *A Continuing Story*, but a better way to describe Faile is that they mock the style of billboards. The brazenness and flair of their works has attracted viewers since 1999 when the team began.

Faile. *A Continuing Story*. 2009. Acrylic, spraypaint, and screenprint on canvas. 62" square.

10

Courtesy of FAILE, by permission.

Some of today's most skillful street art is created by Swoon. She carves large linoleum blocks and makes relief prints from them, usually life-size portraits of everyday people. She prints them on large sheets of cheap (usually recycled) newsprint and pastes them on urban walls, beginning on the Lower East Side of Manhattan, but now in cities on every continent. Her *Untitled* installation at Deitch Projects was a recent indoor work. Against objections that her work is mostly illegal, she replies that her creations are far easier to look at than advertising, that they lack any persuasive agenda, and that they glorify common people. Moreover, the newsprint that she uses decays over time so that her work is impermanent. Although she works mostly outdoors, she sometimes shows in galleries because, she admits, "I have to make a living," but she charges far less for her work than most other artists of wide repute.

Probably the most famous street creator today is the English artist Banksy. His street art is generally witty, as we see in *Stone Age Waiter*. This piece adorns an outdoor location in a Los Angeles neighborhood with many restaurants; a cave man has apparently joined the ranks of the pleasure-seekers. Well-heeled Angelenos who walk the (always short) distance from their cars to their favorite restaurants will pass this stencil-and-spray-paint creation. Banksy is currently one of the most popular artists in his homeland, and many of his outdoor works have been preserved. When a prominent street work of his was recently

mock:

brazenness:

flair:

relief print:

glorify:

repute:

prominent:

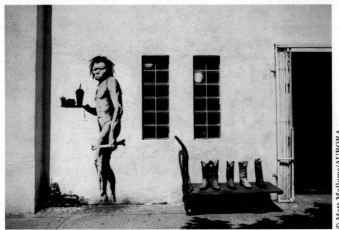

© Matt Mallams/AURORA

Banksy. *Stone Age Waiter*. 2006. Spray paint and stencils. Height 5'6". Outdoor location, Los Angeles.

defaced by another graffiti artist, protests ensued and the defacer was arrested for vandalism! Thus, street artists often blur the line between legal and illegal.

defaced:

ensued:

defacer:

practice it 25.3   Post-Reading Activity

This art textbook includes images to help clarify the ideas presented. Go back through the reading and annotate the images, connecting them to the text that they support. How do the images help you understand the concepts introduced in the reading?

COMPREHENSION QUESTIONS

1. What is public art?

2. What is the role of public art like the *Vietnam Veterans Memorial*?

3. What other ways does public art function, according to the reading?

4. How is public art subsidized?

5. How does street art differ from more traditional art forms?

DISCUSSION QUESTIONS

1. Is public art important? Why or why not?

2. According to Frank, "Many . . . 'street artists' were based in the culture of skateboards and punk music" (para. 8). Is the origin of street art significant? Why or why not?

3. Some street artists like Banksy have achieved widespread fame and recognition, to the point that people protect and even sell their street art. Who owns street art?

4. Should street art be protected or removed as illegal graffiti? Explain.

model reading strategy: Connecting Image to Text

As the founder and artistic director of FORECAST Public Artworks in Minnesota, Jack Becker has been heavily involved in public art and recognized as a leader in the field of public art. In his role as director of FORECAST Public Artworks, he created a statewide grant program for emerging artists and the national journal *Public Art Review*. He holds a Ph.D. in American art and is currently the executive director of the Joslyn Art Museum in Omaha, Nebraska. His writing has been published in both books and periodicals, including the *Utne Reader* and the *Boston Globe*. The following article, published in 2004, is excerpted from the *Americans for the Arts Monograph* series, which is intended mostly for people working in the art world or interested art patrons.

When previewing this reading, you will likely notice a lot of references to famous landmarks, works of art, and cities. Chances are some of them will be familiar to you, but others won't be. To help understand this reading, then, a good strategy would be to do a quick Internet search for images of the landmarks, works of art, or cities that you can't picture in your mind. We have modeled this strategy for you by including a few images in bubbles in the margins as well as some empty bubbles to suggest images you might want to find on your own.

practice it 25.4   Pre-Reading Activity

Preview the article, looking carefully at the section headings as well as the images to try to determine the audience and purpose. What clues provide information about this? What do you expect this reading to be about?

JACK BECKER

Public Art: An Essential Component of Creating Communities

Defining Public Art

A definition of public art is essential to establish ordinances, develop permits, and educate broad audiences. However, as the field grows and evolves at a rapid pace, developing a fixed definition is very difficult. The intention and the desired outcomes of each program vary. For most public agencies, public art may be defined as "work created by artists for places accessible to and used by the public," but the variety of public art encompasses a much broader spectrum of activities and approaches.

It is important to distinguish between public art, which takes into account its site and other contextual issues, and art in public places. Simply placing a sculpture on a street corner is not the same as designing a sculpture specifically for that site by considering its audience, environmental conditions, the history of the site, etc. Regardless, art placed in public can still be quality art and offer the general public an art experience outside a museum or gallery setting.

As more artists have entered the public arena, their art has taken many forms. The field today encompasses place-making, environmental activism, cause-related art, sound installations, interdisciplinary performance events, community-based initiatives, and much more. Indeed, public art is a multifaceted field, open to artists of all stripes, without predetermined rules or a mutually agreed upon critical language. This open-endedness can be a liability for public agencies seeking to serve a diverse community. Artists may view it as an asset, however, liberating them from the constraints imposed by the commercial marketplace.

The process of creating public art necessarily involves interaction among many interests; it is a cooperative, somewhat theaterlike production with many individuals playing a part in creating a common goal. As people of different perspectives and positions seek to make decisions cooperatively, the result can be dynamic, inviting, engaging, and sometimes contentious.

Likewise, the experience of viewing public art is dynamic. The   5
relationship between the work and its site, its audience, and other contextual factors all contribute to its impact. Successful public art evokes meaning in the public realm while retaining a high artistic quality. Perhaps most exciting is the fact that the field is evolving to include different art forms, traditions, and perspectives.

Why Is Public Art Important?

Imagine, if you can, a world devoid of public art: no *Statue of Liberty*, no *Eiffel Tower*, no *Vietnam Veterans Memorial*, no *Tribute in Light*. No murals, memorials, or monuments. What would life be like without fireworks displays, puppet parades, sculpture parks, and visionary roadside folk art? These landmarks and special events enhance our experience of a place and our quality of life. They engender a sense of pride and community identity. They reach audiences outside museums, galleries, and theaters, and they add to the beauty of

Statue of Liberty or Eiffel Tower

Tribute in Light initiative: John Bennett, Gustavo Bonevardi, Richard Nash Gould, Julian Laverdiere, Paul Marantz, Paul Myoda. Produced by the Municipal Art Society and Creative Time, with support from the Battery Park City Authority.

© Songquan Deng/Shutterstock

everyday life. They declare the worth of a place and a time in our shared culture.

How important is the design of our shared public realm? What is the value of a park or plaza, or of a free exchange in a welcoming environment? Public art projects offer us a way to participate in the planning, design, and creation of communal space. For this reason, many refer to public art as a democratic art form. And while democracy can be a messy process, public art is an integral part of the fabric of American culture.

Public art does many things, most of which can be divided into four areas. It can:

- engage civic dialogue and community;
- attract attention and economic benefit;
- connect artists with communities; and
- enhance public appreciation of art.

Engage Civic Dialogue and Community

During the mid-1990s, in a run-down row of shotgun houses in Houston, artist Rick Lowe saw an opportunity to return life and vitality to an endangered part of that city's African American history. *Project Row Houses*, a public art effort involving numerous public and private entities, demonstrated successful community building. In addition to artists in residence, the area around the restored homes

Project Row Houses
Courtesy of Project Row Houses, by permission

featured events and festivals, renewing residents' faith in the power of civic dialogue.

In addition to grand monuments like the *Gateway Arch* or *Mount Rushmore*, which foster pride and contribute to our cultural heritage, strategically executed public art can raise awareness of issues such as racism, gang violence, and environmental degradation. The *AIDS Memorial Quilt*, featuring over 70,000 individual quilts, has been displayed on the National Mall in Washington, D.C. Beyond the spectacle of a colorful, monumental folk art installation, the quilt raises awareness of the AIDS epidemic, generates significant media attention, and leverages increased support for research and education.

10

The AIDS Memorial Quilt
Danny Johnston/APA Photos

Attract Attention and Economic Benefit

Providence, Rhode Island, experienced a revitalization of its downtown due in part to *WaterFire Providence*, a public art event conceived in 1995 by artist Barnaby Evans. While the concept is simple—burning fires in the middle of a restored river channel through downtown, accompanied by original musical compositions from artists around the world—it draws thousands of people several times each year, stimulating the economy and creating pride.

Thanks to Kathleen Farrell and a handful of other artists, Joliet, Illinois, became a mural capital, attracting positive media attention, tour groups, and increased community support for the arts. Many of the murals relate to Joliet's colorful history and connect with the city's Heritage Walk.

Significant funds and attention have been generated by such projects as *Cows on Parade* in Chicago and *Art on the Street* in Cedar Rapids, Iowa, supporting a wide variety of causes. Public art can help visitors navigate a city and can generate cultural tourism. The economic benefits of public art also include the many businesses contributing to the field, such as design, fabrication, engineering, lighting, insurance, and installation. Indeed, public art services are a growth industry in communities such as Los Angeles, Minneapolis, Phoenix, and San Francisco.

Murals in Joliet, IL, *Cows on Parade*, or *Art on the Street*

Connect Artists with Communities

Public art can assume many forms. It is malleable, able to meet the needs of different communities and contribute to many types of projects, from city planning or a river cleanup to a memorial for a lost hero. Artists bring creative perspectives to the strategies and management of such projects, and their efforts often improve the end result.

As an audience development tool, public art provides unparal- 15
leled access to the arts. Street-painting festivals, such as the Italian
Street Painting Festival held annually in San Rafael, California,
encourage audiences to watch as artists create temporary master-
pieces in chalk on the street. The May Day Parade in Minneapolis,
hosted by Heart of the Beast Puppet and Mask Theatre, features
community art-making workshops that invite hundreds of neighborhood residents to create their own contribution to a celebratory
festival that draws an audience of 50,000 annually.

Enhance Public Appreciation of Art

Public art can inspire awe, draw out deep emotions, make us smile,
engage young people, and refresh our perspective. Sometimes,
appreciation of public art is found in the details, the fine craftsman-
ship, and the sheer artistry. Red Grooms's *Tennessee Foxtrot Carousel*
in Nashville, Tennessee, features a rideable Davy Crockett, Kitty
Wells, Chet Atkins, a big catfish, and many more colorful characters
from the region's musical legacy. It's fun, it's educational, and it oozes
creativity.

Artists can deliver messages—unfiltered by galleries, agents, or
the media—to targeted audiences. In fact, every site comes with an
audience. Creative expressions can be directed to businesspeople
downtown; children at a playground; seniors at a community center;
or farmers at a grain elevator, such as Tacoumba Aiken's giant mural
in Good Thunder, Minnesota. Public art can teach us about the
diverse cultures inhabiting our community, and invite us to consider
the role of art and artists in our society.

Great public art reveals its meaning over time, rewarding
repeated visits. Beyond all that, public art has the distinct ability to
add beauty to our shared environment; to commemorate, memorial-
ize, and celebrate; and to transport us, if only momentarily, out of our
daily routine. Public art is for everyone and it is free. Many people
don't visit museums or attend the theater; anybody can experience
public art.

Critical Issues

Given the complexities of developing and managing public art
programs, working as a professional in the field, and connecting
public art with a broad and diverse audience, critical issues abound.
Discussing complex topics such as selection processes, funding,
conservation, contracts, copyright, and insurance could fill a book;
many of these issues will be dealt with in subsequent Public Art

Tennessee Foxtrot Carousel

Tacoumba Aiken mural

Network publications and on its Web site. What follows is intended to illuminate a select number of critical issues facing contemporary public art production and administration, and offer possible solutions or methods for addressing them.

Diversity

Public art reflects the changing demographics of our society, but it could do even more. Creating opportunities for diverse and immigrant populations to participate in public art will strengthen the overall fabric of our culture and inform audiences about the creative impulse found in all cultures.   20

Unlike the traditional world of art museums, diverse artists now figure prominently in the public art field, including such visionaries as Maya Lin, Suzanne Lacy, Mel Chin, Pepón Osorio, and Rick Lowe. These and countless other artists have championed public art as a humanizing force; strengthened our connections to the natural world and to each other; and created a means of communicating ideas and sharing experiences in a changing, culturally diverse world.

Philadelphia's Latino community, for example, recently celebrated the installation of internationally renowned artist Pepón Osorio's *I have a story to tell you . . .*, a set of large-scale photographic images in the newly renovated headquarters of Congreso de Latinos Unidos. The installation was commissioned by the Fairmount Park Art Association [now the Association for Public Art] as part of their groundbreaking New-Land-Marks program. The windows of the main building and the adjacent, more intimate *casita* (little house) are fabricated with photographic images on glass. To create this community photograph album, Osorio collected photographs from community members, seeking images that reflect shared experience and depict local events that have impacted community life.

I have a story to tell you . . . (2003). Pepón Osorio, artist. Photo by Gregory Benson. Courtesy of the Association for Public Art; Photograph: Gregory Benson © 2004

Beyond its empowering attributes for the Latino community, Osorio's project offers the community at large a glimpse at a growing population and with it a sense of their culture and their values.

Critical Language

Shared vocabulary in the public art field urgently needs development. Not everybody is on the same page. Each of us brings a different perspective and a distinct set of criteria when deciding what makes good public art. Can the field develop critical language through shared sets of evaluation criteria?

Few public art programs currently conduct evaluations. Only 27 percent of the programs responding to the field survey stated that they had conducted an evaluation or assessment of an individual public art project; 22 percent had conducted an evaluation or assessment of their entire program. It is interesting to note that the survey found that programs that have completed an evaluation of their entire program have much larger and more aggressively growing budgets than those that have not.

Public art programs can develop their evaluation methods by gathering information from local and national grantmaking organizations about evaluation processes, working with an evaluation consultant, and learning about the evaluations conducted by other public art programs. Reporting back to the field about the evaluation mechanism and results via the Public Art Network, websites, conferences, listservs, and articles is an essential step toward advancing awareness of the need and benefits of evaluation.   25

Critical writing and analysis on public art is scarce, but it is a skill that needs to be fostered among the many talented writers in the United States. Beyond art critics, who tend to be more interested in aesthetics or art historical concerns, investigative journalists, social critics, anthropologists, social workers, and the articulate layperson should all be encouraged to write and talk publicly about public art more often.

Public artists and program administrators, both of whom have the greatest involvement and familiarity with the field, need to gain more objective critical writing skills to effectively share their experiences with public art's larger audience. Public art programs and their parent agencies should consider partnering with foundations and the media to support fellowships for writers and commentators. Newspapers undoubtedly could do a better job covering what's important about public art; many regard it merely as a photo opportunity or a human interest story.

Every project has a story to tell, making film and video and the Internet effective tools for talking about public art. The complex process, the many talented artists, and the wide range of projects can be edited and organized for a broad audience. We can walk around a sculpture, observe it during different seasons, hear the comments of those passing by, and go behind the scenes.

Television programs such as PBS's *Art 21* and segments occasionally aired on *CBS Sunday Morning* are good examples of ways to explore contemporary art and artists, as they are accessible to a broad audience and they don't "talk down" to viewers. Noteworthy films include *Running Fence*, documenting Christo and Jeanne-Claude's struggle to install a 22-mile fabric sculpture in California. More recent documentaries include the Academy Award–winning *A Strong Clear Vision* about Maya Lin's experience creating the *Vietnam Veterans Memorial* and other projects, and the 2003 documentary *Rivers and Tides* about artist Andy Goldsworthy and his persistent struggle to create meticulous, fragile, and ephemeral—and stunningly beautiful—outdoor works of art. These and other records are tremendous resources that begin to break down the language barriers between public art and its many audiences.

Andy Goldsworthy artwork

Controversy

Public art can become a lightning rod, especially in complex capital projects, because it is often the only area where public participation is invited. Public art can also attract controversy because it uses public funds and occupies a prominent place in public spaces. The meaning of great public art is often not grasped immediately upon installation; consider the *Eiffel Tower*, the *Gateway Arch*, the *Statue of Liberty*, and the *Vietnam Veterans Memorial*—all controversial. It wasn't until years—or even decades—later that these projects became valued icons, able to withstand the test of time. It isn't hard to offend someone with nudity, political incorrectness, social commentary, the perceived unnecessary use of public funds, etc. And sometimes public art simply doesn't work.

Let's face it, there's plenty of mediocre art out there, making it difficult to build a case for future support.

Controversy is a magnet for the media, and there are plenty of examples. Dennis Oppenheim's *Blue Shirt* project for Milwaukee's General Mitchell International Airport faced overwhelming opposition after the design was approved by the county's art committee in 2000. The monumentally scaled wall-mounted sculpture of a blue

30

Gateway Arch

work shirt was the subject of a legal dispute, based on the fact that the artist did not complete installation on time. Oppenheim said the problems with the piece were not about timing or money, but about politics. The city government and local press mounted a campaign against the sculpture, characterizing it as a pejorative comment on Milwaukee's reputation as a blue-collar town. The dispute kept the project on hold for months, until a revised installation was approved for completion.

Everyone's a critic. If you want to find fault with a public art project at any point in the process, you can. And, depending on the situation, there may be a need for "damage control." Obtaining written support from key community leaders and project stakeholders early on can help.

Strategic planning and obtaining early feedback helps avoid unwanted controversy. Play your own devil's advocate and determine the risks carefully, then move forward with assurance and conviction. If you consider the examples listed here—all considered great works of public art—controversy can be viewed as a good sign. Controversy and an abundance of attention indicate that people are interested, concerned, or even outraged. This begs the question: why? The root of this question is at the heart of what makes public art so compelling.

Conclusion

Communities that desire meaningful public art need to work at it by reaching out and participating in the effort. After all, the public is the final beneficiary of public art. As the demographics and the economics in our communities change, public art must constantly prove its value to the public.

Based on the significant number of programs, the size of their budgets, and the millions of people affected every day, public art appears to be gaining recognition. As public art infiltrates almost every facet of our culture, in myriad forms, it can help all the arts to regain a position of value and priority in our society. We must continue to support public artists; help them to give shape to our shared identity; and bring their visions, their energy, their spirit, and their creative solutions to the world. Shaping places—with landmarks and landscapes, events and ideologies—sets the stage for a critical part of our existence: our connection with our environment; with our past, present, and future; and with other human beings.

About Public Art Network

PAN is a program of Americans for the Arts designed to provide services to the diverse field of public art and to develop strategies and tools to improve communities through public art. PAN's key constituents are public art professionals, visual artists, design professionals, arts organizations, and communities planning public art projects and programs. For more information about PAN, e-mail pan@artsusa.org or visit the Web site at www.AmericansForTheArts.org/PAN.

practice it 25.5   Post-Reading Activity

Look up two or three of the various artists, programs, and organizations referenced in "Public Art: An Essential Component of Creating Communities." After doing some brief research, add additional information to your annotations.

COMPREHENSION QUESTIONS

1. What is the role of a public art ordinance?

2. What does Becker mean when he says that "the experience of viewing public art is dynamic" (para. 5)?

3. How can public art become a "lightning rod" (para. 30)?

4. Why does the author introduce examples of famous public art projects like the *Eiffel Tower*, the *Gateway Arch*, and the *Statue of Liberty*? How is he using these examples to make a point? Does he succeed?

5. Becker says that "controversy can be viewed as a good sign" (para. 34). Why does he say this? Do you agree? Why or why not?

DISCUSSION QUESTIONS

1. Becker writes that "art placed in public can still be quality art and offer the general public an art experience outside a museum or gallery setting" (para. 2). What does this mean, and is this important? What does public art do for a community? Explain.

2. Why does Becker suggest that public art is a "democratic art form" (para. 7)? What does he mean? Do you agree?

3. The creation of public art requires the cooperation of many: city officials, artists, and the public, among others. How does graffiti art skirt this process? What are the pros and cons of both commissioned public art and graffiti art?

4. What suggestions does the author make about ways that public art can be fostered?

ONLINE ARTICLE

Teresa Palomo Acosta researches and writes about the history of Texas. She is the author of three books of poetry and the coauthor of *Las Tejanas: 300 Years of History* (2003). Her article on the Chicano mural movement was published in the *Handbook of Texas Online*, a publication featured on the Web site of the Texas State Historical Association (TSHA). Founded in 1897 to preserve and promote Texas history, the TSHA publishes books and articles, maintains an online database of state historical records, and offers educational workshops and online resources for students and historians. *Some difficult words have been identified in the margins. Look up those you do not know, and write the definitions in your own words either before or as you read. The first one has been done for you.*

practice it 25.6 Pre-Reading Activity

What is significant about the geographic locations of El Paso, San Antonio, and Houston? Look the cities up on a map if you aren't familiar with them. What do you know about these cities or the state of Texas? Spend a few minutes freewriting on these places before you begin the reading.

tshaonline.org

Chicano Mural Movement
Teresa Palomo Acosta

The Chicano mural movement began in the 1960s in Mexican-American **barrios** throughout the Southwest. Artists began using the walls of city buildings, housing projects, schools, and churches to depict Mexican-American culture. Chicano muralism has been linked to pre-Columbian peoples of the Americas, who recorded their rituals and history on the walls of their pyramids, and Mexican revolutionary-era painters José Clemente Orozco, Diego Rivera, and David Alfaro Siqueiros, collectively known as *los tres grandes*, who painted murals in the United States. Two other Latino **predecessors** were Antonio García and Xavier González, who painted murals in the 1930s under the **auspices** of the Work Projects Administration art projects. In 1933 at San Diego (Texas) High School, García produced *March on Washington*, which has since been moved to the Duval County Museum. It embodies the idea that President Herbert Hoover failed to rebuild the nation's finances after the stock-market crash of 1929 and that President Franklin Delano Roosevelt triumphed in putting Americans back to work. García also painted murals for Corpus Christi

barrios: Spanish-speaking neighborhoods

predecessors:

auspices:

Cathedral and an academy in Corpus Christi. González, who went on to international acclaim as a sculptor, painted a mural for the San Antonio Municipal Auditorium in 1933. It was later removed because of public outcry over the "upraised fist and a palm with a bleeding wound" depicted in it.

During the Mexican-American artistic and literary renaissance that occurred throughout the Southwest in the 1960s and 1970s mural production became part of the effort of Hispanics to reinvigorate their cultural heritage, which was manifested in the rise of the Raza Unida party, the United Farm Workers Union, and the Mexican American Youth Organization, all of which tried to affirm cultural identity and challenge racism. The mural movement depicted such cultural motifs and heroes as Quetzalcoatl from the pre-Columbian era, Francisco (Pancho) Villa from the revolutionary period, and Cleto L. Rodríguez from Tejano history. Nuestra Señora de Guadalupe (Our Lady of Guadalupe) is the only representation of a woman. Around the state, most of the artists, some formally trained and others self-taught, worked in collaboration with community volunteers, often teenagers who were recruited for specific projects, to fashion the murals.

In El Paso more than 100 murals have been painted since the mid-1960s. Manuel Acosta painted *Iwo Jima*, perhaps the earliest of the city's known Chicano murals, at the Veterans of Foreign Wars office in 1966. Carlos Rosas, Felipe Adame, and Gaspar Enríquez usually worked in conjunction with student painters. Mago Orona Gándara, one of the few known female muralists working in El Paso, has painted at least two as a solo artist, *Señor Sol* and *Time and Sand*. Two other women, Irene Martínez and Monika Acevedo, participated in the team that completed *Myths of Maturity* at the University of Texas at El Paso library in 1991. The murals, located throughout the city's various corridors, often depict themes common to Chicano muralism, such as mestizo heritage or social problems, but they also tell unique stories about the "merging of ideas, cultures, and dreams" along the United States–Mexico border. An attempt to preserve the murals, as well as to restore older ones or paint new ones, was sponsored in the early 1990s by the city's artists and the Junior League, which also published a brochure entitled *Los Murales, Guide and Maps to the Murals of El Paso*.

San Antonio also has a strong Chicano mural tradition, with the majority of murals concentrated on the city's predominantly Mexican-American West Side. The Cassiano public-housing project, for instance, has been the site of numerous murals, many of them painted under the direction of the Community Cultural Arts Organization, which was organized in 1979. CCAO chief artist Anastacio "Tacho" Torres has recruited teams of student artists to complete works that depict an array

acclaim:

renaissance:

manifested:

affirm:
motifs:

mestizo:

predominantly:

of subjects: labor leader César Chávez, lowriders, the San Antonio missions, Tejano military and political heroes, and others. More than 130 murals had been completed in the city by the early 1990s. Some have been privately commissioned for a variety of locales such as the convention center, Mario's Mexican Restaurant, and Our Lady of the Lake University. As in El Paso, efforts to record the existence of these works have occurred. In the early 1980s, for example, historian Ricardo Romo developed a slide show on them called "Painted Walls of the Barrio" for the University of Texas Institute of Texan Cultures.

In Houston, Leo Tanguma painted *Rebirth of our Nationality* on the   5
wall of the Continental Can Company. Because of the politically charged content of Tanguma's mural art, several of his works have been erased. In Austin muralist Raúl Valdez has led volunteer teams in painting murals at several public sites on the city's predominantly Mexican-American east side, including the Pan American Recreation Center. Some of his work, like Tanguma's, has been lost in recent years. *Los Elementos*, for instance, which was painted on the exterior of the Juárez-Lincoln University building in 1977, was destroyed in 1983; city officials could not save it when the building was sold to a new owner. Sylvia Orozco, codirector of Mexic-Arte, has also painted murals, among them one for the Chicano Culture Room in the student union building of the University of Texas at Austin. Murals have also been reported in Crystal City, Dallas, Lubbock, Levelland, Lockhart, and other cities. Whether in small or large towns, artists in the Chicano mural movement have offered an opportunity to the barrios' "untrained" painters. Art historians Shifra Goldman and Tomás Ybarra-Frausto call the murals a significant contribution to public art.

Bibliography

Arriba, November 15–December 15, 1989.

Shifra Goldman and Tomás Ybarra-Frausto, *Arte Chicano: A Comprehensive Annotated Bibliography of Chicano Art, 1965–1981* (Chicano Studies Library Publications Unit, University of California, Berkeley, 1985).

practice it 25.7   Post-Reading Activity

Look back at the freewrite you wrote as your pre-reading activity. Has reading the Web article provided you with more information, not only about the topic of mural art, but also about these three cities and the people who live there? Add new information and thoughts to your freewrite based on what you learned from the reading.

COMPREHENSION QUESTIONS

1. What is the historical basis of the 1960s Chicano mural movement?

2. What kinds of topics or scenes did early murals depict?

3. What were the goals of the Mexican American mural movement in the 1960s and 1970s?

4. What kind of mural activity has there been in El Paso, San Antonio, and Houston since the 1960s?

DISCUSSION QUESTIONS

1. What is the significance of mural artists' being self-taught versus formally trained?

2. How might a mural "affirm cultural identity and challenge racism" (para. 2)? How might a mural not be successful in challenging racism? Can you think of any examples of murals you have seen that work to challenge racist attitudes? If so, explain how. If not, explain why they don't.

3. Why are Chicano murals "concentrated on the city's predominantly Mexican-American West Side" (para. 2)? What does that suggest about the intended audience and purpose of the murals? How might the murals function differently in other neighborhoods?

4. What rights should a community have to remove art that the majority of residents find politically objectionable? How should decisions be made about which murals to remove and which to preserve?

Before becoming an intern for NPR's Digital News Desk in Washington, D.C., Paige Pfleger graduated from the University of Michigan with a bachelor of arts degree in communications studies and was a reporter for the *Michigan Daily*, the University of Michigan's campus newspaper, for four years. Her articles and photographs have appeared on Michigan Radio's Web page, in the *Tennessean*, and in *USA Today*. *Some difficult words have been identified in the margins. Look up those you do not know, and write the definitions in your own words either before or as you read. The first one has been done for you.*

practice it 25.8   Pre-Reading Activity

Before you read, scan the article to locate the names of the mural artists and murals mentioned. Then practice the model reading strategy Connecting Image to Text (see p. 486) and find images of them.

npr.org

What Right Do Muralists Have to the Buildings They Paint On?

Paige Pfleger

It took artist Katherine Craig about a year to create her nine-story mural on 2937 E. Grand Blvd. in Detroit. Most people who drive around the city have seen it—one side of the Albert Kahn–designed building is covered in a blanket of electric blue, and a flowing waterfall of multi-colored paint splatters descend from the roof line. It stands in stark contrast to the rest of the landscape of low buildings and muted Mid-western colors.

stark: *extreme or complete*

It's called *The Illuminated Mural* and it's become emblematic of Detroit's North End neighborhood.

This week, it was also on the auction block.

Well, the building is. But what does that mean for Craig's mural? What rights does a muralist have to the wall she painted on?

That's a question that echoes throughout the country right now, as   5
muralists try to lay claim to their artwork under the Visual Artists Rights Act of 1990.

Katherine Craig, *The Illuminated Mural*, Detroit, MI.

Daniel Mears/AP photos

A Massive Loss, a Huge Win

California muralist Kent Twitchell was in a hotel room in Sausalito, Calif., when he got the call—his six-story mural of Ed Ruscha in Los Angeles had been painted over. It was June 2, 2006, a date he remembers vividly because it was the day he lost his mural, and also the day of his daughter's wedding.

Twitchell had worked on the mural over the course of nine years, and it was ruined in one day.

"It's hard to describe," he says. "It's like being kicked in the stomach, I guess. It takes the wind out of you."

So he took the case to court. He sued the U.S. government, which owned the building, and 11 other defendants for damages under the Visual Artists Rights Act, which prohibits the desecration, alteration or destruction of public art without giving the artist at least 90 days' notice.

He won $1.1 million, which is regarded as the largest win under VARA. 10

"If the work is destroyed, it's like part of your resume being destroyed," says Eric Bjorgum, the lawyer who won Twitchell's case, and the president of the Mural Conservancy of Los Angeles.

Many disputes surrounding murals have a lot to do with advertising, Bjorgum explains. When an area of a city is downtrodden, muralists choose highly visible walls for their works to spruce up the space. But

TIP

Try searching online for images of the Ed Ruscha mural. What search terms would you use?

vividly:

desecration:

downtrodden:

spruce up:

when that area is developed, large spaces that are seen easily from the street are ideal real estate for advertisers.

Money is always a motivator—in one of Bjorgum's cases, a brewing company was paying $18,000 per month to have a beer ad on a wall, covering up a mural.

Muralist Robert Wyland knows how that goes all too well. In 27 years, he painted 100 whale-themed murals, called Whaling Walls, in cities around the world. With that many murals, it makes sense that he's run into problems. Some of the murals were painted over, relocated or destroyed.

Others were covered with gigantic, multistory advertisements.   15

That's what happened in his hometown of Detroit. *Whale Tower*, painted in 1997, is on the back side of the 34-story Broderick Tower. The Grand Circus Park area wasn't very populated when he painted the mural, Wyland explained, so when the new stadium, Comerica Park, went up next door in 2000, the wall his mural was on became a hot commodity for advertisers.

In 2006, a gigantic vinyl ad for Chrysler's Jeep Compass was put up over the mural. Verizon Wireless followed suit. Wyland was angry, but knew that even if he sued the companies under VARA, it would only be a "drop in the bucket" in comparison to the ad revenue they were getting from the space. They'd pay him off and keep his mural covered.

"The art doesn't belong to the owner of the building," Wyland says. "It belongs to the community. So it's outrageous that people think they can do whatever they want with public art."

He doesn't always fight back when his works are ruined or covered up. Lawsuits under VARA mean a lot of time and money spent that mural artists like Wyland or Craig don't necessarily have.

"It's harder to save the walls than it was to paint them," Wyland says.   20

Finding Compromise in a Changing City

In Philadelphia, murals reign supreme. Around most corners there are huge, colorful paintings of people, places and things that serve as a walking art tour of the city's culture.

Jane Golden of the Mural Arts Program is the engine that has powered Philly to become the mural mecca it is today.

Golden started painting murals in the 1970s and worked with Kent Twitchell in Los Angeles on her first mural. She moved back to her hometown of Philadelphia because of health problems, and joined in on Mayor Wilson Goode's anti-graffiti effort in the Mural Arts Program. She reached out to graffiti writers in the city and started creating murals with them.

"People started to fall in love with the murals," Golden says. "It was like a mirror held up to them that said, 'Your life counts, you matter.'"

reign:

These murals <u>snowballed</u> from collaborations with taggers, to   25
collaborations with truant kids, then entire communities. Under Golden's
care, the Mural Arts Program has created nearly 4,000 works of art since
1987. She's seen the city undergo a lot of change in the past 30 years, and
she has been striving to have the program change along with it.

A big part of that change is the development of lots that were vacant
or empty—spaces that were once prime placement for murals are now
also ideal for condominiums and parking garages. And when land is
bought that could <u>jeopardize</u> a mural, Golden says the first step is to
communicate with the developer. That's what she did when she found out
that Joe Zuritsky of Parkway Corp. was going to build a high-rise directly
in front of the *Legacy* mural.

"No one would ever give a wall for a mural if they thought they could
never build and cover it up," Zuritsky says. "That would be giving away
the right to the real-estate with no compensation."

And that's just not good business, he says.

Zuritsky and the Mural Arts Program agreed that the *Legacy* mural
shouldn't be completely obscured. The developer plans to install columns
in front of portions of the mural, but the mural will be wrapped around
the columns, so as to not disrupt the flow of the work.

When to Fight, When to Say Goodbye

But sometimes compromises can't be reached. Wyland has a Whaling   30
Wall in Philadelphia as well, on the side of the Marketplace Design Center.
The building is slated for renovation this month—a renovation that could
destroy the *East Coast Humpbacks* painting.

Golden explains that losing murals comes with the territory of
creating art in a city that is rapidly growing. Occasionally the Mural Arts
Program invokes VARA, but it became clear over time that the program
couldn't fight for every mural. Sometimes it had to say goodbye.

"Every time we lose something, we try to create lemonade out of the
lemons," Golden says. "The memory of it should be so <u>profound</u> that it
continually reminds us that art is important in our lives."

So what is a mural artist to do after the loss of a piece?

Keep painting. That's what Kent Twitchell is doing. He's planning a
new Ed Ruscha mural for LA's arts district.

"I'm really enjoying this recovery, this new lease on life," Twitchell   35
says. "To have something lost and then recovered is always a good thing."

Back in Detroit, Katherine Craig is waiting anxiously. The auction on
2937 E. Grand closed on Thursday. She hopes that the winning bidder is a
fan of murals.

Otherwise, she'll be looking for a lawyer.

snowballed:

jeopardize:

profound:

practice it 25.9 Post-Reading Activity

Although VARA gives artists some legal protection over their public art works, what are the "moral" and "aesthetic" rights artists have over their work? Why?

COMPREHENSION QUESTIONS

1. According to the article, what is VARA, and what does it protect?

2. What does Kent Twitchell's lawyer mean when he says, "If the work is destroyed, it's like part of your résumé being destroyed" (para. 11)? How is a mural like a résumé for an artist?

3. Why are spaces that muralists paint on ideally suited for advertisements?

4. Pfleger refers to Philadelphia as a "mural mecca"; explain in your own words what a "mural mecca" is.

5. How did Joe Zuritsky, a building developer, and Jane Golden, executive director of Philadelphia's Mural Arts Program, work together to save the mural titled *Legacy*?

DISCUSSION QUESTIONS

1. The title of this article raises an important question that the article attempts to answer. After reading the article, what right do you believe muralists have to the buildings and walls they paint on? Explain.

2. What is the difference between a wall painted with a mural and a wall covered in advertising images? Is one better than the other for the community? Explain why.

3. Mural artist Robert Wyland argues that "[t]he art doesn't belong to the owner of the building. It belongs to the community" (para. 18). Why does Wyland see mural art this way? Do you agree or disagree with him? Explain.

4. How might programs like Philadelphia's Mural Arts Program help a community?

SCHOLARLY JOURNAL

Koon-Hwee Kan is a practicing artist as well as an associate professor in the art education department at Kent State University's School of Art. She is also the coordinator for the Saturday Art Program, a ten-week outreach program for children in the community. Kan has received several awards for her research and presents nationally and internationally on art education. In addition to publishing this article in the journal *Art Education* in 2001, she has also published numerous articles in other art and art education journals, including a number of studies on art and youth in Singapore. *Some difficult words have been identified in the margins. Look up those you do not know, and write the definitions in your own words either before or as you read. The first one has been done for you.*

practice it 25.10   Pre-Reading Activity

> What kinds of graffiti do you notice in your environment? What locations are most likely to have graffiti? Is the graffiti you see on bathroom walls on campus different from the other graffiti you see on campus? How?

KOON-HWEE KAN

Adolescents and Graffiti

What is graffiti, and why are many adolescents attracted by it? Art teachers recognize that there are great variations of visual art forms nowadays. As conceptions of art change, so will the ideas about art education. Wilson (1997) has proposed an expanded concept of "child art" to include activities that are common to the youth of today. This view could encourage teachers to broaden their curriculums and incorporate new art forms that are more engaging to young people.

curriculums: *programs of study*

This article uses teenage psychology to interpret adolescents' involvement in both private and public graffiti. Graffiti art will be examined in different contexts with its educational implications considered for the secondary school art curriculum and instruction.

implications:

© Olivar Sved/Shutterstock

Private Graffiti

Doodling

Doodling is a form of private graffiti. These scrawls and scribbles are created when attention is supposed to be focused elsewhere, so their completeness and aesthetic quality are seldom recognized. Adolescents' doodling may seem totally formless and meaningless, but it fits perfectly into certain aspects of adolescents' psychology.

Living in multiple realities, including the "daydream reality," is common among adolescents. My personal experience of interviewing and observing adolescents has alerted me that even when they seem to be very engaged in an activity or a conversation, their thoughts can change dimension and direction at any time without warning. This scattered attention continues to puzzle and worry many parents and teachers. However, adolescents' accomplished "divided attention" and "selective attention" can easily allow them to concentrate on different things simultaneously, switching focus instantly to activities that interest them while allowing others to fade into the background (Higgins & Turnure, 1984).

Thus, the elongated concentration span of adolescence that guides   5
curriculum planning has certain limitations. As academic achievement is not valued by many teenagers today (Meyer, 1994), schooling becomes a boring, frustrating, stressful, or anxious experience for them. In such cases, their natural tendency to drift in and out of multiple realities increases. From this perspective, adolescent doodling is a form of escape. It can be interpreted as an unconscious rejection of the kind of

scattered:

learning that is not helping them to construct personal meanings and effectively integrate their inner needs to promote growth.

"Latrinalia"

Another type of private graffiti is "latrinalia," the kind of graffiti found near toilets (Abel & Buckley, 1977). In most civilizations throughout history, its creators were usually <u>suppressed</u> individuals in the society, for example, slaves working in monumental construction or prisoners inside jail cells. In contemporary times, such creation is not the sole responsibility of adolescence; people of all ages are equally likely to perform such acts. Yet, latrinalia is common in school toilets and poses a major vandalism problem.

suppressed:

   Creation of latrinalia satisfies the emotional needs of adolescents in an unusual manner. Adolescence is a stage of life in which the individuals seek <u>autonomy</u>. When trying to secure a sense of personal space and time, the presence of others, especially adults, is often deemed threatening. At home, parents may regularly notice the strange behaviors of their adolescents, either behind frequently locked bedroom doors or during unusually extended times inside the bathrooms. Yet, many such episodes end almost immediately with the flushing of the toilet and a speedy reappearance of their teenagers without clues to what had happened just before. For many adolescents, parents' caring questionings are regarded as tight supervision. Nor is the school community perceived as supportive and accommodating of their unique growing-up experience. Thus, latrinalia in schools may be a form of silence and mindless protest for them against the large educational system that alienates their primary needs. There is evidence that school vandalism decreases or is absent in schools that manage a successful community of learning (Flaherty, 1987).

autonomy:

Public Graffiti

In contrast to private graffiti, public graffiti always makes its debut known. The main distinction between the two types of graffiti is that the latter is often created with an intended audience and special motives, while the former is created more unconsciously. Different forms of public graffiti, like gang graffiti, "tags," and "pieces," provide different means to satisfy the psychology and emotional needs of their creators, who are not exclusively adolescents.

Gang Graffiti

Gang graffiti appeared in the United States in the 1950s. It is the most unacceptable form of public graffiti because of the <u>notorious</u>

notorious:

hierarchy:

reputation of gangs. "These are primitive scrawls focusing on the gang names or symbols adopted to mark territory and war zones" (Gomez, 1993, p. 644). They are often simple alphabets written backwards, numbers marked in sets, or letters intentionally crossed out to send coded messages among gang members or warn away intruders. Usually, these activities are carried out by junior members within the gang hierarchy or by newly recruited young members to prove their worth and courage by entering the territory of another gang and leaving an insulting mark.

Tags

"Tags are simple, stark lettering like signatures . . . that Taggers have adopted for different personal reasons" (Gomez, 1993, p. 645). The invention of magic markers and improvement of spray paint in the late 1960s made tagging possible and popular in the United States, as these two mediums can easily and quickly mark on any surface.

Pieces

Deriving from the word "masterpiece," these are large, elaborate works with refined details often found on the exterior of subway trains and buildings. "Style" of pieces is important since they distinguish how different creators, known as "artists" or "writers" (Gomez, 1993), express their imaginations. Pieces can be a form of political protest or social statement as in the example of works found on the former Berlin Wall (Walderburg, 1990). Many creators of "pieces" consider their work as public art, an improvement to their surrounding environment and com-

commissioned:

munity (Geer & Rowe, 1995). Some families of victims of crime and violence in New York have commissioned graffiti artists to paint murals in memory of the deceased (Cooper & Sciorra, 1994). In the 1970s, a Union of Graffiti Artists (UGA) was formed that organized exhibitions and sales.

How Did Graffiti Become Art?

emergence:
icons:

The 1980s were the Golden Age of graffiti art with the emergence of "wild style," an intertwined and decorative lettering that mixes icons and images from popular culture to form a complex composition

avant-garde:

(Fineberg, 1995). A big avant-garde art show at Times Square in 1980 featured many graffiti artists, including Jean-Michel Basquiat, Futura 2000, Lee Quinones, and Keith Haring. Most of them seemed to become famous overnight. At that time, high art was being criticized as too <u>institutionalized</u> and intellectual. A huge discrepancy existed between art in museums and the experience of common people. Witnessing the gradual decline of Minimalism in the previous decade, art critic Rene Ricard highlighted graffiti art in *Art Forum*, a distinguished high art magazine. Art dealers sought "new blood" to stimulate the art market. Graffiti thus became an art <u>commodity</u> worth investing in.

 Graffiti art was also <u>indebted</u> to the Hip-Hop culture popular at that time, which included rap music, disc jockeys and break dancing (Hager, 1985). This subculture gained attention in the *New Yorker* magazine, films, and movies. American popular culture made heroes of graffiti artists like Jean-Michel Basquiat, portraying in the movie *Break-in* the young talent who died prematurely at age 29. Another young rising star was Keith Haring, who soon became the most widely renowned graffiti artist.

 By the 1990s, Hip-Hop culture had lost its initial <u>vibrancy</u>, but had become known worldwide and accepted as part of mainstream U.S. culture. Graffiti art became commercialized at about this time, appearing in the advertisements of Nike and Sprite, while other marketing strategies targeted at youth culture continued to reinforce the notion of graffiti as an artistic form of expression to the younger generations.

institutionalized:

commodity:

indebted:

vibrancy:

References

Abel, E. L., & Buckley, B. E. (1977). *The handwriting on the wall: Towards a sociology and psychology of graffiti*. Westport, CT: Greenwood Press.

Cooper, M., & Sciorra, J. (1994). *R.I.P. New York spraycan memorials*. London, United Kingdom: Thames & Hudson.

Fineberg, J. (1995). *Art since 1940: Strategies of being*. Englewood Cliffs, NJ: Prentice Hall.

Flaherty, G. (1987). Reducing vandalism by changing the school community. *Trust for Educational Leadership, 16*(5), 28–30.

Geer, S., & Rowe, S. (1995, spring/summer). Thoughts on graffiti as public art. *Public Art Review*, 24–26.

Gomez, M. (1993). The writing on our walls: Finding solutions through distinguishing graffiti art from graffiti vandalism. *University of Michigan Journal of Law Reform, 26*, 633–707.

Hager, S. (1985). *Hip Hop: The illustrated history of break dancing, rap music, and graffiti*. New York, NY: St. Martin's.

Higgins, A., & Turnure, J. (1984). Distractibility and concentration of attention in children's development. *Child Development, 44*, 1799–1810.

Meyer, L. (1994). *Teenspeak: A bewildered parent's guide to teenagers.* Princeton, NJ: Peterson's.

Walderburg, H. (1990). *The Berlin Wall book.* New York, NY: Thames & Hudson.

Wilson, B. (1997). Child art, multiple interpretations, and conflicts of interest. In A. Kindler (Ed.), *Child development in art* (pp. 81–94). Reston, VA: National Art Education Association.

practice it 25.11 Post-Reading Activity

▶ For more on mapping, see Chapter 5, Active Reading Strategies.

Make a map of this article, outlining the various kinds of graffiti Kan discusses. Use the headings as a guide. Include illustrative examples to help fill out the map.

COMPREHENSION QUESTIONS

1. What is art education?

2. What connection does Kan make between adolescence and graffiti?

3. What are the differences between "private" and "public" graffiti?

4. According to the article, what are the differences between "gang graffiti," "tags," and "pieces"?

5. What does it mean that graffiti art has become "commercialized"?

DISCUSSION QUESTIONS

1. How does Kan relate doodling to other forms of graffiti? Do you agree with the comparison? Why or why not?

2. According to Kan, historically writers of latrinalia were usually "suppressed" people, and today "people of all ages are equally likely to perform such acts" (para. 6). Why do people write on bathroom walls? What kind of outlet does it provide?

3. Kan references the former Berlin Wall as a location of works of political graffiti art. Do an online search to learn more about the Berlin Wall, including a search for images. Why might graffiti artists have been drawn to this location?

4. Kan raises the question of whether lessons on graffiti should be included in art curricula for adolescents. What do you think, and why?

WEB PAGE

The Los Angeles Police Department's Web site provides a robust assortment of information for the community. In addition to the 2013 Web article "What Graffiti Means to a Community," the organization offers a "newsroom" with current issues, a blog, and a newsletter published on a quarterly basis called *The Beat. Some difficult words have been identified in the margins. Look up those you do not know, and write the definitions in your own words either before or as you read. The first one has been done for you.*

practice it 25.12 Pre-Reading Activity

Preview the whole article before reading. What can you infer about the topic, audience, and purpose of this Web article? Would you say this article is a credible source? Why or why not?

www.lapdonline.org

What Graffiti Means to a Community
Los Angeles Police Department

The more social disorder and graffiti in a neighborhood, the louder the message is sent that "nobody cares." This sets off a vicious cycle that encourages further crime in affected neighborhoods.

Most vandals are young people, from grade school age to young adults, who damage property for reasons of boredom, anger or revenge. Others vandalize to show defiance toward rules, laws and authority or to draw attention to a "cause." Graffiti is often the first sign that gangs are taking over a neighborhood. Gangs use graffiti as their street "telegraph," sending messages about turf and advertising their exploits. Graffiti identifies territorial boundaries, lists members, and communicates threats to rival gangs.

telegraph: *a system for sending messages in code*

Each year millions of dollars are spent to clean up graffiti. Communities can adopt a zero tolerance policy for vandalism. The first step is to identify locations or objects prone to graffiti and to teach property owners effective removal methods. Participants should include property owners victimized by graffiti, schools, government, businesses, recreation facilities, public transportation, utilities, public works, and shopping malls among others.

zero tolerance:

prone:

Beautification projects such as trash cleanups, landscape enhancements, and gardens also serve as a focus for community organizing.

enhancements:

Community groups working with law enforcement, public works, or parks and recreation staff clean up public areas and abandoned lots. The project may reclaim a public space for neighborhood use, establish new green space, or mark neighborhood boundaries. The Los Angeles Police Department has a number of such projects. For more information, contact your local Los Angeles Police Department Community Relations Office.

A community's first step in taking back its streets is getting rid of   5
graffiti immediately. This power struggle cannot be won overnight, but persistent communities working in partnership with law enforcement almost always emerge as victors. Once the graffiti is gone, use landscape designs (such as prickly shrubs or closely planted hedges), building materials (such as hard-to-mark surfaces), lighting, or fences to discourage vandalism. This philosophy, known as Crime Prevention Through Environmental Design, can help diminish the possibility of graffiti by changing landscaping, lighting, fencing, etc.

Since 1990, the Los Angeles Police Department (LAPD) in an effort to combat graffiti, implemented the Police Assisted Community Enhancement Program (PACE) which coordinates other City agencies to alleviate adverse conditions affecting the quality of life in neighborhoods citywide. Conditions such as graffiti, abandoned cars, vagrants, accumulative trash, street vendors and abandoned buildings are examples of conditions that cause fear among residents and are a sign that residents have lost control of their neighborhood. If minor problems such as broken windows are left unattended, it could foster serious crimes such as robbery, assault, etc. The PACE program is the method by which these problems are addressed and the core of the Department's community based policing efforts.

The PACE program is heavily dependent on the hard work of the Senior Lead Officers (SLOs) who maintain an active liaison with area residents and other City entities. Once a problem has been identified, officers will complete the Community Enhancement Request (CER) form. This form is reviewed by a supervisor who then forwards it to the proper City department that will handle the specified problem.

Public works agencies, such as the City of Los Angeles' Board of Public Works, can supply equipment and staff for larger projects, while landscaping firms or other businesses can donate supplies and plants. Publicity and coordination with other police-advised beautification projects help enhance the success of such efforts. Volunteer patrols help support maintenance, and publicity helps protect areas from future deterioration.

persistent:
emerge:

alleviate:

adverse:
vagrants:

accumulative:

liaison:

enhance:

deterioration:

practice it 25.13   Post-Reading Activity

Compare and contrast the perspective of this article with the perspective of one other reading in this chapter. How are the perspectives similar? Where do they differ? What might account for their differences? Go back to your annotations for each article and add notes about the similarities and differences between the two articles.

COMPREHENSION QUESTIONS

1. How does this Web article portray graffiti and the people who make graffiti? Where in the text do you find evidence of these portrayals?

2. According to the article, how do gangs use graffiti?

3. What are some of the suggestions the article makes for preventing graffiti?

4. What is the PACE program? Why was it created, and whom does it serve?

DISCUSSION QUESTIONS

1. What is the thesis of this Web article?

2. In order to adopt a "zero tolerance policy" toward graffiti, the LAPD suggests uniting "property owners victimized by graffiti, schools, government, businesses, recreation facilities, public transportation, utilities, public works, and shopping malls among others" (para. 3) in the cause. How are each of these groups related to or affected by graffiti?

3. The article cites graffiti as one of the "adverse conditions" (para. 6), along with vagrancy, trash, and abandoned vehicles, that make people fearful. What is graffiti's role in this list of conditions that create fear? Do you agree that it can make people fearful? Why or why not?

4. What is the role of a police department in a community? What position should a police department take on graffiti?

Synthesizing the Readings as Pre-Writing for Your Own Essay

Now that you have read a wide variety of texts on the topic of public art, you have enough schemas, or background information, to begin to synthesize the material and build arguments of your own. It's helpful, though, to pause and discuss how the various readings "converse" with one another before you jump right into a writing assignment. You can use a variety of techniques and activities—alone or with peers—to help your thoughts take shape. Whichever method you choose, it's helpful to have the readings out in front of you so that you can review your annotations. Look for connections across articles as you review. Quite often, you don't see the bigger picture until you take the time to step back and review the material.

DISCUSS TO SYNTHESIZE IDEAS

Talk through the following questions with peers to uncover the connections among readings:

1. Some graffiti art is not only accepted but highly valued and even protected, such as works by the famed street artist Banksy, whereas other graffiti is removed and the artists are prosecuted. What differentiates the two kinds? What effect might this contradictory message have on graffiti artists?
2. What is the meaning of public art? How is public art different from museum art or art sold in galleries?
3. How does the more temporary nature of some public art affect the way people view it?
4. How are graffiti, murals, and other forms of public art related? What connects these forms of public art? What differentiates them from one another?
5. Consider the locations of public art. Some public art is located in plazas, libraries, parks, and yards, or on the walls of buildings and other structures. Does the location determine people's attitude toward the art? Why or why not?
6. How do the readings in this chapter challenge your notions of what qualifies as private and what qualifies as public? Can private property function as public space? Can public function as private?
7. Who decides what makes something "art"? Who decides whether artwork is "good" or "great"?
8. What connections can you make between the readings in this chapter and those in Chapter 26, Fame and Celebrity (p. 520), if you have completed that chapter? Is Banksy a celebrity? Are graffiti artists? If a street artist or a graffiti artist gains some level of fame or notoriety, does this change your estimation of his or her art? Why or why not?
9. What is the meaning of "self-expression"? Do we value self-expression? How does it compare with other needs, rights, or responsibilities?
10. The discussion of graffiti art tends to focus on male artists, but there are female graffiti artists as well. Some of them use spray paint, but others use different materials, like yarn. Does graffiti appeal more to males than females? Why or why not?

CHART TO SYNTHESIZE IDEAS

▶ For more about creating synthesis charts, see pages 71–73 in Chapter 2, Active and Critical Reading, and pages 238–40 in Chapter 10, Pre-Writing.

For many writers, organizing ideas graphically is a vital part of the reading/writing process. Using the method you learned in Chapter 2, make a synthesis chart on one focused topic related to the theme of public art. Remember to include space for your own ideas. Look through your annotations on the texts you have read before filling in the chart.

IDENTIFY SUBTOPICS TO SYNTHESIZE IDEAS

If you're still struggling to settle on a specific focus for your essay after the discussion questions and synthesis charting, you can generate a list of possible subtopics that could be the focus of an essay. Here are a few sample subtopics to spark your thinking:

Public Art Topics
What is art?
Ownership of art
Legal versus illegal art
Public art as community identity

Take a few minutes to add to this list of subtopics, using the following questions to help you generate topics:

1. Which reading did you find most interesting? Why?
2. Which reading did you find most informative? What did you learn?
3. In which reading did you find the most to disagree with? What specific things did you disagree about?
4. In which reading did you find the most to agree with? What specific things did you agree about?
5. Which reading had good examples? List a few of the examples. What are they examples of?

Writing Your Essay

Once you have done some synthesis thinking, you can begin to write your essay. The following steps review how to get into the mind-set to write. These steps are outlined in greater detail in Chapters 2, 3, and 4.

STEP 1: What type of essay are you assigned to write about public art? Look over the question or your instructor's prompt, and write it in your own words.

STEP 2: Which readings from this chapter do you think you will include? List them in your notes, including any quotations that you think you might use. (Don't forget to include the author and page number when you write down the quotation.)

STEP 3: What ideas from class discussion or your own experience and observation would you like to include? Look over your notes, and add those thoughts to your brainstorming for this assignment.

STEP 4: Take a few more minutes to brainstorm in your favorite method: listing, freewriting, clustering, questioning, or group discussion.

STEP 5: Look back at the assignment prompt, and write up a tentative thesis or main idea based on your work so far. Remember, one way to think of the thesis is as the answer to the question posed in the assignment prompt. Don't worry that your thesis has to be perfect or set in stone right now. It's a working thesis that you will probably revise as you make decisions about what you want to say.

STEP 6: Make a bullet-point outline for your essay. Remember to first put the ideas down and then reorganize them into a logical order.

STEP 7: Copy or type up the relevant quotations and examples under each appropriate bullet point.

STEP 8: Pat yourself on the back! You have a lot of material so far.

STEP 9: Write the rough, rough draft, remembering that you'll be revising it.

STEP 10: Reread the assignment sheet one more time, and then make big-picture revisions to your focus, content, and organization. Peer review may help.

STEP 11: Once you are generally satisfied that your work is focused, complete, and organized, edit for sentence-level issues. Remember to use the editing techniques of reading your work out loud, reading "backward," and isolating your common errors. Refer to your Grammar Log frequently during this process. Edit and print your paper again and again until you are satisfied with the way each sentence sounds.

▶ To learn how to use the Grammar Log, see page 575 in Chapter 27, How to Learn the Rules and Apply Them to Your Own Writing.

STEP 12: Take a break.

STEP 13: Proofread your essay one or two more times to correct any minor errors and to make sure your document format is correct.

Writing Assignments

DEFINITION ASSIGNMENT

How would you define *public art* or *street art*? Write an essay that explains what constitutes public or street art. What are the differences between public and private art? What characteristics do they share? What qualities do we associate with those terms, and how do we stretch the labels to include a variety of artworks?

NARRATION ASSIGNMENT

Whether you like them or not, you can probably agree that murals, street art, and graffiti are all the attempt of an individual or community to make a mark on the world. This is a common human desire. For this essay, recall a time—either when you were a child or an adult—when you tried to make some mark on your world. (Make sure you choose a specific event or a focused time period, not a general phase of your life.) Tell the story of that experience, recalling as many vivid details as you can. What happened? Did you feel successful in making your mark? Did others recognize it? How? What were the ramifications or outcomes of the experience? Refer in your introduction or conclusion to at least one of the readings as a touchstone for your own story.

DESCRIPTION ASSIGNMENT

Imagine that you are asked to create a mural for your community or school. What message would you want to present to or about your community or school? What images would you include in the mural to get that message across? What colors would you use? Would you use traditional paint or spray paint? Would you create a mosaic? Where would you locate your mural, and what would be significant about that location? Before you begin, visit some murals in your community or do an online image search for mural art. Consider how the artists use both color and imagery. As a pre-writing activity, sketch out a concept of your mural.

PROCESS ANALYSIS ASSIGNMENT

Considering the complicated nature of street art, how would you design a lesson on street art for a high school class? What would you highlight? What visuals would you include, and why? Is there anything specific about this topic that you would emphasize to this age group? Why or why not? Write a process analysis essay that outlines the steps of the lesson, with explanations and justifications for each step.

COMPARISON AND CONTRAST ASSIGNMENT

Drawing extensively on the examples given in the readings, compare and contrast two of the following: murals, street art, graffiti. What is similar about the art forms and about the artists? What differences do you find?

PROBLEM-SOLUTION ASSIGNMENT

Choose one form of public art (graffiti, sculpture, or murals) and, noting the causes, identify the potential problems in the community with that art form and evaluate a possible solution. For example, if graffiti is considered a blight in your community, discuss the reasons graffiti exists and what problems it causes. Come up with a potential solution for the problem of graffiti. Alternatively, consider a sculpture or mural that the community dislikes.

ANALYSIS ASSIGNMENT

Murals are a very public kind of artwork. The artwork on a mural is not intended to hang in someone's home or sit in a museum; rather, murals, belong to everyone. Some murals are political; others tell a story about the dreams, achievements, and cultural identity of the artist or community. Choose a mural that tells a story or responds politically or socially to the community, and analyze the message of that mural. Explain the importance of that mural's message to the community. How does the mural reflect the identity of the community?

RESEARCH ASSIGNMENT

Walk one square mile near your home and document all the public expressions of creativity you see. Or research the public art in your community, considering civic spaces like city hall, libraries, and schools, and the sculptures or fountains that often adorn business buildings. What kinds of art do you find? What themes emerge from the public art in your neighborhood or city? What is your neighborhood or community's attitude toward public art? Are there any places where installing public art would improve your surroundings? In what ways?

ARGUMENT ASSIGNMENTS

1. Street art, which can include murals as well as graffiti "pieces," "tags," or stenciled art, is often a temporary and publicly shared art form. Using a variety of examples of graffiti art, write an essay about the role of graffiti art in a community. Is it art or vandalism?
2. Is public art important in a community? Write an essay in which you take a position about the role of public art. Use specific examples from the readings to support your position.

Additional Online and Media Sources

The readings in this chapter may spark your thinking and leave you wanting some more information for further study or personal reflection. If so, consult the following online and media sources.

WEB RESOURCES

Banksy (www.banksy.co.uk): The official Web site of street artist Banksy, which includes a sampling of images of his street art.

Blek le Rat (http://bleklerat.free.fr/stencil%20graffiti.html): The robust site of Blek le Rat, a pioneer of street art stencil graffiti; the site includes galleries of images, press, and a personal manifesto.

City of Philadelphia Mural Arts Program (http://muralarts.org): As the largest public art program in the United States, the City of Philadelphia Mural Arts Program offers program information on its Web site, as well as a well-documented history of its murals.

"Female Writers," @149st The Cyber Bench: Documenting New York Graffiti (www.at149st.com/women.html): A brief history of female graffiti artists in New York City, along with images of their work.

Fine Arts Collection (http://www.gsa.gov/fa/#): The U.S. General Services Administration collects, maintains, and makes accessible one of the biggest public art collections in the nation.

Mona Caron (www.monacaron.com): The official site of muralist Mona Caron, with images of her public art murals.

NoLa Rising (http://nolarising.org): The Web site for the nonprofit public art initiative to revitalize a post-Katrina New Orleans.

***Project Row Houses*, Public Art** (http://projectrowhouses.org/public-art): The Web site for the public art community of Houston's Third Ward neighborhood.

San Francisco Arts Commission, Public Art (www.sfartscommission.org/pubartcollection): The Web site for the city agency in San Francisco that oversees the installation and care of public art, as well as education about it.

Street Art Utopia (www.streetartutopia.com): An online gallery of street art from around the world.

FILMS

Basquiat. Directed by Julian Schnabel, performances by Jeffrey Wright, Dennis Hopper, and Gary Oldman, Miramax, 1996.

Bomb It. Directed by Jon Reiss, performances by Cope 2, Kid Acne, and Antonio, Gravitas Ventures, 2008.

Cave of Forgotten Dreams. Directed by Werner Herzog, performances by Werner Herzog and Jean Clottes, Creative Differences, 2010.

Exit through the Gift Shop. Directed by Banksy, performances by Banksy, Mr. Brainwash, and Debora Guetta, Paranoid Pictures, 2010.

Jean-Michel Basquiat: The Radiant Child. Directed by Tamra Davis, performances by Jean-Michel Basquiat, Julian Schnabel, and Larry Gagosian, Arthouse, 2010.

Style Wars. Directed by Tony Silver, performances by Cey Adams, Cap, and Daze, Public Art Films, 2005.

Vigilante Vigilante: The Battle for Expression. Directed by Max Good, performances by Stefano E. Bloch, Joe Connolly, and Michael Dingler, Open Ranch, 2011.

Wild Style. Directed by Charlie Ahearn, performances by Easy A. D., A. J., Almighty K. G., and Lee Quinones, Rhino, 1983.

26
Fame and Celebrity

"I'm not a businessman; I'm a business, man."

—Jay Z

Stephen Lovekin/Getty Images

520

Theme Overview

Everyone wants to be famous, right? Who wouldn't? Fame often brings money and attention, sometimes even adoration. However, as we often see in celebrity gossip news, fame can also bring pain, addiction, and a complete loss of privacy. Many people who gain public fame have private lives that do not match their image. When we look beneath the surface, we begin to ask whether the gains of fame outweigh the losses. Is celebrity worth the price in our media-saturated world? Why do some people want to be famous? Why do others shun attention? How has fame changed as new media outlets have evolved? Most of us don't get even fifteen minutes of fame, but we may yearn for celebrity status or be drawn to those who have achieved it for reasons we don't fully understand.

Drawing on research in psychology, history, and business, the writers in this chapter will get you thinking about the value of fame and celebrity, the values that underlie America's apparent celebrity obsession, and the way new forms of brand marketing help create what might be called a "celebrity culture." This chapter may also help you begin to define what success might mean for you personally.

While you read, it is tempting to get caught up in celebrity gossip. Try not to do so; instead, focus on the overall point of the articles rather than the specific stars under discussion. Also, since celebrity is a short-lived type of fame, the articles in this chapter may not reflect current events. Celebrities' marriages dissolve at an alarming pace, and no textbook could possibly keep current with the latest gossip or fads. Remember, it's not the minute details of a star's clothes, hair, or persona that are so important. Focus instead on the broader arguments that the writers are making about the role of fame and celebrity in American culture.

practice it 26.1   Taking Stock of What You Already Know

Think about your own knowledge and feelings about fame and celebrity. Then try to answer the following questions:

- Have you ever met anyone famous? If so, what was your experience? If you could meet that person again, would you do anything differently? Why or why not?

- What famous people would you like to meet, and why? What do you hope would happen if you met them?

- What are the benefits of fame and celebrity? What are the downsides?

- Do you want to be famous? Why or why not? If so, what would you want to be famous for doing?

readings on
Fame and Celebrity

NEWSPAPER

Andrea Chang is a staff writer who covers retail, business, and technology for the *Los Angeles Times*. This article, published in 2011, shows how the Kardashian family functions as a celebrity brand. The specific details of the Kardashians will quickly become dated, but the article is useful because of the detailed way it describes celebrity self-branding. This year it might be the Kardashians, and next year someone else, but the process of idolizing celebrities and making them into commodities remains similar. Indeed, celebrity self-branding has been going on in Hollywood for as long as films have been around, though one might argue that the Kardashian family has taken the business of self-promotion to a more intense level. *Some difficult words have been identified in the margins of this reading. Look up those you do not know, and write the definitions in your own words either before or as you read. The first one has been done for you.*

practice it 26.2   Pre-Reading Activity

This article about the Kardashian family of reality TV fame was originally published in the Business section of the *Los Angeles Times*, not in one of the sections usually devoted to celebrities and popular culture. Preview the article, thinking about its title, its place in the newspaper, and its lead paragraph: "There are Kardashian boutiques, fragrances, jewelry, apparel, bikinis, skin-care products and candles. And the reality-TV family says it's just getting started. But with a less-than-wholesome image, will the brand have staying power?" What perspective can you predict this article will take on the Kardashians? What types of information do you think you will learn as you read? Write your predictions directly on the article.

ANDREA CHANG

The Kardashians: Cashing in with a Capital K

There are Kardashian boutiques, fragrances, jewelry, apparel, bikinis, skin-care products and candles. And the reality-TV family says it's just getting started. But with a less-than-wholesome image, will the brand have staying power?

Having conquered reality television, the Kardashians are fashioning a celebrity retail powerhouse.

Beyond the glittery red carpets and steamy tabloid fodder, the famous family has transformed itself into a branding machine, quickly leveraging the hype into a retail empire worth tens of millions of dollars.

Unlike other reality-stars-turned-entrepreneurs such as Snooki of *Jersey Shore* fame or Lauren Conrad of *The Hills*, the Kardashians are in a class by themselves and unfazed by skeptics who doubt they can keep it up for the long haul.

There are Kardashian boutiques, fragrances, jewelry, apparel, bikinis, self-tanner, skin-care products, candles—even bottled water, if you're willing to shell out $10 for it.

Whether it's business savvy or shameless self-promotion, it's paid off: 5 Kardashian Inc. raked in an estimated $65 million last year, according to the *Hollywood Reporter*, a trade publication. And with the family signing on to a slew of new projects, it's poised to make even more in 2011.

This year alone, sisters Kourtney, Kim and Khloe released their own "glam pack" of Silly Bandz, the wildly popular rubber-band shapes that kids trade and wear as bracelets. They're also opening Kardashian Khaos, a celebrity retail store at the Mirage in Las Vegas. Kim has been promoting her jewelry line Belle Noel and touting Midori liqueur as a company spokeswoman; she and mother Kris are also the new faces of Skechers Shape-Ups sneakers. Khloe and Laker husband Lamar Odom, who are starring in their own spin-off series on E!, recently released a unisex fragrance called Unbreakable.

The sisters' biggest project this year is the launch of the Kardashian Kollection, an ambitious "shop-within-a-shop" concept that will launch at Sears stores in late August and in international markets.

The global lifestyle brand is Sears' biggest celebrity deal ever. The line will span categories including dresses, outerwear, T-shirts, denim, footwear, jewelry, handbags and lingerie, and will reflect the sisters' individual styles: classic red-carpet glamour for Kim, bohemian chic for Kourtney and edgy rocker for Khloe.

"It's new and exciting and different, and they're going to be a big part of that change," said John Goodman, executive vice president of apparel and home for parent company Sears Holdings Corp. "In order to evolve and move forward, you're going to have to step out of the comfort zone."

Not everything the Kardashians have lent their name to has been a success. 10 In November, the sisters were forced to pull their prepaid debit card, called the Kardashian Kard, amid slow sales and an outcry about high fees. After releasing "JAM (Turn It Up)," a dance-pop-infused single last month, Kim was criticized as having an uneven voice and talking her way through the song.

But for the most part, strong sales have followed their many pursuits. Kim's eponymous perfume was Sephora's No. 1-selling fragrance last year and the sisters' exclusive Bebe collection was a huge success, a company spokeswoman said. Their memoir and style guide, *Kardashian Konfidential,* debuted at No. 4

fodder: material that feeds

leveraging:

entrepreneurs:

unfazed:

savvy:

slew:

unisex:

eponymous:

debuted:

on the *New York Times* bestseller list in December. Unbreakable, available exclusively at Perfumania, has sold out twice since its February launch.

In recent interviews with *The Times*, the Kardashians said they're just getting started.

"There's some days we definitely go crazy," Khloe said during a recent appearance at the Beverly Center, where hundreds of hysterical fans lined up for photos and autographs. Added Kourtney: "There's no way I could do this alone. . . . We all kind of pick up the pieces for each other."

The Kardashians became household names in 2007 with the debut of *Keeping Up with the Kardashians* on the E! channel, which was conceived of by Kris as a modern-day Brady Bunch–esque reality show.

At the time, Kim Kardashian, still the most well-known of the brood, had   15 already made a name for herself as Paris Hilton's sidekick and fellow socialite. And like Hilton, Kim was also facing notoriety over the release of a sex tape made with her then-boyfriend.

The family's less-than-wholesome reputation has earned the Kardashians a fair amount of criticism that retail experts say could hinder the family's long-term viability as a brand.

"The Kardashians are a great example of, in my mind, talentless celebrities or celebrity for celebrity's sake who took advantage of their looks, a sex tape, a lot of pretty raw and low-level stuff that titillated and fascinated the American public," said Eli Portnoy, a marketing and branding expert in Los Angeles.

Led by Kris, who describes herself as the family's "momager," the Kardashian brood includes Kourtney, 32, Kim, 30, Khloe, 26, and Rob, 24, her children with her first husband, former O. J. Simpson lawyer Robert Kardashian, who died of esophageal cancer in 2003.

After divorcing Robert in 1989, Kris married Olympic gold medalist Bruce Jenner, who also had four kids. Kris and Bruce have two daughters together, Kendall, 15, and Kylie, 13.

Also part of the family are Odom, the Lakers basketball player who married   20 Khloe in 2009 after a month of dating, and Scott Disick, Kourtney's on-again, off-again boyfriend and father of her 1-year-old son, Mason.

As a group, the Kardashian-Jenner-Odom-Disick clan is capitalizing on its multi-generational, multiethnic appeal, actively pursuing and inking deals for everyone in the family.

But celebrity branding is a fickle beast. Too many missteps or a slump in popularity could see the Kardashian franchise headed the way of Lindsay Lohan's infamous leggings line or Sarah Jessica Parker's clothing collection at now-defunct Steve and Barry's.

If successful, they could join the elite ranks of celebs-turned-lucrative-designers such as Victoria Beckham, Mary-Kate and Ashley Olsen and Jessica Simpson, whose retail empire is expected to bring in $1 billion in sales this year.

notoriety:

titillated:

brood:

fickle:

defunct:

Whether the nonstop rollout of new products will damage the brand or lead to a bona fide franchise with lasting appeal will depend on the family's ability to maintain product quality and exclusivity, said Howard Davidowitz, chairman of national retail consulting and investment banking firm Davidowitz & Associates Inc.

bona fide:

"If you're everywhere and you become a mass brand, that means you better 25 really be good," he said. "The Kardashians are hot as a pistol, but they're no Oprah. This stuff can dissipate very quickly."

dissipate:

The Sears deal in particular is a curious choice, marketing and branding experts say, given the sisters' sought-after, fashion-forward styles—a stark contrast to Sears' image as a place to buy power tools or a new washing machine.

stark:

"The Sears thing—I have a question mark," Portnoy said. "In my mind, Sears and the Kardashians are not consistent at all. It hurts both properties. That one strictly comes off as about more greed, more money."

Not so, said Bruno Schiavi, president of Jupi Corp., which will produce the Kardashian Kollection.

mavens:

"It's not a one-off collection—this is a long-term goal for us," he said, noting that other celebrity mavens have partnered with Sears. Most notably, Martha Stewart offered an exclusive line for years at Kmart, a Sears Holdings company.

notably:

Another challenge is the fact that the public's fascination still mostly centers 30 on the family's real-life dramas and not the products. For Kim especially, being seen as a serious businesswoman has been a struggle.

At recent Los Angeles events promoting the sisters' various products, the women were mobbed by hordes of paparazzi and tabloid reporters who lobbed a few throwaway questions about whatever the Kardashians were hawking—clothes, shoes, jewelry—before spending most of the time grilling them on what new words Kourtney's baby was saying, Khloe's latest diet tricks and Kim's new boyfriend (she's currently dating Kris Humphries of the New Jersey Nets; previous boyfriends include NFL players Reggie Bush and Miles Austin).

The sisters admit that fame sometimes gets in the way of getting the job done.

In Calabasas, where they opened their first Dash boutique before becoming tabloid fixtures, Khloe said it was no longer possible to swing by and work the cash register or greet customers—"it almost causes a scene where people can't shop."

For the Kardashian sisters, who don't have business backgrounds, running a burgeoning empire has been about being heavily involved and carefully vetting projects. Only Kourtney, who attended the University of Arizona, graduated from college.

"We all approve everything together," Kim said at a recent event at Kitson in 35 Los Angeles, where she and her sisters were promoting their Silly Bandz rubber-band shapes. "I could love something but they hate it, so two out-rule the one."

"We're in every design meeting, we pick everything from the buttons to the fabric to the fit, we pick the fit models," Khloe said. "We're very hands-on."

The companies that are signing the Kardashians say they're not concerned that their own brands might be hurt by the family's sexually charged, drama-driven image.

"This is just nonsense," said Silly Bandz creator Robert Croak. "They're having fun. There's always going to be the naysayers who say someone's famous for nothing, and I really don't see that with the girls."

Not surprisingly, the family is open for even more business ventures. Among the categories they'd like to tackle next include home decor and children's products, Kourtney said; they are also in talks with nail polish maker OPI for a not-yet-announced project.

"We have to, No. 1, make sure that it's something that we really want to spend our time doing," Kim said. "Time is really precious now." 40

So far, the overexposure isn't turning off their fans.

"Get it while you can get it," said Amanda Lopez, 29, after buying a $140 dress at Dash Calabasas recently. "I think it's great that they're branching out. They're hot right now; why wouldn't they?"

naysayers:

practice it 26.3   Post-Reading Activity

You may be familiar with the idea of brands, since you see brands in the products you use all day long, from your morning coffee to your toothpaste at night. What does it mean, though, to suggest that a person—or an entire family, as the Kardashians have shown—can function as a brand? Think of another major celebrity who has his or her own product line. What products are sold with that person's name? Does the person have a well-known logo or look that has been used for selling products unrelated to his or her initial fame? What are that person's admirable qualities? What are his or her flaws? Write a well-developed paragraph that answers these questions.

COMPREHENSION QUESTIONS

1. How does the entrepreneurship of the Kardashians go beyond the marketing of other reality stars?

2. Kris Jenner refers to herself as the "momager" of her client-daughters. What does this mean?

3. What does Chang mean by "celebrity branding is a fickle beast" (para. 22)? How is it fickle?

DISCUSSION QUESTIONS

1. How has the Kardashian family transformed itself into a brand? What is the Kardashian brand?

2. How does the partnership between the Kardashians and Sears benefit each party? Which partner has more to gain or more to lose? Explain.

3. After reading the article, do you think of the Kardashians more as entrepreneurs or as celebrities? Why?

4. Is the celebrity entrepreneur a new role for stars? Can you think of any other celebrity entrepreneurs? How successful have they been at promoting their fame?

5. Have you ever purchased a celebrity-branded product? If so, were you drawn to the celebrity name? Why or why not?

MAGAZINE

Having been trained as a journalist, Carlin Flora worked as a writer and editor for *Psychology Today*, a well-respected magazine for general readers, when she wrote this article, published in 2004. Her journalistic specialty is science, particularly psychological issues such as narcissism, self-representation, and friendship. She has published articles in a variety of health and beauty magazines, and her most recent book is *Friendfluence: The Surprising Ways Friends Make Us Who We Are*. Some difficult words have been identified in the margins of this reading. Look up those you do not know, and write the definitions in your own words either before or as you read. The first one has been done for you.

practice it 26.4 Pre-Reading Activity

Identify the audience, topic, and purpose of this article by using the pre-reading techniques that you have learned so far. Answer these questions:

▶ **For more on identifying audience, purpose, and topic, see Chapter 7, Audience, Purpose, and Topic.**

• What do you think the focused topic is? How do you know?

• Who do you think the audience of *Psychology Today* is? Who do you think the audience for this particular article might be?

• What is the author's purpose, and what clues did you use to figure that out?

Write down your answers in your notes.

CARLIN FLORA

Seeing by Starlight: Celebrity Obsession

From Princess Diana to The Donald, A-listers teach us how to grab life's goodies—or so we're wired to think. What we actually learn from celebrities may surprise you.

A few years ago, Britney Spears and her entourage swept through my boss's office. As she sashayed past, I blushed and stammered and leaned over my desk to shake her hand. She looked right into my eyes and smiled her pageant smile, and I confess, I felt dizzy. I immediately rang up friends to report my

sashayed: *walked as if showing off*

celebrity encounter, saying: "She had on a gorgeous, floor-length white fur coat! Her skin was blotchy!" I've never been much of a Britney fan, so why the contact high? Why should I care? For that matter, why should any of us? Celebrities are fascinating because they live in a parallel universe—one that looks and feels just like ours yet is light-years beyond our reach. Stars cry to Diane Sawyer about their problems—failed marriages, hardscrabble upbringings, bad career decisions—and we can relate. The paparazzi catch them in wet hair and a stained T-shirt, and we're thrilled. They're ordinary folks, just like us. And yet . . .

Stars live in another world entirely, one that makes our lives seem woefully dull by comparison. The teary chat with Diane quickly turns to the subject of a recent $10 million film fee and honorary United Nations ambassadorship. The magazines that specialize in gotcha snapshots of schleppy-looking celebs also feature Cameron Diaz wrapped in a $15,000 couture gown and glowing with youth, money and star power. We're left hanging—and we want more.

It's easy to blame the media for this cognitive whiplash. But the real celebrity spinmeister is our own mind, which tricks us into believing the stars are our lovers and our social intimates. Celebrity culture plays to all of our innate tendencies: We're built to view anyone we recognize as an acquaintance ripe for gossip or for romance, hence our powerful interest in Anna Kournikova's sex life. Since catching sight of a beautiful face bathes the brain in pleasing chemicals, George Clooney's killer smile is impossible to ignore. But when celebrities are both our intimate daily companions and as distant as the heavens above, it's hard to know just how to think of them. Reality TV further confuses the picture by transforming ordinary folk into bold-faced names without warning. Even celebrities themselves are not immune to celebrity watching: Magazines print pictures of Demi Moore and "Bachelorette" Trista Rehn reading the very same gossip magazines that stalk them. "Most pushers are users, don't you think?" says top Hollywood publicist Michael Levine. "And, by the way, it's not the worst thing in the world to do."

Celebrities tap into powerful motivational systems designed to foster romantic love and to urge us to find a mate. Stars summon our most human yearnings: to love, admire, copy and, of course, to gossip and to jeer. It's only natural that we get pulled into their gravitational field.

Exclusive: Fan's Brain Transformed by Celebrity Power!

John Lennon infuriated the faithful when he said the Beatles were more popular 5 than Jesus, but he wasn't the first to suggest that celebrity culture was taking the place of religion. With its myths, its rituals (the red carpet walk, the Super Bowl ring, the handprints outside Grauman's Chinese Theater) and its ability to immortalize, it fills a similar cultural niche. In a secular society our need for

schleppy:

cognitive:
spinmeister:

innate:

jeer:

immortalize:

niche:

secular:

ritualized idol worship can be displaced onto stars, speculates psychologist
James Houran, formerly of the Southern Illinois University School of Medicine
and now director of psychological studies for True Beginnings dating service.
Nonreligious people tend to be more interested in celebrity culture, he's found,
and Houran speculates that for them, celebrity fills some of the same roles the
church fills for believers, like the desire to admire the powerful and the drive to
fit into a community of people with shared values. Leo Braudy, author of *The
Frenzy of Renown: Fame and Its History*, suggests that celebrities are more like
Christian calendar saints than like spiritual authorities (Tiger Woods, patron
saint of arriviste golfers; or Jimmy Carter, protector of down-home liberal
farmers?). "Celebrities have their aura—a debased version of charisma that
stems from their all-powerful captivating presence," Braudy says.

    Much like spiritual guidance, celebrity-watching can be inspiring, or at least
help us muster the will to tackle our own problems. "Celebrities motivate us to
make it," says Helen Fisher, an anthropologist at Rutgers University in New
Jersey. Oprah Winfrey suffered through poverty, sexual abuse and racial discrimi-
nation to become the wealthiest woman in media. Lance Armstrong survived
advanced testicular cancer and went on to win the Tour de France five times.
Star-watching can also simply point the way to a grander, more dramatic way of
living, publicist Levine says. "We live lives more dedicated to safety or quiet
desperation, and we transcend this by connecting with bigger lives—those of the
stars," he says. "We're afraid to eat that fatty muffin, but Ozzy Osbourne isn't."

Don't I Know You?!

Celebrities are also common currency in our socially fractured world. Depressed
college coeds and laid-off factory workers both spend hours watching Anna Nicole
Smith on late night television; Mexican villagers trade theories with hometown
friends about who killed rapper Tupac Shakur; and Liberian and German
businessmen critique David Beckham's plays before hammering out deals. My
friend Britney Spears was, in fact, the top international Internet search of 2003.

    In our global village, the best targets for gossip are the faces we all know. We
are born to dish dirt, evolutionary psychologists agree; it's the most efficient way
to navigate society and to determine who is trustworthy. They also point out that
when our brains evolved, anybody with a familiar face was an "in-group"
member, a person whose alliances and enmities were important to keep track of.

    Things have changed somewhat since life in the Pleistocene era, but our neural
hardwiring hasn't, so on some deeper level, we may think NBC's *Friends* really are
our friends. Many of us have had the celebrity-sighting mishap of mistaking a
minor star—a local weatherman, say, or a bit-part soap opera actor—for an
acquaintance or former schoolmate. Braudy's favorite example of this mistake: In
one episode of the cartoon show *King of the Hill*, a character meets former Texas
Governor Ann Richards. "You probably know me," he says. "I've seen you on TV."

ritualized:

idol worship:

arriviste:

aura:

muster:

enmities:

neural:

mishap:

That's also why we don't get bored by star gossip, says Bonnie Fuller, editorial director of American Media, which publishes *Star* and *The Enquirer*: "That would be like getting bored with information about family and friends!"

The brain simply doesn't realize that it's being fooled by TV and movies,   10 says sociologist Satoshi Kanazawa, lecturer at the London School of Economics. "Hundreds of thousands of years ago, it was impossible for someone not to know you if you knew them. And if they didn't kill you, they were probably your friend." Kanazawa's research has shown that this feeling of friendship has other repercussions: People who watch more TV are more satisfied with their friendships, just as if they had more friends and socialized more frequently. Another study found that teens who keep up to date on celebrity gossip are popular, with strong social networks—the interest in pop culture indicates a healthy drive for independence from parents.

penchant:

The penchant for gossiping about the stars also plays into our species' obsession with status. Humans naturally copy techniques from high-status individuals, says Francisco Gil-White, professor of psychology at University of Pennsylvania. It's an attempt to get the same rewards, whether that's "attention, favors, gifts, [or] laudatory exclamations." Stars get all kinds of perks and pampering: Sarah Jessica Parker was allowed to keep each of her *Sex and the City* character's extravagant getups; Halle Berry borrowed a $3 million diamond ring to wear to the Oscars. Understandably, we look to get in on the game.

laudatory:

The impulse to copy is behind the popularity of celebrity magazines, says Fuller. Regular women can see what the stars are wearing, often with tips on how to buy cheap knockoffs of their outfits. Taken to extremes—which television is only too happy to do—the urge to copy produces spectacles like the MTV reality show *I Want a Famous Face*. By dint of extensive plastic surgery, ordinary people are made to look more like their famous heroes. In one episode, two gangly 20-year-old twin brothers are molded into Brad Pitt look-alikes. The brothers want to be stars, and they've decided that looking more like Pitt is the fastest road to fame. No wonder makeover shows are so popular, points out Joshua Gamson, an associate professor of sociology at the University of San Francisco. These shows offer drab nobodies a double whammy: simultaneous beauty and celebrity. The most fascinating measure of status is, of course, sex. "We want to know who is mating with whom," says Douglas Kenrick, professor of psychology at Arizona State University. He speculates that we look to stars to evaluate our own sexual behavior and ethics, and mistake them unconsciously for members of our prospective mating pool. Given this me-too drive to imitate and adore, why are celebrity flame-outs and meltdowns so fascinating? Even though we love to hear about the lavish rewards of fame—remember *Lifestyles of the Rich and Famous*?—we're quick to judge when stars behave too outrageously or live too extravagantly. We suspect some stars are enjoying society's highest rewards without really

gangly:

drab:

speculates:

lavish:

deserving them, says University of Liverpool anthropologist Robin Dunbar, so we monitor their behavior. "We need to keep an eye on the great-and-the-good because they create a sense of community for us, but also because we need to make sure that they are holding to their side of the bargain."

Diva Alert: Beauty Isn't Everything (Being Nice Helps!)

The beauty bias is well-known. We all pay more attention to good-looking people. Kenrick's eye-tracking research has shown that both men and women spend more time looking at beautiful women than at less attractive women. Babies as young as 8 months old will stare at an attractive female face of any race longer than they will at an average-looking or unattractive female face. Certain human traits are universally recognized as beautiful: symmetry, regularity in the shape and size of the features, smooth skin, big eyes and thick lips, and an hourglass figure that indicates fertility. Men interpret these features as evidence of health and reproductive fitness. Women's responses are more complex, says psychologist and Harvard Medical School instructor Nancy Etcoff, author of *Survival of the Prettiest*. Women stare at beautiful female faces out of aesthetic appreciation, to look for potential tips—and because a beautiful woman could be a rival worth monitoring.

    It's not surprising that gorgeous people wind up famous. What's less obvious is that famous people often wind up gorgeous: The more we see a certain face, the more our brain likes it, whether or not it's actually beautiful. Thanks to what is known as "the exposure effect," says James Bailey, a psychologist at George Washington University, the pleasurable biological cascade that is set off when we see a certain celebrity "begins to wear a neurochemical groove," making her image easier for our brains to process. It begins to explain why Jennifer Aniston—not exactly a classic cover girl—was again named one of *People* magazine's 50 "most beautiful" in the world this year.

    On the flip side, celebrity overload—let's call it the J.Lo effect—can leave 15 us all thoroughly sick of even the most beautiful celeb. With the constant deluge of celebrity coverage, says Etcoff, "they at first become more appealing because they are familiar, but then the ubiquity becomes tedious. That is why the stars who reign the longest—Madonna is the best example—are always changing their appearance." Every time Madonna reconfigures her look, she resets our responses back to when her face was recognizable but still surprising.

    Just as in pageants, personality plays a part in the beauty contest, too. State University of New York at Binghamton psychology professors Kevin Kniffin and David Sloan Wilson have found that people's perceptions of physical appeal are strongly influenced by familiarity and likability. "Almost all of the beauty research is based on subjects looking at strangers in photos or computer-generated images—but we don't live in a world of strangers!" Kniffin points out.

aesthetic:

deluge:

ubiquity:

tedious:

reconfigures:

conversely:

In one of Kniffin's experiments, students worked on an archeological dig together toward a shared goal. Those who were deemed cooperative and likable were rated as more attractive after the project was finished than they were at the outset. Conversely, students who were not as hardworking were rated as less attractive after the chore was done.

propel:

Kniffin believes this same mechanism is at work in our feelings toward celebrities, who rank somewhere between strangers and intimates. Athletes are an obvious example: Team spirit gives even ugly guys a boost. NBA great Wilt Chamberlain might have been a bit goofy-looking, but his astonishing abilities to propel his team to victory meant that he was a hero, surrounded with adoring—and amorous—fans. Kniffin points to William Hung, the talent-free and homely also-ran on the contest show *American Idol*, as evidence of his theory at work. In part because of his enthusiasm and his good-natured willingness to put up with ridicule, Hung became a bigger star after he was kicked off the show: His album, *Inspiration*, sold more than 37,000 copies in its first week. "William doesn't display the traits of universal attractiveness, but people who have seen the show would probably rate him as more attractive because of nonphysical traits of likability and courage. He's even received some marriage proposals." Kniffin's theory also explains why models are less compelling objects of fascination than actresses or pop stars. They're beautiful, but they're enigmatic: We rarely get any sense of their personalities.

amorous:

homely:

enigmatic:

Saved from Oblivion!

What's the result of our simultaneous yearning to be more like celebrities and our desire to be wowed by their unattainable perfection? We've been watching it for the past decade. Reality television is an express train to fame, unpredictably turning nobodies into somebodies. Reality TV now gives us the ability to get inside the star factory and watch the transition to fame in real time.

"The appeal of reality stars is that they were possibly once just like you, sitting on the couch watching a reality TV program, until they leaped to celebrity," says Andy Denhart, blogger and reality TV junkie. "With the number of reality shows out there, it's inexcusable to not be famous if you want to be!" In the past, ambitious young men who idolized a famous actor might take acting lessons or learn to dance. Now, they get plastic surgery and learn to tell their life stories for the camera. In fact, says editor Fuller, the newly minted stars of reality TV are better at the celebrity game than many of the movie and television stars: "They are more accessible, more cooperative. They enjoy publicity. They will open up and offer insight, often more than a 'traditional' celeb, because they want the attention, whereas an actress might have ambivalent feelings about fame and how it is tied in with her 'craft.'" At the same time, shows like *The Simple Life* and *The Newlyweds* (and amateur videotapes like Paris Hilton's) let us gawk at the silly things that stars do in

20

ambivalent:

the privacy of their own home. As a result, the distance between celebrity stratosphere and living room couch dwindles even further.

     Yet there's still something about that magic dust. A celebrity sighting is not just about seeing a star, author Braudy points out, but is about being seen by a star: "There is a sense that celebrities are more real than we are; people feel more real in the presence of a celebrity." It wasn't just that I saw Britney, it was that Britney saw me.

stratosphere:

---

practice it 26.5   Post-Reading Activity

Look back at your predictions about audience, topic, and purpose that you made before you started reading the article. How accurately did you predict them? What, if anything, about the article's audience, topic, or purpose was surprising to you? What did you learn about celebrity watching? What questions do you still have about the topic?

COMPREHENSION QUESTIONS

1. In paragraph 3, what does Flora mean by "cognitive whiplash"?

2. What is the "cultural niche" (para. 5) that celebrity watching fulfills in our society, according to Flora?

3. Flora writes that celebrities provide a "common currency in our socially fractured world" (para. 7). What does she mean by this? Do you agree with her? Can you think of any instances where celebrities provide us with a way to connect?

4. What is the "exposure effect" (para. 14)?

5. Why, according to Flora, are we so drawn to stars?

6. How might a reality TV star and an actor deal with fame differently?

DISCUSSION QUESTIONS

1. In what ways can star watching be inspiring? What inspirational celebrities can you think of who fulfill this role? What needs can celebrity watching fulfill?

2. How does celebrity watching affect your friendships?

3. Using the reading-against-the-grain strategy, can you find any flaws in Flora's argument?

4. Think of a current big celebrity; do Flora's points about our fascination with celebrities apply to this celebrity? Why or why not?

SCHOLARLY ARTICLE

Donna Rockwell is a practicing psychologist, professor, and mindfulness workshop facilitator who specializes in helping people with anxiety and celebrity. British psychology professor David Giles of the University of Winchester has authored five scholarly books and numerous articles on topics related to media and psychology, especially the influence of fame and celebrity on the fans and the stars. Together, Rockwell and Giles studied the impact of celebrity on famous people. The article excerpted below, originally published in the *Journal of Phenomenological Psychology* (2009), reports some of their findings.

---

practice it 26.6   Pre-Reading Activity

This article is excerpted from an academic journal, so it has some of the most difficult vocabulary of any of the readings you will encounter in this book. The terminology that it uses is relevant to psychology, of course, but also to many other fields of study. You will understand the article much better if you do pre-reading specifically to help you with this jargon. First, scan the title, subtitle, and all the subheadings of the article, making a list of the terminology that you do not know. Some difficult words and phrases have been identified in the margins; scan these words as well. Next, look up the words you do not know in a dictionary or, if you are taking a psychology class, the glossary of your psychology textbook. Think about the meanings of the words and try to make sense of them, by yourself or in conversation with your classmates. Finally, write the definitions down in the margins in your own words. The first word in the margin has been defined for you.

DONNA ROCKWELL AND DAVID C. GILES

Being a Celebrity

Most everybody secretly imagines themselves in show business and every day on their way to work, they're a little bit depressed because they're not . . . People are sad they're not famous in America.   —John Waters, 2004

glorified: *given more praise and importance than deserved*

Movie producer John Waters's quotation may not only apply to the United States. Over the last century the mass media have <u>glorified</u>

the exploits of famous people to all corners of the globe, so that being recognized and talked about by millions of people has become a desirable goal for many individuals in contemporary society. But what of the lucky few who actually attain that goal? In this paper we describe the experience of fame for those who have achieved it at some point in their lifetime.

The purpose of the present study was to investigate the experience of fame, effectively asking the question: what is it *like* to be famous? What means of coping do individuals adopt for such situations? Are paparazzi and fan encounters experienced as problematic for famous people? Are the benefits of the celebrity experience worth the loss of privacy and anonymity, meeting cherished expectations of "the big time"? The goal of this study was to present an authentic account of *what it is like* to be famous.

coping:

cherished:

Method

Participants

Interviews were conducted with 15 adults who have at some stage in their lives attained celebrity status in the United States. The sample consisted of 11 males and four females between the ages of 35 and 86. Of the two selection criteria, the main one was public recognition—that the individual was readily identifiable when in the "public eye." As pointed out by Mitchell & Cronson (1987), celebrity families "live under a distinct set of rules dictated by their social status and high public visibility" (p. 236). This visibility involves face recognition and name recall. The second criterion was that the individual had been written about in the public press, which contributed to his or her garnering attention.

criterion:

garnering:

We selected celebrities from a spectrum of categories that reflect American culture: government, law, business, publishing, sports, music, film, television news and entertainment (including morning, daytime, primetime, and late night television personalities). The pool of participants included national and local celebrities. Age and gender were not factors in our selection process. Participants included a TV star, a TV news personality, a state governor, a Hollywood actor, a local TV sportscaster, NHL hockey and NBA basketball athletes, a famous CEO, a celebrity lawyer, a former Rhythm & Blues superstar, and a former child star. Face-to-face interviews lasted from 1 to 1½ hours. Two of the 15 interviews were conducted by telephone due to geographic considerations. A letter of intent was mailed to potential participants, explaining the nature, questions, and aims of the research. A participation-release agreement was signed.

spectrum:

Participants' names and identifying information were changed in order to maintain confidentiality.

Five core questions were used to guide the open-ended inter- 5
views: 1) When considering celebrity and your being-in-the-world, what is the experience of being famous? 2) What is your first memory of being famous? 3) Have you lost or gained anything as a result of being famous? 4) What was your life like before and then after you became famous? 5) Do you have anything else you would like to add?

Findings
Fame as Four-Phase Temporal Design

It is important to look at the way fame is experienced by the celebrity over time. Fame was generally experienced as a progression through four phases: a period of *love/hate* towards the experience; an *addiction* phase where behavior is directed solely towards the goal of remaining famous; an *acceptance* phase, requiring a permanent change in everyday life routines; and finally an *adaptation* phase, where new behaviors are developed in response to life changes involved in being famous. Participants described this temporal aspect as unfolding from the first moment of being famous throughout the rest of the lifespan.

Love/Hate. Relationship-to-world themes are revealed as participants seek effective ways of acclimating to being a famous person. At first, the experience of becoming famous provides much ego stroking. Newly famous people find themselves warmly embraced. There is a guilty pleasure associated with the thrill of being admired in that participants both love the attention and adoration while they question the gratification they experience from fame. "I enjoy parts of it, but I hate parts of it, too," was a generally reported theme.

Addiction. The lure of adoration is attractive, and it becomes difficult for the person to imagine living without fame. One participant said, "It is somewhat of a high," and another, "I kind of get off on it." One said, "I've been addicted to almost every substance known to man at one point or another, and the most addicting of them all is *fame*." Where does the celebrity go when fame passes; having become dependent on fame, how does one adjust to being less famous over time? "As the sun sets on my fame," one celebrity said, "I'm going to have to learn how to put it in its proper place." The adjustment can be a difficult one.

Acceptance. As the attention becomes overwhelming and expectations, temptations, mistrust, and familial concerns come to

temporal:

acclimating:

gratification:

familial:

the fore, the celebrity resolves to accept fame, including its threatening <u>phenomenal</u> aspects. "You learn to accept it," one celebrity said. After a while, celebrities report that they come to see that fame is "just so much the will-o'-the-wisp, and you just can't build a house on that kind of stuff."

phenomenal:

Adaptation. Only after accepting that "it comes with the terri-   10 tory" can the celebrity adaptively navigate fame's choppy waters. "Once you're famous," a participant said, "you don't make eye contact or you keep walking . . . and you just don't hear [people calling your name]." Adaptive patterns can include <u>reclusiveness</u>, which gives rise in turn to mistrust and isolation. "I don't want to go out if I don't feel good about looking forward to meeting anybody or just being nice to people," another celebrity reported.

reclusiveness:

The Experience of Being Famous: A Composite Textual Description

The experience of being famous is something for which no one is prepared. It is a world described as bizarre, <u>surreal</u>, scary, lonely, creepy, <u>daunting</u>, embarrassing, confusing, and <u>invasive</u>. The celebrity life is also described as providing flattery, warmth, ego gratification, adoration, unlimited access, enormous wealth, and membership in an exclusive club in which one is surrounded by other famous people.

surreal:
daunting:

invasive:

Loss of Privacy and Entitization. Many celebrities reported finding themselves ill-equipped for and struggling with the deluge of attention that comes with fame.

Fame 101 is needed to teach people what's coming: the <u>swell</u> of people, the requests, the letters, the e-mails, the greetings on the street, the people in cars, the honking of the horns, the screaming of your name. A whole world comes to you that you have no idea is there. It just comes from nowhere. And it starts to build and build like a small tornado, and it's coming at you, and coming at you, and by the time it gets to you, it's huge and can sweep you off your feet and take you away and put you in a world that has no reality whatsoever because all the people are judging you on what you do for a living, not for who you are.

swell:

The individual is left to find his or her way through an unfamiliar <u>labyrinth</u>-like world. From an initial desire to become successful, the celebrity experiences personal confusion and a loss of ownership of life in a depersonalizing "entitization" process, in which participants reported feeling like a thing rather than a person of unique character. Immediately upon entering the <u>sphere</u> of fame, relationships

labyrinth:

sphere:

with "self" and "other" are profoundly affected. The public wants a piece of them, to touch them, to get an autograph, to have their picture taken with the star. All the while hearing one's name screamed out, the famous person feels as if he or she is not even there. Participants find themselves at a loss when members of the public can "hardly contain themselves" at the sight of them and "make you larger than life." It *is* lonely at the top for persons who find themselves alone and isolated on an island of recognition, where "there's a loneliness that happens because you are separate."

For the former child star at the age of ten, the experience of going from a "neighborhood kid" to a famous TV personality over-night was life-altering. Cast on a hit TV series, he recalls the reaction after the show's debut. "When I went outside the next day, my life was different . . . And the first thing that I knew, 'Holy Toledo, I'm famous!'" The experience of being recognized comes with a person's celebritization. Celebrities become accustomed to looking into a crowd and seeing the adoration "in their eyes." "You know they know who you are." The right to be anonymous is exchanged for all that fame has to offer. The famous person feels exposed, with very few places to experience privacy. There is a tendency to get "peopled out" when approached by those who engage the celebrity "24/7."

There is a feeling that "I can't be left alone," with a lingering fear of tabloid paparazzi around any corner. It can be "a drag," and "a pain in the butt to have to worry about that." Moments of anonymity are relished, moments with family, "with good friends who I knew before I was famous." Privacy becomes a coveted luxury. If the celebrity is not feeling "100%" on a particular day, staying home may be preferable to facing the crowd. If "I'm not feeling all that sociable, I have to put that aside."

This public visibility engenders the celebrity's sense that, "I become a target." When walking down the street, dining at a restaurant, or "sitting alone in a highly public place in America, someone will eventually come up and say, 'Aren't you . . . ?'" The famous person's being-in-the-world is impinged on, in that he or she "can't just go anywhere." The celebrity suffers a loss of personal freedom in relation to the world and develops a heightened capacity to scan his or her environment in a state of alerted attention in order to assess the possibilities of advance or the need to retreat. The experience of being a celebrity compromises the individual's personal space, which was taken for granted before fame hit.

It changes my whole persona and way of being when I am out in public . . . when I am walking into the building, into my office,

15

anonymity:

coveted:

engenders:

impinged:

persona:

people are like, "Oh my God! There's Patty!" I used to want to turn and wave and say "hi" to people, but now sometimes it gets too much, and intrusive.

I've had guys coming up to me while I was using the restroom, standing there wanting to shake my hand. "Could you wait a minute? Could you please wait?" Just the crudeness. Completely impolite.

Mistrust. Eventually, the very others who adore the celebrity evoke mistrust. "There is always a part of you that wonders why they are becoming friendly with you." In an everyday environment, the celebrity wonders, "Do people like me because of who I am or because of what I do? You find out there are millions of people who like you for what you do. They couldn't care less who you are." With the development of this operating belief system, the conditions are set for grave mistrust and problems in interpersonal relating. "In the process of losing trust, I've lost some of the innocence I've had about life, about the world and about people . . ." The famous person seeks to discern the *true* intentions of others. "I just think with time and a trained eye, for the most part, I've learned about certain parasites who want to take advantage of me for whatever reason, whether it's money or simply the association of hanging out with somebody who's . . . famous." The difficulties of such discernment may leave the celebrity feeling confused and alienated. He or she may then seek refuge in physical and/or emotional isolation by becoming more detached.

That trust thing is important. I don't think you trust anybody the same way when you become well-known, because you don't trust being well-known. It is an intrinsically untrustworthy dance partner—it could leave you at any time . . . so it's a very mysterious thing. Anyone who comes through that dance partner to you is also mysterious. Why? Why do they want me? Why are they interested in me? Are they laughing at my jokes because they think I am funny or because it is me saying them? And you start double guessing yourself. I find I put up a kind of a wall around me, and I just deal with people up to that wall but not inside of it.

Demanding Expectations. The celebrity must renegotiate his or her relationship-to-world in order to carve out a new operative awareness and set of strategies for living in the spotlight's penetrating glare. The celebrity copes with intense public scrutiny through character-splitting. He or she divides into two identities by contriving a celebrity entity, a new self-presentation in the "public sphere." This

evoke:

grave:

interpersonal:

discern:

intrinsically:

scrutiny:

contriving:

entity:

abeyance:

sequestered:

confidants:

paradoxically:

"individuating construction of the public personality" (Marshall, 1997, pp. 70–71) allows the famous person to hold his or her more personal "true self" in abeyance, sequestered from all but a trusted inner circle of confidants. "The only way I think you can really handle it is to say, 'That's not really me . . . it's this working part of me, or the celebrity part of me.'. . . So, I am a toy in a shop window."

Participants report that being a famous person "is a full time job." Living up to others' expectations becomes a vicious cycle, in which the celebrity, like a hamster on a wheel, works to satisfy a hungry and demanding public. The famous person feels the need to always "be on." "There's no going out in sweats and sunglasses and a baseball cap and expecting I'll get out and not have to see anybody or say anything, 'cause that usually doesn't happen anymore." There is an obligation to be "nice to everyone, and that becomes exhausting." Famous people worry, while playing the celebrity role, "I'm probably going to disappoint them," so celebrities have "two different dialogues—the one that I'm thinking and the one I'm saying," so one is "not necessarily as authentic as I'd like to be." There is not enough time to "show my true self."

The celebrity experiences being put on a pedestal, "and there are people who love to knock us off the pedestal." Paradoxically, along with all the adulation—gratuitous and genuine, no matter what the celebrity does, someone, somewhere, will be disappointed. In order to create a balanced life, famous persons struggle to maintain their *own* perspective.

> [Fame makes you] extremely vulnerable. And you can really take it to heart and get your feelings tremendously hurt. I stopped reading e-mail very quickly because I couldn't take some of the negative stuff. I wanted to write and say, "You don't know who I am. Why are you doing this?" And it was all about who they thought I was . . . You have to be very thick-skinned.

Gratification and Loss. Celebrities, as they take in the adoration, 20 say that they are "aware of how dangerous it can be" to witness themselves "through the eyes of many watchers." "I mean, the more famous you get in Hollywood, the more close you get to Caligula or Nero."

> You try to put [fame] in its place because otherwise it will swallow up everything else. It will be totally out of control. It could destroy everything you have or it could make you into a monster. We've all heard, and I've seen, people who believe that they are better or bigger or more important than the person next to them . . . There

are famous people who believe: "Do you know who I am? You are treating me this way, and do you know who I am?"

While public admiration is an apparent validation of personal worth, it can evoke self-consciousness and engender a self-serving way of life. "A lot now I am focused on the other peoples' reaction, rather than my reaction to the world . . . I think a lot of my attention is focused on myself." "This whole fame stuff is <u>fraught</u> with problems and pitfalls and I can easily lose perspective on myself, and that's very scary. You can buy into it and think, 'I really am the best thing since sliced bread . . .'" One celebrity describes the tight wire act of balancing <u>narcissistic</u> gratification with interest in and <u>empathy for</u> others.

fraught:

narcissistic:

empathy:

> My life is different in that people kiss my ass, and that's not always a good thing because then you start believing that your ass is worthy of being kissed. You have to constantly stay on guard for that. And I think it's very hard. There are times when I exploit that. I take advantage of people sucking up to me, or the power that I wield.

In a world where the celebrity is hardly ever told "no," a predominantly self-centered orientation can occur. This kind of self-absorbed posture is underwritten by positive feedback from the world. The new relational patterns of fame have the potential to unsteady even the most grounded individuals. Isolation and false entitlement make it easier for the celebrity to start rationalizing choices he or she makes. After all, fame changes the way the world responds to the celebrity, who is no longer hearing intimately related others' honest appraisals "because whether you want to be or not—and there are those who very much want to be, you are larger than life." Flying high on the rush of celebrity, some participants reported that, blinded by fame's sudden flash, they lost sight of "the truly important things."

> I began to forget my family, I began to forget my children, I began to forget my wife. I knew it was me, and it was just bad and I didn't care, and however I needed to comfort myself I was going to comfort myself. I was going to get there and I was going to get it done: the fame, the work, the TV station.
>
> The biggest problem was that I had forgotten those who were the closest to me. So I had to bring them back into the fold, reattach, and have a better understanding of what they went through. And then I had to build myself up again, but, in conjunction with all of them, not in spite of all of them. For me it was a harsh lesson and a tough lesson.

Symbolic Immortality. Those participants who fare best in the world of celebrity assume their position as an opportunity to "give back," "inspire," "role model," or "make a difference" in the lives of others. "You've got to realize that you're just wearing the suit, that someone else wore it before you, that someone will wear it behind you, and that it's only a suit." "If you really think about fame, it should be less about what you get as opposed to what you give."

> Whether you've earned it or not earned it, I think that you have an obligation to use it wisely, to give back, to not have it be just one more situation of take, take, take, take, take, which I think a lot of famous people do. But there are just as many who use it for good and see it as a way to make a difference. So it's weird. [Fame] can fuck you up or it can elevate you, or a little bit of both, depending on your own perspective. And I think you constantly have to reassess who you are, take [the fame] off of you and make sure that you are centered as a person.

This orientation of "giving back," making a lasting mark on humanity, can entail a symbolic meaning of immortality. Most research participants pointed to such in, for instance, the roles they played and in the creative expressions of their professional work, as noted by Loy— "symbolic immortality through reputation" (2002, p. 220). This symbolic sense of self as larger than life was emphasized over and above their interpersonal roles as mother, father, husband, wife, daughter or son. As such ordinary family-oriented roles went unmentioned, the celebrity-self was described as a <u>luminous</u> figure against the ground of "everyman." One way that famous people see themselves making a lasting mark after "the mortal shell is <u>husked</u>" is by effecting change in the world that continues after their death. Although aspiring to immortality appears to rob death anxiety of some of its power, it is experienced as relatively difficult and <u>tenuous</u>.

> Fame while you're alive will probably get you good seats at restaurants. But the only possible way to make your life significantly meaningful is—there are two ways: to positively affect the people around you with love and caring, and to effectuate some change that lives on after you, which is very difficult. Very few people do that.
>
> . . . Fame is . . . one of the mechanisms by which you can obtain immortality, not by virtue of the fame, but by virtue of the achievement.

Wealth. Wealth, as a by-product of fame, provides immediate, <u>tangible</u> evidence of celebrity's distinction and staying power. Fame's

luminous:

husked:

tenuous:

tangible:

windfall goes a long way in lifting financial burdens, opening the celebrity to experiences that are special. Money is no longer a "worry," and provides "the glory side, the financial side of being famous." Some celebrities go from "not being able to afford a home," to multi-million dollar contracts. "They are our royalty." Famous people model conspicuous consumption for an attentive public. "I've gained so many material things. I could look around and start naming stuff, 'Ooh. A video camera, a bunch of cars,' but they all fall under the umbrella of money." "Having that extra money enabled me to dabble in real estate. So it enabled me to pursue other business ventures. That's exciting to me." Money may also buy the privacy famous people need, as some celebrities reported choosing to rent houses rather than stay at hotels and secure their homes with iron gates.

Access. Although famous people try to keep the public out of their personal domain, they are invited freely and openly into an exclusive social world of celebrity. "The fabulous people," as a New York doorman recently referred to celebrities, are ushered into rarefied air where Dustin Hoffman is on the phone, George Steinbrenner is taking the call, or Warren Beatty is free for dinner. Fame is a private club, and famous people are automatic members. "The access is unbelievable." "Suddenly, you're worth something. You're important." In the world of ordinary people, it becomes commonplace for famous people to receive preferential treatment from almost everyone with whom they interact.

> When I get stopped by the police, if I am going too fast, I roll the window down. I give them my license. They say, "Oh. Could you give me an autograph for my son?" I say, "Absolutely," sign the autograph, they just say, "Be careful," and I go on my way.

"You can drop the name and get the table at the restaurant. You can get seats at the sporting event." One research participant noted that, "when you reach a stage financially when you don't need freebies, that's when freebies are thrown to you." Famous people grow accustomed to the privileged world of celebrity.

Temptations. The lure of life's temptations may be the most secret side of celebrity experience, introduced by only a few participants as an unexpected side benefit and also a danger in the world of fame. "We live faster . . . The involvement with different things . . . I know it has to do with fame." Being famous opens up a larger than life world for the larger than life celebrity. Tempting opportunities materialize in the wake left by fame.

windfall:

conspicuous:

dabble:

domain:

rarefied:

fortitude:

conjured:

grist:

baffled:

I live in Hollywood and I'm a middle-aged man, and Miss September keeps throwing herself at me. That wouldn't happen if I wasn't famous. Believe me . . . The average guy turning down Miss September is a tough day. That would show intestinal <u>fortitude</u> that I don't know that I have. I've been to that Playboy Mansion . . . You'd have to be a fairly strong man to not let that kind of thing interfere with your life . . . you could let it abuse your family.

A star athlete describes the off-court world:

I've seen too many guys outside of fame willing to sacrifice and do anything to be a part of it. I've seen too many girls disrespect themselves to be a part of it. I've seen too many celebrities completely abuse it, use it, and abuse anybody in their path.

Concerns about Family Impact. The situations <u>conjured</u> by   25
<u>celebrity life become grist</u> for additional concerns about how fame affects the celebrity's family. Can the celebrity protect his or her spouse and children from the darker side of the celebrity experience? For example, anti-abortion demonstrators make the governor "want to move everybody to the back of the house . . . I want to shield my child's eyes from some of the horrible and violent imagery that is presented." Several research participants bemoaned the fate, beyond their control, of family members living in the shadow of fame. One research participant tearfully gazed out a Manhattan window, concerned with the legacy of his fame on his 15-year-old son.

I worry about my son, because I don't want him to think of me, because I'm famous, as being any more special than he is. And I wonder sometimes if he's going to confuse fame with worthiness or value as a person, that if he doesn't grow up to be someone who has celebrity or fame, he is somehow not recognized or not worthy of people's respect or admiration. I think a lot of people confuse it. In our whole culture, people confuse it. To be rich and famous—the two words go together. There are a lot of challenges; the family dynamic is complicated by fame.

Celebrity families often cannot go out together in public and enjoy uninterrupted time without strangers entering the family circle. The famous person's child, <u>baffled</u> by the celebrity social world, may begin to feel anger, guilt, and resentment.

I think he . . . doesn't like sharing me in public and feeling like other people know me and can come up and talk to me. I think he kind of wanted me for himself and for Mommy. You're ours. You're not the public's.

Whether it is a fan's friendly slap on the child's back, a question asking a son if he is planning on following in his father's footsteps, or a daughter's concern that she will never equal her mother's achievements, fame's impact on children worries celebrity parents. However, there is only so much that parents can do to protect their children from these inevitabilities.

> This is what happens when I go out: I am scanning, I'm looking, I'm trying to evaluate what kind of place this is, what's going on. I am trying to laugh and talk with my daughter and my son, but I am looking the whole time, too. Because too many times I have gone out and it has become something that it shouldn't for my kids and my wife, the intrusion upon them.
>
> I think that can eat children up . . . I try to keep the family separate [from fame] as much as I can. I want to share it and keep it separate. Sometimes those lines are unfair.

The experience of being famous comes with wealth, unlimited access, and gratifying opportunities to contribute something lasting to the world. Learning to contend with being "entitized," a loss of privacy, unrealistic expectations, temptations, mistrust toward others, a falsely inflated self, and impact on the celebrity's family delineates the great challenges in the experience of being famous. The celebrity encounters a world forever changed and must navigate a new course through the unforeseen realities of a famous life.

The Experience of Being Famous

Richard: Stage and Screen Star

Spatiality: Isolation. Richard, an A-list actor, remembers the moment he knew he was famous. He was in an off-Broadway show, playing the gay lover of the lead character. The play was in the sixth month of its run when a group of gay men started waiting at the stage door. One night, as he left the theater, Richard asked them, "Did you see the show?" "For the sixth time!" one excitedly shouted back. "Terrific," Richard laughed to himself. These were his first fans. When it strikes, the effect of becoming famous is immediate and <u>pervasive</u>:

pervasive:

> The first thing that happens is that everything and everybody around you changes . . . And you can feel it filter down to whatever your inner circle of friends is . . . For someone like me who doesn't want to be larger than life, who just was given this gift, who can do this thing that I do called acting—I've chased it up the ladder of levels, and now I'm at the highest level. But in doing that comes this adoration you can see in [everyone's] eyes.

Ultimate stardom came after the huge success of a $120 million motion picture in which Richard starred. His celebrity reached global proportions, making him recognized almost everywhere. "No matter where I go, certainly in the States and maybe most of Europe, they know my name." Celebrity alters a person's way of life, affecting the interpersonal space in which the famous person lives, works, and plays. The celebrity starts to lose the important boundary of personal privacy.

> You are an animal in a cage. If you're sitting at a sporting event in a seat and you're on the aisle . . . all of a sudden you have someone on your left arm kneeling in the aisle. [He or she asks,] "What's [another actor] like?" And you want to push them down the stairs. There are many people who know what's appropriate and what isn't, but there are some that want their piece of you.

Richard's way of coping with this invasion is through behavioral adaptations in which he shuts out others and retreats as much as possible from public spaces. This choice shrinks his world and his ability to move freely. "You can't just go anywhere . . . You walk into [a place], and somebody slapped a sign on your back [that says], 'I'm famous.' That's what it's like."

glaring: The constant recognition from a glaring public can become tiring. In the hope of avoiding interaction, Richard adjusts by acting like "a busy guy on his way somewhere."

> One of the first things you learn once you're famous is that you don't make eye contact and you keep walking. Whether you're down a street or down a hallway, you can feel the heads [turn] . . . so you just don't make eye contact. You steal from [President] Reagan. You suddenly become deaf. You isolate yourself. The more obvious [fans yell things like]: "Oh my God! Who's that?" when you're just three feet away. Those are the ones you literally go, "Fuck! Okay, keep going. Just keep going."

When in public, he feels like a sitting duck. Constant recognition becomes a barrier to being able to enjoy the normal events in everyday life.

> The goal of [acting career success] reached also includes the guy that's going to lean across you at a [hockey] game, drunk, with your 8-year-old boy there, and say, "I hate the fuckin' [hockey team]" into your kid's face, because he wants you—and this is where you get smart—he wants you to shove him or push him so that he can fall down the stairs and call his lawyer. . . . I can't go into bars, because [someone] will pick a fight with me, and they've got a witness that'll back them up. I can go to court, or I can settle. Did I

have anything to do with the fight? No. But to make it go away, here's $100,000, here's $50,000. I'll go to a game . . . but once I'm recognized . . . it bursts the bubble of the experience of just trying to see the game with your family or friends.

Richard can never escape fame completely. In this inner conflict of wanting fame while longing for anonymity, Richard creates a new, second identity—his "celebrity self." He protects his authentic self by what he calls "putting up the vibe."

It's the look . . . the look I give [the public] that says, "Not now." And I get in trouble with [my wife] a little bit sometimes, but I don't care. . . . You try to do the best you can, being nice to people when they approach you, but sometimes it's, "No! Not right now," and the wall goes up.

Temporality: Fame, a Life Changing Moment. Fame is Hollywood's currency, where people make "firestorms around themselves that translate into power and money and importance and fame." This shifts the balance of power in all the celebrity's interactions, personal as well as professional, and over time fame fundamentally changes the celebrity's relationships with friends, family, and business associates. The experience of living life as "the star," separates one from the norm, and begins to weigh on these relationship bonds. This difference from others <u>insinuates</u> emotional distance and   **insinuates:** contributes to isolation. Fame becomes "baggage." When he is socializing with friends, Richard's celebrity lies between them, "like a bloated cod, just sitting there." Fame chases old friends away at the same time that strangers are flocking toward him.

Over the years, fame itself informs all the celebrity's encounters;   30 being "a celebrity" comes to define much of the person's identity, sometimes more significant than the particular talent, artistry or craft for which he or she became famous. Richard's larger-than-life persona interferes with the development of desirable relationships.

Some friends can handle [my fame], and I've lost friends because of it . . . just by all this adoration that comes whenever you're in public, they feel less. They feel inferior . . . You're special and they aren't. You're extraordinary and they're ordinary. All of a sudden, they aren't calling you back and they aren't around. And the next thing you know, they'd really rather not have anything to do with you. And you understand them. You have to.

There is a tendency for famous people to see themselves as celebrities first and authentic selves second. The person adapts to fame by crafting, servicing, and protecting the celebrity self. Every move must

duality:

be considered. A duality between the celebrity's public persona and private self is experienced as a necessary adaptation. While welcoming its monetary riches, Richard rejects fame's more negative trappings. His trust diminishes, his private space shrinks, character-splitting increases, and resentment of personal losses intensifies.

sackcloth:

Once a person has transitioned into fame, as in death, there is no turning back. Celebrity becomes sackcloth that is never shed, a suit of clothing worn at all times. Richard tolerates the glare of fame by returning to his comfort zone, his acting. Work is a refuge where his

recedes:

celebrity status recedes, and he regains a sense of agency in his life. "The only thing I can control is what happens between action and cut. That's what I've been taught. That's the school I went to, the school of acting. I didn't go to star school."

Relationship to Self and Other: Fame, the Sequel. Fame does not last; it is temporary, ephemeral. Fame is fleeting. Richard knows that

ephemeral:

celebrity is a "flavor of the minute today, not week or month. Look at Bennifer. You look at those guys and you just go, 'The clock's ticking.'" Richard tries not to think of himself as a celebrity in order to protect himself from being entirely consumed by fame. "I'm guilty of trying to lead an ordinary life and think of myself as ordinary—simple. Not famous."

In order to put fame in its proper place, Richard has decided to use his fame and wealth for "good works" and community-based causes, creating something that will live on beyond him. In the small town where he and his family live, Richard has paid for the building of high school sports stadiums that are "premiere facilities." These fields exist "because I'm famous," he says. He also supports a local music school. "We can . . . leave the place better than we found it . . . It's a great use of the fame. It's like turning a negative into a positive, I guess." Turning the negative of fame into a positive allows Richard to tolerate the loss of privacy and isolation he faces as a result of being a celebrity.

Conclusions

ideation:

Celebrity experience is the object of much public fascination and fantasy ideation. The ideal of becoming rich and famous has become intricately woven into the cultural tapestry of not only the United States, but also most of the Western world. Celebrities come to represent the hopes and dreams of the average citizen. Therefore, the study of the world of fame, its social relevance, and the role it plays in American culture helps define us as a people. From reality TV, to MTV, to movie star governors and celebrity presidents, America is fascinated with fame. According to *American Idol* host, Simon Cowell

(2003), "There is a fame epidemic!" If our culture is in the midst of an epidemic of fame and a quest to celebrity, as Cowell claims, it behooves the psychological establishment to research the actual lived-experience of the celebrity to assess the emotional impact of fame upon an individual. Most reality shows now routinely offer an option of psychological counseling or psychological referrals to their contestants in an attempt to mitigate the mental health risk of becoming a reality TV star.

behooves:

mitigate:

The data collected in this study have given us insight into the experience of fame through the eyes of celebrities themselves. The set of textural themes indicates that although fame is experienced as providing wealth, access to a privileged world, gratification and symbolic immortality, it also robs the celebrity of privacy; leads to isolation; engenders mistrust of others; introduces temptations; can lead to creating a character-split between the "celebrity entity" and the "private self"; and heightens concern about risks to other family members.   35

Perhaps some findings of this study could have the unintended effect of encouraging fame-seekers. All research participants claimed that despite its negative elements, fame is worth it after all and they would not trade it back. The material rewards of fame confirm the celebrity's being-in-the-world such that neither character-splitting, isolation, mistrust, nor fame's impact on family members, led to celebrity regret over becoming famous. At the heart of the fame experience lies an intrinsic affirmation of individual uniqueness and "specialness" that spurs those who seek celebrity status. Participants distinguished the self-affirmative trajectory of fame from the aspiration to make a difference and leave a mark on history that benefits others, goals often cited by famous people like actor Paul Newman and rock star Bono, who have used their celebrity for philanthropic or altruistic ends. However, inasmuch as fame itself makes possible such impressive altruism, self-expansion and serving others are ambiguously intertwined in the consequent symbolic immortality.

spurs:

trajectory:

aspiration:

philanthropic:

altruistic:

References

Cowell, S. (2003, January 22). *The Conan O'Brien Show* [Television broadcast]. National Broadcasting Company.

Loy, D. R., in Liechty, D. (2002). *Death and denial. Interdisciplinary perspectives of the legacy of Ernest Becker.* Westport, CT: Praeger.

Marshall, P. D. (1997). *Celebrity and power: Fame in contemporary culture.* Minneapolis, MN: University of Minnesota.

Mitchell, G., & Cronson, H. (1987). The celebrity family: A clinical perspective. *American Journal of Family Therapy, 15,* 235–241.

Waters, J. (2004, February 25). *Fresh Air from WHYY: Filmmaker John Waters.* [broadcast on National Public Radio]. Retrieved August 15, 2006, from archived sound file at http://www.npr.org.

practice it 26.7   Post-Reading Activity

To spark your thinking and deepen your participation in class discussion, pick out five to ten quotations from the reading that you really like and copy them out onto a chart like the following one.

Quotation You Find Meaningful (p. no.)	Why Quotation Is Meaningful

It will be helpful to return to these quotes later when you begin to write an essay. For now, reflect on them in writing or share them in class discussion.

COMPREHENSION QUESTIONS

1. What are the main questions Rockwell and Giles are trying to answer in their research?

2. How did Rockwell and Giles conduct their study?

3. What did Rockwell and Giles discover? In other words, what is their thesis? Try to find a specific sentence in the Conclusion section of the paper that might serve as the thesis, and then restate it in your own words.

4. What are the four phases of experiencing celebrity? Name them and describe them in your own words.

5. In paragraphs 6–26, which forms a major part of this article, the authors list and describe some of the characteristics of fame. List each of these characteristics, and give a brief, one-sentence summary of it.

6. The authors provide a detailed case study of the actor Richard. What is Richard's experience of fame?

DISCUSSION QUESTIONS

1. Richard describes the feeling of celebrity as being "an animal in a cage" (para. 27). Having read the article, what other metaphors might you use to describe the experience of being a celebrity?

2. The article describes how famous people get preferential treatment. Have you seen other local "stars" (like high school athletes or cheerleaders) getting similar types of preferential treatment?

3. In their conclusion, the authors write that all the celebrities they studied "claimed that despite its negative elements, fame is worth it after all and they would not trade it back" (para. 36). Why might this be? Given what you have learned about the process of adapting to fame, do you think that the celebrities are thinking clearly and rationally when they make this claim? Why or why not?

4. Given the clear downsides to celebrity that Rockwell and Giles document, would you want to be a celebrity? Why or why not?

BOOK   model reading strategy: Mapping

Jake Halpern is a prolific writer whose works span several genres: magazine journalism, radio, fiction, and book-length nonfiction. Educated at Yale University, Halpern dropped the suit-and-tie cubicle life as a young man to pursue writing. This selection is excerpted from his book *Fame Junkies: The Hidden Truths behind America's Favorite Addiction* (2007), which launched an original radio series on National Public Radio. This chapter posits a difference between "old fame," which was based on accomplishments and talents, and "new fame," which is based on self-promotion and self-branding and not necessarily on accomplishments, outside of sports and acting or modeling.

▶ For about mapping, see pages 135–36 in Chapter 5, Active Reading Strategies.

To help you understand the structure of this reading, we have modeled a mapping strategy that divides the article into chunks based on the main ideas. Before you read, scan the map of the reading, as indicated by the colored brackets in the margins. Note the ideas covered and how many paragraphs are spent on each. Then, after you have finished reading the text, examine the mapping in more detail to help you understand the text's structure. As you read, look up the words you do not know and write their definitions in your own words in the margins.

practice it 26.8 Pre-Reading Activity

Make a list of ten to fifteen famous people and then group them into two categories: those born before 1950 and those born after 1950. If you don't have any born before 1950, brainstorm a few more people. What do you notice about the two groups? What types of things are the pre-1950 people famous for doing? What types of things are the post-1950 people famous for? Reflect on the list you have generated. What does your list tell us about contemporary fame?

Jake Halpern

THE DESIRE TO BELONG: WHY EVERYONE WANTS TO HAVE DINNER WITH PARIS HILTON AND 50 CENT

I got a chance to talk on the phone with one of my longtime heroes, "the Edge," who is the lead guitarist for the band U2. His ambivalence about

Introduction: The Edge anecdote

Introduction: The
Edge anecdote
continued

celebrity struck me immediately. "After our *Joshua Tree* album, we were as famous as you could be in music," he said, "and frankly, it was kind of overpowering for a while, but it really wasn't that interesting. If anything, it was something we tried to downplay. I don't think we ever *really* wanted celebrity, in and of itself, because we came out of the whole punk-rock thing, which was all about tearing that system down."

More than anything else, he said, fame was a kind of psychological torment for the band, especially in the beginning. "Early on, we were kind of overwhelmed by it," he explained. "At the big U2 concerts we were really just hanging on to make it through. There was an element of desperation in which we were just trying to focus on our music. And if we got seduced by fame, I think our version of that was being too self-conscious, taking ourselves a little too seriously, and wondering, *Did we measure up? Were we a good enough band? Were we really able to do this?*" According to the Edge, fame's effect on the band was the opposite of a high—it induced a kind of low in which they constantly questioned themselves. Apparently, it had taken them years to outgrow this.

"I think now we are a little older, and we don't beat ourselves up quite so much," he said. "We feel extremely fortunate to have such great fans and to have written some great songs. Now, without being complacent, we're really enjoying what we're doing in a way that we probably wouldn't have earlier on, when there was an element of struggle, and nothing was ever good enough. We were always trying to reach beyond our abilities. We still do that now, but we also accept that we have certain limitations. It just gets to a point where you go, 'This is me. I am not everything I would like to be as an artist, but that doesn't mean I don't have anything worth saying.'"

We chatted about celebrity and the emptiness of fame for almost an hour. The irony of this whole episode was that as soon as our conversation was over, I felt compelled to call a number of my friends and tell them I had just talked with the Edge. I was especially excited because he had offered me two tickets and backstage passes for U2's concert in Boston the following evening. For the next thirty-six hours I actually walked around under the blissful delusion that he and I were on the verge of becoming pals. On some level I realized that I was falling into the very trap I was meant to be objectively observing, but it made no difference. In my heart I admit that I felt thrilled, privileged, and special.

The following evening, before the concert started, I made my way 5 backstage. It was a mob scene. The small concrete room was crawling with people—doctors, business executives, schoolteachers, fashion models, and more than a few squealing children, all of whom had a connection to someone in the band. Needless to say, I never got even close to the Edge. I felt completely deflated. I also worried about what I would say to the friends I'd told about my budding rapport with him.

Eventually I shook off my <u>malaise</u>, and enjoyed one of the best concerts I've ever attended. Still, somewhere deep down, well beyond the reach of rational thought, lurked a hunger that left me feeling supremely uncomfortable.

Why was I so desperate to talk to the Edge that night? For that matter, why did people in general <u>pine</u> to bond with and befriend celebrities? The answer may be found in something called Belongingness Theory. Some research psychologists have come to believe that the need to belong is every bit as urgent as the need for food and shelter. Supporters of this theory contend that the desire to belong is actually humankind's driving psychological force. As they see it, Freudian theories about sexuality are compelling, but not nearly as important as the <u>primal</u> yearning for social acceptance.

Belongingness Theory is rooted in evolution. It holds that humans who formed groups in ancient times increased their chances of survival and reproduction. When it came to hunting large animals or defending the campfire against <u>marauders</u>, groups fared better. Anthropologists point out that groups were <u>resilient</u> in a way that individuals weren't, because their members could spread out and offer a number of services, such as hunting, firewood gathering, and even healing. Groups are especially important for children. Those who stayed close to the group probably received more food, care, and protection. Perhaps most important, at least in terms of evolution, adults in groups were more likely to find mates, reproduce, and form long-term parental relationships, increasing the chances that their children would reach maturity and reproduce themselves.

Belongingness Theory posits that over time, evolution has created a sort of internal mechanism that makes us crave social acceptance. This mechanism prompts us to feel stressed when we are isolated and pleased when we interact with others. Some psychologists, including Jaak Panksepp, of the Medical College of Ohio at Toledo, claim that the formation of social relationships actually stimulates the production of opioids—chemicals in the brain that make us feel pleasure. Panksepp goes so far as to say that "social affect and social bonding are in some fundamental neurochemical sense opioid addictions." In other words, what started as a basic survival mechanism has evolved into an addiction to natural chemicals that our bodies release whenever we socialize.

This has direct implications for how we react to famous actors and even to the fictional characters they portray on television and in the movies. I've always been a fan of the TV show *Cheers*. In fact, not far from where I live in Boston, there is a sign for the bar Cheers, and I'm frequently tempted to stop in and have a beer at the place where Norm, Cliff, Carla, and Sam hung out—only it's not the place where

Belongingness Theory

they hung out, because *that place* never really even existed except on
some Hollywood back lot.

Evidently, I've formed what research psychologists call a "para- 10
social" relationship with the characters on the show. The notion of
such a relationship was first discussed by two psychologists, Donald
Horton and R. Richard Wohl, in a 1956 article for the journal *Psychiatry*.
They argued that television gives viewers "the illusion of a face-to-face
relationship with the performer." Over the course of many episodes,
viewers come to feel that they know a given performer or a fictional
persona. Horton and Wohl write:

> The persona offers, above all, a continuing relationship. His appear-
> ance is a regular and dependable event, to be counted on, planned
> for, and integrated into the routines of daily life. His devotees "live
> with him" and share the small episodes of his public life—and to
> some extent even of his private life away from the show. Indeed,
> their continued association with him acquires a history. . . . In time,
> the devotee—the "fan"—comes to believe that he "knows" the per-
> sona more intimately and profoundly than others do.

Para-social relationships

There are numerous examples of this phenomenon. Soap-opera
viewers send flowers and condolence cards to TV studios when a favorite
character is injured or killed in a tragic episode. Hordes of "Trekkies"
obsess over Captain Kirk, Mr. Spock, and the other fictional personae
on *Star Trek*. Perhaps the most extreme example involves Robert Young,
the actor who starred in the series *Marcus Welby, MD*. In the early 1970s,
during his first five years on the show, he received some 250,000 letters
from viewers, most of them asking for medical advice.

One important thing that has changed since the 1950s, when Horton and Wohl introduced their theory, is that we (the public) can now
know as much about the personal lives of our favorite stars as we do
about the fictional lives they portray on TV and in the movies. In the
early 2000s, for example, fans could follow the romantic entangle-
ments of Rachel Green on the TV show *Friends*, and they could also
then watch *Access Hollywood*, or pick up a copy of *Us Weekly*, to catch
up on the love life of Jennifer Aniston, who played Rachel. According
to Robert Thompson, of Syracuse University, the upshot of this is it is
now easier than ever to form para-social relationships—-not just with
fictional personae but with actual celebrities as well. It all comes down
to access, Thompson says, and the venues that offer glimpses into the
lives of celebrities—magazines, books, Web sites, online chat rooms,
radio and TV talk shows—seem endless.

"Just look at the rise in TV talk shows," Thompson says. "In the six-
ties you had just a few TV talk-show hosts, like Johnny Carson and Dick
Cavett, who interviewed celebrities, whereas nowadays—especially

with cable and satellite channels—you've got dozens of these hosts interviewing every last celebrity. You've got Oprah Winfrey, David Letterman, Jay Leno, Carson Daly, Conan O'Brien, Ellen DeGeneres, Jon Stewart, Martha Stewart, Jenny Jones, Jimmy Kimmel, Montel Williams, Maury Povich, Jerry Springer, Ricki Lake, Rosie O'Donnell, Sally Jessy Raphael, Tony Danza, Tyra Banks—and the list goes on." All these hosts offer us a chance to meet celebrities "being themselves," he says.

Another major change since the 1950s is that Americans now appear to be lonelier than ever. In his book *The Loss of Happiness in Market Democracies*, the Yale political scientist Robert Lane notes that the number of people who described themselves as lonely more than quadrupled in the past few decades. We have increasingly become a nation of loners—traveling salesmen, Web designers, phone-bank operators, and online day traders who live and work in isolation. According to the U.S. Census Bureau, we also marry later in life. In 1956 the median age for marriage was 22.5 for men and 20.1 for women; by 2004 it was 27.4 for men and 25.8 for women. This helps to explain something else the Census Bureau has noted: Americans are increasingly living alone. The share of American households including seven or more people dropped from 35.9 percent in 1790, 5.8 percent in 1950, and 1.2 percent in 2004. Meanwhile, the number of households consisting of just one person rose from 3.7 percent in 1790 to 9.3 percent in 1950 and 26.4 percent in 2004. Nowadays, one out of four American households consists of a single person. In recent years this trend has been especially discernible among young people. Since 1970 the number of youths (ages fifteen to twenty-five) living alone has almost tripled, and the number of young adults (ages twenty-five to thirty-four) living alone has more than quadrupled.

> **Loneliness**

The combination of loneliness and our innate desire to belong 15 may be fueling our interest in celebrities and our tendency to form para-social relationships with them. Only a few research psychologists have seriously explored this possibility, among them Lynn McCutcheon and Dianne Ashe. McCutcheon and Ashe compared results from 150 subjects who had taken three personality tests—one measuring shyness, one measuring loneliness, and one measuring celebrity obsession, on something called the Celebrity Attitudes Scale, or CAS. The CAS asks subjects to rate the veracity of statements such as "I am obsessed by details of my favorite celebrity's life" and "If I were lucky enough to meet my favorite celebrity, and he/she asked me to do something illegal as a favor, I would probably do it." McCutcheon and Ashe found a correlation among scores on loneliness, shyness, and the CAS. Their results led McCutcheon to observe in a subsequent paper, "Perhaps one of the ways [we] cope

> **Studies about para-social relationships with celebrities**

Studies about
para-social
relationships
with celebrities
continued

with shyness and loneliness is to cultivate a 'safe,' non-threatening relationship with a celebrity."

Another investigation, led by Jacki Fitzpatrick, of Texas Tech University, looked at the correlation between para-social relationships and actual romantic relationships. Fitzpatrick asked forty-five college students to complete a questionnaire containing several psychological measures, including one that gauged para-social relationships (the Para-social Interaction Scale) and another that gauged romantic relationships (the Multiple Determinants of Relationship Commitment Inventory). She and her colleague, Andrea McCourt, discovered that subjects who were less invested in their romantic relationships were more involved in para-social relationships. They concluded, "It makes sense that individuals may use para-social relationships as one way to fulfill desires or address needs (e.g., for attention, companionship) that are unmet in their romances."

The Rochester survey, too, provides evidence that lonely teenagers are especially susceptible to forming para-social relationships with celebrities. Boys who described themselves as lonely were almost twice as likely as others to endorse the statement "My favorite celebrity just helps me feel good and forget about all of my troubles." Girls who described themselves as lonely were almost three times as likely as others to endorse that statement.

Another survey question asked teens whom they would most like to meet for dinner: Jesus Christ, Albert Einstein, Shaquille O'Neal, Jennifer Lopez, 50 Cent, Paris Hilton, or President Bush. Among boys who said they were not lonely, the clear winner was Jesus Christ; but among those who described themselves as lonely, Jesus finished last and 50 Cent was the clear winner. Similarly, girls who felt appreciated by their parents, friends, and teachers tended to choose dinner with Jesus, whereas those who felt underappreciated were likely to choose Paris Hilton. One possible interpretation of these results is that lonely and underappreciated teens particularly want to befriend the ultimate popular guy or girl.

For the older generation, that guy was Steve McQueen; nowadays he appears to be 50 Cent. Regardless of who exactly this figure is at a given time, it's clear that many of us—lonely people in particular—yearn to belong to the popular crowd.

I also got to know a Hollywood publicist named Michael Levine. I'd 20 first seen Levine on television as Michael Jackson's publicist during Jackson's first child-molestation scandal, in the early 1990s. He'd been in the business more than twenty years, representing quite a few stars, and had written a number of books on public relations, including *Charming Your Way to the Top: Hollywood's Premier PR Executive Shows*

You How to Get Ahead, and *Raise Your Social I.Q.: How to Do the Right Thing in Any Situation.*

Levine and I met for tea one afternoon at the Century Plaza Hotel in Los Angeles. We found each other in the hotel's soaring, sun-drenched lobby, where a pianist in a tuxedo played soft jazz while a svelte waitress whose nametag read "Queenie" served drinks to tourists laden with Gucci and Versace shopping bags. Levine was a tall, handsome man in his midfifties with watery blue eyes, an aquiline nose, and a shock of gray hair slicked back with gel.

When we shook hands, he greeted me loudly, as if he were greeting everyone in our section of the lobby. I quickly discovered that Levine had two modes of speaking. The first was his broadcast mode, in which he spoke with the volume and authority of a courtroom lawyer. The second was his intimate mode, in which he drew close, made unwavering eye contact, and spoke in a hushed manner as if letting me in on a secret that was far too sensitive for public consumption. His intimate voice was rare, and when he used it, I had the impression I might be speaking with Michael Levine the person.

"Are you familiar with my Tiffany's theory?" he asked as we sat down.

I told him I wasn't.

Levine cleared his throat and explained. "If I visit you today and 25 give you a present, and I give it to you in a Tiffany's box, in your mind the gift that I gave you has a higher perceived value than if I gave it to you in *no* box or a box of lesser prestige. The reason that's true is not because you are a psychological jackass"—he smiled briefly, presumably to convey that no offense was intended—"but because you and I and your wife and this waitress live in a culture in which we gift-wrap everything. We gift-wrap our politicians, our corporate heads, our TV and movie stars, and even our toilet paper."

"So you see yourself as gift-wrapping celebrities?"

"Yes," he replied. "That is the analogy."

When I asked him to clarify one aspect of his theory, he responded by asking which of the ninety-nine words I wanted him to repeat. I said I'd like to hear the entire theory again. Levine nodded, gathered himself for a minute, and then repeated his words verbatim, with the same seemingly nonchalant facial expressions and hand gestures he'd used before. Clearly, this was a man who had perfected the art of speaking in sound bites; I began to worry that he wasn't going to tell me anything he hadn't already composed, edited, and delivered dozens of times before.

Nonetheless, I pressed on, and asked Levine how he had become, as his books claimed, "Hollywood's premier PR executive."

Levine
anecdote

Levine anecdote *continued*

"The arc of anyone's career . . . ," he began, and then paused to ³⁰ reconsider his approach. "Scratch that," he said. "Yours is a multi-dimensional question. Is it luck? Is it timing? Is it skill? I'm not sure, but I have represented some of the most successful people in the world." He paused again and then rattled off the following names in rapid-fire succession: "Michael Jackson, Charlton Heston, Nancy Kerrigan, Demi Moore, Michael J. Fox, Sandra Bullock, David Bowie, Prince, Kareem Abdul-Jabbar, Jon Stewart, Dave Chappelle, Cameron Diaz, Bill O'Reilly, Ozzy Osbourne, Bob Evans, and Barbra Streisand. I learned something very important when I was working for Barbra Streisand on New Year's Eve. It was an event at the MGM in Las Vegas, and she hadn't performed in many years—two decades, actually—and right at midnight, or perhaps twelve-thirty, she asked me whether I could find her some plum sauce. Plum sauce—like you get in a Chinese restaurant. And I figured something out real quick. When Barbra Streisand asks you for plum sauce on New Year's Eve in Las Vegas, 'No' is a really bad answer. And 'I don't know' is a really bad answer. 'Yes,' however, is a really good answer. You've got to figure that out! And the higher you get, the harder it gets. The demands get more intensified."

I asked him how he, as a professional at the top of his field, coped with such demands.

"This is a question that goes through your head at the beginning of your career," he admitted in a quiet voice. "But I want you to understand: Getting someone plum sauce in Las Vegas at midnight on New Year's Eve is challenging, but it's not murder. It's not so ludicrous. And professionals who work at the top of their field in the fame game realize that this is simply part of the game."

In the end, Levine said, any misgivings he had about occasionally being asked to fetch plum sauce were far outweighed by the status he gained in performing such duties. "Look," he said, "I've seen strangers look at Mike Tyson and say, 'What a scumbag, what a vermin, what a douche bag.' Then, as he gets closer, they start getting excited. And then, three minutes later, they want their picture taken with him. Fame is a validator. The conflict is that I want it. You want it. We all want it—or want to be close to it. But what is the price? It's the Faustian bargain. You see what I mean? Celebrities offer you the drug of validation, but you can't talk straight to the pusher, or you won't get your drag. That's the deal."

Hollywood, like Washington, D.C., is known for being an insular company town where everybody competes for recognition, status, and, above all, proximity. In Washington it is commonly said that your status can be measured by how many degrees of separation exist between you and the president; in Hollywood the same is often said of Jack Nicholson or Steven Spielberg.

One could argue that this fight for proximity, in which we strive to ₃₅ ingratiate ourselves with famous and prestigious people, goes well beyond those power vortexes and plays itself out in many corners of America. Perhaps the best example of this can be found in studies on the social dynamics of cheerleaders. According to the sociologists Pamela Bettis and Natalie Adams, 3.3 million people participate in cheerleading each year. They observe, "Numerous scholars have documented that cheerleading is often perceived as the highest-status activity for girls in middle school, and girls who cheer often occupy positions of power, prestige, and privilege in their schools."

In a landmark study Donna Eder examined the social dynamics of cheerleaders at an unspecified middle school in the Midwest. Eder and several research assistants spent more than a year interviewing students during lunch, between classes, and at special after-school events such as dances and picnics. In the process Eder identified an elite group—composed primarily of cheerleaders—that most of the other girls wanted to join. The members of this elite group were typically referred to as the "popular girls" by the rest of the students. According to Eder, these girls commanded the school's attention. Eder observed that girls throughout the school discussed the activities of the popular girls, but the popular girls paid almost no attention to anyone but themselves. She also noted that non-cheerleaders often went to great lengths to ingratiate themselves with the cheerleaders:

> Many of the girls wanted to sit with the cheerleaders at lunch and made special attempts to be friendly toward them. For example, when it looked as though cheerleading might be eliminated from the school budget, Sylvia made a point of telling Carrie, one of the new cheerleaders, that she had written a letter to President Reagan telling him how important cheerleading was for school spirit and how hard some of her friends had worked to become cheerleaders. Also, if one of the new cheerleaders was upset about something, there were usually many girls around to comfort her.

Eder concluded that there were "two main avenues for mobility into the elite group—becoming a cheerleader or becoming a friend of a cheerleader." But few cheerleading positions were ever available, so all the other girls engaged in a desperate race to befriend the school's pompom-toting elite. The upshot of all this, observed Eder, is that teenage girls often become more self-conscious and preoccupied with being liked.

The social lives of cheerleaders and celebrities are strikingly similar. Both groups consist of and are defined by two types of people: the "stars," who appear talented, glamorous, and popular; and the

Cheerleaders

"acolytes," who strive to endear themselves to the stars. The question is: What exactly motivates the acolytes? To a certain extent, Belongingness Theory explains why so many of us yearn to belong to groups in general, but not why we prefer these highly prestigious groups above all others, or why we toil to ingratiate ourselves with the leaders of these groups.

Prestige Theory

Francisco Gil-White, an evolutionary anthropologist at the University of Pennsylvania, offers one explanation. In 2001 he and a colleague, Joseph Henrich, of Emory University, proposed the idea of Prestige Theory. The core of the theory is based on the notion that humans—unlike chimps, orangutans, and other primates—have the unique ability to learn and perfect highly nuanced skills. Perhaps the best example of this involves an experiment conducted by two Emory primatologists, Josep Call and Michael Tomasello, who tested and compared the learning abilities of adult orangutans and four-year-old humans. According to Call and Tomasello, orangutans have a reputation among primatologists for being skillful problem solvers. To test just how clever they were, the researchers built a small contraption that dispensed M&M chocolate candies. It had a long steel handle that could be pushed, pulled, or rotated. During the experiment a researcher would manipulate the handle in a combination of ways, and if the orangutan successfully mimicked this motion, it received an M&M. Call and Tomasello discovered that the adult orangutans were not nearly as successful as the four-year-old humans at doing this. They concluded that orangutans "did not use imitative learning to help them solve the problem presented," whereas children "did use their observations of the demonstrations to help them solve the task."

Gil-White and Henrich relied on experiments like this one to 40 argue that only humans have the ability to observe and then mimic complex behaviors. They claim that this uniquely human ability eventually created "prestige hierarchies" in which those with the most valuable skills sat at the top. So when a truly talented hunter emerged in prehistoric times, he was revered both because he brought home food and because his skill could be learned. Disciples soon gravitated toward this hunter. They "paid" for access by doing favors for him, excusing him from certain obligations, and siding with him politically. Posses of studious disciples eventually formed. According to Gil-White and Henrich, these posses served as beacons, allowing hungry tribe members to identify a mentor, learn a skill, and begin feeding themselves as quickly as possible.

The premise of Prestige Theory is that it has been evolutionary advantageous for human beings to identify prestigious people and befriend them in order to gain skills. In ancient times the disciple of a successful hunter stood a better chance of surviving, having children, and then feeding them. By this rationale, over the millennia astute disciples have flourished. But perhaps even more interesting is the notion that human beings have developed a conditioned response to entourages. In theory, at least, we are genetically predisposed to identifying posses of admirers and gravitating toward the leaders (or people with the skills) because historically this is how our ancestors survived and reproduced. So when Michael Levine fetches plum sauce for Barbra Streisand, or Sylvia tries to ingratiate herself with a "skilled" cheerleader, the invisible hand of evolution is simply pushing them along.

These instincts still help us in modern-day scenarios. In many work settings, for example, it pays to identify and endear oneself to the man or woman at the center of a posse of admirers. This allows one to learn valuable skills—today's equivalent of hunting school. But according to Gil-White, whom I interviewed, this goes all wrong when it comes to celebrities. When we see them on TV, we sense that they are at the center of a truly enormous entourage, so our conditioned "posse response" is activated, and we gravitate toward them. A few savvy operators, like Michael Levine, can actually find their way into the posse and become disciples or insiders. The overwhelming majority of us, however, can't. And we are the real losers in this scenario because we subconsciously attempt to ingratiate ourselves with our idols—buying Paris Hilton's jewelry and Nicole Kidman's perfume—without really gaining anything. In essence we are still chasing the great hunters; but, of course, most of these hunters have no interest in teaching us, and worse yet, many of them have little of real value to teach.

Whatever motivated Michael Levine to run errands for his famous clients, he at least had the satisfaction of knowing that he had been invited to the party.

Conclusion

---

practice it 26.9   Post-Reading Activity

This reading begins with Halpern's anecdote about his own brush with a celebrity. What other types of evidence does he give to support his points? Which types of evidence do you find most effective, and why?

COMPREHENSION QUESTIONS

1. What is Belongingness Theory? Find the definition in the chapter, and then rephrase it in your own words, using your own example.

2. What is a "para-social" relationship (para. 10), and how do we form para-social relationships with television characters or other celebrities?

3. According to Halpern, how does our loneliness contribute to our love of celebrities?

4. What is Prestige Theory? How does it apply, according to Halpern, to understanding the power of celebrity?

5. Why are we the "real losers" in our attempt to "ingratiate ourselves with our idols" (para. 42)? What do we lose, according to Halpern?

DISCUSSION QUESTIONS

1. Reflect on Halpern's book title, *Fame Junkies: The Hidden Truths behind America's Favorite Addiction.* What do you think of the metaphor of addiction? How does celebrity addiction compare and contrast to more physical addictions?

2. Does the evidence Halpern gives convince you that, as he says, "Americans now appear to be lonelier than ever" (para. 14)? What types of evidence does he provide? How do you value that evidence, as compared to your own personal experiences and observations?

3. Think back to your own experience of high school. How effective is Halpern's comparison between celebrities and cheerleaders?

4. Presuming you agree with Halpern's argument that celebrity worship is caused by our desire to belong, what could be done to change our culture of celebrity worship? What else besides celebrity worship might help us feel like we "belong"?

Synthesizing the Readings as Pre-Writing for Your Own Essay

Now that you have read a wide variety of texts on the topic of fame and celebrity, you have enough schema, or background information, to begin to synthesize the material and build arguments of your own. It's helpful, though, to pause and discuss how the various readings "converse" with one another before you jump right into a writing assignment. You can use a variety of techniques and activities—alone or with peers—to help your thoughts take shape. Whichever method you choose, it's helpful to have the readings out in front of you so that you can review your annotations. Look for connections across articles as you review. Quite often, you don't see the bigger picture until you take the time to step back and review the material.

DISCUSS TO SYNTHESIZE IDEAS

Talk through the following questions with peers to uncover the connections among readings.

1. What are the key themes of the readings in this chapter? How do these themes intersect with one another?
2. Compare and contrast the effects of fame and celebrity on people of different ages (young children, teens, young adults, and older adults). What are the similarities and differences in the impacts fame and celebrity have on their lives?
3. How deep of a problem is the celebrity culture in America? If you think it is a large problem, how might we address it in our families or communities? Should this become a nationwide issue?
4. Do local heroes or other "old fame" figures still exist in our communities? How do they compare and contrast to "new fame" celebrities?
5. Compare the ideas about fame in Halpern's and Rockwell and Giles's articles. On what points would they agree? On what points would they disagree?
6. Thinking back to the quotation from Jay Z that opened this chapter, which authors best support Jay Z's quote?

CHART TO SYNTHESIZE IDEAS

For many writers, organizing ideas graphically is a vital part of the reading/writing process. Using the method you learned in Chapter 2, make a synthesis chart on one focused topic related to the theme of fame and celebrity. Remember to include space for your own ideas. Look through your annotations on the texts you have read before filling in the chart.

▶ For more about creating synthesis charts, see pages 73–73 in Chapter 2, Active and Critical Reading, and pages 238–40 in Chapter 10, Pre-Writing.

IDENTIFY SUBTOPICS TO SYNTHESIZE IDEAS

If you're still struggling to settle on a specific focus for your essay after the discussion questions and synthesis charting, you can generate a list of possible subtopics that could be the focus of an essay. Here are a few sample subtopics to spark your thinking:

Fame and Celebrity Topics

- What does it mean to be famous?
- Problems associated with fame
- Benefits associated with fame
- Branding of a celebrity
- Attraction to fame or famous people

Take a few minutes to add to this list of subtopics, using the following questions to help you generate topics.

1. Which reading did you find most interesting? Why?
2. Which reading did you find most informative? What did you learn?
3. In which reading did you find the most to disagree with? What specific things did you disagree about?
4. In which reading did you find the most to agree with? What specific things did you agree about?
5. Which reading had good examples? List a few of the examples. What are they examples of?

Writing Your Essay

Once you have done some synthesis thinking, you can begin to write your essay. The following steps review how to get into the mind-set to write. These steps are outlined in greater detail in Chapters 2, 3, and 4.

STEP 1: What type of essay are you assigned to write about fame and celebrity? Look over the question or your instructor's prompt, and write it in your own words.

STEP 2: Which readings from this chapter do you think you will include? List them in your notes, including any quotations that you think you might use. (Don't forget to include the author and page number when you write down the quotation so that you don't have to find it again later.)

STEP 3: What ideas from class discussion or your own experience and observation would you like to include? Look over your notes, and add those thoughts to your brainstorming for this assignment.

STEP 4: Take a few more minutes to brainstorm in your favorite method: listing, freewriting, clustering, questioning, or group discussion.

STEP 5: Look back at the assignment prompt, and write up a tentative thesis or main idea based on your work so far. Remember, one way to think of the thesis is as the answer to the question posed in the assignment prompt. Don't worry that your thesis has to be perfect or set in stone right now. It's a working thesis that you will probably revise as you make decisions about what you want to say.

STEP 6: Make a bullet-point outline for your essay. Remember to first put the ideas down and then reorganize them into a logical order.

STEP 7: Copy or type up the relevant quotations and examples under each appropriate bullet point.

STEP 8: Pat yourself on the back! You have a lot of material so far.

STEP 9: Write the rough, rough draft, remembering that you'll revise it.

STEP 10: Reread the assignment sheet one more time, and then make big-picture revisions to your focus, content, and organization. Peer review may help.

STEP 11: Once you are generally satisfied that your work is focused, complete, and organized, edit for sentence-level issues. Remember to use the editing techniques of reading your work out loud, reading "backward," and isolating your common errors. Refer to your Grammar Log frequently during this process. Edit and print your paper again and again until you are satisfied with the way each sentence sounds.

▶ To learn how to use the Grammar Log, see p. 573–75 in Chapter 27, How to Learn the Rules and Apply Them to Your Own Writing.

STEP 12: Take a break.

STEP 13: Proofread your essay one or two more times to correct any minor errors and to make sure your document format is correct for this assignment.

Writing Assignments

DEFINITION ASSIGNMENT

What do *fame* and *celebrity* really mean? Write an essay in which you offer your own extended definition of *fame* and/or *celebrity*. You may want to distinguish between fame and celebrity as a way to help make your points. Be sure to use specific examples to illustrate your points.

DESCRIPTION ASSIGNMENT

Think of a celebrity who, like the Kardashians, functions as a brand. What is the celebrity's brand identity? Describe in specific detail the image, products, and values associated with this celebrity.

COMPARISON AND CONTRAST ASSIGNMENT

Drawing on Jake Halpern's book chapter "The Desire to Belong: Why Everyone Wants to Have Dinner with Paris Hilton and 50 Cent" from *Fame Junkies*, write an essay that compares and contrasts one person who has "new fame" with one person who had "old fame." You may need to use outside library sources to research your people. Use these examples to make a larger point about new and old fame.

ANALYSIS ASSIGNMENT

Choose a popular magazine from the past or from today. (Older magazines are available in libraries, and many are now archived online.) Look at all the facets of the magazine, including the cover, articles, regular columns, photo spreads, and advertisements. Analyze how the magazine presents fame and/or celebrity. In developing your thesis, realize that magazines might not offer one coherent "message" but instead might offer contradictory messages about fame and celebrity.

RESEARCH ASSIGNMENT

Choose someone famous and research the path he or she took to achieve fame and the contributions this person made to his or her field or the world at large. What did this person actually do to achieve fame? What were the critical moments in the development of his or her career? What is or was the value of fame to this person and to those around him or her?

ARGUMENT ASSIGNMENT

As the authors in this chapter have shown, celebrities have a hold on us. We obsessively watch them on TV, follow their lives in gossip magazines and on Twitter, and buy the trendy clothes and gadgets they promote. Why are we so obsessed with celebrity watching? Is there any value in it, or does it have a solely negative impact? Drawing on the readings by Halpern and Rockwell and Giles, write an essay in which you take a position on the psychological and/or social impact of celebrity culture on America as a whole or on some segment of the population.

Additional Online and Media Sources

The readings in this chapter may spark your thinking and leave you wanting some more information for further study or personal reflection. If so, you might also want to consult the following online and media sources.

WEB RESOURCES

Check your college library's online databases to see if you have access to the Biography Resource Center or other databases that provide information about famous people. You might also familiarize yourself with the various fan and gossip sites, if you haven't seen them previously. In addition, you can consult the following:

Andy Warhol Museum (www.warhol.org): The robust Web site of the Andy Warhol Museum, which offers information about Warhol along with images of his art.

Bio. (www.biography.com): Biographies of a wide variety of famous people and celebrities.

CelebYouth (www.celebyouth.org): An online research project from the United Kingdom that explores the impact of celebrities on youth.

Federal Resources for Educational Excellence, U.S. History Topics: Famous People (http://free.ed.gov/subjects.cfm?subject_id=172): Research resources for famous people in American history.

Museum of Modern Art, Learning: Pop Art (www.moma.org/learn /moma_learning/themes/pop-art/celebrity): Art, discussion questions, and activities about celebrity culture and art that reflects on celebrity.

FILMS

Almost Famous. Directed by Cameron Crowe, performances by Billy Crudup, Frances McDormand, and Kate Hudson, Columbia, 2000.

Bamboozled. Directed by Spike Lee, performances by Damon Wayans, Savion Glover, and Jada Pinkett Smith, New Line Cinema, 2000.

The Bling Ring. Directed by Sofia Coppola, performances by Katie Chang, Israel Broussard, and Emma Watson, American Zoetrope, 2013.

Consuming Kids: The Commercialization of Childhood. Directed by Adriana Barbaro and Jeremy Earp, performances by Daniel Acuff, Enola Aird, and Michael Brody, Media Education Foundation, 2008.

Exit through the Gift Shop. Directed by Banksy, performances by Banksy, Mr. Brainwash, and Debora Guetta, Paranoid Pictures, 2010.

The Hunger Games. Directed by Gary Ross, performances by Stanley Tucci, Jennifer Lawrence, and Liam Hemsworth, Lionsgate, 2012.

I Love Your Work. Directed by Adam Goldberg, performances by Marisa Coughlan, Judy Greer, and Shalom Harlow, Cyan Pictures, 2003.

The Joneses. Directed by Derrick Borte, performances by David Duchovny, Demi Moore, and Amber Heard, Echo Lake Productions, 2009.

Notting Hill. Directed by Roger Michell, performances by Julia Roberts, Hugh Grant, and Richard McCabe, Polygram, 1999.

Somewhere. Directed by Sofia Coppola, performances by Stephen Dorff and Elle Fanning, Focus, 2010.

"Tennessee Williams: Wounded Genius." *Biography.* Produced by Paul Budline, performances by Tennessee Williams, Helena Carroll, and Candy Darling, A&E, 9 June 1998.

The Truman Show. Directed by Peter Weir, performances by Jim Carrey, Laura Linney, and Noah Emmerich, Paramount, 1998.

The chapters in Part 4 emphasize specific topics and common problems in grammar, style, and mechanics. Whether you need an in-depth introduction or a refresher, these chapters can help you practice your editing skills.

part four

How Do I Make My Sentences Say What I Mean? Grammar, Style, and Mechanics

27

How to Learn the Rules and Apply Them to Your Own Writing

Understanding Editing and Proofreading

Writing involves more than just stringing words together correctly. Writing involves generating ideas, forming logical arguments, and organizing thoughts, among other things. Correcting your sentence-level errors—sometimes referred to generally as errors in "grammar"—is a key part of writing, but often problems with sentences occur because your ideas are not yet clear and focused. For this reason, it's important to work on idea development and larger concerns before you attend to sentence-level issues. Also, make sure you understand the difference between editing and proofreading:

- *Edit:* When you edit your work, you find and fix grammar errors and make changes to improve sentence clarity and style.
- *Proofread:* When you proofread your work, you find and fix typos, minor punctuation errors, and misspellings, as well as correct document format.

That said, when you spend time on your sentence-level errors, you want that time to be productive. Too often, students spend hours doing multiple-choice exercises that don't really help them improve. So how do you learn to find and fix your own errors in your own writing?

Correcting grammar is a process much like working out to get into shape: You have to work on it repeatedly to get the results you want. It also helps to be organized about noting what kinds of errors you make. One of the best ways to track these errors so you can find them and fix them is to keep a Grammar Log of the kinds of errors you are prone to make. This chapter will show you how to do that. If you take the time to learn the rules and correct your errors, eventually you will write fluently and correctly.

As you work to improve your grammar, you will most likely make progress yet have some setbacks. That's completely normal. (In dieting or working out, it's called a plateau.) In writing, you might plateau for a while because you still need to master some basic rules and apply them in a disciplined, consistent way. You might also plateau in the area of grammar because you are focusing on and progressing in other areas of the reading and writing processes. As you move through your college English course, you will be asked to read increasingly difficult texts and write and think in more and more sophisticated ways. Often, when you are reaching a new level intellectually, you will make a few more errors for a while. Try not to see this as a negative thing. Instead, realize that your grammar is suffering because you are hitting new highs intellectually. This is the growth mentality that Carol S. Dweck describes in her work (see Chapter 1, pp. 6–13). You will have to spend more time than usual, perhaps, in the editing stage of writing on a particular assignment, but the end result will be well worth the effort.

So what is the process of correcting grammar errors?

STEP 1: First, you need to figure out exactly what your problems are.   Do you repeatedly write fragments? Comma splices? Do you use commas incorrectly? The more you can pinpoint and identify the exact errors you make, the easier it will be to fix them.

STEP 2: Next, you need to learn the rules for the specific errors you make.   After you feel confident with the rules, you can test yourself.

STEP 3: Finally, you need to apply your knowledge to your own writing by finding and fixing those errors in your own papers.

Note that this process does not involve trying to memorize every aspect of American English grammar. We don't think that is an effective or efficient way to learn to read and write well. So we won't ask you to diagram random sentences, but you will need to turn a microscope on your own work.

Pinpointing Your Errors

Let's look in depth at the first step, identifying your particular errors. How do you do that? Your English instructor is your best resource here. She or he will review your writing and comment in the margins about the errors you make, sometimes correcting those errors to show you how it

▶ **For more help finding your own errors, see Chapter 18, Giving and Receiving Feedback.**

should be done. Take the time to make a list of all the errors your instructor marks. You might also think back to past classes to remember what other instructors have told you about your writing.

| practice it 27.1 | Compile a List of Your Errors

Start to compile a list of your common errors in your notebook.
Include examples from your writing of each error you make frequently.

Once you have a list of the errors you tend to make, you will likely need to prioritize them, especially if you make many errors. Now, this may come as a surprise, but the spelling and apostrophe errors that your high school teachers might have constantly corrected—while common—are not the worst errors you can make. Let's take a look at the most common types of errors, in order of importance.

ERRORS THAT MAKE YOUR WRITING UNREADABLE

First, we have the major errors, those that make your writing unreadable:

- verb problems
- fragments
- run-ons and comma splices
- mixed constructions

Tackle these problems first because they hide the meaning of your sentences. If you make these mistakes frequently, your reader won't understand what you are trying to say.

ERRORS THAT MAKE YOUR WRITING UNCLEAR

Next up, we have the errors that make your writing unclear or difficult to follow:

- pronoun problems
- some comma errors
- parallelism errors
- misplaced and dangling modifiers
- overuse of passive voice
- wordiness and other style problems

In some cases, these errors occur because you are trying to do something more sophisticated with your work but aren't quite getting it right. In other cases, these are errors of style. If you focus on being clear and concise, your work will have more impact.

ERRORS THAT MAKE YOUR WRITING DISTRACTING

Last, but not least, we have the errors that make your writing distracting:

- apostrophe errors
- some comma errors
- most punctuation errors
- spelling and capitalization errors

These errors concern minor issues, but they make your writing unpolished and unprofessional and can easily distract your reader from your ideas. Errors like these may seem minor, but they add up and undermine your credibility.

If your list of errors includes one or two from each of these categories, begin with the errors that make your writing unreadable, and work your way down to the other categories.

CREATING A GRAMMAR LOG

Copy the following chart into your notebook. Add rows to the chart as needed.

GRAMMAR LOG

My Error	The Rules in My Own Words	Example of Corrected Error	My Notes

Here, list your most common errors, in order of priority.

Write the rules for finding and fixing the error. Putting the rule in your own words will help you understand the rule.

Write an example of a sentence with the error corrected.

Add any notes that will help you understand or remember how to fix the error.

practice it 27.2 Prioritize Your Errors

Look back over the list of your common errors in your notebook. Prioritize your errors based on the categories above. Then write the name of your two or three most important errors in your Grammar Log. These are the errors you will begin to address first this semester.

IDENTIFYING AND PRIORITIZING ERRORS: ONE STUDENT'S PARAGRAPH

Let's take a look at a sample student's writing. This student, Andrea, wrote a paragraph about budgeting and financial literacy.

> Financial literacy is important for everyone. Like college students, young couples, and retired people. Most people think that having a budget is enough but they do not realize that budgeting is just the first step. Making long-term plans, setting goals, and building an emergency fund as well. Their are so many resources available to help. Such as Web sites, books, government publications, and even online lessons for children. The U.S. council on economic education has one of the best Web sites i have seen for children. (My little Sister even liked it!) Starting young makes all the difference in the world. If people start thinking about finances when they are little they will do it regularly when they actually have a job later in Life. From that point on the road to success is certain.

This student made many errors. This is just a quick rough draft, however, so she probably knows how to correct some of these errors but just hasn't fixed them yet. Based on the preceding paragraph, though, we can list the following errors (they are color-coded to correspond to the paragraph):

- fragments (-*ing* and example fragments)
- commas (after introductory element and when joining two main clauses with a coordinating conjunction)
- capitalization ("i")
- commonly confused words (*there/their/they're*)

Now, when we look at the list, the most important errors are the fragment errors, followed by the comma errors. The capitalization problems and the commonly confused–word problem are distracting and make the writing look unprofessional, but the fragment and comma errors make it hard to follow. Most likely, too, the student made the capitalization and commonly confused–word errors out of haste or laziness, and that means she needs to edit more carefully. She might already know the rules for these.

This student's instructor would advise her to work on the fragments first, but some comma rules might help her fix the fragments, so she should probably address the commas at the same time or shortly afterward. Most likely, when the student lists her errors, she will realize that she knows to spell *I* with a capital letter, so she can omit this error from her Grammar Log. Her personalized Grammar Log, then, will look something like the example on the top of page 575.

GRAMMAR LOG

My Error	The Rules in My Own Words	Example of Corrected Error	My Notes
fragments, especially with –*ing*			
fragments with examples			
comma rules			
there/their/they're			

Remember, you probably won't be able to pinpoint all your own errors yourself. Look over comments and corrections made on your past work, and ask your instructor for help.

Learning the Rules

Once you figure out what you need to work on, how do you learn the rules? A few students do well with self-study—they can read the chapters in a grammar handbook and figure it out pretty well. Most students, though, learn best in an interactive way, either with classmates outside of class or through in-class instruction. Though your instructor may devote class time to the major errors that appear frequently in student work, you will probably need some one-on-one help also. Make sure to read and study the relevant material in Chapters 28–41 of this book, and try your hand at the Practice It activities. One good way to check your understanding of a particular rule is to test how well you can explain it in your own words. Try teaching the rule to another student, or at least repeat it back in your words to your tutor or instructor. Then, when you are sure you have the right idea, write it down in your Grammar Log.

Don't be surprised if you have some trouble figuring out the rules by yourself. You may need to see a tutor or your instructor for personalized help. If so, come prepared with samples of your own writing where the error appears.

practice it 27.3   Define the Rules

Read the appropriate chapters (see Chapters 28–41) and fill in the column labeled "The Rules in My Own Words" in your Grammar Log for the errors you have identified. Seek help from a tutor or instructor if you don't fully understand the rules.

Applying What You've Learned to Your Own Writing

Once you are confident that you know the rules pertaining to the errors you make, it's time for the final step: finding and fixing the errors in your own work. Follow these steps.

STEP 1: Take out one or two current pieces of your own writing, preferably writing that has *not* been corrected by an instructor.

STEP 2: Read your writing out loud, looking for one specific error at a time. For instance, if you make fragments and comma errors, read through it once looking just for fragments. Then read through it a second time looking just for comma errors. As you read, underline any problem sentences, but don't stop to fix them now.

STEP 3: When you have finished reading the whole paper, go back and fix your errors. You might find it helpful to have this book open to the relevant chapter.

STEP 4: Have a tutor or your instructor check your corrections to be sure you are editing correctly. Make sure you show them the original and the corrected versions.

STEP 5: Repeat this process until you find that you are no longer making these errors. Then move on down your list to the other errors that you need to correct.

Remember, learning to write without errors is a process. You get better in time if you study, test yourself, and apply what you know. Regularly taking the time to check your work for errors will reduce the number of errors you make.

Study ⟶ Test yourself ⟶ Apply what you've learned ⟶ Repeat

practice it 27.4 Find and Correct Your Errors

Find in your own writing one common example of each error you make. Copy it out exactly in your Grammar Log. Then, with a different-colored pen, correct the sentence. Do not erase the mistake. You need to see the original error and the way it was fixed when you study in the future.

Here's what Andrea's Grammar Log looked like after she had reviewed all the rules, found examples from her own writing, and corrected them:

My Error	The Rules in My Own Words	Example of Corrected Error	My Notes
fragments, especially with -ing	You can't have an -ing verb all by itself as a sentence.	Financial literacy includes making ~~Making~~ long-term plans, setting goals, and building an emergency fund as well.	Look out for any -ing words starting a sentence.
fragments with examples	Examples should be attached to the thing they are giving an example of.	Financial literacy is important for everyone, like ~~Like~~ college students, young couples, and retired people.	Double-check sentences that start with like or such as.
comma rule before conjunction	Two sentences joined by and or but need a comma before the and or but.	Most people think that having a budget is enough, but they do not realize that budgeting is just the first step.	Use the cover-it-with-your-hand technique to check.
comma rule after introductory material	Use a comma after any introductory word or phrase that is separate from the main part of the sentence.	From that point on, the road to success is certain.	You can hear this one when you read it out loud.
there/ their/ they're	They're over there in their underwear.	There ~~Their~~ are so many resources available to help.	Use the Find feature to check while proofreading.

chapter review

In the following chart, fill in the second column to record in your own words the important skills included in this chapter. Then assess yourself to determine whether you are still developing the skill or feel you have mastered it. If you are still developing the skill, make some notes about what you need to work on to master it in the future. If you believe you have already mastered it, explain why.

Skills and concepts covered in this chapter	Explanation in your own words	I'm developing this skill and need to work on . . .	I believe I have mastered this skill because . . .
Understanding the difference between editing and proofreading			
Understanding different types of errors			
Identifying and prioritizing errors			
Keeping a Grammar Log			
Learning the rules			
Fixing errors by applying the rules			

28

Parts of Speech

Any word used in a sentence fits into one of eight *parts of speech*. The parts of speech are defined by how they function *grammatically*—in other words, by what their job is in a sentence. Because many words can play the role of more than one part of speech, you won't be able to identify what part of speech a word is until you see how it is used.

Why is it important to know the parts of speech? For starters, to build strong, clear sentences, you need to understand how words function in sentences. You also need a basic understanding of the major parts of speech in order to communicate *about* writing. You can't understand the explanations for how to fix your grammar errors if you don't know this basic vocabulary. It would be like trying to learn how to hit a baseball without knowing what *swing* means.

You have probably heard of the parts of speech before, but you may have forgotten what they are or why it's useful to know them.

LaunchPad Solo
macmillan learning

Visit **LaunchPad Solo for Readers and Writers > Overview: Parts of Speech** for extra practice in the skills covered in this chapter.

Part of Speech	Purpose	Example
Noun	person, place, thing, or idea	Professor Peacock, teacher, library, candlestick, honesty
Pronoun	stands for a person or thing	he, she, it, they, my, that, which
Adjective	modifies nouns	purple, cold, awesome
Verb	action or state of being	sat, thinks, is

(continued)

Part of Speech	Purpose	Example
Adverb	modifies verbs, adjectives, or other adverbs	quietly, very
Preposition	links nouns and phrases to the rest of a sentence; often indicates location	to, in, by, through, after
Conjunction	joins complete sentences or ideas	and, but, or
Interjection	expresses emotion	No! Wow! Huh?

Dictionaries are a great resource for determining a word's part of speech. After every word in a dictionary entry, you will find its part(s) of speech listed. Here, for example, is the beginning of the definition of *check* found at Merriam-Webster.com:

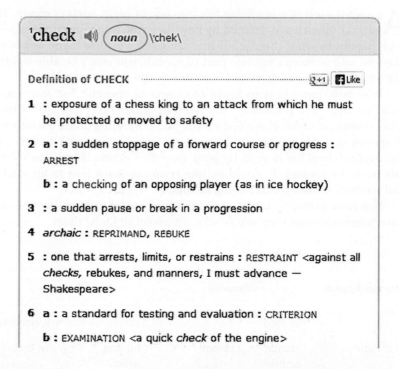

¹**check** ◄)) (*noun*) \chek\

Definition of CHECK .... 8+1 ▯ Like

1 : exposure of a chess king to an attack from which he must be protected or moved to safety

2 **a** : a sudden stoppage of a forward course or progress : ARREST

   b : a checking of an opposing player (as in ice hockey)

3 : a sudden pause or break in a progression

4 *archaic* : REPRIMAND, REBUKE

5 : one that arrests, limits, or restrains : RESTRAINT <against all *checks*, rebukes, and manners, I must advance — Shakespeare>

6 **a** : a standard for testing and evaluation : CRITERION

   b : EXAMINATION <a quick *check* of the engine>

In English, many words are used—sometimes with a slight change—for more than one purpose, so they serve as different parts of speech. For example, as you can see in the following excerpt of the rest of the definition, the word *check* can also be used as a verb and as an interjection.

²check (verb)

Definition of CHECK

transitive verb

1 : to put (a chess king) in check

2 *chiefly dialect* : REBUKE, REPRIMAND

3 **a** : to slow or bring to a stop : BRAKE <hastily *checked* the impulse>

    b : to block the progress of (as a hockey player)

4 **a** : to restrain or diminish the action or force of : CONTROL

    b : to slack or ease off and then belay again (as a rope)

5 **a** : to compare with a source, original, or authority : VERIFY <needs to *check* her facts>

    b : to inspect, examine, or look at appraisingly —usually used with *out* or *over* <*checking* out new cars>

    c : to mark with a check as examined, verified, or satisfactory —often used with *off* <*checked* off each item>

6 **a** : to consign (as luggage) to a common carrier from which one has purchased a passenger ticket <*checked* our bags before boarding>

³check (inter)

Definition of CHECK

    —used to express assent or agreement

If someone asked you what part of speech the word *check* was, you couldn't answer until you saw how it was used in a sentence. In the following sentences, it's used as a noun, a verb, and an interjection.

Verb	Noun		Interjection	

I check my check every payday to see if there's an error. Check! No error.

Nouns and Pronouns

WHAT ARE NOUNS AND PRONOUNS?

TIP

If you can put *a, an,* or *the* in front of a word, it is most likely a noun. Some examples:

an athlete, a beach, the dream, a car, the loyalty

A *noun* is a person, place, thing, or idea. Nouns are the most basic building blocks of writing. Examples of nouns include *athlete, beach, dream, car,* and *loyalty*. In the following sentence, all the underlined words are nouns:

It was the Olympic athlete's dream to own a house at the beach.

A *proper noun* is the name of a specific person, place, or thing and always begins with a capital letter regardless of where it is in a sentence. In the following sentence, all the underlined words are proper nouns:

<table>
<tr><td>Specific Person</td><td>Specific Place</td><td>Specific Place</td></tr>
</table>

The statue of Abraham Lincoln at the Lincoln Memorial in Washington, D.C., is massive in size and dramatic when lit up at night.

A *pronoun* is a word that stands in for a noun. (Hint: Imagine that its job is to "play" a noun; it is a professional—or "pro"—noun.) Examples include *I, you, he, she, it, we, they, everybody,* and *one*.

Pronouns are helpful because they allow us to avoid repeating the same noun over and over, which can get tedious.

The bus was so crowded, the bus looked like a can of sardines; I still had to get on the bus though.

The bus was so crowded, it looked like a can of sardines; I still had to get on it, though.

Notice how much smoother the sentence is with pronouns in the place of the noun *bus?*

To avoid a common pitfall in using pronouns, be aware that pronouns must clearly refer back to a particular noun in order for a sentence to make sense.

Mike and Paul ran to the store, but he didn't go in.

Which *he* didn't go in? In this case, repeating the noun (either *Mike* or *Paul*) is essential.

Mike and Paul ran to the store, but Mike didn't go in.

IDENTIFYING NOUNS AND PRONOUNS

▶ **For more on fixing pronoun problems, see Chapter 34.**

Both nouns and pronouns can be used as the *subject* of a sentence—generally speaking, the person, place, thing, or idea that performs the action of the sentence.

> Clarence feels bad.

To identify the subject, ask yourself: Who or what feels bad? In this case, *Clarence* is the one who feels bad, so *Clarence* is the subject. You could also write this:

> He feels bad.

Again, who or what feels bad? *He* feels bad, so *he* would be the subject. Here's another example:

> For Americans, freedom is a founding principle of government.

Ask yourself: Who or what is a founding principle? *Freedom* is, so *freedom* is the subject. Let's look at one final example:

> It is also the subject of a song Janis Joplin made famous.

Ask yourself: Who or what is also the subject? *It* is also the subject. Don't get fooled by the fact that this sentence has a person's name in it. The subject isn't necessarily a person.

Nouns and pronouns can also serve as the *object* of the action in the sentence, as the object of a *preposition*, or as part of a *subordinate clause*.

> Janis Joplin sang the song. [What did she sing? The *song*, the object of the action.]

> Janis Joplin sang it. [What did she sing? *It*, the object of the action.]

> Janis Joplin sang about freedom. [What did she sing about? About *freedom*, the object of the preposition *about*.]

> Janis Joplin died young because she abused drugs. [*She* and *drugs* are part of a subordinate clause, *because she abused drugs*, which is subordinate because it can't stand on its own as a sentence.]

▶ **For more on subordinate clauses, see Chapter 30, Sentence Structure.**

What else do you need to know about nouns and pronouns? Nouns and pronouns are *modified* (a fancy word for "described") by adjectives, which we'll discuss in the next section.

Adjectives

WHAT ARE ADJECTIVES?

An *adjective* is a word that modifies or describes a noun. Adjectives answer three questions about nouns or pronouns:

1. What kind/kinds?
2. How many/much?
3. Which one/ones?

Adjectives are an interesting part of speech because they add description. Adjectives are also immensely helpful to us because they provide clarifying information about the nouns in a sentence. You may be familiar with the lyrics to the old tune "How Much Is That Doggie in the Window?" Of course, if you worked in a pet store and someone asked you this question, you wouldn't know which dog the customer was referring to. But the second line of the song goes: "The one with the waggly tail." Okay, now it's clear which dog the customer is interested in: the pup wagging its tail. It wouldn't be enough to just say "the one with the tail"; since the majority of dogs have tails, this wouldn't be enough information. In this case, *waggly* gives us more information about the noun *tail* by answering the question, what kind of tail?

IDENTIFYING ADJECTIVES

Adjectives answer one or more of the three questions listed previously about nouns and pronouns. Here are some examples:

I ended up buying an old car.

This answers the question, what kind of car? An *old* car.

My feet are tired.

I have tired feet.

Both of these sentences answer the question, what kind of feet? *Tired* feet.

Raisin Bran has two scoops of raisins.

This answers the question, how many scoops? *Two* scoops.

I have little homework to do this weekend.

This answers the question, how much homework? *Little* homework.

Use the sharp scissors.

This answers the question, which ones? The *sharp* scissors.

Now, let's see how nouns, pronouns, and adjectives might appear in a sentence together:

adj.   adj. noun   pron. noun   adj. noun
The quick, brown fox jumped carefully over his friend, the lazy dog.

What kind of fox? A *quick* and *brown* fox. Which dog? The *lazy* dog.

DEFINITE AND INDEFINITE ARTICLES

A, *an*, and *the* are adjectives that have a special function. They are called **articles** and are sometimes considered a separate part of speech.

They are typically used before nouns and are used to show whether you are referring to a specific or a general noun. Articles are divided into two categories: definite (*the*) and indefinite (*a/an*).

A *definite article* is used when you are referring to specific nouns or pronouns.

Can you pass the bread?

Here, you are not referring to any bread, but some specific bread you have your eye on, probably sitting at the other end of the table just out of reach.

The pipes in the sink are leaking again; I need to call the plumber.

This sentence refers to specific pipes (not just any pipes in the house), a specific sink (not all the sinks, thankfully), and a specific plumber (your regular plumber).

An *indefinite article* is used when you aren't referring to a specific noun or pronoun.

I would love a piece of fruit.

In this example, it's not clear what kind of fruit the speaker wants. No specific fruit has been specified.

A pipe is leaking somewhere; I need to call a plumber.

In this sentence, it's not clear which pipe is leaking, and there is no specific plumber needed—any plumber will do.

TIP

Generally, native speakers of English don't misuse definite and indefinite articles. Using the correct one comes automatically from years and years of speaking English. However, if English is not your first language, it's important to understand the difference between them so you know when to use *a*, *an*, or *the*.

Verbs

WHAT ARE VERBS?

A *verb* indicates an action or state of being. Examples include *laugh*, *laughing*, *is laughing*, *laughed*, *is*, *was*, *were*, *has been*, and *seems*.

▶ **For more help with verbs, see Chapter 31, Finding and Fixing the Major Verb Errors.**

IDENTIFYING VERBS

To find the verb, look for what is happening in a sentence.

Lydia goes to the movies.

What is the action? What is Lydia doing? She *goes* to the movies. Is *going* an action? Yes.

Lydia loves silent films.

What is happening in this sentence? The action is *loves*. That's what Lydia is doing; she *loves*. Although *love* may not seem like an action because you can't see her doing it, it is. Think of *love* this way: Is it something you can do or not do? Can she not love? Yes, she can. Therefore, *loving* is an action.

In the next example there is more than one action. What are the actions?

Lydia buys popcorn and sits in the front row.

What is Lydia doing? She *buys* and *sits*, so these are the verbs in the sentence.

Often action verbs get a little help from their friends, the *helping verbs*.

Helping Verbs

is, am, are, was, were, be, being, been	may, might, must	shall, should
do, does, did	can, could	will, would
have, has, had		

Memorize these or keep a list of them, and when you see them, know they are part of the main verb.

A noisy couple was sitting behind her.

In this case, the verb includes the helping verb *was* and the action *sitting*.

In some sentences, the verb is not an action but a state of being. This means that something simply exists—something is or was—as in the following sentence:

The movie was in black and white.

When looking for the verb in this sentence, you might have difficulty at first because there is no action. The movie didn't do anything. It just existed; the movie *was*. Here are some more examples of verbs that show state of being:

The sky is a cloudless, perfect blue.

The traffic on the freeway was at a standstill.

There are two sides to every story.

I am optimistic about the new semester.

What else do you need to know about verbs? Verbs are modified by (described by) adverbs, which we'll discuss in the following section.

Adverbs

WHAT ARE ADVERBS?

An *adverb* is a word that describes a verb, an adjective, or another adverb. Adverbs answer the following five questions:

1. Where?
2. How?
3. Why?
4. When?
5. To what extent?

Adverbs are similar to adjectives in that they both describe or provide more information about another word; but remember, adjectives modify nouns and pronouns, and adverbs modify verbs, adjectives, and other adverbs. In the following examples, the adverbs are underlined twice and the word being modified is underlined once.

Verbs   Melanie ran tirelessly.

How did she run? She ran *tirelessly*.

Adjectives   The sky at sunset was extremely pretty.

To find the adjective, ask: What kind of sky was it at sunset? It was *pretty.* Then ask the adverb question about the adjective. How pretty was it? It was *extremely* pretty.

Other Adverbs   If you make errors, you should proofread more cautiously.

How should you proofread? *Cautiously.* How cautiously should you proofread? *More* cautiously.

IDENTIFYING ADVERBS

Adverbs answer the five questions listed previously. Many adverbs end in *-ly*, but not all do. In the following examples, the word being modified is underlined.

Lydia laughed loudly during the movie.

Ask yourself: How did Lydia laugh? Lydia laughed *loudly*.

The movie was over too soon.

Ask yourself: When was the movie over? *Soon.* How soon? *Too* soon. In this case, as you can see, there are *two* adverbs. The first modifies the verb *was*; the second modifies the adverb *soon*.

The movie was very good.

How good was the movie? *Very* good.

Sometimes Lydia will <u>see</u> a double feature.

When will she see a double feature? She'll see a double feature *sometimes*.

Now let's see how nouns, pronouns, adjectives, verbs, and adverbs might appear in a sentence.

art. adj.   adj. noun verb   adverb   pron. noun art. adj. noun
The quick, brown fox jumped carefully over his friend, the lazy dog.

Wow—we've learned the function of almost all the words in the sentence. What about the word *over*, though? We'll cover that on page 590.

Conjunctions

A *conjunction* is a word that joins other words and phrases and sentences together and shows the relationship between them. There are four kinds of conjunctions: coordinating conjunctions, correlative conjunctions, subordinating conjunctions, and conjunctive adverbs. Let's take a look at each of these.

COORDINATING CONJUNCTIONS

Coordinating conjunctions join words, phrases, or clauses that are parallel in structure. In the following example, *but* joins two complete sentences, each with a subject (underlined once) and a verb (underlined twice).

The <u>desserts</u> here <u>are</u> delicious, *but* the <u>coffee</u> <u>is</u> on the weak side.

There are only seven coordinating conjunctions, and you can remember them easily by the catchword "FANBOYS":

Coordinating Conjunctions
For
And
Nor
But
Or
Yet
So

CORRELATIVE CONJUNCTIONS

Correlative conjunctions come in pairs and, like coordinating conjunctions, join parallel grammatical structures, as shown in the following sentences. In the first sentence, the conjunctions join nouns that function as subjects. In the second sentence, the conjunctions join two verb phrases. The conjunctions are underlined.

> Both the apple pie and the pecan pie are outstanding.

> We should either share a piece or skip dessert.

Here's the full list of correlative conjunctions:

Correlative Conjunctions
as/as
both/and
either/or
neither/nor
not only/but also
whether/or

SUBORDINATING CONJUNCTIONS

Subordinating conjunctions, also referred to as subordinators, introduce a clause. They are great words to help relate the ideas of the clause to the rest of the sentence, but these words make a powerful change to the clause they are attached to: They make it a *dependent clause*, which means it can no longer stand on its own. In the following example, the dependent clause is underlined.

> Because I am trying to cut down on sugar, I think I'll skip dessert after all.

Common Subordinating Conjunctions		
after	if	unless
although	now	until
as	once	when
as if	provided that	where
because	since	whereas
before	so that	which
even	than	while
even if	that	who
even though	though	whoever

▶ For more on subordinators, see Chapter 30, Sentence Structure.

CONJUNCTIVE ADVERBS

These are mostly used as transition words leading from one sentence to the next, as in the following example:

> I'll skip dessert. However, coffee might be nice.

When joining two complete sentences together, use a semicolon before the conjunctive adverb and a comma after it:

I really enjoyed the whole dining experience; <u>nevertheless</u>, I now regret that I didn't order dessert.

Common Conjunctive Adverbs

also	consequently	however	on the other hand
altogether	finally	meanwhile	similarly
as a result	further	moreover	then
besides	furthermore	nevertheless	therefore

Prepositions

A *preposition* is a word that shows location in time or space. Prepositions are always part of a *prepositional phrase*, which begins with a preposition and ends with a noun or pronoun.

The troll lived <u>under the bridge</u>.

Under is the preposition; *bridge* is its object; and the underlined portion is the prepositional phrase.

Common Prepositions

about	besides	in regard to	over
above	between	in spite of	since
according to	beyond	inside	through
across	by	instead of	throughout
after	by way of	into	till
against	down	like	to
around	during	near	toward
at	except	of	under
because of	for	off	until
before	from	on	up
behind	in	on account of	upon
below	in addition to	out	with
beneath	in front of	out of	without
beside	in place of	outside	

TIP

Any word you can put in the blank of the following sentence is probably a preposition:

The ant ran _____ the picnic basket.

There are prepositions that won't work in this sentence, but many will.

Prepositional phrases add interesting material to a sentence, but they are never the main subject or main verb of the sentence. In the examples that follow, the prepositional phrase is underlined.

Ellie surfs the Internet <u>in her spare time</u>.

The prepositional phrase *in her spare time* adds information, but it's not the subject. Who surfs? Ellie does, so *Ellie* is the main subject. What does

Ellie do? She surfs, so *surfs* is the main verb. *In her spare time* tells us when Ellie surfs.

Once you get the hang of prepositional phrases, you can see that you can use them to add all kinds of information to the sentence:

> In the morning, Ellie surfs the Internet.

> Ellie surfs the Internet after school at the school's computer lab.

> Instead of writing her paper, Ellie surfs the Internet.

Still, the subject is *Ellie*, and she's still surfing.

Interjections

An *interjection* is a word like *Aha!*, *Oh!*, *Wow!*, or *Whoops!* used to indicate emotion. Here are a few examples:

> Darn! There is no more milk left!

> Hey! Hold the elevator!

Now let's see how nouns, pronouns, adjectives, verbs, adverbs, conjunctions, prepositions, articles, and interjections might all appear in a single sentence.

> interj. art. adj.   adj. noun verb   adverb prep. pron. noun art. adj. noun
> Wow! The quick, brown fox jumped carefully over his friend, the lazy dog.

That's almost all eight parts of speech. (Did you notice that there were no conjunctions?) Well done!

practice it 28.1   Identifying the Parts of Speech

In the paragraph on p. 592, identify the parts of speech for the words in bold. Either write the part of speech above the word or use the number of the part of speech to identify it.

1. noun
2. pronoun
3. verb
4. adjective
5. adverb
6. preposition
7. conjunction
8. interjection

continued ❯

Not all **penguins** live **among** ice and snow. **Although** the penguins of Antarctica are the most famous, only five species of penguin **live** on that icy continent. There are twelve other **species** of penguin that live elsewhere **in the** Southern Hemisphere from the Galapagos Islands to the **very southern tip** of the African continent. Many of these African penguins live **on** islands off the coast of mainland Africa, although several colonies of the African penguins live **contentedly** on the actual continent. **They were** the first penguins that **European** explorers encountered, **and** by the middle of the twentieth century much of the African penguin population had died out. **Wow! Both** the birds **and** their eggs **were used** for food **or** their habitats were destroyed. Since then, the African penguin population has been dwindling; **consequently**, unless there is more effort to save these lovable birds, **their** future **is** in peril.

practice it 28.2   Using Parts of Speech

In this Mad Libs–style activity, fill in the blanks with the appropriate part of speech.

When I am prepping for a test, I have a series of strategies that I practice in order to get ready. First, I make sure to _____ (adv.) take notes in class. This helps _____ (verb) my anxiety when it comes to studying. Second, I always meet with a _____ (noun) because _____ (pronoun) knows a lot about _____ (noun), which can usually help me add to my knowledge. If I can, I also get a group of _____ (plural noun) together so we can _____ (verb) and _____ (verb). This often results in clearing up any confusion I may have had _____ (prepositional phrase). These are _____ (adj.) ways to make sure I am as prepared as I can be. I also make sure to get a _____ (adj.) night's sleep and eat a _____ (adj.) breakfast on the day of the _____ (noun). When I'm done, I can shout _____ (interjection) in relief.

chapter review

In the following chart, fill in the second column to record in your own words the important skills included in this chapter. Then assess yourself to determine whether you are still developing the skill or feel you have mastered it. If you are still developing the skill, make some notes about what you need to work on to master it in the future. If you believe you have already mastered it, explain why.

Skills and concepts covered in this chapter	Explanation in your own words	I'm developing this skill and need to work on . . .	I believe I have mastered this skill because . . .
Identifying nouns and pronouns			
Identifying adjectives			
Identifying verbs			
Identifying adverbs			
Identifying conjunctions			
Identifying prepositions			
Identifying interjections			

in this chapter

- What Is a Sentence?
- What Are Verbs?
- What Are Subjects?
- What Are Phrases?
- What Are Clauses?

29
Basic Sentence Components

What Is a Sentence?

LaunchPad Solo
macmillan learning

Visit **LaunchPad Solo for Readers and Writers > Overview: Sentences** for more about basic sentence components.

At the minimum, a sentence is made up of a subject and a verb, and it must express a complete thought or idea. However, most sentences you write are more complex. While it's not necessary to understand how every word is working in a sentence to write well, knowing the basic components of sentences will help you understand how to fix grammar errors when they occur and will also help you avoid making them.

Verbs

A verb (sometimes called a *predicate*) is a word that is an action or a state of being or existence. In sentences that express actions, the verb tells us what the subject of the sentence is doing. Because actions are usually easier to spot in a sentence than some of the other sentence components, for many students it is easier to find the verb first and then work backwards to find the subject.

Not all verbs describe actions. Some verbs, *helping verbs* (sometimes called *auxiliary verbs*), accompany main verbs to show tense. Still others, *linking verbs*, often express states of being or connect subjects to the words that describe them. These verbs may not always be immediately recognizable as verbs, but it is important to know how to find them in a sentence.

- Action verbs are the things that someone or something can do—for example, *laugh*, *jump*, or *run*.

- Helping verbs, also called auxiliary verbs, are used with other verbs, as in *is running* or *had been*. Often, when we talk about the main verb in a sentence, we actually mean two or more verbs together, also called the *verb phrase*. The helping verbs don't necessarily look like verbs, but there are only twenty-three of them, so they are easy to learn and recognize.

Helping Verbs		
is, am, are, was, were, be, being, been	may, might, must	shall, should
do, does, did	can, could	will, would
have, has, had		

- Linking verbs link the subject with a word that describes the subject.

Linking Verbs and State-of-Being Verbs
is, am, are, was, were, be, being, been
become, seem
feel, taste, touch, smell, sound, look, seem, appear, grow, remain, stay, turn

Verbs are important building blocks of a sentence, so being able to locate the main verb in a sentence will help you avoid many kinds of sentence errors in addition to verb errors. How can you locate the main verb in a sentence? Let's look at an example. In the following sentence, the main verb is underlined:

Regina is going to the art studio after lunch.

What is Regina doing? She *is going*. Both of the underlined words are verbs, and together they make up the main verb of the sentence.

Let's look at another example, one without a clear action:

Wayne was a little ill from the roller coaster.

What was Wayne doing? Well, nothing—he just *was*. In this case, the verb is the state-of-being *was*. The state-of-being verbs are linking verbs, and they are not very action packed as verbs go, but they are still verbs.

Let's try another:

Marjorie seems upset again.

Seems isn't an action, but in a way it is what Marjorie is doing: She is seeming. In this sentence, *seems* links Marjorie with the word *upset*.

Let's try one more:

Gabriel appears angry.

TIP

Think of a linking verb as an equal (=) sign. Marjorie = upset. The equal sign is a good way to check if a verb is linking or not. If you can use the equal sign instead of the verb, it's a linking verb.

What is the verb? Ask yourself: Can you appear? Yes. Can you angry? No. So *appears* is the verb. This method won't always work, but it will often help you locate the verb.

Sentences can include multiple clauses, so there might be more than one verb in a sentence, but there will only be one main verb. Remember, a clause is a group of words that has a subject and a verb. (For more on clauses, see pp. 603–4 later in this chapter.) Here's an example, with the subjects underlined once, the verbs underlined twice, and the subjects and verbs that go together linked by arrows:

The books that I need for this class are in the campus bookstore.

Both *need* and *are* are verbs in this sentence. The word *are* is the main verb. The verb *need* is part of the clause *that I need*, which modifies *books* but can't stand on its own.

To review, a verb can be an action or link the subject to a descriptive word. A sentence can have more than one verb. To correct sentence structure errors, such as fragments and run-ons, you need to figure out which verb is serving as the main verb of the sentence.

TIME-TESTING TO FIND THE VERB

Since looking for the action will only help you part of the time, you need a more surefire way of finding the main verb in a sentence. Luckily there is a fairly easy way to do this, which we call "time-testing."

Let's use this sentence as an example:

The Grand Canyon seems to go on forever.

STEP 1: Put the words *last week* at the beginning of the sentence, and see what word you have to change as you read it out loud.

Last week, the Grand Canyon seemed to go on forever.

STEP 2: Put the words *next week* at the beginning of the sentence, and see what word you have to change as you read it out loud.

Next week, the Grand Canyon will seem to go on forever.

STEP 3: Put the word *today* at the beginning of the sentence, and see what word you have to change as you read it out loud.

Today, the Grand Canyon seems to go on forever.

Aha! In our three time tests, the only word we had to change from the original sentence was *seems*. (Not in every case, but in two of three.) That tells us that *seems* is the verb of the sentence. *Seems* is not an action; it's a linking verb connecting *Grand Canyon* with *to go on forever.*

Let's try another example. In this case, there are two sentences. Each sentence needs to have its own verb. You do the time test to see if you can find them.

It doesn't look real. It looks like a painting.

The first sentence has a slightly more complicated verb situation. When you did the time test, what words did you change? Did you notice that the contraction *doesn't* had to change to either *didn't* or *won't*? The part of each of those words that did not change is the *n't* part of the contraction. This is because *n't* is not actually part of the verb. *Doesn't* is a contraction for *does not*, and the word *not* is an adverb modifying *does*, so *not* is not actually part of the verb. The verb here is really *does look*. *Look* is an action verb and *does* is the helping verb that goes with it. Together, they make up the main verb.

The second sentence is a bit easier. Did you find *looks* as the verb? If so, good job! *Looks* is a linking verb, and linking verbs aren't always easily recognizable as verbs.

Try the time test with these next two sentences to locate the verbs.

The Grand Canyon is about a mile deep and eighteen miles wide.

It boasts some of the most beautiful sunsets in the world.

In the first sentence, did you identify *is* as the verb? If you did, great job. *Is* is one of those verbs you'll learn to identify right away as a verb. It's probably the most commonly used verb in the English language, and it is always used as a verb. For the second sentence, you should have picked *boasts* as the verb.

Here's another one to try:

Running along the floor of the canyon, the Colorado River stretches over 1,400 miles.

This sentence is trickier because there are two words that right away seem like actions: *running* and *stretches*. If you do the time test, you discover that the only word that has to change is *stretches*. There's the verb.

TIP

When you see a word that looks like a verb and ends in *-ing*, check whether it's accompanied by a helping verb; if it isn't, it's not functioning as a verb in the sentence.

---

practice it 29.1   Time-Testing to Find Verbs

Time-test to find the verb in the following sentences:

1. Up close to a mural, you might notice some interesting details that you hadn't seen from farther away.
2. Grace feels excited to be on a boat in the bay because she has always loved sailing.

continued ◯

3. Martha and Bill spent their honeymoon camping rather than staying at a fancy hotel.
4. Even with all the hills, Norm loves walking around the city watching all the people hustling and bustling about.
5. Luckily Jean's favorite Italian restaurant also happens to be right down the block from where we live.

COMPOUND VERBS

In some sentences, more than one action is expressed, and therefore there is more than one main verb. We write sentences like this all the time. A sentence with more than one main verb has a *compound verb*.

> The hikers climbed the steep trail, admired the view, and guzzled plenty of water before heading back down the mountain.

What is the action of this sentence? *Climbed, admired,* and *guzzled.* There are three verbs in this sentence.

Locate the verb(s) in the following sentence; don't forget to use the time test to find the verb(s).

> Instructors work hard planning and grading and care deeply about their students.

Did you find two verbs? You should have found *work* and *care* as the compound verb. (*Planning* and *grading* don't have helping verbs, and they don't change when you time-test.)

Grammar and sentence syntax (the way words are strung together to make meaning) are endlessly fascinating for English instructors, but many of those details don't really affect day-to-day writers. If you are interested in the workings of parts of speech or sentence components, consider taking a grammar class. It's fascinating to poke around under the hood of sentences. For now, though, know that finding the main verb is extremely important, because the main subject(s) and main verb(s) are the fundamental components of the sentence. You can add other information to sentences in the form of prepositional phrases, modifiers, or clauses, but as long as you can find the main subject and verb, you can tackle (and avoid) a lot of the major sentence errors.

practice it 29.2 Finding Compound Verbs

Underline all of the compound verbs in the following paragraph:

Buying a house that is a fixer-upper can result in a beautiful, affordable

home but can also be a lot of work. Many people skip right over fixers

when they are looking to purchase a home because they don't have the experience or desire to do a lot of work on a house. This means that fixers can usually be purchased for a good price. First, you have to have someone inspect and verify that the structure is sound. Also, check the plumbing and fix anything necessary. Another important necessity is making sure the electrical wiring is up to code and safe. Once these foundational elements of a house are in good working order, the fun part begins. With a fixer-upper, you can add a new kind of flooring and repaint all the rooms to your liking. You might update the bathroom or renovate the kitchen too. Depending on your budget, you can make an old house totally new again.

Subjects

The subject of a sentence is the person or thing doing the action of the verb. Think of the subject as the star of the sentence, so to speak. The subject is essentially what the sentence is about. The easiest way to find the subject of the sentence is to first find the verb and then ask: Who or what is doing the action?

Take a look at this sentence:

The Grand Canyon became a national park in 1919.

Okay, let's find the verb. What is the action in this sentence? *Became* is the only action here, so that must be the verb. So who or what *became*? The *Grand Canyon* became, so *Grand Canyon* is the subject and *became* is the verb.

Let's try another:

Rafting is fun on this river.

First, locate the verb *is*, and then ask: Who or what *is*? *Rafting* is, so *rafting* is the subject, even though it might not look like a noun.

SENTENCES THAT BEGIN WITH *THERE IS* OR *THERE ARE*

Consider the following sentence:

There are many outdoor activities at the Grand Canyon.

In sentences starting with *there is* or *there are*, the subject follows the verb. In the preceding sentence, we've underlined the subject once, and the verb twice.

TIP
If the verb is *are*, look for a plural subject; if the verb is *is*, look for a singular subject.

A good way to check that you have the correct subject is to turn the sentence around, beginning with the word you think is the subject and ending with *there is* or *there are*.

> Many outdoor activities at the Grand Canyon <u>are there</u>.

It might sound awkward, but does the sentence make sense? Ask yourself the subject-finding question now: Who or what are there? *Activities* are there, so *activities* is the subject. Here's another example:

> <u>There are</u> some trails you can hike from the top to the bottom of the canyon.

> Some trails you can hike from the top to the bottom of the canyon <u>are there</u>.

Who or what are there? *Trails* are there, so *trails* is the subject.

VERBALS: THE VERBS THAT AREN'T VERBS

Verbals are verbs that function as nouns, adjectives, or adverbs, in terms of parts of speech. In a sentence, verbals that function as nouns may be used as a subject. Verbals used as adjectives might modify a subject or other noun in the sentence.

> **Verbals as Nouns/Subjects**
> *Swimming* is Jean's favorite exercise.
>
> The *waiting* was the hardest part.
>
> *To eavesdrop* is rude.

> **Verbals Used as Adjectives or Adverbs**
> Every *waking* hour should be spent studying. [adj.]
>
> The *swimming* pool is a perfect 80 degrees. [adj.]
>
> *To impress* his boss, Bob worked over the weekend. [adv.]

COMPOUND SUBJECTS

Sentences can have more than one subject, just like they can have more than one verb. This is called a *compound subject*. In these sentences, ask yourself: Who or what is doing the action of the verb? If there are two answers, there is a compound subject.

> The icy roads and strong winds keep me off the roads during winter storms.

After locating the verb *keep*, ask: Who or what keep? *Icy roads* and *strong winds* keep, so both are the subjects of the sentence and make up a compound subject. Here's one more example:

> Both my history class and my English class challenge me in a good way this semester.

Who or what challenge? *History class* and *English class* challenge, so they are the compound subject of the sentence.

practice it 29.3   Finding Subjects

Underline all of the main subjects in the following paragraph. There are 19 subjects to underline.

Fads are ever-present. There are clothing fads, home-design fads, and even dessert fads. Cake-pops are a recent dessert fad. Although having a bite-sized dessert on a stick is convenient, when it comes to cake, a bite-sized serving doesn't quite satisfy. Clearly many people, however, disagree with my opinion because you can still find cake-pops at cafés, as an alternative to wedding cakes, and, of course, in bakeries. Pies have also had their day in the spotlight. Pie shops seem to be opening up throughout major cities, selling full pies, slices, and hand pies that are reminiscent of Hostess pies: small, individual pies to eat with your hands. But any discussion of dessert trends would be remiss without recognizing the trend of boutique ice cream shops. Almost everywhere you look, you can find small mom-and-pop ice cream shops making their own unique flavors of ice cream. Olive oil, green tea, honey-lavender, sweet cream, and even maple-bacon are some of the flavors you might find. There are as many unique flavors as ice cream makers. Often made of organic ingredients, these ice cream shops put a lot of thought into their craft. Eating your way through the various dessert fads is not a bad way to keep up with trends.

practice it 29.4   Finding Subjects and Verbs I

Find all the subjects and verbs in the following paragraph. Circle the subjects and underline the verbs.

The Grand Canyon is a great place for people who love the outdoors and crowds. About five million people visit the park every year. Visitors come from all over the world. They camp, hike, raft, backpack, and visit archaeo-logical ruins. Spring and summer are the most crowded seasons. In the

continued ❯

summer, it seems less like nature and more like a busy city. Still, you will see many animals when visiting the park, especially if you wake up early or stay up late. At sunrise, visitors regularly see elk around the lodges. People who camp can hear the animals scurrying through the campsite at night.

practice it 29.5 Finding Subjects and Verbs II

Find all the subjects and verbs in the following paragraph. Circle the subjects and underline the verbs.

Yellowstone National Park offers visitors a glimpse into the Earth's past. The park sits on a series of giant underground volcanoes. Some of these volcanoes are under Yellowstone Lake. Other evidence of the volcanoes can be seen in all the lava flows, known as mudpots, around the park and the hot springs in the north end near Mammoth Hot Springs. These spectacular features look wonderful but smell awful. Of course, the most famous feature of Yellowstone is the geyser Old Faithful. It erupts very regularly, so visitors can wait and watch for it. Even though Old Faithful is spectacular, any visit to Yellowstone would be incomplete without a trip to some of the other amazing sights.

Phrases

A phrase is a group of words that can't stand on its own as a complete thought; therefore, a phrase is not a sentence, although it may be part of a sentence. There are prepositional phrases, verb phrases, adverb phrases, adjective phrases, and noun phrases. Most of the time, native English speakers use all the different phrases correctly, so for the purposes of writing, keep doing what you are doing. However, the one phrase that gives writers trouble is the prepositional phrase. This is the most important kind of phrase for you to know because it can muddle up your writing.

PREPOSITIONAL PHRASES

We use prepositional phrases all the time to add more information to a sentence. Prepositional phrases always begin with a preposition and always end with a noun or pronoun. In the following examples, prepositions are underlined and prepositional phrases are bold.

▶ **For a definition of prepositions, see Chapter 28, Parts of Speech.**

I am going **to the gym in the morning**.

During the power outage, I had to study **by candlelight**.

On Saturday, I am going to be moving, **with help from friends**.

Notice that in each of these examples, the prepositional phrases stick together as a kind of word unit.

- to the gym
- in the morning
- during the power outage
- by candlelight
- on Saturday
- with help
- from friends

Prepositional phrases are essential sentence components when writing essays. Without them, we couldn't say things like this:

In her article, Olivia Mellan writes **about couples and their attitudes toward money**.

The three bold phrases are prepositional phrases (the prepositions are underlined). See how much they add to academic writing? Without them, all this sentence could say is "Olivia Mellan writes." That is a complete sentence, but it says nothing valuable about her article or her ideas.

Sometimes, however, prepositional phrases get in the way. If you use them incorrectly, you will have trouble writing clear, well-constructed sentences. If this is the case, see Chapter 30, Sentence Structure.

---

practice it 29.6 Finding Prepositional Phrases

Take a look at a paragraph you have written and underline all the prepositional phrases you used. How are they being used in your sentences? What kinds of information do the prepositional phrases add?

Clauses

A clause is a group of words that has a subject and verb. (This is the main difference between a phrase and a clause: Phrases don't have subjects and verbs.) There are two kinds of clauses, *independent clauses* and *dependent clauses*. An independent clause is a complete sentence. A dependent clause can't stand on its own. Left by itself, a dependent clause makes a fragment, which is a major grammar error.

▶ To learn more about fragments and how to avoid them, see Chapter 32, Fragments.

Here are some examples of independent clauses; the subjects are underlined once and the verbs are underlined twice.

Our bodies are 75 percent water.

Water is the healthiest drink for you.

Here's an example of a dependent clause; again, the subject is underlined once and the verb is underlined twice.

Although people can go weeks without food

This may look like a sentence, but it's not. It's a dependent clause because although it has a subject and verb, it does not complete a thought. In order to do so, it needs to be attached to an independent clause.

Although people can go weeks without food, they can survive only a few days without water.

Because all organs require water to function, it is recommended that you drink sixty-four ounces a day.

The bold parts of the sentence are dependent clauses. Read them by themselves to hear how dependent they are on the rest of the sentence: They can't stand alone even though they have a subject and verb.

> **practice it 29.7**   Identifying Phrases, Dependent Clauses, and Sentences (Independent Clauses)
>
> Examine the following sentences to determine which are sentences (independent clauses) and can stand alone, which are dependent clauses, and which are phrases.
>
> 1. Fall is my favorite time of year
> 2. Because I love the beautiful colors
> 3. Drinking warm apple cider is a tradition
> 4. Visiting pumpkin patches
> 5. If you love Halloween, fall is for you
> 6. From September through Thanksgiving
> 7. Though winter is a lot of fun too
> 8. Ever since I was a kid
> 9. Anticipating all the fun of the holidays
> 10. There's so much to look forward to

Knowing how to identify the basic components of a sentence will not only help you avoid common sentence errors like fragments and run-ons, but also help you tackle the next chapter, Sentence Structure, which will show you how to use this knowledge to build more sophisticated sentences (like this one!).

chapter review

In the following chart, fill in the second column to record in your own words the important skills included in this chapter. Then assess yourself to determine whether you are still developing the skill or feel you have mastered it. If you are still developing the skill, make some notes about what you need to work on to master it in the future. If you believe you have already mastered it, explain why.

Skills and concepts covered in this chapter	Explanation in your own words	I'm developing this skill and need to work on . . .	I believe I have mastered this skill because . . .
Finding verbs			
Finding subjects			
Identifying phrases			
Identifying clauses			

30
Sentence Structure

in this chapter

- What Is Coordination?
- What Is Subordination?
- What Are the Four Types of Sentences?
- How Do You Create Variety in Your Sentences?

Sentence structure refers to the way you build, or structure, your sentences. You can build very simple sentences or very complex ones. Complex sentences can convey more sophisticated information and relationships between ideas than simple sentences can, but they are also more prone to sentence errors. One reason to learn about sentence structure is to give your writing some variety. If you write only simple sentences, your writing will sound choppy and repetitive, but if you mix them up and vary the kinds of sentences that you write, you will give your writing more rhythm and interest. The key to using good sentence structure is to understand the basic building blocks of a sentence as discussed in Chapter 29—subjects, verbs, phrases, and clauses (including independent and dependent clauses)—and then to study this chapter to learn the foolproof ways to build on those basics using coordination and subordination.

Coordination to Create Compound Sentences

Coordination is a way of connecting words and ideas in a sentence or between sentences. The most common way to coordinate sentences is by using the *coordinating conjunction*, sometimes better known as **FANBOYS** words. When we use these words to connect two simple sentences, we create compound sentences. Look at these two sentences:

I am tired. I got plenty of sleep.

The two sentences are grammatically fine just as they are, but the sentences are choppy, and the relationship between them is unclear. We can guess at what the writer means, but we shouldn't have to do that work (and we might guess wrong). Take a look at this version:

I am tired, but I got plenty of sleep.

Now, with the word *but* combining these sentences, we see that the writer is ruling out lack of sleep as the cause of his or her tiredness. The word *but* is a coordinating conjunction connecting two complete sentences into a compound sentence and showing the opposing or negative relationship between them. Each of the FANBOYS coordinating conjunctions expresses a particular kind of relationship between the components it connects:

F	**For** indicates cause and effect
A	**And** indicates addition of two things
N	**Nor** indicates addition of two negatives
B	**But** indicates opposition or negation
O	**Or** indicates alternatives
Y	**Yet** indicates opposition
S	**So** indicates cause and effect

You can use these coordinating conjunctions to join words, phrases, or independent clauses. Note that when you use a FANBOYS word to combine two independent clauses, you need to add a comma before the coordinating conjunction. Here's an example:

> Each hour-long episode is like watching a short movie. You don't have to stand in line.

> Each hour-long episode is like watching a short movie, but you don't have to stand in line.

practice it 30.1 Combining Sentences Using Coordination

Use the technique of coordination to combine the sentences provided into a longer, compound sentence that is correctly punctuated. Feel free to add transition words if necessary to make the sentences work.

1. De-extinction is the act of bringing extinct species back from extinction. People have mixed opinions about de-extinction.
2. Some scientists see it as a dream. Other scientists see it as a potential nightmare.
3. There are ethical issues to be considered. Even if it is ethical, it might not be the best use of scientific funding.

continued ❯

4. De-extinction can be done through cloning. It can be done through selective breeding.

5. Many people think cloning should be used to save species that are on the verge of extinction. The idea of cloning extinct animals from thousands of years ago concerns many people.

6. Scientists cannot currently clone dinosaurs. There is really very little danger of a real-life Jurassic Park.

7. Ice Age animals, such as the woolly mammoth, are more likely to be cloned. We have mammoth specimens that were frozen in ice.

8. We have dinosaur fossils. We do not have actual dinosaur flesh preserved anywhere.

9. DNA from the passenger pigeon could be used to bring that species back. Scientists would use another type of pigeon to help them re-create the passenger pigeon.

10. Having a similar species that is roughly the same size as the extinct species makes de-extinction much more feasible. We do not have any animals now that resemble a T-rex.

FINDING AND CORRECTING CHOPPY SENTENCES

Placing multiple short sentences one after the other in a paragraph produces a choppy effect. Read the following two paragraphs to see which one sounds better.

Paragraph 1

Television shows seem to be getting better and better. I used to love TV dramas like *Dallas* and *Charlie's Angels*, which were fun. They were not very realistic. After a number of years, okay, decades, TV shows have become more true to life. Now there are more great dramas on TV, especially HBO and Showtime. There are police dramas like *CSI*, *Law & Order*, *The Closer*, and *Criminal Minds*. The TV dramas like *Breaking Bad* and *True Blood* keep viewers on the edges of their seats. The production quality of the shows is terrific. Each hour-long episode is like watching a short movie. You don't have to stand in line. You don't have to pay the high prices of the movie theaters. Shows like *CSI*, *The Wire*, *The Sopranos*, and *Law & Order* all deal with emergencies or crime in the same way a blockbuster film might. All the shows have excellent writing, action-packed scenes, and good actors.

Paragraph 2

Television shows seem to be getting better and better. I used to love TV dramas like *Dallas* and *Charlie's Angels*, which were fun, but they were not very realistic. After a number of years, okay, decades, TV shows have become more true to life, and now there are more great dramas on TV, especially HBO and Showtime. There are police dramas like *CSI*, *Law & Order*, *The Closer*, and *Criminal Minds*. The TV dramas like *Breaking Bad* and *True Blood* keep viewers on the edges of their seats. The production quality of the shows is terrific, so each hour-long episode is like watching a short movie, but you don't have to stand in line, nor do you have to pay the high prices of the movie theaters. Shows like *CSI*, *The Wire*, *The Sopranos*, and *Law & Order* all deal with emergencies or crime in the same way a blockbuster film might. All the shows have excellent writing, action-packed scenes, and good actors.

Which paragraph sounds smoother and flows better from one idea to the next? If you aren't sure, read them each again before continuing on.

If you chose the second paragraph, we agree. Why? What makes the first paragraph harder to read? If you look back, you'll see that the first paragraph has lots of short, choppy sentences. Reading it is like driving along a series of short streets, each ending with a stop sign. You can get to the end of the paragraph eventually, but the journey is not an easy one. The second paragraph has the same information, in the same order, but it combines the shorter sentences together, not only to provide better flow, but also to show the relationship between the ideas of the sentences.

In order to combine short, choppy sentences into smoother-sounding sentences, you need to understand the rules for avoiding run-on sentences and fragments. You also need to be able to recognize what you want your sentences to say. Let's look at two of the ways you can combine short sentences.

▶ For more on fragments, see Chapter 32, Fragments. For more on run-on sentences, see Chapter 33, Run-Ons: Fused Sentences and Comma Splices.

OPTION 1: **Use a FANBOYS word to combine short sentences.** (For examples, see p. 607.)

OPTION 2: **Use a semicolon (;).** Semicolons have a unique function in English grammar. The semicolon's main job is to join independent clauses (sentences) together without needing a FANBOYS conjunction or a capital letter.

| **Choppy** | Some TV shows have remained popular even after decades. The show *The Simpsons* is one example. |
| **Better** | Some TV shows have remained popular even after decades; The show *The Simpsons* is one example. |

practice it 30.2 Combining Choppy Sentences through Coordination

Rewrite the following choppy paragraph to express the logical relationships between sentences and ideas and to create a smoother paragraph.

continued ❯

Traveling is not only a luxury. It is an education as well. When visiting the eastern United States, you can learn about the Pilgrims. You can learn about early American life by visiting Plymouth Rock in Massachusetts. If you want to travel back in time, you can also visit the Jamestown Settlement in Virginia and Colonial Williamsburg in Virginia. They both have re-created outdoor living-history areas you can walk through. The states of the Midwest boast picturesque, small-town American life in towns throughout Ohio, Illinois, Michigan, Nebraska, Missouri, and Minnesota. You can really get a feel for the importance of farming by driving through these bountiful states. You have your choice when visiting the Pacific Northwest to get a peek into America's logging. Another choice is you can get a peek into the local fishing industry. It would be a shame to leave without learning about the culture of the indigenous people of this region. Don't miss it. The western and southwestern states offer more than just sunshine. They offer interesting historical lessons about the Gold Rush. You won't find any gold there, unless you buy it. The southern states of America provide a rich opportunity to learn more about and understand the history of the civil rights movement. You can visit some very important locales such as the Civil Rights Memorial and Center in Montgomery, Alabama. The Lorraine Hotel in Memphis, Tennessee, where Martin Luther King Jr. was assassinated, is not to be missed. Of course, traveling to our nation's capital, Washington, D.C., is a must for anyone interested in educational travel. This city is home to dozens of museums where you can learn about history, art, and culture all in one place.

Subordination to Create Complex Sentences

Understanding subordination is crucial to understanding how we build sentences in English. Once you get this concept and can recognize the common subordinating words, it will be much easier to notice and fix your errors with fragments, commas, and sentence structure.

If something is subordinate, that means it's on a lower level. In writing, subordination shows a relationship between ideas or sentences in which one idea is "lower" or deserves less emphasis. If you take a regular sentence and attach a subordinating word or phrase to it, it can no longer stand alone as a sentence. It becomes a *dependent clause* or *subordinate clause*. For example, take a perfectly good sentence like this:

Mel got a car.

Now add the subordinating word *after*:

After Mel got a car

This is no longer a perfectly good, complete sentence. It's a *subordinate clause*. (It's a clause because it has a subject and verb, and it's subordinate because it can no longer stand alone.) When we read this, we are left wondering what happened after Mel got a car. The thought is not complete. We could attach this clause to some new information, which might look like this:

After Mel got a car, he stopped taking the bus.

Now this is a complete sentence again. Notice that the emphasis in this sentence is placed on the second half: *he stopped taking the bus.* The subordinate part of the sentence, *After Mel got a car*, tells us when he stopped taking the bus.

COMMA PLACEMENT WITH SUBORDINATING WORDS OR PHRASES

Some of the most common comma mistakes have to do with subordination. While there are always exceptions, you can generally follow these rules:

RULE 1: When you begin a sentence with a subordinate clause, put a comma after it.

Subordinate Clause   Main Clause
When I graduate, I will throw a huge party.

Notice that the comma comes after the entire subordinate clause, not right after the word *when*. You might notice a natural pause between the subordinate clause and the main sentence when you read it out loud.

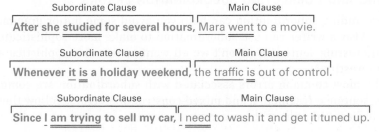

Subordinate Clause   Main Clause
After she studied for several hours, Mara went to a movie.

Subordinate Clause   Main Clause
Whenever it is a holiday weekend, the traffic is out of control.

Subordinate Clause   Main Clause
Since I am trying to sell my car, I need to wash it and get it tuned up.

RULE 2: **When the subordinate clause comes after the main sentence, do not use a comma to separate them.**

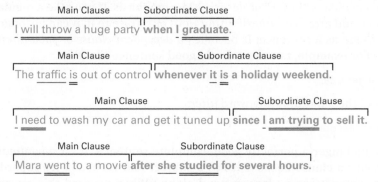

In this sentence, the subordinate clause can come either before the main sentence or after it and have the same meaning.

> **practice it 30.3**   Combining Choppy Sentences through
> Subordination
>
> Rewrite the following choppy paragraph by using subordination
> meaningfully to combine sentences and create a smoother paragraph.
> For a list of common subordinators, see page 613. Try not to use any
> subordinator more than once.
>
> I forgot my new smartphone password. I had to reboot the whole thing.
>
> Maybe I will lose all my contacts and calendar appointments. I rarely sync
>
> my phone. Smartphones are supposed to make my life easier. I'm spend-
>
> ing far too much time taking care of my device. I wish I hadn't forgotten my
>
> new password. That was pretty careless of me.

FINDING AND CORRECTING SUBORDINATION ERRORS

Understanding subordination can help you avoid some major grammar
errors. Also, a writer can use subordination to make more sophisticated
and interesting sentences. (Don't we all want to be more sophisticated
and interesting?)

The most common errors associated with subordination are comma
errors, sentence fragments, and mixed-construction errors. Follow these
steps to find and correct these errors.

STEP 1: Learn to recognize subordinating conjunctions (sometimes called subordinators). Memorize this list if necessary, or at least memorize the subordinators that tend to show up in your mistakes. Add those to your Grammar Log. Whenever any of the subordinators begin a sentence, you should check carefully to make sure you have a complete sentence.

▶ For more on keeping a Grammar Log, see page 575 in Chapter 27, How to Learn the Rules and Apply Them to Your Own Writing.

Common Subordinators

after	since	whereas
although	so that	wherever
as	than	whether
as if	that	which
because	though	whichever
before	unless	while
even if	until	who
even though	whatever	whom
ever since	when	whose
however	whenever	why
if	where	

STEP 2: Learn how to tell the difference between a sentence and a fragment. Here's an example:

Fragment   As long as each person takes one step toward reducing greenhouse gases.

How do we know this is a fragment? Ask yourself: Do we know what will happen as long as each person takes one step toward reducing greenhouse gases? Nope. The sentence doesn't tell us that, so the subordinator *as long as* makes this a fragment. Because it adds an independent clause to the dependent clause, the following sentence is complete:

▶ For more on fragments, see Chapter 32, Fragments.

Correct   As long as each person takes one step toward reducing greenhouse gases, we can greatly reduce the threat of climate change.

Notice that we added the comma *before* we added the independent clause.

practice it 30.4 Editing for Errors with Subordinators

In the following paragraph, look for subordinate-clause fragments and comma errors. When you find an error, fix it. There are four errors.

When you think of freshly baked cookies or cakes. What person comes to mind? If it is Mrs. Fields or your mother or grandmother you are not alone.

continued ❯

Many people associate baking with women and the home kitchen. Although there are plenty of male chefs who, along with female chefs, excel in the pastry arts. Baking is a perfect blend of science and art, and contemporary bakers have taken baking to new heights. Because it relies on chemical changes in the oven you have to be very exact with your measurements and ingredients. Having a background in food chemistry is almost a necessity with baking these days. While there used to be only shows focused on cooking savory appetizers and entrées. There are now several competition cooking shows dedicated strictly to desserts. These shows highlight some of the most intriguing and artistic sweet creations I have ever seen. No longer focused on traditional desserts like cookies, cakes, and pies, these chefs have truly broken the mold when it comes to reinventing dessert. Some of the creations look like modern art pieces—too incredible to eat. Even though they certainly look like they would taste amazing. The proof in this case is not in the pudding, for we never get a chance to try them. We have to instead rely on the culinary wisdom of the celebrity chef judges. Lucky ducks.

Sentence Variety

Just as you would get bored listening to music that all had the same beat or tempo, your reader would find your essay monotonous if your sentences were all the same length and constructed the same way. For example, a shorter sentence among longer sentences may give that sentence some emphasis. You can improve your overall writing quality by getting comfortable with more complex sentence constructions. However, despite all of the variety in what people say, how they can structure their sentences is fairly limited. There are really only four kinds of sentences.

SIMPLE SENTENCE: **One independent clause made up of a subject and a verb and a complete thought**

Independent Clause

The dog ate my homework.

Independent Clause

I always order popcorn at the movies.

Independent Clause

Murals often display culturally or historically significant themes.

COMPOUND SENTENCE: Two or more independent clauses joined by a coordinating conjunction and a comma or by a semicolon

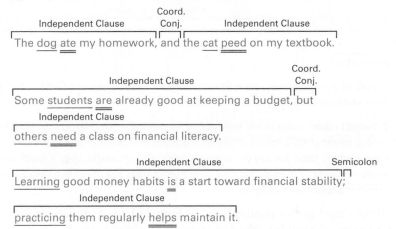

| | Coord. | |
| Independent Clause | Conj. | Independent Clause |

The dog ate my homework, and the cat peed on my textbook.

| | Coord. |
| Independent Clause | Conj. |

Some students are already good at keeping a budget, but

Independent Clause

others need a class on financial literacy.

| Independent Clause | Semicolon |

Learning good money habits is a start toward financial stability;

Independent Clause

practicing them regularly helps maintain it.

▶ **For more about conjunctions, see pages 588–90 in Chapter 28, Parts of Speech.**

COMPLEX SENTENCE: One independent clause and at least one dependent clause

| Independent Clause | Dependent Clause |

The dog ate my homework because he was hungry.

| Dependent Clause | Independent Clause |

Since most jobs require strong writing skills, learning to improve writing in

college is a smart career move.

| Dependent Clause | Independent Clause |

Although you can't choose your siblings, they can be a source of great

comfort and support.

▶ **For more about phrases and clauses, see Chapter 29, Basic Sentence Components.**

COMPOUND-COMPLEX SENTENCE: Two or more independent clauses and at least one dependent clause

| | | Coord. | Independent |
| Independent Clause | Dependent Clause | Conj. | Clause |

The dog ate my homework because he was hungry, and the cat peed on my

textbook.

Independent   Coord.   Independent
Dependent Clause   Clause   Conj.   Clause

Unless it is fostered, curiosity can dwindle, so it is important for parents to

be curious role models for their children.

Independent Clause   Dependent Clause

Celebrities' status is fickle because their fame depends on the whims of

Coord.
Conj.   Independent Clause

their fans, and these fans often lose interest and move on to follow the next

rising star.

Let's look at a paragraph from Susan Engel's "The Case for Curiosity" to see how sentence variety can add interest to a text:

> It doesn't mean much to value a quality like curiosity in children if you never assess whether it's present. What we measure is what we'll teach. In class-rooms where teachers are deliberately cultivating curiosity, they should see more of it in May than September, and they should see their own responses becoming more encouraging.

Note how Engel uses a combination of long and short sentences as well as a mixture of complex (shaded in purple), simple (shaded in green), and compound-complex (shaded in yellow) sentences to add emphasis and complexity to her ideas.

practice it 30.5   Finding the Four Types of Sentences I

Label each of the sentences in the following paragraph by Ken Ilgunas from his essay "Out of Debt, on the Road" by type:

- simple
- compound
- complex
- compound-complex

Then reread the paragraph to get a sense of how sentence variety adds to the impact of what he is writing about.

> It was then that I began to realize that I was getting a very different educa-tion than I'd gotten in college. Jeffrey Williams, in his illuminating essay "The Pedagogy of Debt," calls student debt a "mode of pedagogy." Williams says the university experience teaches students that debt is not

something to be avoided, but normal and expected; it's how things are done. To buy something, we learn to swipe our credit or college ID card and worry about the bill later. Policies like compulsory campus housing and ridiculously priced dining plans force students to go deeply into debt. And, most tragically, the university experience influences how we think about and handle money for the rest of our lives. College does not teach us to save, live frugally, or work our way through school. It teaches us how to be debtors.

practice it 30.6 Finding the Four Types of Sentences II

Look over a paragraph of your writing and label each of your sentences by type:

- simple
- compound
- complex
- compound-complex

How much variety do you have in your writing? Is there a sentence type that you are more prone to using than others? How can you add more variety to your writing?

practice it 30.7 Varying Your Sentence Structure

You have learned all the basic parts of a sentence, so you should now be able to construct all four kinds of sentences: simple, compound, complex, and compound-complex. Try your hand at sentence variety by writing a short paragraph on one of the following topics. Be sure to practice writing at least two of each kind of sentence.

Suggested Paragraph Topics

Your favorite TV show
The last meal you cooked
Your study plan for the week or month
A summary of the last article you read

chapter review

In the following chart, fill in the second column to record in your own words the important skills included in this chapter. Then assess yourself to determine whether you are still developing the skill or feel you have mastered it. If you are still developing the skill, make some notes about what you need to work on to master it in the future. If you believe you have already mastered it, explain why.

Skills and concepts covered in this chapter	Explanation in your own words	I'm developing this skill and need to work on . . .	I believe I have mastered this skill because . . .
Using coordination			
Using subordination			
Identifying the four sentence types			
Varying sentence structure			

in this chapter

- What Is Subject-Verb Agreement?
- What Is Verb Tense?
- What Are Irregular Verbs?

31

Finding and Fixing the Major Verb Errors

Verbs are especially important parts of speech because they are half of the basic requirements for a sentence. (What do you need to have a complete sentence? A subject and a verb!) But verbs can appear in various places in a sentence, and once you've mastered the basics of sentence construction, you might still have some nagging verb errors. The three areas that can get you into trouble with verbs have to do with *subject-verb agreement*, *verb tense*, and *irregular verbs*. It's no wonder that verbs are some of the hardest things for people to get right when they are learning English—and that even those who grew up speaking only English still make mistakes. Verbs are downright tricky sometimes.

So, if you are making mistakes with verbs, your first job is to figure out what sort of mistakes you are making. Are your errors mostly with subject-verb agreement? Verb tense? Incorrect usage of irregular verbs? It's possible that you are making all three errors, but most likely you make one error more than the others. Try to pinpoint your problem areas, if possible, by looking over your past work or asking a tutor or instructor to help you identify them.

LaunchPad Solo
macmillan learning

Visit **LaunchPad Solo for Readers and Writers > Verb Tense** and **> Subject-Verb Agreement** for extra practice in the skills covered in this chapter.

Finding and Fixing Errors in Subject-Verb Agreement

Let's start with subject-verb agreement. Your instructor might write "s/v agr" on your paper, and what he or she means is that you have a verb that doesn't match the subject you used. Let's look at an example:

Jennifer laugh at the comedian.

What's wrong here? The verb *laugh* doesn't agree with—or match—the subject *Jennifer*. We can't really change the subject because only Jennifer is performing the action, so we have to change the verb to match the subject.

Jennifer laughs at the comedian.

Can you hear the difference between *Jennifer laugh* and *Jennifer laughs*? If you can't, then you probably grew up—as many of us did—hearing this error frequently, and you are likely to make it when you write. You will need to pay special attention while editing your writing, using the specific strategies described here.

Errors in subject-verb agreement are serious because they can make a sentence confusing. So how do you get a handle on subject-verb agreement once you have pinpointed it as one of your trouble areas? If you have studied French or Spanish, the following conjugation chart will look familiar:

	Singular	**Plural**
First person	I _____	we _____
Second person	you _____	you _____
Third person	he _____	they _____
	she _____	
	it _____	

This chart provides a basic format for conjugating a verb. When you fill in the chart with a nice, normal, regular verb, it looks like this:

	Singular	**Plural**
First person	I dance	we dance
Second person	you dance	you dance
Third person	he dances	they dance
	she dances	
	it dances	

What do you notice? Most of the forms of *to dance* are the same, except the *he/she/it* form, which we call the third-person singular. That verb form has the letter *s* on the end: *dances*. That box in the chart is always the one that changes.

If the verb ends in a vowel (*a, e, i, o, u*), then add *-es* instead of just *-s* to that third-person singular form. Here's an example with the verb *to do*:

	Singular	Plural
First person	I do	we do
Second person	you do	you do
Third person	he does	they do
	she does	
	it does	

Nice and regular, right? Remember, though, there are three things you have to know about verbs: subject-verb agreement, tense, and irregulars. What happens when we try to figure out the subject-verb agreement for a really irregular verb? Take a look at the verb *to be*:

	Singular	Plural
First person	I am	we are
Second person	you are	you are
Third person	he is	they are
	she is	
	it is	

This is a truly funky irregular verb. It's also one that we use all the time. What do you notice? Take a minute to look at the boxes again. Which one is the most different? The lower left. Granted, they are all pretty bizarre. None of them even start with the letter *b*. The *he/she/it* verb form is the oddest, though. To have subject-verb agreement with the verb *to be*, you have to make sure the verb you are using matches with the subject. You say, "I am," not "I be" or "I are."

▶ **For more about irregular verbs, see pages 632–35 in this chapter.**

Most of the time, if you make subject-verb agreement errors, it's not with simple sentences. Most adults wouldn't say, "I are ready for a nap." Rather, most adults mess up subject-verb agreement in two scenarios:

1. The subject is very complicated.
2. There are words between the subject and the verb.

Let's look at these two scenarios in greater depth.

COMPLICATED SUBJECTS

Here are two simple sentences:

> José dances. He dances.

That's pretty straightforward, and the subject-verb agreement is easy to hear and see. What happens, though, when the subject is a lot more complicated?

> My older sister Sally's ancient VW still gets twenty miles to the gallon.

Trickier, isn't it? You might start to second-guess yourself. What's the subject? *Sister*? *Sally*? *VW*? All of the above? The full subject, really, is the entire phrase *My older sister Sally's ancient VW*; the main subject is *VW*. The verb is *gets*. Do subject and verb agree? Yes, but you may not be as sure as you were with the simpler *José dances*.

So how do you know for sure if your subjects and verbs agree? One way to double-check or fix your subject-verb agreement is to replace the subject with its corresponding pronoun.

STEP 1: Figure out what you're really talking about in the sentence. In this case,

> My older sister Sally's ancient VW = a car

STEP 2: Figure out which pronoun from the conjugation chart for *to be* fits best. Would you replace *car* with *I, we, you, he, she, it,* or *they*? In this case,

> a car = it

STEP 3: Think about how you would rewrite the sentence using the pronoun. In this case, it would read:

> It still gets twenty miles to the gallon.

Once you see the sentence this way, it's easier to hear and see that the subject and verb agree.

Subjects That Are Indefinite Pronouns. Some tricky subjects might seem like a *they* or a *we* when they really aren't, so be on the lookout for these. The following *indefinite pronouns* should be treated as singular:

another	either	no one
anybody	everybody	one
anyone	everyone	somebody
anything	everything	someone
each	neither	something

For example, even though *everybody* sounds like many people, it is treated like a third-person singular (*he/she/it*) form.

Everybody [every individual he/she] hopes for love and success.

There are other indefinite pronouns that can take a singular or plural verb, depending on the context:

all
any
most
none
some

These words take a singular verb unless they refer to something that has countable components. In general, they are used as singular subjects.

All of my chores are done. [*all* refers to *chores* = plural]

All of the ice cream is gone. [*all* refers to *ice cream* = singular]

Most of my homework is done. [*most* refers to *homework* = singular]

Most of my video games are interesting. [*most* refers to *video games* = plural]

Singular Nouns That End in -*s*.   There are also some strange nouns that look plural because they end in the letter *s* but that actually function as the third-person singular (*it*) form. These include words like the following:

athletics	mumps
civics	news
economics	physics
genetics	series
mathematics	United States
measles	

For example, *United States* would be replaced by the pronoun *it*, not *we*— even if the writer is American.

The **United States** [it] plays a major role in the global economy.

Nouns That Take a Plural Verb.   And, of course, some words seem singular but take a plural verb:

both	pliers
few	scissors
jeans	several
many	shears
pants	trousers

For example, *jeans* would be replaced by the pronoun *they*.

> My **jeans** [they] fit like a glove.

Did you notice how many words in this list are things that come with two legs or points? It's probably not a coincidence. Perhaps these words came to be treated as plural because they have two parts.

Collective Nouns as Subjects.   The following words are usually treated as singular, but they may be treated as plural depending on context. These are known as *collective nouns*:

audience	group	posse
class	jury	team
crowd	media	
family	orchestra	

Let's look at an example:

> The crowd was cheering wildly when the band came back out for an encore.

Here, *the crowd* refers to one group acting together, so it's treated as singular. Here's another example:

> My family have always argued about politics.

Here, *family* refers to a group made up of individuals, so it's treated as plural.

WORDS BETWEEN THE SUBJECT AND VERB

The other common reason people make errors in subject-verb agreement is that other words come between the subject and verb, which causes confusion. Consider the following example:

> My physics professor, who has been here since the college first opened and serves on the boards of several internationally ranked academic journals, loves to salsa dance in his spare time.

This sentence conveys a lot of information, but to check the subject-verb agreement, you have to temporarily get rid of some of the information. Look at all the words that come between the subject and verb:

> My physics professor, ~~who has been here since the college first opened and serves on the boards of several internationally ranked academic journals,~~ loves to salsa dance in his spare time.

Once we cut those words out of the sentence, we then see that the subject and verb match:

> My physics <u>professor</u> . . . <u>loves</u> to salsa dance in his spare time.

If you are still confused, you can always change *My physics professor* into the corresponding pronoun:

> <u>He</u> . . . <u>loves</u> to salsa dance in his spare time.

Often, one or more prepositional phrases are between the subject and the verb. Prepositional phrases seem to throw students off because they end with a noun or pronoun, and this sometimes causes confusion about which noun is the subject. For example, take a look at this sentence:

> The bank with the free checking accounts is my favorite.

Accounts is doesn't sound right if you read just those two words together, but in this case you shouldn't read those two words together. *Accounts* is part of the prepositional phrase *with the free checking accounts*. What happens if you eliminate that prepositional phrase temporarily?

> The <u>bank</u> ~~with the free checking accounts~~ <u>is</u> my favorite.

Now it's easier to see that the subject is *bank* and the verb is *is*. *The bank is* sounds right. The subject and verb do agree.

Simple, right? In fact, simplicity is your best tool for correcting errors in subject-verb agreement. Once you change the subject into a simple pronoun and temporarily eliminate any extra words or phrases, you can simplify the sentence and check its subject-verb agreement.

---

practice it 31.1   Editing for Subject-Verb Agreement Errors I

The following paragraph has only subject-verb agreement errors. You should find and fix six errors.

According to Carol S. Dweck, we have the fixed-mind-set students, who approaches their learning by just doing the bare minimum. On the other hand, there is students who have a growth mind-set. Having a growth mind-set mean you are more eager to learn. A student who has a growth mind-set always try to achieve a lot more. In my opinion, having a growth mind-set is the best way to progress in life. This way of thinking about life show that you believe in yourself and have hope for the future. My sister, who is successful in her career and makes my family proud, have a growth mind-set all the way. I am working hard to be like her.

practice it 31.2 Editing for Subject-Verb Agreement Errors II

Find and fix ten subject-verb agreement errors in the following paragraph.

If you have studied French or Spanish, then you might be able to figure out that the word "parasol" come from the prefix "para," which mean to stop or shield, and the root "sol," which means sun. So a "parasol" shield you from the sun. However, "para" can have totally different meanings in other words. For instance, in an English word like "paramedic" or "paralegal," the prefix "para" means someone who are slightly less trained. A paralegal have less training and fewer responsibilities than an actual lawyer. "Para" can also means abnormal or beyond, as in "paranormal" or "paranoia"; in this case, the "noia" part of the word come from the Greek "noos," which means "mind." If the root "graph" means something drawn or written, what do you thinks the prefix "para" means in the word "paragraph"? You would have to know something about the history of how books were made to get that answer correct. In the earliest days when books were hand-made, the bookmakers would mark a break in the text with a paragraph symbol in the margins. So in this case, the "para" in "paragraph" literally mean beside the writing. In fact, any annotations written in the margins were originally referred to as paragraphs. The word have since evolved to mean the break, usually a tab space but sometimes a line space, that we leave between sections of writing about different topics.

Finding and Fixing Errors in Verb Tense

The second major type of verb error you might make has to do with verb tense. Tense indicates time. So when we speak of verb tense, we mean the time period in which the action happened—past, present, or future. It happens; it happened; it will happen—all of these are different verb tenses. If your instructor writes "tense" or "tense shift" while correcting your paper, then you have problems with verb tense.

Let's start with the present tenses. On page 627, we list verb tenses that refer to the various ways you can do something in the **present**.

Present	Jane smiles when she serves ice cream.
Present Progressive	Jane is smiling because she likes serving ice cream.
Present Perfect Progressive	Jane has been smiling while serving ice cream for three hours.

Now, let's look at a few of the ways you can indicate something happened in the **past**, or at least started in the past:

Past	Jane smiled at me at the ice cream shop yesterday.
Past Progressive	Jane was smiling when I walked in the door.
Past Perfect	Jane had smiled when I ordered a chocolate malt, but then she frowned when she realized I had no money.
Past Perfect Progressive	Jane had been smiling at me for three minutes when I finally admitted I'm lactose intolerant.

Finally, there are a number of ways you can talk about **future** actions:

Future	Jane will smile at Bob if he comes for ice cream tonight.
Future Progressive	Jane will be smiling when Bob drops his ice cream cone.
Future Perfect	Jane will have smiled at 287 customers by the end of the day.
Future Perfect Progressive	Jane will have been smiling for eight hours by the time her shift is over tonight.

Each verb tense has a name, and if you are learning English as a second language, you may need additional instruction in these tenses. Mostly, though, the goal is to understand the implied time difference enough so that you can figure out from context when something happened or when it happened in relation to another event. For instance, the complicated verb tense *had been smiling* implies that Jane was smiling in the past and had been doing it for some time until something else happened. Both actions are over now. Verb tense becomes a problem when you use the wrong tense or—more commonly—when you shift from one tense to another inappropriately.

Instead of memorizing grammatical terms for each verb tense, concentrate on asking yourself the following key questions:

- Did the action happen in the past, present, or future?
- Is the action ongoing, or is it finished or will it finish?
- If there is more than one action happening, which one happened first?

Since the proper use of verb tense is always context specific—meaning it depends on what exactly you are saying—you have to check verb tense on a case-by-case basis. Generally, reading out loud is a good strategy to edit for verb tense if you are a native speaker of English.

USING THE WRONG VERB TENSE

Remember, verb tense means verb *time*. Let's say, for instance, you are describing what happened at a birthday party yesterday. Since the party is in the past, and it is not still going on, you use *simple past*:

> We had a great time at Samantha's birthday party. She served twenty-five different kinds of cupcakes.

How would that sound in the *simple present* tense?

> We have a great time at Samantha's birthday party. She serves twenty-five different kinds of cupcakes.

Not quite right, huh? If the party was still going on, and, let's say, we called a friend to brag about it while we were still there, we would put it this way, using the *present progressive*, which is used when something is currently happening.

> We are having a great time at Samantha's birthday party. She is serving twenty-five different kinds of cupcakes.

A bit conceited, but grammatically correct. Now, what about the future tense? How would that sound?

> We will have a great time at Samantha's birthday party. She will serve twenty-five different kinds of cupcakes.

That sounds okay. The question is, did the party already happen or not? Only you, the author/guest, know what you are trying to say. Choose the right verb tense so that your reader knows when the party took place. The verb tense is the only indication of this information in the sentence.

THE LITERARY PRESENT

One unusual thing about academic writing is the use of the "literary present tense." What this means is that we are expected to write in the present tense when writing about what happens in literature, films, and other creative works. Why? It's a convention, or a rule. It does have some logic to it as well: Every time you open a book, the characters are always doing the same actions—Huck's always going down the river; Harry Potter's always battling Voldemort. They always exist in the present; frozen in the literary present, they never change. This same logic applies when referring to the author writing the text. Here's what it looks like:

> As <u>Mark Twain</u> <u>writes</u> in *Huckleberry Finn*, "We went to a clump of bushes, and Tom made everybody swear to keep the secret, and then showed them a hole in the hill, right in the thickest part of the bushes" (9).

Sure, Mark Twain has been dead for over a century, but in academic writing we still say "Mark Twain writes . . ."

SHIFTING INCORRECTLY BETWEEN TENSES

Most verb-tense errors are actually verb-tense-shift errors. The rules for these can be complex because the correct verb tense always depends on the context. Let's look at a couple of common student verb-tense errors, starting with this example:

| Incorrect | She **was** in a bad mood because she **is** in an awkward position between her bickering friends. |

Here the writer shifts from *was* to *is*—from past to present—a shift for which there is no reason in the sentence.

| Correct | She **was** in a bad mood because she **was** in an awkward position between her bickering friends. |

OR

| Correct | She **is** in a bad mood because she **is** in an awkward position between her bickering friends. |

Only the writer knows whether past or present is preferable; the important thing is to stay consistent, since there is no logical reason to shift tenses. Here's another example:

| Incorrect | Yesterday, he **was** being weird because he **gets** too little sleep. |

Here, we clearly have a time marker, the word *yesterday*. So we know this action took place in the past.

| Correct | Yesterday, he **was** being weird because he **got** too little sleep. |

When you write a paragraph, you often need to shift from one verb tense to another because of what you are trying to say, which is appropriate. On page 630 look at the short paragraph that shifts from one verb tense to another correctly.

> Financial literacy <u>used</u> to be taught in most high schools, but it <u>has</u> not been <u>taught</u> since school boards <u>cut</u> home economics classes in order to focus more on English, math, and science. They <u>might have moved</u> the financial literacy component of the curriculum into the math classes, but for some reason they <u>didn't</u>. Unfortunately, most students <u>are</u> no longer <u>taught</u> how to read a contract, balance a checkbook, or make a home budget.

As you can see, the basic verb tense is past (*used, cut, didn't*). The verb tense shifts when appropriate, though, to more complicated tenses like *has been taught*. In fact, there are many appropriate verb tense shifts in the paragraph.

So, then, how do you shift verb tense appropriately while writing? Try following these steps.

STEP 1: Figure out what time frame you want to use throughout the piece of writing: past, present, or future. For example:

> It **was** August 29, 2016, the first day of my college career. I nervously **took** a seat in the front row of my English class. [time frame: past]

OR

> It **is** August 29, 2016, the first day of my college career. I nervously **take** a seat in the front row of my English class. [time frame: present]

STEP 2: When something happens outside of your basic time frame, change the verb tense. Be sure to return to your basic time frame immediately afterward. In the following example, the basic time frame is the simple past, and most of the verbs are in the simple past (they are in bold italic so you can see them). However, some of the verbs (the ones that are underlined) indicate actions that happened prior to August 29, 2016, so the verb tense shifts appropriately.

My College Career by Joe Mangaro, February 2017

> It ***was*** August 29, 2016, the first day of my college career. Just a few days earlier, I <u>had decided</u> to quit my job and register for classes at City College. I nervously ***took*** a seat in my first class, English 100. For the past ten years, I <u>had been working</u> in a small factory, bored out of my skull. Now, all of a sudden, I ***found*** myself ***crammed*** into a chair too small for me, ***surrounded*** by a bunch of teenagers. I ***felt*** too old to be in college, and they ***looked*** too young to ever be my friends. I ***found*** out that I ***had*** more in common with them than I <u>had thought</u>.

If the tense shifts in this paragraph are confusing, it might help to make a time line of the events. It would look like the example on page 631.

2006–2016	approx. August 23, 2016	August 29, 2016	February 2017
working in a factory, bored	decided to quit job and register for college	first day of college	writing this essay

Having a clear sense of the time line makes it much easier to get your verbs right, so take the time to draw one if you find that you are not sure about what happened when.

practice it 31.3 Editing for Verb-Tense Errors I

Verb-tense errors are context specific, so there will be more than one way to fix the following paragraph. Maintain consistent simple past tense unless specific time markers require you to shift to another tense. You should find and fix sixteen verb errors.

On April 23, 1967, Bobby McGregor, who was then seventeen, stolen fifteen dollars from the home of his aunt and uncle, Mr. and Mrs. Neal McGregor. Since Bobby was a family member, the McGregors do not press charges. Now, looking back on it after all these years, the McGregors wishing they had. Perhaps, they might stop Bobby from developing into one of the worst petty thieves in town history. For on April 24, 1967, thrilling at how easy it would be to take the fifteen dollars, Bobby breaked into the local general store and stolen some perfume for his little sister, Kate, and a baseball glove for his brother, Sammy. Two days later, he was slipping into the school cafeteria after the lunch period and walked off with fourteen chocolate chip cookies. From there, things are going downhill quickly: A lawn mower was pilfer from the local hardware shop, a historical brass bell was remove from the town museum, and fourteen glass rabbit figurines vanish from the mayor's wife's personal collection. No one could quite identify the thief, but everyone in town had their suspicions. The McGregor name was tarnish forever. Little Kate had no friends at school, and Sammy's dream of becoming president is crushed. Ashamed but silent, Bobby left town when he turned eighteen, never to be seen or hearing from again.

practice it 31.4   Editing for Verb-Tense Errors II

Verb-tense errors are context specific, so there will be more than one way to fix the following paragraph. Maintain consistent simple present tense unless specific time markers require you to shift to another tense. Find and correct twelve errors in verb tense in the following paragraph.

The typical American suburban lawn today had one type of grass, with each blade the same bright green, cut to a uniform height. Many Americans obsess over their lawns, trying to eradicate every weed and bit of clover. They pulled weeds and sprayed weedkiller. They will fertilize several times a year. In warmer climates, they even reseeding their lawn so it stays green all year round. The American lawn, however, hasn't always been like this. In fact, this stereotypical lush green lawn will come about in the 1950s, a time of economic success and social conformity. People have the money to buy all the new lawn mowers that were being invented and they will want to keep up appearances compared to their neighbors in the new suburban communities. Before the 1950s, lawns usually are a mixture of grasses and clovers. The clover actually provide nutrients to the grasses, so homeowners didn't have to apply chemical fertilizers much, if at all. Lawn mowers are hand-pushed machines with a rotating blade, which didn't result in that perfect uniformity. Of course, spending a lot less time taking care of the lawn might have meant that people have more time to enjoy their summers.

Finding and Fixing Errors with Irregular Verbs

The third tricky thing about verbs is that even if you master the rules for verb use, many common verbs in English don't follow the rules. Linguists debate why this is true, but it happens in many languages. For example, the verb *to give* doesn't follow the pattern of a regular verb; in the past tense, we say *she gave me an extra slice of cake*, not *she gived me an extra slice of cake*. Of course, anyone who has ever been around small children will remember laughing at their occasional errors, such as this:

"Billy <u>gived</u> me his truck and I <u>hitted</u> him with it!"

This sentence actually uses the logical past tense of *give* and *hit*, but it doesn't follow accepted usage. A parent would probably repeat back the corrected sentence to the child:

> "Billy gave you his truck and you hit him with it? That's not very nice!"

The child then hears the verb tense in its irregular form—*gave* instead of *gived* and *hit* instead of *hitted*—and eventually, after hearing this a few times, learns the irregular form. (Though who knows how long it might take to work out the problem with Billy and the truck!)

As adults, many of us—even those whose first language is English—still make errors with certain irregular verbs, though not ones so obvious as those in the previous example. More likely, our errors emerge in more complicated verb forms, especially when a form of the verb *to be* is involved. In fact, the verb *to be* is the most frequently used verb in the English language, so it's a good idea to just memorize the various forms of the verb so you can recognize them when you see them. Here are some of them:

	Singular	**Plural**
First person	I am	We are
Second person	You are	You are
Third person	He/She/It is	They are

There are many other irregular verbs. Most of the time, it's the past tense that is irregular—*gave* instead of *gived*, *bought* instead of *buyed*. Sometimes, as with *to be* or *to have*, all the forms of the verb are oddballs. Take care to keep track of the verbs you tend to use incorrectly, and pay attention to the ways that irregular verb forms contribute to your problems with subject-verb agreement or verb tense.

To fix errors with irregular verbs, begin by writing up a list of the verbs that you use incorrectly. Then make flash cards with their proper usage and spend time memorizing them. For instance, if you have trouble with forms of the verb *to be*, write out the conjugation chart a few times. We rarely suggest that you use rote memorization to solve your grammar problems, but this is one of those times when it might be necessary to drill the right information into your head through constant repetition.

Most likely, if you struggle with irregular verbs, it is because English is your second (or third) language, or because you grew up hearing the "wrong" verb over and over. For example, in many regions of the country, people might say, "He *snuck* into the movie theater." This is a regionalism that probably sounds just perfect to you if you live in the American South or parts of the Midwest. It is, however, not proper grammar. The correct way to say it is, "He *sneaked* into the movie theater." But if you grew up hearing *snuck*, then it's going to be a hard habit to break.

Constant repetitive practice, such as making and practicing with flash cards, may be necessary to break the habit.

    If you regularly make one or two errors like this, people will consider it a cute regionalism. If you make many such errors, they will start to question your grasp of the English language. Certain errors also attract more unwelcome attention than others. Simply using *snuck* instead of *sneaked*, for example, will fly below most people's radar, but using *gived* instead of *gave* will not. So target your most serious errors and practice correcting them. Start by looking at the errors your instructor has marked on your papers. Be sure to add those errors to your Grammar Log with some of your own sample sentences.

▶ **For more on keeping a Grammar Log, see page 573 in Chapter 27, How to Learn the Rules and Apply Them to Your Own Writing.**

---

practice it 31.5   Editing for Multiple Errors in Verb Use I

Correct the following paragraph, which has various types of verb problems. Remember, there is more than one correct way to rewrite the paragraph. Check with your instructor or tutor if you get stuck. There are sixteen verb errors.

    Portable music are not a recent invention. It used to be common to see teens with transistor radios, which are small and easy to carry around, but you couldn't play your own music on them. With radios you can only listen to what the station played. Then came boom boxes blasting the latest new music. The problem is that boom boxes were bulky and everyone could have to hear your music. In the eighties, Sony invented the Walkman, which is a small, portable tape player. This was a good change because you could have played any music you wanted. They even made a waterproof version that you could take to the beach or pool. The main problem with a Walkman is that the sound quality of tapes were pretty bad. Sony eventually made a Discman that was the same idea, but it played CDs instead of tapes. The Discman were an improvement from the Walkman, but songs skipped a lot when the Discman gets bumped. With more recent technology came the MiniDisc player, which was a huge improvement, but it didn't last long because even better technology are just around the corner: the MP3 player. The MP3 player's strongest feature was that you could store tons of songs in a compact player. Now it seems like everyone have a smartphone. My phone can hold up to six thousand songs, and it's tiny! It has a long battery life, and I can even watch movies or TV shows on it. Portable music did really evolved over the years, and I can't imagine what's next: probably a microchip that you would drop into your ear.

practice it 31.6 Editing for Multiple Errors in Verb Use II

Correct the following paragraph, which has various types of verb problems. Remember, there is more than one correct way to rewrite a paragraph. Check with your instructor or tutor if you get stuck. There are ten verb errors.

Exploring different majors during your first year or two of college is a good idea even if you think you knew what you want to study. About half of all college freshman has a declared major when they begin college, but some of those students will change their minds along the way. Taking general education courses that were required in the first couple of years can expose you to new subjects that you may have never study before. You may enter college with the idea that you want to major in business, but after taking a marine biology course you decided that tracking the migration patterns of blue whales are what you are born to do. Then again, you might really love business but realized that you have a real aptitude for numbers and decide to focus on financial management instead of marketing. Economics are another related major with a financial focus. Having an open mind while you take a range of classes to give you a chance to find what you enjoy and what you are good at.

chapter review

In the following chart, fill in the second column to record in your own words the important skills included in this chapter. Then assess yourself to determine whether you are still developing the skill or feel you have mastered it. If you are still developing the skill, make some notes about what you need to work on to master it in the future. If you believe you have already mastered it, explain why.

Skills and concepts covered in this chapter	Explanation in your own words	I'm developing this skill and need to work on . . .	I believe I have mastered this skill because . . .
Fixing errors in subject-verb agreement			
Fixing errors in verb tense			
Fixing errors in irregular verb usage			

32

Fragments

What Exactly Is a Fragment?

Fragments are a very common sentence error, and they can seriously affect the meaning of your writing. A fragment is also sometimes called an incomplete sentence, and that's a good way to think about it. Fragments occur when you have a partial sentence that is missing something. You can also think of them as thoughts that aren't completely finished. The three main causes of fragments are

- A missing subject
- A missing verb or part of a verb
- An incomplete thought—a "cliffhanger," so to speak

Your readers care about sentence fragments because without the verb or subject they don't know what the action of the sentence is, or who performs the action. That's why instructors consider sentence fragments major errors. Instructors will usually take points off your grade for them, so you definitely want to learn how to edit to fix fragments. Luckily, learning a few rules and practicing them can help you tackle this problem.

Take a look at the following example:

> **Fragment**   Going to the bookstore to get my textbooks.

This is a fragment because we don't know who is going to the bookstore. In other words, we don't know the subject of the sentence. Now, you may think, "Well, anybody could figure it out—I am the one going to the bookstore," and that fragment would be fine if you were just talking, but in written English, it's important to say what you mean completely.

> **Correct**   <u>I am</u> going to the bookstore to get my textbooks.

For a sentence to be complete, it needs to have all these things: a subject, a complete verb, and a complete thought. An incomplete-thought fragment might occur when you begin to write what seems like

LaunchPad Solo
macmillan learning

Visit **LaunchPad Solo for Readers and Writers > Fragments** for extra practice in the skills covered in this chapter.

a sentence but don't quite finish it. Basically, this fragment occurs when your sentence does not complete your thought. The sentence leaves the reader hanging on to hear the rest of the thought; this type of fragment is sometimes referred to as a "cliffhanger." Sometimes authors write fragments on purpose because they are acceptable in certain kinds of writing like newspaper headlines, magazine articles, literature, or children's picture books. Fragments in these cases are produced intentionally for stylistic purposes, but in academic writing, fragments are always considered errors.

FRAGMENTS THAT ARE MISSING A SUBJECT

TIP

To find the subject of a sentence, ask "Who or what is doing the action of the verb?"

Typically, if there's a problem with a fragment's subject, it's simply that you left it out. This error usually happens when the subject is in the previous sentence or when the subject seems obvious. Most of the time, you can't get away with this type of fragment. Without a subject, you don't have a complete sentence. Take a look at the following example of a fragment:

> **Fragment**   Gave up playing pro basketball to coach.

Ask yourself: Who or what gave up playing basketball? Let's say Samantha did.

> **Correct**   Samantha gave up playing pro basketball to coach.

Let's examine another fragment:

> **Fragment**   Interesting to compare the two readings.

What is interesting to compare? Think about what your sentence is about. What are you trying to say? In this case, you are basically saying *it* is interesting or *comparing* is interesting. Either of these could be the subject.

> **Correct**   It is interesting to compare the two readings.
>
> **OR**
>
> **Correct**   Comparing the two readings is interesting.

When you find fragments that are missing subjects, the solution is to add a subject. Sometimes the subject is actually in the sentence before or after the fragment, and the best fix is to combine the fragment with that sentence. Remember that when you use a semicolon, the parts that come before and after it must be able to stand as complete sentences.

> **Fragment**   Jeremy loved the beach and ocean; also wanted to learn to scuba dive.

Who wanted to learn to scuba dive? *Jeremy.* You can join the fragment to the independent clause to avoid repeating the same subject, or add a subject to the fragment after the semicolon.

▶ **For more on independent clauses, see Chapter 29, Basic Sentence Components.**

Correct   Jeremy loved the beach and ocean <u>and</u> also wanted to learn to scuba dive.

OR

Correct   Jeremy loved the beach and ocean; <u>he</u> also wanted to learn to scuba dive.

Now, let's take a look at a special kind of sentence:

Not **a Fragment**   Finish your coffee before entering the computer lab.

Although this sentence begins with a verb and there is no subject visible in the sentence, it is not a fragment. This sentence is a command, and most command sentences have an implied *you* as the subject even though it won't appear in the sentence.

(Hey, you:) Finish your coffee before entering the computer lab.

practice it 32.1   Finding a Fragment

Find an example from your own writing of a fragment that is missing a subject. Jot it down in your Grammar Log and correct it. If you can't find any, try to make one up, and then correct it.

▶ **For more on keeping a Grammar Log, see page 573 in Chapter 27, How to Learn the Rules and Apply Them to Your Own Writing.**

practice it 32.2   Editing for Fragments Missing Subjects

1. Read the following paragraph and underline all the fragments you find. You should find five problem sentences.
2. Decide how to fix the parts you've underlined. Remember, you can combine sentences, add words, or totally rewrite. Make your corrections by hand in the space above the sentence you are fixing.

Fast Food Nation by Eric Schlosser is an eye-opening book about the fast-food industry in America. Not just about fast-food restaurants, but is revealing about the entire industry from cattle ranching to marketing. The book taught me a lot. Didn't know what went on behind the scenes at a slaughterhouse. The way employees are treated at many fast-food

continued ❍

restaurants was disappointing to read about. McDonald's doesn't want any of its employees to belong to a union. Preferring to close down a restaurant sometimes instead of allowing the employees to create a union to protect workers' rights and wages. What was most surprising, though, was learning about how bad for you the food is. Of course, never thought cheeseburgers and fries were healthy, but I had no idea that they caused so much obesity in people. Not only is the fat bad for you, but there's lots of sugar in the food too. Causing childhood obesity. I will never look at another McBurger the same way again after reading this book.

FRAGMENTS THAT ARE MISSING A VERB OR PART OF A VERB

▶ For more help finding verbs, see "Time-Testing to Find the Verb," page 596 in Chapter 29, Basic Sentence Components.

Sometimes sentences have words that look like verbs, but the verb is not complete or isn't actually a verb at all. Two common causes of fragments are using an *-ing* verb all by itself or using the *to* _____ form of the verb. Watch out for words ending in *-ing* that look like verbs but are not complete on their own. If they do not have a helping verb, then the sentence won't be complete. Also look out for *to* verbs, which are in their infinitive form and can't work as the main verb of the sentence.

Take a look at the following fragment:

Fragment   The waiter carefully balancing several plates on the way back to the kitchen.

▶ For a list of helping verbs, see page 586 in Chapter 28, Parts of Speech.

Can the waiter *balancing*? No, he *was balancing* or maybe he *balanced*. Either add a helping verb to make the verb complete, or turn *balancing* into a verb on its own. In this case, either works.

Correct   The waiter <u>was</u> carefully <u>balancing</u> several plates on the way back to the <u>kitchen</u>.

OR

Correct   The waiter carefully <u>balanced</u> several plates on the way back to the kitchen.

Let's look at another sample fragment:

Fragment   Maya for mayor.

Is there a verb here? Can you *for*? Nope. You can be for something or run for mayor, but you can't *for*. This is a popular campaign slogan, and it fits easily on election posters, but in writing this phrase is considered a fragment. Add a verb.

| Correct | Maya <u>ran</u> for mayor. |

Here's another example:

| Fragment | My history professor to return our exams today. |

Is there a verb here? In this sentence, *to return* seems like a verb (action), but the *to* form can never be the verb. Either add a verb to the sentence, or change the *to* form into a verb.

| Correct | My history professor <u>promised</u> to return our exams today. |

OR

| Correct | My history professor <u>returned</u> our exams today. |

practice it 32.3 Finding a Fragment

Find an example from your own writing of a fragment that is missing a verb or part of a verb. Jot it down in your Grammar Log, and then correct it. If you can't find any, try to make one up, and then correct it.

practice it 32.4 Editing for Fragments Missing Verbs

1. Read the following paragraph and underline all the fragments you find. You should find five problem sentences.
2. Decide how to fix the parts you've underlined. Remember, you can combine sentences, add words, or totally rewrite. Make your corrections by hand in the space above the sentence you are fixing.

Everybody knows the three Rs of waste disposal: reduce, reuse, and recycle, right? Recycling is easy to do. So why don't more people recycle? People are busy and stressed in their daily lives. People feeling inconvenienced. Recycling takes effort, and so people don't do it. An increase in recycling bins around town. However, the problem is also created by our impatient lifestyle. People buy lots of disposable products. For example, plastic razors, disposable cleaning products, and, disposable diapers, which account for a large amount of the landfill waste. Instead, we could shop smarter to reduce the amount of disposables and packaging that gets thrown away. Also, so much food and yard waste that ends up in landfills that could be composted instead. You probably never thought of recycling your old coffee grounds or banana peels, but you can. The end result makes soil. Composting, an easy solution.

FRAGMENTS THAT ARE INCOMPLETE THOUGHTS

▶ **For more on subordinators, see Chapter 28, Parts of Speech, and Chapter 29, Basic Sentence Components.**

Another kind of fragment is an incomplete-thought fragment, also known as a "cliffhanger." This type of fragment occurs when the idea or thought is not complete. These fragments may look a lot like sentences, but they do not complete a thought—they are cliffhangers, because they leave us needing more information. This kind of fragment has several variations. Cliffhangers might be a phrase adding information to another sentence or beginning with a preposition or a subordinator.

With these kinds of fragments, it's often easiest to look at the sentence before or after the fragment to figure out what is missing. In some cases, cliffhanger fragments need both subjects and verbs, as in the following example:

>   **Fragment**   Wishing he had more time to study.

Wishing seems like a verb, but it's not complete without a helping verb because an *-ing* verb alone can't be the main verb of the sentence.

>   **Fragment**   Was wishing he had more time to study.

Okay, that fixes the verb problem, but the sentence is still a fragment because it needs a subject. *Who* was wishing? Let's say *Carlo*.

>   **Correct**   Carlo was wishing he had more time to study.

Now that we have added enough information to make the thought complete, this is no longer a cliffhanger; it's now a complete sentence.

practice it 32.5   Finding and Fixing Fragments

Find the fragments in the following paragraph that are missing subjects or verbs or that do not complete a thought. Rewrite the paragraph to fix the fragments. There are six fragments.

> Elephants a familiar animal but much about them not widely known. For
> example, their great intelligence, their practice of living in close-knit,
> maternal communities, and their complex emotional life. Elephants have a
> very well-defined social structure that is headed by a matriarch—a female,
> usually the oldest of the group, an older elephant. Will be better able to
> lead the herd to water and food sources from memory. The rumor about
> elephants having a terrific memory is true. Elephant babies, called calves,
> are raised communally. Male elephants leave the herd at about twelve
> years old when they go off to live on their own or in bachelor communities.

Living separately from the matriarchal herd for the rest of their lives, returning only to mate. Elephants are also one of the most intelligent animals on the planet and can communicate from one herd to another through stamping on the ground and making a low rumbling sound that humans can't hear. In addition to being smart, elephants have some of the most complex emotional lives of animals. Have a sense of humor, show compassion for other animals, are playful and exhibit cooperation. It is well documented that elephants express grief over the death of other elephants, even ones they don't know. Some scientists believe that elephants' fascination with death suggests an awareness of their own mortality and thus, their own existence. Although they may be a familiar sight in zoos or in movies. There is much more to this magnificent creature than meets the eye, and elephants in the wild are in danger of extinction and must be protected.

Fragments That Begin with Prepositions.   Beware of sentences that begin with prepositional phrases. They often add a bunch of words to a sentence and give you the illusion that it's a complete thought. Don't fall for it! Learn to recognize a prepositional phrase so it doesn't trick you.

▶ **For more on prepositions, see Chapter 28, Parts of Speech, and Chapter 29, Basic Sentence Components.**

Common Prepositions		
after	by	into
among	for	like
as	from	since
before	in	with

Let's look at an example. Here, the second sentence, which is actually a fragment, begins with a prepositional phrase.

Fragment   The author starts off making an argument. *For increasing the number of healthy snacks available to school kids, who are currently at the mercy of fast-food manufacturers.*

The prepositional phrase "For increasing the number of healthy snacks available to school kids, who are currently at the mercy of fast-food manufacturers" cannot stand alone; it is not a complete thought. It should be a part of the previous sentence because it tells us what kind of argument the author is making. Fix this fragment by removing the period after *argument* and making the *F* in *For* lowercase.

> **Correct**   The author starts off making the <u>argument for</u> increasing the number of healthy snacks available to school kids, who are currently at the mercy of fast-food manufacturers.

Here's another example:

> **Fragment**   In an attempt to impress the other guests.

What happened in an attempt to impress the other guests? You need to explain what happened.

> **Correct**   <u>Cynthia wore a fancy hat</u> in an attempt to impress the other guests.

Fragments can often occur when you use a preposition to introduce an author or quote. Be especially on the lookout for fragments like this one:

> **Fragment**   In the beginning of his essay "The Fifteen Appeals of Advertising," states that the appeal for affiliation—friends, family, and romantic relationships—is actually more common than most people would think.

Who is doing the stating? The author, Jib Fowles.

> **Correct**   In the beginning of his essay "The Fifteen Appeals of Advertising," <u>Jib Fowles</u> states that the appeal for affiliation—friends, family, and romantic relationships—is actually more common than most people would think.

---

practice it 32.6   Editing for Fragments That Begin with Prepositions

Make a list of prepositions that you often use and want to keep an eye on in your own writing. Find an example from your own writing of a fragment that begins with a preposition. Jot it down in your Grammar Log, and then correct it. If you can't find any, try to make one up, and then correct it.

▶ **For more on subordinates, see Chapter 28, Parts of Speech, and Chapter 29, Basic Sentence Components.**

Fragments That Begin with Subordinators (Dependent Words). Even if you've never heard of a subordinator or think it sounds like an engine part, don't let this grammar word confuse you. As we discuss in Chapter 28, a subordinate is someone who is lower than someone else; for instance, an employee is the subordinate of the boss.

Some Common Subordinators		
after	even	when
although	if	whenever
anywhere	since	whereas
as	so that	wherever
because	though	while
before	unless	

A subordinating word is a word that makes one part of the sentence "lower" in rank, or dependent on the main sentence. In this position, this part of the sentence can't stand alone; it becomes a fragment. You make a fragment if you put a subordinator on a sentence and don't add anything else to the sentence. This would be a bad idea, as we can see in the following example.

Fragment   *Unless there is a great demand for change.* The school district won't improve the snacks or lunches it provides for students.

What won't happen unless there is great demand for it? *The school district won't change the snacks or lunches.* In this case, it makes the most sense to simply combine the fragment with the sentence following it, since they are really two parts of the same thought.

Correct   Unless there is a great demand for change, the school district won't improve the snacks or lunches it provides for students.

Let's take a look at another example:

Fragment   *Although TV news programs can provide video footage and up-to-the-minute information on developing news stories.* News on the Internet is updated even more frequently throughout the day and night.

Can the first sentence here stand on its own? Does it complete a thought? No. Words like *although* set up a two-part sentence kind of like *if ... then ...* You need both parts for the sentence to make sense and to complete the thought. Here, the second part of the two-part thought is in the next sentence. In this case, combine the two thoughts by replacing the period with a comma. Any time you begin a sentence with a dependent word, you need a comma to separate the first part of the sentence from the rest of the sentence.

Correct   Although TV news programs can provide video footage and up-to-the-minute information on developing news stories, news on the Internet is updated even more frequently throughout the day and night.

Which of the following sentences is a fragment?

Fragment   To me, this party is boring. Since my best friend just met a cute guy. Maybe we'd better stay a while longer.

The fragment is *Since my best friend just met a cute guy*. *Since* is a subordinator, and it creates a cliffhanger because we are left wanting to know what will happen since the best friend just met a cute guy. Once again, you can use a comma to combine the two thoughts.

Correct   To me, this party is boring. Since my best friend just met a cute guy, maybe we'd better stay a while longer.

---

practice it 32.7   Finding a Fragment

Make a list of subordinators that you often use and want to keep an eye on in your writing. Find an example from your own writing of a fragment that begins with a subordinator and jot it down in your Grammar Log. If you can't find any, try to make one up, and then correct it.

Fragments That Add Additional Information: *Who, When, Like,* and *Which* Fragments.   Some fragments are created when you write a phrase that might be adding more information or explanation to a previous sentence, but the phrase can't stand alone. Often, these phrases begin with words like *who, like, when,* and *which*. These fragments are usually best fixed by combining the additional information to another existing sentence. Here's an example:

Fragment   Cosmetic ads especially appeal to teens. *Who might feel insecure about their appearance.*

To whom does *Who might feel insecure about their appearance* refer? *Who* refers to *teens* in the previous sentence and should be a part of that sentence.

Correct   Cosmetic ads especially appeal to <u>teens who might feel insecure</u> about their appearance.

Here's another instance where added information can't stand alone:

Fragment   Of course we are going to have high standards for beauty. *When advertisers only use young, beautiful models to sell their products.*

What is going to happen *When advertisers only use young, beautiful models to sell their products? We are going to have high standards for beauty* when that happens, so this fragment is really finishing the thought of the previous sentence and should be joined with it.

> **Correct**   Of course we are going to have high standards for beauty when advertisers only use young, beautiful models to sell their products.

The word *like* at the beginning of a sentence is almost always an indication that you have made an additional-information type of fragment. Watch out for fragments like the one in this example:

> **Fragment**   To do well this semester, I have mapped out all my major assignments. *Like my art history term paper, my English semester project and paper, and all my final exams.*

Like suggests that you are going to provide examples of something. What are the art history term paper, the English semester project and paper, and the final exams examples of? They are examples of *major assignments.* A list of examples cannot stand on its own as a sentence, because there is no subject. In this case, it should be joined with the sentence before it.

> **Correct**   To do well this semester, I have mapped out all my major assignments, like my art history term paper, my English semester project and paper, and all my final exams.

Similarly, the word *which* at the beginning of a declarative sentence often signals an additional-information fragment:

> **Fragment**   Barney is a great guy and a really fantastic dancer. *Which is why he always gets invited to parties.*

Why does he always get invited to parties? He always gets invited to parties because he is a great guy and a really fantastic dancer. Connect the *which* clause to the previous sentence with a comma to make it complete the thought.

> **Correct**   Barney is a great guy and a really fantastic dancer, which is why he always gets invited to parties.

practice it 32.8   Words That Lead You to Write Fragments

Look at papers you have gotten back from your instructors. In your Grammar Log, make a note about what kinds of words might trigger fragments for you. It's likely that there is a pattern to the types of fragments you write. Once you see your fragment pattern, it's easier to find and fix the errors. (If there is a pattern, your instructor can help you find it too.)

> ▶ **For more on keeping a Grammar Log, see Chapter 27, How to Learn the Rules and Apply Them to Your Own Writing.**

Finding and Fixing Incomplete-Thought Fragments

Find seven sentence fragments in the paragraph below. Correct the sentence fragments by determining which surrounding sentences they fit best with and properly connecting them to eliminate the fragment.

Ebola is a deadly zoonotic virus that crosses from animals to humans. Like rabies. Even though the news media has claimed that Ebola was passed to humans from bats. Scientists still have not conclusively proven that bats were responsible for transmitting the virus to humans. Much research has been done testing hundreds of types of bats. Indeed, bats often do spread diseases, but even the leading expert who did the research only claims that the bats may be responsible for the recent Ebola outbreak. He is not completely sure. Scientists do know that Ebola has been around. Since at least the 1970s. It tends to emerge in a horrible outbreak, killing many people. Then, medical personnel manage to isolate it, and it seems to disappear for years. When it returns it usually has not mutated. Like other viruses. Scientists are still in search of the animal, plant, or insect. That might be the "reservoir host" of Ebola. A "reservoir host" can incubate and pass on a virus but usually does not die from it. Depending on the virus. A human might have to eat an infected reservoir host or just touch it to get infected. If scientists were to determine for sure the reservoir host for Ebola. They could help people living in Africa avoid infection.

Recognizing Fragments in Your Own Writing

The trick to identifying fragments in your own writing is to know what a complete sentence needs and then make sure each sentence has all the necessary parts. When in doubt, ask yourself the following three questions:

1. Does it have a subject?
2. Does it have a verb?
3. Does it complete a thought?

If the answer to any of these questions is "no," you've found a fragment.

Most often, we end up with fragments when the sentence seems long enough to be complete, but isn't. Just because a sentence is long does not mean it is complete; even a long sentence can be a fragment. Look at the following example:

> Cleaner-burning fuels, hybrid cars, and better public transportation have led to improved air quality, which continues to improve. Because older cars are removed from the roads and no longer pollute the air with harmful carbon dioxide.

This seems like two sentences when we read them together, but one is actually a fragment. See what happens when we read them separately:

> Cleaner-burning fuels, hybrid cars, and better public transportation have led to improved air quality, which continues to improve.

Ask yourself: Does it have all the necessary parts?

1. Does it have a subject? Yes: *fuels, cars, and transportation*
2. Does it have a verb? Yes: *have led*
3. Does it complete a thought? Yes: *They've led to improved air quality.*

So that one checks out. How about the next one?

> Because older cars are removed from the roads and no longer pollute the air with harmful carbon dioxide.

1. Does it have a subject? Yes: *cars*
2. Does it have a verb? Yes: *are removed*
3. Does it complete a thought? No: *What happens when older cars are removed from the roads?*

So the second "sentence" is not a sentence at all, but a fragment. Generally, you have two choices when fixing a fragment:

1. Add the missing necessary part.
2. Combine the fragment with the previous or following sentence to complete the thought or to add the necessary part.

In this case, the missing part (what happens when older cars are removed from the roads) is in the previous sentence (air quality will continue to improve).

> **Correct**   Cleaner-burning fuels, hybrid cars, and better public transportation have led to improved air quality, which continues to improve because older cars are removed from the roads and no longer pollute the air with harmful carbon dioxide.

You can learn to fix fragments, but it will take practice. The best way to catch sentence errors like fragments is to read your essay out loud, slowly. Often you can "hear" when a sentence is not complete. Not all fragments are easy to spot, so we've provided some good tips for finding them on the next page.

- **Keep a list of words to look out for** and check your paragraph or essay for sentences that begin with them. When you find them, pay careful attention to whether or not you have created a fragment.

- **Look for sentences that begin with verbs** in your writing and check to make sure you haven't created a fragment.

- **When you edit, get into the habit of reading your writing from back to front.** This helps because you often blend sentences together in your mind when reading. In the case of "cliffhanger" fragments, you won't always be able to tell when a sentence is really missing information without isolating it. To do this, begin at the last sentence of the paragraph or essay and read it through. Check to see if it has a subject, verb, and complete thought. If it does, great, move to the next-to-last sentence and repeat this process all the way through your writing. This trick is a bit time-consuming, but it really helps you find cliffhangers.

- **Don't think that a long sentence is always a complete sentence, or a short sentence is necessarily incomplete.** Fragments can be long or short, and so can sentences. Length is not a good way to determine if something is a fragment or not.

practice it 32.10 Editing for Fragments

1. Read the following paragraph and underline all the fragments you find. You should find eight problem sentences.
2. Decide how to fix the parts you've underlined. Remember, you can combine sentences, add words, or totally rewrite. Make your corrections by hand in the space above the sentence you are fixing.

Most of the time, Americans spend more money than they earn. Which leads them into debt. However, every so often, you end up with extra money in your pockets from a sudden windfall, like a birthday. Or if you're lucky, a tax refund. Wondering what the best use for that money is? A quick trip to Vegas. Sounds like fun, but most of us know there are better ways to spend it. So what should you do with that extra cash? The first thing to do is to pay off your debt or any money you borrowed from someone else. If you have more than one type of debt, you should pay down the one with the highest interest rate first. Usually your credit card. After that, you should try to save a good chunk of change for emergencies. It's smart to imagine what types of emergencies you might have. For instance, a flat tire or a broken cell phone. Maybe even living expenses for three to six months if you live on your own. Then you can decide how much you need to save for emergencies. Once your emergency fund is as full as necessary, then you can start to save for those little luxuries you want, like that trip to Vegas. Knowing what to do with extra cash is the first step toward not having to worry about money.

practice it 32.11 Applying What You've Learned

Take out a draft of your writing and use one or more of the techniques you have learned to search for fragments. If you don't have a current piece of writing, try looking through an older essay or paragraph that you have written. If your instructor has told you that you tend to make fragment errors in your writing, then be especially careful in your search for them.

chapter review

In the following chart, fill in the second column to record in your own words the important skills included in this chapter. Then assess yourself to determine whether you are still developing the skill or feel you have mastered it. If you are still developing the skill, make some notes about what you need to work on to master it in the future. If you believe you have already mastered it, explain why.

Skills and concepts covered in this chapter	Explanation in your own words	I'm developing this skill and need to work on . . .	I believe I have mastered this skill because . . .
Understanding the difference between a fragment and a complete sentence			
Finding fragments with missing subjects			
Finding fragments with missing verbs			
Finding fragments that are incomplete thoughts			
Recognizing and fixing fragments in your own writing			

33

Run-Ons: Fused Sentences and Comma Splices

What Are Fused Sentences and Comma Splices?

LaunchPad Solo
macmillan learning

Visit **LaunchPad Solo for Readers and Writers > Run-Ons** for extra practice in the skills covered in this chapter.

The terms *fused sentence* and *comma splice* refer to sentence errors where two or more sentences are joined incorrectly, creating a *run-on* sentence. (Be aware, however, that some instructors use the term *run-on* to refer to fused sentences only.) Fused sentences and comma splices are errors that can get in the way of your meaning. For instance, take a look at the following fused sentence:

My car broke down yesterday I took the bus to school.

Which does it mean?

My car broke down yesterday, so I took the bus to school.

OR

My car broke down. Yesterday, I took the bus to school.

It gets even more confusing when you have a longer, more involved thought that you are trying to express. Some writers even pile more than two sentences together without any clear indication of where one stops and the next starts:

Run-On   It might be necessary to take the bus drivers usually can help you find the route you need to give him or her the correct change.

Should we take the bus or the drivers? Do I need to give them the correct change or do they help me find the route I need? This sentence is confusing, isn't it?

In the case of a *fused sentence*, the error is that the writer has run one sentence into another without any punctuation between them. Take a look at the following example:

Fused   I will have to make my mom's birthday present the mall is closed.

There are two complete sentences smushed together here. Can you find them?

[I will have to make my mom's birthday present] [the mall is closed.]

Each of these could stand on its own as a complete sentence because each one contains

- A subject (underlined once)
- A verb (underlined twice)
- A complete thought or idea

Let's look at another example:

Fused   I saw *The Hunger Games* I also read the book.

Because the subject of each sentence, *I*, stands out, this fused sentence is probably easier to spot.

[I saw *The Hunger Games*] [I also read the book.]

Here's one final example:

Fused   Some think charter schools may solve the problems of public education they have their own problems.

This fused sentence may be trickier to spot because the sentence is longer.

[Some think charter schools may solve the problems of public education] [they have their own problems.]

▶ To learn how to join two independent clauses with a comma and coordinating conjunction, see Chapter 30, Sentence Structure and Chapter 35, Commas.

Some people think they can fix any fused sentence by inserting a comma into it. But just throwing in a comma usually results in another type of error, a *comma splice*. Commas are great, but on their own they are not strong enough to join complete sentences. Take a look at the following example:

Comma Splice   I will have to make my mom's birthday present, the mall is closed.

This comma splice is essentially the same as the first fused-sentence example; the only difference is the comma between the two sentences.

[I will have to make my mom's birthday present], [the mall is closed.]

The following sentences are also comma splices:

> [Baseball is the de facto national sport of America], [football and soccer are gaining in popularity.]

> [Regular exercise is great for weight loss], [it is even better for heart health.]

Finding and Fixing Fused Sentences and Comma Splices

▶ To review how to find the subject or verb in a sentence, see Chapter 29, Basic Sentence Components.

In order to find and fix fused sentences and comma splices, you have to find the subject and verb in a sentence. These are the basic sentence components, and knowing them makes it possible for you to determine if a sentence is complete or not.

Also, you need to understand what an *independent clause* (complete sentence) is and be able to recognize it. Knowing how to find the subject and verb of a sentence allows you to identify independent clauses, which helps you see if there is more than one sentence joined together in a fused sentence or comma splice.

Here are some steps to follow for fixing fused sentences and comma splices.

STEP 1: **Locate the subject-verb pairs.**

> I remember the first teacher I had she was the same teacher my older sister had.

STEP 2: **Identify the complete independent clauses.** Double-check that both actually express a complete thought coherently (as they do in this example). The double slashes below separate the two complete independent clauses.

> I remember the first teacher I had // she was the same teacher my older sister had.

STEP 3: **Pick a method from the following list to fix the problem.**

- **Add a period and begin each sentence with a capital letter.** This is a good method, but it can lead to two short, choppy sentences, so you need to learn the other methods as well.

  > I remember the first teacher I had. She was the same teacher my older sister had.

- **Add a semicolon (;).** This is a good method to use when the sentences are both short and related in meaning.

I remember the first teacher I had; she was the same teacher my older sister had.

- **Add a comma after the first sentence and a FANBOYS word (*for, and, nor, but, or, yet, so*).** This solution clarifies the relationship between the two ideas.

   I remember the first teacher I had, **and** she was the same teacher my older sister had.

- **Start one of the independent clauses with a subordinating word (*because, since, although, when,* and so on).** This solution makes your sentence more sophisticated.

   I remember the first teacher I had **because** she was the same teacher my older sister had.

With practice, you'll be able to avoid fused sentences and comma splices. Often, these errors happen during the flurry of drafting, when your ideas are coming fast and furious and you don't pay as much attention to sentence structure as you do to your ideas, and that's okay. There are so many things to keep track of during the writing process that sentence problems are common; however, this means that taking enough time to edit and proofread your sentences carefully is essential.

TIP

Just using a FANBOYS word alone to join two sentences is not enough. All FANBOYS words must also have a comma before them to correctly join complete sentences.

▶ **For more on subordinating words, see Chapter 29, Basic Sentence Components.**

practice it 33.1 Editing for Fused Sentences and Comma Splices I

1. Read the following paragraph and underline all the fused sentences and comma splices that you find. You should find five problem sentences.
2. Decide how to fix the parts you've underlined. Remember, to fix the fused sentences and comma splices, you can use a

   - period
   - semicolon
   - comma plus a FANBOYS word
   - subordinating word

   Make your corrections by hand in the space above the sentence you are fixing. To do your best, read slowly and look at every word. If you don't find five errors when you go through the paragraph the first time, try reading the last sentence first. Then read the second-to-last sentence, and so on. You will probably find more errors when you read it "backwards" like this because you will be focusing on the sentence itself instead of on the meaning of the paragraph.

continued ❯

The word *style* is hard to define it means so many different things to different people. Most people think about fashion when they think about style, but it means so much more than that. Style can be the way you walk, style can be the way you talk. Most of all, style is the way you carry yourself. Sometimes your personal style reflects your values when you wear a T-shirt with a political slogan, people assume you believe in that idea. This isn't always true, though, lots of people who aren't hippies wear tie-dyed shirts nowadays, whereas in the old days wearing tie-dye really meant that you were antiwar and into peace, love, and happiness. We shouldn't judge people by their style, sometimes we do, though, especially when someone has no style.

practice it 33.2 Editing for Fused Sentences and Comma Splices II

Follow the instructions for Practice It 33.1 (p. 655) to find and fix five problem sentences in this paragraph.

My mom is a medical doctor she practices at the Johnson Family Care Center in a small town forty miles west of our home. Although it takes her almost an hour to get there from our house, she thinks it's worth it to serve that community. Apparently, very few physicians and nurses live near there so they have difficulty staffing the center adequately. My mom feels like she is making a huge difference in the community by providing medical care to the residents who might otherwise have to drive quite far to see a doctor. When you're sick, you're not in the mood to drive, you sometimes don't get the care you need. Some of her patients are rather poor, too the cost of gas alone might deter them from going to the doctor. Even though the drive is far, the medical center makes it worthwhile, they provide my mom with a pretty nice car and pay her gas and maintenance costs. She told me that they are willing to pay for medical school for any student from the town who would study to be a doctor and commit to living there long term. That sounds like a pretty good deal to me.

practice it 33.3   Editing for Fused Sentences and Comma Splices III

Follow the instructions for Practice It 33.1 (p. 655) to find and fix five problem sentences in this paragraph.

When you think of unicorns, do you think about children's cartoons, rainbows, and fairies, in popular culture today, unicorns are often associated with cuteness and children. Ask any kindergarten classroom full of children to name their favorite animal, and chances are good at least one youngster will say the unicorn, however, the unicorn has played an interesting role in history. The Greeks thought the unicorn was a real animal living in India, as they had seen pictures and sculptures of it in Indian art. In Denmark, the royal throne is supposedly made of unicorn horns unicorns appear on many royal crests across Europe. Over the centuries, many stories have been told about how difficult it is to catch a unicorn, some stories said that if you chased a unicorn, it would jump off a cliff and land headfirst on its horn, which would cushion the blow and allow it to escape. Other stories said that only a pure and beautiful maiden could catch a unicorn indeed, people have been so fascinated with unicorns that early scientists even claimed to have discovered unicorn fossils, though they were probably a mixture of fossils from different animals. Most likely, stories of the unicorn have emerged out of sightings of other one-horned animals, like the rhinoceros, the oryx, and the narwhal, or because of goats whose horns were made to grow together to look like a single horn.

chapter review

In the following chart, fill in the second column to record in your own words the important skills included in this chapter. Then assess yourself to determine whether you are still developing the skill or feel you have mastered it. If you are still developing the skill, make some notes about what you need to work on to master it in the future. If you believe you have already mastered it, explain why.

Skills and concepts covered in this chapter	Explanation in your own words	I'm developing this skill and need to work on . . .	I believe I have mastered this skill because . . .
Understanding fused sentences			
Understanding comma splices			
Finding and fixing fused sentences			
Finding and fixing comma splices			

34
Pronouns

in this chapter

- What Exactly Is a Pronoun?
- What Is an Antecedent?
- What Are Common Pronoun Errors?
- How Do You Fix Pronoun Errors?

What Exactly Is a Pronoun?

Pronouns are words that can be used in place of nouns. Their job is to fill in for nouns, sort of like a stunt double fills in for the movie star in certain scenes. We use pronouns all the time without thinking about them. Understanding how they work will help you avoid making certain sentence errors, though, so they're worth paying attention to. We'll start by discussing the different types of pronouns and their purposes.

LaunchPad Solo
macmillan learning

Visit **LaunchPad Solo for Readers and Writers > Pronouns** for extra practice in the skills covered in this chapter.

SUBJECT PRONOUNS

Some pronouns can be used as a subject.

Subject Pronouns	
I	we
you	you
he/she/it	they

We use these pronouns to replace nouns so that we can avoid repeating the noun over and over again. Consider the following example:

> Professor Pippilini talks too quickly when lecturing. Professor Pippilini always lectures for hours and hours too.

Using *she* rather than *Professor Pippilini* a second time would make the sentences much easier to read or say.

> Professor Pippilini talks too quickly when lecturing. She always lectures for hours and hours too.

POSSESSIVE PRONOUNS

Some pronouns are used to show ownership. These are known as the *possessive pronouns*, but we don't use an apostrophe with them.

Possessive Pronouns	
my/mine	his
our/ours	its
your/yours	their/theirs
her/hers	whose

Here's an example:

> That shirt is <u>mine</u>, not <u>yours</u>!

INDEFINITE PRONOUNS

Some pronouns don't look very much like pronouns, but they function that way by standing in for nouns. The following is a list of pronouns used when you are stating a general principle or idea and not referring to a specific person or thing:

Indefinite Pronouns		
anybody	everybody	no one
anyone	everyone	nothing
anything	everything	somebody
each	neither	someone
either	nobody	something

Here's an example:

> Anybody who wants to board a plane must bring his or her proper identification.

DEMONSTRATIVE PRONOUNS: *THIS/THESE/THAT/THOSE*

Although they do not look or act much like the other pronouns, the words *this*, *that*, *these*, and *those* are, technically speaking, pronouns. When you use one of these words, known as demonstrative pronouns, you are usually using it to replace a group of words. For example, if you and your friend were walking through a neighborhood looking at murals, you might point to one and say, "That is artfully painted." The word *that* replaces the word *mural*, and as long as your friend knows what you're talking about, everything's fine. In writing, we want to be as specific as possible, so we try to avoid overusing *that* in this manner. In other words, we prefer to make *that* or *this* function more as an adjective than a pronoun. So, instead of writing, "That is artfully painted," you should say, "That mural is artfully painted." Since unclear demonstrative pronoun usage is more a clarity issue than a pronoun issue, you will find more examples of how to address this problem in Chapter 39, Clear and Focused Language.

Antecedents

Another important term to know if you want to understand pronouns is *antecedent*. Think of the antecedent as the "ancestor" of the pronoun: The antecedent is the thing that a pronoun replaces, usually a noun or a phrase that acts like a noun. Take a look at the following sentence:

> Stefanie changes the oil in her car every six months because she wants to keep it running.

What does *her* refer to? What does *it* refer to? In this sentence, *Stefanie* is the antecedent for *her*, and *car* is the antecedent for *it*. Take a look at another example:

> Going to the mechanic takes a lot of time, but it is worthwhile.

What does *it* refer to? In this case, the entire phrase *Going to the mechanic* is the antecedent for *it*.

Common Pronoun Errors

Pronoun errors are fairly common, and they tend to fall into the following three major categories:

1. *Pronoun reference*: It's not clear what your pronoun refers to.
2. *Pronoun agreement*: You picked the wrong pronoun to go with the noun it is replacing.
3. *Pronoun shift*: You shift from one pronoun to another when you shouldn't.

PRONOUN-REFERENCE ERRORS

If your reader can't tell which word your pronoun replaces, this problem is called unclear pronoun referent, and you need to fix it. Take a look at this example:

Unclear   Gabriel took his dog for a walk because he was restless.

TIP

Did you notice how the pronoun agreement and shift errors sound a lot like two major verb errors? People who tend to make subject-verb-agreement errors sometimes also make pronoun-agreement errors, and people who make verb-tense-shift errors sometimes make pronoun-shift errors, so watch out for these patterns as you try to pinpoint your own personal grammar errors. You might even try studying the errors together.

Who was restless, the dog or Gabriel? It's not clear who the *he* in this sentence is supposed to replace.

Correct   His dog was getting restless, so Gabriel took him for a walk.

OR

Correct   Gabriel was getting restless, so he took his dog for a walk.

Here's another example:

Unclear   The San Francisco Giants and the Detroit Tigers played against one another in the 2012 World Series, and they ultimately won.

The reader can't tell from this sentence who won. Does *they* refer to the Giants or the Tigers? Did they tie? In this case, you can't replace the noun with a pronoun because the reader can't tell from the context which team name the pronoun replaces. Here's a possible revision:

Correct   The San Francisco Giants ultimately won when they played against the Detroit Tigers in the 2012 World Series.

In this revised sentence, *they* clearly refers to the Giants, so there is no confusion.

practice it 34.1   Editing for Pronoun-Reference Errors

1. Read the following paragraph and underline all the pronoun-reference errors you find. You should find five problem sentences.
2. Decide how to fix the parts you've underlined. Make your corrections by hand in the space above the sentence you are fixing.

The Monterey Road Citizens Committee (MRCC) has been given the tasks

of evaluating possible street designs, gathering input from the residents

and other stakeholders, and making a recommendation about what, if

anything, to change about the street. The MRCC has fifteen members,

including the architect Mrs. O'Malley, who lives on Monterey Road, and

Mr. Watson, who uses his wheelchair to get to the Metro line a block away

from Monterey Road. The redesign was prompted by the street's non-

compliance with the Americans with Disabilities Act. They are obstructed

by light poles and utility boxes. People riding in wheelchairs or pushing baby strollers have great difficulty going down the sidewalk. The street is uneven and badly in need of a new asphalt surface. Mr. Ono, the city planner, recommends the MRCC consider whether bike lanes would be a good addition to the street. Since it has to go to the expense to pave and redesign the sidewalks, other changes should be considered at this time. At the first meeting, they agreed that wheelchair access, bike lanes, and an overall slower traffic pattern are the top priorities. Much to Mr. Ono's surprise, parking is not a high priority on the street. They would prefer to have a bike lane and a quieter street instead of the current number of on-street parking spots. It quickly arrived at a consensus on their goals. The next step is to bring in an engineering consultant to determine the viability of it.

PRONOUN-AGREEMENT ERRORS

The other common pronoun error involves agreement. If you use the wrong pronoun, one that does not agree with the noun it is replacing, you create an error. Usually, the error is that you used a singular pronoun when you should have used a plural one, or vice versa. For instance, if you replace the word *Americans* with a pronoun, you should choose the pronoun *they*—or perhaps *we* if you include yourself in the group. If you replace the phrase *American way of life*, you should choose the pronoun *it*. A way of life is one thing, singular. Look at the following example:

> **Unclear**   Leila liked the songs Eric wrote about her. It made her feel loved.

Here, the pronoun *her* matches with *Leila*, but the pronoun *it* doesn't agree with *songs*. To fix this error, you need to change either the word *songs* or the pronoun.

> **Correct**   Leila liked the song Eric wrote about her. It made her feel loved.

OR

> **Correct**   Leila liked the songs Eric wrote about her. They made her feel loved.

Agreement with Indefinite Pronouns and Collective Nouns. Two categories of words are particularly tricky when it comes to antecedent agreement: *indefinite pronouns* and *collective nouns.* (Both groups should be familiar friends if you have worked on subject-verb agreement at all, since they are some of the biggest hurdles with subject-verb agreement too.) If you recall, the indefinite pronouns are the words beginning with *any-/every-/no-/some-* and ending in *-body/-one/-thing*, plus their friends *each*, *either*, and *neither* (p. 660). These pronouns should all take a third-person singular pronoun: *he, she,* or *it.* Here are some examples:

Everything in my studio is ready for its shipping container.

Something under the bushes is growling and showing its fangs.

Neither car is available with its original 1964 engine.

▶ For more on subject-verb agreement, see Chapter 31, Finding and Fixing the Major Verb Errors.

Collective nouns should also look familiar if you have studied subject-verb agreement. These are words like *couple* and *jury.* The pronoun you use to replace one of these nouns depends upon the context of the sentence. Do you want to stress the "group-ness" of the word, or do you want to emphasize the individual members of the group?

The couple celebrating its first anniversary is so cute.

The couple dividing up their assets are nearly finished with their divorce proceedings.

The first example stresses the togetherness of the couple; the couple functions as one item, an *it.* The second example stresses the separateness of the two people in the couple; the couple function as a *they,* so we use the possessive pronoun *their.*

Gender Agreement. One of the most difficult issues with pronouns is gender agreement. Historically, *he* was used to refer to any person; this was called the "generic *he.*" The generic *he* led to sentences like "When an American wants to vote, he must register." (Huh? Didn't women earn the right to vote nearly a hundred years ago?) Most people avoid this usage today because it's sexist and just plain inaccurate. Instead, we say "he or she," "his or her," and so on, as in the following example:

A student should bring his or her books to class every day.

Eliminating sexist language is great. Figuring out which pronoun to use so that you are not being sexist is sometimes a challenge. The truth is that we aren't used to the sound of gender-neutral pronouns quite yet, so our tongues tend to trip over the "his or her" or the "he or she." While the preceding short sentence about a student's books sounds okay, sentences can become unwieldy pretty quickly.

> **Awkward**   A dog trainer must have patience, for his or her client may need to have his or her basic assumptions about dogs challenged.

Frequently, writers just give up and rewrite such sentences, which usually works.

> **Revised**   A dog trainer must have patience, for the client may need to have basic assumptions about dogs challenged.

Rewriting may work beautifully, as in the preceding example. Because it doesn't always work so well, it's a good idea to learn a few strategies for avoiding sexist language:

- **Switch singular nouns to plural.** This allows your pronouns to shift to the gender-neutral *they*.

  > Dog trainers must have patience, for their clients may need to have their basic assumptions about dogs challenged.

- **Use the generic *one* pronoun.** This can work when the situation is formal; be aware, though, that *one* needs to be used consistently in the sentence. For instance:

  > One must have patience to train dogs, for one is often training one's clients as well.

  Sentences with *one* can sound stiff, so use this strategy judiciously.

In everyday speech, the desire to be gender-neutral has triumphed over correctness with the indefinite pronouns. For example, it is grammatically correct to say:

> Everyone in the tour group to France must be responsible for his or her own luggage.

However, in speech, most people use the incorrect version:

> Everyone in the tour group to France must be responsible for **their** own luggage.

By the time your grandchildren are in college, the language will have probably evolved out of this conundrum, but for now at least, in writing, you should err on the side of correctness and use "his or her" to replace the indefinite pronouns.

▶ **For more about reducing biased language, see Chapter 39, Clear and Focused Language.**

practice it 34.2 Editing for Pronoun-Agreement Errors

1. Read the following paragraph and underline all the pronoun-agreement errors you find. You should find seven problem sentences.
2. Decide how to fix the parts you've underlined. Make your corrections by hand in the space above the sentence you are fixing.

Julia Alvarez's epic novel In the *Time of the Butterflies* tells the story of the four Mirabal sisters, Patria, Dedé, Minerva, and María Teresa. Tracing her lives from girlhood until her tragic end, and even beyond, the story follows the events of her attempts to overthrow the dictator Trujillo. Readers fall in love with the girls, taking sides in our arguments and rooting for them in their romantic and religious quests. No more realistic portrait of sisters has existed in fiction since the March girls sprang from Louisa May Alcott's pen. Alvarez drew on their own family's connection to her parents' homeland in writing this novel, and readers can't help but wonder if he is meant to be the journalist who bothers Dedé, asking all those questions about the girls. *In the Time of the Butterflies* makes readers laugh and cry—and call her sisters.

PRONOUN-SHIFT ERRORS

A pronoun-shift error occurs if you move from one pronoun to a different pronoun (and sometimes back again) when you should not. Take a look at the following example:

Incorrect When one intends to purchase a house, you should always get an inspection.

This sentence leaves the reader confused: Are *one* and *you* the same person? In addition to being unclear, shifting the pronouns like this is odd for a couple of reasons. First, *one* is very formal and *you* is informal. Second, *one* is a third-person pronoun, and *you* is a second-person pronoun. (Did you notice that the verb *intends* ends in *s*? That is the third-person form, which you use with *he*, *she*, or *it*.) Correct this pronoun shift by replacing one or the other of the pronouns to stay consistent:

Correct When one intends to purchase a house, one should always get an inspection.

TIP
When you switch a pronoun to second person (*you*), you also need to double-check the verb. Pronoun and verb problems often go hand in hand, which is why you need to take the time to carefully reread any sentence after you make a change.

OR

Correct   When <u>you</u> intend to purchase a house, <u>you</u> should always get an inspection.

---

practice it 34.3 Editing for Pronoun-Shift Errors

1. Read the following paragraph and underline all the pronoun-shift errors you find. You should find three problem areas, both within and between sentences.
2. Decide how to fix the parts you've underlined. Make your corrections by hand in the space above the sentence you are fixing.

One might think that children's literature is a simplistic form intended only for kids, but the reality is that children's literature is just as sophisticated and rich as literature for adults. Sure, there are plenty of poorly written fairy-tale books out there, but there are probably more badly written romance novels. You cannot judge the genre by its worst examples; we must judge based on the best the field has to offer. Children's classics like *The Wind in the Willows* have endured over time and have probably touched as many minds and hearts as the classics of adult literature. *The Hunger Games* is written so well that you must read it all in a day—or be haunted by nightmares about Katniss in the arena.

Fixing Pronoun Errors

You are likely to make pronoun errors when you rewrite a sentence and don't go back to double-check your writing. Sometimes we change our minds about what we are going to say while we are writing the sentence, and pronouns are usually the biggest casualty. If we change one sentence, this change can have an impact on pronouns later in the paragraph. Therefore, if you don't go back and edit the entire paper at least a couple of times, you are likely to miss pronoun errors.

Often, pronoun errors require some rewriting of the entire sentence structure, and there's usually more than one way you can fix the error. Experiment a little to find the best way to edit the sentence. Editing specifically for pronoun errors is worth the time, especially if your instructor has noted that you make pronoun errors on your papers. Follow these steps, which will help you eliminate most of your mistakes.

STEP 1: **Print out the paper so that you are not working from a computer screen.**   This allows you to write on the draft and to see it all at once.

STEP 2: **Starting at the beginning, read over the draft with a highlighter in hand.**   Highlight every pronoun you find.

STEP 3: **When you have finished highlighting all the pronouns, look at each one individually.**   Ask yourself: What does this pronoun replace? If you can't find the exact word(s) it replaces, that's a red flag that you may have a pronoun-reference problem. If you can find the word(s) it replaces, ask yourself: Does my pronoun match its antecedent? (Remember, the antecedent is what the pronoun replaces.) For example, if your pronoun is *it*, does that fit well with the noun *it* refers back to?

STEP 4: **Check for pronoun shifts by looking at all the highlighted words.**   Did you change from *it* to *he* when you shouldn't have? Did you change from *you* to *one* and back again? Look for these shifts and correct them so you are consistent.

---

practice it 34.4   Editing for Mixed-Pronoun Errors

Find and fix each of the pronoun errors in this paragraph. There are five errors.

Collecting things can be a rewarding hobby. I had an aunt who collected teapots from around the world. It reminded her of different places she had been. Her collection was enormous; they lined the special shelves she had built all over her house. She could remember where she purchased each teapot and when. Collecting stamps, coins, or baseball cards is quite popular, but any interest could inspire a collection; everyone has something he is interested in. A former professor of mine collected elephant figurines. He explained once that he had started his collection as a child after visiting an elephant sanctuary. His office was filled with glass, ceramic, porcelain, and wooden elephant figurines of all sizes. Once you start a collection, going to garage sales or flea markets becomes a treasure hunt for that perfect item to add to one's collection. Since it is a very personal hobby, it is a great way to highlight your personality.

chapter review

In the following chart, fill in the second column to record in your own words the important skills included in this chapter. Then assess yourself to determine whether you are still developing the skill or feel you have mastered it. If you are still developing the skill, make some notes about what you need to work on to master it in the future. If you believe you have already mastered it, explain why.

Skills and concepts covered in this chapter	Explanation in your own words	I'm developing this skill and need to work on . . .	I believe I have mastered this skill because . . .
Understanding pronouns			
Finding and fixing pronoun-reference errors			
Finding and fixing pronoun-agreement errors			
Finding and fixing pronoun-shift errors			

35

Commas

What Is a Comma?

Visit **LaunchPad Solo for Readers and Writers > Commas** for extra practice in the skills covered in this chapter.

The comma (,) is the punctuation mark that makes a speaker or reader pause when reading. It helps the reader figure out what groups of words go together, and it helps establish the rhythm of the sentence. For instance, read the following sentences out loud:

Too fat to jump the cat Mr. Boots just sat and stared.

Difficult, isn't it? Now try it again, pausing where there is a comma:

Too fat to jump, the cat, Mr. Boots, just sat and stared.

In this example, a reader can barely make out what the sentence is saying without the commas. These are very necessary commas. Other times, the commas may not be so absolutely necessary, but they force the reader to pause where you want him or her to pause. For example:

Hey, Marco, where did you put your hat?

has a slightly different rhythm than

Hey Marco, where did you put your hat?

Can you hear the difference when you read these sentences? If not, try reading them again out loud, emphasizing the pauses where there are commas. Controlling the rhythm of the language means you can control the reader's pacing and emphasis, which in turn influences the tone of the language. That little comma has a lot more power than at first glance.

So, how do you use commas correctly? Read on!

Rules for Using Commas

USE A COMMA TO SEPARATE ITEMS IN A LIST

Use a comma after each item in a list. Most American writers also use a comma after the second-to-last item (before *and* or *or*), as in the following examples:

> Siblings may be best friends, enemies, caretakers, or strangers.

> I like punk music, ferocious dogs, and romantic sunsets.

This rule applies whether the list is made up of single words or phrases. For instance, in the following example the items in the list are phrases:

> I spent much of my summer camping among the redwoods, reading great works of literature, hiking until my feet hurt, and waking up with the sunrise.

If you struggle with this rule, one simple trick is to imagine a number on each item in the list:

>   1   2
> Trixie likes playing tug-of-war with her favorite rope taking long walks in the
>
>   3
> forest and seeing her family at the end of the day.

Once you figure out where the numbers go, simply add a comma after each numbered item:

> Trixie likes playing tug-of-war with her favorite rope, taking long walks in the forest, and seeing her family at the end of the day.

When you have *only two* items in a list joined by *and* or *or*, *don't* use a comma, no matter how long the items in the list might be. Here's a list with two short items (underlined):

> I like chocolate and vanilla.

Here's an example where each item in the list is very long:

> I like traveling on my summer vacations to exotic locales like the Galápagos and spending my rather short winter breaks at my brother's house in Maine.

You'll notice that the list is still made up of only two items joined by the word *and*. No comma is used, even though there are many words in the sentence.

USE A COMMA TO SEPARATE PLACE NAMES, DATES, AND PEOPLE'S TITLES

Your teachers no doubt tried to drill this comma rule into your head in elementary school. (You may have been more interested in recess at the time, so here it is again, for old time's sake.) Use a comma in the following situations:

- Between city and state and between city and country
- Between day and year
- Between a person's last name and any official letters (such as Ph.D., M.D., or Esq.)

Here are two examples:

> Brian May, Ph.D., lives in Surrey, England.

> I visited Washington, D.C., on Tuesday, July 15, 2014, and Richmond, Virginia, on Wednesday, July 16, 2014.

USE A COMMA WHEN YOU INTRODUCE A QUOTATION, *UNLESS* YOU USE THE WORD *THAT*

Commas are required most of the time when you use quotation marks, whether you are writing dialogue or quoting from a source.

Dialogue	The waiter asked, "Would you like cheese with that?"
Quotation from Source (with Comma)	The syllabus for my math course reads, "Students who arrive late will not be allowed to take the final exam."

▶ **For more on using source material in your own writing, see Chapter 17, Quotation and Paraphrase; Chapter 22, MLA Documentation; and Chapter 23, APA Documentation.**

Remember, when using source material, you must cite it to give credit to the original source.

Sometimes when you use quotation marks, the material you are quoting is integrated fully into the grammar of your sentence. Usually such sentences include the word *that* shortly before the quotation. In these cases, do *not* use a comma.

Quotation from Source (No Comma)	The banker said that "a 529 plan is the best college savings vehicle for most middle-class families."

As you read this sentence out loud, notice that you don't naturally pause after the word *that*.

USE A COMMA WHEN YOU HAVE TWO OR MORE ADJECTIVES IN A ROW

When describing a person, place, thing, or idea, sometimes you want to stack up the adjectives to add more detail to the description. In almost all cases, you should use commas to separate the words, even if there are only two adjectives in the list.

> Chad is the <u>kindest, strangest</u> friend I have ever had.

> Children should learn to develop <u>positive, respectful</u> relationships with their siblings.

As you might notice, this rule is different from the earlier rule about a list of items using the word *and* or *or*. The lists in that rule usually consist of nouns or of phrases that stand in for nouns. The lists here consist of adjectives.

The exception to this rule is when one adjective modifies an adjective/noun combination, rather than the noun alone. For example:

> The <u>ratty old</u> toy should have been thrown out.

In this case, the *old toy* is ratty, not the *toy*. Try using an exaggerated pause where the comma would go to judge the difference between sentences that follow the rule about using a comma to separate adjectives and those that represent an exception.

practice it 35.1   Editing for Basic Comma Errors

The following paragraph is missing commas of the following types:

- commas separating items in a list
- commas separating place names and dates
- commas that introduce a quotation
- commas between two or more adjectives in a row

Add all the necessary commas. You should add eleven commas altogether.

Genealogy is the study of family history, and it's never been easier to find out who you are and where you come from. Millions of scanned preserved historical documents are available online: census reports from as early as the 1800s marriage and death certificates passenger manifests from ships that crossed the oceans and military records. Genealogy Web site Ancestry.com provides another members-only feature: the ability to share and search other family trees. CEO Tim Sullivan says "Family history is truly social." You can find long-lost ancestors and also connect with living relatives by sharing family trees through the site. Doing serious

continued ❯

genealogical research twenty years ago meant traveling to the National Archives in Washington D.C. to spend hours reading microfilm of census and military records. Now all the exciting investigative work of finding out who your ancestors were can be done in the comfort of your home in your free time without the travel dusty old microfilm or expense. You may even find an interesting ancestor like the sixth great-grandmother from Plymouth MA born on January 18 1743.

USE A COMMA WITH INTRODUCTORY ELEMENTS

Using the comma appropriately with introductory elements clarifies the meaning of your sentence. In many cases, a missing or misplaced comma makes it hard to understand what you're trying to say. For instance, if you leave out the comma in the following sentence, your reader won't be sure exactly what you mean.

After playing mahjong for several hours I felt sick.

The sentence could mean:

After playing mahjong, for several hours I felt sick.

Or it could mean:

After playing mahjong for several hours, I felt sick.

Without the comma, the reader cannot be sure what you mean. Avoid such errors by using a comma after words or groups of words (phrases or clauses) that introduce the main sentence.

However, Aaron is the better goalie.

On Valentine's Day, I hope to get some flowers.

Read these sentences out loud, and you can hear the pause. Here are some additional examples:

Without more funding for education, schools will continue to struggle with limited resources.

After trying for several hours, Maria finally mastered her math homework.

Finding and Fixing Comma Errors with Introductory Elements. Most of the time, you can read the sentence out loud, slowly and clearly, to determine where to place the comma after introductory material. In addition, as you revise, be on the lookout for typical "introductory" words.

Common Introductory Words		
after	even if	in conclusion
although	first/second/third	once
as	furthermore	since
because	however	when
before	if	while
despite	in	

When you see one of these words or others like it, stop and reread the sentence to see if you can remove any words from the start of the sentence and still have a complete sentence. If you can, then you probably need a comma. Consider this example:

> When I miss the bus I am late for work.

If we remove the introductory material, what we are left with could still stand alone as a sentence:

> ~~When I miss the bus~~ I am late for work.

So we definitely need the comma:

> When I miss the bus, I am late for work.

Beware of the Word *Although*. The word *although* is the source of one common error, because *although* does not function in the same way as the word *however*. *However* can be used in more ways than *although*. For instance, both of the following sentences are correct:

> Correct   However, I like macaroni and cheese.

> Correct   However much I like macaroni and cheese, I get sick of eating it every day.

With *however*, the introductory material can be just the one word or a whole phrase. Either way, the sentences are complete as written. But you can't do the same thing with *although*. *Although* is never a one-word introductory phrase. When you see the word *although* at the start of a sentence, the whole phrase it's attached to is the introductory phrase:

> Incorrect   Although, I like macaroni and cheese.

> Correct   Although I like macaroni and cheese, I get sick of eating it every day.

practice it 35.2	Editing for Comma Errors with Introductory Elements

In the following paragraph, insert the seven missing commas after introductory words, phrases, or clauses:

> Fairy tales can tell us about what is universal in the human experience, and they can also tell us how different cultures have expressed universal truths across different historical periods. For instance the story that Americans know as Cinderella has many variations. In most of them nature is a theme, and the main character goes to a magical tree, bird, cow, or talking horse for help. In many stories Cinderella wears special shoes, though they are not always made of glass; in fact the use of the glass slipper is rather recent. Surprisingly many of the stories have more to do with sisterhood than romance. In one version the main character and her sisters are left to die in a forest, and they fight an ogre to escape. Whether or not the Cinderella character kills her sisters in revenge for their meanness or forgives them and allows them to live seems more important than marrying the prince in most of the stories. According to experts in children's literature studying several different versions of the same fairy tale can help us understand different cultural values as well as how those values have changed over time.

USE A COMMA WHEN JOINING TWO SENTENCES WITH A COORDINATING CONJUNCTION

If you have trouble with fragments, run-ons, or comma splices, this is the comma rule for you. Understanding this comma rule is fundamental to making clear, correct, compound sentences. Imagine that you have two short, choppy sentences:

> The tree is beautiful. The flowers are dead.

Now, imagine you don't like the sound of these short, choppy sentences. You want to combine them:

> The tree is beautiful. + The flowers are dead.

You need to do more than just throw in the word *and*. You have to include a comma as well:

> The tree is beautiful, and the flowers are dead.

Here's another example:

> I like physics, but my educational plan requires chemistry.

I like physics could be a sentence by itself. *My educational plan requires chemistry* could be a sentence by itself. When you join them with the word *but*, you have to put a comma before *but*.

Notice that you don't use a comma *every* time you use a FANBOYS word. Only use a comma if both halves of the sentence can stand on their own. In the following example, you should *not* use a comma:

> My choice was clearly between physics and my educational plan.

The words *my educational plan* can't stand alone as a sentence, so you don't put a comma before the word *and* in this case.

Finding and Fixing Comma Errors with FANBOYS. While editing your paper, stop every time you see one of the FANBOYS words in the middle of a sentence. Take your hand and cover up the FANBOYS word and all the words that come after it. The underlined words in the following example indicate the portion of the sentence you would cover.

> I love pizza <u>so I'm going to eat it every day this week.</u>

Is that first half a complete, correct sentence? The answer is yes, so cover up the first half of the sentence and check the second half.

> <u>I love pizza so</u> I'm going to eat it every day this week.

Is that a complete sentence? The answer is yes, so you need a comma before the FANBOYS word *so*.

> **Correct**   I love pizza, so I'm going to eat it every day this week.

Simple? Yes—but you have to take the time to read each sentence carefully, and you have to be able to tell if a sentence is complete and correct or not.

TIP
Coordinating conjunctions are also known as the FANBOYS words: *for, and, nor, but, or, yet, so.* If you haven't memorized these words yet, do it now. You'll need them for lots of grammar rules.

▶ **If the whole sentence is incomplete, it is a fragment. For more about fragments, see Chapter 32, Fragments.**

practice it 35.3   Editing for Comma Errors with Coordinating Conjunctions

The following paragraph has several errors where commas are used to join two independent clauses with a coordinating conjunction. Add or delete commas as necessary to punctuate correctly. Do not rewrite any words. You will make seven changes.

Why is it that many Americans are willing to buy a three-hundred-dollar

continued ❯

purse or a two-hundred-dollar pair of headphones but they would not be willing to spend the same amount on an original work of art to hang in their home? The purse will wear out, or become unfashionable and technological advances will make the headphones outdated in a couple of years. The artwork, however, would be timeless, may even grow in value, and could be enjoyed for generations. Apparently, many people think of art as a luxury, for the rich and only the rich. Many seem to think that "regular people" just don't collect art or they believe that they can only purchase things that are useful. However, such reasoning is not entirely consistent. A designer purse costs ten times what a regular purse costs yet it is not ten times more useful. Clearly, we are buying the item because we like the way it looks or how it makes us feel. Why is it that we don't get the same buzz from buying a beautiful photograph, or a painting?

USE COMMAS WITH SENTENCE INTERRUPTERS

The last major comma rule has to do with words that interrupt the flow of a sentence or that are tacked on to the end of a sentence. You can think of such words as nonessential information—material you could take out and still be left with a complete sentence. The rule is that you need to use commas to set off words or groups of words that interrupt the flow of the sentence. Take a look at the following example:

My brother, who graduated with a chemistry degree last June, has a high-paying job with great benefits, which is why he's paying for dinner.

In this example, the main sentence is "My brother has a high-paying job with great benefits." The words *who graduated with a chemistry degree last June* and *which is why he's paying for dinner* are extra pieces of information that interrupt or are added onto the main sentence. Try reading this sentence out loud, and listen for the pauses before and after you read those parts. You could take out either piece of information and the sentence would still make sense:

My brother, who graduated with a chemistry degree last June, has a high-paying job with great benefits.

OR

My brother has a high-paying job with great benefits, which is why he's paying for dinner.

You could even take out both parts:

> My brother has a high-paying job with great benefits.

Another type of extra information is a short description of a noun, usually a person, that comes directly after the noun. Take a look at the following example:

> My cardiologist, <u>Dr. Nathan Flowers</u>, appeared on the news yesterday.

Here, the cardiologist is Dr. Nathan Flowers. The information between the commas is called an *appositive*. It gives details about the subject, in this case his name.

Sometimes it might be a little difficult to tell whether some information is truly essential to the sentence. To test whether or not this information is essential, ask yourself if you need it to understand who or what you are talking about. Take a look at these two examples:

> Mr. Ross, who has spent more than a few years in jail, is not exactly my mother's idea of a role model.

> The banker who has spent more than a few years in jail is not exactly my mother's idea of a role model.

In the first example, the phrase *who has spent more than a few years in jail* is interesting, but the reader doesn't need it to know who we are discussing because the person's name is given. There can be no confusion that we are talking about Mr. Ross. Therefore, we use commas around the nonessential information to set it off from the main sentence. In the second example, however, we don't know which banker is being described without the phrase *who has spent more than a few years in jail*. The additional information is necessary to distinguish one banker from all the other possible bankers. Here we do not use commas since that information is part of the main sentence.

Finding and Fixing Comma Errors with Interrupters.   When looking for this particular error in your writing, look for phrases (word groups) that come before or after the subject and verb of the sentence. These phrases often—but not always—begin with:

that	who
when	whom
where	whose
which	

Look out for these words to see if the information that follows them is essential to the meaning of the sentence or not. If it isn't, add commas to set the nonessential information apart from the sentence.

practice it 35.4   Editing for Comma Errors with Sentence Interrupters

The following paragraph is missing numerous commas with sentence interrupters. Add twenty-three necessary commas.

The American K-12 school system a relatively young institution can be categorized in a variety of ways. One major division is between public education which is considered "free" because it is paid for through government taxes, and independent schools also known as private schools which are supported by tuition and usually some other types of institutional support. Public schools can be further divided into neighborhood schools such as the local Lincoln Elementary which enroll the students who live in the immediate vicinity; charter schools such as the KIPP Academies which have more freedom in how and what they teach and usually draw students from across a school district sometimes through a lottery system; and magnet or specialty schools such as the Los Angeles County High School for the Arts which usually have a specific focus such as a performing arts magnet or a science magnet school. Independent schools can also not surprisingly be divided into categories. The usual breakdown whether or not they are religiously affiliated can have important financial implications. Religiously affiliated schools such as Trinity Catholic School frequently get some financial support from the churches with which they are associated. Many nonreligious private schools like Green Valley Country Day School have what is known as an endowment an investment that generates interest every year which helps pay expenses and sometimes provides scholarships to needy students. Private schools are sometimes all-female or all-male; public schools rarely offer single-sex education.

practice it 35.5   Editing for a Variety of Missing Commas I

The following paragraph lacks commas altogether. Add the missing commas to the following paragraph using all the comma rules you have learned. You will need to add fourteen commas.

I was born in Baldwin Park California on January 1 1986. The attending

physician was Nidia Rivera M.D. My mother screamed "Get this baby out!"

One nurse says that I "spit up in her face smiled and fell asleep." Everyone

says I was the cleverest most beautiful baby in the maternity ward.

However my musical talent was not recognized until I was four. On my

fourth birthday I received my first drum set. I loved my drums but my mom

began getting intense headaches. My choice was clearly between the

drums and my mom's sanity. My love for my mom who is the best mom

ever made me switch to the guitar which is why I am now the rock goddess

that I am.

practice it 35.6   Editing for a Variety of Missing Commas II

Again, this paragraph is missing various different types of commas. Add all necessary commas. You should add twenty-eight commas altogether.

The first United States Census which was taken in 1790 identified the

population of the original thirteen states as well as the districts of Kentucky

Maine Vermont and what is now Tennessee as close to 4 million people.

Since then the census has been taken every ten years with the most

recently updated census done in April of 2010. The U.S. population recorded

at the most recent census was over 300 million—seventy-five times the size

of the first census. At the time of the first census New York City was the

largest city with a population of just over 33,000 people and today New York

City at over 8 million residents has a population larger than the entire first

census report of 1790. Of course the census is much more than just a count

of the population. Census reports have collected data about a wide range of

things including the economy health employment education housing and

living arrangements among other topics. The questions added or removed

from each census can reveal a lot about the country at the time. For

example the 1860 census on the eve of the Civil War had separate slave and

continued ❯

free person questionnaires. The questions on the 1940 census aimed to find out how the Great Depression affected the population and the 1980 census included questions about commuting to and from work. Far more than just a record of population the U.S. Census is a window into history.

---

practice it 35.7   Editing for a Variety of Missing Commas III

Again, this paragraph is missing a variety of different types of commas. Add all necessary commas. You should add eleven commas altogether.

Baseball is considered America's favorite pastime but you may not know that its athletes are among the most superstitious. These superstitions range from pregame rituals to in-game practices and one of the most well-known pregame rituals was Hall of Famer Wade Boggs's habit of eating chicken before every game. In-game rituals include jumping over the foul lines between innings and taking the exact same number of practice swings when up at bat. When a pitcher is pitching a no-hitter the superstitions intensify. His teammates who are watching with excitement will not sit next to him or even talk to him in order to avoid jinxing such a rare feat. It is also taboo to even mention the fact that a no-hitter is in progress. When a player is doing really well such as having a prolonged hitting streak he may continue to wear the same socks or undershirt while the streak lasts and when a team is doing really well the players may go without shaving to keep the winning streak going. As long as baseball is played one thing is certain: Superstitions will be a part of the game.

Building Sentences Using These Comma Rules

Once you have mastered the comma rules, you can see how they help you build more sophisticated sentences. Take a basic sentence:

The orange cat is purring.

Now add information and set it off with commas:

> The orange cat, <u>who is the oldest of my pets</u>, is purring.

Now add even more information:

> The orange cat, <u>who is the oldest of my pets</u>, is purring, <u>thinking he's going to be fed soon</u>.

We can even add information to the start of the sentence, as in the introductory-material comma rule:

> <u>At the moment</u>, the orange cat, <u>who is the oldest of my pets</u>, is purring, <u>thinking he's going to be fed soon</u>.

This sentence is now quite long, but it is not a run-on sentence. In fact, its grammar is perfect. As you can see, once you gain control of commas, you can express more complicated ideas in a single sentence.

Editing Your Work for Comma Errors

Like most punctuation errors, comma errors are best fixed during the editing and proofreading stages of the writing process. Figure out which comma errors you tend to make, and read through the paper looking for just those comma errors. As you practice fixing your own errors, correct comma usage will become part of how you write, and you will break the rules less and less frequently. Pretty soon you'll put the commas in the right place without even thinking about it.

In the meantime, since many students seem to believe myths about commas, it might be useful to dispel a few of the common ones. The truth is:

- There is no set number of commas that a sentence is allowed to have or not allowed to have.
- A run-on cannot be fixed simply by throwing in a comma. In fact, that's just making a comma splice, another type of error.
- Whether you use a comma before the final *and* in a list is up to you, but be consistent. Most American writers use the comma in this case.

chapter review

In the following chart, fill in the second column to record in your own words the important skills included in this chapter. Then assess yourself to determine whether you are still developing the skill or feel you have mastered it. If you are still developing the skill, make some notes about what you need to work on to master it in the future. If you believe you have already mastered it, explain why.

Skills and concepts covered in this chapter	Explanation in your own words	I'm developing this skill and need to work on . . .	I believe I have mastered this skill because . . .
Understanding what commas do			
Understanding how commas affect the rhythm of a sentence			
Using commas with lists, place names, dates, and people's titles			
Using commas with quotations			
Using commas with two or more adjectives			
Using commas with introductory elements			
Using commas with coordinating conjunctions			
Using commas with sentence interrupters			
Fixing comma errors in your own work			

36
Parallelism

What Is Parallelism?

Perhaps you have identified a problem you have with parallelism. More likely, your instructor made a note to you about a parallelism problem, and you—being the successful college student that you are—looked it up. Maybe you thought parallelism had something to do with geometry. It sure sounds like it: parallel lines, parallelograms, that sort of thing. Actually, if you're thinking along those lines, you aren't far off. Parallel lines are lines that go in the same direction and never cross. They match, in a way.

In grammar, an error in parallelism means that you have a list of things, but they don't all follow the same path. One or more of the items in the list do not match the others in form. They're not parallel. Here's an example:

Incorrect   At the gym, I rotate between cycling, weightlifting, kickboxing, and to go swimming.

Notice how awkward that last part of the sentence is? One of the things that you do at the gym is not in the same grammatical format as the others. The first three items—cycling, weightlifting, and kickboxing—are simply *-ing* words, but *to go swimming* is an oddball. It has *to go* before the *-ing* word. It just doesn't fit. So how do you fix it? Make that oddball parallel with the other words in the sentence by changing its form:

Correct   At the gym, I rotate between cycling, weightlifting, kickboxing, and swimming.

Another solution is to change the first three items in the list to fit the last item, but this involves some rewriting:

At the gym, I like to do cycling, to practice weightlifting, to engage in a bit of kickboxing, and to go swimming.

LaunchPad Solo
macmillan learning

Visit **LaunchPad Solo for Readers and Writers > Parallelism** for extra practice in the skills covered in this chapter.

685

The first possible correction is much cleaner. You can always try revising the sentence a couple of different ways; read each version out loud to see which you prefer.

Correcting errors in parallelism looks pretty easy when you see it like this, right? As with most things grammatical, though, you usually won't make only simple errors. Sure, writers might make the preceding error, but they would probably catch it pretty quickly if they edited the sentence. It's the trickier, more complicated errors in parallelism that may stump you.

Let's try another, trickier example:

> **Incorrect**   College has improved my study habits by helping me to organize my time, taking better notes, and get help from my instructor when I don't understand something.

It can be difficult to figure out where the list of items that need to be parallel starts. In this case, not all items in the list start with the word *to*, so this is not a list of phrases that begin with *to*. You might notice that each item starts with a verb: *organize*, *taking*, and *get*. However, the verbs aren't all parallel. *Taking* is in the *-ing* form, and that doesn't fit with the others. The fix, in this case, is simple:

> **Correct**   College has improved my study habits by helping me to organize my time, take better notes, and get help from my instructor when I don't understand something.

Often, only a slight change in wording will correct an error in parallelism. It's one of those errors that are harder to notice than to fix.

Common Parallelism Errors

Most real-life parallelism errors occur when it's not quite so obvious that you are using a list of things in your writing, such as when the items in the list are each quite long or when the ideas are complicated. The trick is to notice that the items are in a list, figure out what each item is, and make sure that each item uses the same grammatical structure.

LISTS WITH COLONS

Sometimes writers use a colon to indicate a long pause before a list. This is great, so long as you do it correctly and maintain parallel structure. Take a look at this example:

> **Incorrect**   Puppies need several important things to be healthy and happy: proper veterinary care, nutritious puppy food, to be loved and petted by their new owners, and when you get a new puppy, you have to exercise it frequently.

In this example, the items in the list are seriously mismatched, and the sentence seems to go on past the end of the list, which further confuses the reader. The writer needs to decide on the best way to rewrite, and whether or not to move that last part—*and when you get a new puppy, you have to exercise it frequently*—into the list or toward the front of the sentence. Take a look at some possible solutions:

Minor Revision   Puppies need several important things to be healthy and happy: proper veterinary care, nutritious puppy food, loving affection, and frequent vigorous exercise.

Major Revision   When you get a puppy, you must realize that it needs several important things to be healthy and happy: proper veterinary care, nutritious puppy food, and a loving new home.

Both of these options sound good and are grammatically correct; they use the colon, end the sentence with the list, and have parallel forms. The option you choose will depend on what you try to emphasize. The minor revision changes very little, while the major rewrite shifts the focus of the sentence from the puppy to the owner.

LIST INTERRUPTERS

Another tricky but fairly common parallelism problem happens when a writer puts a thought into the middle of the list that shouldn't be there at all. Here's one example:

Incorrect   My girlfriend plays video games all day, I even complain about it, and never takes me out to dinner.

Here we have three things that look like they are in a list, but it's not a parallel list.

My girlfriend plays video games all day, I even complain about it, and never takes me out to dinner.

Actually, the girlfriend does two things:

1. plays video games all day
2. never takes me out to dinner

Who is complaining? Not the girlfriend. She seems pretty happy. That bit in the middle about complaining shouldn't even be in the list. We can move it to the front of the sentence and rewrite it like this:

Correct   Even though I complain about it, my girlfriend plays video games all day and never takes me out to dinner.

Much better! *Plays video games all day* and *never takes me out to dinner* are parallel, and the misfit phrase has been moved out of the list. (Now all that's needed is a new girlfriend.)

THAT TRICKY WORD *THAT*

Often, when your sentences include phrases with the word *that*, you can lose track of your ideas and create a problem with parallelism. Here's an example:

> **Incorrect**   My instructor promised that she would grade our essays within two weeks, that we would be happy with the results, and she was really nice about it.

Where does the list begin?

> **Incorrect**   My instructor promised <u>that she would grade our essays within two weeks</u>, <u>that we would be happy with the results</u>, and <u>she was really nice about it</u>.

Notice how the first two items in the list begin with the word *that* followed by a complete thought. The last item doesn't fit, though, does it? It's not parallel. In fact, it's a comment on the other two things in the list. We might decide to take it out and put it elsewhere, like this:

> **Correct**   My instructor <u>was really nice when</u> she promised <u>that she would grade our essays within two weeks</u> and <u>that we would be happy with the results</u>.

If we want to keep the item in the list, some rewriting would be necessary:

> **Correct**   My instructor promised <u>that she would grade our essays within two weeks</u>, <u>that we would be happy with the results</u>, and <u>that she would be kind to us</u>.

This doesn't work as well, for a couple of reasons. First, it sounds repetitive. Saying "we would be happy" and "she would be kind" is practically the same thing. More important, it's probably not what the writer originally intended.

MAINTAINING PARALLELISM WHEN QUOTING

▶ **For help integrating quotations into your own writing, see Chapter 17, Quotation and Paraphrase.**

Probably the trickiest parallelism problem is how to integrate a quotation into your sentence and keep the writing parallel. Read the following passage from Susan Engel's article "The Case for Curiosity," which describes one of her suggestions for improving the experience of teaching and learning.

How do we judge whether someone is truly curious? A teacher's thirst for finding out should be evident in what he or she has done or in how he or she behaves. Sometimes a teacher with plenty of curiosity has done scientific research or spent years studying some topic of personal interest (such as butterflies or architecture). Sometimes their curiosity is expressed as an urge to know more about their students. Often teachers of young children excel because of their unending interest in early development. Either way, the teacher who knows what the itch to find out feels like is in a better position to foster that itch in students. (462)

Most likely, if you were writing an essay about this topic, you would not want to include the entire paragraph in your essay. Instead, you would pick and choose the details you would want to stress. However, when you do that, you have to be careful to maintain good parallel structure.

First Attempt   Engel suggests we should hire teachers who have "plenty of curiosity, . . . spent years studying some topic of personal interest, [and] . . . an urge to know more about their students" (462).

What's wrong with the way that sounds? Read it out loud, and you'll probably hear the problems with parallelism. Let's take a closer look, this time by underlining the elements of the list:

Engel suggests we should hire teachers who have "plenty of curiosity, . . . spent years studying some topic of personal interest, [and] . . . an urge to know more about their students" (462).

Even though these phrases were fine in Engel's original passage, the way they have been selected and introduced with the signal phrase makes the grammar a mismatch. The first phrase begins with a noun (*plenty*), as does the third (*an urge*), but the middle item begins with a verb (*spent*). It's probably best to go with the majority in this case, so you can fix the passage by eliminating or changing part or all of the middle phrase. You may need to add back in some words from the original passage to make it meaningful.

Revised   Engel suggests we should hire teachers who have "plenty of curiosity, . . . ~~spent years studying~~ some topic of personal interest (such as butterflies or architecture), [and] . . . an urge to know more about their students" (462).

Here's the final result:

Correct   Engel suggests we should hire teachers who have "plenty of curiosity, . . . some topic of personal interest (such as butterflies or architecture), [and] . . . an urge to know more about their students" (462).

Always go back and read the sentence out loud to double-check its parallelism.

Another way to solve the problem of parallelism when quoting is to take the phrases you want to quote and list them to check for parallelism before you write your signal phrase. Then you can work backwards to devise the most grammatically appropriate signal phrase. For example, imagine you wanted to stress the following ideas from Engel's original paragraph:

- "a teacher with plenty of curiosity has done scientific research or spent years studying some topic of personal interest (such as butter-flies or architecture)"

- "the teacher who knows what the itch to find out feels like is in a better position to foster that itch in students"

Take a look at those bits of Engel's writing. How could you make them parallel? What would you need to cut out to make them parallel (making sure you don't change the meaning at all)? You might decide to start by focusing on verbs:

- "has done scientific research or spent years studying some topic of personal interest"

- "knows what the itch to find out feels like"

Then you can put the subject (*a curious teacher*) into your signal phrase, like this:

> As Engel suggests, a curious teacher usually "has done scientific research or spent years studying some topic of personal interest [and therefore] knows what the itch to find out feels like" (462).

Always read the sentence out loud one last time to check for parallel language.

Finding and Fixing Parallelism Errors

Most likely, you make parallelism errors when you are struggling to say something that you haven't fully articulated yet. That's okay. Take some time to think through what you really mean to say, and then be willing to rewrite the sentence. Quite often, sentences that have parallelism problems are clunky sentences that would benefit from serious editing.

Keep an eye out for any sentences that introduce or explain two or more examples, reasons, actions, or ideas. Sometimes, when we start writing a list like that, we can only think up two good ideas, but we feel compelled for some reason to have three, so the third one that we make up is the clunker that is not parallel. Check over your sentence a few times to see if you can cut something.

TIP
If you are prone to making errors in parallelism, double-check for parallelism each time you use the words *and* and *or*. This could help you locate your own parallelism errors.

Reading your writing out loud is very effective for finding errors in parallelism because parallelism is related to the rhythm of language, so be sure to use this editing strategy as you look over your papers.

Remember, errors in parallelism often do not have only one right solution. Play around with the sentence a little to discover a few different options, and then choose the one that sounds best to you.

---

practice it 36.1 Editing for Parallelism I

1. Read the following paragraph and underline all the errors in parallelism. You should find seven errors.
2. Go back to the errors that you underlined and decide how to fix them. Remember, you can either make minor changes or rewrite entirely. Make your corrections by hand in the space above the sentence you are fixing.

Richard Louv's *Last Child in the Woods: Saving Our Children from Nature-Deficit Disorder* makes a convincing argument that American culture has made childhood too safe and kids are too clean. In his book, Louv shows that children are no longer allowed to have a free and open relationship to nature because their parents won't let them climb trees or play in the woods, their teachers won't let them take any real risks on the playground, and many children live in high-crime neighborhoods. Even those who don't are often kept inside because the parents fear kidnappers and child predators. These fears, Louv demonstrates through statistical evidence, are not logical; rather, they are created by the media and enhanced by new styles of hands-on parenting that may not be for the best. Louv is right. We need to allow children to climb trees, getting dirty, and run around their neighborhoods a little bit more often. The environmentalist groups also need to lighten up their attitudes toward fishing, being hunters, and the principles of "leave no trace." Sure, we want kids to respect nature, but many children who grow up fishing and hunt do have more respect for nature than those who grow up playing video games. Hunters are, ironically, some of the best caretakers of natural lands. "Leave no trace," while good in theory, can go a little overboard. If a child picks up a stick or plucking a flower, maybe he

continued ❯

or she will remember that day and enjoying the beauty of nature forever. If all the child hears is "don't touch that," do you think that child will grow up to care about the natural world? Definitely not.

practice it 36.2   Editing for Parallelism II

1. Read the following paragraph and underline all the errors in parallelism. You should find four problem sentences.
2. Go back to the errors that you underlined and decide how to fix them. Remember, you can either make minor changes or rewrite entirely. Make your corrections by hand in the space above the sentence you are fixing.

Richard Louv's book *Last Child in the Woods: Saving Our Children from Nature-Deficit Disorder* argues that the current generation of American children has literally lost touch with nature and knowing a lot about environmental issues. While he has tons of great facts to support his argument, his personal anecdotes, especially when he compares his childhood to his son's life, are the most convincing. For example, Louv opens the book with a description of a conversation he had with his son, who asked him why life was more fun when his dad was growing up (1). Louv reflects on this and concluding that "[a] kid today likely will tell you about the Amazon rain forest—but not about the last time he or she explored the woods in solitude, or lay in a field listening to the wind and watching the clouds move" (1–2). In this scene, Louv does not seem like a scientist or philosophical; he seems like a dad who is trying to do his best to raise his son. He is really listening to his son and thoughts are about what his son has to say. You have to admire him for that.

chapter review

In the following chart, fill in the second column to record in your own words the important skills included in this chapter. Then assess yourself to determine whether you are still developing the skill or feel you have mastered it. If you are still developing the skill, make some notes about what you need to work on to master it in the future. If you believe you have already mastered it, explain why.

Skills and concepts covered in this chapter	Explanation in your own words	I'm developing this skill and need to work on . . .	I believe I have mastered this skill because . . .
Identifying errors in parallelism			
Making lists with colons parallel			
Using parallel structures with list interrupters			
Making parallel sentences while using the word *that*			
Maintaining parallelism when quoting			
Fixing parallelism errors in your own writing			

in this chapter

- What Is a Mixed Construction?
- What Are Predication Errors?
- How Do You Find and Fix Mixed Constructions?

37
Mixed Constructions

▶ **For more about sentences, see Chapter 29, Basic Sentence Components**

Have you ever had the experience of finding sentences in your writing that just didn't seem to make sense or work well, but you weren't sure exactly what was wrong or how to fix them? You are not alone. The English language is complex, and when you express your sophisticated ideas in writing, you are bound to create some messy sentences along the way. This chapter covers mixed constructions, an important category of grammar errors that can make your writing difficult to follow. In order to get the most out of this chapter, you should have a good understanding of the basic sentence components and how to find the subject and verb in a sentence.

What Is a Mixed Construction?

Mixed constructions occur when you begin a sentence with one kind of structure and then switch to a different structure partway through. This happens sometimes when you edit sentences as you write. It can also happen in long sentences, in sentences including quotations, or in sentences with certain verbs or phrases. Terms like *sentence structure* or *sentence pattern* refer to the basic building blocks of a sentence. Although there is plenty of room for creativity in writing, once you begin a sentence, you are limited in the number of ways you can finish it. For example, suppose a sentence begins:

In her essay . . .

There are limited ways to go from here; logically, you need to tell the reader what the author says or does in her essay.

In her essay, the author claims . . .

At this point, this sentence is on a clear trajectory. Now that you have said *the author claims*, you have to say *what* she claims. This can come in the form of a summary, quotation, or paraphrase.

Prepositional Phrase Showing *Where* the Author Makes Her Claim	Subject and Verb Showing *What* the Author Is Doing	Phrase Stating *What* the Author Is Claiming
In her essay,	the author claims	**that balloon animals are art**.

Prepositional Phrase Showing *Where* the Author Makes Her Claim	Subject and Verb Showing *What* the Author Is Doing	Quoted Clause Stating *What* the Author Is Claiming
In her essay,	the author claims,	**"Balloon animals are a craft that few people recognize as art, but they are."**

Notice that we have many choices in terms of which author we put in this sentence and which quote or paraphrase we add, but once we begin with a prepositional phrase, we're limited as to how we structure the rest of the sentence. We could, of course, start the sentence by taking the prepositional phrase out, but we'd end up right back where we started.

	Subject and Verb Showing *What* the Author Is Doing	Phrase Stating *What* the Author Is Claiming
Correct	The author claims	**that balloon animals are art**.

	Subject and Verb Showing *What* the Author Is Doing	Quoted Clause Stating *What* the Author Is Claiming
Correct	The author claims,	**"Balloon animals are a craft that few people recognize as art, but they are."**

In a mixed-construction sentence, the structure of the sentence doesn't make sense logically—the parts don't match.

Incorrect   In her essay, balloon animals are art.

To see the mismatch, read each sentence part carefully:

Incorrect   In her essay, balloon animals are art.

The balloon animals are not art *in her essay*, but that's what this sentence suggests.

The following sentence is a common type of mixed construction.

Incorrect   Even though unauthorized graffiti is technically vandalism, it can also be expensive to remove.

This sentence begins one way and then shifts gears in the middle. The words *Even though* are setting up the sentence to suggest something about graffiti despite the fact that it is vandalism, but the second part of the sentence doesn't continue in that direction. To fix this mixed construction, change the conjunctions:

Correct   Unauthorized graffiti is technically vandalism, <u>and</u> it can be expensive to remove.

WHAT ARE PREDICATION ERRORS?

A predication error is a common mixed-construction error that happens when the subject and the predicate (verb part of the sentence) don't match. This often occurs when you use a form of the verb *to be*, which functions like an equals sign between sentence parts. If the two parts connected by the verb *to be* are not equal, you have created a predication error.

Incorrect   <u>Summer vacation</u> is where I get to travel.

What this sentence is saying: Summer vacation = where.

Summer vacation is not a place, so you can't use *where* to refer to it. Summer vacation is a time period, however, so you can fix it by changing the word *where* to *when*.

Correct   Summer vacation is when I get to travel.

Here is an example of another common predication error:

Incorrect   <u>The reason to have charter schools</u> is because they have more autonomy over their budgets and their teachers' salaries.

Using *reason . . . is because* this way is common but incorrect. The word *because* is not a reason. In this instance, the word *because* is actually getting in the way of your reason. A better solution is to use *reason . . . is that . . .* and then to fill in the reason:

Correct   The reason to have charter schools is that they have more autonomy over their budgets and their teachers' salaries.

Let's look at another example of a common error:

Incorrect   <u>Another way that education is in trouble today</u> are not enough supplies for their classes.

In this example, the first part of the sentence (the subject part) does not match the second part (the predicate part). The first part sets up a *way* that education is in trouble, but *not enough supplies* is not a *way* education is in trouble; it is an example of the result of not having enough funding. How could you fix this sentence?

practice it 37.1   Editing for Predication Errors

There are five predication errors in the following paragraph. Underline or highlight the errors and rewrite them to avoid this kind of error.

Test anxiety can really make your life miserable, but there are ways to reduce anxiety that help significantly. Test anxiety is where you get so nervous before a test that you might not be able to sleep or eat or concentrate. The reason someone might get test anxiety is because they are extremely afraid of failing or maybe they did horribly on a test in the past and are constantly afraid they will repeat that failure on every test. Although important, in most classes tests aren't the entire grade, and remembering that might take some of the pressure off. Another way to combat test anxiety is to prepare well in advance of the test because "cramming" right before a test is more likely to make you anxious. Preparing makes sure you know the material. Knowing that you know the material well is how you can feel confident going into the test. And although it might seem counterintuitive, putting the books and notes away early and tuning out thoughts of the exam will help you get a good night's sleep, which will enable you to concentrate when you really need it.

Finding Mixed Constructions

The best way to find mixed-construction sentences is for you or someone else to read your essay aloud while you listen for parts that sound awkward or don't make sense. It's important to hear these kinds of errors because when you read something silently, your brain will "fix" mistakes as you read in order to make broader sense of the sentence or paragraph. Of course, this does not actually fix the mistake in your paper. Another strategy for finding mixed-construction sentences is to look for sentences that

- include quotations
- begin with a prepositional phrase
- are long
- use *reason* and *because* together
- use *is when* or *is where*

These may not be the only places mixed-construction errors pop up, but they are the most common. Of course, if your instructor or a tutor has commented on this error in your writing before, be especially on the lookout. Ask for examples of places in your essays where you have made this error if they aren't already marked; this will give you a good idea of where you run into trouble.

Don't be discouraged if you create mixed constructions. Often they emerge in a piece of writing when the writer is trying to express something slightly beyond his or her skill level. This sort of stretching is great. You just have to challenge yourself to make the grammar of the sentence appropriate to the level of your ideas. The worst thing is to simply delete the problematic sentence. Take the time to fix it. The idea in the sentence might be one of your best!

Fixing Mixed Constructions

So, then, how do you fix those awkward sentences? What it boils down to is understanding the basic sentence parts and making sure the compatible sentence parts match. Start with the subject and verb. Being able to identify the subject and verb of the sentence will help you unravel the mixed construction. Slowly read through your sentences one at a time. Circle or underline the subject of each sentence, and then underline the main verb of each sentence twice. After you do this for every sentence in your paragraph, look more closely at each sentence. Do the subject and the verb make sense together?

Incorrect   Increases in bus fare make it harder to ride the bus.

The subject and verb are identified in this sentence. Read just the subject and verb together. Do they make sense? Do *increases* make it *harder to ride the bus*? No. Maybe they make it more expensive to ride the bus, or they make it harder to afford riding the bus, but *increases* don't make it *harder to ride the bus*. One way to rewrite the sentence might be:

Correct   Increases in bus fare make it harder to afford riding the bus.

Another way to check for mixed construction is to underline the phrases or word groups that go together in the sentence.

Incorrect   In the article "Chicano Mural Movement," says that Chicano murals are depictions of Mexican American culture.

Check to see if the underlined parts work together. Do they make sense? In this example, who *says that Chicano murals are depictions of Mexican American culture*? Does *In the article* say? No, *the author* says this. But the author is not in the sentence. Now you know what to add to make this sentence make sense.

Correct   In the article "Chicano Mural Movement," Teresa Palomo Acosta says that Chicano murals are depictions of Mexican American culture.

Much better! Let's look at another example.

Incorrect	My favorite memory was when I walked across the stage at graduation.

By looking at the underlined parts, we can see that the first part of the sentence starts off fine, but the second part goes in a different direction by saying *was when*. When you use *when*, you refer to a time, but a memory is not a time, so you can't refer to it using *when*. How can we fix this sentence?

Correct	My favorite memory was walking across the stage at graduation.

OR

Correct	I remember when I walked across the stage at graduation.

Notice that the second sentence changes the meaning. The sentence is no longer about a "favorite" memory; now it is just about remembering. When you fix your sentences, think about what point you want to get across.

Another way to fix sentences with structure problems is to learn the basic sentence structures and practice using them when you write. There are four basic sentence constructions:

1. *Simple sentence:* an independent clause that makes up the basic sentence unit. It is made up of a subject and a verb and expresses a complete thought. Here are some examples:

   I always order popcorn at the movies.

   Murals often display culturally or historically significant themes.

   A good education is important.

2. *Compound sentence:* two independent clauses joined by a coordinating conjunction (FANBOYS: *for*, *and*, *nor*, *but*, *or*, *yet*, *so*). In the following examples, the conjunction and the second independent clause are bold.

   Some students are already good at keeping a budget with their money, **but others need a class on financial literacy.**

   Learning good money habits is a start toward financial stability, **and practicing them regularly helps maintain it.**

   Public schools are overcrowded, **so students get too little time from their teachers.**

3. *Complex sentence:* an independent clause joined with a dependent clause. In the following examples, the dependent clause is in italics.

   Because most jobs require strong writing skills, learning to improve writing in college is a smart career move.

Although you can't choose your siblings, they can be a source of great comfort and support.

4. *Compound-complex sentence*: two independent clauses joined by a coordinating conjunction and at least one dependent clause. In the following examples, the conjunction and the second independent clause are bold, and the dependent clause is in italics.

Unless it is fostered, curiosity can dwindle, **so it is important for parents to respond when children ask questions.**

A celebrity's status is fickle *because his or her fame depends on the whims of the fans*, **and these fans often lose interest and move on to follow the next rising star.**

---

practice it 37.2 Editing for Mixed-Construction Errors

There are four mixed-construction errors in the following paragraph. Underline or highlight the errors and rewrite them to avoid this kind of error.

Public art is a way for a community to express its pride. Public art is when a community has sculptures, murals, decorative fountains or installments, or even buildings. All communities have public art of some kind. Murals are a common kind of public art, often painted on school walls or in libraries or, in parks. With people in the community helping to decide what art is displayed makes them invested in both the art and the community. In his article "Public Art: An Essential Component of Creating Communities" by Jack Becker says, "[public art] engender[s] a sense of pride and community identity" (487). Public art helps people feel connected to their community because it's something they share. In some communities, the public art is so famous that people travel from all over the world to come and see it. Examples of some of these famous works of public art are where buildings are so iconic that they are recognized around the world, like the Eiffel Tower in Paris, France, or the Opera House in Sydney, Australia.

chapter review

In the following chart, fill in the second column to record in your own words the important skills included in this chapter. Then assess yourself to determine whether you are still developing the skill or feel you have mastered it. If you are still developing the skill, make some notes about what you need to work on to master it in the future. If you believe you have already mastered it, explain why.

Skills and concepts covered in this chapter	Explanation in your own words	I'm developing this skill and need to work on . . .	I believe I have mastered this skill because . . .
Understanding mixed constructions			
Understanding predication errors			
Finding and fixing mixed constructions			

in this chapter

- What Is a Modifier?
- What Are Misplaced Modifiers?
- What Are Dangling Modifiers?
- How Do You Find and Fix Misplaced and Dangling Modifiers?

38

Misplaced and Dangling Modifiers

Visit **LaunchPad Solo for Readers and Writers > Modifier Placement** for more practice in the skills covered in this chapter.

Who says grammar can't be fun? Or funny? This chapter covers errors related to misplaced and dangling modifiers. When you make an error with a modifier, your sentences often end up sounding downright ridiculous. While cracking people up can be fun, we would hope that your humor would come from the quality of your jokes, not your grammar. Read on to find out how to recognize and fix modifier problems.

What Is a Modifier?

A **modifier** is a word or group of words that adds to or changes the meaning of another word. Adjectives and adverbs are modifiers; they describe or add to the meaning of nouns, verbs, adjectives, and other adverbs. Essentially, you have two parts to the modifying equation: the word or group of words being modified and the modifier.

The black cat, Zeus, is fat and likes to eat broccoli.

In this sentence, all the underlined words or phrases are modifying the word *cat*.

What kind of cat? black, fat, likes to eat broccoli

Modifiers can either be single words (*black*) or phrases (*likes to eat broccoli*). Either way, modifiers should appear next to the word they are modifying in the sentence (or at least very close).

MISPLACED MODIFIERS

A misplaced modifier happens when the word being modified is not close enough to the modifier, so it ends up modifying the wrong word in the sentence.

> **Misplaced**   Jake saw a roach taking out the trash.

Wait, what? He saw a roach carrying garbage? Of course not. This is just a case of a misplaced modifier. In this sentence, *taking out the trash* is the modifier, meaning it gives more information about what Jake was doing. Modifiers end up modifying the words closest to them, and in this case the modifier is seriously misplaced! This phrase is about Jake, not the roach, so it needs to be placed next to the word *Jake* in the sentence. Let's try that again:

> **Correct**   Taking out the trash, Jake saw a roach.

Now that makes a lot more sense. Here's another example of a misplaced modifier:

> **Misplaced**   Raquel served birthday cake to the guests on paper plates.

This sentence reads as though the guests were on paper plates. What part of the sentence is the modifier? And what word is it modifying?

The underlined part of the sentence is the modifier, giving us more information about the birthday cake. To fix this, move this part of the sentence closer to the word it modifies.

> **Correct**   Raquel served birthday cake on paper plates to the guests.

practice it 38.1   Correcting Misplaced Modifiers

Rewrite the following sentences to correct the misplaced modifiers.

1. Ben kicked a goal wearing only one cleat.
2. Decorating an otherwise decrepit wall, the graffiti artist painted a large, abstract flower arrangement.
3. Brian cheered on his favorite team jumping up and down.
4. Norm hiked through the hills bundled up for warmth.
5. Valentina went down the slide squealing with delight.
6. Nereida and her friends danced along with the music video waving their hands in the air.

DANGLING MODIFIERS

A dangling modifier occurs when only half of the modifying equation is in the sentence. In the case of a misplaced modifier, the word being modified is in the sentence but is separated from the modifier. In the case of a dangling modifier, the word being modified is missing from the sentence entirely.

Dangling Modifier   Raised in a very large family, the house was too small for us.

The house was not raised in a very large family. What or who was? It's not clear from this sentence. *Raised in a very large family* is modifying something, but that something is not in the sentence and needs to be added.

Correct   I was raised in a very large family, and the house was too small for us.

OR

Correct   Raised in a very large family, I always thought our house was too small for us.

There is no single correct way to fix a dangling or misplaced modifier; the key is to identify what is misplaced or dangling and rewrite the sentence so that the modifier modifies the right word.

---

practice it 38.2   Correcting Dangling Modifiers

Rewrite the following sentences to correct the dangling modifiers.

1. With the idea of improving the vacant lot, the graffiti was painted with bright colors and a sleek design.
2. After watching *Lifestyles of the Rich and Famous*, a career in Hollywood seemed desirable.
3. Searching for ways to be more curious, the idea of asking questions somehow never came up.
4. Despite having read the entire book, his storytelling is rather bland.
5. When taking out a loan, interest rate is everything.

Finding and Fixing Misplaced and Dangling Modifiers

To find misplaced and dangling modifiers, follow the same careful proofreading techniques outlined earlier in this book: Slowly read your essay out loud with a pencil in hand so you can mark sentences that don't sound quite right. Keep a lookout for prepositional phrases or *-ing* words that begin sentences, as these are likely places for misplaced modifiers. If you find a sentence that doesn't sound right, underline the sentence parts to see if they work together. If not, see if there is a part of the sentence that provides more information. Read it carefully a few times to decide whether the word or phrase is modifying the right part of the sentence.

Modifiers aren't picky; they modify anything you put next to them. For this reason, you should keep your modifiers close to the word they modify—right next to them is the best place. When you separate the modifier from the word or group of words that it modifies, confusion and sometimes hilarity ensue, and unfortunately the meaning of your sentence is compromised. In the case of a dangling modifier, the word being modified is actually missing from the sentence.

Dangling Modifier	While jogging along the trail, a mountain lion frightened the couple.

Although a jogging mountain lion would frighten most people, this is not what the writer intended to say here. The modifier *while jogging along the trail* should be modifying the couple, not the mountain lion. The fix is to move this phrase next to *the couple*.

Correct	A mountain lion frightened the couple, who were jogging along the trail.

Here's another example:

Dangling Modifier	The cake was ruined, having forgotten to add baking powder.

The cake did not forget to add baking powder, but the person who did is not in the sentence. To fix this, add the person in the sentence where he or she belongs.

Correct	Having forgotten to add baking powder, Don ruined the cake.

practice it 38.3   Finding Misplaced and Dangling Modifiers I

Underline the misplaced or dangling modifiers in the following sentences. Then rewrite the sentence to fix the problematic modifiers.

1. To be good at baking, following recipes exactly is crucial.
2. The mailman left a package outside our house dripping wet from the rain.
3. The sweater once belonged to my grandmother full of moth holes.
4. Cynthia ran out to the scene of the car accident wearing pajamas and a robe.
5. Preparing for the long car ride, the cat paced.

practice it 38.4   Finding Misplaced and Dangling Modifiers II

Underline the misplaced or dangling modifiers in the following sentences. Then rewrite the sentence to fix the problematic modifiers.

1. Pouring millions of gallons over the waterfall, Bill marveled at Niagara Falls.
2. While walking down the street, a football smashed into my head.
3. Slithering smoothly down the trail, Martha and Jean came across a rattlesnake.
4. Reading the directions while driving, the map looked confusing.
5. Nathaniel saw the Rocky Mountains looking out the airplane window.
6. We ordered a sundae from the waiter with extra whipped cream.
7. Hanging on a lamppost Allegra saw the parade banners.
8. Walking through the door, the dog jumped up and licked Brian's face in welcome.
9. Zola saw a family of ducks on the way to the hospital.
10. Hungry after a day of yard work, the steaks looked mouthwatering.

chapter review

In the following chart, fill in the second column to record in your own words the important skills included in this chapter. Then assess yourself to determine whether you are still developing the skill or feel you have mastered it. If you are still developing the skill, make some notes about what you need to work on to master it in the future. If you believe you have already mastered it, explain why.

Skills and concepts covered in this chapter	Explanation in your own words	I'm developing this skill and need to work on . . .	I believe I have mastered this skill because . . .
Understanding modifiers			
Finding and fixing misplaced modifiers			
Finding and fixing dangling modifiers			

39

Clear and Focused Language

What Is Clear and Focused Language?

Your instructor may have written comments on your paper saying you need to work on clarity or focus, but perhaps you aren't entirely sure what this means. If your writing lacks clarity, your reader can't understand what you are trying to say about the topic. Similarly, lack of focus means the topic itself is too vague. The most fundamental purpose of writing is to communicate, and if your language lacks clarity or focus, you aren't communicating. For instance, can you get a clear sense of what the following sentence is saying?

> Whether it is from the latest trends in fashion or the way people behave, you will come across numerous celebrity obsession stories that all too often hook us in.

How about this one?

> Children with older siblings can affect the behavior of children in many ways.

Neither of these sentences is very clear or focused. After reading them several times, you might get a sense of what the author means, but you don't want your reader to have to work that hard to understand you. Writing clear, focused language from the beginning makes you and your ideas stand out in a good way.

Lack of clarity and focus may have any number of causes, but the most common ones in student writing are wordiness, vague or unclear pronouns, passive voice, and poor vocabulary choices (clichés, empty phrases, and slang).

LaunchPad Solo
macmillan learning

Visit **LaunchPad Solo for Readers and Writers** for extra practice in the skills covered in this chapter. See the units Wordiness, Pronouns, Active and Passive Voice, and Appropriate Language.

Avoid Clichés, Empty Phrases, and Slang

Clichés are literary shortcuts that would be great if they weren't so overused. For example, how many times have you heard the phrase *sweep it under the rug* to describe someone who hides a problem? Avoid clichés in your writing; instead, come up with a fresh way of describing things or at least attempt to use newer analogies to make your point. Think for a moment about what you are actually trying to say. Often, just saying exactly what you mean is the best choice. Take a look at this example:

Cliché	Here's some food for thought: Almost 25 percent of students who begin high school never make it to graduation.

What is this writer really trying to say here? The point is that this statistic might be information you didn't already know. Okay, so how about writing that?

Revised	Surprisingly, almost 25 percent of students who begin high school never make it to graduation.

Now the reader can focus on the information, not the worn-out cliché.

Common Clichés

as luck would have it	a breath of fresh air
bored to tears	chip off the old block
few and far between	crying over spilled milk
food for thought	don't rock the boat
larger than life	good to go
up in arms	missed the boat

Like clichés, empty phrases don't really say anything. Using them is like adding packing peanuts to your essay; they take up space but provide no valuable content. Most of the time, you can cut out the empty phrases or replace them with a simpler expression. For instance:

Empty Phrase	In today's society, women and men both attend college.
Empty Phrase Deleted	Women and men both attend college.
Replaced and Revised	Since the late 1970s, both women and men have attended college in equal numbers.

Common Empty Phrases

the fact of the matter is
I, myself
I, personally
in my opinion
in today's society
since the dawn of time
throughout time
we, as humans

Slang words or phrases are very informal or not considered part of Standard English. Avoiding slang language in an academic paper is important because you want instructors to take you seriously, and using slang makes writing at best informal and at worst sloppy. We often use more informal, slang language when talking with friends or even when e-mailing or texting. But for the same reason that you talk differently with your friends than you do during a job interview, you use more formal language when writing for academic or job-related purposes than you do when writing e-mails or text messages to friends.

Common Slang Expressions

24/7
back in the day
for sure, for real
LOL, OMG (any text abbreviations)
stuff
u (for "you")

Avoid Wordiness

Another common problem with language clarity and focus has to do with wordiness. Instructors write "wordy" on your paper when you use too many words to say something that could be said in fewer words. Often, wordy sentences also have an overly complicated sentence structure that can be simplified for clarity and focus. Let's look at an example:

Wordy   It is the best way to see a car at the auto show because the auto show is where you can really see what is going to be coming out in the new line of cars.

Sounds wordy, doesn't it? What is the point of this sentence? From reading the sentence a few times, we can see that the real point made here is that car makers reveal their new cars at auto shows. Here's one possible revision:

Revised   The auto show introduces the new line of cars to the public.

This gets to the point more quickly with fewer words and less confusion.

Fortunately, you already have the tools you need to correct wordiness. Mostly, you need to be willing to cut out unnecessary words or replace those words with better ones.

Strategy 1: Try to eliminate *there is*, *there are*, and *it is* from the beginning of your sentences. Once you delete these phrases, you'll need to rewrite the sentence a little, which usually makes the verbs stronger.

Wordy   There are several cures for a hangover, but no cures for hangover have been scientifically proven.

Better   Several cures for a hangover exist, but no cures for hangover have been scientifically proven.

Strategy 2: Look for redundant words (words used twice) in the sentence, or synonyms (words that mean the same thing). Rewrite the sentence to delete these repetitions.

Repetitive   Several cures for a hangover exist, but no cures for hangovers have been scientifically proven.

Better   Several cures for a hangover exist, but none have been scientifically proven.

Strategy 3: Make the verbs in the sentence as strong as possible. Don't turn perfectly good verbs (such as *avoid*) into nouns (like *avoidance*). Try to avoid *-ing* verbs if you can too.

Wordy   One sure way for hangover avoidance is spending more time on the dance floor instead of drinking so much when you go to a club.

Better   To avoid a hangover, when you go to a club, dance more and drink less.

Strategy 4: Figure out who or what is really doing the action of the sentence, and put that at the beginning of the sentence. This often forces you to make your verbs stronger, as suggested in the previous strategy.

Wordy   The winner of the contest will be the person who has the best dance moves.

Better	The person with the best moves will win the dance contest.

Strategy 5: Eliminate inflated or empty language. Sometimes students use big words and fancy phrases when a simple word will do. Of course, having a good vocabulary is great, but an inflated vocabulary just makes you seem like you're trying to impress, which is, well, not impressive.

Wordy	In the event that the executive in charge of production deems it necessary to call for a work stoppage for the day, we will resume our duties in a timely fashion tomorrow.
Better	If the production manager thinks we need to stop work today, we will start again early tomorrow.

While the first sentence might seem better to some because it sounds official, most readers will find it wordy.

The following is a short list of phrases you should avoid whenever possible, as well as some suggested substitutions:

Avoid	Substitute
due to the fact that	because
in the event that	if
in society today, *or* nowadays	in Texas since the mid-1990s (or other specific time and place)

Wordiness makes your writing hard to understand, and sometimes makes it look like you're trying to sound important, which usually ends up just sounding silly. Avoiding wordiness is the key to having a clear, concise, college writing style.

Avoid Vague or Unclear Pronouns

Vague or unclear pronouns create unclear or unfocused sentences. Although this can happen with almost any pronoun, the following pronouns are most likely to cause trouble:

▶ **For more on pronouns, see Chapter 34, Pronouns.**

Pronouns That Refer to People	
he	she
hers	their
his	they
one	

> ### Pronouns That Refer to Things
>
> it
> that
> this

Here's an example:

> **Unclear**   The instructor gave the student his essay.

Whose essay did the instructor give the student? Was it the student's essay or the instructor's essay? It's not clear who *his* refers to in this sentence.

> **Revised**   The student received his essay back from the instructor.

Now we know whose essay it was: the student's. Let's look at another sentence:

> **Unclear**   Taking the bus or walking is a great way to get around the city; this also helps reduce traffic on the streets.

What does *this* refer to? Taking the bus, walking, or both?

> **Revised**   Taking the bus and walking are great ways to get around the city and to reduce traffic on the streets.

Good, now it's clear that *both* methods of transportation reduce traffic on the streets. Here's another example:

> **Unclear**   In the trilogy *The Lord of the Rings,* it creates a fantasy world that is very complex.

What does *it* refer to? What creates a fantasy world that is very complex? *The Lord of the Rings* trilogy creates the fantasy world, but in this case it would be too wordy to repeat the title and too vague to use the pronoun *it* to replace it.

In some cases, the best solution is to rewrite the sentence to focus on what you are trying to say. In this instance, the point is that the books create a complex fantasy world. So let's rewrite the sentence with that point as the focus:

> **Revised**   The trilogy *The Lord of the Rings* creates a very complex fantasy world.

Much clearer!

Using the pronoun *one* is sometimes necessary to avoid a lengthy explanation of whom *one* refers to, but overuse of this pronoun leads to a vague sentence or paragraph, as in the following example:

> **Unclear**   If one recycled all of one's plastics and cans, one could get by with a smaller garbage can.

This sentence sounds really awkward because of the use of the vague pronoun *one*. It's not clear to whom the writer is referring. The general population? A specific audience? Us? If you know whom you are referring to in the sentence, use a concrete subject instead of the vague pronoun *one*. The following sentence is much clearer:

Revised   If the tenants of the apartment building recycled all of their plastics and cans, they could get by with smaller garbage cans.

Can you see how this sentence becomes clearer and more focused when we replace the vague pronoun with a concrete subject? The use of the pronoun *they* in the second half of the sentence works fine because now that we have clarified the subject (*tenants of the apartment building*), we know exactly to whom that pronoun refers. Essentially, if you can't tell what the noun is, then you have an unclear pronoun referent.

> **TIP**
> In addition to vague or unclear pronouns, the word *things* can be vague or unclear as well. Be sure to make it clear in your sentence what thing or things you are referring to when you use this word.

Use Active Voice Whenever Possible

An active-voice sentence occurs when the subject of the sentence is doing the action. For example:

Active   Financial literacy programs make sense.

In this sentence, the subject *programs* is doing something; it is making.

In contrast, the action of a passive-voice sentence is done by someone not named in the sentence. For example:

Passive   Financial literacy programs should be taught.

Who should teach financial literacy programs? It's not clear because the person or thing doing the action (teaching) is not in the sentence. Passive-voice sentences can really reduce the clarity of your writing. Here's another example:

Passive   The problem of having different financial styles is solved through talking.

Who is doing the solving through talking? Couples, maybe? Now look at the following sentence, written in the active voice:

Active   Couples can solve the problem of having different financial styles through talking.

Much better! Let's look at another sentence:

Passive   Yosemite has been visited by many tourists over the years.

This sounds awkward. If it's tourists who are doing the visiting, *tourists* should be the subject.

| **Active** | Many tourists have visited Yosemite over the years. |

Sometimes the passive voice is necessary, especially when you don't know who is doing the action or the doers of the action are too large and varied a group to name. However, if you know who is doing the action of the sentence, it is generally better to avoid the passive voice and keep the verb active.

| **General Group Doing the Action** | The Nike "swoosh" symbol is recognized around the world. |

In this case, the group recognizing the "swoosh" symbol is so general that it is not necessary to name it.

| **Unclear Who Is Doing the Action** | Diamonds can now be manufactured in labs. |

It's not clear who is doing the manufacturing; the point is that this technology exists.

| **To Avoid Naming Who Is Doing the Action** | During the group obstacle course, mistakes were made. |

In this case, the passive voice is used intentionally to protect the identity of the person or people who made mistakes.

---

practice it 39.1   Editing for Clarity and Focus I

Edit the following paragraph using the information and skills you learned in this chapter:

- remove clichés, empty phrases, and slang
- reduce wordiness
- avoid vague or unclear pronouns
- use active-voice verbs

In society today, one problem with public schools is the lack of funding. The lack of funding, especially in low-income areas, makes it harder for students to achieve success. It is harder for students to achieve success because the schools don't have a lot of things. They don't have enough books or computers for each student to use. The test scores are very low because when students can't study, they score very low on the test. They can't study because they don't have enough books or materials. The children are suffering. They are not to blame.

practice it 39.2 Editing for Clarity and Focus II

Edit the following paragraph using the information and skills you learned in this chapter:

- remove clichés, empty phrases, and slang
- reduce wordiness
- avoid vague or unclear pronouns
- use active-voice verbs

Clashes between celebrities and paparazzi are frequent occurrences in the news. A lack of privacy is the result of photographers following celebrities everywhere they go. After one incident between a celebrity photographer and a bodyguard, it was claimed that the bodyguard took his camera. The allegation was denied by the bodyguard. It was also stated that the reputation of the celebrity was on the line when photos of him being arrested for drunk driving emerged. There are those who blame them for invasion of privacy, and there are others who say that it is a right that celebrities forfeit in exchange for their fame. Shows like *TMZ* (OMG, so funny) always follow celebrities around asking stuff until the celebrities finally get mad, and then the celebrities usually get in a car and drive away. Sometimes they show other paparazzi getting into arguments with celebs. Although I envy their fancy clothes, cars, and vacations, I am glad I don't have anyone following me around with a camera.

practice it 39.3 Editing for Clarity and Focus III

Edit the following paragraph using the information and skills you learned in this chapter:

- remove clichés, empty phrases, and slang
- reduce wordiness
- avoid vague or unclear pronouns
- use active-voice verbs

Despite how expensive college is, there are ways to afford your college tuition when it's time to go to college. Back in the day, college tuition was

continued ⊚

much less expensive and so was the cost of living. However, in today's society, today, everything is more—housing, food, textbooks, and tuition. As luck would have it, saving money has never been easier. U can use any of the tons of online money management Web sites or apps that help you keep a budget. Your spending and earnings should be tracked so you can see where your money is going. In order to save, you'll have to reduce your spending or increase your earnings. By following one of these, your savings will grow. Working on campus is another way to help pay for college. Campus jobs are geared toward student workers so they generally have flexible hours and decent pay. There are also lots of scholarships that are available to help students pay for school. Scholarships are not always based on GPA; there are also need-based scholarships and some scholarships that are based on a person's qualities, heritage, or group affiliation. These aren't easy, but they can sure make a big dent in the cost of college.

Reduce Bias

Bias is another important language consideration. Although your writing most certainly should reflect your perspective, it should not contain insensitive or offensive language. Becoming aware of how language can reinforce stereotypes is the first step in avoiding them. Biased language can be offensive, does not reflect the preferences of the subject, or suggests "normal" or "abnormal" status. Because language changes over time, it is important to use the language that reflects current preferences.

RACIAL OR CULTURAL LANGUAGE

Words used to identify one's race or culture should reflect how that group prefers to be identified. An example would be references to Hispanic or Latino individuals, who often prefer to be referred to by their families' countries of origin (Puerto Rican, Mexican, Guatemalan) rather than by a broader, more generic ethnic label.

GENDERED LANGUAGE

Other kinds of biased language include using the pronoun *he* as the standard or default when the gender is unknown. In this case, do not replace *he* with *he or she* or other awkward substitutions. Instead, attempt to rework the sentence to avoid use of a pronoun, or use the plural *they* and *their*. When referring to job titles that have traditionally been masculine through the suffix *-man* (*fireman, congressman, mailman*), use a gender-neutral substitute (*firefighter, congressperson, letter carrier*). Gender-neutral language is intended to remove any expectation of or emphasis on one gender over another. Of course, when the gender of the person is known or the reference to gender is necessary, using a gendered pronoun is acceptable.

chapter review

In the following chart, fill in the second column to record in your own words the important skills included in this chapter. Then assess yourself to determine whether you are still developing the skill or feel you have mastered it. If you are still developing the skill, make some notes about what you need to work on to master it in the future. If you believe you have already mastered it, explain why.

Skills and concepts covered in this chapter	Explanation in your own words	I'm developing this skill and need to work on . . .	I believe I have mastered this skill because . . .
Understanding clear and focused language			
Avoiding clichés, empty phrases, and slang			
Fixing wordy sentences			
Avoiding vague or unclear pronouns			
Understanding passive and active voice			
Using active voice whenever possible			
Using nonbiased language			

40

Apostrophes

What Is an Apostrophe?

Visit LaunchPad Solo for Readers and Writers > Apostrophes for extra practice in the skills covered in this chapter.

The apostrophe—that little thing that looks like a comma but hangs above the line—is one of the most incorrectly used punctuation marks in the English language. People who make signs and banners seem particularly confused by this tiny demon. You, however, can master the apostrophe. The first step is to recognize that it has two totally different purposes: to show a contraction and to show ownership. Next, you need to figure out how to use it correctly. This is pretty easy with contractions, but more difficult with ownership. Luckily, a few simple possession tests can tame this punctuation mark.

USING APOSTROPHES TO MAKE CONTRACTIONS

When something contracts, it shrinks. It pulls together. Your muscles can contract while you run and give you a cramp or a muscle spasm, which is why you should stretch before you jog.

In language, a contraction is the pulling together of two words. You smush them together and leave out a few letters. We do this constantly in spoken English, often in a sloppy, informal way: "Bobby, gimme the shovel." What we really mean is "Bobby, give me the shovel," but we run *give* and *me* together and say it quickly: *gimme.* This is not good English. You can get away with it with Bobby, but definitely not on a job application or a college paper.

Some contractions are acceptable in written English, if you make them properly and spell them correctly. Common acceptable contractions are shown in the list on page 719.

TIP

Some instructors request that you never use contractions in formal papers. Look at the course syllabus and assignment sheets, and listen to your instructor's verbal instructions, to find out his or her preference. When in doubt, leave them out.

Common Contractions

do not	becomes	*don't*
is not	becomes	*isn't*
she will	becomes	*she'll*
we are	becomes	*we're*
it is	becomes	*it's*

To make a contraction properly, you have to know which words you are trying to contract (or pull together), and you have to know how to spell them. Then, when you pull them together, simply insert the apostrophe where you leave out the letters. Let's look at some examples in closer detail:

1. Begin with the words: do not
2. Run them together: → donot ←
3. Replace the second *o* with an apostrophe: don't

Sometimes you leave out more than one letter. That's okay too.

1. Begin with the words: she will
2. Run them together: → shewill ←
3. Replace *wi* with an apostrophe: she'll

A FEW EXCEPTIONS

Of course, it wouldn't (would not) be the English language if there weren't (were not) some exceptions, which you'll (you will) just have to memorize if they don't (do not) come naturally to you. Here are some exceptions:

will not	→	won't
shall not	→	shan't

Some contractions have more than one meaning, which can make things a bit tricky. For these, the reader has to use context to figure out which one the writer means. Turn the page to see a few examples.

TIP

Contractions with the word *is* are the ones that give people the most trouble. To figure out if a word is a contraction with *is*, try reformulating it as a question by reversing the two words that you are contracting. Here's an example: "She's going to call me." Is she? Yes, she is. Here's another example: "It's raining outside." Is it? Yes, it is.

Contractions That End in -'s

he's	can mean	he is	OR	he has
that's	can mean	that is	OR	that has
there's	can mean	there is	OR	there has

Contractions That End in -'d

he'd	can mean	he had	OR	he would
you'd	can mean	you had	OR	you would

practice it 40.1   Using Apostrophes to Make Contractions

Read the sentences below and underline any word groups where you could form a contraction. (In some cases, a word is inserted between the two words that you will combine into a contraction, so some rewriting is necessary.) Then rewrite the sentences, inserting apostrophes in the appropriate places to make contractions. Read both versions out loud and compare how they sound.

1. Let us get to the field. The game is about to start, is it not?
2. No, I do not think it starts for another hour.
3. Do you not want to have a barbecue in the parking lot?
4. I am not hungry.
5. True, but it is so fun to stand around in the cold and talk to our friends.
6. I do not really agree. Standing around in the cold does not sound so fun when we could just have them meet us here.
7. I promised my friend I would meet him there, so I have got to go.
8. I did not promise anyone that I would be there.
9. You promised me, did you not?
10. I do not remember agreeing to do that. See you at the game.

practice it 40.2   Editing for Contractions

Look at the last essay you wrote for this class. Circle all the contractions on one page. How many contractions did you use? How formal is this piece of writing expected to be? Does the number of contractions seem appropriate? Correct any errors that you see in any of the contractions you found.

USING APOSTROPHES TO SHOW OWNERSHIP

As we have seen, the first reason to use an apostrophe is to make a contraction. The second reason is to show ownership—also known as possession. In other words, you use an apostrophe to show that one person, place, or thing (one noun) belongs to another person, place, or thing (another noun). For instance:

> my iguana's cage = the cage that belongs to my iguana

Of course, my iguana didn't buy the cage. He got it as a gift. Still, it's his, and he lives there, all by himself, so I use an apostrophe to show ownership.

The tricky part of using apostrophes to show ownership always seems to involve the letter *s*. Let's look at a few more examples. As you read, pay special attention to the word endings. Reading each example twice might help.

> my iguana's cage = one iguana, one cage

Now, say my iguana had two babies, and I'm keeping them all in the same cage. I need to make *iguana* plural (because there are more than one now), but I can keep *cage* singular, since I still have only one cage. So I add an *s* to *iguana* to make it plural, and then I hang the apostrophe on the outside, like this:

> my iguanas' cage = more than one iguana, one cage

Now, say the babies got too big to share a cage, and I bought each of them its own cage. I now have three iguanas and three cages. I need to make both words—*iguana* and *cage*—plural. Then I need to hang the apostrophe after the *s* on *iguanas*. Here's what it looks like now:

> my iguanas' cages = more than one iguana, more than one cage

Tricky, right? It gets even tougher when the first word ends in an *s*. Let's start with the word *witness* and imagine our witness has a story about what happened in an accident.

> the witness's story = one witness, one story

For singular nouns that end in *s*, add an apostrophe and an *s*.

If more than one witness was there, but they all remembered seeing the same thing, I would need to add *-es* to *witness* and write it like this:

> the witnesses' story = more than one witness, one story

If, however, the witnesses had different recollections of the accident—different stories—it would look like this:

> the witnesses' stories = more than one witness, more than one story

We agree that this can get confusing. Luckily, there is a very simple rule to follow to avoid making mistakes with the possessive. Here it is, in two easy steps.

STEP 1: Make the noun showing ownership singular or plural *first.*

STEP 2: Hang an apostrophe + *s* (if it is singular or if it is plural and ends in any letter except *s*) or an apostrophe (if it is plural and ends in *s*) on the word that is demonstrating ownership of something.

Let's look at one more example:

I have three female siblings, and they own a house together.

      Plural   Singular

My sisters own a house.

Since *sisters* already ends in the letter *s*, to make it possessive, just hang an apostrophe on the end:

My sisters' house

Now, let's say they go into a real estate business together and start buying up houses. Now we would say:

My sisters' houses

But if two of them moved to France and left all the houses to one of the sisters, we would say:

My sister's houses

But then let's say she decided to sell all the houses and move into a condo. We would say:

My sister's condo

The mighty apostrophe in combination with the letter *s* certainly can convey a lot of information, right? Unfortunately, though, in English, there is no way to determine from the apostrophe *how many more than one* we have. The reader or listener has to figure that out from the context.

Sometimes nouns form irregular plurals. For instance, *radius* becomes *radii* when you have more than one of them. More than one *life* would be *lives*. Here are some other common examples:

deer = one deer AND more than one deer
mouse = one mouse
mice = more than one mouse

Handle irregular plurals with the same rules given earlier: Make the noun that owns something singular or plural first, and then add the apostrophe or the apostrophe + *s* as necessary.

the mouse's cheese = one mouse, one piece of cheese

the mice's cheese = more than one mouse, one piece of cheese

---

practice it 40.3   Using Apostrophes to Show Possession I

Insert missing apostrophes to show possession in the paragraph below. You will add six apostrophes.

My cars fan belt needs to be replaced. The mechanic says that his shop can do it tomorrow. However, my grandmothers birthday is tomorrow, and I want to visit her in the nursing home, which is far away. My grandmothers nurse said that they will have a cake for her. If my car is in the shop, I will miss her celebration. Maybe I will call my cousin Billy. If he could take me, then maybe the nursing homes van could bring me back when it goes on the seniors weekly shopping trip. I will have to call my aunt to see if Billys schedule is free tomorrow morning.

Finding and Fixing Apostrophe Errors with Possessives

Sure, the spell checker on your computer can catch some apostrophe errors, but that doesn't help you when you're taking an essay exam or doing the sort of on-the-spot report writing common in so many professions. Plus, the spell checker is notoriously wrong much of the time when it comes to apostrophes. You need to learn how to eliminate apostrophe errors from your writing to gain a level of polish and sophistication in your work.

Many times, we've seen students who are trying to fix their apostrophe errors take something that was correct and rewrite it the wrong way. There are so many weird words in English, and it's easy to get overwhelmed. That's why the best way to find and fix your own errors is by repeating this simple rule to yourself while you are editing:

Make the noun showing ownership singular or plural first. Then hang an <u>apostrophe + *s*</u> or an <u>apostrophe</u> on it to make it possessive.

One more time:

Singular or plural first. Then think about the apostrophe.

It's sort of like the order of operations in math problems. As long as you follow that order, you'll be right every time.

▶ **For help with forming plurals, see page 730 in Chapter 41, Spelling and Capitalization.**

To edit carefully for apostrophes, you may want to read your writing "backwards" by starting at the last sentence and ending with the first. You could use a piece of blank paper to cover the words so you are only looking at one sentence at a time. Some writers like to read out loud as they proofread. Proofreading works best from the printed page, not the computer screen.

practice it 40.4 Using Apostrophes to Show Possession II

Practice using the apostrophe correctly by making possessives with the following:

- Your family name
- The first name of everyone in your family
- The names of all your pets
- Objects you see in the room
- Your favorite dessert
- Your favorite animal
- Your favorite sport

practice it 40.5 Correcting Apostrophe Errors I

The following paragraph is missing eleven apostrophes. In some cases, the missing apostrophe is part of a contraction; in other cases, the missing apostrophe shows possession. Proofread the paragraph with a pen or pencil in hand, correcting the apostrophe errors as you go.

You cant deny that Juan Carlos new job is amazing. Hes going to be the lead computer engineer of a team that is building the next generation of robots for space exploration. Hes hoping that hell be able to hire his old neighbors, twin brothers whose technical skills will be helpful. The twins, Jeremy and Jerome, used to fix their bikes brakes when they were seven years old. Those boys can fix anything: broken toasters, the nozzles of sprinklers, and even the pools overflow pump. Many college-educated engineers have the mathematical skills, but they lack the twins hands-on experience. Juan Carlos hopes for the future are high. With the help of Jeremy and Jerome, he imagines building NASAs next Mars Rover. Wont their mothers be proud of them?

practice it 40.6   Correcting Apostrophe Errors II

The following paragraph contains twelve apostrophe errors. Some are contraction errors, and some are possession errors. The words might be missing an apostrophe or might have it in the wrong place. Proofread the paragraph with a pen or pencil in your hand. Circle each apostrophe error as you find it. Then go back and fix the errors, using this chapter to help you.

Yesterday I went to a seminar on time management. Its about time I went to something like this. My sisters boyfriend told me about it, and he's really smart, so I figured Id give it a try. I wasn't exactly thrilled to go at first, but now I'm totally glad I went. I feel like it will completely change my life. If I can apply some of the strategies' the lecturers were talking about, I can save myself so much time and get so much more done. For instance, they showed us how to make a weekly schedule with a to-do list. They said we should do it every Saturday morning so we have a sense of what our whole week's will look like. They also gave a lot of simple suggestions' that seem so easy. I don't know why I did'nt think of them before. They said that we should pack our backpack for school the night before class. Ive never bothered to do that, which is probably why I'm always rushing and forgetting things every morning. It sure would be nice to have time to have a bowl of cereal in the morning instead of rushing around like mad looking for all my books. Im going to start small and try those two strategies', and then once I've become good at those Ill try some of the other stuff they mentioned, like stopping procrastination, getting all the details' of my life organized, and finishing my homework before I go out to have fun.

chapter review

In the following chart, fill in the second column to record in your own words the important skills included in this chapter. Then assess yourself to determine whether you are still developing the skill or feel you have mastered it. If you are still developing the skill, make some notes about what you need to work on to master it in the future. If you believe you have already mastered it, explain why.

Skills and concepts covered in this chapter	Explanation in your own words	I'm developing this skill and need to work on . . .	I believe I have mastered this skill because . . .
Understanding contractions			
Using apostrophes to make contractions			
Using apostrophes to show ownership (make words possessive)			
Making a word singular or plural before making it possessive			

41

Spelling and Capitalization

in this chapter

- What Are the Most Commonly Confused Words?
- What Are Some Tricky Spelling Rules?
- When Do You Capitalize?

Spelling

Computers have spell checkers that can fix your typing or spelling errors, sometimes without your even realizing you've made an error. Such technology can help writers reduce errors and make the finished product look much more polished. However, relying on your spell checker alone can be dangerous for a couple of reasons. First, spell checkers won't alert you if you use the wrong word. For instance, most computers can't tell when you should use *their*, *there*, or *they're*. Such errors are actually the most common spelling mistakes. Second, and more important, not all the writing you do is on a computer, so you won't have your spell checker with you everywhere. In fact, in college some of the most important types of writing you do—midterms and finals—are still handwritten, so you need to find and fix spelling errors yourself.

LaunchPad Solo
macmillan learning

Visit **LaunchPad Solo for Readers and Writers > Spelling** and **> Capitalization** for extra practice in the skills covered in this chapter.

Commonly Confused Words

Let's start with the most common errors, the ones that make your writing look sloppy but are, thankfully, easily fixed.

Confusion between *it's* and *its* is reported to be the most common mistake in English.

> ***it's*** is a contraction that means "it is": It's raining.

> ***its*** is a possessive pronoun: The dog chased its tail.

One way to tell whether to use *it's* or *its* is to ask yourself the question "Is it?" and see if you can create an answer. For instance, look at the sentence at the top of page 728.

It's raining.

Ask yourself: Is it raining?

Answer: Yes, it is.

Therefore, use *it's* to mean *it is*.

Now, try it with this sentence:

The dog chased its tail.

Ask yourself: Is it?

Answer: There's no answer that makes sense to that question. We could say "Did it?" but "Is it?" doesn't fit.

Therefore, use *its* in this sentence.

Another way to remember the difference is to memorize the following sentence:

It's time that the apostrophe took its place at the start of the sentence.

Other commonly confused words are *their*, *there*, and *they're*:

> *their* refers to a person
> *there* refers to a place
> *they're* means "they are"

Fortunately, there are some helpful memorization tricks you can use to remember these words. If you create a sentence that uses all three words in alphabetical order, you can figure out which word to use:

Their car is over there, but they're not in it.

Have a little fun creating your own sentence, one that you might remember better, making sure to keep the words in alphabetical order. Here are a few more examples of commonly confused words:

> *accept* is a verb that means to receive or agree to something
> *except* indicates that one was left out

The cashier accepted all my coupons except for the one that had expired.

> *advice* is a noun that means the words of wisdom someone gives
> *advise* is what people do while they are delivering advice

Good advice is rare; I advise you to take it.

> *affect* is usually a verb that means to impact or influence
> *effect* is usually a noun that means the result of something

He suffered from seasonal depression and was affected by the lack of sunshine in the winter. The effect was that he slept all the time and rarely ate.

loose is the opposite of tight
lose is what happens when you can't find something

My pants are loose; I hope I don't lose them when I round third base!

prejudice is a noun that refers to the state of being biased
prejudiced is an adjective that describes something that has prejudice

Racial prejudice is a terrible thing; I won't date anyone who is prejudiced.

quiet is the opposite of loud
quite means "very"

Being quiet is quite important in libraries.

than is used when comparing things
then refers to time or place (now and then)

I'd rather make dinner at home than eat out, but then after dinner I'd like to go out for ice cream.

to serves as a preposition (to the store) or as part of an infinitive (to dance)
too means "also" or "in addition" (I want a million dollars too!)
two is the number (No, I want two million dollars!)

To dance too much is impossible for those two.

weather is the snow, rain, sunshine, and so on
whether refers to possibilities, choices, or alternatives

The weather will determine whether the baseball game is called off.

we're is a contraction that means "we are" (We're going to buy books.)
were is the past tense of the verb *to be* (They were going to buy books.)
where refers to a place (Where are you going to buy books?)

We're lucky because we were just driving on the road where the avalanche hit, but it missed us by a minute.

your is an adjective that means belonging to you
you're is a contraction of two words: *you are*

You're going to love your new car.

Tricky Spelling Rules

The commonly confused words discussed in the preceding section cause most spelling errors among adults. Three types of words seem to cause the majority of the rest of the errors: plurals, words ending in silent *e*, and words for which people are not sure whether to double the final consonant when adding suffixes.

PLURAL ENDINGS

Turning a singular word into a plural causes many spelling errors. The three rules are pretty simple:

1. For regular words, most of the time you simply add *s* to the end to make them plural.

Singular		Plural
bird	→	birds
book	→	books
house	→	houses

Remember, though, there are some irregular plurals, like *woman* → *women* and *mouse* → *mice*.

2. For regular words ending in *s*, *sh*, *ch*, *x*, or *es*, add *es* to the end to make them plural.

Singular		Plural
dress	→	dresses
dish	→	dishes
lunch	→	lunches
box	→	boxes

3. For most words ending in *f* or *fe*, change the ending to *ves* to make it plural.

Singular		Plural
thief	→	thieves
knife	→	knives

Note that *safe* (meaning a place to store valuables) does not follow this rule. Its plural is *safes*.

SILENT *E*

Silent *e* is the letter at the end of a word that changes the sound of the vowel in the middle but does not have a sound itself.

For example, take the word *tap* and add silent *e* and you get *tape*. When we say *tape*, it sounds like "tayp," not "tay-pee," right? That's silent *e* in action.

If you need to add a suffix like *-ing*, *-ed*, or *-en* to a word that ends in silent *e*, drop the silent *e* before adding the suffix.

chase + ed = chased

chase + ing = chasing

take + en = taken

take + ing = taking

If the word ends in *ce* or *ge*, keep the *e* when adding the suffix *-able* or *-ous*.

replace + able = replaceable

advantage + ous = advantageous

TO DOUBLE OR NOT TO DOUBLE THE FINAL CONSONANT

Knowing whether or not to double a final consonant before adding a suffix is another tricky spelling situation. The rule is that you double the consonant if the word is only one syllable and the final consonant comes after a single vowel, as in the following examples:

stop + ed = stopped

bug + ing = bugging

The same rule applies if the word has more than one syllable and the final syllable is stressed.

submit + ed = submitted

regret + able = regrettable

If a word has more than one vowel, don't double the consonant.

feel + ing = feeling [not *feelling*]

look + ed = looked [not *lookked*]

FOREIGN WORDS

Like many languages, English has words that don't follow the rules. Often, this happens when a word enters English from another language. This list includes words like *bourgeois*, *entrepreneur*, *caveat*, *faux pas*, *avant-garde*, and *llama*. You need to memorize these words or look them up in a dictionary. Keeping a list in your Grammar Log may help.

▶ **For more on keeping a Grammar Log, see page 573 in Chapter 27, How to Learn the Rules and Apply Them to Your Own Writing.**

practice it 41.1   Proofreading for Spelling Errors and Commonly Confused Words I

The following paragraph contains eleven spelling errors. Proofread the paragraph with a pen or pencil in your hand. Correct each spelling

continued ❯

error you find. You may find it easier to read "backwards," going sentence by sentence from the end of the paragraph.

Being an enterpeneure sounds great, right? The idea of being you're own boss seems amazing cuz of the freedom and flexibility. However, they're are many factors that you have to consider before taking the plunge into self-employment. First, you will be giving up the security you might have in your current job. Their's no unemployment insurance for the self-employed. Second, you do not have quiet the same vehicles to save for your retirement. In many cases, 401(k)s are free money. Some employers match all or part of your contributions, and at the very least you should concider the tax-free contributions an automatic return on your investment. The types of retirement savings plans for the self-employed are not as generous. Finally, you have to factor in the cost of health insurance, which will be determined by you're age, health, and smoking habits. Its wise to comparison shop for health insurance before you decide to quit your regular job and start your own business. Overall, the life of an entrepreneur does have many advantages, but their are significant drawbacks as well. Make sure you carefully weigh the costs and benefits and have enough cash to carry you over lean times before you except the challenge of starting your new business.

practice it 41.2 Proofreading for Spelling Errors and Commonly Confused Words II

The following paragraph contains seventeen spelling errors and incorrect words. Proofread the paragraph with a pen or pencil in your hand. Correct each spelling error you find. You may find it easier to read "backwards," going sentence by sentence from the end of the paragraph.

People say to travel while your young, but they're are advantages to traveling when your older as well. For starters, once you get established in your carreer you will probably have a bit more money in your pocket to spend on plain tickets and dinning out at local restaraunts. Its true that you may not have as much free time to spend on vacation, but you'll really savor the break from your work life. Another advantage to travelling later in life is having plenty of time to think about where in the world you really want to go. When you are younger, you might be limited in were you go based on the cost. If you wait until you are a bit older, you will have time to save up for the expensive expedition to Antarctica or the pricey cruise to the South Seas. But don't weight to long to go on that trip to India were the whether might be too hot or rainy for your comfort once you hit middle-age. Luckily, you're not limited to one or the other. The best advise for those wanting to see the world is to travel when you are younger and a bit older. Afterall, it's a pretty big place and it will take awhile to see the whole thing.

Capitalization

As we become more reliant on digital communication in which capitalization rules are often ignored, our knowledge of capitalization rules seems to be slipping. You will need to watch out for proper capitalization while proofreading, and probably you will need to review some basic rules from time to time. Capitalize words at the beginning of sentences, proper nouns, and the first and major words in titles. The devil, as they say, is in the details. What counts as a proper noun? Which words in a title are considered major? When in doubt, you can check a good dictionary, of course, but you should also learn a few specific techniques to help you figure out whether to capitalize or not to capitalize.

PROPER NOUNS

Proper nouns are capitalized because they refer to important things: specific names of people, places, and events. Take, for example, Niko the cat. The word *cat* is a common noun. It refers to all four-legged furry felines. The word *Niko* is a proper noun because it is the name of one specific cat. Most nouns work this way, as you can see in the examples on page 734, where the proper nouns are capitalized and the corresponding common nouns are not.

I think Saturday is my favorite day of the week.

Most people believe Earth is the best planet.

The writer Jane Austen is the best novelist.

That guy says Nirvana is the most influential band of all time.

Who knew Paris was the most beautiful city?

Is Halloween the most fun holiday?

Sometimes, though, a word can be either a proper or a common noun, so you capitalize it or don't capitalize it depending on whether or not it refers to a specific person, place, or thing. Look at these examples:

A new study reported that the average mom does twenty-seven hours of housework a week.

I sure hope my mom has some help with all that work.

"Hey, Mom, did you wash my soccer jersey?"

In the first example, the word *mom* refers to the general category of mothers. In the second example, someone is referring to his or her mother but not using the word as a name. In the third example, the person is using *Mom* in place of a name, so it is capitalized. Here's another example:

Any college you attend should be accredited.

Pasadena City College is an accredited institution.

TITLES

The rule for titles is that you capitalize the first and last words in any title or subtitle, plus all the major words. What counts as a major word? Anything except articles (*a, an, the*), coordinating conjunctions (*for, and, nor, but, or, yet, so*), and prepositions (*of, on, with*, and so on) needs to be capitalized. Here are some examples:

I'm Dancing as Fast as I Can

Of Human Bondage

Home to Harlem

All the Pretty Horses

▶ For more on formatting titles, see Chapter 22, MLA Documentation, and Chapter 23, APA Documentation.

These minor capitalization rules do change from one publication style to the next, so MLA may capitalize something that APA does not. Remember, too, that book titles are italicized in MLA style, and essay and short story titles are in quotation marks. Check with your instructor in each class to determine which documentation style you should use, but keep in mind that generally MLA is used in the humanities and APA is used in the social and health sciences.

practice it 41.3 Proofreading for Capitalization in Titles

The following paragraph contains nine titles that need proper capitalization. Proofread the paragraph and make the necessary corrections.

Although nothing replaces reading books, there are lots of books that have been made into very popular films. *to kill a mockingbird* was a huge success in print and on the screen and netted Gregory Peck an Academy Award. *interview with the vampire* helped launch Brad Pitt's career as the vampire Louis de Pointe du Lac. *the war of the worlds* by H.G. Wells was famously broadcast on the radio in the 1930s and created a widespread panic when confused listeners thought the Earth was being invaded by Martians. Wells's book was so popular that it was also made into a movie twice. Another classic work of literature, *the great gatsby*, has been captured on film more than once. In recent years, the super-popular Harry Potter book series by J.K. Rowling was made into an equally popular series of movies beginning with *harry potter and the sorcerer's stone* all the way through *harry potter and the deathly hallows, part 2*. There are some good but lesser-known books that have made it on-screen as well, such as *the fault in our stars* by John Green, *water for elephants* by Sara Gruen, and *unbroken: a world war II story of survival, resilience, and redemption* by Laura Hillenbrand. Although films can't capture all the details of a good book, they do go well with popcorn.

practice it 41.4 Proofreading for Capitalization Errors I

The following paragraph contains numerous capitalization errors. Proofread the paragraph with a pen or pencil in your hand. Correct each capitalization error you find. You may find it easier to read "backwards," going sentence by sentence from the end of the paragraph.

The local Public Radio Station, Kacg, has a weekly talk show program about personal finance called *Money Matters And me.* This week, the host,

continued ❯

Janice million, was joined by a guest expert on financing a college education, Mr. Edward Most. He explained the difference between student loans backed by the Government and private loans, and he argued that parents should always put their retirement savings ahead of their children's college savings goals. When a college student called in and asked Mr. Most what she should do if her Parents hadn't saved enough for college, he gave her a very informative answer about various options, like work-study, post-graduation work opportunities that forgive part or all of your student loan debt, and, of course, the Military, which has the gi bill for veterans as well as some excellent training programs for active duty military personnel. The radio program made a compelling case that parents and students need more education about College Financing, and that most americans probably are not aware of the full array of options available.

practice it 41.5   Proofreading for Capitalization Errors II

The following paragraph contains numerous capitalization errors. Proofread the paragraph with a pen or pencil in your hand. Correct each capitalization error you find. You may find it easier to read "backwards," going sentence by sentence from the end of the paragraph.

In 2015, the united states supreme court ruled in favor of an American muslim woman who had been denied a job with clothing store abercrombie & fitch because she wore a headscarf. The supreme court ruled almost unanimously in her favor, saying that she should be considered for employment with her headscarf, which is an expression of her religious practice and therefore is protected under freedom of religion. Abercrombie & fitch had argued that she did not fit the ivy league collegiate look that they wanted all their staff to have and that she had not informed them that her desire to wear the headscarf was religious in nature. The court ruled that it was obviously an Expression of Religion and that she should not have to inform them of that fact. This case has interesting implications for other corporations that try to limit whom they hire based on a specific appear-

ance. while they might still be able to reject a job candidate because of

piercings, unnaturally colored hair, or tattoos, they will not be able to

discriminate against people with headscarves or other Religiously Related

Types of Attire.

chapter review

In the following chart, fill in the second column to record in your own words the
important skills included in this chapter. Then assess yourself to determine whether
you are still developing the skill or feel you have mastered it. If you are still developing the skill, make some notes about what you need to work on to master it in
the future. If you believe you have already mastered it, explain why.

Skills and concepts covered in this chapter	Explanation in your own words	I'm developing this skill and need to work on . . .	I believe I have mastered this skill because . . .
Spelling commonly confused words			
Turning singular words into plural words			
Adding suffixes to words with silent *e*			
Adding suffixes to words with a final consonant			
Capitalizing proper nouns			
Capitalizing the correct words in titles and subtitles			

ACKNOWLEDGMENTS

Teresa Palomo Acosta. "Chicano Mural Movement," *Handbook of Texas Online* (http://www.tshaonline.org/handbook/online/articles/kjc03), accessed September 4, 2013. Published by the Texas State Historical Association. Used by permission.

Jack Becker. "Public Art: An Essential Component of Creating Communities," Americans for the Arts/Monograph, March 2004 with permission by Americans for the Arts, www.AmericansForTheArts.org and author Jack Becker, Forecast Public Art, www.forecastpublicart.org. Used by permission.

Kathleen Stassen Berger. Education in the U.S. infographic from *Invitation to the Life Span*, 3rd ed., p. 409. New York: Freeman, 2016. Used by permission.

Paul J. Campbell. Excerpt from Chapter 22, pp. 805–808 and portions of pp. 820, 821, 822, 826, 827 from *For All Practical Purposes: Mathematical Literacy in Today's World*. 9th ed. New York: Freeman, 2013. Used by permission.

Andrea Chang. "The Kardashians: Cashing in with a Capital K," *LA Times*, April 24, 2011. Used by permission.

Theresa Cramer. "Would You Quit Social Media if You Could?" EContent, April 22, 2014. Reprinted by permission.

KJ Dell'Antonia. "Disney Limits Junk-Food Ads," *The New York Times*, June 5, 2012. Copyright © 2012 *The New York Times*. All rights reserved. Used by permission and protected by the Copyright Laws of the United States. The printing, copying, redistribution, or retransmission of this content without express written permission is prohibited.

Carol S. Dweck. "The Perils and Promises of Praise." From the Oct. 2007 issue of *Educational Leadership*, 65(2), pp. 34--39. Copyright © 2007 by ASCD. Reprinted with permission. Learn more about ASCD at www.ascd.org.

Susan Engel. "The Case for Curiosity." From the February 2013 issue of *Educational Leadership* 70(5), pp. 37–40. Copyright © 2013 by ASCD. Reprinted with permission. Learn more about ASCD at www.ascd.org.

Richard Erdoes and Alfonso Ortiz, eds. "Sun and Moon in a Box (Zuni)," from *American Indian Trickster Tales*. Copyright © 1998 by Richard Erdoes and the Estate of Alfonso Ortiz. Used by permission of Viking Books, an imprint of Penguin Publishing Group, a division of Penguin Random House LLC.

Carlin Flora. "Seeing by Starlight," *Psychology Today*, July/Aug 2004. Reprinted with permission from *Psychology Today* Magazine. Copyright © 2004 Sussex Publishers, LLC.

Patrick L. Frank and Sarah Prebles. *Prebles' Artforms*, 10th ed. © 2011. Reprinted by permission of Pearson Education, Inc., Upper Saddle River, NJ.

Andrew Friedland, Rick Relyea and David Courard-Hauri. Excerpts and figure 4.35 from the section "The Open Ocean," p. 112 in *Environmental Science: Foundations and Applications*. New York: Freeman, 2011. Used by permission.

Bruce Gervais. Excerpt from Chapter 14, p. 5, "About Volcanoes," from *Living Physical Geography*, 1st ed. New York: Freeman, 2015. Used by permission.

Katie Allison Granju. "A Parenting Secret I Am No Longer Willing to Keep." Babble.com, May 1, 2010. Used by permission of the author.

Jake Halpern. "The Desire to Belong: Why Everyone Wants to Have Dinner with Paris Hilton and 50 Cent" from *Fame Junkies: The Hidden Truths Behind America's Favorite Addiction*. Copyright © 2007 by Jake Halpern. Reprinted by permission of Houghton Mifflin Harcourt Publishing Company. All rights reserved.

Higher One and Everfi. Excerpt and infographic from 2015 *Money Matters on Campus* report. www.moneymatterssoncampus.org. Used by permission.

Sherie Holder and Kenneth Meeks. "Teach Your Children the Building Blocks of Finance," *Black Enterprise*, Feb. 1, 2006. Used by permission.

Ken Ilgunas. "Out of Debt, on the Road," *The Chronicle Review*. May 06, 2013. Used by permission.

Koon-Hwee Kan. "Adolescents and Graffiti." *Art Education*, Jan. 2001, Vol. 54, No. 1, p. 18. © 2001. Used with permission of the National Art Education Association.

Paul Krugman and Robin Wells. "Economics in Action: Failure to Launch" graph with accompanying text from *Macroeconomics*, 4th ed. New York: Freeman, 2015. Used by permission.

LA Times Editorial Board. "How Can We, How Should We, Regulate Hobby Drones?" Sept. 20, 2015. Used by permission.

Littleton, C. Scott. "Amaterasu" from *World Mythology: The Illustrated Guide*, edited by Roy Willis. © 2006. By permission of Oxford University Press.

Los Angeles Police Department. "What Graffiti Means to a Community," http://www.lapdonline.org/get_informed/content_basic_view/23481. Used by permission.

Ian Leslie. Excerpts from pp. ix-xxii in the Introduction to *Curious: The Desire to Know and Why Your Future Depends On It*. Basic Books. Used by permission.

Patrick McCrystal and Andrew Percy. "Factors Associated with Teenage Ecstasy Use," *Drugs: Education, Prevention, and Policy*, Vol. 17, No. 5, pp. 507-527, 2010. Copyright © 2010, Informa Healthcare. Adapted with permission of Informa Healthcare.

Olivia Mellan. "Men, Women and Money," *Psychology Today*, Jan. 1, 1999. Reprinted by permission of the author.

Dave Myers. Excerpt from *Psychology*, 11th ed., p. 17. New York: Freeman, 2015. Used by permission. "Intelligence" from *Psychology*, 11th ed., pp. 384–395 and p. 416. New York: Freeman, 2015. Used by permission.

Amy T. Peterson and David J. Dunworth. "Pandora." pp. 140–141 in *Mythology in Our Midst: A Guide to Cultural References*. Greenwood Press, 2004. Used by permission.

Paige Pfleger. NPR news report titled, "What Right Do Muralists Have to the Buildings They Paint On?" Originally published on NPR.org on June 27, 2015, and is used with the permission of NPR. © 2015 National Public Radio, Inc. Any unauthorized duplication is strictly prohibited.

Christina A. Roberto, et al. "Influence of Licensed Characters on Children's Taste and Snack Preferences," *Pediatrics*, June 21, 2010. Used by permission.

Rockwell, Donna and David C. Giles, excerpts from "Being a Celebrity: A Phenomenology of Fame." *Journal of Phenomenological Psychology*, Vol. 40, No. 2, pp. 178–210. 2009. Used by permission.

Beth Shapiro. "How to Clone a Mammoth: The Science of De-Extinction." Reproduced with permission of Princeton University Press in the format Book via Copyright Clearance Center.

Janna Malamud Smith. "Income Inequality within Families is emerging as a Major Issue." *Newsweek*, Jan. 19, 2013. All rights reserved. Used by permission and protected by the Copyright Laws of the United States. The printing, copying, redistribution, or retransmission of this Content without express written permission is prohibited.

Jim Whitehurst. "How I Hire: Intellectual Curiosity Required," from LinkedIn, Sept. 24, 2013. Reprinted by permission.

Daisy Yuhas. "Curiosity Prepares the Brain for Better Learning." *Scientific American*, Oct. 2, 2014. Used by permission.

Index

A

a, basics of, 584–85
Abbreviations, for note taking, 378
-able, adding, 223, 731
Abstract page, 419, 423
accept/except, 728
Accuracy, checking, 22, 334
Acosta, Teresa Palomo, 496–99
Action verbs. *See also* Verbs
    definition of, 587
    identifying, 585–86
    in sentence structure, 594
Active reading, 3, 14. *See also* Reading critically
Active voice, 713–14
Adjectives
    adverbs and, 587
    basics of, 579, 583–84
    commas between, 672–73
    verbals as, 600
"Adolescents and Graffiti" (Kan), 204, 337–38, 339, 343, 347–48, 505–10
Adverbs
    basics of, 580, 587–88
    conjunctive, 589–90
    verbals as, 600
advice/advise, 728
affect/effect, 728
although, 268, 675
"Amaterasu" (Littleton), 155, 444–48
American Psychological Association. *See* APA style
an, basics of, 584–85
Analysis assignment, example of, 518, 566
Analysis questions, 368
analyze, meaning of, 79
and. See also Coordinating conjunctions
    comma before, in list, 671, 673
    for compound sentences, 607, 615
    as coordinating conjunction, 606–7
    for run-on sentences, 655
anecdote, meaning of, 79

Anecdotes
    in introduction and conclusion, 331
    as introductory hook, 320–21
    strengthening evidence with, 260, 286
Annotating
    Cornell method of note taking and, 378–80
    of fiction, 151–52
    to outline, 292–96
    of textbooks, 159
    while reading, 14–19
    writing summary after, 24–26
Antecedents, of pronouns, 661
Anthology, article in
    APA format for, 428
    MLA format for, 408
APA style, 399
    capitalization and, 734–35
    components of, 416–32
    document format, 417, 423–24
    in-text citations, 430–32
    References page, 417, 424–30
APA Template, 417, 423–24
Apostrophes, 718–26
    to show possession, 721–24
Application, high-level thinking and, 368
Appositives, commas with, 679
argue, meaning of, 79
Argument, 257–72
    components of, 257
    concession words in, 267–69
    counterarguments and rebuttals in, 265–67
    examples of assignment for, 101, 475–76, 518, 566
    sample for analyzing, 270–72
    sample thesis statements for, 255
    taking position in, 258–59
Art, public, readings on, 335–36, 478–519
    graffiti as art, 203, 258–59, 261, 505–13
Articles *(a, an, the),* basics of, 584–85
as/as if, 589

Index of Readings